Clinical Neuroscience

Clinical Neuroscience offers a comprehensive overview of the biological bases of major psychological and psychiatric disorders, and provides foundational information regarding the anatomical and physiological principles of brain functioning. In addition, the book presents information concerning neuroplasticity, pharmacology, brain imaging, and brain stimulation techniques. Subsequent chapters address specific psychological disorders and neurodegenerative diseases, including major depressive and bipolar disorders, anxiety, schizophrenia, disorders of childhood origin, and addiction, as well as neurodegenerative disorders, such as Parkinson's and Alzheimer's diseases. This highly readable textbook expands case examples and illustrations to discuss the latest research findings in clinical neuroscience from an empirical, interdisciplinary perspective.

Lisa L. Weyandt, Ph.D., is a professor of psychology at the University of Rhode Island (URI). She is an active member of the University of Rhode Island Interdisciplinary Neuroscience Program and faculty member of the George and Anne Ryan Institute for Neuroscience. Professor Weyandt is recognized internationally and nationally as an expert on the assessment and treatment of attention deficit hyperactivity disorder (ADHD). She has published numerous peer-reviewed articles covering an array of clinical neuroscience topics ranging from the use and misuse of prescription stimulants, brain imaging techniques, Tourette's disorder, Alzheimer's disease, and executive functions in clinical and non-clinical populations. She is also a licensed psychologist and works with children and adults with a variety of psychological conditions. Dr. Weyandt is the recipient of several awards; has presented at numerous regional, national, and international conferences; and has authored four books in addition to *Clinical Neuroscience: Foundations of Psychological and Neurodegenerative Disorders.*

Clinical Neuroscience

Foundations of Psychological
and Neurodegenerative Disorders

SECOND EDITION

Lisa L. Weyandt, Ph.D.

Routledge
Taylor & Francis Group

NEW YORK AND LONDON

Second edition published 2019
by Routledge
52 Vanderbilt Avenue, New York, NY 10017

and by Routledge
2 Park Square, Milton Park, Abingdon, Oxon, OX14 4RN

Routledge is an imprint of the Taylor & Francis Group, an informa business

First edition published by Routledge 2005

Library of Congress Cataloging-in-Publication Data
Names: Weyandt, Lisa L., author.
Title: Clinical neuroscience : foundations of psychological and
    neurodegenerative disorders / Lisa L. Weyandt.
Other titles: Physiological bases of cognitive and behavioral disorders.
Description: 2nd edition. | New York, NY : Routledge, 2019. | Preceded
    by The physiological bases of cognitive and behavioral disorders /
    Lisa L. Weyandt. 2006. | Includes bibliographical references and index.
Identifiers: LCCN 2018031153 (print) | LCCN 2018031940 (ebook) |
    ISBN 9781315209227 (E-book) | ISBN 9781138629790 (hardback) |
    ISBN 9781138630758 (pbk.) | ISBN 9781315209227 (ebk)
Subjects: | MESH: Mental Disorders—physiopathology | Neurocognitive
    Disorders—physiopathology | Brain Diseases—physiopathology |
    Cognitive Neuroscience—methods
Classification: LCC RC455.4.B5 (ebook) | LCC RC455.4.B5 (print) | NLM
    WM 140 | DDC 616.89—dc23
LC record available at https://lccn.loc.gov/2018031153

ISBN: 978-1-138-62979-0 (hbk)
ISBN: 978-1-138-63075-8 (pbk)
ISBN: 978-1-315-20922-7 (ebk)

Typeset in Minion Pro
by Apex CoVantage, LLC

To my son, Sebastian, an extraordinary young man, and to
Andrew who has taught me the true meaning of tenacity.

Contents

Acknowledgments

I would like to express my gratitude to the University of Rhode Island (URI), College of Health Sciences, and the Department of Psychology for supporting my professional leave so that I could devote my time to formulating and writing *Clinical Neuroscience: Foundations of Psychological Disorders and Neurodegenerative Disease*. I would also like to express my deepest appreciation to Megan Keith, an undergraduate student enrolled in the nursing program at the University of Rhode Island, who served as my research assistant during the writing stage. Megan was responsible for typing the reference section of the text—a formidable task given the extensive number of citations and the attention to detail required to complete this section of the textbook. Megan's enthusiasm for the project and her unwavering work ethic inspired me to continue writing into the late evening and early morning hours. Thank you, Megan. I would also like to thank Aaron Doerflinger, an undergraduate URI student who helped to create tables for the initial chapters of the text and who also assisted with references early on in the project, despite being enrolled as a full-time student and working two jobs. Thank you, Aaron.

I would also like to thank my editor, Lillian Rand, for her support throughout the writing and publication process, as well as her assistant, Olivia Powers. Bruce Blausen, CEO and president of Blausen Medical Scientific and Medical Animations; the project coordinator and medical illustrator Katherine Henning; illustrator Joseph Ewing; and the entire Blausen team deserve special recognition for their professionalism, commitment to the project, and for creating the internal images, as well as the exquisite cover for the text.

I would like to acknowledge the scientists and their research participants who have contributed their expertise and time toward the advancement of knowledge. I extend my thanks to my undergraduate and graduate students whose questions and insights over the years have continued to fuel my interest in the field of physiological psychology and clinical neuroscience.

I am particularly grateful to my partner, Andrew, who saw relatively little of me for the past year and a half yet whole-heartedly supported my efforts on this project. I would especially like to thank him for venturing down the rabbit holes with me and discussing obscure facets of neuroscience, and sharing my awe of life. Lastly, I would like to express my gratitude to my 18-year-old son, Sebastian, who day after day observed me reading, researching, and writing, and unfortunately too often heard me say, "Not now, I'm working on my book". Thank you, Sebastian, for your patience, your love, and your encouragement. I hope that all your dreams come true.

Foreword

In his seminal work, *The Structure of Scientific Revolutions*, Thomas Kuhn distinguished the two modes in which science occurs: incremental step-by-step "puzzle-solving" and revolutionary changes in perspective and fundamental assumptions, which he termed "paradigm shifts". Kuhn noticed that all the sciences, like all human endeavors, are built on an implicit framework of shared and unspoken assumptions. These include tenaciously defended views on what questions can legitimately be posed, the methods that can be used to address those questions, and the criteria by which answers are judged to be valid or not. This is the "paradigm" that organizes what we know at any point in time. Working within a paradigm provides the basis for the true alchemy of science: the emergence of profound insights from the accumulation of individual findings, each of them nearly insignificant when considered in isolation. Inevitably, Kuhn observed, knowledge accumulates within the accepted paradigm until a tipping point is reached, beyond which newly acquired data no longer fit the previously accepted framework/mosaic. This conflict between data and theory is first resolved by rejecting the data, which are always flawed and subject to multiple interpretations. Eventually, as data in conflict with the dominant paradigm continue to accrue, theories are altered ad hoc. Such improvised fixes can continue indefinitely, but their progressive esthetic and predictive deficiencies inevitably accumulate. Following a period of fertile but disturbing confusion, new paradigms emerge, encompassing prior observations and providing additional conceptual space for continued scientific exploration. And so on.

Just over 100 years ago, Albert Einstein published three papers that led to the paradigm shifts that became known as the theory of relativity and quantum mechanics. Although it took several decades for these fundamental ideas to take hold within the physics community, now it is difficult to take seriously the perseverative attempts to measure the ether through which the earth was supposedly moving or Euclidian definitions of space and time. Despite these achievements, even physics, the "hardest" of the sciences, continues to struggle with incipient paradigm shifts, as demonstrated by continuing failed attempts to formulate a unified theory of gravity and electromagnetism.

However, the most challenging, fascinating, and necessary task before the community of 21st-century scientists is arguably the attempt to understand the physiological bases of psychiatric disorders and neurodegenerative diseases. This endeavor began in the 19th century, but every generation since has made its hard-won contributions. However, it has only been in the past three decades that the tools to study the living brain with reasonable spatial and temporal resolution have become available. The human brain is the most complex object in the universe, with more than 100 billion neurons integrating inputs from up to tens of thousands of other neurons dozens of times a second. Fortunately, the pace of discovery in brain sciences continues to accelerate so that we can be confident that new paradigms will emerge that will dramatically alter the way in which we understand brain function and dysfunction. The elements of this vast mosaic are emerging from clinics in which the suffering of individual patients is systematically cataloged, thus improving our diagnostic systems. Other elements are increasingly provided by the panoply of emerging neuroimaging technologies, including positron emission tomography, magnetic resonance imaging, electroencephalography, magnetoencephalography, and near infrared spectroscopic imaging. The exuberant enthusiasm about decoding the human genome has been replaced by awareness that nearly all diseases are complex, resulting from the interplay of hundreds or thousands of genetic and environmental factors, in variegated space (where in the brain) and developmental time. Still, the clues continue to accumulate as the cultural shifts of Big Data and Open Science continue to be powered by the apparently inexorable increase in computational power predicted by Gordon Moore in 1965. This is the landscape that this text surveys, with a specific focus on methods of studying the brain and on the major classes of psychopathology. Neurodegenerative disorders of aging are well covered, as are schizophrenia, mood and anxiety disorders, addiction, and the prototypical disorders of childhood origin. Continuing studies of these conditions will inevitably lead to the new paradigms of brain function that we so badly need. Ironically and wonderfully, it is much more likely that those new paradigms will be conceived by the generation of students who will be introduced to these topics by this comprehensive text, rather than by one of the authors cited in its list of references. And that is as it should be.

Francisco Xavier Castellanos, MD
Brooke and Daniel Neidich Professor of Child and Adolescent Psychiatry;
Professor of Radiology, Neuroscience and Physiology
Hassenfeld Children's Hospital at NYU Langone
NYU School of Medicine
New York, NY USA

Preface

Clinical neuroscience is a branch of neuroscience that involves the scientific study of mechanisms that underlie disorders and diseases of the brain and central nervous system. The focus of this text is on psychological disorders and neurodegenerative diseases that affect a startling percentage of the population. The World Health Organization recently reported that depression is the leading cause of disability and ill health worldwide, with approximately 300 million people living with depression (WHO, March, 2018). In the United States, the National Institute of Mental Health (NIMH) recently reported that one in six adults live with a mental illness, representing 18.3% of the adult population. According to NIMH, approximately 50% of adolescents experience any level of mental health disorder (mild, moderate, severe), and 13% of children age 8–15 experience a *severe* psychological disorder prior to adulthood. When these figures are examined further, they reveal that rates of psychological disorders are higher among women and adults age 18–25 years, and among adults reporting two or more races. Rates of mental health disorders are particularly high among vulnerable populations, including the homeless, prisoners, and juveniles involved with the justice system. With regard to treatment, the majority of children and adults living with psychological disorders do not receive appropriate mental health services, and minority populations are less likely to have access to needed services. For example, NIMH reported that African Americans and Hispanic Americans use mental health services at about one-half the rate of Caucasian Americans (NIMH; Noonan, Velasco-Mondragon, & Wagner, 2016). Clearly, a greater understanding of the etiology of psychological disorders is needed in order to develop appropriate preventative and treatment programs for all segments of the population, particularly those most at risk.

With regard to neurodegenerative disease, Alzheimer's disease is the most common form of dementia in those over the age of 65. Alzheimer's disease is a progressive disease, and current treatments do not reverse or cure the disease. Alzheimer's is estimated to affect 44 million individuals worldwide, and the numbers of patients with this disease are expected to double nearly every 20 years. In the United States, approximately 5.3 million Americans have the disease, and this number is projected to increase to 13.8 million by 2050 (Du, Wang, & Geng, 2018). The economic cost of the disease is substantial; approximately $226 billion was spent for long-term care, hospice, and general health care of patients 65 and older with dementia in 2015, according to the Alzheimer's Association. Parkinson's disease is also a progressive neurodegenerative disease and is estimated to affect seven to ten million individuals worldwide (Aarsland et al., 2010). Parkinson's disease is classified as movement disorder, although most patients with the disease exhibit a wide variety of non-motor symptoms, including cognitive impairment, depression and anxiety, psychotic symptoms, fatigue, urinary problems, and sleep disorders (Santiago, Bottero, & Potashkin, 2017). Although genetic factors play a role in the pathophysiology of Alzheimer's disease and Parkinson's disease, the etiologic underpinnings of both diseases remain a mystery.

Psychological and neurodegenerative disease affect all our lives at a personal and global level. Scientists from a variety of disciplines, such as molecular genetics, biology, psychology, neuropsychology, neuroimaging, neurophysiology, engineering, communication disorders, pharmacy, neurology, and more, have helped to further our understanding of brain functioning and pathology. The level of knowledge that is currently available, however, is at a rudimentary level relative to that which is yet to be discovered about the brain. The purpose of this text is to provide foundational information regarding the anatomical and physiological principles of brain functioning, as well as information concerning neuroplasticity, pharmacology, brain imaging, and brain stimulation techniques, followed by chapters addressing specific psychological disorders and neurodegenerative diseases from an empirical, interdisciplinary perspective. This text is designed for undergraduate and graduate students enrolled in traditional liberal arts programs, interdisciplinary neuroscience programs, medical programs, psychology and clinical neuroscience courses, and professional degree programs.

What makes this text unique is the focus on clinical neuroscience—i.e., psychological disorders and neurodegenerative disease. Numerous biopsychology textbooks are available; however, these texts are often designed for undergraduate courses and typically include only one chapter concerning pathological conditions. Only a handful of clinical neuroscience texts are available in the market, and these texts lack the depth and resources presented in the present text. This text is also unique for its coverage of brain imaging techniques as well as brain stimulation techniques and their applied use for various disorders. The references provided are extensive and will aid the student and the professional in obtaining additional information regarding topics, disorders, and diseases covered in the text. In relation to the 2006 publication (*The Physiological Bases of Cognitive and Behavior Disorders*), the current version offers expanded and more in-depth content of previously covered topics. New content is included regarding multicultural findings, genetic information, and molecular findings. Each chapter now contains hundreds of new citations, color images, additional tables, summaries, and chapter review questions. An overarching objective of the text is to encourage the reader to think scientifically, to consider information from various perspectives, to carefully consider both supporting and non-supporting evidence, and to be open to interdisciplinary ways of thinking.

one

Neuroanatomy, Brain Development, Protection, Metabolic Needs of the Brain, and Neuroplasticity

Clinical neuroscience is a branch of neuroscience that focuses on the fundamental mechanisms that underlie disorders and diseases of the brain and central nervous system, and on scientifically based approaches to diagnosis and treatment. Clinical neuroscience has made its way into the mainstream media with daily headlines claiming, "Rewire your brain, overcome your addictions", "train your mind, change your brain", and online programs that offer personalized brain training programs to improve memory and cognition. This textbook will provide students with a foundation in neuroscience that will enable students to differentiate neuroscience fact from fiction and to navigate and decipher the clinical neuroscience literature. This chapter presents foundational information by reviewing the anatomy of the brain: the structures and associated functions of the forebrain, midbrain, and hindbrain, and lateralization of the hemispheres. It also covers glial cells and neurons, and addresses the processes involved in prenatal and postnatal brain development, including neurulation, dendritic arborization, and myelination. Sex differences in brain morphology are also explored. Finally, the concept of neuroplasticity is introduced with respect to the brain's capacity to change in response to environmental stimulation, including cerebral stroke, developmental conditions, deprivation, limb amputation, and enrichment.

Chapter 1 Learning Objectives

- Identify the major divisions and subdivisions of the brain and nervous system.
- Describe the brain's major structures and associated functions.
- Identify the major anatomical directional terms and planes of section.
- Distinguish between two main types of brain cells.
- Explain the process of brain development from prenatal to young adulthood.
- Distinguish between synaptogenesis, necrosis, and apoptosis.

- Define neuroplasticity and provide examples of plasticity.
- Explain physiological mechanisms of plasticity.
- Explain brain lateralization and provide specific examples of lateralization.
- Discuss brain morphology and sex differences.
- Identify protective layers of the brain.
- Discuss blood supply and metabolic needs of the brain.

Overview of the Nervous System

The nervous system has two main divisions: the peripheral nervous system (PNS) and the central nervous system (CNS) (Figure 1.1). The PNS is located outside the skull and spine,

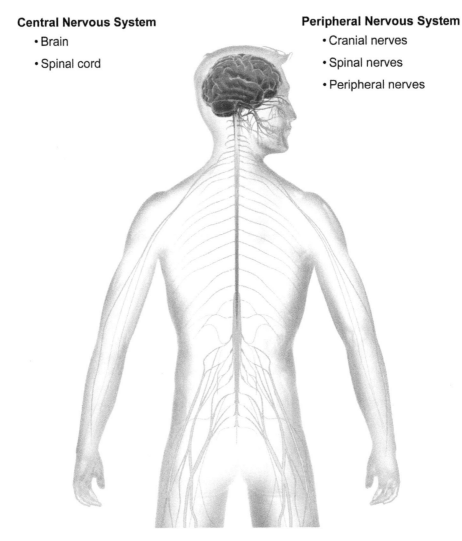

Central Nervous System
- Brain
- Spinal cord

Peripheral Nervous System
- Cranial nerves
- Spinal nerves
- Peripheral nerves

FIGURE 1.1.   Organization of the Nervous System

Copyright Blausen Medical Communications. Reproduced by permission.

and detects environmental information via sensory receptors. It then transmits this information to the CNS by way of sensory nerves known as *afferent* nerves (from the Latin for carry information *to* the CNS). The PNS also transmits information from the CNS to muscles, glands, and internal organs by way of motor nerves known as *efferent* nerves (from the Latin for carry information *away* from the CNS) (Figure 1.2). The PNS is subdivided into the somatic and autonomic nervous systems. The somatic division includes both sensory and motor nerves, and controls skeletal and voluntary movement. The autonomic division controls glands and muscles of internal organs, and regulates internal bodily processes. The autonomic division consists of three main parts: the sympathetic (arousal, "fight or flight") and parasympathetic (restoration) nervous systems, as well as the enteric nervous system (ENS) that governs the function of the gastrointestinal system. The ENS receives sympathetic and parasympathetic input but is also capable of acting independently to affect the functions of the gastrointestinal tract. The gastrointestinal tract has recently been implicated in depression symptoms. Major depressive disorder will be covered in detail in Chapter 6.

Spinal Cord Roots

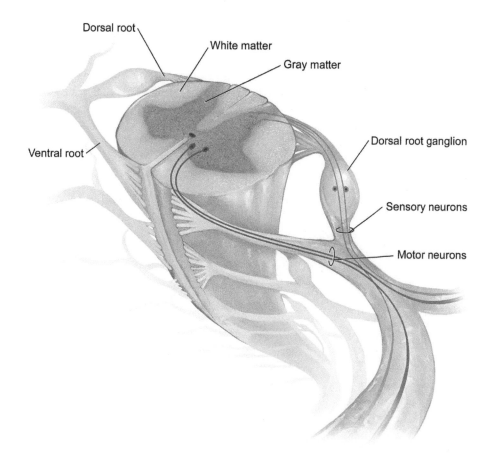

FIGURE 1.2.   Afferent and Efferent Nerves

Reproduced by permission.

BOX 1.1   Can Probiotics Help Lessen Depression Symptoms?

The human gastrointestinal (GI) tract consists of a large number of microorganisms. Research has found a bidirectional relationship between the brain and the GI tract that involves neural, hormonal, and immunological pathways. Preliminary evidence suggests that these microbes may play an important role in the development and maturation of brain systems that are associated with stress responses. Recently, Slykerman et al. (2017) found that women who were treated with a probiotic for six months following childbirth reported significantly less depression and anxiety symptoms relative to women who were randomly assigned to a placebo condition. In patients with irritable bowel syndrome (IBS), Pinto-Sanchez and colleagues (2017) found probiotic treatment was associated with a significant reduction in depression and increased quality of life in patients with IBS compared to patients taking a placebo. Furthermore, the clinical improvements were associated with changes in brain activation patterns—i.e., reduced limbic reactivity to negative emotional stimuli. Although additional studies are needed, researchers hypothesize that probiotics lead to a reduction in GI inflammation while simultaneously increasing brain levels of serotonin.

The CNS is located in the skull and spine, and consists of the brain and the spinal cord. Twelve pairs of cranial nerves and 31 pairs of spinal nerves connect the PNS to the brain and spinal cord. As shown in Figure 1.3, cranial nerves are located on the

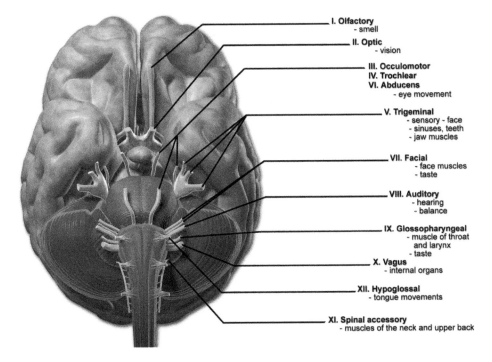

FIGURE 1.3.   Location and Function of Cranial Nerves

Copyright Blausen Medical Communications. Reproduced by permission.

ventral surface of the brain and involve numerous functions of the head, neck, and face. Cranial nerves I and II (olfactory and optic) are located in the forebrain, while cranial nerves III and IV (oculomotor, trochlear) are located in the midbrain. The final eight pairs of cranial nerves, which are found on the ventral surface of the brain stem, are important in tongue and neck movements, as well as regulating internal organs and vital functions.

Brain Regions, Structures, and Functions

Directionality and Terminology

The brain can be viewed from various anatomical directions based on three axes: anterior-posterior, dorsal-ventral, and medial-lateral. *Anterior* refers to the front (also known as rostral in four-legged animals) and *posterior* refers to the rear or tail (also known as caudal). *Dorsal* refers to the back or top and *ventral* toward the belly or ground. *Lateral* refers to the side and *medial* the midline (Figure 1.4). *Ipsilateral* refers to the same side of the body and *contralateral* to the opposite side of the body. The structures of the brain can also be viewed from several sections ("cuts"): horizontal, sagittal, and coronal planes. A *horizontal* plane runs parallel to the top of the brain, a *sagittal* plane runs parallel to the midline of the brain, and a *coronal* plane runs parallel to the front of the brain, dividing the nervous system from front to back ("frontal cut"). A section that divides the brain into two equal halves is known as a *midsagittal* section. This directional terminology will be important for understanding the information to follow (Tables 1.1 and 1.2) as well as understanding and interpreting the scientific literature.

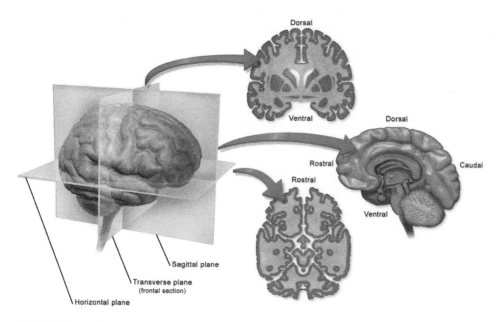

FIGURE 1.4.   Directionality and Planes

Copyright Blausen Medical Communications. Reproduced by permission.

Table 1.1 Major Structures and Functions of the CNS

Cerebrum	The cerebrum is the largest part of the human brain. It is associated with higher brain functions and is divided into four lobes: frontal, parietal, occipital, and temporal.
Frontal Lobe	The front lobes are involved in executive functions, planning, speech production, motor movements, emotional regulation, and complex problem solving.
Parietal Lobe	The parietal lobes are involved in somatosensation, spatial orientation, and sensory integration.
Occipital Lobe	The occipital lobes are involved in processing and perception of visual stimuli.
Temporal Lobe	The temporal lobes are involved in perception and processing of auditory stimuli, memory, speech pattern recognition, and receptive language.
Cerebellum	The cerebellum, like the cerebrum, has two hemispheres. The cerebellum is involved in numerous functions, including memory, coordination of movement, posture, and balance.
Limbic System	The limbic system is a set of interconnected structures involved in emotions, learning, motivation, memory, and the four Fs.
Thalamus	The thalamus functions as the major relay station of the brain for sensory-motor information and is involved in sleep and arousal.
Hypothalamus	The hypothalamus is involved in hormonal regulation and numerous homeostatic functions, such as temperature regulation, circadian rhythms, thirst, and hunger.
Amygdala	The amygdala is involved in memory, processing and formations of emotion, and motivation.
Hippocampus	The hippocampus is involved in memory formation and memory retrieval, as well as spatial navigation.
Brain Stem	The brain stem connects the cerebrum to the spinal cord, has numerous ascending and descending sensory-motor pathways, and is involved in maintaining vital functions.
Midbrain/ Mesencephalon	The midbrain is the most rostral part of the brain stem. It includes the tectum and tegmentum, and is involved in vision, hearing, eye movement, and voluntary body movement.
Pons	The pons is part of the hindbrain and is involved in motor control, posture, and sensory-motor functions.
Medulla	The medulla is in the most caudal part of the brain stem located between the pons and spinal cord, and is involved in regulating autonomic functions, such as breathing, heart rate, and blood pressure.

Brain Divisions

The brain consists of three major divisions with further subdivisions: 1) prosencephalon, telencephalon, and diencephalon; 2) mesencephalon; and 3) rhombencephalon, metencephalon, and myelencephalon. The prosencephalon refers to the forebrain, mesencephalon the midbrain, and the rhombencephalon the hindbrain (Figure 1.5).

Table 1.2 Major Divisions of the Brain: Structures and Ventricles

Telencephalon	**Cerebral Cortex** **Major Fissures** **Major Gyri** **Four Lobes** **Limbic System** **Basal Ganglia** **Cerebral Commissures**	Lateral Ventricle
Diencephalon	**Thalamus** **Hypothalamus** **Optic Chiasm** **Pituitary Gland**	Third Ventricle
Mesencephalon	**Tectum** **Tegmentum**	Cerebral Aqueduct
Metencephalon	**Reticular Formation** **Pons** **Cerebellum**	Fourth Ventricle
Myelencephalon	**Reticular Formation**	

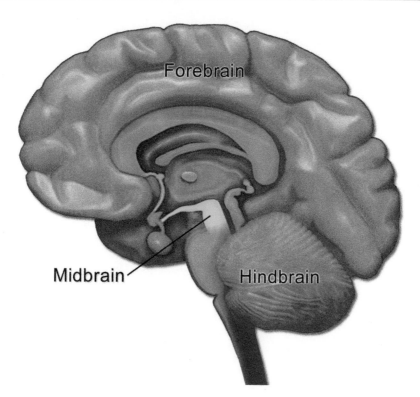

FIGURE 1.5. Sagittal Section Depicting Three Primary Divisions of the Brain

Copyright Blausen Medical Communications. Reproduced by permission.

Forebrain and Lateralization

The prosencephalon—i.e., the forebrain—consists of the telencephalon and diencephalon. The *telencephalon* is the largest division of the human brain and is involved in developing complex cognitive and behavioral processes, such as initiating movement, interpreting sensory stimulation, and higher-level cognition such as planning and problem solving (i.e., executive functions), and language. The telencephalon is made up of two cerebral hemispheres—the right and the left (Figure 1.6)—which are connected by a number of bundles of nerve fibers (i.e., commissures), including the corpus callosum, anterior, posterior, hippocampal, and habenular commissures. The commissures act as a conduit through which the right and left hemispheres exchange information and function interdependently (Springer & Deutsch, 1993). The hemispheres are asymmetrical and vary in size depending on specific structures or regions (e.g., left frontal is larger in size than right frontal; Watkins et al., 2001). The hemispheres traditionally have been described as specialized in function (*lateralization*), and functions traditionally ascribed to the left hemisphere include language-related functions, logical thinking, and writing; visuospatial, musical, and artistic abilities have been ascribed to the right hemisphere (Springer & Deutsch, 1993). Early evidence of these processing hemispheric differences derived largely from individuals with

Cerebral Hemispheres

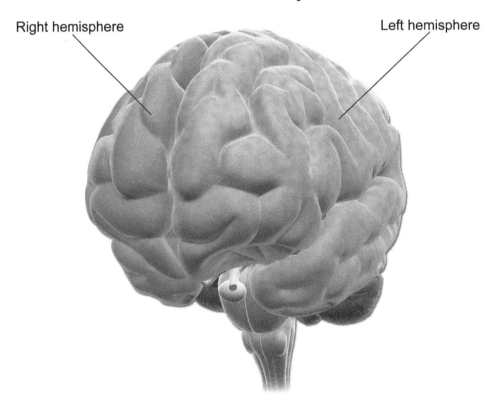

Right hemisphere

Left hemisphere

FIGURE 1.6. Left and Right Hemispheres of the Brain

Copyright Blausen Medical Communications. Reproduced by permission.

brain damage, surgically cut corpus callosum ("split-brain patients"), and neuropsycholog-ical studies. For example, damage to the left frontal lobe (Broca's area) or left temporal lobe (Wernicke's area) can result in difficulties with language production and comprehension (Damasio, 1991); however, this is not always the case and variability exists among patients. Damage to the right hemisphere can result in spatial reasoning difficulties, such as judg-ing line orientation (Benton, Hannay, & Varney, 1975) and interpreting facial expressions (D. Bowers et al., 1985). Patients with uncontrollable forms of epilepsy who have had their corpus callosum surgically severed have been studied extensively by Michael Gazzaniga of UC Santa Barbara. Gazzaniga's work has further substantiated lateralization of cognitive functions (e.g., Gazzaniga, 2005). Many other deficits have been attributed to left and right hemisphere damage and vary depending on the cortical and subcortical regions involved, as well as factors such as age, sex, intelligence, location, and severity of the damage (Kolb, 1989; Kolb & Whishaw, 1996).

More recently, brain imaging technology has been used to explore lateralized functions in healthy individuals across a spectrum of cognitive processes. For example, studies have found that in most people, the left hemisphere is primarily activated when viewing static emotional facial expressions, particularly positive emotions, while the right hemisphere is correlated with negative emotions and dynamic facial expressions (Baeken et al., 2010). Spatial movements, particularly global movements are largely right hemisphere dominant (Floegel & Kell, 2017). Language and reading are largely, although not exclusively, left hemisphere dominant in both males and females, particularly in right-handed individuals (Nenert et al., 2017; Waldie et al., 2017). Interestingly, in congenitally blind individuals, a reduction is found in left hemisphere lateralization when performing language-related tasks (Lane et al., 2017). These findings support that the neurobiology of language can be modified by experience and are consistent with the previous discussion of neuroplasticity. Additional cognitive processes (e.g., musical ability, memory) have been investigated with respect to lateralization, and the current view is that constructs such as language, mem-ory, and emotion consist of an array of individual cognitive processes that often require involvement of *both* hemispheres. The relative contribution of each hemisphere involved in various cognitive processes remains under investigation, however, as well as factors that may mitigate hemispheric involvement. In terms of hemispheric control of the body, the left hemisphere generally controls the right side of the body and the right hemisphere controls the left side of the body (i.e., contralateral control).

The hemispheres are covered by the *cerebral cortex* and separated by the longitudinal fis-sure (Figure 1.7). The cerebral cortex is approximately 3 mm thick, convoluted, and consists of six layers of cells (of varying thickness) running parallel to its surface (Martini, 1998; List et al., 2013; Tamnes et al., 2017). Because the cortex consists mainly of cell bodies, it has a grayish appearance and is commonly referred to as "gray matter". Extensions of the cell body of neurons (*axons*) project to other areas of the cortex and to subcortical regions of the brain, and are often covered in myelin. Myelin consists of fats and proteins, has a whitish appear-ance, and is commonly referred to as "white matter". According to Martini (1998), the total surface area of the cortex is roughly equivalent to 2.5 square feet of flat surface. The size and shape of the skull cause the cortical structure of the brain to fold inward. Hence much of the brain is hidden within the grooves. These folds or bumps are called *gyri*, and the grooves are known as *sulci* (smaller grooves) and *fissures* (major grooves). The largest fissure is the longitu-dinal fissure that separates the left and right hemispheres. The lateral fissure divides both the frontal lobe and parietal lobe from the temporal lobe. During evolution, the human brain

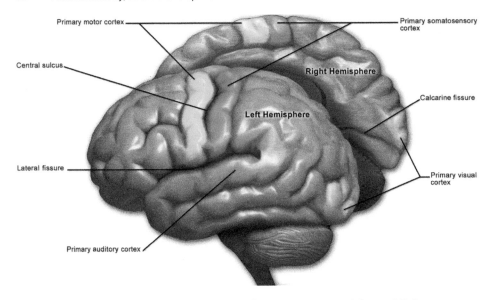

FIGURE 1.7. Left and Right Hemispheres, Corti, Fissures, and Central Sulcus

Copyright Blausen Medical Communications. Reproduced by permission.

increased in size, in particular the volume of the cerebral cortex. Rakic (1995) has suggested that a genetic alteration may have played a significant role in the large surface size of the cortex in humans relative to other animals.

The **telencephalon** also includes the frontal, parietal, temporal, and occipital lobes (Figure 1.8). The frontal lobe is the most anterior, and the parietal lobe is posterior and dorsal to the frontal lobe. Located on the lateral surface, the temporal lobe is separated from the frontal and parietal lobes by the lateral fissure. The occipital lobe is the most posterior of the four lobes. Although each lobe is associated with primary functions, the four lobes are highly interconnected.

The *frontal lobe*, the largest of the four lobes, contains the *motor cortex* that is involved in planning, control, and execution of voluntary movement. The motor cortex consists of three areas; the premotor cortex, primary motor cortex, and supplemental motor cortex, with each believed to contribute to different aspects of motor functions, the details of which are not fully understood. A specialized region important in language production, known as *Broca's area*, is found in the frontal lobe of the left hemisphere. Other higher-order cognitive processes associated with the frontal lobes, in particular the anterior region (prefrontal cortex), include strategic planning, impulse control, and flexibility of thought and action. Collectively, these processes are known as executive functions (Fletcher, 1996). A number of clinical disorders are characterized by executive function deficits, including attention deficit hyperactivity disorder (ADHD), Alzheimer's disease, schizophrenia, obsessive compulsive disorders, and others (Weyandt, 2004).

The frontal lobes have three primary circuits: dorsolateral, orbitofrontal, and anterior cingulate (Burruss et al., 2000). The dorsolateral circuit is postulated to be specifically involved in executive functions and the orbitofrontal circuit in regulation of emotions and socially appropriate behavior. The anterior cingulate circuit is thought to mediate motivation and wakefulness and arousal. As described by Burruss and colleagues, damage to this

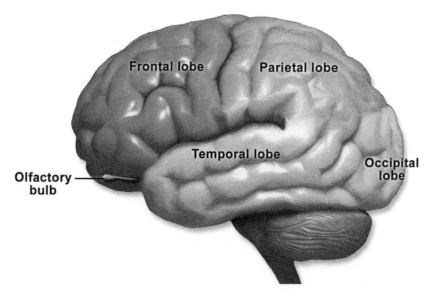

FIGURE 1.8.   Olfactory Bulb and Four Lobes of the Brain

Copyright Blausen Medical Communications. Reproduced by permission.

circuit can result in profound apathy, immobility, and absence of behavior. Brain imaging studies have recently demonstrated that executive functioning extends beyond the frontal lobes and involves subcortical structures (e.g., putamen, thalamus) in both hemispheres, and is related to the extent of gray and white matter in regions beyond the frontal lobes (Ardila, Bernal, & Rosselli, 2017; Bettcher et al., 2016).

The *parietal lobe* contains the somatosensory cortex that processes and integrates information concerning the body's position in space and sensory information from the skin, such as touch, pressure, and pain (see Figure 1.8). Stimulating any part of the skin—for example, on the nose, finger, or foot—leads to activation of neurons in the somatosensory cortex that represent that area. Damage to the parietal lobe from head injury, stroke, and so on can result in a number of effects depending on the location and severity of the damage. For example, damage to the right parietal lobe can result in contralateral neglect—that is, complete lack of awareness of visual, auditory, and somatosensory stimulation on the left side of the body (McFie & Zangwill, 1960). Damage to the parietal lobe can also result in anosognosia, a lack or self-awareness or inability to recognize a disorder or defect that is clinically evident (Vossel et al., 2012). Disorders of tactile function, spatial ability, and drawing are also associated with damage to the parietal lobe (Kolb & Whishaw, 1996).

BOX 1.2   Alien Hand Syndrome (AHS)

Alien hand syndrome is a rare neurological condition in which one hand functions involuntarily and is often purposeful in action. For example, individuals with this condition have reported that the affected hand antagonizes the other hand, grasps or tears at clothing, and, in extreme cases, inflicts self-harm. In some cases, individuals with AHS perceive that the affected hand is not theirs (Josephs and Rossor, 2004). The underlying neural mechanisms of AHS are not well understood. Alfaro and colleagues (2017) recently described a case of a 65-year-old professional pianist who showed uncontrolled levitation with her right arm while playing the piano. The pianist reportedly perceived her hand as if it had a "mind of its own". When she moved her left hand, her right hand raised involuntarily, which prevented her from playing. As part of the evaluation, the patient underwent magnetic resonance imaging (MRI diffusion tensor tractography) and a brain perfusion scan using SPECT. MRI results revealed severe atrophy in the left parietal lobe (anterior and posterior regions, as well as the left posterior postcentral gyrus). SPECT supported damage to the left parietal lobe as reduced blood flow was found in the left posterior parietal-occipital cortex. Although it may be tempting to conclude that parietal lobe involvement is characteristic of AHS patients, damage to other areas of the brain without parietal lobe involvement have also resulted in AHS (Bartolo et al., 2011).

Like the other lobes, the *temporal lobes* are rich in afferent and efferent pathways that connect to cortical and subcortical regions of the brain. The primary auditory cortex located in the temporal lobe plays a critical role in hearing and the processing of sounds. The left hemisphere of the temporal lobe contains a region known as *Wernicke's area* that is critical to understanding spoken language. Damage to the temporal lobe can result in a variety of disturbances affecting auditory sensation and perception, long-term memory, personality, and language comprehension (e.g., Scoville & Milner, 1957; Squire, 2017). The primary function of the *occipital lobe* is the analysis of visual information, and damage therein can result in a number of visual perception disturbances (*agnosias*). Two different categories of visual object agnosia have been identified: apperceptive agnosia and associative agnosia. Apperceptive agnosia involves failing to recognize a visual stimulus due to a perceptual impairment, while associative agnosia involves correctly perceiving a stimulus but failing to recognize the object because of faulty memory. Examples of agnosias include prosopagnosia (for faces), alexia (for words), or topographagnosia (for landmarks), akinetopsia (for movement), and orientation agnosia (for the placement of objects in space) (see Martinaud, 2017 for a review).

Additional structures located in the telencephalon include the *limbic system* and basal ganglia (Figure 1.9). The limbic system is actually a set of interconnected structures that form a ring around the thalamus and include the limbic cortex, hippocampus, amygdala, and fornix. Other structures are sometimes included as part of the limbic system (e.g., olfactory bulb, cingulate cortex). The limbic system is involved in motivated behaviors, such as sexual behavior, eating, and aggressive behavior, as well as learning, memory, and recognition and expression of emotion. Research has implicated part of the limbic cortex, the anterior cingulate cortex, in a variety of cognitive and emotional functions as well as addiction. Bush, Luu, and Posner (2000) described two main subdivisions of the anterior cingulate cortex: the cognitive and affective subdivisions. They suggested that connections with the lateral prefrontal cortex, parietal, and motor corti are tied to cognitive processing, such as the modulation of attention, motor control, pain aversiveness, and higher-order

The Limbic System

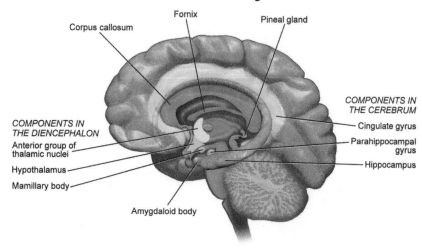

FIGURE 1.9. Limbic System

Copyright Blausen Medical Communications.

cognitive processes. Alternatively, the affective subdivision is connected to structures, such as the hippocampus, hypothalamus, amygdala, and nucleus accumbens, and is involved in the interpretation and regulation of emotional responses. Bush and colleagues also suggested that the cingulate cortex undergoes a long developmental process, and the volume of the cingulate cortex is related to regulation of emotional and behavioral responses.

Heimer (2003) noted that the interconnections among limbic-related structures are so complex that it is a misconception to regard the limbic system as a separate system from the basal ganglia. He described additional circuits within the limbic region and explained how these pathways project from the cerebral cortex, hippocampus, amygdala, and other structures to the basal ganglia. Quirk and Gehlert (2003) suggested that the *amygdala* plays an important role in the development of anxiety disorders and drug-seeking behaviors. Specifically, they hypothesized that the neuronal pathways that extend from the amygdala to the prefrontal cortex are deficient in inhibitory tone (i.e., overactivity), and thus drugs targeting these pathways could prevent addiction relapse and anxiety disorders. More recent research has implicated connections among the lateral hypothalamus, amygdala, and ventral tegmental areas of the brain in drug-seeking behavior due to an abundance of dopamine-releasing neurons in this region. Substance abuse and addiction will be covered in Chapter 8.

The *basal ganglia* are a complex group of subcortical cell bodies that play a critical role in movement. They consist of the caudate nucleus, putamen, globus pallidus, subthalamic nucleus, and substantia nigra (Figure 1.10). The caudate nucleus and putamen together are known as the *striatum*. The striatum receives input from the cortex and other structures (e.g., thalamus and amygdala) and projects information to widespread regions, such as the brain stem and the prefrontal cortex (van Dongen & Groenewegen, 2002). The nucleus accumbens is a group of cell bodies located adjacent to the striatum. One pathway known as the nigrostriatal system extends from the substantia nigra to the striatum. Parkinson's

Basal Ganglia

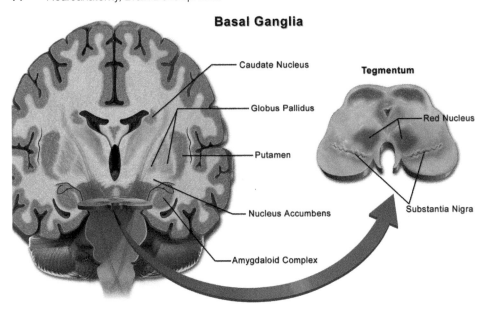

FIGURE 1.10.   Basal Ganglia

disease is associated with degeneration of cell bodies of the substantia nigra that affect functioning of the nigrostriatal system and, consequently, movement. A second pathway, the mesolimbic system, extends from the tegmentum (midbrain cell bodies) to the nucleus accumbens, amygdala, and hippocampus. This pathway has been implicated in rewarding brain stimulation (i.e., rat lever pressing to receive a drug) and clinical disorders, such as schizophrenia and addictive behavior (Dubol et al., 2017; Koob & Nestler, 1997; Soares & Innis, 1999). Heimer (2003) discussed additional pathways that connect the cerebral cortex, limbic system, and basal ganglia, and suggested "all major telencephalic disorders are, to some extent at least, disorders of the basal ganglia" (p. 1737). These topics and pathways will be examined in greater detail in subsequent chapters (see Nicholson & Faull, 2002, for additional information about the basal ganglia).

The *diencephalon*, also part of the forebrain, consists of the thalamus and the hypothalamus. The thalamus consists of cell bodies that receive, process, and transmit sensory input to appropriate areas of the cortex. For this reason, it is often referred to as a "relay station" for visual, auditory, and somatosensory information. The hypothalamus also consists of a group of cell bodies and is located below the anterior portion of the thalamus. It plays a critical role in regulating the autonomic nervous system as well as numerous survival behaviors, such as eating, drinking, emotional regulation, and mating, as mentioned previously. The hypothalamus is also involved in functioning of the endocrine system and releasing hormones that stimulate the pituitary gland, which in turn controls other endocrine glands. The pituitary gland is located on the ventral surface of the hypothalamus near the optic chiasm and mamillary bodies (Figure 1.10). The *optic chiasm* is the point at which the nerves extending from each eye come together. The *mamillary bodies* are a collection of cell bodies located posterior to the pituitary gland and are part of the hypothalamus. These

CSF System

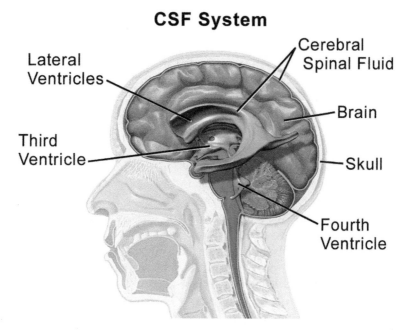

FIGURE 1.11.   Sagittal Section Showing the Pituitary Gland, Ventricle System, Corpus Callosum, and Additional Brain Structures

Copyright Blausen Medical Communications. Reproduced by permission.

regions along with the limbic system, sensorimotor cortex, and areas of the brain stem are characterized by greater structural development (e.g., white matter) and functional activity in infants compared to other areas of the cortex (Chugani, 1998). Recent brain imaging research has substantiated that different regions of the brain mature at different rates and this level of brain maturation is associated with age-related changes in cognition during childhood, adolescence, and young adulthood (Lebel, Treit, & Beaulieu, 2017).

Midbrain

The *mesencephalon*, also known as the *midbrain*, contains numerous ascending and descending pathways that project from the subcortical to cortical regions. The midbrain is involved in maintaining alertness as well as many basic behavioral reactions. It consists of two subdivisions: the tectum and the tegmentum. The tectum is composed of two pairs of bumps: the superior and the inferior colliculi. The superior colliculi are involved in vision and the inferior colliculi are involved in hearing. The inferior colliculi, for example, are involved in localizing sounds in our surroundings and orienting the body toward those sounds. The tegmentum lies ventrally to the tectum and contains a number of structures that play an important role in attention, arousal, sleep, sensitivity to pain, and movement. These structures include the reticular formation, red nucleus, substantia nigra, and the periaqueductal gray matter (PAG) (Figure 1.9).

The periaqueductal gray separates the tectum from the tegmentum and plays a critical role in the perception of pain (the PAG is rich in opioid receptors and endogenous opioids). Descending pathways projecting from the PAG have been implicated in relaying modulatory responses to brain stem, cerebellum, and spinal cord, and have been shown to have profound effects spinal pain transmission. For example, deep brain stimulation in the area of the PAG has been found to lessen pain in patients with intractable neuropathic pain syndromes. Interestingly patients with a gastrointestinal disorder known as *functional dyspepsia* who have an abnormality of pain processing and disruption of emotion processing have been found to have decreased connectivity between the PAG and other regions of the brain (Donaldson & Lumb, 2017; Henricus, Domburg, & Donklaar, 1991; Liu, Wang, et al., 2017).

Hindbrain

The *metencephalon* and *myelencephalon* comprise the *hindbrain* (Figure 1.5). The metencephalon consists of the pons and the cerebellum. The myelencephalon contains one structure: the medulla oblongata. The pons lies between the midbrain and the medulla oblongata, ventrally to the cerebellum. The pons also serves as a relay station from the cortex to the cerebellum and contains a portion of the reticular formation. The reticular formation extends from the brain stem to the forebrain and consists of pathways rich in cell bodies that help to regulate arousal, wakefulness, and sleep (Jones, 1993). The pons is believed to play a role in a wide variety of abilities as demonstrated by diseases that affect the pons. For example, *central pontine myelinolysis*, a condition in which the fatty substance that covers part of the neurons of the pons is destroyed, is characterized by muscle weakness, tremor, poor balance, swallowing difficulties, and speech problems.

The cerebellum is attached to the pons by bundles of axons called cerebellar peduncles. The cerebellum receives information from other parts of the brain and projects information throughout regions of the brain. It plays a critical role in movement, and damage to the cerebellum impairs coordinated movements as well as standing and walking. Research suggests that the cerebellum is involved in additional functions such as language, memory, and emotions and may play a role in a variety of disorders such as schizophrenia, autism spectrum disorder (ASD), fetal alcohol syndrome, and bipolar disorder (Boronat et al., 2017; Caplan et al., 2002; Herb & Thyen, 1992; Laidi et al., 2017; Leroi et al., 2002; Martin & Albers, 1995; Shinn et al., 2016; Vokaer et al., 2002).

The myelencephalon consists of the medulla oblongata and structures therein. The medulla oblongata is the hindmost portion of the brain and appears as a bulge at the upper end of the spinal cord. Contained within the medulla is a complex network of cell bodies and pathways that project to the midbrain. This network is known as the *reticular formation*, and as noted previously, it is important in a variety of functions, such as attention, arousal, sleep, and certain reflexes that are necessary for survival (cranial nerves 9–12 are located on the medulla oblongata).

BOX 1.3   Brain Eating Amoeba: Up the Nose?

Naegleria fowleri is a single-celled organism found in warm freshwater lakes, streams, rivers, hot springs, and ponds throughout the world. It enters the body through the nose when an individual accidentally inhales water while swimming or diving. The amoeba then travels up the nasal passages and enters the brain through the olfactory nerve, producing a highly virulent condition known as primary amoebic meningoencephalitis (PAM). Symptoms, including severe headache, fever, vomiting, stiff neck, seizures, and, possibly, coma, typically begin within one to ten days after infection. Once in the brain, the organism begins to "eat" the brain and destroy brain tissue. There have been approximately 138 cases in the United States since 1950, with a fatality rate of 97%. There is hope for future cases, as an adolescent male from the state of Florida was recently quickly diagnosed with PAM and successfully treated with Miltefosine (Miltex), a broad spectrum antimicrobial agent (Bellini, Santos, et al., 2018; Jamerson et al., 2017; Lindsley, 2016).

Brain Development

Penfield (1958) and Luria (1973) were among the first to advance models of functional brain systems, and, today, researchers continue to try to unravel the intricacies of normal as well as abnormal brain functioning. Luria suggested that posterior and subcortical regions of the brain that are associated with early survival behaviors (e.g., sucking, swallowing) are more developed at birth than cortical regions that are involved in higher-order cognitive processes (e.g., executive functions, problem solving). Hynd and Willis (1988) and others extrapolated on Luria's theory of functional brain units and postulated that various regions and structures of the brain are specialized in function yet function interdependently. Indeed, structural and functional imaging studies of the brain have found a consistent pattern of evolving changes with greater cellular activity in the brain stem and subcortical structures shortly after birth and gradual increase in cortical activity during the first two years (Tokumaru et al., 1999). In addition, neuroimaging studies have found that as development progresses, activity at the level of the cerebral cortex changes from more diffuse involvement to greater localization of brain activity. Just et al. (1996), for example, studied adults using functional magnetic reasoning (fMRI) and found that more regions of the brain were activated during a complex sentence comprehension task, and fewer regions were activated as the task decreased in complexity. Longitudinal studies with children have found similar findings, supporting the view that different regions and networks of the brain are specialized in function, and these functions are related to stages of brain development and behavioral functioning (Geng et al., 2017). Neuroimaging studies among adults also suggest that higher-level cognitive functions, such as abstract reasoning, problem solving, and planning are processed at the level of the cortex and the pattern of activation for these tasks may vary greatly among individuals and with age (e.g., Derbyshire, Vogt, & Jones, 1998). In summary, research clearly indicates that during early development, a relationship exists between brain development and behavior, and that the brain develops in a hierarchical fashion (Huttenlocher, 2002; Yuan et al., 2016). Brain development begins shortly after conception with the onset of neurulation.

Prenatal Brain Growth

Neurulation

The first prenatal period of development is the *germinal period* and is characterized by the union of egg and sperm, division of cells, and implantation of this group of cells in the uterine wall. The second prenatal period begins around the 14th day of gestation and is known as the *embryonic period*. At approximately two weeks gestation, a portion of the embryonic tissue (*ectoderm*) begins to thicken and forms the neural plate. In the middle of the neural plate is a fissure that continues to deepen and fold inward, forming the neural groove. The folds of the neural groove eventually fuse and form the neural tube. A portion of the tube later becomes the brain's ventricles and spinal canal. At approximately three weeks gestation, the ectoderm separates from the neural tube, and cells from the ectoderm migrate laterally and eventually form the spinal and cranial nerves. Between the third and fourth weeks of gestation, the anterior and posterior ends of the neural tube fuse, and the posterior end develops into the spinal cord. The anterior end of the neural tube gives rise to brain vesicles that later develop into the structures that form the major subdivisions of the brain (forebrain, midbrain, hindbrain; see Swanson, 2003, for more information). During the fetal period, which lasts from the beginning of the third month gestation until birth, the brain continues to develop at a rapid pace, at a rate of 250,000 neurons per minute (Cowan, 1979). This growth is associated with functional abilities in the fetus (e.g., somatosensory, hearing, movement) as well as noticeable morphological changes (e.g., gyri and sulci form around the seventh month) (Kolb & Whishaw, 2001, p. 242). By five months gestation, most nerve cells (neurons) have formed but are morphologically immature. By the end of the fetal period, all of the brain's structures have formed and become functional. A number of cellular events contribute to brain maturation, including cell birth, migration, differentiation, synaptogenesis, myelination, synaptic pruning, and cellular death.

Brain Cells and Brain Maturation

Neurons and Glial Cells

The brain consists of two main types of cells: neurons and glial cells (Figures 1.12–1.14). For decades, glial cells were reported to substantially out number neurons (i.e., 10:1); however, more recent findings support a 1:1 ratio (von Barthheld, Bahney, & Herculano-Houzel, 2016). Neurons are specialized for communication, and in general, glial cells serve a number of ancillary functions, such as providing structure and support to neurons. Recent research suggests that glial cells also play a role in a number of cellular processes, such as facilitating communication among neurons, plasticity, and production of substances that nourish neurons and enhance their survival (*neurotrophins*; Otten et al., 2001). Glial cells are subdivided into two main classifications: macroglia and microglia. Macroglia are the larger glial cells, and in the brain, they include *astrocytes* and *oligodendrocytes*. Astrocytes are the largest and most abundant type of glial cell and provide structural support for neurons. In addition, they are in physical contact with blood vessels and form a protective barrier so toxic substances do not penetrate the brain. Astrocytes also transport substances from the blood to and from neurons. Evidence suggests that astrocytes are involved in the production of chemicals that neurons use to communicate with each other and that the interaction between astrocytes and neurons may be impaired during degenerative brain diseases such as dementia (Hertz et al., 2000). Evidence also suggests that astrocytes react to injury of the brain in a number of ways, including the formation of scar tissue that serves to reduce further inflammation of the brain but also interferes with axonal regeneration. Interestingly, the pattern of astroglial scarring in the brain appears to differ depending on the source of the brain injury. For example, preliminary findings suggest that military personnel suffering

Table 1.3 Types of Glial Cells Found in CNS and Associated Functions

Glial Cells	Glial cells assist with neural communication by serving a number of important functions, including modulation of neurotransmission, structural support, providing sustenance, removal of waste and debri, and reuptake of neurotranmsitters. Glial cells are categorized into two types: smaller cells known as microglia and larger cells known as macroglia.
Macroglia: Astrocytes	Astrocytes are the largest and most abundant glial cells in the CNS. Astrocytes perform a variety of functions, including providing nutrients to neurons and removal of waste products, providing support to cells that form the blood-brain barrier, and releasing neurotrophins and neuromodulators.
Macroglia: Oligodendrocytes	Oligodendrocytes provide structural support for neurons and insulate axons by ensheathing axons with concentric layers of myelin. Myelin consists of ~80% lipids and 20% protein, and facilitates the rapid transduction action potentials down the axon.
Microglia Cells	Microglial cells play a major role in phagocytosis, as microglia are scavengers that remove waste and debris, including dead neurons. These cells act as the brain's primary active immune defense system against any pathogen threatening the brain.

brain injury as a result of blast exposure have a particular pattern of astroglial scarring that may predict psychological outcomes such as post-traumatic stress disorder (Shively et al., 2016). Recent findings have revealed the presence of N-methyl-D-aspartate (NMDA) receptors on astrocytes, receptors previously thought to be found only on neurons (Kirchhoff, 2017). NMDA receptors play a critical role in memory formation and will be discussed in more detail in Chapter 4. Research also suggests that astrocytes may strengthen signaling among neurons by releasing substances that amplify the effects of neurotransmitters (Do et al., 2004). In contrast to the traditional view of glial cells as exclusively "nurse cells", current research suggests that glial cells often serve to modulate neurotransmission and are also capable of releasing neurotransmitters that activate receptors on neurons, other glial cells, and vascular cells (Bellot-Saez et al., 2017; Fields, 2010).

A second type of macroglial cell, oligodendrocytes form a protective sheath, known as *myelin*, around part of the neuron: the axon. Myelin consists of lipids and proteins, and helps to insulate and facilitate the transduction of messages sent from one neuron to another. Interestingly, the brain contains approximately 20% of the body's total cholesterol and about 70% of it is found in myelin. The remaining 30% is found in the membranes of glial cells and neurons where it is used for neuronal repair. Oligodendrocytes biosynthesize cholesterol from acetate (cholesterol does not cross the blood-brain barrier), and this process involves a specific pathway (apoE) that is implicated in Alzheimer's disease (discussed in Chapter 4) (Mahley, 2016).

Many, but not all, axons are myelinated in the CNS. A single oligodendrocyte can myelinate multiple neurons via extensions that wrap around the axon of neurons. Microglia

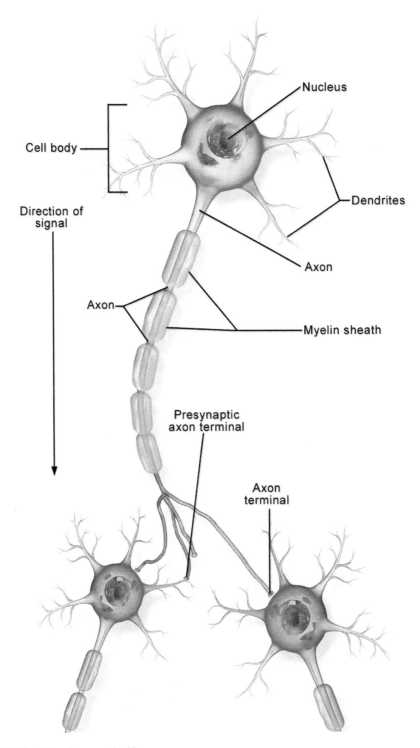

FIGURE 1.12. Image of a Neuron

Copyright Blausen Medical Communications. Reproduced by permission.

Classification of Neurons

Anaxonic Neuron	Bipolar Neuron	Unipolar Neuron	Multipolar Neuron

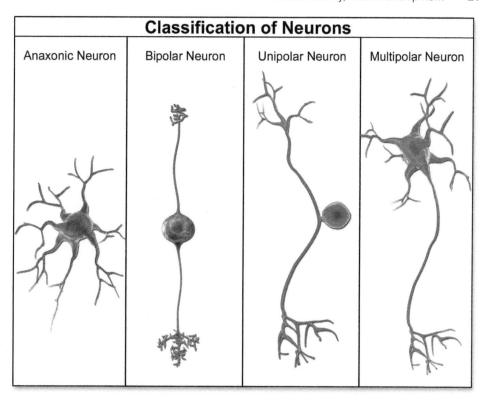

FIGURE 1.13. Types of Neurons

Copyright Blausen Medical Communications. Reproduced by permission.

are smaller in size and are phagocytic—i.e., they engulf and digest brain debris. Recent findings suggest that microglia may play a role in neurodegenerative disease, epilepsy, cerebral palsy, and autistic spectrum disorder due to their release of substances that are associated with inflammation of brain tissue (e.g., cytokines, chemokines, reactive oxygen species, nitric oxide) and inactivity associated with increasing age (Kaur, Rathnasamy, & Ling, 2017; Salters & Stevens, 2017).

In summary, glial cells (a) participate in the uptake and breakdown of chemicals that neurons use for communication; (b) act as scavengers and remove waste products and debris, including dead neurons; (c) take up ions from the extracellular environment; (d) provide proteins and other substances to neurons; (e) segregate groups of neurons from one another; and (f) modulate neuronal signaling (Levitan & Kaczmarek, 1997, p. 25; Sykova, Poulain, & Oliet, 2004).

Neurons

Neurons come in different shapes, sizes, and types, and are located differentially throughout the brain. Neurons can be categorized according to functional or structural features (Figure 1.13). As reviewed by Thompson (2000), there are four main functional classifications of neurons: motor, sensory, principal, and interneurons. *Motor* neurons have axons that project to the spinal cord where they communicate with other motor neurons that innervate muscles and glands. *Sensory* neurons convey information from the peripheral

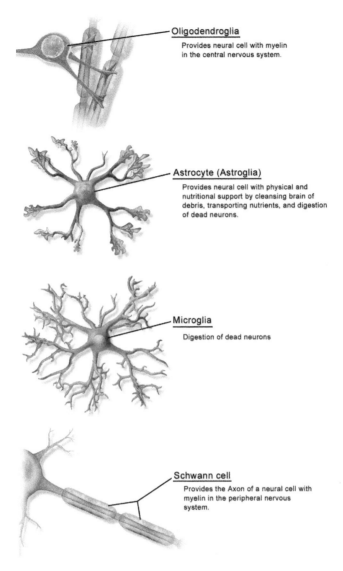

FIGURE 1.14. Types of Glial Cells

nervous system to the CNS, such as sights, sounds, taste, and tactile information. Within the brain are principal neurons and interneurons. *Principal* neurons have long axons that extend to other locations in the brain, whereas *interneurons*, the most abundant neurons, have shorter axons that communicate messages to nearby cells and convey information between sensory and motor neurons. For example, habitual behaviors (e.g., nail biting) are behaviors that are often completed without thought and are difficult to terminate. Recently, O'Hare and colleagues (2017) found that a particular type of interneuron ("fast spiking") located in a particular area of the basal ganglia (dorsolateral striatum) modulated habitual behavior in mice and may have implications for human behaviors. The role of interneurons in epilepsy, addiction, and other human conditions is also being studied (Librizzi et al., 2017; Yu, Lan, et al., 2017).

The basic components of a neuron include a cell body (*soma*), dendrites, and an axon. The cell body contains the nucleus and other structures that help a neuron process and transmit information. Dendrites are very thin structures that emerge from the cell body of the neuron and are formed in a variety of shapes and sizes. They receive messages from other neurons while axons transmit messages to other cells. Dendrites continue to develop and mature postnatally, and are believed to play an integral role in neuroplasticity (Kennedy, 2000; Chen et al., 2002). Axons of neurons extend from the cell body and transmit information via the terminal button to other neurons, a process known as *neurotransmission*. Internal components of neurons and the process of neurotransmission are covered in detail in the Chapter 2.

Cell Migration

Neurons and glial cells originate prenatally from stem cells. Stem cells line the cerebral ventricles—i.e., ventricular zone—and give rise to progenitor cells that in turn produce neuroblasts and glioblasts. *Neuroblasts* are immature neurons and *glioblasts* are immature glial cells; the formation of these cells is known as *neurogenesis* and *gliogenesis*, respectively. Factors that regulate the processes of neurogenesis and gliogenesis are not well understood, but neuroscientists are studying the role of genes and various proteins that trigger cellular change and maturation. In recent years, a number of factors have been identified, including proteins that promote the division of neural stem cells, neurotrophic substances (e.g., brain-derived neurotrophic factor [BDNF]) that critically affect the survival and maturation of these cells, and intracellular as well as extracellular substances (e.g., neurogenin, oxygen, glucocorticoids, retinoic acid) that may further enhance their survival (Conti et al., 2001; Odaka, Adachi, & Numakawa, 2017; Ortega et al., 2017; Sun et al., 2001). This continues to be an active area of research in which future studies will likely reveal the complexities involved in the formation of neurons and glial cells.

Once neuroblasts and glial cells have been created, they migrate from the ventricular zone to other brain locations with the assistance of radial glial cells. Radial glial cells extend from the ventricular zone to various parts of the brain, including the cortex. Developing cells migrate by moving along the radial glial fibers until they reach their destination. The mechanisms that govern the migration process are under investigation but involve an interaction between genetic and environmental factors. For example, Rakic (1995) hypothesized that in addition to building scaffolding, glial cells offer chemical trails for neurons to follow to their destinations. Indeed, several types of extracellular molecules have been identified in other animals and insects that attract, repel, or help form migrating neurons form connections with other neurons, including cadherins, integrins, netrins, ephirins, semiphorins, slit molecules, SYG-1, and SYG-2 (Frei & Stoeckli, 2017; Mueller, 1999; Shen & Bargmann, 2003; Hirano & Takeichi 2012).

Migrating neurons (i.e., neurites) are not fully formed and have a structure that extends from the tip of the axon called a *growth cone*. The cones have long fingerlike extensions known as filopodia that move forward and pull the neurite along. The growth cones are believed to contain proteins (i.e., receptors) that are attracted to and repelled by other proteins released by glial cells along the migration path (Ma et al., 2014; Terman & Kolodkin,

1999). Thus, the developing neuron moves along a particular pathway, led by the growth cone that moves forward and turns in response to molecules that attract or repel the cell. Once the cell's destination is reached, the growth cone is replaced by an axon terminal that forms connections (*synapses*) with other cells (Mueller, 1999). Substances on the surface of cells have been found to facilitate synaptic connections among neurons, and these substances are known as *cell adhesion molecules*. The process of formation of synapses with nearby or distant neurons is known as *synaptogenesis*.

Synaptogenesis

After the developing neurons have migrated, they differentiate into different sizes and shapes, and align themselves with other neurons in the same vicinity to form networks, a process known as *aggregation*. The initial process of aggregation is believed to be under genetic control, but chemicals surrounding neurons appear to be involved in the maturation and functional role of neurons. For example, research has found that if pre-differentiated cells are removed from one brain region and placed in another, they will serve the same functions as those in their new vicinity (Bosworth & Allen, 2017; Schlaggar & O'Leary, 1991). After developing neurons reach their destinations, synaptogenesis occurs—they form communication networks with nearby or distant neurons, and this process continues throughout the prenatal period. By five months gestation, neurogenesis is mostly complete, and many neurons have migrated to their correct location where they continue to mature morphologically and form connections with other neurons. Subcortical structures, such as the hippocampus, continue to undergo neurogenesis, and synaptogenesis occurs here earlier than in cortical regions (Kolb & Gibb, 2011; Kostovic et al., 1989).

After birth, during the first one to two years, synaptogenesis increases dramatically and is followed by a substantial reduction, or pruning phase. Different regions of the cortex increase in synaptic density and experience pruning at different times. The visual cortex, for example, increases in synaptic connections after birth during months 2–4, while other areas of cortex increase in synaptic connections during the first 12 months. Huttenlocher (1979) explored synaptic density in the frontal cortex of 21 postmortem normal human brains ranging from newborn to 90 years. Results indicated that synaptic density in newborns was similar to the density level in adults. The morphology of the connections was immature, however, and did not resemble adult appearance until approximately 24 months. Synaptic density continued to increase from birth until one to two years, at which time the level was about 50% above the adult mean. The synaptic and neuronal density levels slowly declined from ages 2 to 16, but then remained constant throughout adulthood. These data suggest that neurons establish their synapses during the first one to two years of life, followed by loss of connections until late adolescence. Abnormalities in synaptic density found in individuals with autism spectrum disorder intellectual impairment, and schizophrenia suggest that the synaptic elimination process is crucial to normal brain development (Armstrong et al., 1995; Cragg, 1975; Feinberg, 1982; Murray et al., 2017; Packer, 2016).

The synaptic pruning process depends on genetic and non-genetic factors, and it has been purported that those synaptic connections that are used and reinforced will evolve, while other idle synapses will not survive—i.e., *Hebbian Synapses* (Hebb, 1949). Using brain imaging (fMRI), Pallier et al. (2003) found that adults exposed to a native language during childhood, but were adopted and subsequently reared with a second language, did not show specific cortical activation when exposed to their native language. They interpreted these findings as supporting the notion that brain plasticity for language progressively closes as networks for language stabilize. In other words, plasticity for language is available during childhood, but if the language is not used, the brain does not appear to show evidence of exposure to the language over time. Similar assertions have been made with regard to the ability to play a musical instrument. The Suzuki method, for example, stresses the importance of training in early childhood. Elbert et al. (1995) compared the size of the area of the right hemisphere somatosensory cortex that controls finger movements on the left hand and found that this region was significantly larger in adults who had begun playing the violin in childhood. These studies suggest that there is a relationship between size and function of a given area of the cortex and that early childhood experiences can facilitate the synaptic connections among neurons. As will be seen in a discussion of brain plasticity to follow, early childhood experiences such as neglect and deprivation can also result in loss of synaptic connections as originally proposed by Donald Hebb (1949).

It has been estimated that the human brain contains more than 100 trillion synapses, and the number of synapses for both men and women declines as part of the normal aging process. Synaptic decline is also characteristic of neurodegenerative disorders and will be discussed in Chapter 4. Several factors have been found to affect neurogenesis and synaptogenesis throughout the life span in other animals and possibly humans, including regular aerobic exercise, neurotrophins, dietary sufficiency, sleep deprivation, and others (Dietrich, Andrews, & Horvath, 2008; Simor et al., 2017). A direct relationship does not exist, however, between anatomical brain size and function. For example, on average, male brains tend to be 10% larger than female brains, but larger brains are not predictive of higher cognitive capabilities, such as intelligence. Albert Einstein's brain was in the low average range for weight (Diamond et al., 1985), and some individuals who have had an entire hemisphere removed remain of average to superior intelligence (Smith & Sugar, 1975; St. James-Roberts, 1981).

Apoptosis

In addition to an excessive production of synapses followed by synaptic pruning, neurons are overproduced prenatally and subsequently die off before and after birth, a process known as *apoptosis*. Neuronal cell death takes place both cortically and subcortically, although factors triggering and determining the extent of specific neuronal loss in each region is not well understood. It has been estimated that approximately 50% of neurons follow a programmed cell death, and this process continues during childhood and puberty (Durston et al., 2001). A number of factors appear to contribute to cell death, including lack of exposure to neurotrophic factors. When synapses are not established, neurons are deprived of neurotropic factors, substances believed to alter gene expression and regulate protein synthesis, and cell death follows (Cheng et al., 2014; Huang & Reichardt, 2001; Pettmann & Henderson, 1998). The purpose of programmed cell death and synaptic pruning is not fully understood, although scientists have hypothesized that an overproduction of neurons and subsequent competition for synapses increase the likelihood that an appropriate number and degree of complexity among synapses will be achieved (Gordon, 1995). Huttenlocher (2002, p. 80) suggested that apoptosis removes unnecessary cell populations, resulting in more efficient connections among neurons.

Environmental factors are also thought to contribute to cellular changes and apoptosis. For example, current research suggests that general anesthetics during infancy are associated with increased apoptosis, pathological neurogenesis, alterations in dendritic formation, and possibly memory changes in adulthood (Loepke & Soriano, 2008). In an ongoing longitudinal study, McCann and de Graff (2017), however, did not find neurocognitive differences in children at 2 years of age who had been exposed to general versus regional anesthesia during infancy, although possible longer-term effects are yet to be determined. Researchers are, however, actively exploring ways to prevent and reduce the neurotoxic effects of general anesthesia. Hua and colleagues (2016), for example, found that neonatal rat pups pretreated with a flavonoid (naringenin) prior to a commonly used general anesthetic in children and adults (isoflurane) had substantially less apoptosis and significant improvements in learning capacity and memory retention. These findings may aid in the development of strategies to lessen the neurotoxic effects of anesthesia in both children and adults.

Postnatal Brain Growth and Neuroplasticity

During prenatal development, the brain produces approximately 250,000 neurons per minute (Cowan, 1979), and at birth, the brain has accumulated billions of neurons and glial cells. Glial cells continue to reproduce throughout childhood and adulthood (von Bartheld, Bahney, & Herculano-Houzel, 2016). Reproduction of neurons (neurogenesis) was believed to be complete before birth; however, Eriksson and colleagues (1998) discovered neurogenesis in the hippocampus of adult humans. More recent research has substantiated that neurogenesis also occurs in the olfactory bulb of humans after birth (Angelova, Tiveron, Cremer, & Beclin, 2018; Hanson et al., 2017). It is possible that scientists will discover neurogenesis in other brain regions, and efforts are underway to develop methods to promote neurogenesis, which would have obvious implications for treatment of neurodegenerative diseases as well as psychiatric disorders, such as anxiety and depression.

At birth, the newborn's brain is nearly two-thirds the adult size but only 25% of the adult weight. After age 5, however, total brain size does not increase significantly. The brain's weight, however, increases fourfold from birth to 10 years (Webb, Monk, & Nelson, 2001). The postnatal increase in the brain's volume and weight is due to a number of factors, including proliferation and maturation of glial cells, synaptogenesis, myelination of axons, and maturation of neurons characterized by axonal development and dendritic expansion. As noted by Huttenlocher (1979), the morphology of neurons and the connections among neurons, especially at the level of the cortex, are immature at birth, and these connections increase dramatically shortly after birth. For example, Webb et al. (2001) reported that the length of dendrites in the prefrontal cortex increases five to ten times during the first six months (postnatal). Buell and Coleman (1981) found that dendrites continue to grow and elongate throughout adulthood, even late adulthood, and Petanjek and colleagues (2011) found that elimination of dendritic spine density continues into adulthood. Growth of axons and increased complexity of synaptic connections also characterize cell maturation. Different regions of the cortex mature at different rates and, based on anatomical and neuroimaging studies, the prefrontal cortex appears to be the last region to mature, and maturation plays an important role in the development of memory formation (Huttenlocher, 1979; Tang, Shafer, & Ofen, 2017). Synaptogenesis is also associated with brain function during child development, including memory formation and language abilities (Kozuka et al., 2017; Tang et al., 2017). Changes in the motor system is obviously correlated with brain maturation as infants and toddlers pass through predictable developmental milestones, such as sitting unassisted, crawling, walking, and so on.

Developmental changes also occur with respect to the ratio of white matter (*myelinated axons*) to gray matter (*cell bodies*). Webb et al. (2001), for example, reported that whereas at birth 50% of the total brain volume is composed of gray matter, gray matter decreases substantially with age due to neuronal death and pruning of synapses. During early childhood and into adolescence, there is a rapid increase in the percentage of gray matter, peaking at puberty and followed by selective elimination (Rapoport et al., 1999; Luby et al., 2013). White matter has been found to increase substantially prenatally, and according to Huppi et al. (1998), there is a fivefold increase in prenatal white matter between 29 and 41 weeks. The trajectory of the development of white and gray matter, however, is influenced by a number of factors, including genetics, sex, IQ, hormonal, and environmental factors (Lenroot et al., 2009).

Postnatally, myelination of axons increases in the cortex throughout childhood and adolescence, and levels off during late adolescence, but continues throughout life (de Faria, Pama, Evans, Luzhynskaya, & Káradóttir, 2018; Klingberg et al., 1999; Sowell et al., 1999; Tokumaru et al., 1999). MRI studies have shown that several areas of the cortex are myelinated at birth and myelinate rapidly within a few months after birth (e.g., visual system, somatosensory cortex). Other regions, such as the prefrontal cortex, myelinate more slowly, and the process continues into young adulthood (de Faria et al., 2018; Kinney et al., 1998). Recently, Friedrichs-Maeder and colleagues (2017) advanced a computation model describing the interdependent relationship between the development of white and gray matter extending in a hierarchical manner from subcortical to cortical regions. These findings support that myelination and gray matter are clearly related to brain function in infancy and childhood are may also be associated with cognitive capabilities later in life. Green, Kaye, and Ball (2000) and Cai, Dong, and Niu (2018), for example, examined the postmortem brains of 19 men and women ages 85–104 years and reported that those who remained cognitively unimpaired showed very few changes in white matter, neuronal, and glial cell density.

Factors Influencing Brain Development

It is generally accepted that prenatal brain development is initiated as a result of genetic factors, but environmental factors play a significant role during prenatal and postnatal development (Huttenlocher, 1994). The relative contributions of genetic and environmental influences on brain development remain unclear. For example, the appearance and functional organization of the brain from the cortex to subcortical structures are similar across individuals. Humans vary tremendously, however, with respect to their personalities as well as their cognitive and behavioral capabilities. As Joseph LeDoux (2002) suggested, "The key to individuality, therefore, is not to be found in the overall organization of the brain, but rather in the fine-tuning of the underlying networks" (p. 36). In other words, the connections between neurons may define individuality, and these connections are influenced greatly by environmental experiences, particularly after birth. Research has demonstrated that environmental experiences can have profound negative *and* positive effects on the structure of the brain. For example, it has been well established that toxic substances, such as alcohol, can have deleterious effects on a developing embryo or fetus, interrupt normal brain functioning, and perhaps permanently damage the corpus callosum, as is seen in fetal alcohol syndrome (Bookstein et al., 2002; McEwen and Sapolsky, 1995). Others have postulated that children who are maltreated may have elevated levels of stress hormones (e.g., cortisol) that are toxic to the hippocampus due to the large number of cortisol receptors located on this structure, as well as chronic alterations in hypothalamic-pituitary axis (Heim et al., 2010). Kolb and Gibb (2011) concluded that sensory stimuli, diet, stress, hormones, and drugs all affect the developing brain in very different ways and across individuals. Recently, Luby and colleagues (2016) conducted a longitudinal brain imaging study with preschoolers and followed them up approximately 11 years later into their school-aged years and assessed their brain morphology as well as their psychological functioning. Results revealed significant decreases in thickness of cortical gray matter and volume loss in children with significant symptoms of depression at nearly twice the rate of children without depression symptoms. These findings suggest that psychological and emotional factors, such as depression, may alter brain development.

Environmental experiences can also have positive effects on brain development. Research with other animals, for example, has shown that rats reared in enriched, complex environments show increased complexity of neuronal connections as well as superior task performance compared to rats reared in less stimulating environments (Greenough & Black, 1992). With regard to humans, Elbert and colleagues (1995) found that the area of the cortex that subserves the fingers is larger in musicians who play string instruments than in non-musicians. Certainly, the concept of rehabilitation following brain injury is based on the notion that environmental stimulation can affect brain functioning. The process of the brain's ability to change in response to environmental experience, whether positive or negative, is known as *plasticity* (Konorski, 1948) or *neuroplasticity*. Brain plasticity is often characterized by structural and functional changes at both the cellular (e.g., increased dendritic spines) and global (e.g., increased blood flow) levels (Greenough, 1988). During various periods of brain development, the brain is believed to be more plastic as more synapses are available to support developing functions. Plasticity declines in adulthood, but the brain remains capable of responding to environmental experiences throughout the life span (Stiles, 2000; Pascual-Leone, 2011).

Neuroplasticity

Kennard (1936) was among the first to systematically study plasticity with regard to the behavioral effects of brain injury in monkeys, and based on these studies, she concluded that the earlier in life brain damage occurs, the less severe the behavioral effects. Subsequent research challenged the Kennard doctrine and demonstrated that although in some cases brain injury in early childhood is associated with better outcome, usually the outcome depends on a variety of modulating factors other than age. For example, Kolb (1989) was among the first to identify and study factors such as intelligence, handedness, sex, location and severity of the damage, environmental experiences, and type of assessment techniques and concluded that all of these factors can influence the behavioral effects of the brain damage. Kolb's work as well as others substantiated that individuals can suffer the same type of brain damage but the effects resulting from the damage may vary significantly due to mediating variables.

For decades, the bulk of information on neuroplasticity derived from studies of other animals. These studies were conducted with monkeys, chimpanzees, rats, mice cats, dogs, rabbits, and other animals. Plasticity research with other animals has decreased relative to years past; however, animal models continue to be used in the study of brain plasticity. Although a variety of methods are used, studies often involve molecular or genetic alterations, lesioning part or parts of the brain, and/or altering the environment, and observing the subsequent anatomical, physiological, and/or behavioral effects. In general, results from these studies have demonstrated that the brain has the ability to reorganize its connections depending on a large number of factors, such as the age and sex of the animal, location and severity of the damage, and environmental conditions. A limitation with this body of literature is that the brains of other animals are not morphologically or functionally the same as the human brain. As Huttenlocher (2002, p. 113) stated, "The newborn monkey brain is not a good model in which to study the likely effects of cortical lesions in human neonates", and further added, "the results obtained in lesions made in a 2 or 3 month old monkey therefore have limited relevance to the study of plasticity related to perinatal brain lesions in humans". Therefore, although voluminous information is available concerning neuroplasticity in other animals, the following section focuses primarily on the human literature to date.

Traumatic Brain Injury

According to the Centers for Disease Control (CDC), everyday 153 people in the United States die from injuries that involve a traumatic brain injury (TBI) (Taylor et al., 2017). Men have more than twice the rate of TBI-related deaths than women, and the causes of injury associated with TBI-related deaths vary by age group. For example, TBI-related deaths in children 0–4 years are primarily associated with assault (42.9%) and automobile accidents (29.2%). Motor vehicle accidents account for a majority of TBI-related deaths in youths 5–14 years (55.8%) and nearly half (47.4%) of TBI-related deaths in young adults 15–24 years. In adults 65 years of age and older, falls account for the majority (54.4%) of TBI-related deaths (CDC, 2016). Unfortunately, TBI is a relatively common injury experienced by military service members (Armistead-Jehle et al., 2017). Teenagers are also at increased risk for TBI, as Veliz (2017) recently reported that one out of five teenagers have had one concussion in their lifetime, and 5% have had two or more concussions.

A TBI is an insult to the brain that disrupts normal brain functioning and results in temporary or sustained impairments in cognitive, emotional, behavioral, or physical functioning. TBI is classified by severity level (mild, moderate, severe) based on a number of criteria, including the level of consciousness, the presence of post-traumatic amnesia, and the Glasgow Coma Scale (Werner and Engelhard, 2007). The Glasgow Coma Scale uses a 3- to 15-point scale to assess a patient's level of consciousness and neurologic functioning. Scoring is based on best motor and verbal response, as well as eye opening (e.g., opening upon command). Mild TBI, typically characterized by short-term memory and attention impairments, accounts for the majority of TBI cases; however, recent research supports that repetitive mild TBIs (e.g., contact sports and military events) can lead to significant long-term emotional and cognitive disabilities (Levin & Robertson, 2012).

During TBI, secondary injury effects emerge that include cellular injury mechanisms and systemic complications that occur over the course of hours to several weeks following the primary injury. Systemic complications may include swelling of brain tissue leading to increased intracranial pressure (ICP) and bleeding or hemorrhaging. All of these complications can lead to decreased blood flow to the brain (ischemia) leading to a poor supply of oxygen and nutrients needed for proper cellular function. Restricted blood flow can result in cerebral infarction or ischemic stroke, leading to the death of brain cells. Impaired blood flow in turn initiates a cascade of harmful events, including excessive release of glutamate and calcium, ions that can be toxic and ultimately fatal to other neurons and glial cells (Stein, Brailowsky, & Will, 1995). Internal structural processes of neurons are also affected by TBI, including mitochondria function and structural stability of the cytoskeleton, both of which can lead to cell death (Singleton, 2004). As cells die, free radicals are released into the extracellular fluid, causing further damage to surviving neurons and glial cells, leading to the release of inflammatory proteins. TBI can also result in demyelination and structural damage to axons as well as abnormal reactivity of astrocytes leading to blood-brain barrier dysfunction (Burda, Bernstein, & Sofroniew, 2016; Julliene et al., 2016). TBI-induced inflammation can also result in overactivity of phagocytic microglial (autophagy), leading to the death of healthy cells as well as reduced production of neurotrophic factors (Cherry, Olschowka, & O'Banion, 2014). These processes can result in rapid neuronal and glial cell death through programmed and necrotic cell death.

The effects of the injury vary depending on the location and severity of the injury as well as other factors such as age and timing of treatment interventions (Watanabe, Miller, & McElligott, 2003). Taylor et al. (2002) reported that the behavioral and academic outcomes were poorer for children with moderate to severe TBI. They also found that family factors moderated the long-term effects of TBI, and unfavorable family circumstances (high stress, economically disadvantaged) were associated with a poorer prognosis. More recently, brain imaging techniques have allowed the detection of white matter tract damage in even mild to moderate cases of TBI that may be associated with longer-term cognitive effects observed repetitive mild TBI cases (Bramlett & Deitrich, 2015; Ojo et al., 2016).

Research indicates that participation in a rehabilitation program enhances the rapidity and extent of recovery following TBI (Cope, 1995). As with plasticity in general, the precise mechanisms responsible for recovery are not well understood, and there is tremendous variability in methods used in rehabilitation programs to treat TBI. One method, constraint induced movement therapy (CIMT), has been found to improve the functional capabilities of brain injury victims (Taub et al., 1993). CIMT involves constraining the unaffected extremity and gradually inducing patients to use the affected limb. Kunkel et al. (1999), for example, investigated cortical activity of stroke patients following CIMT. Results indicated substantial reorganization of motor areas in the hemisphere that controlled the unaffected limb, and this was correlated to recovery of movement in the affected limbs. Modified versions of CIMT have recently been studied and found effective in increasing limb function short and long term (Doussoulin et al., 2017). Bilateral training has also been used with stroke victims to avoid loss of strength and range of motion in the unaffected limb. Results by Whitall et al. (2000) have supported the use of this rehabilitation technique at improving strength and range of motion in both the affected and unaffected limbs. Regardless of the intervention method, research indicates that rehabilitation should begin shortly after the injury to increase the likelihood of greater recovery (Gonzalez-Rothi, 2001). The neurophysiological basis of rehabilitation is uncertain, but as Gonzalez-Rothi described, recovery of behavioral and cognitive function is likely the result of focusing on specific and desired behaviors, and providing a stimulating, enriched environment that leads to synaptic and neuronal changes (see Dobkin, 2003 for a review). Taub, Uswatte, and Elbert (2002) noted that although historically the field of rehabilitation has been disconnected from neuroscience, recent discoveries in behavioral neuroscience—particularly with regard to plasticity—will likely lead to more effective intervention techniques to enhance recovery following brain injury. Galetto and Sacco (2017) recently conducted a systematic review of studies published between 1985 and 2016 concerning functional neuroplasticity induced by cognitive rehabilitation following TBI and concluded that rehabilitation results in neural reorganization of brain networks regardless of the severity of the injury.

Brain Injury—Stroke

Strokes are sudden disruptions to the blood supply to the brain by either a blockage or hemorrhage that cause damage to brain cells. Bleeding in the brain (cerebral hemorrhage) can result from structural problems in the brain's arteries, hypertension, rupture of aneurysms, exposure to toxic chemicals, or blood disease. Blockage of blood vessels in the brain is due to thrombosis or embolism. Thrombosis occurs when a substance forms a plug that blocks blood flow. When a plug moves to a different location and forms a blockage, it is known as an embolism. The loss of blood flow to the brain restricts the supply of oxygen and glucose to brain tissue and consequently results in damage and death of brain cells. In addition, neurons in damaged areas tend to fire excessively, releasing the neurotransmitter glutamate. This excessive release of glutamate is toxic to neurons, triggers a cascade of molecular events, and results in further cellular death. Dying cells spill their contents into the affected region, causing additional damage. Tissue plasminogen activator (t-PA), a medication approved by the FDA in 1996 for the treatment of ischemic strokes, dissolves blood clots and helps to restore blood flow to the brain. The medication also diminishes the subsequent degree of brain damage if administered properly. In order to be effective, t-PA needs to be administered within three hours of the onset of the stroke (Katzan et al., 2000).

The specific effects of a stroke vary depending on the region of the brain affected and the severity of the stroke. Compared to adults who suffer a stroke, children tend to have fewer long-lasting behavioral effects such as facial weakness and difficulties with walking (Lenn & Freinkel, 1989). Approximately 50% of children experience chronic problems with speech, movement, and learning, but the effects tend to be mild relative to adult impairment (Walsh & Garg, 1997). Using neuroimaging, Blasi and colleagues (2002) discovered that the right hemisphere is capable of performing language tasks when the language-related areas of the left hemisphere in adults are damaged by stroke. They also found that, similar to healthy patients, individuals who had suffered a stroke in the left hemisphere became more efficient with language tasks over time, and this was reflected in decreased activity in the right hemisphere. The cognitive and behavioral effects of the stroke appear to vary significantly among individuals, however, as Delsing, Catsman-Berrevoets, and Appel (2001) were unable to identify a relationship between etiology, age, or gender and stroke outcome. According to Thirumala, Hier, and Patel (2002), the most powerful predictor of recovery is the severity of the stroke (Burda et al., 2016). A large study of stroke outcome found that patients reached their maximal improvement by three months regardless of the initial severity of their symptoms (Jorgensen et al., 1999). The mechanisms responsible for varying levels of recovery are not completely understood but likely include reorganization of neuronal pathways at the cortical and subcortical levels, modulation of new and existing synapses, generation of new cells (neurogenesis and gliogenesis) and blood vessels (angiogenesis), sprouting and growth of new axons, and the development of new motor networks (Azari & Seitz, 2000; Carmichael, 2006; Thirumala et al., 2002). The role of epigenetics in brain plasticity is also receiving attention among scientists who are studying cellular mechanisms following a stroke that may modify gene expression and ultimately lead to greater recovery (e.g., Felling & Song, 2015). Overall, research with stroke victims suggests that depending on the severity of the stroke, recovery is possible, and the physiological factors associated with recovery of function differ in children and adults. In general, children are less likely to suffer from chronic behavioral and cognitive effects of stroke, and their symptoms are often milder than adults. Child and adolescent brains are still developing and are therefore more plastic than the mature adult brain. Recent research has also found that the patient's and family members' attitudes and stroke knowledge were predictive of outcome, with patients' intention of independence positively affecting motor recovery, while family members' positive attitudes promoted cognitive regain (Fang et al., 2017). These findings suggest that age-related differences may exist in younger and older patients with respect to outcomes, and positive family attitudes toward independence may play a critical role in the recovery process.

Developmental Conditions

Lesions are injury-related changes in brain tissue that may affect functioning at various levels of development. A large number of factors may produce lesions early or later in life, and the timing of the lesions may have different behavioral effects. Brain injury that severely damages language-related regions results in permanent or transient language deficits in adults, but the prognosis is more positive in young children. Research indicates brain lesions that occur in infancy, prior to the onset of language, are associated with normal development of receptive language. Productive language (i.e., speaking) is usually delayed but subsequently progresses normally (Bates, 1999b).

Children who have had a hemisphere completely or partially removed (known as *anatomical* and *functional hemispherectomy*, respectively) due to drug-resistant epilepsy or brain diseases have been found to develop language in the intact hemisphere (Sperry, 1974). The degree of recovery and nature of impairment are variable, however (Curtiss & Schaeffer, 1997; de Bode & Curtiss, 2000). Research also indicates that children who have had the left hemisphere removed tend to have more problems acquiring and restoring their language, and the course is more prolonged than for children who have had the right hemisphere removed (de Bode & Curtiss, 2000). In adults, hemispherectomy leads to more severe language-related deficits (Ogden, 1996; St. James-Roberts, 1981). The physiological reasons for the disparity between child and adult outcomes of hemispherectomy are unclear, although several hypotheses have been advanced. Several studies have found, for example, that children tend to process language more diffusely, and language is not yet localized in the left hemisphere as is typically characteristic of adults (e.g., Mills, Coffey-Corina, & Neville, 1993; Ojemann & Schoenfield-McNeill, 1999). In addition, the child brain, relative to the adult brain, is thought to have more synaptic connections available for recovery and reorganization (Huttenlocher, 1979). Holloway et al. (2000) used fMRI to investigate sensorimotor functions of 17 children and adolescents (1–19 years) who had either part or the complete left or right hemisphere removed due to congenital or acquired brain disease. Results indicated that the somatosensory cortex of the remaining hemisphere was activated with both hands in all children regardless of the onset of the brain damage. These findings demonstrated that ipsilateral pathways had become activated, but the source of these pathways was unknown. Holloway et al. speculated that the ipsilateral pathways may have been present since early childhood but silent. After the hemispherectomy, however, the silent pathways may have become activated and strengthened due to demand. Alternatively, intact neurons may have sprouted projections from intact axons and created new pathways. Ivanova et al. (2017), using fMRI, found that following hemispherectomy in children, the right hemisphere revealed a functional network that strongly resembled right-hemisphere networks observed in controls. In other words, evidence was found for substantial reorganization of the right hemisphere that supported newly acquired language functions as well as previous functions ascribed to the right hemisphere.

Other evidence of plasticity comes from studies of individuals who were born deaf or blind, and those with reading disabilities. Neville, Schmidt, and Kutas (1983) examined cortical activity among adults who were congenitally deaf and of normal hearing, and results indicated that areas that were normally devoted to hearing were now devoted to vision in these individuals. Sterr, Elbert, and Rockstroh (2002) reported that the area of the somatosensory cortex that controlled the fingers was significantly larger in blind adults who were experienced Braille readers than a group of sighted adults who did not read Braille. They also compared the somatosensory arrangement in one-finger versus multi-finger Braille readers and found that the cortical arrangements were different in these groups. In a related study, Sadato and colleagues (1998) used PET to study the areas of the cortex that were activated during Braille reading in blind and sighted subjects. As predicted, findings indicated that different areas were activated in the two groups. Specifically, areas of the occipital cortex (primary visual cortex) were activated in the blind subjects during Braille reading, whereas areas of the somatosensory cortex were activated in sighted subjects. Sadato et al. (2002) later discovered that the age at which sight was lost was associated with areas of cortical activation in blind subjects during a tactile task. Specifically, an area of the visual cortex was activated in blind subjects who lost their sight prior to age 16, but this same area was suppressed in blind subjects who lost their sight past that age. Debowska and colleagues (2016) recently trained normal vision individuals for three weeks to read Braille exclusively by touch. Participants in the study underwent a brain scan before and after training, while performing a same-different discrimination task on Braille characters and meaningless characters. Findings revealed a large training-induced effect in the primary somatosensory cortex, including increased white matter and cellular activity.

The results of these studies support Ramachandran's (1993) hypothesis that reorganization of synapses at the level of the cortex is capable in the adult brain and that these changes can occur in response to environmental demands but may be mediated by other variables such as age. For example, Temple et al. (2003) investigated brain activation in children with reading disability before and after a remediation program that focused on auditory training and oral language training. Using fMRI, Temple and colleagues found increased activity in brain regions associated with reading following the remediation program. In fact, the investigators reported that the level of brain activation approximated that of normal-reading children, and these changes were correlated with improvement on oral language and phonological awareness tasks. These findings as well as those from other studies provide evidence of brain plasticity in childhood and adulthood in response to congenital or environmentally induced brain changes.

Amputation—Phantom Limb

A substantial body of research supports that amputation of upper or lower limb can induce functional reorganization in the sensory and motor cortices. Ramachandran (1993) was among the first to report that adults who had a limb amputated experienced sensations as if the limb were still present when part of their face was touched ("phantom limb"). The sensations reported by the amputees are diverse and may include feelings of warmth or cold, itching, tingling, and painful sensations (i.e. "phantom limb pain"). Ramachandran hypothesized that areas of the cortex devoted to the face invaded and took over the area of the cortex that had previously been devoted to the limb and hypothesized that "silent" synapses are present in the surrounding region of the cortex, and these synapses become activated or "unmasked" (Ramachandran, 1993).

Since that time, neuroimaging studies have documented morphological and functional changes at the level of the somatosensory cortex in phantom limb patients (e.g., Jiang et al., 2015; Ramachandran & Rogers-Ramachandran, 2000; Simoes et al., 2012; Yao et al., 2015). These changes emerge in amputees who report and do not report phantom limb pain and the extent of reorganization varies among individuals (Simoes et al., 2012). Studies have not found sex differences in reported phantom pain, although females have been found to report greater overall average pain intensity than males (Hirsh et al., 2010). In 2007, Ramachandran reported transgender individuals often describe their untreated sexed body parts as incongruent and aversive, and many experience phantom body parts of the sex they identify with (Ramachandran & McGeoch, 2007). Case and colleagues (2017) recently used brain imaging (magnetoencephalography) to record brain activity during somatosensory stimulation of a body part that felt incongruent to presurgical female-to-male transgender (FtM) individuals compared to a body part that felt congruent. Results supported Ramachandran's earlier reports as differences were found between transgender and nontransgender individuals with respect to brain activation patterns and in white matter connectivity in congruent versus incongruent cortical regions. The authors concluded, "The dysphoria related to gender incongruent body parts in FtM individuals may be tied to differences in the neural representation of the body and altered white matter connectivity" (2017, p. 1223). Phantom sensations have also been reported for other amputated body parts, including breasts, internal organs, and the rectum (Björkman et al., 2017; Dorpat, 1971; Ovesen et al., 1991).

What accounts for the phantom sensations? A number of morphological and functional changes, particularly in the somatosensory and motor systems, are believed to underlie phantom sensations, including cortical reorganization, white matter cortical thinning, axonal sprouting, synaptogenesis, microstructural changes in the corpus callosum and commissural fibers connecting the premotor cortices, and increased activation in brain regions involved in integrating multisensory information (Andoh et al., 2017; Brozzoli, Gentile, & Ehrsson, 2012; Jiang et al., 2015; Simoes et al., 2012; Yao et al., 2015). Preliminary findings also suggest that neurochemical changes at the cellular level may affect the integrity of the cell, including cellular metabolism following limb amputation (Cirstea et al., 2017). These cellular changes may contribute to the structural and functional changes, as well as the somatosensory sensations observed in phantom limb cases.

Deprivation Studies

Relative to other animals, few studies are available on the structural and functional brain effects of sensory deprivation in humans. Heron (1957) was among the first to study the behavioral effects of depriving young adults of nearly all sensory input. In this study, college students were paid to remain in an isolated, soundproofed room, lying on a bed with their eyes, ears, and extremities covered. Most participants became distressed after a few hours and very few could remain for the duration of the study. Several of the students who participated the longest (not more than 24 hours) reported having visual hallucinations. Grassian (1983) has written about the pathological effects of prisoners held in solitary confinement—perceptual distortions, hallucinations, delusions, generalized anxiety, and impulsive, violent behavior. Clark (2017) has recently argued that solitary confinement of juveniles is a form of child abuse.

Research on the physiological effects of deprivation in children is limited, but the available studies suggest that there are brain changes in response to reduced environmental stimulation. White and Held (1966), for example, studied reaching behavior and attentiveness in institutionalized infants reared in non-stimulating environments. By simply introducing a visual stimulus at 1 month of age, the infant's reach and visual attentiveness nearly doubled relative to infants not exposed to the stimulus. Chugani et al. (2001) used PET to study brain activity in human infants who had been reared in deprived conditions. Specifically, Chugani and colleagues studied 10 children (average age of 8) who had been placed in Romanian orphanages 4–6 weeks after birth and had resided in the orphanage for a mean of 38 months before being adopted. PET scans taken during an awake, resting state found that these children had decreased metabolism in several areas of the cortex, particularly the prefrontal cortex, relative to 7 children with epilepsy and 17 healthy adults. In addition, the Romanian children demonstrated mild neuropsychological, attention, impulsivity, and social skill deficits. The researchers hypothesized that these deficits may be a result of early and pervasive sensory deprivation that altered the development of the limbic system and the circuits that project to and from limbic structures.

Glaser (2000) reviewed the literature on child abuse and neglect, and concluded that child maltreatment induces stress in victims that may result in permanent dysregulation of brain structures and systems. Specifically, he suggested that child maltreatment can disrupt normal brain development in the region of the hypothalamic—pituitary—adrenal axis and the parasympathetic system. Impairments in these systems are associated with increased levels of stress hormones (e.g., cortisol, adrenaline) and over time may be toxic to hippocampal and other neurons. Carlson and Earls (1997) and Davies (2002), for example, found that children who were reared in Romanian orphanages showed abnormal cortisol levels, and these levels were associated with poorer performance on developmental screening tests. De Bellis (2001) argued that child maltreatment should be regarded as "an environmentally induced complex developmental disorder" (p. 558) that is often characterized by profound and long-lasting physiological as well as emotional effects. Bugental, Martorell, and Barraza (2003) reported that "subtle" forms of maltreatment (e.g., frequent spanking or emotional maternal withdrawal) during infancy and toddlerhood may alter the hypothalamic—pituitary—adrenal axis in ways that foster social-emotional problems, immune disorders, cognitive deficits, and sensitization to later stress. Balbernie (2001) suggested that childhood maltreatment interferes with normal development of the limbic system and connections with the prefrontal cortex, which in turn results in an impaired ability to regulate emotion and behavior. Supportive of Balbernie's work was a study by Opel et al. (2014) that found a strong relationship between child maltreatment and reduced hippocampal volume and depression in adulthood. Recent findings by Lutz et al. (2017) and others suggest that a history of child abuse has devastating and long-lasting changes to DNA and gene expression, and is associated with decreased myelin and cortical thickness in adults with a history of child abuse. This body of literature supports the implementation of early prevention and intervention programs for infants and children who are at risk for abuse or who have been abused to capitalize on the brain's plasticity and decrease the likelihood of abnormal brain development and possible long-term psychological effects later in life (Blair & Raver, 2016).

Enrichment Studies

The effect of enriched environments has been investigated in other animals for decades. Overall, the results indicate that complex environments, relative to simple environments, are associated with increased connections among synapses, dendritic and axonal expansion, and increased white and gray matter (e.g., Greenough, Withers, & Anderson, 1992; Fares et al., 2013). These physiological changes are associated with improved behavioral performance on learning and memory tasks in other animals and in humans. For example, studies have found that mice who had sustained brain damage and were then reared in complex environments performed significantly better on behavioral tasks than brain-damaged rats who were reared in standard, non-stimulating laboratory cages, and others have found increased production of neurotrophins in mice reared in enriched environments (Grinan-Ferre et al., 2016; Kolb & Elliott, 1987).

With regard to humans, Diamond and Hopson (1998) suggested that an enriched environment is one that is characterized by consistent and positive emotional support, stimulation that is multisensory, relatively stress-free, promotes exploration and active learning, is reasonably challenging, encourages social interactions, and practices good health care. Although these suggestions make intuitive sense, little empirical information is available about the relative contribution of enriching experiences to physiological changes in the human brain. For example, it is well established that the brain develops in a hierarchal fashion and that substantial growth occurs during early childhood and slower growth continues during adolescence and to a lesser extent during adulthood. The types, nature of experiences, and combinations of experiences that would facilitate optimal brain development at different stages of brain development are largely speculative, leading to a gap between neuroscience research and empirically based pedagogy. A number of researchers are attempting to bridge this gap by studying environmental-educational stimulation and behavioral and/ or cognitive gains. Campbell and Ramey (1994), for example, studied the effects of enrichment programs on the intellectual and academic achievement of at-risk children and found substantial positive behavioral effects. Huttenlocher and colleagues (1998) compared the language growth of children when school was in session versus summer vacation periods. Results indicated that there was a significant difference in language growth with greater performance during the school session (i.e., enrichment period). Physiological measures of brain functioning were not included in these studies, however.

More recently, brain imaging studies have revealed changes in brain morphology and function in response to educational interventions. For example, using fMRI, Dehaene (2013) studied brain responses to spoken and written language in adults of variable literacy (10 were illiterate, 22 became literate as adults, and 31 were literate in childhood). Results revealed that as literacy increased, increased activation and reorganization occurred in specific regions of the left hemisphere as well as the occipital cortex. These findings supported that both childhood and adult education targeting reading and writing can profoundly change cortical activity and organization. Executive function training and plasticity have also been investigated in children and adults. For example, Adnan et al. (2017) found that executive function training in adults 60–85 years resulted in improved attention and memory performance, and these improvements were associated with a pattern of enhanced activity in right frontal, parietal and temporal brain regions from pre- to post-training. Similarly, Park et al. (2015) examined the effects of an arts education on executive functions in children using fMRI and reported increased cortical thickness in the left postcentral gyrus and superior parietal lobule following the intervention. Other studies have investigated a variety of interventions on brain morphology including arithmetic, mindfulness, and social skills training (Peters & De Smedt, 2017; Tang et al., 2017; Valk et al., 2017). The morphological and functional brain changes associated with game playing have also been investigated in a large number of studies, including chess, video games, and juggling, as well as others (Gerber et al., 2014; Hänggi et al., 2014; Gong, Ma, et al., 2017). Cognitive training programs have become exceedingly popular for elderly care (e.g., retirement and nursing homes), although findings have been mixed in terms of effectiveness (see Tardif & Simard, 2011, for a review). Preliminary studies suggest that specific memory training programs can result in changes in brain activation patterns and may be effective at improving cognitive functioning in adults with mild cognitive impairment (MCI) or those at risk for cognitive impairment (e.g., Belleville et al., 2011). In terms of mobile application programs and cognitive remediation, in a recent review, McDonnell, Agius, and Zaytesva (2017) concluded that there is insufficient empirical evidence for any of the apps to be specifically recommended for cognitive remediation.

In summary, as a result of the recent discoveries in neuroscience concerning brain development and plasticity, numerous websites, apps, videos, and books have become available, touting methods to enhance brain functioning in general and specific processes, such as attention and memory. These methods are marketed at parents of infants, children, adolescents, and adults who are healthy or suffering from clinical disorders. Although the quest to optimize brain health has become a global business, empirical studies are sorely needed to explore the effectiveness of these methods.

Mechanisms of Neuroplasticity

Glial Cells, Dendritic Arborization, Axonal Sprouting, and Synaptogenesis

As mentioned previously, physiological studies concerning brain plasticity have been conducted with other animals, postmortem human brain tissue, and more recently with humans using a variety of physiologic and neuroimaging techniques. The mechanisms contributing to brain plasticity are not well understood but, as discussed in previous sections of this chapter, appear to involve a number of factors, including white and gray matter changes, proliferation of glial cells, dendritic arborization, increased dendritic spine density, axonal sprouting, increased myelination, cell metabolism changes, increased production and release of neurotrophins, altered neurotransmitter systems, synaptogenesis, neurogenesis, angiogenesis, and epigenetics (Table 1.4). Collectively, these factors result in the modification of existing synaptic connections and/or foster the development of new synaptic connections.

Unlike neurons, glial cells continue to reproduce postnatally and serve a number of functions that promote the development, maturation, and sustenance of neurons, including the production and release of neurotrophins. Glial cells have also been implicated in modulating neurotransmission through release of neurotransmitter substances. Dendritic arborization is characterized by increases in dendritic length, branching, and increased density of dendritic spines. Dendritic spines are located on dendrites and are the preferred sites for axon-dendrite synapses. Greenough and Chang (1988) demonstrated that dendritic spines show remarkable plasticity and can form synapses in hours and possibly even minutes after some enviromental experiences. Axonal sprouting occurs when neighboring neurons send off shoots to the damaged region and form synapses with remaining neurons that no longer have synaptic connections. This process is also known as *collateral sprouting*, and evidence of this process has been substantiated in humans and other animals (e.g., Ramachandran,

1993; Fritschy & Grzanna, 1992). As collateral sprouting advances, increased myelination occurs as well as increased synaptogenesis. Neurogenesis occurs in the hippocampus and olfactory bulbs, and angiogenesis involves the formation of new blood vessels that supply oxygen and nutrients to brain cells. The role of genetic factors in brain plasticity (epigenetics) is a relatively new but promising area of research.

The specific cellular mechanisms responsible for brain plasticity, specifically learning and behavioral adaptation are poorly understood. Research suggests that stimulation of synaptic pathways facilitates the maturation and strength of these pathways. The process by which this strengthening occurs is unclear but has been linked to *long-term potentiation* (LTP). LTP has been studied primarily in the hippocampus of other animals and refers to the increased excitability of a neuron in response to repeated stimulation. Increased excitability of cells over time is thought to result in more efficient communication among neurons. More efficient communication among neurons is associated with enhanced learning and memory (see Levitan & Kaczmarek, 1997, for a review) and has been described as a major factor in neural plasticity during childhood as well as adulthood (Huttenlocher, 2002). McEachern and Shaw (2001) have argued that the case for LTP and plasticity is weak; however, LTP may also be involved in neuronal pathology. As an example, they suggested that LTP in the adult brain may arise in response to injury or gene dysfunction and produce pathological changes in neuron numbers or connections. McEachern and Shaw also proposed that plasticity is the result of interactions across multiple levels of neural organization; however, these relationships and dynamics are poorly understood. More recently, researchers have begun to focus on proteins (e.g., Drebrin) that are involved with LTP and the regulation of dendritic spines and cytoskeleton of cells, and how the presence of these proteins may affect plasticity (e.g., Sekino et al., 2017). Neurotransmitters, such as serotonin, are also a focus of research due to other animal studies that have found that antidepressants (fluoxetine) result in increased excitability of cells, enhances axonal and dendritic reorganization, and promotes neurogenesis and angiogenesis (Sun et al., 2017). Finally, studies with mice indicate that sleep plays a crucial role in fostering synaptic connections and that these connections increase and decrease in size during sleep in response to daily learning (Tononi & Cirelli, 2014). Future studies will likely continue to unravel specific molecular factors involved in the brain plasticity as well as the complex relationships among these factors.

Table 1.4 Mechanisms of Neuroplasticity

- White and gray matter changes
- Proliferation of glial cells
- Dendritic arborization
- Increased dendritic spine density
- Axonal sprouting
- Collateral sprouting
- Increased myelination
- Cell metabolism changes
- Increased production and release of neurotrophins
- Synaptogenesis
- Neurogenesis within the hippocampus
- Angiogenesis
- Epigenetic changes

Medication, Neurotrophins, and Neurogenesis

Researchers have explored the role of various medications in facilitating plasticity with regard to recovery from brain injury (TBI). These medications include β-Adrenergic receptor blockers, acetylcholine agonists, stimulants, antihypertensives, hormones, erythropoietin (used to treat severe anemia), and a number of investigation drugs under clinical and preclinical trials. Although some of the medications are associated with decreased morbidity (Ko et al., 2016), and improved attention of children with pediatric brain injury (Kajs-Wyllie, 2002; Williams, Ris, & Ayangar, 1998), none have emerged as reliably effective at promoting neuroplasticity (Xiong et al., 2015).

Antidepressant medications have been found to promote *neurogenesis* in other animals as well as humans (Eliwa et al., 2017), although their role in promoting brain plasticity is unclear. Zhang and colleagues (2002) at the Henry Ford Health Science Center in Detroit, for example, discovered that mice that were treated with sildenafil (Viagra) for six days following an induced stroke showed new blood vessel growth and an increase in dendritic arborization, as well as synaptic connections. Compared to mice that had not received the drug, Viagra-treated mice performed significantly better on behavioral and health measures. More recently, Uthayathus and colleagues (2013) found enhanced synaptic plasticity and memory performance in mice treated with sildenafil, and Zhang et al. (2012) found that sildenafil enhanced neurogenesis and oligodendrogenesis in middle-age mice who endured ischemic stroke. Although there were approximately 1.7 million prescriptions for Viagra/sildenafil in the United States in 2015, the implications of this drug for brain plasticity in humans are unknown. Scientists will likely continue to strive to develop medications that promote neurogenesis, angiogenesis, oligodendrogenesis, and synaptogenesis in an effort to foster brain plasticity following TBI or in the treatment of neurodegenerative disease.

Neurotrophins

Neurotrophins are substances that are thought to play an important role in brain plasticity by promoting the sustenance-surviving neurons and synaptogenesis. Several types of neurotrophins have been identified such as nerve growth factor (NGF), neurotrophin 3 (NT-3), transforming growth factor (TGF), epidermal growth factor (EGF), and Mesencephalic astrocyte-derived neurotrophic factor (MANF) but perhaps the most widely studied is brain-derived neurotrophin factor (BDNF) (Kowiański et al., 2017). Neurotrophins are produced by neurons and glial cells but relatively little is known about the dynamics of neurotrophins or the factors that regulate their production and release (Schuman, 1999). Altar and colleagues (1997) demonstrated that BDNF is widely distributed in the rat brain and in nerve terminals, and is produced in the cell body and transported to the nerve terminals where it is released. Thoenen et al. (1991) found that drugs that increased the amount of a certain neurotransmitter (GABA) reduced basic levels of NGF and BDNF, suggesting that the regulation of neurotrophins is at least partially mediated by the brain's neurotransmitter systems. Neurotrophins have been found to facilitate the development of immature neurons and to enhance functioning of mature synapses. For example, research with other animals and insects has found that neurotrophins help to regulate ongoing neurogenesis in young and adult rats (Wagner, Black, & DiCicco-Bloom, 1999), and speed up the neurotransmission process in hippocampal neurons (Messaoudi et al., 1998). Mice that have been genetically altered so that BDNF is reduced demonstrate learning deficits (Linnarsson, Bjorklund, & Ernfors, 1997), implicating neurotrophins in learning and memory. King, Heaton, and Walker (2002) found that chronic ethanol intake led to learning and memory deficits in mice, and these deficits were correlated with a significant reduction of neurotrophins in the forebrain and hippocampus. King and colleagues argued that compromised levels of neuro-trophins interfered with synaptic connections in the hippocampus and other regions of the forebrain, resulting in memory and learning deficits. Currently, the study of neurotrophins in other animal models of Alzheimer's, Parkinson's disease, and other neurodegenerative disease is a highly active area of research (Chen, Zhang, et al., 2017).

With regard to humans, a large number of studies have found reduced levels of neuro-trophins in postmortem brains of individuals with various disorders such as Alzheimer's disease, Parkinson's disease, and depression (D'Sa & Duman, 2002; Fahnestock et al., 2002; Momose et al., 2002). D'Sa and Duman (2002) suggested that medications used to treat depression may increase neurogenesis and modulate processes associated with the pro-duction and release of neurotrophins. Garzon, Yu, and Fahnestock (2002) suggested that decreasing levels of neurotrophins (BDNF) is an early symptom of Alzheimer's disease. Siuda and colleagues (2017) recently investigated BDNF blood serum levels in patients with Alz-heimer's, MCI, and healthy controls. Patients with AD had significantly lower BDNF serum levels compared to MCI and controls. An association was not found between depression symptoms and BDNF levels; however, age and education were associated with BDNF levels. BNDF levels were positively correlated with cognitive impairments. Galvez-Contreras and colleagues (2017) recently promoted the use of BDNF and other neurotrophins as clinical markers for the diagnosis and prognosis of ASDs and ADHD. Although a growing body of research is available concerning the role neurotrophins might play in the etiology of psychi-atric and neurodegenerative diseases, their use in treatment remains equivocal.

Protection and Metabolic Needs of the Brain

In addition to being encased in the skull, the brain is protected by three layers of mem-branes known as meninges. The outer most layer located closest to the skull is the dura mater ("hard mother" in latin). Just below the dura mater is the arachnoid layer—a layer that appears more delicate and weblike, hence the name. The third most inner layer that adheres to the surface of the brain is the pia mater. The space between the arachnoid and pia mater is the sub ("below") arachnoid space and this area contains cerebral spinal fluid (CSF). CSF is a clear colorless fluid that circulates within the brain and spinal cord, and consists primarily of proteins, glucose, and electrolytes. Its primary role is to protect, or cushion, the brain, but CSF is also involved in circulating nutrients and chemicals filtered from the blood and removing waste products from the brain. CSF is produced from mate-rial found in the arterial blood that filters through specialized cells (choroid plexuses) lining the ventricles of the brain (particularly the lateral and fourth ventricles).

The brain's blood vessels are surrounded by perivascular spaces that resemble tunnels. Extensions of astrocytes (feet) completely surround the outer wall of the perivascular space. Research has found that when arteries pulsate, they drive large quantities of CSF through the perivascular space. Some of the CSF enters through the feet of the astrocytes and is then propelled in the areas between cells, weaves through the brain, and picks up waste products from cells. This waste-filled fluid then moves into the perivascular space surrounding veins where it is absorbed and removed from the brain and enters the general blood circulation. This intricate cleansing system is known as the "glymphatic system" (Jensen et al., 2016). The rate of fluid flow through the glymphatic has been found to increase during sleep, and the malfunctioning of this cleansing system has been implicated in neurodegenerative dis-orders (Yulug, Hanoglu, & Kilic, 2017).

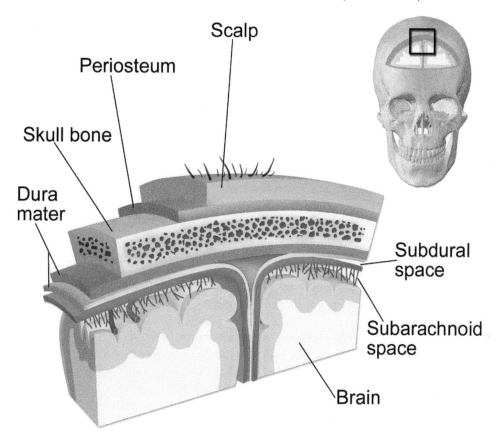

Scalp

Periosteum

Skull bone

Dura mater

Subdural space

Subarachnoid space

Brain

Layers covering the Brain

FIGURE 1.15.   Protective Layers of the Brain

Copyright Blausen Medical Communications. Reproduced by permission.

BOX 1.4   Brain Drain, Water on the Brain

CSF is circulated throughout the brain and is eventually reabsorbed into the body through a network of veins within the brain. In cases where the CSF is not reabsorbed at a normal rate, CSF builds up within the brain's ventricles, causing pressure, a condition known as normal pressure hydrocephalus. If the pressure is not alleviated, damage can occur to brain tissue, including neuronal networks. Cognitive and behavioral symptoms result, including mobility and urinary incontinence problems, as well as concentration, memory, and executive function deficits. Treatment requires decreasing the level of CSF within the skull and can be achieved with surgical placement of a shunt (catheter) into the lateral ventricle. The catheter is typically attached to a valve behind the ear, and another catheter extends down the neck into the chest or abdomen where the fluid is released and reabsorbed by the body (Saito, 2011).

The adult brain weighs approximately 3 pounds and comprises about 2% of the body's weight. Due to its high metabolic activity, it uses approximately 20% of the body's oxygen consumption in an adult (Sokoloff, 1989). Blood is supplied to the brain through the arteries on either side of the neck and up through the back of the skull (carotid and vertebral arteries). At the base of the brain, the carotid and vertebral arteries form a circle of communicating arteries known as the Circle of Willis. From this circle, other arteries arise and travel to all parts of the brain. Most of the brain's metabolism is used for cellular processes involved in neuronal communication. This high level of oxygen consumption continues 24 hours a day with very little decrease during sleep. If the cerebral blood flow delivering the oxygen is interrupted, then loss of consciousness occurs within seconds, and cessation of blood flow for a few minutes, can result in irreversible damage to the brain. Blood flow rates vary throughout the brain, with four to five times greater blood flow to gray matter compared to white matter regions, and altered blood flow patterns is associated with cortical thinning in cerebral vascular disease (Marshall et al., 2017).

Cerebral oxygen consumption changes with development, characterized by low levels at birth and unusually high levels during childhood. For example, Sokoloff reported that the brain's oxygen consumption at age 5 is greater than that of an adult brain. Specifically, the cerebral oxygen consumption of a child of 5 or 6 equals more than 50% of his or her total body basal oxygen consumption. This high level of oxygen consumption steadily declines during childhood and levels off during adolescence. Cerebral oxygen consumption corresponds to cellular activity, and the brain's primary fuel is glucose. Consistent with the high demand for oxygen during childhood, Chugani and Phelps (1991) and Van Bogaert et al. (1998), using neuroimaging (PET), reported that glucose consumption nearly triples during the first few years of life. Between the ages of 3 and 8, the consumption levels off and is reduced to approximately 30% above the initial high levels, and changes continue into adulthood. This high rate of glucose metabolism has been correlated with regions of brain development and behavior. Specifically, at birth, the sensorimotor cortex is highly active corresponding to survival behaviors, such as sucking and mobility of limbs. The prefrontal cortex is the last to mature and is associated with higher-order cognitive skills, such as hypothetical thinking, abstract reasoning, planning, and problem solving (Hemmingsen et al., 1999; Kolb et al., 2012).

Brain Metabolism and TBI

The role of brain metabolism indices has been studied in gauging brain metabolic response to illegal drug abuse (Bodea, 2017; Volkow et al., 1991) and as a predictor of outcome after moderate or severe head injury. Glenn and colleagues (2003) compared the cerebral metabolic rate of oxygen and glucose consumption, as well as mean cerebral blood flow in 49 patients with TBI. Results indicated that during the first 6 days following the injury, cerebral metabolic rate of oxygen consumption was one of the best predictors of neurologic outcome. These results support an earlier study by Kelly et al. (1997), who reported that an acute elevation in cerebral blood flow after TBI is necessary for recovery of cognitive and behavioral functions. However, it is also the case that after TBI, the ability of cerebral vessels to appropriately react to changes in arterial blood pressure (pressure reactivity) can be impaired, leaving patients vulnerable to increased or decreased arterial blood pressure. Research has also attempted to predict factors that lead to successful outcomes for individuals with TBI, with differences found between males and females in terms of cognitive, emotional, and vocational outcomes (Bounds et al., 2003). Recently, Chan and colleagues (2017) found that females with TBI, particularly females > 65 years, were more likely to have comorbid mental health and physical conditions than males. The most common comorbidities among *male patients*, regardless of age, were disorders of multiple injury and trauma (40.6%), the circulatory system (34.5%), mental health (31.8%), and the nervous system (29.8%). Among *female patients*, regardless of age, the most common comorbidities are related to the circulatory system (50.4%), multiple injury and trauma (39.7%), the nervous system (35.0%), and the musculoskeletal system (32.8%). An increased risk of psychosis has also been reported in patients with moderate to severe head injuries, with males at greater risk (Arciniegas, Harris, & Brousseau, 2003). In general, studies have found that individuals with mild or moderate/severe TBI are at increased risk for developing a psychiatric condition during the first year post-injury, and affective disorders are associated with poor functional outcomes in both males and females. Studies have also found differences between males and females with respect to brain anatomy and processing.

Sex Differences in Brain Morphology and Function

Prior to the development of noninvasive brain imaging technology, such as fMRI, studies focused on morphological differences between males and females with respect to overall brain size and specific structures. Regarding brain size, Durston et al. (2001) reported that on the average, the male brain is 10% larger than the female brain; however, males on the average are larger in body weight and size than females. Size differences between males and females have also been found with regard to specific brain structures. Although a complete review of these findings is beyond the scope of this chapter, studies have found, for example, that boys tend to have larger total brain size than girls beginning prenatally, and this difference continues postnatally (Giedd et al., 1996). Structural size differences have been reported between males and females, with some studies finding larger caudate, hippocampus, and globus pallidus in females and larger amygdala and greater gray matter percentage in several cortical regions in males (Dekaban, 1978; Schlaepfer et al., 1995). Females have been found to have a larger corpus callosum and greater gray matter percentages in several cortical regions relative to males (Shiino et al., 2017). Recently, Gennatas and colleagues (2017) published findings from the Philadelphia Neurodevelopmental Cohort Study investigating age-related brain changes and sex differences in a large sample of youth ranging in age from 8 to 23 years. Results revealed that gray matter density increased from childhood to young adulthood and females had lower gray matter volume but higher gray matter density than males throughout the brain.

Not all studies have found morphological differences between males and females, however. Witelson (1989), for example, examined 50 postmortem brains of males and females, and found that females did not have an overall larger corpus callosum than males. Size differences were found between males and females, however, in specific areas of the corpus callosum (males had larger genu and females had larger isthmus). Recent meta-analyses reported the left and right amygdala and the hippocampus in males and females did not differ in size, contrary to what is often reported in the literature (Marwha, Halari, & Eliot, 2017; Tan et al., 2016).

Some researchers have speculated that structural differences between the brains of males and females are related to functional cognitive differences (i.e., language and spatial reasoning) that have been found between the sexes. For example, Harasty et al. (1997) found that language-associated areas of the cortex were larger in females compared to males. Functionally, girls on average learn to read earlier than boys, which may be related to language-related brain processing differences or environmental factors or a combination of both factors. Shaywitz et al. (1995) investigated regions of the brain that were function-ally activated in males and females during a language task (rhyming). Results indicated that compared to males, females had greater bilateral activation of areas of the frontal lobe. Additional studies have also supported functional brain differences between males and females regarding reading. Although these findings may be due to a number of factors, they do suggest that males and females may process language differently, at least on some types of language tasks.

Others have speculated that structural brain differences may underlie other cognitive processes as well. For example, Frederikse et al. (1999) found that males had larger gray matter volumes of a particular area in the left parietal lobe (inferior parietal lobule). In females, however, this same area was larger in the right hemisphere relative to the left hemi-sphere. The meaning of this anatomical difference is unclear, but researchers have specu-lated that this region of the parietal lobe plays a role in spatial and mathematical reasoning. Recent neuroimaging studies have supported this hypothesis and have specifically impli-cated the intra-parietal sulcus in the perception of numbers and performance of arithmetic (Schel & Klingberg, 2017).

During the past decade there has been an exponential increase in the number of studies exploring functional brain differences between males and females, and a review of these studies is beyond the scope of this chapter. However, a large number of studies have reported sex differences in resting states, neural connectivity, fear conditioning, emotion recogni-tion, and visuospatial abilities. Differences in working memory performance have also been found between males and females, and have been correlated with differences in brain activation patterns (Zilles et al., 2016). A recent meta-analysis across 56 emotion-eliciting studies revealed distinct differences in activation in the medial prefrontal cortex, anterior cingulate cortex, frontal pole, and mediodorsal nucleus of the thalamus in men relative to women, while women showed distinct activation in bilateral amygdala, hippocampus, and regions of the dorsal midbrain, including the periaqueductal gray/superior colliculus and locus coeruleus (Filkowski et al., 2017). However, Scherf, Elbich, and Motta-Mena (2017) recently investigated the influence of biological sex on the behavioral and neural basis of face recognition in healthy, young adults, given that face recognition is an essential skill for navigating human social interactions equally in men and women. Findings revealed similar activation patterns in men and women, and the authors concluded that face recognition behavior is *not* inherently sexually dimorphic.

It is important to note that many studies investigating structural and functional differ-ences between the brains of males and females are fraught with methodological problems. Indeed, many of the studies are conducted with small samples, include only one sex or unequal numbers, do not address multicultural factors and ethnicity, and differ radically in the types of tasks and measures used to assess brain anatomy and functioning. In addition, anatomical differences often do not reflect functional differences as described previously in this chapter, and the origin of morphological differences is uncertain. Indeed, Luders and Toga (2010) noted that the presence, magnitude, and direction of brain-based sex differences strongly depend on a number of factors, such as the brain structure examined (cerebral cor-tex, corpus callosum, etc.), the specific brain feature assessed (cortical thickness, cortical convolution, etc.), the degree of regional specificity (global gray matter volume, voxel-wise gray matter volume, etc.), and whether measurements were adjusted for individual brain size. Given the previous discussion of neuroplasticity, daily living experiences likely affect the developing brain in ways that remain obscure but may influence findings of structural and functional studies. Lastly, it is crucial to note that structural or functional brain differences between the sexes are correlational findings and do not reflect causal relationships. In other words, it would be erroneous to conclude that morphological differences lead to behavioral differences when it is entirely possible that behavioral differences contribute to morphological (or functional) differences observed between males and females. Clearly, more research is needed to explore potential structural and functional brain differences *and similarities* between males and females, as well as the relevance of these findings.

Chapter Summary

The brain can be divided into three main regions: the forebrain, midbrain, and hindbrain. Brain development begins prenatally with the onset of neurulation and continues hierarchically postnatally. During the first two years of life, the brain has an overabundant number of connections among neurons, and these connections rapidly decrease in number during childhood and adolescence. Internal and environmental factors are believed to contribute to postnatal brain growth, including reproduction of glial cells, synaptogenesis, increased complexity of connections among neurons, angiogenesis, dendritic arborization, myelination of axons, and production and release of neurotrophins. The brain has the capacity to change structurally and functionally in response to stimulation or deprivation, a process known as neuroplasticity. Plasticity occurs throughout the life span, but, in general, the brain is more plastic prior to adulthood. Morphological brain differences have been found between males and females, but the meaning of these differences is unclear. Although there is no universally accepted theory of precisely how the brain functions, it is generally understood that the left and right hemispheres are lateralized in function, and the brain works as an interdependent system. The basis of this system is cellular communication, the details of which will be explained in the next chapter.

Chapter Summary: Main Points

Identify the major divisions and subdivisions of the brain and nervous system.

- The nervous system consists of the central nervous system (brain and spinal cord) and peripheral nervous system (somatic and autonomic divisions).
- Twelve pair of cranial nerves and 31 pair of spinal nerves connect the CNS to the PNS.
- The brain can be divided into anatomical directions and planes of section.
- The major divisions of the brain include the prosencephalon (forebrain), mesencephalon (midbrain), and rhombencepalon (hindbrain).
- The left and right hemispheres are connected by commissures.
- The forebrain is the largest division and contains the four lobes including the frontal lobe that contains the motor cortex.
- The parietal lobe contains the somatosensory cortex.
- The temporal lobe is involved in comprehension of language.
- The occipital lobe is involved in perception.

■ The limbic system is a set of interconnected structures involved in motivated behaviors.
■ The basal ganglia are involved in regulating movement and specific pathways are involved in Parkinson's disease.
■ Prenatal brain development is regulated by genetic and environmental factors.
■ Postnatal brain growth is characterized by structural and functional changes.
■ Neurons and glial cells are the two main types of brain cells.
■ Neuroplasticity refers to the brain's ability to change structurally and functionally in response to environmental stimuli.
■ Sex differences have been found in brain structure and function.
■ The adult brain weighs approximately 3 pounds and comprises 2% of the body's weight and uses 20% of the body's oxygen consumption.
■ The brain is protected by three layers of meninges: the dura, arachnoid, and pia matter.

Review Questions

1. What are the major structures found in the prosencephalon, mesencephalon, and rhombencephalon? What functions are associated with each of these structures?
2. Describe hemispheric lateralization. Describe evidence supportive of lateralization.
3. Distinguish between oligiogenesis, neurogenesis, synaptogenesis, and angiogenesis.
4. Define brain plasticity and discuss implications for stroke, TBI, amputation, deprivation, and enrichment.
5. Imagine you were asked to close your eyes and feel an object placed in your lap. You gently place your hand on the object and discover what appears to be the soft fur of a kitten against your fingertips. This information is sent via the peripheral nervous system via what type of neuron and which specific root of the spinal cord?
6. What is the name and number of the cranial nerve that is affected if you were unable to move your tongue?
7. Explain the difference between the brain's *gyri*, *sulci*, and *fissures*.
8. What is *contralateral neglect* and damage to which lobe is associated with contralateral neglect?
9. Where in the brain are the superior and inferior colliculi found? What role do they play in brain function?
10. Research supports that during the first one to two years after birth, synaptogenesis increases dramatically and is followed by a substantial reduction, or pruning phase. What are the implications of this information for parents, educators, and health care providers?

two

Cellular Function, Neurotransmission, and Pharmacology

This chapter reviews the principles of cellular function and explains the process of neurotransmission. Information is also presented on the specific types and general functions of neurotransmitters. The chapter concludes with an overview of psychopharmacology and its use in the treatment of psychological disorders.

Chapter 2 Learning Objectives

- Identify the major internal and external components of a neuron.
- Describe the main functions of the internal and external components of a neuron.
- Identify the major ions involved in the development of the action potential.
- Distinguish between depolarization and hyperpolarization.
- Identify types of presynaptic and postsynaptic receptors.
- Identify the main types of neurotransmitter substances.
- Describe factors that affect the release of neurotransmitters.
- Describe reuptake.
- Distinguish between exocytosis, pinocytosis, and endocytosis.
- Distinguish between agonists and antagonists.
- Define pharmacokinetics.
- Identify the main classes of drugs.
- Distinguish between agonists and antagonists.
- Describe the mode of action of commonly prescribed psychotropic medications.

Intracellular Components and Functions

As depicted in Figure 2.1, each internal component of a cell serves a particular function. The main structures include the cell membrane, nucleus, ribosomes, smooth and rough endoplasmic reticulum, mitochondria, golgi complex, cytoskeleton, and synaptic vesicles. The cell body is encased in a semipermeable membrane consisting of a double layer of lipid molecules. Embedded in the membrane are proteins that have a number of functions and serve an essential role in communication between neurons. The intracellular space of

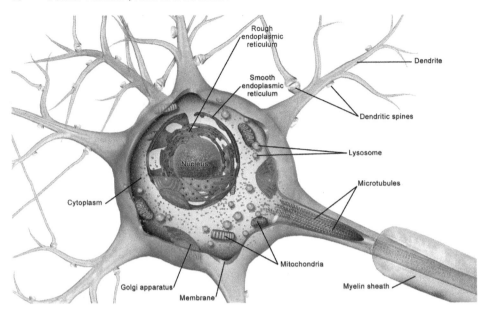

FIGURE 2.1. Internal Components of a Cell

Copyright Blausen Medical Communications. Reproduced by permission.

the cell is filled with cytoplasm; within the cytoplasm is the nucleus of the cell containing the chromosomes and nucleolus. Chromosomes consist of strands of DNA, and portions of the DNA—the genes—initiate production of messenger ribonucleic acid (mRNA). The nucleolus produces ribosomes, and ribosomes interact with the mRNA to synthesize proteins for the cell. The endoplasmic reticulum is of two forms: rough and smooth. Rough endoplasmic reticulum contains ribosomes that produce proteins to be transported within and out of the cell. The smooth endoplasmic reticulum plays an important role in the production of lipids and transports proteins produced by the rough endoplasmic reticulum to the golgi complex (or apparatus). The main function of the golgi complex is to assemble proteins and package them to be sent to other destinations. For example, some proteins are transported to the cell membrane, others are transported out of the cell, and larger molecules, such as neurotransmitters, are packaged in vesicles that are transported to the terminal button for release. The cell's energy supply is produced by mitochondria. Mitochondria produce adenosine triphosphate (ATP), which the cell uses as an energy source.

BOX 2.1   Rare Diseases: Role of Endoplasmic Reticulum

Heredity Spastic Paraplegias (HSPs) are a group of neurodegenerative conditions characterized by weakness and spastic paralysis of the legs due to degeneration of the axons of specific motor tracts in the brain. HSPs are caused by genetic mutations that encode proteins that formulate the structure of the endoplasmic reticulum. These mutations lead to degeneration of axons of motor neurons that form the corticospinal tract. Motor neurons of the corticospinal tract descend from the level of the cortex and extend the length of the spinal cord and are essential for proper limb movement. Degeneration of axons of these motor neurons leads to abnormal gait, difficulty walking, and progressive spasticity of the lower limbs (Fowler & O'Sullivan, 2016).

Strands of proteins maintain the internal structure of a cell by forming the *cytoskeleton*, and these proteins range in size from large to thin. The large strands are known as microtubules, and they extend from the cell body through the axon to the terminal button. Microtubules consist of tubulin proteins. Various substances and organelles are transported from the cell body by specialized proteins down the microtubules to the terminal button, a process called *anterograde transport*. Substances are also transported from the terminal button to the cell body along these same microtubules (*retrograde transport*). For example, mitochondria, lysosomes, and vesicles filled with neurotransmitter substances are transported down the microtubules to the terminal button via anterograde transport. Specific motor proteins (e.g., kinesin and dynein) bind to and transport substances down the microtubule to the terminal button and back to the cell body (Craig et al., 2017; Morris & Hollenbeck, 1995). According to a review by De Camilli, Haucke, et al. (2001), the movement of substances within a neuron via anterograde and retrograde transport can take anywhere from hours to several weeks depending on a variety of factors.

Proteins have also been found to stabilize the microtubules within the cytoplasm of the cell. One such stabilizing protein is tau protein. Overexpression of tau protein has been found to interfere with the internal trafficking processes of cells and significantly slows the transport of substances down the microtubules (Ebneth et al., 1998). Elevated levels of tau protein and mislocated tangled filaments of tau protein are believed to cause a gradual degeneration of microtubules and ultimately neurons, leading to cognitive impairment. Patients with Alzheimer's disease as well as other neurodegenerative diseases, for example, have been found to have neurofibrillary tangles of tau protein and elevated levels of tau protein compared to adults without the disease (Ji, Tang, & Johnson, 2017; Kahle et al., 2000). Felipo and colleagues (1993) also studied the role of microtubules in neuronal degeneration and found that toxic substances (e.g., ammonia) can interfere with the integrity and functioning of microtubules and the transport process. Tau protein is believed to play a critical role in stabilizing microtubule structures, and these networks become compromised in neurodegenerative diseases, including Parkinson's disease and Alzheimer's disease (Kurian, Obisesan, & Craddock, 2017).

The terminal button, located at the end of the axon, contains many of the structures found in the cell body (Figure 2.2). The terminal button contains vesicles filled with substances that are released by the cell and cause a reaction in nearby and, in some cases, distant cells. This process, known as *exocytosis*, will be covered in detail later in the chapter. At the other end of the cell body are dendrites. *Dendrites* are very thin, treelike structures of various shapes and sizes that emerge from the cell body of the neuron and receive messages from other neurons. Located on the dendritic branches are protrusions known as *dendritic spines*. Dendritic spines consist of a head-like structure, attached to the dendrite via a thinner stem or "neck". Dendritic spines change in shape and number depending on a number of factors, including neural activity (Torres et al., 2017).

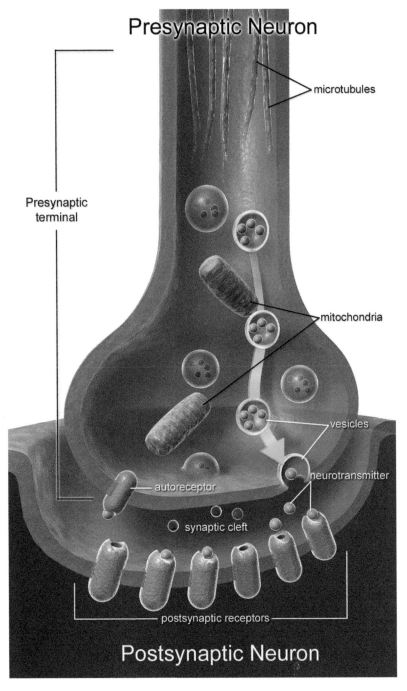

FIGURE 2.2. Terminal Button of Presynaptic Neuron and Cell Membrane Depicting Receptors of Postsynaptic Neuron

Dendrites and Synapses

As mentioned in the previous chapter, dendrites continue to develop and expand through-out the life span (i.e., neuroplasticity), and help to establish connections among neurons. As the principal reception sites for information from other neurons, each dendrite receives thousands of inputs from other neurons via synapses. The term *synapse*, first identified by Sherrington in 1897, refers to the site at which axons make functional contact with their target cells (Cowan, Sudhof, & Stevens, 2001, page vii). Specifically, a synapse is the space between the terminal button of a neuron sending a message and the area of a neuron that is receiving the message. Most synapses occur on mushroom-shaped dendritic spines that protrude from the shaft of the dendrite (Kennedy, 2000). Synapses can also occur on the dendrites soma, axon, or nonspecifically into the extracellular fluid; these synapses are known as axodendritic, axosomatic, axoaxonic, and axoextracellular, respectively. Other types of synapses are also possible, for example, when an axon terminal forms a synapse with a small blood vessel and releases chemicals such as hormones into the bloodstream (i.e., axosecretory synapse; Cowan & Kandel, 2001) (Figure 2.3).

BOX 2.2   Dendritic Spine Pathology

Abnormalities in the shape, size, and density of dendritic spines has been implicated in a variety of disorders, including Williams Syndrome, Fragile X, Rett's Syndrome, and Down Syndrome. A number of studies have found decreased density of dendritic spines as well as abnormally short and long dendritic spines in adults with Down Syndrome, and in those with Down syndrome who later developed Alzheimer's disease (Roizen & Patterson, 2003; Torres et al., 2017). It is estimated that 90% of adults age 60 and over with Down syndrome will develop Alzheimer's disease (Zis & Strydom, 2017). Defects in the shape of dendritic spines as well as increased density of spines is purported to affected normal synaptogenesis and is correlated with memory and learning ability in other animals. Genetic mutations such as deletions and truncations are associated with intellectual disability in a variety of conditions; however, the ways in which these mutations lead to alterations in brain development, such as dendritic morphology and cognitive functioning, are uncertain (Ka et al., 2016). No treatment currently exists to treat dendritic spine abnormalities. Torres and colleagues (2017) are currently investigating a protein secreted by astrocytes (thrombospondin-1) as a potential therapeutic agent to ameliorate dendritic spine pathology and improve cognitive functioning in individuals with Down syndrome.

Features of the synapse include the terminal button of the neuron ("presynaptic") that releases vesicles filled with neurotransmitter, the space ("synaptic cleft") between the pre-synaptic and postsynaptic neurons, and the receptor of the neuron that receives the message ("postsynaptic"). The synaptic cleft is small, with an average width of 20 nm, and contains protein filaments that are thought to stabilize the synaptic connections (Südof, 2001). Studies have found that synaptic connections change in size and appearance during specific cellular events (e.g., stimulation and long-term potentiation), and that the changes in the presynaptic

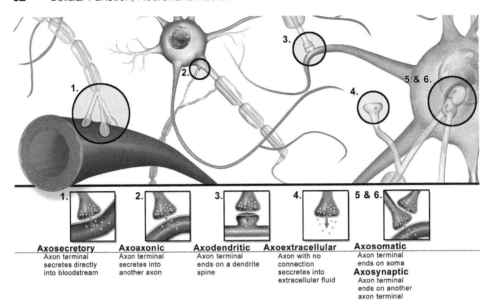

FIGURE 2.3.   Types of Synapses

Copyright Blausen Medical Communications. Reproduced by permission.

and postsynaptic sides are coordinated—that is, they enlarge and contract together (Toni et al., 1999). The molecular factors that mediate these synchronized changes and maintain synaptogenesis are fully not understood but appear to involve cell adhesion molecules, neurotrophins, and various enzymes (e.g., protein kinase, postsynaptic density-95) that promote synapse stability (Rothwell et al., 2017; Südof, 2001; Taft & Turrigiano, 2014).

Located on the dendritic spines are the receptors that respond to specific neurotransmitter substances and consist of protein channels that change shape (i.e., open and close) to allow the exchange of substances across the cell membrane (Figure 2.4). The pattern and distribution of these channels are diverse. For example, in some neurons, channels that respond to particles in the extracellular fluid, such as ions (particles that have a positive or negative charge, e.g., $Na+$, $K+$, Ca_2+), are evenly distributed along the dendrites. In other neurons, however, these channels may be present along the cell body but occur in very low density along the dendrites (Häusser, Spruston, & Stuart, 2000). Historically, dendrites have been recognized for their structural role in synaptic connections, but dendrites are now known to play an active role in processing the thousands of inputs they receive from other neurons (Häusser et al., 2000). For example, the distribution and density of dendritic spines and ion channels likely affect neuronal signaling, although the mechanisms are not well understood. Matus (2000) reported that the production of dendritic spines is influenced by environmental experiences, and that increased numbers of dendritic spines are associated with brain development, plasticity, and learning. Robinson and Kolb (2004) reported that exposure to drugs such as cocaine, nicotine, and morphine alters the functioning of neurons and neuronal systems by inducing changes in the structure of dendrites and dendritic spines. Recently, researchers have established that aerobic exercise increases dendritic spine density and is also capable of reversing dendritic spine loss in mice (Chen, Zhang, et al., 2017). Although many questions remain about the role of dendrites in neuronal processing of information, it

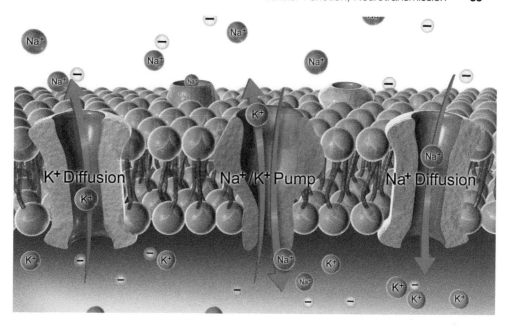

FIGURE 2.4. Exchange of Ions Across Cell Membrane

Copyright Blausen Medical Communications. Reproduced by permission.

Table 2.1 Structural Features of the Synapse

Presynaptic Neuron	Neuron sending message via neurotransmitter release.
Postsynaptic Neuron	Neuron receiving message.
Synaptic Cleft	Area between presynaptic and postsynaptic neuron across which neurotransmitter diffuses.
Dendritic spine	Protuberance on dendrite containing receptors in which neurotransmitter attaches.
Dendrite	A branched extension of a neuron along which impulses are received and transmitted to the cell.
Terminal Button	Bulbous structure located at the end of the axon from which neurotransmitter is released.

is well established that dendrites receive messages from other neurons and that these messages affect the distribution of energy across the cell's membrane. If the sum total of all of the synaptic inputs changes the cell membrane to a degree that an action potential develops, then the recipient neuron will send a message to other neurons.

Development of the Action Potential

Electrostatic Pressure and Diffusion

A neuron that is not actively communicating with other neurons is said to be at rest. When a neuron is at rest, particles called ions, which have either a negative (*anion*) or positive (*cation*) charge, are unevenly distributed in the intracellular and extracellular fluid (refer to Figure 2.4). Specifically, ions are distributed in such a way that the inside of the cell has a negative charge (–70 mv) relative to the outside of the cell. This is because the intracellular fluid contains organic anions not found in the extracelluar fluid (A–), which largely accounts for the negative charge inside the cell relative to the outside of the cell. The intracellular fluid also contains more potassium ions (K+) than the extracellular fluid and smaller amounts of cloride ions (Cl–) and sodium (Na+). The extracellular fluid contains larger amounts of Na+ and Cl– and smaller amounts of K+, and has a positive charge relative to the intracellular fluid. Because of this distribution, the positive ions outside the cell (Na+ and K+) are attracted to the intracellular fluid (with its negative charge). Negative ions such as Cl–, however, are repelled by the negative charge of the intracellular fluid. Within the intracellular fluid, negative ions (A–) are attracted to the positive charge of the extracellular fluid but cannot leave the cell because of their large size. Intracellular positive ions (K+) are repelled by the positive charge of the extracellular fluid. This attraction between positive and negative ions and the repulsion between like-charged ions produce energy in the form of electrostatic pressure.

Because ions are unevenly distributed inside and outside the cell, they try to *diffuse*. Diffusion refers to the tendency of molecules to move from areas of higher concentration to lower concentration until they are distributed equally (for example, think of a substance that is sprayed in the air—at first the concentration and odor is quite pungent or fragrant; however, the molecules quickly diffuse and are less noticeable). The only ion that is more abundant in the extracellular fluid *and* is also attracted to the intracellular fluid is Na+. Because of electrostatic pressure and diffusion, Na+ enters the intracellular fluid when the neuron is at rest. However, Na+ is pushed back out of the cell by the sodium potassium pump. The sodium potassium pump consists of proteins located in the cell membrane that actively and efficiently pump out the extra Na+ that has entered the cell and retrieve K+ ions that have leaked out of the intracellular fluid. To function properly, the sodium potassium pump uses a considerable amount of the cell's energy supply. Abnormalities of the sodium potassium pump as well as elevated levels of extracellular sodium have been implicated in clinical disorders such as bipolar disorder (Looney & El-Mallakh, 1997; Huff et al., 2010).

Depolarization and Hyperpolarization

An action potential develops as a result of stimulation to the cell that changes the permeability of the membrane to sodium and potassium ions. Specifically, a single neuron receives thousands of messages from other neurons. If these messages selectively open the Na+ channels on one or many parts of the cell membrane, then sodium enters the intracellular fluid (due to diffusion and electrostatic pressure), and the intracellular fluid becomes less negative—that is, it becomes more positive (*depolarization*). This reduction in the negative charge of the intracellular fluid is known as excitatory postsynaptic potential (EPSP) because it increases the likelihood that an action potential will develop. On the other hand, if K+ channels are selectively opened and K+ exits the inside of the cell, the intracellular fluid becomes even more negative. This increase in the negative charge of the inside of the cell—inhibitory postsynaptic potential (IPSP)—hyperpolarizes the cell because it decreases the likelihood that the neuron will develop an action potential. These excitatory and inhibitory potentials occur at thousands of places on the cell. Their net effect is integrated at the junction between the cell body and the axon known as the *axon hillock*, or the area adjacent to the axon hillock, the *axon initial segment* (Kole & Stuart, 2012). If the sum of the total depolarizations and hyperpolarizations is sufficient to depolarize the cell membrane to a certain point called the threshold of excitation (−65 mv), an action potential will develop. An action potential is a rapid and complete reversal of the neuron's membrane potential from −70 mv to approximately +50 mv, meaning that the inside becomes positive relative to the extracellular fluid, mainly because of the influx of Na+ (Figure 2.5).

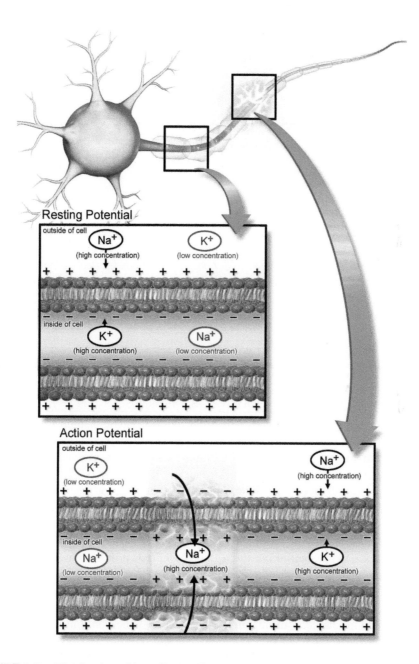

FIGURE 2.5. Distribution of Ions During Resting and Action Potentials

Copyright Blausen Medical Communications. Reproduced by permission.

An action potential lasts less than 1 millisecond until neurons are quickly restored to the resting potential. This is achieved by the outflow of K+ ions to the extracellular fluid after the threshold of excitation is reached. In fact, the outflow of K+ ions result in the membrane overshooting the −70 mv resting potential for a brief period during which another action potential cannot develop (*absolute refractory period*). Within a millisecond or two, the sodium potassium pump removes the extra Na+ ions from the intracellular fluid and retrieves the K+ ions from the extracellular fluid and the resting potential is then restored. In summary, an action potential is the result of a neuron receiving inputs from many presynaptic cells. The likelihood of a neuron developing an action potential is the net result of excitatory and inhibitory inputs to that cell. Once the action potential develops, the role of the neuron as a recipient of information changes to one of a transmitter of information.

BOX 2.3   Capital Punishment: Lethal Injection

According to the National Conference of State Legislatures (2017), capital punishment is legal in 31 states in the USA. Lethal injection for capital punishment was first implemented in 1982 in the state of Texas and is the primary method of execution. In most cases, lethal injection uses a combination of three drugs: (a) a sedative that induces unconsciousness such as sodium thiopental, (b) a muscle relaxer that induces paralysis and stopping respiration (e.g., pancuronium bromide), and (c) potassium chloride. It is actually the rapid influx of potassium chloride into the extracellular fluid ("hyperkalemia") that produces death by altering the membrane potential and inducing cardiac arrhythmia, and, subsequently, resulting in cardiac arrest (Parham et al., 2006).

Process of Chemical Neurotransmission

Transmission of information between cells occurs by two general methods: electrical synapses and chemical synapses. Electrical synapses involve the rapid movement of ions or molecules from the cytoplasm of one cell to another via gap junctions, such as are found in tissues of the liver and the lens of the eye (Levitan and Kaczmarek, 1997). More prominent in the central nervous system are chemical synapses, the focus of this chapter. Chemical synapses involve the release of transmitter substances that result in the depolarization or hyperpolarization of the postsynaptic membrane, as discussed. Neurotransmitter synapses also differ with respect to the number of synapses on a neuron; the type and number of receptors specific to the neurotransmitter; the biosynthesis process of neurotransmitters; the size of the neurotransmitter molecule; the type of neurotransmitter that is released from the terminal button, whether more than one type of transmitter substance is found within the cell; and the reuptake/deactivation process associated with the neurotransmitter.

As discussed in Chapter 1, during prenatal development, neurons migrate to a destination and immediately form synapses with other neurons. Within the axons of these immature neurons are synaptic vesicles containing neurotransmitter fluid. These vesicles coalesce in areas of the axon that will later form the presynaptic terminal button (De Camilli, Haucke, et al., 2001). According to Huttenlocher (2002), a developing neuron releases a neurotransmitter from a growth cone, and this neurotransmitter then induces a morphological change on part of the dendritic membrane of neighboring neurons. This part of the dendritic membrane develops into a receptor, and, according to Huttenlocher, the receptor will continue to respond to the neurotransmitter in the future. According to De Camilli, Haucke, et al. (2001), clusters of vesicles will not remain in areas of the axon that do not form synapses. Interestingly, neurons may be flexible with regard to the type of neurotransmitter that they will ultimately produce and release. Patterson (1978), for example, found that neurons that normally use dopamine as their neurotransmitter could instead produce and release acetylcholine if they matured in an environment that contained an extract of muscle that relied on acetylcholine. Craig and Lichtman (2001) described in more detail the maturational events that lead to the formation of receptors on neurons, which are found on all parts of the cell but primarily on dendritic spines.

Although the general process of neurotransmission is fairly well understood, many of the specifics processes remain theoretical. For example, questions remain concerning the details (a) by which vesicles fuse and release a neurotransmitter, (b) methods by which transmitter substances may interact and affect cellular communication, (c) how the terminal button membrane maintains it size and shape, (d) the formation and maturity of synapses in the human brain, (e) the role of neurotrophins in cellular communication, and (f) the ways in which lesser-known neurotransmitters contribute to cellular communication and brain function. Questions also remain about the role of genes and epigenetics in neurotransmission. For example, Cravchik and Goldman (2000) proposed that genetic diversity among human dopamine and serotonin transporters and receptors leads to neurochemical individuality, which can be seen in behavioral differences among humans. Others have suggested that maternal prenatal nutrition can affect gene expression, which in turn can lead to abnormalities in brain development thereby increasing the likelihood of schizophrenia in offspring (e.g., Kirkbride et al., 2012). Ideas such as these will certainly continue to be explored and unfold as technology advances our understanding of the interactions between genetics, epigenetics, environmental experiences, and cell communication.

The following section provides an overview of the processes involved in neurotransmission, followed by a discussion of transmitter substances and the effects of several classes of drugs at the level of the synapse.

Exocytosis

Traditional explanations concerning communication among neurons usually describe the release of neurotransmitters from the ends of the axon at the terminal button. More numerous, however, are neurotransmitters that are released from areas on branched axons called axonal varicosities (Vizi et al., 2010). These neurotransmitters diffuse and affect cells elsewhere in the brain and do not require close synaptic arrangements. From these axonal varicosities, described as beadlike in appearance, neurotransmitters, such as catecholamines (e.g., norepinephrine, dopamine), are released (Cooper, Bloom, & Roth, 2003). According to von Bohlen und Halbach and Dermietzel (2002), a single dopamine-releasing neuron can form up to 100,000 varicosities that synapse with other neurons.

When an action potential is produced, it is propagated down the axon through a process known as *saltatory conduction*. Saltatory conduction refers to the movement of an action potential from the node of Ranvier to the next node of Ranvier. Nodes of Ranvier are unmyelinated portions of the axon, and the action potential is regenerated at these nodes. When the action potential reaches the terminal button, a number of events occur that facilitate the release of a neurotransmitter. This process of release is known as *exocytosis*. First, the membrane of the terminal button depolarizes with the arrival of the action potential, triggering calcium (Ca+) to enter the intracellular fluid. The entry of calcium initiates a process that results in neurotransmitter release from vesicles contained within the terminal button. Large and small vesicles filled with transmitter substances (i.e., peptides and neurotransmitters) are located throughout the terminal button but are most abundant near the membrane. According to Betz, Bewick, and Ridge (1992), synaptic vesicles are adaptable and can merge to form large clusters. Typically vesicles filled with larger transmitter substances (*peptides*) are packaged in the soma and transported to the axon terminal, while vesicles that contain smaller substances (e.g., catecholamines) are biosynthesized and packaged in the terminal button (e.g., Gervasi et al., 2016). Their containment in the vesicles helps to protect neurotransmitters from degrading enzymes in the intracellular fluid.

Although the specifics of the neurotransmitter release process are still under investigation, research supports that areas of the terminal button membrane are *active zones*—i.e., some vesicles are believed to be "docked" at the membrane and ready for release (Lübbert et al., 2017). Entry of Ca+ and subsequent protein reactions are believed to cause the docked vesicles to fuse completely with the membrane and for at least one vesicle to spill its contents into the synaptic cleft (von Bohlen und Halbach & Dermietzel, 2002). Proteins (e.g., synaptotagmin) and believed to be important in facilitating fusion of a synaptic vesicle with the cell membrane by forming long and short tethers (Chen, Li, et al., 2017; Wang et al., 2001). Meanwhile, other vesicles migrate to the active zone area in preparation for release (Greengard et al., 1993). Although the details of this process are under investigation, it has been hypothesized that proteins play a critical role in providing structural support and serve as scaffolding for the reserve vesicles (Pieribone et al., 1995). Murphy et al. (2000) reported that a particular family of proteins (synuclein proteins) are involved in maintaining reserve pools of synaptic vesicles in the terminal button of neurons and suggested that pathologies in the synuclein proteins could lead to impaired synaptic function and degeneration of neurons. These findings may be particularly relevant to understanding neural degeneration in Parkinson's and Alzheimer's diseases, as studies have found synuclein proteins in plaque deposits in the brains of individuals with these diseases (Baba et al., 1998; Flores-Cuadrado et al., 2017).

Table 2.2 Neurotransmitter Precursors

Neurotransmitter	Precursor
Dopamine	Tyrosine
Serotonin	Tryptophan
Aetylcholine	Choline
Glutamate	Lysine

Neurotransmitter Regulation

Factors that help regulate the amount of neurotransmitter produced and released by a cell include *rate-limiting enzymes, autoreceptors, heteroreceptors,* and *vesicular transporters.* Rate-limiting enzymes are enzymes that essentially control the amount of neurotransmitter that can be produced. For example, when dopamine is biosynthesized by the cell, tyrosine is converted to dopamine by tyrosine hydroxylase. Tyrosine hydroxylase is found in all catecholamine neurons and is essential for the synthesis of dopamine. Increasing the level of tyrosine itself does not result in increased levels of dopamine. Manipulation of tyrosine hydroxylase by drugs, however, can affect the levels of dopamine that is produced. Thus, tyrosine hydroxylase is a rate-limiting enzyme. More detailed information concerning the biosynthesis of dopamine is presented later in this chapter.

Autoreceptors, special proteins embedded in the cell membrane and located on the presynaptic terminal membrane, cell body, and/or dendrites, respond to neurotransmitter released by that neuron. They moderate the amount of neurotransmitter released and generally decrease the synthesis and release of neurotransmitter (Hunt, 2000; Schlicker & Feuerstein, 2017). For example, when autoreceptors located on the terminal button are stimulated, they trigger feedback mechanisms to the cell (i.e., second-messenger systems) and transmitter production, and release is reduced. Drugs have been developed, for example, that target the dopamine system and stimulate autoreceptors. The result is that dopamine synthesis and release is inhibited. Drugs that block these autoreceptors increase dopamine synthesis and release (Cooper et al., 2003). The role of autoreceptors located on the soma and dendrites is less well understood, and their effect on neurotransmitter release is dependent on a variety of factors (von Bohlen und Halbach et al., 2002; Webster, 2001a).

Heteroreceptors are also located on the presynaptic membrane but respond to different neurotransmitters than the one released by the neuron on which they are located. According to Carvey (1998), heteroreceptors modulate the activity of neurons by influencing the increased or decreased release of neurotransmitters. Most research with autoreceptors and heteroreceptors has been conducted in other animals; their role in human brain functioning is not well understood. Schlicker colleagues (1998, 2017) for example, suggested that autoreceptors and heteroreceptors have complex interactive effects on neurons. Raiteri (2001) noted, "Due to the multiplicity of the proteins that seem to be involved in the exocytotic process, understanding their interactions with presynaptic receptors will be a formidable task" (p. 674). What can be concluded is that the regulation of neurotransmitter release is clearly influenced by presynaptic receptors, and these receptors play a role in psychiatric and neurodegenerative disorders. Neuroimaging methods are currently available that make it possible to study receptor distributions in the brain of living individuals by using substances tagged with tracers. These studies have provided valuable information concerning normal distribution of receptors, areas of neuronal degeneration, and target sites for therapeutic drugs for psychiatric conditions (Amato, Vernon, & Papaleo, 2017; Fritze, Spanagel, & Noori, 2017; Sedvall et al., 1986).

Vesicular Transporter Proteins

Small molecule transmitters are synthesized in the cytoplasm and then transported into the synaptic vesicles via vesicular transporters that are specific for each neurotransmitter substance (McIntire et al., 1997). Compared with transporter proteins that assist in the reuptake of neurotransmitters into the terminal button, less is known about vesicular transporters. *Vesicular transporters* are proteins that move neurotransmitters from the cytoplasm into the vesicles. Studies that have genetically altered the expression of these transporter proteins have found significant reductions in the amount of neurotransmitter stored in vesicles and released with exocytosis (Reimer, Fon, & Edwards, 1998). Vesicular transporter proteins exist for classes of neurotransmitters—for example vesicular monoamine transporters

(VMAT) for dopamine, norepinephrine, epinephrine, and for other types of neurotransmitters such as glutamate. The addictive properties of some types of central nervous system stimulants have been attributed in part to their interference with VMAT functions (Wimalasena, 2011). A recent study by Horváth et al. (2017) found that mice genetically altered to lack a particular type of glutamate vesicular transporter displayed heightened anxiety and fear relative to wild type (control) mice. Drugs such as methamphetamine rapidly decrease dopamine uptake into the vesicles and contribute to abnormal levels of dopamine within the cytoplasm, while MDMA (ecstasy) disrupts the vesicular storage of serotonin (Lizarraga et al., 2014; Sandoval et al., 2003). Chen et al. (2003) suggested that newly synthesized neurotransmitters (e.g., dopamine) are preferentially taken up into vesicles by transporters rather than preexisting neurotransmitters in the cytoplasm. The precise mechanisms involved in vesicular functioning including packaging and reuptake processes are currently not well understood, but vesicular transporters appear to play a role in understanding and treating psychiatric and neurodegenerative conditions.

Postsynaptic Receptors

After a neurotransmitter is released from the terminal button, it diffuses across the synaptic cleft and attaches to postsynaptic receptors. Postsynaptic receptors can be classified into two types: ionotropic and metabotropic. Activation of ionotropic receptors results in rapid, shorter-lasting effects, whereas activation of metabotropic receptors results in slower, longer-lasting effects. For example, the opening of an ion channel can occur in less than 5 milliseconds while activation of metabotropic receptors may take 30 milliseconds or longer (Hunt, 2000).

When activated by a neurotransmitter substance, ionotropic receptors directly open membrane ion channels, resulting in a rapid change in the membrane potential. Metabotropic receptors do not open channels directly but instead activate a series of intracellular biochemical events that may result in opening or closing of ion channels. Each metabotropic receptor is attached to a serpentine-shaped protein known as a signal protein. On the other end of the signal protein, located in the intracellular fluid, is a G protein. When a neurotransmitter (the first messenger) attaches to the receptor, it causes the G protein to break away, and this detached subunit either moves to a nearby ion channel, attaches, and causes it to open, or the G-protein may instead activate the synthesis of a second messenger. If the first option occurs—i.e., G-protein moves to a nearby ion channel and attaches—then the cell membrane will either become slightly depolarized (i.e., excitatory postsynaptic potential) or hyperpolarized (i.e., inhibitory postsynaptic potential). Depending on the effects of neural integration—that is, temporal and spatial summation—an action potential may or may not develop, and the neuron may or may not fire. Alternatively, if the G-protein subunit activates a second messenger, chemicals will diffuse throughout the cytoplasm and initiate changes in the cell's DNA or metabolic activity, or cause ion channels on the membrane to open or close (Figure 2.6). Examples of second messengers include cyclic AMP, cyclic GMP, and calcium, all of which can trigger changes in the cell, such as increased protein production, structural and functional changes in cell membranes, and apoptosis.

Research has found that postsynaptic receptors are adaptive and can increase in number ("up-regulation") if a substance such as a drug blocks the receptor for an extended period of time (e.g., a dopamine antagonist such as an antipsychotic) (Cooper et al., 2003). Postsynaptic receptors (and presynaptic) can also decrease in number ("down-regulation") if a stimulus is frequently or chronically present, such as cocaine or methamphetamine, both

Example of a Second-Messenger System

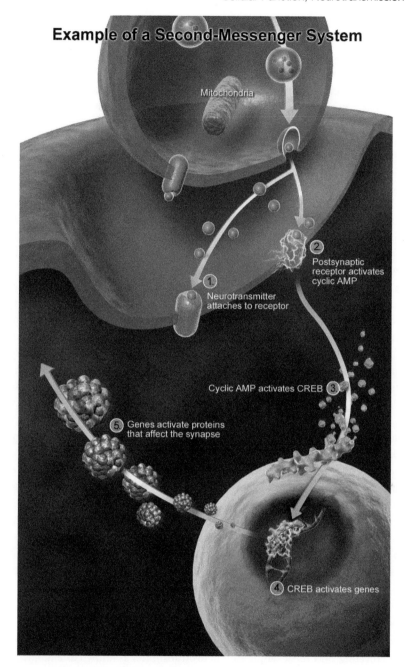

Mitochondria

(1.) Neurotransmitter attaches to receptor

(2) Postsynaptic receptor activates cyclic AMP

Cyclic AMP activates CREB (3)

(5) Genes activate proteins that affect the synapse

(4.) CREB activates genes

FIGURE 2.6.   Second-Messenger System

Copyright Blausen Medical Communications. Reproduced by Permission

of which are dopamine agonists (Ashok, Mizuno, Volkow, & Howes, 2017; Volkow et al., 2001). Studies have also reported up-regulation of serotonin receptors in acutely suicidal patients relative to healthy controls in some areas of the brain but not in other areas (e.g., Rao et al., 1998; Sullivan et al., 2015). Some antidepressant medications (SSRIs) increase the amount of serotonin that remains in the synaptic cleft, and this increase is associated with a down-regulation of serotonin receptors and improvement in behavioral symptoms (Meyer et al., 2001; Morton, Yanagawa, & Valenzuela, 2015; Stahl, 1998). It is critical to note, however, that although up- and down-regulation of receptors may correlate with drug effects, they are not necessarily causally related to changes in behavior, emotion, or cognition.

Termination of Neurotransmission

Neurotransmitters bind and detach from receptors rapidly and return to the synaptic cleft where their signaling effects are terminated by four main processes: reuptake, enzymatic deactivation, diffusion of the neurotransmitter into the extracellular fluid, and reuptake by glia cells. *Reuptake* is the removal of the transmitter substance from the cleft by the protein pumps that are located on the presynaptic membrane. These proteins are specific to the neurotransmitter and are known as transporter proteins. For example, SERT is the transporter protein that removes serotonin from the cleft; the transporter proteins that remove dopamine and norepinephrine are known as DAT and NET, respectively. In other animals, different types of transporters have been found for a single neurotransmitter. For example, four types of GABA transporter proteins have been identified in the mouse (von Bohlen und Halback & Dermietzel, 2002). Although the precise mechanisms by which the transporter proteins function in humans are not well understood, various drugs developed to inhibit these proteins are associated with certain behavioral effects. For example, Prozac, a commonly prescribed antidepressant blocks the transporter protein for serotonin thereby preventing it from transporting serotonin back into the terminal button. As a consequence of this blockage, serotonin remains longer in the synaptic cleft, and its effects are prolonged (Schloss & Williams, 1998). Once the neurotransmitter is taken up by the presynaptic neuron, various theories exist concerning the method by which it is repackaged (see pinocytosis, to follow).

In addition to reuptake, other factors are involved in clearing neurotransmitters from the cleft. *Enzymatic deactivation* occurs, for example, when an enzyme breaks down the neurotransmitter while it remains in the cleft. For example, acetylcholinesterase (AchE) breaks down Ach into choline and acetate. *Diffusion* occurs when neurotransmitters drift away from the receptor sites and are no longer capable of activating the receptors. Finally, research suggests that glia cells (astrocytes) take up neurotransmitters (or their metabolites) and assist in the recycling process of neurotransmitters (Danbolt, Furness, & Zhou, 2016; Kettenmann & Ransom, 1995).

Endocytosis and Pinocytosis

The process of release of a neurotransmitter is known as *exocytosis*, while the process of reuptake, recycling, and repackaging of a neurotransmitter is known as *endocytosis*. Once the neurotransmitter has been released, there are several theories about the process by which the vesicle is recycled and the membrane maintains its shape (*pinocytosis*). Two main theories are the "budding" and "kiss-and-run" theories (De Camilli, Slepnev, et al., 2001). The *budding theory* proposes that a vesicle fuses with the membrane, releases its neurotransmitter filled contents into the synaptic cleft, and then completely collapses with the presynaptic membrane. A number of specialized proteins (e.g., stoning-2, clathrin, dynamin) are located in the area where the vesicle has fused with the presynaptic membrane. After fusion, these specialized proteins form clusters near segments of the presynaptic membrane. This clustering of proteins results in invagination of the membrane, leading to formation of a vacuole. Another specialized protein, dynamin, is believed to form rings at the neck of the vacuole, resulting in a newly formed vesicle that then "buds off" from the membrane (Takei et al., 1996; Watanabe & Boucrot, 2017). The newly formed vesicle is then refilled with neurotransmitter inside the terminal button and ready for re-release. This entire process is estimated to take between 4 and 90 seconds (Sankaranarayanan et al., 2000). Recently researchers have proposed an ultra-fast process in which vesicles can be reformed and repackaged with neurotransmitter 50–100 milliseconds after release (Watanabe & Boucrot, 2017).

Alternatively, the *kiss-and-run* theory suggests that after a vesicle fuses with the presynaptic membrane and releases its neurotransmitter, it does not collapse with the presynaptic membrane as proposed by the budding theory; instead, it reseals, remains intact, and is released back into the terminal button. After various staging processes, the vesicles are refilled with neurotransmitters and transported to reserve areas in the terminal button where they will remain until needed. At that point, the vesicles will once again migrate, fuse with the membrane, and release their contents. The entire process of release, recycle, and repackaging is hypothesized to occur within 60 seconds (De Camilli, Slepnev, et al., 2001; Levitan & Kaczmarek, 1997). A number of factors have been found to facilitate or hinder the vesicle recycling process, including the protein snyaptojanin. Synaptojanin plays a critical role in regulating the clathrin coating of synaptic vesicles. Molecular studies have found that mutations in genes that are involved in the expression of synaptogin result in a significant depletion of synaptic vesicles and in abnormal accumulations of clathrin (Verstreken et al., 2003). Other studies have implicated additional proteins in the recycling of synaptic vesicles; however, the interactive effects of these proteins are not currently understood (e.g., Bloom et al., 2003; Harris et al., 2000).

It is important to note that the budding and kiss and run theories are not mutually exclusive and have been found coexist (Harata, Aravanis, & Tsien, 2006). Although the details of the budding and kiss and run theories are not fully elucidated, both theories currently remain viable (Chanaday and Kavalali, 2017).

Neurotransmitter Substances

Neuroscientists estimate that the brain contains hundreds of different neurotransmitters; many of which may yet to be identified. According to Werman's classic definition (1966), chemicals found in the brain are considered to be a neurotransmitter if

- They are synthesized in the neuron;
- They are released, occupy a receptor, and result in an effect in another cell;
- They are cleared from the synaptic cleft following release; and
- Their effects can be replicated by an experimental substance.

Neurotransmitters can be classified in a number of ways, but the simplest is a breakdown by size into three categories: transmitter gases, large molecule transmitters, and small molecule transmitters (Webster, 2001b). Small molecule transmitters have molecular weights less than 200, while large molecule transmitters have molecular weights ranging from 200 to 5,000 (Beart, 2000). Different types of transmitter substances can coexist in neurons and may be co-released and have interactive effects (von Bohlen und Halbach & Dermietzel, 2002). Transmitter substances are unequally distributed throughout the brain and are found in higher and lower concentrations depending on the type of substance and on processes, such as biosynthesis and axoplasmic transport (von Bohlen und Halbach & Dermietzel, 2002). For example, large molecule transmitters are most concentrated in the nuclei of the hypothalamus; glycine, a small molecule transmitter, is the most abundant inhibitory neurotransmitter in the spinal cord; and dopamine, a small molecule transmitter, is heavily concentrated in the substantia nigra and surrounding systems (Ashwell, Tancred, & Paxinos, 2000).

Transmitter Gases

Unlike large and small molecule transmitters, once transmitter gases are synthesized in various locations by the cell, they easily cross the cell's membrane, diffuse across the cleft, and enter other cell membranes. After they enter other cells, transmitter gases are short-lived and are believed to exert their effects by activating internal processes within the cell (second-messenger systems). Relative to what is known about large and small molecule transmitters, the role of transmitter gases in brain function is poorly understood. Examples of transmitter gases include hydrogen sulfide (H2S), carbon monoxide (CO), and nitric oxide (NO). Nitric oxide is involved in the dilation of the brain's blood vessels and has been hypothesized to play a mediating role in learning and memory (Levitan & Kaczmarek, 1997). The role of carbon monoxide is unclear but may be involved in regulating functions in olfactory neurons and stimulating neurons in the hypothalamus (Kim & Rivier, 2000; Snyder, Jaffrey, & Zakhary, 1998). Wang (2002) implicated hydrogen sulfide (H2S) in brain development and long-term potentiation in the hippocampus. Kimura (2002) reported that H2S is produced in response to neuronal firing and that it plays a role in the release of hormones from the hypothalamus. Recently, Sestito and colleagues (2017) advocated for the use of H2S in drug development for neurodegenerative diseases. More empirical information is available, however, on large and small molecule transmitters.

Large Molecule Transmitters

Large molecule transmitters include a variety of peptides that consist of two or more amino acids connected by peptide bonds. Peptides are synthesized by neurons and released from the terminal button. Leng and Ludwig (2008) reported that over 100 peptides have been identified, each with different contributions and functions. For example, some peptides attach to receptors and influence changes on the postsynaptic membrane while others exert indirect effects on cells by diffusing throughout the extracellular fluid and are referred to as neurohormones (e.g., follicle-stimulating hormone). As reviewed by von Bohlen und Halbach and Dermietzel (2002), peptides, unlike small molecule neurotransmitters, are involved in a number of processes, such as immune responses and physiological growth and development.

Examples of peptides include angiotensin, cholecystokinin, somastostatin, oxytocin, and vasopressin (Hökfelt, 1991). Vrontakis (2002) reviewed the role of galanin and indicated that this peptide alters the release of several neurotransmitters and has multiple biological effects. He suggested that drugs that interfere with the effects of galanin may be beneficial in the treatment of eating disorders, depression, and Alzheimer's disease, among others. The peptide oxytocin has been found to have a modulatory effect on pain perception, and vasopressin is believed to play a role in face processing and social responses in humans (Boll et al., 2017; Price et al., 2017). Perhaps the most well-studied peptides are the endogenous opioid peptides (e.g., endorphins). Opiate drugs, such as morphine and heroin, bind to these naturally occurring opioid receptors and activate pain suppression (i.e., analgesia), and they are involved in reinforcement or "pleasure" systems.

Relative to small molecule transmitters, peptides have slower, longer-lasting effects. They can augment or reduce the effect of small molecule transmitters when they are released. Peptides can be present in the same terminal button as small molecule transmitters but are located in separate vesicles. Peptides differ from small molecules in a number of ways (Fairchild, 2011; Belzung et al., 2006; Cooper et al., 2003):

- Synthesis and packaging of peptides occurs in the soma, and the vesicles containing the peptides are delivered via microtubules to the terminal button.
- Once released, peptides are deactivated by enzymes and are not taken up by the terminal button and recycled.
- Peptides are released in larger amounts from various regions of the terminal button.
- Peptides diffuse throughout the extracellular fluid and are capable of modulating the activity of neurons in a wider region.
- Peptides can increase the sensitivity of postsynaptic receptors to small molecule transmitters.

Small Molecule Transmitters

The three classes of small molecule transmitters are amino acids, monoamines, and acetylcholine. The amino acids include aspartic acid, gamma-aminobutyric acid (GABA), glutamate, and glycine. The monoamines include catecholamines—for example, dopamine (DA), epinephrine (EP), and norepinephrine (NE)—and indolamines (serotonin [5HT], melatonin). Amino acids are the building blocks of proteins and are widely distributed throughout the brain. They contain both a carboxyl group and an amino group attached to the same carbon. The amino acids are the major transmitters in the brain, while the remaining neurotransmitters account for a relatively small percentage of synapses (Cooper et al., 2003; Griffin & Bradshaw, 2017).

Aspartate

Although abundant in the brain, relatively little is known about aspartate (aspartic acid). Both aspartate and glutamate serve as building blocks for proteins and peptide synthesis, and are involved in intracellular metabolism (Cooper et al., 2003). Aspartate typically produces an excitatory effect (depolarizes) on the membrane and is closely related to glutamate. According to von Bohlen und Halbach and Dermietzel (2002), aspartate and glutamate are synthesized in the terminal button, attach to similar postsynaptic receptors (NMDA), and produce comparable effects. Receptor dysfunction for both amino acids has been implicated in schizophrenia (Kim, Kaufman, et al., 2017; Olney & Farber, 1995). Ketamine, a drug that blocks NMDA receptors, has produced schizophrenia-like symptoms in healthy adults, providing further evidence that glutamate is involved in psychotic symptoms (Kokkinou et al., 2017; Morgan et al., 2003). Information regarding schizophrenia will be covered in Chapter 5.

Glutamate

Glutamate is the principal excitatory neurotransmitter in the brain, accounting for approximately 50% of synapses (Snyder & Ferris, 2000). Glutamatergic neurons are widely distributed—in subcortical structures, throughout the cortex, and in other areas of the brain. Glutamate is biosynthesized in the cell via a series of enzymatic changes beginning with precursors (e.g., ammonia, lysine) and is stored in synaptic vesicles (Papes et al., 2001; Yelamanchi et al., 2016). Several types of glutamate receptors have been identified, including NMDA, AMPA, and the Kainate receptor. Ionotrophic as well as metabotrophic receptors specific to glutamate have been identified (Sheng, 2001; Petralia, Al-Hallaq, & Wenthold, 2009; Pittenger, 2015). These receptors consist of complex subunits that interact with intracellular proteins, but the specific functions of the subunits are not fully understood. For example, the NMDA receptor has been found to have at least seven different binding sites that have varying effects when occupied (Dickenson, 2001; Hansen et al., 2017). The NMDA receptor has been implicated in a variety of psychiatric disorders as well as neurodegenerative diseases (Hansen et al., 2017). The AMPA and kainate receptors are thought to control sodium channels. When glutamate binds to these receptors, depolarization results (i.e., EPSPs). Glutamate receptors are usually located on parts of the dendrite and less commonly near or on the cell body (see von Bohlen und Halbach & Dermietzel, 2002 for a review).

Glutamate is cleared from the cleft primarily by glia cells (astrocytes) via transporter proteins found on the glial cell membrane. Glutamate is also reclaimed from the synaptic cleft by transporter proteins located on the presynaptic neuron (Albrecht & Zielińska, 2017; Cooper et al., 2003). Several subtypes of glutamate transporter proteins have been identified. After glutamate is cleared from the cleft by glial cells enzymes convert it into glutamine. Glutamine is then transported to neuronal terminal buttons, where it serves as a precursor for the biosynthesis glutamate. The reuptake process is particularly important, as high levels of extracellular glutamate can be toxic to other neurons and glia cells, as discussed in Chapter 1.

Glutamate has been implicated in learning and memory (e.g., Riedel, Platt, & Micheau, 2003) as well as a variety of psychiatric illnesses. For example, Michael and colleagues (2003) reported that adults suffering from bipolar disorder and mania had significantly elevated levels of glutamate in the region of the prefrontal cortex. Schiffer (2002) reviewed molecular genetics findings and concluded that mutations in glutamate receptor genes might increase the risk of developing schizophrenia, bipolar disorder, or depression. Levine and colleagues (2000) compared cerebral spinal fluid glutamate metabolites in adults with depression (unipolar and bipolar) relative to control subjects and found that those suffering from depression had higher metabolite concentrations. Glutamate has also been found to influence the release and inhibition of other neurotransmitters such as serotonin. Marek (2002), for example, reported that drugs that stimulate glutamate autoreceptors suppress the release of glutamate, which in turn reduces the release of serotonin in the prefrontal cortex. Recent research has focused on the role of glutamate and glutamate agonists in major depressive disorders (Abdallah et al., 2017; Lang et al., 2017). One of the difficulties in determining the role of glutamate or other neurotransmitters in pathological conditions is that the complexities of these neurotransmitters systems in the normal brain are not yet understood.

Y-Amino Butyric Acid (GABA)

GABA is the principal inhibitory and most common neurotransmitter in the brain, expressed in approximately 30% of all synapses (Cooper et al., 2003). Widely distributed throughout the brain, it is found in higher concentrations in the limbic system, basal ganglia, and cortex. GABA is biosynthesized from glutamate by GAD (glutamic acid decarboxylase), an enzyme that removes a carboxyl group Three main types of GABA receptors have been identified: GABAa, GABAb, and GABAc receptors. GABAc receptors are found primarily in the retina and therefore will not be included in the following discussion. GABAa and GABAb receptors are located throughout the brain and are implicated in a wide variety of functions and behaviors. GABAa is an ionotropic receptor, and when occupied by GABA, the chloride channel opens. Some of the most effective medications to treat insomnia target the GABAa receptor (Wisden, Yu, & Franks, 2017). GABAb is a metabotropic receptor, and when occupied, potassium channels open and a cascade of intracellular events follow. GABAb receptors are implicated in the pathophysiology and treatment of anxiety and will be discussed in more detail in Chapter 7. In addition, GABA autoreceptors have been identified on the membrane of the terminal button and on the axon, where they appear to play a role in both inhibiting the release of GABA and in increasing excitability of other neurons (de San Martin et al., 2015; Sarup, Larsson, & Schousboe, 2003).

GABA is cleared from the cleft primarily by reuptake via GABA transporters (GAT) found on the presynaptic membrane of the terminal button and the glia cell membrane. Several types of GABA transporters have been identified. Cooper et al. (2003) suggested that different types of transporter proteins may serve as co-transporters for other types of amino acids or that they may have the capacity to function in an outward direction, "serving as a paradoxical mechanism for release, rather than the removal of GABA" (p. 114). Like most neurotransmitters, GABA has been implicated in psychiatric disorders, including epilepsy, Tourette's disorder, anxiety disorders, and neurodegenerative disease. Sepkuty and colleagues (2002), for example, reported that a specific glutamate transporter protein (EAAC1) found on the soma and dendrites of many neurons plays a critical role in GABA synthesis. Specifically, they found excessive neuronal activity and seizures were induced in rats treated with a drug that blocked the EAAC1 transporters. In addition, a 50% loss of GABA in the hippocampus demonstrated that GABA synthesis is partially dependent on glutamate transporter proteins (i.e., GABA is biosynthesized from glutamate). Sepkuty et al. (2002) hypothesized that epilepsy can result from a disruption in the process of EAAC1 reuptake and GABA metabolism. Drake et al. (2003) reported that a drug (Baclofen) that activates GABA postsynaptic receptors was effective at decreasing symptoms of post-traumatic stress disorder (PTSD) in patients with PTSD due to combat. Recent research has reported that alterations in the expression of GABA transporters in various regions of the brain were present in patients with Alzheimer's disease (Fuhrer et al., 2017). Additional studies have implicated the GABA system in psychiatric and neurodegenerative disorders, and are discussed in subsequent chapters.

Monoamine Neurotransmitters

The monoamine neurotransmitters fall into two main groups: catecholamines and indolamines. The catecholamines include dopamine (DA), epinephrine (EP), and norepinephrine (NE). Indolamines include serotonin and melatonin.

Dopamine

Dopamine cell bodies are heavily concentrated in the basal ganglia, substantia nigra, and tegmentum and have widespread projections to the frontal regions of the brain, and to a lesser extent, other regions of the brain. Several complex dopaminergic systems have been identified, and these systems originate in the midbrain and forebrain, and include the nigrostriatal, mesolimbic, and mesocortical systems (Figure 2.7). Each system is associated with specific functions, and the morphology and density of the neurons vary among the systems (Cooper et al., 2003). Dopamine is involved in numerous functions (e.g., movement,

Dopamine Pathway

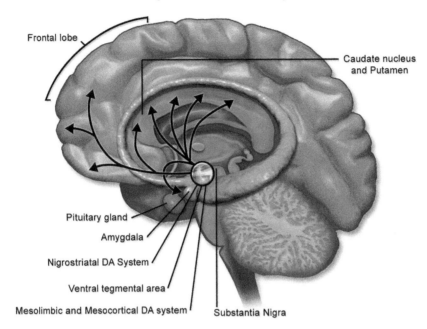

FIGURE 2.7.   Dopaminergic Pathways and Projections

Copyright Blausen Medical Communications. Reproduced by permission.

attention, motivation, learning) and has been implicated in a variety of disorders, such as schizophrenia, obsessive compulsive disorders, Tourette's disorder, Parkinson's disease, and addiction (e.g., Ghorayeb et al., 2017). These disorders and the role of the dopaminerigic systems, as well as other neurotransmitter systems, are addressed in subsequent chapters.

The pathway involved in the biosynthesis of dopamine was first proposed in 1939 by Blaschko (1939), and according to Meiser (2013), this process is highly complex, with many unanswered questions remaining. The traditional pathway begins with the precursor amino acid tyrosine. Tyrosine is found in various foods (cheese, eggs, turkey, nuts, etc.) and can be manufactured by the body from phenylalanine. Tyrosine is converted into L-DOPA by the enzyme tyrosine hydroxylase (which adds a hydroxyl group to the tyrosine). The enzyme DOPA decarboxlyase then removes a carboxyl group from the L-DOPA, which results in dopamine. Dopamine is stored in synaptic vesicles located in the terminal button to prevent breakdown by the enzyme monoamine oxidase (MAO), which is present in the intracellular fluid (Bhagvat, Blaschko, & Richter, 1939).

Five families of dopamine receptors have been identified, all of which are metabotropic receptors. According to Greengard (2001), the second-messenger pathways involved in these metabotropic receptors are enormously complicated. In addition, dopamine receptors vary in their distribution throughout the brain, and, depending on the receptor, dopamine can have an excitatory, inhibitory, or modulating effect on the cell (Cooper et al., 2003). This variance in distribution of receptors is consistent with the large number of brain functions in which dopamine appears to be involved. The synthesis and release of dopamine are also regulated by presynaptic autoreceptors. In general, drugs that stimulate autoreceptors tend

to inhibit dopamine release; drugs that block autoreceptors tend to elicit its production and/
or release. As Shin, Adrover, and Alvarez (2017) recently found, however, dopamine signals
can be modulated by dopamine autoreceptors in conjunction with other neurotransmitters,
such as acetylcholine, and this complex process is currently under investigation.

Dopamine is cleared from the synaptic cleft primarily by transporter proteins, known as
DAT, found on the dendrites, terminal button, and soma of the presynaptic neuron (Kuhar,
1998). According to Cooper et al. (2003), 80% of dopamine is retrieved from the extracellular fluid by reuptake. Different DAT levels are found in among dopamine neurons,
however, suggesting that diffusion is also involved in removing dopamine from the synaptic
cleft. Drugs such as cocaine and methylphenidate selectively target and block DAT, thereby
prolonging dopamine's effects in the synaptic cleft (Volkow et al., 1999). In addition, meta-
analytic findings indicated that cocaine and methamphetamine users have been found to
have lower DAT density compared to non-drug users (Ashok et al., 2017). Drugs with a high
affinity for DAT also have been used by neuroimaging researchers to measure DAT density
in patients who suffer from Parkinson's disease. Neuroimaging studies revealed that the disease is often characterized by a loss of DAT in the striatum (Oh et al., 2016; Varrone et al.,
2001). DAT levels also appear to change developmentally and to be associated with cognitive performance. For example, Mozley et al. (2001) measured DAT levels in 30 men and 36
women, and reported age as well as sex differences, with women and younger subjects having higher DAT availability in the striatum (caudate and putamen). For women and younger
participants, increased DAT availability was associated with better neuropsychological task
performance. Studies are currently underway to better understand the role of DAT in normal cognitive functioning as well as neurodegenerative and psychiatric conditions.

Dopamine is broken down by monoamine oxidase (MAO) and catechol-o-methyl transferase (COMT) into homovanillic acid (HVA). HVA levels in the cerebral spinal fluid have
been used as an index of dopamine activity in the brain. For example, levels of HVA have
been reduced in patients with epilepsy as well as Parkinson's and Alzheimer's diseases (Gibson, Logue, & Growdon, 1985; Laxer et al., 1979). Morimoto and colleagues (2017) recently
suggested that HVA level may serve as a reliable biomarker for dementia. In contrast,
increased levels of HVA have been found with patients with Tourette's syndrome (Cohen
et al., 1978) and bipolar disorder (Swann et al., 1983). Interestingly, deep brain stimulation (discussed in Chapter 3) has been found to increase HVA levels in patients with OCD
(Figee et al., 2014). Lastly, developmentally, children have been found to have higher levels
of cerebral spinal fluid HVA and other neurotransmitter metabolites compared to adults
(Leckman et al., 1980), while children with autism disorder have been found to have higher
HVA levels compared to children without the disorder (Kaluzna et al., 2010). More research
is needed to understand the significance of HVA levels among patients with psychiatric and
neurodegenerative disorders.

Norepinephrine and Epinephrine

Norepinephrine is differentially distributed in the brain, with most cell bodies contained in
the brain stem in the locus coeruleus (Figure 2.8). These neurons form tracts and project
to many areas, such as the hypothalamus, thalamus, and the cortex. Neurons that release
norepinephrine are referred to as *noradrenergic*, while neurons that release epinephrine are
referred to as *adrenergic*.

Norepinephrine is biosynthesized in the terminal vesicles from dopamine by the enzyme
dopamine B-hyroxylase. In some cells, norepinephrine is not released but instead is further

Norepinephrine Pathway

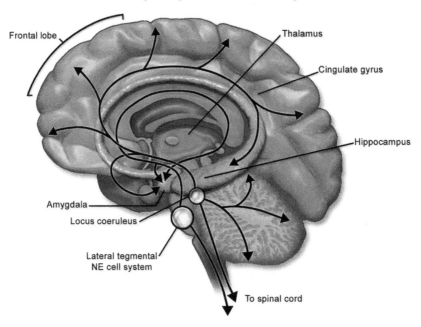

FIGURE 2.8.   Norepinephrine Pathways and Projections

Copyright Blausen Medical Communications. Reproduced by permission.

metabolized to create epinephrine. Norepinephrine is released both from the terminal button and from swellings located along branches of the axon known as varicosities (von Bohlen und Halbach & Dermietzel, 2002). Epinephrine is released by the adrenal glands located above the kidneys. The adrenergic receptors in the brain respond to epinephrine as well as norepinephrine. Like dopamine and other neurotransmitters, norepinephrine release is partially regulated by autoreceptors. Several types of norepinephrine postsynaptic receptors (i.e., adrenergic receptors) have been identified and all are metabotropic. Norepinephrine is cleared from the extracellular fluid by norepinephrine transporters (NET). Densities of NET vary in the brain, with the highest concentrations found in the locus coeruleus and the lowest in the caudate and putamen (Charnay et al., 1995). NET density has been implicated in major depressive disorders and using brain imaging (PET) Yatham et al. (2017) recently reported significantly lower NET density of patients with depression compared to those without the disorder, and a 50% *increase* in NET occupancy in the hypothalamus following a two-week treatment with an antipsychotic medication (quetiapine). Norepinephrine that is taken back into the cell is either repackaged into synaptic vesicles or broken down by MAO or COMT and recycled.

Norepinephrine has been implicated in a number of psychiatric disorders, in particular anxiety and mood disorders (Charney, 2003; Moriguchi et al., 2017). For example, some, but not all, studies have reported lower urinary metabolites of norepinephrine in patients with bipolar disorder relative to control participants (Wehr, Muscettola, & Goodwin, 1980). Bhanji et al. (2002) suggested that hyperactivity of norepinephrine systems is likely implicated in mania episodes as mirtazapine, a drug that increases levels of norepinephrine in the brain, was found to induce mania in adults. Norepinephrine has also been implicated in ADHD, panic disorder, major depressive disorders, and other psychiatric conditions (Sand et al., 2002; Biederman & Faraone, 2002; Montoya et al., 2016). More about the role of norepinephrine in psychiatric conditions will be discussed in subsequent chapters.

Serotonin

Serotonin (5-hydroxytryptamine; 5HT) is categorized as an indolamine. It is also differentially distributed throughout the brain, with higher concentrations located in the brain stem (i.e., raphe nuclei) and midbrain. Similar to dopamine, the projection systems for serotonin are complex and widespread (Figure 2.9). The precursor for serotonin is the amino acid tryptophan, and it is converted to serotonin via enzymatic reactions with tryptophan hydroxylase. Although serotonin's role in the brain is not fully understood, studies indicate that it is involved in a vast array of behaviors and functions. For example, serotonin helps to regulate arousal, wakefulness, sleep, appetite and eating behavior, stress response, mood, and motor behavior (Stanford, 2001b; Brummelte et al., 2017). Developmentally, serotonin synthesis is substantially higher in children than adults, and during ages 5–15, there is a gradual decline in synthesis values toward adult levels (Blummelte et al., 2017; Chugani et al., 1999). Serotonin appears to interact with other growth factors and neurotransmitter systems to facilitate brain and bone growth (Cirmanova et al., 2017; Sodhi & Sanders-Bush, 2004).

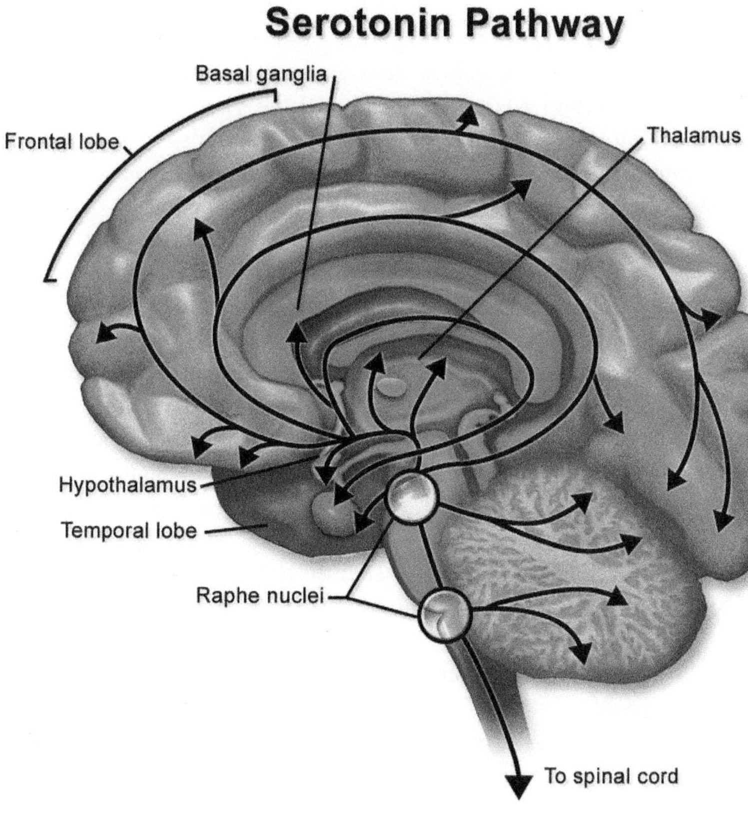

FIGURE 2.9. Serotonergic Pathways and Projections

Copyright Blausen Medical Communications. Reproduced by permission.

Serotonin is synthesized from a precursor-amino acid tryptophan. The first step of serotonin synthesis in neurons is that the enzyme tryptophan hydroxylase adds a hydroxyl group to the tryptophan, resulting in 5-hydroxytryptophan (5-HTP). Next, the enzyme 5-HTP decarboxylase removes a carboxyl group from the 5-HTP, producing serotonin. Serotonin is stored in synaptic vesicles, and its synthesis and release are regulated by a number of factors, including autoreceptors and heteroreceptors. Serotonin autoreceptors are found on the terminal button as well as the cell body of neurons. Like other neurotransmitter autoreceptors, their function is primarily inhibitory. The role of heteroreceptors in serotonin synthesis and release is poorly understood. Harsing and colleagues (2004) speculated that glutamate-releasing neurons possess serotonin heteroreceptors that inhibit glutamate release, thereby influencing serotonin synthesis and release. Other studies have implicated additional mediating factors in the release of serotonin, including stress and corticotropin-releasing factor (Mo et al., 2008).

With regard to serotonin postsynaptic receptors, 15 different serotonin receptors have been identified and classified into seven family types (N. M. Barnes & Sharp, 1999; Visser et al., 2011). Most postsynaptic serotonin receptors are metabotropic, and the effects of serotonin can be excitatory or inhibitory depending on the receptor. The reason for multiple receptor types for serotonin is unclear. Stanford (2001b) hypothesized that the variety of receptors allows for greater flexibility and refinement of response to serotonin. Serotonin is deactivated by reuptake from the cleft by the serotonin transporter (SERT) and further degraded by MAO. The final metabolite of serotonin, 5-hydroxyindolic acid (5-HIAA), is similar to other neurotransmitter metabolites in that it can be detected and measured in the urine, blood, and CSF; however, metabolites are considered an unreliable measure of brain levels of neurotransmitters (Potter, Hsiao, & Goldman, 1989; Visser et al., 2011). Abnormalities of the serotoninergic system, including regulatory genes, transporter proteins (SERT), and presynaptic and postsynaptic receptors, have been implicated in a number of psychiatric conditions and will be discussed in subsequent chapters.

Acetylcholine

Acetylcholine (Ach) was the first neurotransmitter discovered and is in its own class. Acetylcholine is widespread throughout the central (Figure 2.10) and peripheral nervous systems. Neurons that release Ach are referred to as *cholinergic*. Ach is synthesized from choline found in various foods and is a by-product when fats are broken down. As the enzyme acetylcholinetransferase transfers an acetate ion to choline, this process results in Ach. Ach is then stored in synaptic vesicles, and similar to other neurotransmitters, the synthesis and release of Ach are partially regulated by autoreceptors. Two main types of postsynaptic receptors have been identified for Ach: nicotinic (ionotropic) and muscarinic (metabotropic) receptors. They were so named after the drugs that were found to stimulate or inhibit the receptors—namely, nicotine, found in cigarettes, and muscarine, found in the poisonous mushroom *amanita muscaria* (Sabec et al., 2018).

The nicotonic receptor is complex, consisting of several subunits. Binding Ach to one of the subunits alters the conformation of the receptor—a change that opens the ion channels and depolarizes the membrane. The roles of each of the subunits of the nicotinic receptor are not fully understood. Nicotonic receptors (i.e., heteroreceptors) are found on GABA, dopamine, and glutamate-releasing neurons, and, according to von Bohlen und Halbach and Dermietzel (2002), activation of these receptors by Ach can increase the synthesis and release of these neurotransmitters. The muscarinic receptor functions quite differently than

Acetycholine Pathway

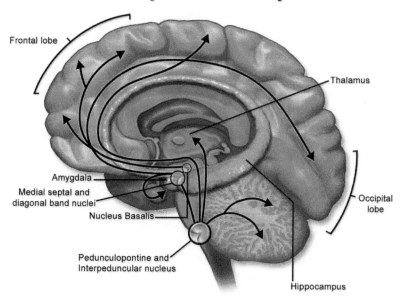

FIGURE 2.10. Acetylcholine Pathways and Projections

Copyright Blausen Medical Communications. Reproduced by permission.

the nicotonic receptor and is coupled to second-messenger systems. Different classes and subtypes of the muscarinic receptor have been identified; they differ in their distribution in the brain as well as their second-messenger pathways. After release from the terminal button, Ach is not terminated by reuptake but instead is broken down by acetylcholine esterase into its constituents (acetate and choline) that are cleared from the cleft by diffusion a choline transporter (von Bohlen und Halbach & Dermietzel, 2002).

Acetylcholine has been implicated in complex cognitive functions, such as attention, memory, and learning, as well as a variety of psychiatric disorders and dementias (Haig et al., 2017; Mihailescu and Drucker-Colin, 2000). The role of Ach in Alzheimer's disease and other neurodegenerative disorders has been studied extensively and is covered in Chapter 4.

Psychopharmacology

Drugs have been used to treat psychiatric conditions since the early 1900s, but the first major breakthrough in psychopharmacology occurred during the 1950s with the release of the anti-psychotic drug Thorazine (chlorpromazine). Thorazine was used to reduce psychotic symptoms and to calm patients with schizophrenia and mania. Tofranil (imipramine), the first tricyclic antidepressant, was released during the mid-1950s. Librium, a benzodiazepine, was made available during the late 1950s and the mood stabilizer lithium during the early 1960s (Stanford, 2001c). Drugs prescribed to treat the cognitive and behavioral symptoms of psychological/psychiatric disorders are known as *psychotropic* medications (Table 2.3). Psychotropic drugs are commonly prescribed to treat a wide range of disorders such as anxiety disorders,

Table 2.3 Psychotropic Medications: Brand and Drug Names

Antidepressants (SSRIs)
- Celexa (citalopram)
- Lexapro (escitalopram)
- Luvox (fluoxamine)
- Paxil (paroxetine)
- Prozac (fluoxetine)
- Vilazodone (Viibryd)
- Zoloft (sertraline)

Antidepressants (SNRIs)
- Effexor (venlafaxine)
- Remeron (mirtazapine)
- Cymbalta (duloxetine)
- Savella (milnacipran)
- Fetzima (levomilnacipran)

Antidepressant (NDRI)
Wellbutrin (Bupropion)

MAO Inhibitors
- Deprenyl (selegilene)
- Manerix (moclobemide)
- Marplan (isocarboxazid)
- Nardil (phenylzine)
- Parnate (tranylcypromine)

Tricyclic Antidepressants
- Anafranil (clomipramine)
- Asendin (amoxapine)
- Aventyl (nortriptyline)
- Desyrel (trazodone)
- Elavil (amitriptyline)
- Ludiomil (maprotiline)
- Norpramin (desipramine)
- Sinequan (doxepin)
- Surmontil (trimipramine)
- Trofranil (imipramine)
- Vivactil (protriptyline)

Antianxiety

Benzodiazepines
- Atarax (vistaril)
- Ativan (lorazepam)
- Centrax (prazepam)

Antipsychotic
- Abilify (aripiprazole)
- Chlorpromazine (thorazine)
- Clozapine (clozaril)
- Geodon (ziprasidone)
- Haldol (haloperidol)
- Loxapa (loxapine)
- Mellaril (thioridazine)
- Moban (molindone)
- Navane (thioxthixene)
- Orap (pimozide)
- Permitil (fluphenazine)
- Quide (piperacetazine)
- Risperdal (risperidone)
- Serentil (mesoridazine)
- Stelazine (trifluoperazine)
- Seroquel (quetiapine)
- Taractan (chlorprothixene)
- Tindal (acetophenazine)
- Trilafon (perphenazine)
- Zyprexa (olanzapine)

Mood Stabilizers
- Depakote (divalproex)
- Eskalith (lithobid)
- Lamactil (lamotrigine)
- Neurontin (gabapentin)
- Tegretol (carbamazepine)
- Topamax (topiramate)
- Lithium

Anticonvulsants
- Depakene (valproate)
- Tegretol (carbamazepine)
- Lamotrigine (lamictal)
- Gabapentin (neurontin)
- Topiramate (topamax)
- Oxcarbazepine (trileptal)
- Zonisamide (zonegran)

Stimulants
- Adderall (amphetamine + dextroamphetamine)

- Klonipin (clonazepam)
- Serax (oxazepam)
- Tranxene (clorazepate)
- Valium (diazepam)
- Xanax (alprazolam)

Anxiolytic

- BuSpar (buspirone)
- Catapres (clonidine)
- Librium (chlordiazepoxide)
- Alprazolam (Xanax)
- Bromazepam (Lectopam)
- Clonazepam (Klonopin)
- Clorazepate (Tranxene)
- Diazepam (Valium)
- Flurazepam (Dalmane)
- Lorazepam (Ativan)

- Dexedrine (dextroamphetamine)
- Ritalin (methylphenidate)
- Cylert (pemoline)

Nonstimulant, Prostimulant

- Strattera (atomoxetine)

Vyvanse (lisdexamfetamine dimesylate)

major depressive disorders, and behavioral disorders. It is critical to note that psychotropic medications are palliative in nature, not curative. In other words, psychotropic medications can improve cognitive and behavioral symptoms in many individuals, but they do not cure the underlying cause of psychological disorders.

In 2017, Moore and Mattison reported that one in six adults in the United States reported taking psychotropic medication at least once during 2013. The most commonly used medications were antidepressants and antianxiety medications, and eight out of ten reported using the medications long term. Moore and Mattison also found large differences in race/ethnicity, with 20.8% of white adults reporting use of psychotropic medications versus 8.7% of Hispanic adults. Medication rates for African American and Asian adults were also lower than those for white adults, but not statistically significantly different from Hispanic adults. Women were more likely than men to report taking psychotropic medications and use also increased with age (25.1% of adults aged 60–85 years versus 9.0% of those aged 18–39 years). Psychotropic medications are reportedly widely prescribed among the elderly, particularly individuals living in nursing homes (Ryan et al., 2002).

Psychotropic medication use has also increased among children of all ages. In a recent study involving 16 countries, Hálfdánarson and colleagues reported that antipsychotic medications use increased in 10 of the 16 countries studied between 2005 and 2014. The highest rates of use among children and adolescents were in Taiwan (30.8 out of every 1,000) and the lowest rates were in Lithuania (0.5/1,000). Antidepressant use among children and adolescents has also increased globally despite 2004 government blackbox warnings of increased risk for suicidality within this population (Bachmann et al., 2016). Prescription stimulant use primarily for the treatment of ADHD increased sharply in the United States during the 1990s from 0.6% to 2.7% in 1997 (Olfson et al., 2003). Since that time, rates appear to have leveled off among Caucasian children and adolescents, declined in preschoolers, and increased in children from racial and ethnic minority groups (although the rate remains lower than in non-Hispanic white children) (Zuvekas & Vitiello, 2012). Stimulants are commonly prescribed among more children with more severe behavioral difficulties as Safer, Zito, and dosReis (2003) found that over 20% of outpatient youths treated in community mental health centers and over 40% of youth treated in inpatient facilities were given more than one psychotropic medication. Overall, recent findings indicate that off-label use of stimulants is at least 40%, and stimulant prescriptions are higher for adults than children and adolescents, and more adult women are prescribed stimulants than adult men (Safer, 2016).

In the United States, psychotropic medications such as antidepressants are prescribed by primary care physicians more often than specialty care physicians (Mojtabai & Olfson, 2011). Relatively recently psychologists have been granted prescription privileges and currently have prescription privileges in five states, including New Mexico, Louisiana, Illinois, Iowa, and Idaho (DeAngelis, 2017). According to the American Psychological Association, legislators in Arizona, Hawaii, Montana, New Jersey, Ohio, Oregon, Tennessee, and Utah have also recently considered bills that would allow prescription privileges for psychologists. These measures are frequently opposed by professional medical organizations, including the American Medical Association and American Psychiatric Association, reportedly due to patient safety concerns.

Despite the widespread use of psychotropic medications among children, adolescents, and adults, the precise mode action of most drugs used to treat psychiatric disorders is unknown. Cooper et al. (2003) stated, "At the molecular level an explanation of the action of a drug is often possible; at the cellular level, an explanation is sometimes possible; but at the behavioral level, our ignorance is abysmal" (p. 2). Part of the difficulty in understanding the precise effects of drugs is the complexity of cellular processes involved and the significant variation among individuals with respect to drug response and sensitivity. For example, *pharmacogenomics* is a relatively new field of study of how genes affect a person's response to drugs and in the future may result in "personalized drug treatments". Indeed, a large number of studies have supported that genetic factors are associated with drug response in children as well as adults, including individuals with psychiatric conditions such as ASD, mood disorders, and others (Amare, Schubert, & Baune, 2017; Nuntamool et al., 2017; Petit et al., 2017; Health Quality Ontario, 2017). Currently, research is actively seeking to unravel the complexity of individual drug response by exploring a vast array of pharmacological areas, including (a) the role of genes and genetic mutations in drug response; (b) how genes are activated or suppressed by exposure to drugs; (c) the structure and function of post-synaptic receptors, autoreceptors, and heteroreceptors, and the effects of drugs on these receptors; (d) neurotrophic factors involved in neurotransmission and the effects of drugs on these trophic factors; and (e) the role of glial cells in neuronal signaling and the effects of drugs on glial cell functioning. These topics as well as others are likely to shed light on basic principles of drug action as well as individual drug, responsivity.

Although a plethora of questions remain concerning the mode of action of psychotropic drugs and factors that may influence these mechanisms, basic information is available about the pharmacology of medications used to treat psychiatric and psychological conditions. The following section reviews the basic principles of pharmacology and describes the purported mode of action of commonly prescribed psychotropic medications. Additional details on the use, effectiveness, and side effects of these medications are discussed in subsequent chapters.

Pharmacokinetics

The process of drugs being absorbed, distributed, metabolized, and excreted by the body is known as pharmacokinetics. Oral administration is a common means of administering psychotropic medications, however, other means are also available, such as injection, patches, and nasal sprays. Drugs taken orally are absorbed in the gastrointestinal system and a number of factors can determine the degree of absorption (e.g., food in digestive system, drug concentration, effects of other drugs). After a drug is absorbed into the bloodstream, it is distributed to various sites throughout the body, such as the kidneys, liver, heart, brain, fat tissue, and muscle. Distribution of a psychotropic drug is influenced by blood flow, diffusion of the drug from the blood to the target area, and the degree to which the drug can pass through membranes (i.e., lipid soluble; Carvey, 1998). Some psychotropic drugs, such as antipsychotic and tricyclic antidepressant medications, collect in muscle and fat tissue, and are slowly released into the bloodstream. This storage and slow release process helps to explain why individuals with schizophrenia or depression who stop taking their medications sometimes remain symptom-free for several weeks (Agid et al., 2006; Perrine, 1996).

Metabolism (or biotransformation) of psychotropic medications occurs primarily in the liver, but also in the brain and blood, through a complex system of enzymatic processes. The by-products of drug metabolism are known as *metabolites*, the actions of which can have therapeutic effects. For example, the main metabolites of some antipsychotic drugs (e.g., risperidone) have been found to contribute to the therapeutic effects of the drug (Caccia, 2000a; Takeuchi et al., 2015). During metabolism, metabolites can interact and produce a range of effects from toxicity to canceling out desired drug effects. Trenton, Currier, and Zwemer (2003) reported that toxic doses of psychotropic drugs, such as antipsychotics, are highly variable and may be increased by co-ingestion of other drugs. For example, some prescription drugs can inhibit the enzymes that metabolize antipsychotic drugs and consequently may increase the probability of toxic effects of these antipsychotic medications. Drug metabolites can also be toxic to other cells resulting in neuronal cell death and has been documented with the antipsychotic haloperidol (Kang et al., 2006). Unfortunately, as noted by Caccia (2000a), information is scarce concerning the effects of drug metabolites as well as the interactive effects of these metabolites with other drugs.

The process by which drugs are eliminated from the body is called *excretion*. Excretion occurs primarily in the kidneys, and the by-products are passed in urine. The gastrointestinal system, sweat glands, skin, lungs, and saliva also participate in drug excretion. Differences among individuals in their ability to metabolize psychotropic medications are likely related in part to their genetic makeup. Given that some genetic markers are now available as tests, Eum and colleagues (2016), as well as others, have suggested that these tools may help select optimal medication strategies for individuals with psychiatric conditions.

Medication Effects

The amount of psychotropic drug needed to attain a therapeutic effect can vary widely among individuals, as can the undesirable side effects of psychotropic drugs (Iwata et al., 1999; Trenton et al., 2003). Common and uncommon side effects of psychotropic medications have been well documented. For example, emotional blunting has been reported in approximately 50% of patients taking antidepressant medications for depression and is associated with poorer prognosis (Goodwin et al., 2017). Other side effects associated with antidepressants include constipation, dry mouth, headache, sweating, and reduced libido; rare effects could include seizures and severe allergic reactions (Physicians' Desk Reference [PDR], 2017). Edwards and Anderson (1999) completed a meta-analysis of five SSRIs and reported that although there was no difference in efficacy among the antidepressant medications, the degree of side effects varied widely. As noted previously, genetic variations (e.g., transporter genes) are associated with patients' response to the antidepressants (Eum et al., 2016; Yoshida et al., 2004), although additional studies are needed to better understand the role of genes and therapeutic medication response.

Disparities in medication treatment exist, however, as patients from minority backgrounds typically have poorer access to and use mental health care services at a lower rate than Caucasians, and are less likely to be prescribed and to fill prescriptions for newer antidepressants compared to Caucasians (Neighbors et al., 2007). In terms of the efficacy of antidepressants, research indicates that patients from minority groups have outcomes that are similar to those of Caucasians (Lesser et al., 2010). Studies are needed to explore access and efficacy of antidepressants and other psychotropic medications among additional race and ethnic populations.

Agonists and Antagonists

Drugs can be classified into two broad categories: those that facilitate or enhance the effects of neurotransmitters are known as *agonists*, whereas drugs that interfere with or reduce the effects of neurotransmitters are known as *antagonists* (Figure 2.11). Although not the focus of this chapter, drugs also can be partial agonists (bind to a receptor and produce a partial effect rather than a full effect) and inverse agonists (binds to the receptor but has the opposite effect of an agonist) (see Kowalski, Dowben, & Keltner, 2017).

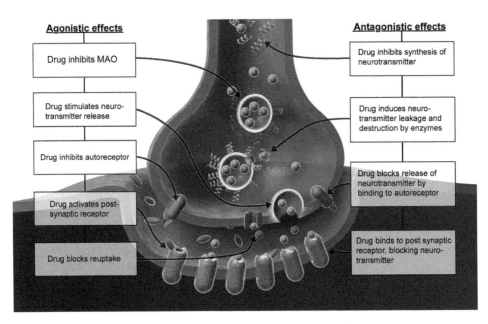

FIGURE 2.11.   Agonistic and Antagonistic Drug Effects

Copyright Blausen Medical Communications. Reproduced by permission.

Agonists may facilitate neurotransmission in a number of ways, including (a) serving as a precursor, (b) stimulating the release of neurotransmitter, (c) occupying and activating the postsynaptic receptors, (d) blocking the autoreceptors, (e) blocking reuptake by inhibiting the transporter proteins, (f) inhibiting deactivating enzymes, or (g) facilitating postsynaptic affinity. Conversely, antagonists may interfere with transmission by (a) preventing storage of neurotransmitter in the vesicles, (b) preventing the release of neurotransmitter, (c) occupying and blocking postsynaptic receptors, (d) activating autoreceptors, (e) preventing synthesis of the neurotransmitter, or (f) deactivating enzymes that naturally inhibit the synthesis of neurotransmitters (Figure 2.11).

Neurotoxins are a good example of substances that can produce either antagonistic or agonistic effects. For instance, curare, which is derived from a plant berry, occupies acetylcholine receptors and blocks acetylcholine from attaching to the receptor. By blocking the receptor, curare prevents the release of acetylcholine from the cell. Curare is therefore an acetylcholine antagonist, and large doses can prevent movement and respiration. In contrast, black widow spider venom increases the amount of acetylcholine released by the terminal button and is therefore an acetylcholine agonist. Other neurotoxins inhibit the breakdown, prevent their release, and/or stimulate the production of neurotransmitters (Webster, 2001b). Many analgesics are considered antagonists because they block receptor sites involved in pain regulation. Antipsychotic medications often target and block dopamine receptors, and hence are considered dopamine antagonists. Drugs can also have both antagonistic and agonistic effects, such as opioid analgesics, that act as an agonist at one receptor and an antagonist at another (e.g., nalbuphine).

Hundreds of drugs have been developed to treat psychological and psychiatric disorders, and various systems exist to classify these medications. Five main types of psychotropic drugs include antianxiety, antidepressants, antipsychotic, mood stabilizers, and stimulants. The next section provides an overview of the mode of action of each these classes. Drugs also will be discussed in subsequent chapters as they pertain to the disorders covered therein.

An Overview of Psychotropic Drugs and Mode of Action

By pharmacologically altering the cell structure and function, and ultimately the process of neurotransmission, medications affect behavior, mood, and cognition. For example, psychotropic drugs can improve symptoms of anxiety, alter or stabilize mood, enhance attention and concentration levels, and decrease symptoms that interfere with daily living such as compulsions, hallucinations, and delusions. Although other classification systems exist, the categorical approach to defining disorders of the American Psychiatric Association, the *Diagnostic and Statistical Manual of Mental Disorders, 5th Edition* (*DSM-V*) will be used in this and subsequent chapters.

Antianxiety Medications

Anxiety disorders are a heterogeneous group of conditions that have been categorized by the American Psychiatric Association in the *DSM-V* as sharing features of excessive fear, anxiety, and related behavioral disturbances. Examples include generalized anxiety disorder (GAD), separation anxiety disorder, specific phobia, social anxiety, and panic disorder. Obsessive compulsive and related disorders are no longer classified as a subtype of anxiety disorder (APA, 2013). Anxiety disorders are the most prevalent psychiatric disorder worldwide, occur more commonly in women, and tend to decrease in prevalence later in life (APA, 2013; Canuto et al., 2018). It has been purported that most individuals who suffer from anxiety do not seek treatment (Lepine, 2002). Anxiety disorders affect children as well as adults and frequently co-occur with depression, adding to the level of disability experienced by individuals with these disorders (Lecrubier, 2001). Ceri and colleagues (2017) studied rates of psychiatric disorders in second-generation immigrant children in Turkey and found that they had higher rates of depression, anxiety, PTSD, and comorbid disorders than native children. In the United States, the CDC reported that 3% of children ages 3–17 were identified as having a current diagnosis of an anxiety disorder (Bitsko et al., 2016). Medications used to treat anxiety disorders include benzodiazepines, antidepressants, antihistamines, and beta-blockers.

Benzodiazepines

Benzodiazepines are used to a variety of conditions, including insomnia, muscle relaxation, seizure disorders, and anxiety. Benzodiazepines are often prescribed to treat acute symptoms of anxiety, such as panic attacks, and are not recommended for longer-term treatment due to their addiction potential and possible heightened risk of mortality (Patorno et al., 2017). Examples of benzodiazepines include Ativan, Xanax, Valium, and Klonipin (see Table 2.1).

Benzodiazepines are GABA agonists, as they modulate neurotransmission by attaching to part of the GABAa receptor (Figure 2.12). When a benzodiazepine occupies this site, GABA attaches to a different part of the receptor more frequently. When GABA attaches to the receptor, chloride (Cl–) channels open and the cell membrane hyperpolarizes, leading to decreased excitability and a calming effect on the brain (Stanford, 2001a). As the principal inhibitory neurotransmitter, GABA is distributed throughout the brain, particularly in the cortex and limbic systems.

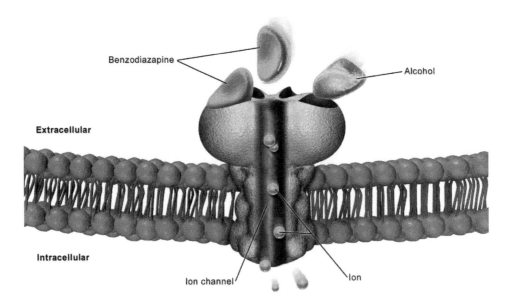

FIGURE 2.12.   GABA Receptor Depicting Attachment of Benzodiazepine and Alcohol

The GABA receptor is complex and consists of multiple subunits. Other drugs such as over the counter sleeping aids, barbituates, and alcohol attach to a different part of the GABA receptor and mimic the effects of GABA. Specifically, the Cl– channels remain open significantly longer, even in the absence of GABA. The end result of these drugs is similar to benzodiazepines in that neural inhibition is increased throughout the brain, however, when used in combination with benzodiazepines, they produce an additive and potential deadly effect (Griffin et al., 2013). Additional information concerning the physiological effects of antianxiety medications is included in Chapter 7.

Antidepressant Medications

Antidepressants are used to treat a number of conditions such as anxiety disorders, chronic pain, migraines, ADHD, and OCD but are most often used to treat individuals suffering from depressive disorders (e.g., major depressive disorder, persistent depressive disorder, premenstrual dysphoric disorder). Major depressive disorder is the most common of the depressive disorders. The 12-month prevalence of major depressive disorder in the United States is approximately 7% and 1.5–3 times higher rates in females than males (APA, 2013). According to the American Psychiatric Association, up to 80% of individuals with a mood disorder respond to treatment that typically involves antidepressants and some form of psychotherapy. The majority of patients respond to antidepressant treatment, and many show improvement with combinations of antidepressants (Safer, 2017; Stahl, 2000a). In 2004, the US Food and Drug Administration (FDA) reviewed 24 trials involving over 4,400 children and adolescents treated with nine antidepressant drugs (or placebo) for OCD, major depression, or other psychiatric disorders. Results revealed an average suicide risk of 4% compared to 2% for placebo (no suicides actually occurred during the trials). As a result of these findings, the FDA directed manufacturers of all antidepressant drugs to include a boxed warning statement about the increased risk of suicidal thinking or behavior among children and adolescents treated with these medications. In December 2006, the Psychopharmacologic Drugs Advisory Committee of the US Food and Drug Administration (FDA) conducted its own meta-analyses on the 77,382 adults from 295 randomized controlled clinical trials that evaluated treatments for major depressive disorder and other psychiatric disorders. The FDA defined suicidality as suicidal ideation, preparatory acts, attempts, or completions, and findings revealed that approximately 70% of the suicidality reported was suicidal thoughts; however, there were eight suicide deaths in the adult trials (five in participants randomized to the investigational agent, one to an active comparator, and two to placebo). Additionally, findings supported a protective effect of antidepressants for ages ≥65 years and a statistically nonsignificant elevation in risk of suicidality for ages 18–25 years. On the basis of these findings, the FDA issued a revised blackbox warning for *all antidepressants* in May 2007, thereby extending the coverage of the 2004 warning that applied to children and adolescents to include patients under 25 years of age. The warning label currently reads, "Antidepressants increased the risk compared to placebo of suicidal thinking and behavior (suicidality) in children, adolescents, and young adults in short-term studies of major depressive disorder (MDD) and other psychiatric disorders" (FDA, Revisions to product labeling).

Recent research has found significant changes in antidepressant prescription practices in the USA and abroad, particularly dosing, among children and adults following the blackbox warning (Abbott et al., 2003; Bushnell et al., 2016). Five broad categories of antidepressants are used to treat depression: monoamine oxidase inhibitors, tricyclic antidepressants, selective serotonin reuptake inhibitors (SSRIs), serotonin and norepinephrine reuptake inhibitors (SNRIs), and atypical antidepressants. The mode of action differs with each type of antidepressant.

Monoamine Oxidase Inhibitors (MAOIs)

Monoamine oxidases are enzymes (MAO-A and MAO-B) that metabolize serotonin, dopamine, and norepinephrine. Research has found that MAO activity varies greatly in the normal population (Brunner et al., 1993). Monoamine oxidase inhibitors are drugs that prevent monoamine oxidase from breaking down neurotransmitters within the terminal button. The first MAOIs produced inhibited both MAO-A and MAO-B, but newer MAOIs target one or the other of these enzymes and are used to treat psychiatric (MAO-A) or neurodegenerative disorders (MAO-B) (Finberg & Rabey, 2016). Some MAOIs have a weak affinity for blocking serotonin and norepinephrine presynaptic transporter proteins and inhibit reuptake to some degree (e.g., Nardil, Iproniazid; Stanford, 2001a, 2001b, 2001c). The end result of both cases is that more neurotransmitter is available for release and for activating postsynaptic receptors. Monoamine oxidase inhibitors are prescribed less frequently than other depressants due to their negative interaction with the amino acid tyramine, commonly found in foods such as cheese, coffee, chocolate, and other items. Specifically, when MAO is inhibited, tyramine is not broken down and consequently accumulates in the intracellular and extracellular fluid (*"cheese effect"*). The accumulation of tyramine elevates blood pressure and can result in hypertension and stroke; however, Gillman (2011) noted the likelihood of consuming tyramine levels large enough to cause a fatal or damaging reaction is quite low.

Tricyclic Antidepressants

Tricyclic antidepressants (e.g., imipramine, desipramine) block the reuptake of norepinephrine and, to a lesser degree, serotonin by binding to the presynaptic transporter proteins. The major limitation of tricyclic antidepressants is their adverse side effects. Singhal et al. (2002) reported that in rare instances, tricyclic antidepressants can produce sudden-onset headaches, seizures, and stroke, a condition known as Call-Fleming syndrome. In addition to blocking reuptake of norepinephrine and serotonin, tricyclic antidepressants attach to acetylcholine and histamine receptors. The consequence of attaching to these receptors is sedation, dry mouth, blurred vision, and dizziness, among other symptoms (PDR, 2017).

SSRIs and SNRIs

Selective serotonin reuptake inhibitors (SSRIs, e.g., Prozac, Paxil) and serotonin norepinephrine reuptake inhibitors (SNRIs, e.g., Pristiq, Cymbalta, Effexor) are used to treat a variety of psychiatric conditions, including anxiety, eating, obsessive compulsive, and, particularly, depressive disorder. SNRIs are also used to treat chronic pain. These medications relative to tricyclic antidepressants produce fewer side effects, have a greater compliance rate, and can be used to treat a larger number of conditions. Although the mode of action of SSRIs is not completely understood, research supports that SSRIs and SNRI immediately attach to the serotonin and transporter (SSRIs) or the serotonin and norepinephrine transporter and prevent the reuptake of serotonin/norepinephrine, resulting in increased levels of these neurotransmitters in the synaptic cleft. In response to increased levels of serotonin of norepinephrine, autoreceptors become desensitized and over time down-regulate resulting in a greater production and release of these substance (Gray et al., 2013). Increased levels of serotonin and norepinephrine in the synaptic cleft correspond with increased postsynaptic signaling and ultimately symptom improvement. SSRIs have also been found to promote intracellular changes that lead to an increased expression of nerve growth factors, dendritic expansion, and neurogenesis in restricted brain regions, such as the hippocampus (Glover & Clinton, 2016; Manji, 2003; Molendijk et al., 2011), although the manner in which these cellular changes relate to symptom improvement is unclear (Tanti and Belzung, 2010). It is also important to note that intracellular changes are not unique to antidepressants. For example, antipsychotic medication, mood stabilizers, and prescription stimulants have been associated with glial cell expansion, synaptogenesis, neurogenesis, and changes in gene expression (Bütefisch et al., 2002; Chen, Hasanat, et al., 1999; Coyle & Duman, 2003; Schmitt et al., 2004)

Although antidepressants are typically prescribed to treat or help remediate depression (or other conditions), some have suggested they be used prophylactically. Wittchen (2002), for example, suggested that antidepressants may play a role in *preventing* the development of major depression in individuals who suffer from GAD, and a more recent meta-analysis reported a 40% reduction in the incidence of depression among individuals receiving treatment for hepatitis C (Udina et al., 2014; Kokkinou et al., 2018). Additional information concerning antidepressants is provided in Chapter 6.

BOX 2.4   Personalized Medication—Swab My Cheek

It has been estimated that more than 40% of patients discontinue their psychotropic medication within 90 days due to adverse effects or lack of response. It has also been reported that approximately 50% of hospital patients are given drugs that can cause serious side effects due to their genetic makeup. In an effort to improve compliance as well as medication efficacy and safety, neuroscientists have looked to our DNA to provide clues, giving birth to the field of pharmacogenetics. Pharmacogenetics involves tailoring medication treatment based on an individual's genetic makeup. Companies such as GeneSight® examine an individual's DNA, and based on the presence of genetic markers (specific polymorphisms or mutations), predict how effective a drug (e.g., antidepressants, psychostimulants) will be for that individual. Recommendations may include dosing suggestions or information regarding frequency of physician monitoring (e.g., typical use, use with caution, frequent monitoring). For example, DNA analysis can identify whether an individual has a specific genetic mutation of the CYP2D6 gene—a gene that encodes specific enzymes (e.g., CYP2D6, CYP2C19) that metabolize SSRIs and breaks down codeine into morphine. Some individuals have genetic polymorphisms that result in too little or too much of the enzyme CYP2D6 that breaks down SSRIs or codeine into morphine. Individuals who are classified as "poor CYP2D6" metabolizers are often recommended to receive a smaller starting dose of an SSRI or codeine. Other genes associated with psychotropic medication response include CYP2D6, CYP2C19, SLC6A4, HTR2A, BDNF, GNB3, FKBP5, and ABCB1. To receive personalized genetic medication, testing must be ordered by a physician and patients must consent to a cheek swab. Companies then provide a report to the physician explaining the genetic findings and offer specific medication recommendations (Brenner & Holubowich, 2017).

Antipsychotic Medications

Antipsychotic medications are typically used to treat psychotic disorders, although they are also used to treat nonpsychotic disorders such as Tourette's disorder, borderline personality disorder, ASDs, anxiety, and bipolar disorder (Gaffney et al., 2002; Handen et al., 2017; Marston et al., 2014). Research has revealed that antipsychotic medications, such as chlorpromazine, clozapine, and haloperidol, primarily lessen psychotic symptoms but have a minimal effect on negative symptoms. One of the most disturbing side effects of antipsychotic medications is tardive dyskinesia, characterized by involuntary muscle movements, primarily in the facial region. The risk of tardive dyskinesia differs among the antipsychotic medications; overall, 20% to 40% of patients will develop the condition (Jest et al., 1999). According to Webster (2001c), tardive dyskinesia can take months or years to develop, and the symptoms may continue or even worsen after the medication is ceased.

With regard to mode of action, antipsychotic medications primarily block the dopamine (D2) receptors (Li et al., 2016). Depending on the drug, however, one or several types of dopamine receptors may be blocked. For example, chlorpromazine blocks D2 receptors, while clozapine is believed to block D4 and serotonin autoreceptors (Peng et al., 2016; Strange, 2001). Grunder et al. (2003) reported that in addition to blocking dopamine postsynaptic receptors, antipsychotic medications reduce the level of dopamine that is synthesized by neurons. Contrary to popular belief that response to antipsychotics is "delayed", research indicates that antipsychotics often result in *immediate* improvement of symptoms, and the greatest symptom relief often occurs within the first two weeks of treatment (Agid et al., 2006).

Mood Stabilizers

Mood stabilizers are primarily used to treat bipolar disorder. Mood stabilizers also have been used to augment antidepressants or antipsychotics in patients who do not respond to standard medication treatment for major depressive disorder or schizophrenia (Bertschy et al., 2003; Conley & Kelly, 2001). For example, Birkenhager and colleagues (2004) reported that a combination of imipramine and lithium was superior to treatment with an antidepressant (fluvoxamine) in individuals with severe depression. Two main types of mood stabilizers are used in the treatment of bipolar disorders—lithium and anticonvulsants (e.g., Carbamazepine, Divalproex). The precise mode of action of lithium is poorly understood, but current research suggests that it may result in molecular changes within specific neural pathways, inhibit second-messenger systems in glial cells and neurons, and have widespread effects on multiple neurotransmitters systems (Malhi et al., 2013; Pardo et al., 2003). In 2000, Lenox and Hahn reviewed the progress in understanding the mode of action of lithium during the past 50 years and concluded, "We are currently still at the stage of identifying the pieces of the lithium puzzle; within the next 50 years, we will be putting the puzzle together" (p. 12). Nearly 20 years later, current understanding of the mode of action of lithium remains limited. Despite this lack of understanding, lithium clearly produces beneficial effects, and recently, Post (2017) recommended that lithium be used prophylactically after the first manic episode of bipolar disorder to lessen the likelihood of additional episodes. The mode of action of anticonvulsants is also unclear, but studies suggest that similar to lithium, they have multiple effects, such as triggering gene expression, altering intracellular processes, inhibiting norepinephrine reuptake, blocking sodium channels, and enhancing the action of GABA (Perrine, 1996; Rosenberg, 2007). Additional information concerning mood stabilizers is provided in Chapter 5.

Psychostimulants

Stimulant medications, including methylphenidate and amphetamine derivatives, have been widely used for decades in the United States and abroad, and remain the first-line pharmacotherapy for children, adolescents, and adults with ADHD (nonstimulant medications have been approved for ADHD and will be discussed in Chapter 9) (DuPaul, Weyandt, et al., 2011; Martinez-Raga et al., 2017). ADHD is estimated to affect 3% to 7% of the school-age population and 4% of adults worldwide (APA, 2013; Weyandt, 2001). Like most medications, the precise mode of action of stimulants is unclear (Safer, 2016). Although variations occur depending on the specific type of stimulant, stimulants typically disrupt the reuptake process by blocking the transporter protein for dopamine (DAT) (and to a lesser extent, norepinephrine). This blockade results in more dopamine available in the synaptic cleft and helps to regulate dopaminergic systems, particularly in the regions of the prefrontal cortex and basal ganglia (Joyce, 2007; Schulz et al., 2017; Volkow et al., 2001). Additional information concerning the effects of prescription stimulants is provided in Chapter 9.

Chapter Summary

This chapter reviewed the processes involved in neurotransmission, including exocytosis, endocytosis, and pinocytosis. Neurotransmitter classifications and neurotransmitter systems were also reviewed, including acetylcholine, aspartate, dopamine, GABA, glutamate, and serotonin. An overview of psychopharmacology was provided as well as a general description of the purpose and mode of action for various classes of psychotropic drugs. Although medications can often improve cognitive and behavioral symptoms of various disorders, it is important to note that they do not remedy the underlying physiological condition that contributes to the expression of the disorder.

Chapter Summary: Main Points

- The nervous system consists of the central nervous system (brain and spinal cord) and peripheral nervous system (somatic and autonomic divisions).
- The cell is encased in a semipermeable membrane embedded with protein channels.
- The major internal components of a cell include the nucleus, ribosomes, endoplasmic reticulum, mitochondria, golgi complex, microtubules, cytoskeleton, and synaptic vesicles.
- The major external components of a neuron include the soma, dendrites, dendritic spines, axons, and terminal button.
- The neuron sending a message is the presynaptic cell; the neuron receiving a message is the postsynaptic cell.
- The space between the pre- and postsynaptic cell is the synaptic cleft.
- Electrostatic pressure and diffusion contribute to the resting potential.
- An action potential develops once a cell membrane reaches the threshold of excitation.
- Action potentials travel down the axon and trigger exocytosis at the terminal button.
- The terminal button maintains its shape through pinocytosis.
- Endocytosis is achieved through the process of reuptake.

- Postsynaptic receptors are ionotropic or metabotropic.
- Neurotransmitter substances include gases, peptides, and small molecule transmitters.
- Glutamate is the principal excitatory neurotransmitter; GABA is the principal inhibitory neurotransmitter.
- Monoamine neurotransmitters include catecholamines (dopamine, norepinephrine, epinephrine) and idolamines (serotonin, melatonin).
- Pharmacokinetics is the process of drugs being absorbed, distributed, metabolized, and excreted from the body.
- Medication effects vary widely among individuals and are influenced by genetic factors.
- Psychotropic drugs include antianxiety, antidepressants, stimulants, mood stabilizers, and antipsychotic medication.
- The mode of action of psychotropic drugs varies at the level of the receptor.

Review Questions

1. What are the major internal and external structures of a cell? What functions are associated with each of these structures?
2. Describe the development of an action potential.
3. Differentiate between agonists and antagonists. Provide examples of each.
4. Distinguish between exocytosis, pinocytosis, and endocytosis.
5. Explain the role of each of the following: vesicular transporter proteins, reuptake transporter proteins, and enzymatic degradation.
6. Describe the general mode of action of each of the following: antianxiety, antidepressants, stimulants, mood stabilizers, and antipsychotic medication.

three

Techniques of Brain Imaging and Brain Stimulation

This chapter reviews techniques that are commonly used to study brain structure or functioning in psychiatric disorders including computed tomography (CT), electroencephalogram (EEG), magnetic resonance imaging (MRI), functional magnetic resonance imaging (fMRI), real-time functional magnetic resonance imaging (rtfMRI), positron emission tomography (PET), and near infrared spectroscopy (NIRS). Although additional physiological techniques are available to monitor brain functioning such as event-related optical signal (EROS), magnetoencephalography (MEG), single photon emission tomography (SPECT), and magnetic resonance spectroscopic imaging (MRSI), compared to other methods they are used less frequently in the study of psychiatric disorders and will not be discussed here. Background information regarding basic principles of brain activation is reviewed, followed by specific neurophysiological and neuroimaging techniques. The final section of the chapter examines brain stimulation techniques, many of which are currently being used in the treatment of mental health disorders.

Chapter 3 Learning Objectives

- Describe fundamental principles of brain activation and measurement.
- Describe important design issues faced by neuroimaging studies.
- Differentiate between structural and functional imaging techniques.
- Define the "default mode network".
- Identify and explain major structural imaging techniques.
- Identify and explain major functional imaging techniques.
- Identify and explain major brain stimulation techniques.

Fundamental Principles of Brain Activation and Measurement

Brain activation is reflected in neuronal signaling and neurotransmission, glucose metabolism, and changes in blood flow. Neuronal signaling refers to the movement of ions across the cell membrane, the process of neurotransmission, and includes receptor studies. These processes of metabolism, blood flow, and signaling occur continually in the brain, but their rate of activity varies across brain regions and during different states (e.g., sleeping, awake, cognitive demands) (Magistretti & Allaman, 2015). Some of these cellular changes produce patterns of electromagnetic signals that radiate to the outside of the brain and can be detected by measurement devices. Other cellular changes, such as increased glucose consumption, can be tracked and measured with radioactive substances that are attached to glucose molecules and taken up by active neurons. Blood flow increases with metabolic demand and therefore changes in regional cerebral blood flow can be used to infer greater cellular activity. Thus, neuroimaging techniques measure either metabolism (glucose, oxygen consumption, or changes in blood volume) or neural signaling (flow of ions, release of neurotransmitters, or density of receptors). Other techniques, such as CT and MRI, measure brain structure, not function, and provide information about the morphology of the brain. Physiological techniques, such as EEG, measure the summed postsynaptic activity of many individual neurons at the level of the cortex.

In general, there are two main purposes of brain imaging techniques. The first is to compare *structural* images of a normal brain to determine whether certain structural changes are characteristic of various diseases. With regard to psychiatric conditions, these types of images are useful for exploring ventricle enlargement, tissue loss, and volumetric differences in structures. A second purpose is to determine whether *functional* changes are associated with different psychiatric disorders or with cognitive processes. For example, epilepsy is characterized by excessive neuronal firing, and Parkinson's disease is characterized by death of neurons in the substantia nigra leading to different patterns of activation in the basal ganglia (Dostrovsky et al., 2000). Studies have also reported, albeit inconsistently, that schizophrenia and major depression are characterized by reduced activity in the frontal regions (Ito et al., 1996; Li et al., 2013; Penades et al., 2017). In order to better understand normal brain functioning, scientists often explore whether certain regions of the brain become more or less activated during various cognitive tasks in healthy participants. Cognitive psychologists, for example have identified brain activation patterns in healthy adults presented with emotional visual information, and a host of studies have explored activation patterns during attention, working memory, and additional cognitive processes (Kuniecki et al., 2017). The focus of this text, however, is on structural and functional findings of participants with various psychiatric and neurodegenerative disorders relative to healthy control participants.

Measurement Design Issues

It is important to note that the structural and functional images of the brain produced by CT, MRI, fMRI, PET, SPECT, and so on are actually reconstructed computerized images. Each method varies with respect to the mathematical formulas used for the reconstruction of these images. Depending on the purpose of the imaging technique, different procedures are used to produce and interpret the brain image. For example, for structural questions, images of a brain of a person with a particular psychiatric disorder can be compared to a normal brain, or the same brain can be imaged over time and compared temporaneously. For questions pertaining to brain function, brain activity measurements of an individual who has been diagnosed with (or is suspected of having) a disorder such as schizophrenia, Parkinson's disease, or Alzheimer's disease can be compared to those taken while a healthy individual is at rest. Alternatively, measurement of brain activity can be taken while an individual is at rest. These measurements can be used as a baseline for comparison to brain activity measurements of the same individual while they are engaged in a task. These comparisons can therefore be used to target brain regions that are likely involved in various cognitive tasks. This same comparison method can be repeated across numerous participants, and the data can be collapsed to identify general areas of increased activation among participants during specific tasks. In addition to providing structural or functional information about the brain, the techniques also differ with regard to (a) time required to complete the image(s), (b) use of radioactive substances, (c) degree of resolution, and (d) expense.

BOX 3.1   Communicating With the Uncommunicative

Patients who have sustained traumatic brain injuries sometimes awaken from a comatose state but appear to lack awareness of anything in their environment. Those who do not show signs of voluntary response to stimuli are often diagnosed as being in a vegetative state. Some patients show inconsistent signs of awareness but are unable to communicate and are diagnosed as minimally conscious. Monti and colleagues wondered whether fMRI would be useful in determining whether patients in a minimally conscious or vegetative state would be able to reliably communicate awareness by modulate their brain activity. As such, the investigators studied 54 patients, 31 in a minimally conscious state, 23 in a vegetative state, and 16 control participants while in the fMRI scanner and were asked to perform two imagery tasks: (a) to imagine standing still on a tennis court and to swing an arm to "hit the ball" back and forth to an imagined instructor and (b) during the spatial imagery task, patients were instructed to imagine navigating the streets of a familiar city or to imagine walking from room to room in their home and to visualize all that they would "see" if they were there. Results indicated that four of the vegetative and one of the minimally conscious patients could willfully and reliably modulate their brain activity as indicated by sustained activation in the supplemental motor cortex during the motor imagery task and parahippocampal region during the spatial task following verbal instructions. These findings are startling and indicate that some patients, although unable to communicate awareness motorically or verbally, retain a level of awareness that can be revealed with brain imaging technology (Monti et al., 2010).

Brain Imaging Techniques: Structural Imaging

Computed Tomography (CT)

The two most common techniques for gathering information about brain structure are computed tomography (CT) and magnetic resonance imaging (MRI). A CT scan is diagnostic imaging test used to create detailed images ("tomographic images") of internal organs, bones, soft tissue, and blood vessels. The scan generates cross-sectional and three-dimensional images that can be viewed on a computer monitor, printed on film, or transferred electronically. A CT brain scan is achieved by an X-ray tube and detector placed around an individual's head. The tube moves in a circular process and passes beams through

Table 3.1 Brain Imaging Techniques

Technique	Description	Purpose
Computed Tomography (CT)	Series of X-ray images taken from different angles to create cross-sectional images of the brain.	Brain Structure
Magnetic Resonance Imaging (MRI)	Magnetic field and radio waves used to produce detailed images.	Brain Structure
Diffusion Tensor Imaging (DTI)	Measures three-dimenstional diffusion of water molecules to estimate white matter connectivity.	Brain Structure
Functional MRI (fMRI)	Magnetic field and radio waves used to identify areas of increased brain activation inferred from changes in blood flow.	Brain Function
Positron Emission Tomography (PET)	Radioactive tracer used to identify areas of increased activation based on glucose metabolism or regional cerebral blood flow.	Brain Function
Single Photon Computed Emission Tomography (SPECT)	Use of gamma-emitting radioisotope to produce three-dimensional, cross-sectional slices of the brain based on blood flow.	Brain Function

the head at different angles. The X-ray tube and detector are located opposite each other, and, after the X-ray beam passes through an individual's head, the detector records the amount of radioactivity that passes through. A computer translates the information from the detector into pictures of the brain and skull. Based on a mathematical formula incorporating density and corresponding voxels, various shades of black, gray, or white can then be assigned to the image. Cerebral spinal fluid appears nearly black on the image, bone appears white, and brain tissue appears gray. Compared to MRI, the resolution of the CT images is low, and, consequently, it is difficult to differentiate between gray (tissues rich in cell bodies) and white matter (myelinated axons) (Hollister & Boutros, 1991; Hsieh, 2009).

Computed tomography has been used to research a number of psychiatric and neurodegenerative diseases, such as schizophrenia, anxiety disorders, and Alzheimer's disease. Johnstone and colleagues (1976) were among the first to use CT with patients with schizophrenia and healthy controls, and found that patients with schizophrenia had enlarged ventricles and smaller cortical gyri than individuals without the disorder. Since that time, hundreds of CT studies have been conducted with clinical disorders. For example, O'Brien et al. (2000) investigated CT images in two groups of patients with two types of dementia and a group with major depression. Results indicated that CT scans did not differentiate between types of dementia but did distinguish between individuals with major depression and dementia. According to Colohan et al. (1989), brain morphology as examined by CT can vary depending on the age of the participant, and occasionally CT scans appear falsely abnormal. Furthermore, CT scan findings, laboratory testing, EEG, physical exam, and psychiatric status often correlate poorly (Colohan et al., 1989). Similarly, Ghaziuddin and colleagues (1993) reported that the widespread use of CT in child and adolescent psychiatry was unfounded because not only do very few of these patients have abnormal CT scans but also changes in diagnoses or treatment are rarely the result of such scans. More recently, Goulet and colleagues (2009) conducted a systematic review of the literature exploring the use of CT and MRI in patients with first-time psychosis and concluded that CT (and MRI) were of little benefit in identifying brain abnormalities. Collectively, these studies suggest that the use of CT in psychiatric structural and diagnostic studies and practice is of limited use. Techniques with greater resolution such as MRI and those that provide information about brain functioning are more suitable for identifying structural and functional patterns in participants with clinical disorders relative to healthy controls.

Magnetic Resonance Imaging (MRI)

Magnetic resonance imaging provides more detailed images than CT scans with more distinct contrasts between gray and white matter and cerebral spinal fluid. MRI does not use X-rays; instead, a strong magnetic field is passed through the skull, and the MRI scanner detects the movement of hydrogen molecules in response to the magnetic field. The details of this process are complex, but, essentially, the nuclei of hydrogen molecules are protons and act as tiny magnets. When the MRI scanner sends a magnetic field through the head, the protons align in one direction. When the scanner delivers a pulse of radio waves, the protons move to a different orientation, and this movement is detected by the MRI scanner. Once the radiofrequency pulse is stopped, the protons return to their original orientation. These protons are present in different concentrations in the brain (e.g., cerebral spinal fluid versus myelinated axons), and the scanner uses this information to produce the MRI image (see Papanicolaou, 1998; Westbrook, 2016, for additional information).

A plethora of studies has been published concerning the use of MRI in dementia, Parkinson's disease, and mental health disorders. It is important to emphasize that MRI produces structural images and does not provide information concerning brain functioning. Nevertheless, MRI brain scans have found morphological deviations in individuals with schizophrenia (e.g., enlarged lateral and third ventricles, reduction of total brain volume, reduction of size of prefrontal and temporal lobes, basal ganglia enlargement (Lawrie & Abukmeil, 1998; Shenton et al., 2001). Volume and size differences have also been found in various brain structures in participants with a wide range of clinical and neurodegenerative disorders (see upcoming chapters). It is important to note, however, that results across studies are highly variable and many studies have not reported structural differences based on MRI scans between individuals with and without psychiatric disorders. MRI, however, has been quite useful in providing information about the normally developing brain. Overall, these developmental studies have revealed changes in structural brain volume, including gray and white matter beginning in infancy and continuing throughout young adulthood in normally developing, healthy individuals (Gennatas et al., 2017; Meng et al., 2017).

Diffusion Tensor Imaging (DTI)

Diffusion tensor imaging analyzes the movement of water molecules in the white matter—i.e., myelinated axons of the brain. Special software enables the MRI scanner to track the degree to which water molecules move about, reflecting changes at the cellular and microstructural level. In the brain, water molecules are typically constrained by white matter tracts (bundles of myelinated axons) and therefore move along the length of the axon (path of least resistance). When completely unrestrained, however, water molecules move in a spherical shape. DTI assesses movement of water molecules within a particular region of the brain. When damage has occurred to white mater, water molecules move more freely—i.e., diffuse. DTI, therefore, measures the white matter connectivity patterns and does so three dimensionally (Alexander et al., 2007). Numerous DTI studies have been conducted with participants with most psychiatric disorders, including neurodegenerative disorders, addiction, schizophrenia, OCD, major depressive disorder, bipolar disorder, ADHD, ASD, and others (Kubicki et al., 2002). Although white matter findings to date have not been specific to a particular disorder, Shizukuishi, Abe, and Aoki (2013) recommended routine use of DTI to assess white matter abnormalities in patients with psychiatric disorders.

Brain Imaging Techniques: Functional Imaging

Functional Magnetic Resonance Imaging (fMRI)

Since its inception in the early 1990s, functional magnetic resonance imaging (fMRI) has been used in an exceptionally large number of medical, psychiatric, and psychological studies (Figure 3.1). In contrast to CT and MRI, which provide information about brain structure, fMRI provides information about brain functioning indirectly based on changes in blood flow and oxygen consumption. When performing a task (e.g., cognitive or motor task), neurons in a specific brain region become more active, and the cell's mitochondria require more glucose for production of cellular energy: ATP. Glucose and oxygen are delivered to cells via the brain's vascular system; consequently, changes in regional blood flow reflect areas of increased neuronal activation (Papanicolaou, 1998). The amount of oxygenated blood that is delivered to brain tissue depends on the rate of metabolism in that region. Following increased metabolic activity, the amount of oxygenated blood delivered to the area increases, although this relationship is not perfectly linear. Instead, the amount of oxygenated blood that is delivered to an active area *exceeds* that of the amount that was actually used, and this process can take up to several seconds. Therefore fMRI does not measure blood flow per se, but instead detects the increase in oxygenated blood relative to deoxygenated blood in the area of increased neuronal activity, and this change is reflected in the BOLD contrast (Blood Oxygenation Level Dependent) (Glover, 2011). It is important to keep in mind that recent research indicates that even at rest, considerable fluctuations in activity exist across brain regions, and these fluctuations vary substantially across individuals (Shine, Koyejo, & Poldrack, 2016).

It is important to note that fMRI has good spatial resolution, as it can distinguish between metabolic activity in the area of interest relative to nearby locations. However, because there is a time delay (3–6 seconds) between the actual onset of neuronal activity and delivery of blood flow to the region of increased neuronal activity, fMRI does not *directly* measure brain activity and consequently has poor temporal resolution (i.e., the smallest time period of neural activity reliably identified) (Foged et al., 2017; Glover, 2011). Recently, studies have begun combining EEG and fMRI to take advantage of the high temporal resolution of EEG and high spatial resolution of fMRI (Cunningham et al., 2008; Foged et al., 2017).

An advantage of fMRI is that it does not require the use of radiation and is considered safe for both adults and children. Although previously MRI and fMRI were exceedingly difficult to use with infants, particularly neonates, fMRI and MRI equipment is currently available for use with newborns (Cusack, McCuaig, & Linke, 2017; Erberich et al., 2003).

With regard to normal patterns of brain functioning in children, adolescents, and adults, longitudinal fMRI studies are currently underway to understand variability in brain development and whether these structural and functional changes correspond with cognitive processes and development (e.g., Gied et al., 1999; Volkow et al., 2017). Other studies have

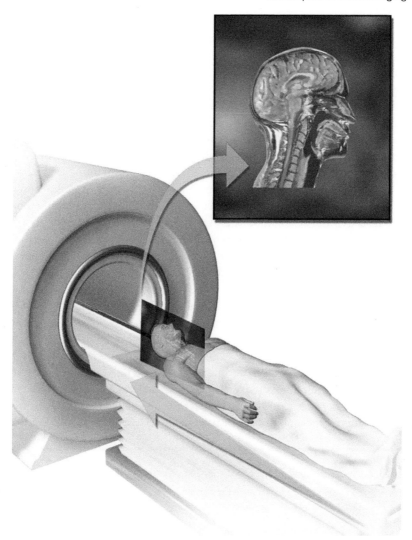

FIGURE 3.1. Functional Magnetic Resonance Imaging Machine

Copyright Blausen Medical Communications. Reproduced by permission.

focused on changes in structural brain networks during the normal aging process (Wu et al., 2013). A plethora of studies have explored various structural and functional aspects of cognitive functioning, including processing of affective information, attention, memory, and basic sensorimotor pathways and processes. Maestu et al. (2003) reviewed the status of neuroimaging studies of cognition and noted that most studies attempted to locate brain regions associated with particular cognitive functions when, in fact, most cognitive processes are widely distributed throughout the brain.

With regard to clinical disorders, the use of fMRI to explore functional differences in psychiatric populations relative to healthy controls has increased dramatically during the past two decades. Clinical fMRI studies are plentiful and usually involve comparison between individuals with a specific disorder relative to healthy control participants and/or a second clinical comparison group. Findings from these studies are discussed in subsequent chapters with regard to schizophrenia, major depressive disorder, bipolar disorder, OCD, childhood onset disorders, neurodegenerative disorders, and addiction.

Default Mode Network

A major concern in interpreting the fMRI literature is that most studies focus on changes in brain activity but relatively little information is available regarding baseline activity of the brain. Gusnard and Raichle (2001) have suggested there may be a baseline or normal resting state of brain function that involves consistent activity in some areas and less activity in others. For example, even at rest, the brain is involved in a continuous process of monitoring the environment (e.g., for potential predators), and this monitoring is correlated with neuronal activity in certain brain regions. Brain regions that are active while a person is not engaged in an activity or is daydreaming have been coined as the "default mode network" (Raichle et al., 2001). The default mode network (also known as the task negative network) includes the posterior cingulate cortex as well as numerous brain regions and has been found to be less active during goal-oriented tasks requiring focused attention and working memory (McGuire et al., 1996; Uytun et al., 2017).

It is important to note that the default mode network is not universally accepted, and many have been critical of the concept (Craig et al., 2017; Fair et al., 2008). In addition, Kosslyn (1999) has argued that simply observing which brain regions are activated during task performance is unlikely to lead to a better understanding of brain functioning. Instead, Kosslyn proposed that scientists develop a taxonomy of questions concerning the manner in which cognitive processes occur in the brain, design tasks that capitalize on the strengths of neuroimaging techniques, and then offer specific hypotheses based on the research questions. Relative to other neuroimaging techniques (i.e., PET), fMRI is less expensive, does not require radiation exposure, and can be used safely with children as well as adults.

BOX 3.2   Something Fishy?

In 2010, Craig Bennett and colleagues published a paper "Neural Correlates of Interspecies Perspective Taking in the Post-Mortem Atlantic Salmon: An Argument for Multiple Comparisons Correction". Bennett et al. presented fMRI findings from one subject, a mature Atlantic Salmon, that was reportedly 18 inches long, weighed 3.8 pounds, and was not alive at the time of scanning. The salmon was shown a series of photographs depicting humans in social situations with a specified emotional valence. The salmon was then "asked to determine what emotion the individual in the photo must have been experiencing". A total of 15 photos were individually presented for 10 seconds followed by 12 seconds of rest. Total scan time was 5.5 minutes. A t-contrast was used to test for regions with significant BOLD signal change during the photo condition compared to the rest condition. Results revealed several active voxels in a cluster located within the salmon's brain. This finding was startling because the salmon was clearly dead! What contributed to these "active" regions in the dead salmon, and what is the takeaway from this analysis? As the authors noted, statistical analyses may yield spurious (and misleading) results if multiple comparisons are not controlled for statistics. The authors argued that fMRI studies should routinely incorporate multiple comparison corrections as standard practice in statistical computations.

Positron Emission Tomography (PET)

As discussed previously, neurons use a variety of organic molecules to function and these molecules (e.g., glucose, water) are delivered in the blood. The concentration of these substances in a particular region of the brain varies depending on the activity of neurons in that region. The constituents of these substances (e.g., hydrogen, oxygen, nitrogen) do not emit electromagnetic signals and therefore cannot be tracked or measured with neuroimaging devices. Organic substances, such as oxygen and glucose, however, can be bombarded with radioactive isotopes and combined with other substances to create compounds, such as glucose or water (e.g., [18F]fluorodeoxyglucose). These compounds can then be inhaled or injected into a person's bloodstream and then pass the blood-brain barrier and enter the brain. These compounds are "radioactive" and shed positively charged particles (*positrons*) that can be traced in the brain with neuroimaging techniques. Two methods are used to measures neuronal activity: glucose metabolism and blood flow.

Glucose is the primary source of energy for neurons and, as neuronal activity increases, increased amounts of radioactive glucose are taken up by neurons. Alternatively, as discussed with fMRI, blood flow is correlated with increased metabolic activity of neurons and organic molecules, such as oxygen or carbon, can also be tagged and traced in the blood. The time required for the positrons to be shed varies among isotopes; the amount of time it takes for half of the positrons to be shed is known as the *half-life*. As positrons are shed, they collide with electrons, which results in photons. These photons pass through the skull and are detected by the PET scanner (Figure 3.2). The exit location of the photos reflects the distribution of the radioactive compound in the brain and represents the level of brain activity in various regions. The PET scanner records the photon signals and a mathematical algorithm is applied to the data. A computerized image is then projected in shades of gray or color *representing* the neuronal activity changes in the brain. PET images can also be superimposed on an MRI scan. The MRI scan shows the brain anatomy in detail, whereas PET reveals cerebral blood flow (CBF), metabolic rate of oxygen consumption (CMR02), or the metabolic rate of glucose consumption (CMRglc) (Be´langer et al., 2011). Areas of increased blood flow, oxygen consumption, or glucose metabolism are considered "active" and comparisons can be made between levels of activity at rest, during tasks, following tasks, or during drug administration (Newberg et al., 2011; Hung, 2013).

PET studies also use radioactive drugs that bind to neurotransmitter receptors, such as dopamine, serotonin, opiate, and muscarinic receptors. By tracing the attachment of these drugs to the receptors, the density of receptors and transporter proteins in particular regions can be determined. For example, decreased density of dopamine receptors in the striatum and substantia nigra has been found in Parkinson's disease as well as decreased density of nicotinic receptors. The latter finding is curious, as cigarette smoking is associated with a lower incidence of Parkinson's disease (Kas et al., 2017). Density of neurotransmitter receptors will also be addressed in subsequent chapters.

The degree of occupancy of receptors can also be determined by tracer studies and helps to determine medication affinity, efficacy, and therapeutic response (Frost, 1992; Parsey & Mann, 2003). For example, dopamine antagonists tagged with a radioactive tracer (e.g., [11C]raclopride) can identify areas high in a specific type of dopamine receptor (D2). This information is important as it helps to identify sites of drug action as well as degree of binding to these receptors with various drugs (e.g., antipsychotics, cocaine, antidepressants). For example, Drevets et al. (1997) used PET and a radioactive ligand that binds to serotonin receptors ([11C]WAY-100635) to determine the extent of binding in individuals

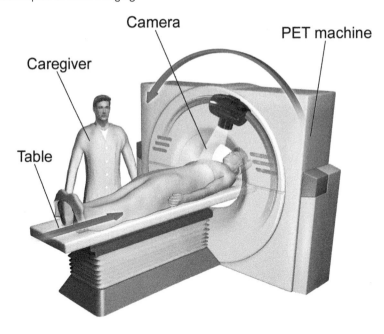

Positron Emission Tomography Scan

FIGURE 3.2. Positron Emission Tomography Machine

Copyright Blausen Medical Communications. Reproduced by permission.

with bipolar disorder and major depression. Results indicated that binding was significantly reduced in individuals with both disorders, but the magnitude of the reduction was greater in those with bipolar disorder. In 1968, Sedvall, Farde, Persson, and Wiesel suggested that quantitative neuroreceptor measurements may one day be used as a biochemical diagnostic tool for neuropsychiatric disorders. Today, neuroreceptor measurements are not yet used as biomarkers for mental health disorders, although they continue to be important in pharmacology, substance abuse research, and neurodegenerative disease (e.g., Prescott, 2013; Volkow, Fowler, and Wang, 2003).

PET has been used in thousands of studies of participants with psychiatric conditions compared to healthy controls. These findings—as well as the limitations of the studies—are discussed in subsequent chapters. Interestingly, direct comparison studies of PET and fMRI have reported similar rCBF response to brain activation (Feng et al., 2004; Scheibler et al., 2012).

Methodological Limitations of Functional Neuroimaging Studies

A number of scientists have expressed skepticism regarding the use of fMRI in understanding cognitive processes and clinical disorders. Concerns pertain mainly to methodological factors, statistical analyses, and lack of standardized procedures. For example, many fMRI studies use small samples, lack adequate statistical power, and rarely report effect size. This is especially problematic in terms of statistical analyses, as most fMRI studies conduct numerous, uncorrected statistical analyses that can lead to Type I errors (claiming a difference exists when it does not) and erroneous interpretations (Bennett et al., 2010; Vul et al., 2009). Indeed, Eklund, Nichols, and Knutsson (2016) reported statistical software packages typically used in fMRI studies resulted in Type I errors more than 50% of the time! A second criticism is that fMRI designs are rarely replicated and available test-retest reliabilities are typically poor (< 0.7) (Vul et al., 2009). A third criticism is that fMRI studies are inherently correlational in design yet findings are often interpreted as causal (e.g., Farah, 2014; Lyon, 2017). Furthermore, recent studies have demonstrated that the BOLD response in circumscribed areas of the brain can be increased or decreased volitionally with training (Sepulveda et al., 2016), thereby raising questions about the construct validity of the images.

In order to address many of the criticisms of fMRI, methodological experts have suggested that (a) statistical analyses should be theoretically based and determined a priori to avoid multiple unplanned comparisons that contribute to spurious findings, (b) statistical corrections procedures need to be implemented to avoid spurious findings and inflated correlation coefficients, (c) the field of cognitive neuroscience should move away from a strong focus on localization of function to understanding patterns of activation, (d) a standardized set of approaches for fMRI connectivity modeling needs to be developed and implemented, and (e) improvement of sample size and statistical power, multi-site, and data-sharing studies should be conducted (Poldrack, 2012, 2015; Vul et al., 2009).

Additional methodological issues need to be considered when interpreting the results of fMRI and PET neuroimaging studies. A major concern involves the validity and reliability of the images. For example, a critical assumption is that the particular brain activity observed actually represents the cognitive or behavioral function that the study was intended to measure—which may not be the case. As noted by Papanicolaou (1998), a study's intent may be to measure glucose metabolism, but the resultant brain activity representing oxygen use and increased blood flow does not necessarily co-vary with the pattern of metabolism. Furthermore, participants may approach tasks differently, and various memories may be triggered while a subject is performing a task. Consequently, the results may not reflect a specific cognitive process (e.g., semantic memory) but instead additional brain functions. Hence, measurement of complex constructs such as "personality" and "novelty seeking" using PET or other neuroimaging techniques is questionable, and terms such as neuronal "connectivity" and "efficiency" are equally problematic (e.g., Horwitz, 2003; Park, Park, & Kim, 2016). When attempting to measure such constructs with PET or fMRI, simplification of concepts and use of operational definitions are crucial. In addition, replication of studies and findings would help support the reliability and validity of results but are rare in the literature.

A related methodological issue is whether similar imaging results would be found over time (i.e., reliability). Currently there is substantial variability across studies in terms of tasks, design, ages of participants, comorbidity, inclusion criteria for clinical disorders, and standardized measures for procedures and tasks could improve measurement validity and reliability. Additionally, many studies do not include information concerning intelligence, ethnicity, or comorbidity. Inclusion of individuals with two or more disorders (comorbidity) makes it difficult to determine whether the findings of the study are related to one disorder or a combination of disorders. Some studies only include females (or males) and/ or include participants within a restricted age range; hence, it remains unknown whether the results of these studies apply to individuals of different ages, sex, and ethnicity. It is also important to emphasize that both PET and fMRI are indirect measures of cellular function and do not directly measure neural communication.

Finally, it is critical that neuroimaging findings be considered in a broader context to help determine the clinical relevance of the findings. For example, hypoperfusion (decreased blood flow) of the frontal lobes, and in particular the prefrontal cortex, has been found in individuals with violent criminal offenses and clinical disorders, including schizophrenia, ADHD, Alzheimer's disease, Parkinson's disease, and borderline personality disorder, as well as others (Archer et al., 2015; Di Tommaso, 2012; Lin, Chen, Huang et al., 2017; Soloff et al., 2003). It would be incorrect, therefore, to conclude that decreased activity in the frontal lobes causes any of these disorders or that hypoperfusion is unique to a specific disorder.

Electroencephalogram (EEG and qEEG)

An EEG is a recording of the postsynaptic cortical activity of groups of neurons while an individual is at rest, sleeping, or during a specific sensory stimulation task (e.g., a flash of light). During an EEG, electrodes are placed on the scalp over different regions of the brain such as the occipital, parietal, temporal, and frontal cortices. Specific systems exist for the placement of electrodes (Nuwer et al., 1994), and the number of electrodes placed on the scalp can vary from approximately 15–125 (Gevins, 1998). In conditions in which a stimulus is presented, the recording is called a sensory-evoked potential or an event-related potential. For example, Molfese (1984) was among the first to use EEG and an auditory stimulus to demonstrate that the left hemisphere in adults, but not the right, responds to consonant sounds. Molfese et al. (2003) later reported that the brain of infants reliably discriminates between familiar and unfamiliar words, based on auditory-evoked responses. Recently, Schermerhorn, Bates, Puce, and Molfese (2017) using EEG discovered that children who were exposed to greater inter-parental conflict showed a distinct pattern of response relative to children who were exposed to less inter-parental conflict.

According to Martin (1991), EEGs are based on frequency and amplitude domains; frequencies of the potentials vary from 1 to 30 Hz and amplitudes from 20 to 100 MV. Several dominant frequency and amplitude bands characterize EEG recordings: alpha (8–13 Hz), beta (13–30 Hz), delta (0.5–4 Hz), and theta (4–7 Hz). Alpha waves are associated with relaxed wakefulness, beta waves with alter wakefulness, and delta and theta waves are associated with sleeping states. Several studies, however, suggest that all of these EEG bands may be involved in various physiological brain states, and thus their usefulness for understanding brain activity is questionable (Klimesch, 1999; Sand et al., 2013). EEG recordings are of value in pathological conditions such as epilepsy (Besio et al., 2014); however, they are of limited value in mental health disorders. Quantitative methods have been developed (qEEG), however, that analyze frequency, amplitude, and spatial changes of potentials that are used more frequently in psychiatric research (Haghighi et al., 2017; Martin, 1991).

Among the recent quantitative methods developed is qEEG mapping. The technique involves the creation of a multidimensional matrix that provides a topographic representation of qEEG parameters, enabling dynamic changes to be observed as they take place during the EEG. Statistical methods are then used to analyze the data to help identify areas of normal and abnormal brain activity (e.g., Bosch-Bayard et al., 2001). As Raichle (2000) noted, qEEG is not an imaging tool like PET and fMRI, and the source of the cortical activity recorded by EEG is difficult to determine. In addition, artifacts and errors in measurement can influence the results and interpretation of qEEG (Lawson et al., 2003). Raichle (2000) advocated the combined use of EEG and neuroimaging techniques such as PET and fMRI to gain a truer picture of brain functioning. Patterns of cortical activation have been found, however, in individuals with various disorders relative to individuals without the disorders. For example, several studies using qEEG have found that individuals with schizophrenia show an increase in delta and theta waves (slow waves) as well as beta (fast) waves (e.g., Itil, 1977). This pattern has not been found in all studies, however, and these findings are not necessarily unique to schizophrenia (Gruzelier, Galderisi, & Strik, 2002; Harris et al., 2001; Sponheim et al., 2000). In addition, not all patients with schizophrenia have abnormal qEEG findings (Kirino & Inoue, 1999).

Studies have also used EEG and qEEG to investigate a wide range of clinical and cognitive disorders, such as anxiety disorders, mood disorders, ADHD, autism, dementia, learning disorders, and PTSD (e.g., Cook et al., 2002; Jokic-Begic & Begic, 2003; Nystrom, Matousek, & Hallstrom, 1986; Oluboka et al., 2002; Shagass et al., 1984; Roh et al., 2016). Tot and colleagues (2002), for example, found that adults with OCD had higher qEEG frequencies of slow-wave bands and lower frequencies of alpha waves (mainly in the left frontal-temporal region) relative to control subjects. Other studies have found EEG pattern differences between individuals with OCD and controls in the anterior regions of the cortex (Blair Simpson et al., 2000; Molina et al., 1995). Interestingly, Leuchter and colleagues (2002) investigated depressed individuals who were classified as medication or placebo responders. Over a nine-week period, several qEEG recordings were performed and results revealed no pretreatment qEEG differences between participants. The authors concluded that placebo effects can induce changes in brain function that are different from those associated with antidepressant medication.

With regard to childhood-related disorders, Gasser, Rousson, and Schreiter Gasser (2003) reported that children with learning disabilities and intellectual disability showed an increase in slow qEEG waves relative to children without these disorders. Others have reported different qEEG patterns in the left anterior and right frontal regions of the cortex in children with ASD (Dawson et al., 1995; Harrison et al., 1998; Machado et al., 2015). Willis and Weiler (2005) reviewed the EEG literature concerning children with ADHD and concluded that, in general, EEG patterns of activity differ between children with and without ADHD. Furthermore, boys and girls with ADHD tend to have different EEG profiles and different patterns sometimes also emerge for different subtypes of ADHD. In a longitudinal study, Otero and colleagues (2003) explored whether psychosocial risk was associated with alteration of the CNS based on EEG findings. Forty-two preschool-age children living in a socially, economically, and culturally disadvantageous environment in a developing country were evaluated several times over a six-year period and compared to a group of low-risk children. The EEG patterns of the at-risk group showed higher delta and theta values in the frontal regions and less alpha activity in the posterior regions of the cortex. The authors interpreted these results as supporting the hypothesis that insufficient environmental stimulation is associated with developmental lag in children.

Despite the multitude of studies that have found EEG differences between groups of individuals with a specific type of disorder relative to control subjects, EEG and qEEG studies are limited in several ways. First, as Gruzelier et al. (2002) noted, measures such as EEG have good temporal resolution but suffer from poor spatial resolution compared to neuroimaging techniques such as PET and fMRI. Second, EEG measures only cortical activity and cannot reveal the subcortical changes that may have affected or produced the cortical activation patterns. Finally, EEG and qEEG have limited diagnostic utility with psychiatric disorders as distinct profiles are not unique to the many different types of disorders. Coutin-Churman et al. (2003) evaluated the incidence, sensitivity, and specificity of abnormal quantitative EEG measures in individuals with and without psychiatric conditions. Results revealed abnormal qEEG findings in 83% of patients and 12% of control participants. The most frequent abnormality was a decrease in delta and/or theta bands, a finding not evident in the control group. However, no qEEG pattern was uniquely characteristic of a disorder and, in many cases, patients with the same disorder had different qEEG profiles. Nevertheless, scientists continue to explore the diagnostic utility of EEG and qEEG and whether patterns of recordings can serve as biomarkers for disorders and/or treatment outcomes (e.g., Leuchter et al., 2014; Olbrich & Arns, 2013).

Real-Time Functional Magnetic Resonance Imaging (rtfMRI)

Technology has recently enabled the use of faster, immediate, "real-time" functional imaging combined with neurofeedback to help individuals decrease or increase areas of activation in the brain. For example, when an individual is placed in the scanner, rtfMRI collects data regarding the BOLD signal, processes the information, and displays the information on a computer screen within one to two seconds or faster (Brühl, 2015; Weiskopf, 2012). When rtfMRI is combined with neurofeedback, participants, while being scanned, are instructed to either increase or decrease the BOLD signal. Most neurofeedback programs use visual instruction such as bar graphs, thermometers, change in colors, or objects being lifted or lowered. Studies have supported that with minimal practice (e.g., 30 minutes or less), participants are indeed able to alter the BOLD signal (Brühl et al., 2014; Thibault, Lifshitz, & Raz, 2016). Recently, rtfMRI treatment studies have increased substantially and included patients with major depressive disorder, ADHD, OCD, PTSD, Parkinson's disease, and others (e.g., Alegria et al., 2017; Gonçalves, Batistuzzo, & Sato, 2017; Zotev et al., 2016). Controlled clinical trials are lacking, however, as are longitudinal studies to assess the long-term effectiveness of rtfMRI neurofeedback at improving symptomatology. It is also important to keep in mind that fMRI findings are correlational and does not substantiate that increased activation in a particular or region of the brain "causes" symptoms associated with a particular disorder. Additionally, studies are needed to determine whether "decreasing" or "increasing" the BOLD signal in the clinical setting generalizes to ecological symptom improvement. In other words, research is needed to establish the internal and external validity of rtfMRI neurofeedback in the treatment of clinical disorders.

Optical Imaging: Near Infrared Spectroscopy (NIRS)

NIRS is an optical technique for measuring blood oxygenation at the level of the cortex. NIRS involves a process of projecting light (in the near infrared part of the spectrum—700–900 nm) through the skull and measuring the degree to which the re-emerging light is reduced. Participants wear an fNIR sensor mounted to their forehead that detects changes in concentrations of oxygenated blood (hemoglobin), oxygenated hemoglobin, and total hemoglobin as the participant is at rest and/or performs tasks (Ohmae et al., 2006; Takamiya et al., 2017). Compared to fMRI, fNIR is portable, less expensive, has higher temporal resolution (100 ms or faster), has greater ecological validity, and can be used with higher risk populations, such as infants (Liu, Cui, et al., 2015).

Although less empirical information is available concerning the use of NIRS with clinical disorders relative to fMRI, preliminary studies have reported differences between patients with various disorders and healthy controls. For example, a recent multi-site study found NIRS patterns of activity differentiated participants with major depressive disorder, schizophrenia, bipolar disorder, and healthy controls with 75% to 85% accuracy (Takizawa et al., 2014). Recently, the use of NIRS has also been advocated in the diagnosis of ASD and to measure the effects of cannabis on prefrontal functioning and working memory (Keles et al., 2017; Yanagisawa et al., 2016). Additional studies are needed to further investigate the clinical and diagnostic utility of NIRS with children, adolescents, and adults.

Brain Stimulation Techniques

A number of brain stimulation techniques have been developed to influence neuronal functioning and behavior, including deep brain stimulation (DBS), electroconvulsive therapy (ECT), magnetic seizure therapy (MST), transcranial magnetic stimulation (TMS), rapid TMS (rTMS), transcranial electrical stimulations (tES), vagus nerve stimulation (VNS), and optogenetics. Information concerning the use of ECT with psychiatric disorders is plentiful, but relatively fewer studies are available concerning the remaining techniques and their application in psychiatric treatment (Table 3.2).

Table 3.2 Brain Stimulation Techniques

Technique	Description
Deep Brain Stimulation (DBS)	A neurosurgical procedure involving the implantation of a medical device under the skin in the chest that sends electrical impulses to electrodes surgically placed in specific locations in the brain.
Repetitive Transmagnetic Stimulation (rTMS)	A noninvasive procedure that involves the placement of a magnetic coil to the scalp that delivers repetitive magnetic pulses to the brain.
Electroconvulsive Therapy (ECT)	A noninvasive procedure that involves the delivery of small electric currents to the brain to induce a brief seizure.
Vagus Nerve Stimulation (VNS)	A neurosurgical procedure involving the implantation of a medical device under the skin in the chest that sends electrical impulses to electrodes surgically attached to the vagus nerve in the neck.

Electroconvulsive Therapy (ECT)

Electroconvulsive Therapy (ECT) was developed in the 1930s as a treatment for schizophrenia (Rudorfer et al., 1997). ECT is used primarily with adults; however, research supports its effectiveness with children and adolescents, although use in this population is controversial (e.g., Fink & Coffey, 1998; Shoirah & Hamoda, 2011). ECT involves the placement of electrodes on the scalp to deliver electricity to the brain, inducing a grand mal seizure. Bolwig (2003) reported that seizure activity of at least 20 seconds is a prerequisite for therapeutic efficacy, and the number of ECT sessions required for improvement of symptoms ranges from 6 to 12. Tremendous variability exists among individuals with respect to the amount of stimulus intensity necessary to produce a seizure. For example, according to Abrams (2000), some individuals have such a high seizure threshold that delivery of maximal stimulus intensity may not be sufficient to achieve a therapeutic response. Children typically have a much lower threshold (Fink & Coffey, 1998). The efficacy of ECT depends on a number of patient factors (e.g., age, severity of illness) as well as technical factors, such as stimulus dosage and electrode placement (Sackheim, 1997).

According to the APA Task Force Report (2001), the mortality rate of ECT is approximately the same as that of minor surgery. The most common side effect of ECT is headache, occurring in 45% of individuals. Nausea, muscle soreness, and temporary memory loss are also commonly reported following ECT. Less common side effects include mania, delirium, prolonged amnesia, and, rarely, cardiovascular complications and prolonged seizures (APA Task Force Report, 2001). Zink and colleagues (2002) suggested that the drug rivastigmine, an acetylcholinesterase inhibitor, could protect against unfavorable cognitive side effects associated with ECT.

Leiknes, Schweder, and Høie (2012) studied use of ECT worldwide and reported that in Western countries, the majority of ECT patients were older women with depression. In Asian countries, the majority of ECT patients were younger men with schizophrenia. Breakey and Dunn (2004) reported that Caucasians were more likely than African Americans to be treated with ECT based on a review of hospital records over the period 1993–2002. Leikness et al. also found procedural differences with many countries administering ECT without anesthesia (e.g., Asia, Africa, Latin America, Russia, Turkey, Spain). The preferred electrode placement was bilateral.

Since the 1940s, ECT has been found to improve symptoms associated with a host of disorders—major depression, bipolar disorder, and schizophrenia, as well as bulimia, Parkinson's disease, and various medical conditions (Hoffman et al., 1985; Uesugi, Toyoda, & Iio, 1995). According to the APA Task Force Report, a substantial body of literature supports the use and effectiveness of ECT in the treatment of major depression, mania, and schizophrenia. Less information is available on the use of ECT in treating other psychiatric disorders, although several studies have been published concerning the use of ECT in the treatment of OCD, Tourette's disorder, and anorexia nervosa. For example, Maletzky, McFarland, and Burt (1994) and Thomas and Kellner (2003) reported that ECT was effective at improving symptoms of OCD, while Rapoport, Feder, and Sandor (1998) and Trivedi, Mendelowitz, and Fink (2003) found that ECT improved symptoms characteristic of Tourette's disorder. In a study by Ferguson (1993), two females with anorexia nervosa responded favorably to ECT while a third patient did not.

Bolwig (2003) described ECT as the most effective and most controversial treatment for severe depression. Gorman (2003) noted that although the majority of patients suffering from depression respond favorably to ECT, the effects are short-lived and relapse rates are high. Antidepressant medication begun immediately after a course of ECT has been found to help maintain remission of symptoms (Gorman, 2003).

ECT also has been used to treat physical symptoms (e.g., motor tremor) in addition to psychiatric symptoms. For example, Fall et al. (1995) reported that ECT improved motor symptoms associated with advanced Parkinson's disease. The period of symptom improvement varied greatly among patients, however, from a few days to over a year. In 2003, Kennedy, Mittal, and O'Jile reviewed the literature from 1990 to 2000 regarding ECT and movement disorders. Most of the studies investigated the use of ECT with patients with Parkinson's disease, although a few studies included patients with progressive supranuclear palsy (PSP), multiple system atrophy (MSA), Wilson's disease, Huntington's disease, tic disorder, and Meige's syndrome. Many of the patients in the studies also suffered from major depression. The authors concluded that ECT is an effective treatment for depression that co-occurs with movement disorders and may also improve the motor manifestations of movement disorders.

Mode of Action

The mechanism by which ECT alleviates depression and in some cases improves motor symptoms is uncertain. Several hypotheses have been presented in the literature. For example, ECT has been found to effect dopaminergic, noradrenergic, and serotonergic transmission (Baldinger et al., 2014; Fall, Ekman, Granerus, & Granerus, 2000; Kapur & Mann, 1993; Kennedy, Mittal, and O'Jile 2003). Indeed, studies support a relationship between improvement of depression symptoms and serotonergic transmission changes, as well as improvement in motor symptoms and dopaminergic changes following ECT (e.g., Bolwig, 2014; Hoffmann et al., 1985).

A second hypothesis supported by neuroimaging studies is that ECT may facilitate dopamine binding to postsynaptic receptors (Andrade et al., 2002; Balldin et al., 1982; Fall et al., 2000; Henry et al., 2001; Kennedy et al., 2003). Others have suggested ECT enhances transmission among GABA-releasing neurons and triggers genetic expression of nerve growth factor production, as well as neurogenesis in subcortical regions, such as the hippocampus (Bolwig, 2003, 2014). However, in a recent review of the literature, Bolwig (2014) concluded that due to the variability across ECT studies, a unified explanation of the mechanism(s) of ECT is lacking.

Although ECT remains controversial, given the empirical support for ECT and symptom improvement, in 2015, the U.S. Food and Drug Administration (FDA) Office of Device Management proposed reclassification of ECT devices in the United States into the less restrictive category II for the treatment of severe major depressive disorder or bipolar disorder in treatment resistant patients 18 years of age or older. The proposal stipulated that ECT devices remain in a more restrictive category (i.e., class III) for patients with schizophrenia or mania (McDonald et al., 2016). Should the FDA approve of the reclassification, ECT may be available to more patients in the United States in need of treatment.

In summary, ECT historically has been used to treat mood disorders and schizophrenia but is currently used to treat a variety of psychiatric disorders as well as motor symptoms characteristic of Parkinson's disease. Although critics claim that ECT causes brain damage (Read & Bentall, 2010), evidence suggests that the memory impairments that are often induced by ECT are temporary, and ECT may actually contribute to neuronal plasticity (Bouckaert et al., 2014). Gorman (2003) noted, "An affluent person in the United States is much more likely to receive ECT for depression than a poor person, quite unusual for something that is truly harmful" (p. 475). The mechanisms responsible for the effectiveness of ECT are not well understood but are thought to involve several neurotransmitter systems and possibly neuroplastic changes in subcortical structures.

Transcranial Magnetic Stimulation (TMS) and Repetitive TMS (rTMS)

TMS and rTMS are noninvasive brain stimulation techniques that can be used to stimulate specific areas of the cortex while an individual is awake. TMS and rTMS uses head-mounted wire coils that deliver strong magnetic pulses to wide or specific areas of the scalp. The coils are of two types: round and figure of eight. According to Grunhaus, Dannon, and Gershon (2002), the round coil is more common in TMS, while the figure-of-eight coil is used more commonly in rTMS studies. TMS was approved by the FDA in 2013 for treatment resistant depression, while rTMS was approved in 2008. TMS is painless and can be applied safely for single or multiple sessions over a period of several weeks (Loo et al., 2001).

TMS and rTMS deliver magnetic pulses that are generated by electricity but, unlike ECT, the magnetic field can be highly focused on specific locations (Crivelli & Balconi, 2017). TMS uses a type of coil that allows for wider and deeper stimulation of the brain, approximately 1.7 cm beneath the surface of the skull (the magnetic field declines logarithmically with distance from the coil). Repetitive TMS (rTMS) involves a different type of coil and repeated delivery of pulses to an approximated depth of 0.7 cm below the skull and for lengthier periods of time (e.g., 20 minutes versus 40 minutes) (Crivelli & Balconi, 2017).

The magnetic pulses last for less than a millisecond and induce changes in the ion distribution across the cell's membrane. Specifically, the magnetic field produces electrical currents in the brain by depolarizing neurons at the level of the cortex and with TMS, possibly subcortical structures (George et al., 2003). Repetitive TMS (rTMS) involves the delivery of magnetic impulses in rhythmic succession, at an adjustable rate. Stimulation frequencies higher than 25–30 Hz increase the risk of seizures, however, so lower Hz are used (George et al., 2003). When comparing TMS and rTMS, both are effective and neither appears to be superior in terms of improvement of symptoms of depression (Grunhaus et al., 2002; Padberg et al., 1999). Chen recently compared rTMS and ECT for the treatment of depression and found that rTMS was the most well tolerated and had the most favorable balance between efficacy and acceptability (Chen, Zhao, et al., 2017).

Mode of Action

According to one of the pioneers in TMS research, Mark George (2003), TMS does not have a single mechanism of action but instead induces different effects depending on several factors: the activity an individual is engaged in while receiving TMS or rTMS the region stimulated by the techniques, and parameters of the devices (e.g., intensity, frequency, coil angles) as well as individual differences among participants. Unlike other brain stimulation techniques, TMS and rTMS can produce immediate effects such as limb movement or cessation of speech. For example, Epstein et al. (1996) demonstrated that TMS applied directly over Broca's area (left frontal lobe) resulted in the immediate cessation of fluid speech, for which the physiological reason is unknown.

TMS is believed to affect multiple neurotransmitter systems but the details of this process are poorly understood. It is plausible that TMS and rTMS have multiple effects: at the level of the synapse and on neural networks, neurotransmitters, gene expression, and glia cell functioning. To help unravel the physiological effects of TMS, researchers have begun to study TMS in combination with fMRI and PET to measure blood flow changes and extracellular neurotransmitter changes in the brain after TMS or rTMS are applied. For example, Strafella et al. (2003) and Strafella et al. (2001) used PET to measure changes in extracellular dopamine concentration after repetitive TMS of the dorsolateral left prefrontal cortex in healthy human participants. Results revealed that TMS induced the release of dopamine in the caudate nucleus in the ipsilateral hemisphere only. The reason for this finding was unclear, but the authors speculated that descending pathways (corticostriatal) extend from the prefrontal cortex and project predominantly to the ipsilateral striatum. By stimulating neurons at the level of the cortex with TMS, other neurons within this pathway are likely activated, including glutamate-releasing neurons, which in turn activate dopamine-releasing neurons in the caudate. Studies also suggest that rTMS and TMS promote neuroplasticity and recent evidence supports their use in rehabilitation following brain injury (e.g., stroke) (Huang, Lu et al., 2017; Pascual-Leone et al., 1999; Ziemann, Corwell, & Cohen, 1998; Watanabe, Kudo, et al., 2018).

Efficacy and Exploratory Use

Findings from meta-analyses concerning the effectiveness of TMS and rTMS have been mixed, suggesting that the techniques have short-term antidepressant effects but questionable long-term effects (Brunoni et al., 2017; Burt, Lisanby, & Sackeim, 2002; Martin et al., 2003; McNamara et al., 2001). Other studies suggest rTMS is as effective as antidepressants at improving depression symptoms (Berlim, Van den Eynda, & Daskalakis, 2013b). Recent meta-analytic findings, however, suggest substantial placebo effects for TMS and rTMS in the treatment of major depressive disorder (Razza et al., 2018).

Exploratory uses of TMS and rTMS include treatment of movement disorders, seizures, bipolar disorder, Tourette's disorder, eating disorders, OCD, schizophrenia, and enhancement of memory and learning (George & Belmaker, 2000; Greenberg et al., 1997; Sachdev et al., 2001; George et al., 2001; Guo, Li, & Wang, 2017b). Following a review of the literature on the use of TMS in treating schizophrenia, Nahas et al. (2000) advocated its use in treating schizophrenia, but acknowledged that, given the chronicity and nature of schizophrenia symptoms, the therapeutic applications of TMS and rTMS are limited with this population. In a recent systematic review, Wang, Li, et al. (2017) concluded that rTMS is effective at improving positive and negative symptoms of schizophrenia when used in combination with antipsychotic medication.

BOX 3.3   Can I Improve My Memory With rTMS?

*One of the classic symptoms of Alzheimer's disease is impaired memory. A number of studies have reported that rTMS improves memory performance in patients with Alzheimer's disease (Liao et al., 2015; Nguyen et al., 2017). Alan Pearce from the Cognitive and Neuroscience Unit at Deakin University in Melbourne, Australia, wanted to explore whether rTMS would improve memory performance in **healthy** adults using multiple bouts of rTMS. Pearce also wondered whether the location of rTMS in the brain would affect memory performance. To conduct the study, Pearce et al. (2014) recruited 20 healthy adults and randomly assigned 10 to receive rTMS in the area of the dorsal lateral prefrontal cortex, and 10 participants received rTMS in the posterior parietal cortex. All participants received six sessions of rTMS every other day for two consecutive weeks. Memory performance—namely, spatial working memory—was evaluated prior to the start of the study and following the sixth session of rTMS. The memory task resembled a video game and participants were required to locate an object that was hidden within a box, among other boxes, on the computer screen. Participants were required to complete several trials with increasing difficulty. Results revealed that participants who received rTMS in the posterior parietal cortex demonstrated significant enhancement of spatial working memory skills, but participants who received rTMS in the dorsolateral prefrontal cortex did not show memory improvement. No significant side effects were reported in either group. The study needs to be replicated with larger samples (as well as a sham group) but these preliminary findings suggest that rTMS may enhance neurocognitive functioning in healthy adults. Perhaps rTMS will one day be available over the counter at your local pharmacy.*

Transcranial Electrical Stimulation (tES)

Transcranial electrical stimulation (tES) involves the delivery of weak electrical currents to the brain via electrodes placed directly on the scalp. The stimulation varies from 5 to 30 minutes and results in changes in the membrane potential of neurons The technique is not thought to induce action potentials but instead to modulate spontaneous neuronal firing rates (Woods et al., 2016). Relative to TMS little is known about the mode of action of tES. The mode of action of tES is unknown, although glutamate is implicated as receptor antagonists have been found to prevent the effects of tES (Nitsche et al., 2003). Several studies indicated tES leads to minimal side effects (Crivelli & Balconi, 2017).

Transcranial electrical stimulation is currently used in the treatment of motor symptoms of Parkinsons's disease, memory impairment in Alzheimer's disease, chronic pain, and epilepsy (e.g., Antal et al., 2017; Marceglia et al., 2016). Recent preliminary findings also support the use of tES in the treatment of mild to moderate depression. Pavlova and colleagues (2017) explored whether 20–30 minutes of tES combined with an antidepressant (sertraline) was effective at decreasing depression symptoms. Meta-analyses also support the use of tES in the treatment of ADHD, ASD, major depressive disorder, and bipolar disorder (Berlim, Van den Eynda, & Daskalakis, 2013a; Dondé et al., 2017; Nejati et al., 2017; Wilson et al., 2017).

Optogenetics

Optogenetic stimulation involves the use of light to activate specific ion channels in cells. Research with mice has found that stimulation by laser or LED light at specific wavelengths can activate dopamine neurons in the ventral tegmental area (VTA) of the brain and can improve depression-like behavior (P. R. Albert, 2014; Lohani et al., 2017). Although this technique holds promise for humans in the future, additional research is needed to better understand the mode of action of optogenetics and its application to human psychiatric conditions.

Vagus Nerve Stimulation (VNS)

Additional stimulation methods that involve the delivery of electrical currents to the brain include vagus nerve stimulation (VNS) and deep brain stimulation (DBS). VNS was first approved by the FDA for treatment of pharmacological resistant epilepsy, but is currently approved for treatment resistant major depression, obesity, and episodic cluster headache (Carreno & Frazer, 2017; Garamendi-Ruiz & Gómez-Esteban, 2017; Roslin & Kurian, 2003). VNS involves the surgical placement of an electrode wrapped around the left vagus nerve located in the neck. The vagus nerve is one of the 12 pairs of cranial nerves and extends from the brain stem through the neck. The vagus nerve lies between the jugular vein and the carotid artery in the neck and contains both ascending sensory (afferent) and descending motor (efferent) pathways; however, nearly 80% of the nerves are sensory in nature (Bolwig, 2003). The lead and electrode are connected to a battery-operated pulse generator implanted in the left side of the chest. The generator is programmed to deliver electrical pulses to the brain via the vagus nerve that projects extensively to many parts of the brain (Henry, 2003).

The known side effects of VNS are minimal. Due to the location of the nerve, vocalization is usually altered by VNS but, according to Kemeny (2003), this is reversible by altering the electrical output. Other possible, but less likely complications include infection, nerve lesions, blood clots, and lead breakage. One of the major disadvantages of VNS concerns its invasiveness (Kosel & Schlaepfer, 2003).

With regard to efficacy, VNS has been found to reduce seizure reduction in patients with epilepsy, reduce the severity of seizures, improve mood, and abort impending seizures when a supplemental magnet is used correctly (Henry, 2003; Oliveira et al., 2017). A number of studies have supported the effectiveness of VNS at diminishing symptoms of major depression (Muller et al., 2017) and recently has been recommended as adjunctive treatment for developmental disorders, including autism (Engineer, Hays, & Kilgard, 2017; Park, 2003). Preliminary findings do not support efficacy of VNS in the treatment of other mental health disorders, including schizophrenia, Alzheimer's disease, OCD, panic disorder, and PTSD (Cimpianu et al., 2017).

Mode of Action

The precise mechanisms responsible for the effects of VNS are unknown. Hypothesized modes of action include modulation of synaptic activity in the locus coeruleus, thalamus, limbic structures and cerebellum, and increased excitability of noradrenergic, serotonergic, and GABA projections throughout the brain (Ben-Menachem et al., 1995; Garamendi-Ruiz & Gómez-Esteban, 2017; Oliveira et al., 2017). Partial support for these hypothesized mechanisms of action is provided by neuroimaging studies. For example, Henry and colleagues (1998) used PET to explore changes in regional cerebral blood flow prior to and during VNS treatment in patients with epilepsy. Results indicated that VNS induced significant increases in blood flow in the medulla and thalamus, as well as many other regions. Significant decreases in blood flow in the amygdala and hippocampus were also associated with VNS in this study. More recent studies support increased rCBF in the prefrontal cortex and decreased blood flow in limbic regions following VNS (Kosel et al., 2011). A few studies have compared the blood flow effects of VNS administered acutely versus chronically. In general, the results have been mixed, with some studies reporting similar areas and degree of CBF changes while other studies have reported differences between acute and chronic VNS activation (Hammond et al., 1992; Henry, 2003; Kosel et al., 2011). It remains unclear if the brain adapts to chronic stimulation of the left vagus nerve and, if so, what the ramifications of this adaptation might entail. Additional research is needed to determine the cellular mechanisms responsible for the therapeutic effects of VNS.

Deep Brain Stimulation (DBS)

The FDA approved DBS in 2002 for treatment of Parkinson's disease (Gardner, 2013), and its efficacy at improving symptoms in a variety of disorders is widely studied. The technique involves surgical insertion of a small lead with an electrode in specific target areas of the brain (e.g., globus pallidus, thalamus). The lead and electrode remain in the brain and are connected to a programmed, battery-operated pulse generator implanted in the chest. Similar to VNS, the generator sends electrical impulses, but in DBS, the impulses are sent directly to the target region of the brain (Figure 3.3). Studies support the use of DBS in epilepsy, brain injury, chronic pain, and other medical conditions (Boccard et al., 2017; Greenberg & Rezai, 2003). A large number of studies have substantiated that DBS improve tremors characteristic of movement disorders, such as Parkinson's disease (Kundu et al., 2017; Vingerhoets et al., 2002). Similar physiological pathways have been implicated in Parkinson's disease and OCD (i.e., cortico-striato-pallido-thalamo-cortical), and many studies report that DBS is often effective at decreasing obsessive-compulsive behavior in treatment

Deep Brain Stimulation

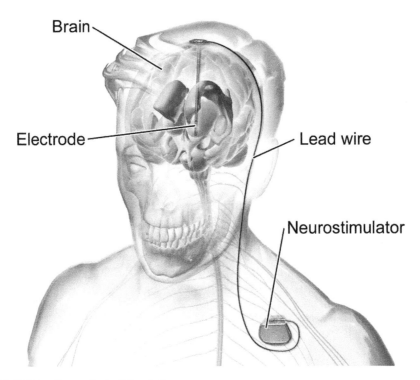

FIGURE 3.3. Deep Brain Stimulation

Copyright Blausen Medical Communications. Reproduced by permission.

resistant cases (Aum & Tierney, 2018; Mallet et al., 2002; Nuttin et al., 1999; Tass et al., 2003; Zhang, Li, et al., 2017).

More recently, DBS is being studied for treatment-resistant depression with findings supporting its efficacy in symptom improvement (Merkl et al., 2018; Zhang, Li, et al., 2017). Use of DBS in the treatment of addiction, including opioid addiction and alcoholism, is currently being explored in other animal studies and preliminarily in human studies (Martínez-Rivera et al., 2016; Muller, Sturm, et al., 2016; Nicolaidis, 2017). Kuhn and colleagues (2014) hypothesized that DBS in the area of the nucleus accumbens can facilitate opioid abstinence by promoting neuroplastic changes in dopaminergic neurons.

Similar to VNS, the side effects and potential complications of DBS are those associated with surgery (e.g., infection, hemorrhage) and actual stimulation. Many of the stimulation-related side effects are temporary and/or can be reduced by varying the electrical output of the generator. The mode of action of DBS is unknown (Agnesi, Johnson, & Vitek, 2013). Greenberg (2002) suggested that DBS may interfere with ("jam") neural circuits or block synaptic transmission by imposing a meaningless pattern of neuronal activity in the target region that produces a "functional" but not morphological lesion. Alternatively, DBS might enhance rather than inhibit communication among neurons that ultimately results in improved motor, mood, or cognitive function (Agnesi et al., 2013; Montgomery & Gale, 2008). Greenberg and Rezai identified a number of variables that could affect the outcome of DBS, including orientation of the electrode, the morphology of the brain structure receiving stimulation, and DBS technical factors, such as device characteristics, duration, and frequency of stimulation.

Chapter Summary

A variety of techniques that are currently available to study brain structure or brain functioning in patients with psychiatric disorders including computed tomography (CT), electroencephalogram (EEG), magnetic resonance imaging (MRI), functional magnetic resonance imaging (fMRI), real-time functional magnetic resonance imaging (rtfMRI), positron emission tomography (PET), and NIRS among others. In general, brain imaging techniques are used to explore structural and/or functional images of the brain, while physiological techniques, such as EEG, measure the summed postsynaptic activity of many individual neurons at the level of the cortex. This chapter reviewed the basic principles associated with structural and functional brain imaging techniques and discussed measurement and methodological limitations of these techniques when used with patients with psychological and psychiatric conditions. The final section of the chapter examined brain stimulation techniques, many of which are currently being used in the treatment of mental health disorders.

Chapter Summary: Main Points

- A number of physiological techniques have been developed to assess brain structure and brain function, for example, CT, EEG, qEEG, MRI, DTI, fMRI, rtfMRI, NIRS, and PET.
- Brain activation is reflected in neuronal signaling and neurotransmission, glucose metabolism, and changes in blood flow.
- Processes of metabolism, blood flow, and signaling occur continually in the brain, but their rate of activity varies across brain regions and during different states.
- Neuroimaging techniques can be categorized as structural or functional.
- A CT scan is diagnostic imaging test used to create detailed images ("tomographic images") of internal organs, bones, soft tissue, and blood vessels.
- MRI produces structural images and does not provide information concerning brain functioning.
- Diffusion tensor imaging analyzes the movement of water molecules in the white matter—i.e., myelinated axons of the brain.
- fMRI detects the increase in oxygenated blood relative to deoxygenated blood in the near vicinity of increased neuronal activity, and this change is reflected in the BOLD contrast (Blood Oxygenation Level Dependent).
- PET measures cerebral blood flow, metabolic rate of oxygen consumption, or the metabolic rate of glucose consumption.
- An EEG is a recording of the postsynaptic cortical activity of groups of neurons while an individual is at rest, sleeping, or during a specific sensory stimulation task.
- qEEG parameters enable dynamic changes to be observed as they take place during the EEG.
- NIRS is an optical technique for measuring blood oxygenation at the level of the cortex.

- The use of brain stimulation techniques such as ECT, TMS, rTMS, tES, VNS, and DBS has been studied in clinical populations.
- ECT involves the placement of electrodes on the scalp to deliver electricity to the brain, inducing a seizure.
- VNS was first approved by the FDA for treatment of pharmacological resistant epilepsy, but is currently approved for treatment resistant major depression, obesity, and episodic cluster headache.
- TMS and rTMS are noninvasive brain stimulation techniques that can be used to stimulate specific areas of the cortex while an individual is awake.
- DBS involves surgical insertion of a small lead with an electrode in specific target areas of the brain (e.g., globus pallidus, thalamus). The lead and electrode remain in the brain and are connected to a programmed, battery-operated pulse generator implanted in the chest.
- The efficacy of DBS for intractable movement disorders is well established.
- Given the significant number of individuals who do not respond to medication interventions, there is a rapidly growing interest in the use of DBS for treatment of severe psychiatric disorders.

Review Questions

1. What types of techniques are used to measure brain structure? Under what conditions are these techniques employed?
2. What types of techniques are used to measure brain function? Under what conditions are these techniques employed?
3. Discuss major criticisms of the use of fMRI in psychological and psychiatric research. How can each of these criticisms be addressed?
4. If you were to undergo brain stimulation, which technique would you choose and why?
5. Compare and contrast four neuroimaging techniques and four brain stimulation techniques.
6. Suggest three ideas for future research with respect to neuroimaging and brain stimulation techniques.

four

Neurocognitive Disorder Due to Dementia of Alzheimer's Type and Parkinson's Diseases

This chapter summarizes background information concerning diagnostic criteria, prevalence, gender, ethnicity, and other findings relevant to two neurodegenerative disorders: neurocognitive disorder due to dementia of Alzheimer's disease and Parkinson's disease. Research findings concerning the etiology of Alzheimer's and Parkinson's diseases are discussed, including information pertaining to genetic, structural, and functional findings. Physiologically based interventions for both diseases are reviewed, including pharmacological approaches, ablative procedures, and brain stimulation techniques. Lastly, information is summarized pertaining to strategies of lowering the risk of developing Alzheimer's and Parkinson's diseases.

Chapter 4 Learning Objectives

- Distinguish between Alzheimer's disease and Parkinson's disease according to symptomatology.
- Describe structural brain findings associated with both diseases.
- Describe functional brain findings associated with both diseases.
- Describe genetic findings pertaining to early and later onset Alzheimer's disease.
- Describe genetic findings pertaining to early and later onset Parkinson's disease.
- Explain the role of environmental factors in the development of both diseases.
- Identify the pharmacological interventions available for both diseases.
- Identify non-pharmacological, physiologically based interventions for both diseases.
- Identify strategies for decreasing risk of developing Alzheimer's and Parkinson's diseases.

Alzheimer's Disease

Background Information

Diagnostic Criteria

The American Psychiatric Association currently classifies Alzheimer's disease as Major or Mild Neurocognitive Disorder due to Alzheimer's disease (APA, *DSM-V*, 2013). Alois Alzheimer, a German neurologist, first described the disease in 1907 (Alzheimer, 1907). For a diagnosis of Alzheimer's disease, patients must meet criteria for major or mild neurocognitive disorder as well as additional criteria. For example, mild cognitive disorder involves evidence of modest cognitive decline in one or more cognitive domains (e.g., learning and memory, attention) however the deficits do not interfere with independence in daily living. In contrast, major neurocognitive disorder involves evidence of significant cognitive decline and the deficits interfere with independence in daily living activities and the term "dementia" is subsumed under this umbrella (APA, 2013). In late stages of life, Alzheimer's disease is the most common cause of dementia and accounts for 50–70% of the cases (Peavy et al., 2012).

For a diagnosis of *probable* Alzheimer's disease in patients with mild neurocognitive disorder, a family history or genetic mutation must be present, while those with *possible* Alzheimer's disease do not have genetic evidence but do evince a steady and progressive decline in cognition, memory, and learning in the absence of other neurodegenerative conditions. In contrast, patients with major neurocognitive disorder, probable Alzheimer's disease have evidence of genetic mutation *or* a steady and progressive decline in cognition, memory, and learning. Patients with major neurocognitive disorder, possible Alzheimer's disease do not have a family history or genetic mutation but display an insidious onset of symptoms and progressive cognitive impairment (APA, 2013, *DSM-V*, p. 611). It is important to note that current research suggests that pathophysiologic process of Alzheimer's disease that manifests in later adulthood begins years or decades before detectable cognitive changes emerge—i.e., "pre-clinical Alzheimer's disease".

Prevalence, Sex, Ethnicity, and Comorbidity

Prevalence estimates of Alzheimer's disease vary depending on the participants sampled, definition, severity of impairment, and countries or regions of the world studied; however, it is estimated that one new case of AD develops every 33 seconds and nearly 13.8 million people worldwide have the disease (Thies & Bleiler, 2013). The World Alzheimer's Report estimates that approximately 46 million people live with some form of dementia worldwide. By 2050, this number is projected to increase to more than 131 million with a worldwide cost of $818 billion (Prince et al., 2016).

In the USA, approximately 5.5 million are living with Alzheimer's disease and 5.3 million of these individuals are age 65 and older. In addition, recent studies indicate that, in 2017, 46.7 million Americans met criteria for preclinical Alzheimer's disease (Brookmeyer et al., 2018). The disease rises sharply with increasing age. For example, according to the American Psychiatric Association, 7% of diagnosed cases affect those between 65 and 74 years of age, while 53% of diagnosed cases involved individuals between the ages of 74 and 84 years of age (APA, 2013). As one might expect, rates of Alzheimer's disease are higher among nursing home residents around the world, even in countries such as Japan that have fewer nursing homes relative to the United States (Obadia et al., 1997; Baiyewu, Adeyemi, &

Ogunniyi, 1997; Meguro et al., 2002). Worldwide, the number of deaths attributed to Alzheimer's disease has increased substantially from a global ranking of 44th to 29th in 2013 (Alzheimer's Dement, 2016).

Sex Differences

The Alzheimer's Association (www.alz.org) reports that two-thirds of Americans with Alzheimer's disease are women. Meta-analytic studies from across United States, Europe, and Asia also indicate that women are at significantly greater risk of developing Alzheimer's disease (Gao et al., 1998); however, in a longitudinal study of Catholic priests, nuns, and brothers, L. L. Barnes et al. (2003) reported that the incidence of Alzheimer's disease did not differ between men and women. Recent findings suggest, however, that the disease appears to affect women more severely than men with respect to cognitive functioning (Laws, Irvine, & Gale, 2016).

Race and Ethnicity

Studies exploring rates of Alzheimer's across race and ethnicity have found considerable differences between groups. Mayeda and colleagues (2016), for example, conducted a landmark study and explored rates of dementia (Alzheimer's disease, vascular dementia, and nonspecific dementia) across six racial and ethnic groups. Results revealed that dementia incidence was highest for African Americans (26.6/1,000 person-years) and American Indian/ Alaska Natives (22.2/1,000 person-years), followed by Latinos (19.6/1000 person-years), Pacific Islanders (19.6/1,000 person-years), and whites (19.3/1,000 person-years). Lowest rates were found among Asian Americans (15.2/1,000 person-years). Overall, risk was 65% greater for African Americans versus Asian Americans and these inequalities were observed for both males and females. The magnitude of risk however, tended to be stronger for men. Specifically, dementia rates were 60% higher among African American women compared with Asian American women; however, dementia rates were 93% higher among African American men compared with Asian American men. An important finding was that dementia incidence rates were similar for women and men until ages 90+ years, when rates tended to be higher for women. Similar findings were reported by Mehta and Yeo (2017) who found prevalence rates for Alzheimer's disease were lowest for Japanese Americans (6.3%) and highest for African Americans (7%–20%) and Caribbean Hispanic Americans (12.2%). Collectively, these findings support that over one in four Americans who survive to age 65 will likely be diagnosed with dementia in their lifetime and that prevalence rates vary among men and women, as well as race and ethnicity (Mayeda et al., 2016).

Comorbidity

In addition to cognitive decline, behavioral and psychological symptoms also commonly occur in patients with Alzheimer's disease. Hart et al. (2003), for example, investigated the prevalence of non-cognitive symptomology in patients with a three-year or greater diagnosis of Alzheimer's disease and found that apathy occurred in 88% of the patients, aggression in 66%, sleep disturbances in 54%, irritability and appetite changes in 60%, 56% suffered from depression, 55% had delusions, and 52% experiences significant anxiety symptoms. McCurry and colleagues (2004) found that 56% percent of patients with Alzheimer's disease suffered from anxiety symptoms that positively correlated with nighttime behavioral disturbances, such as awakenings. Neuropsychological impairments, particularly deficits in executive function, also commonly occur in Alzheimer's disease (Swanberg et al., 2004).

A number of studies have found that performance on specific types of neuropsychological tests, such as episodic and semantic memory tasks, may predict preclinical Alzheimer's disease with considerable accuracy, perhaps as high as 95% to 97% (e.g., Blackwell et al., 2004). Recently, Mortby and colleagues (2017) reported that neuropsychiatric symptoms are associated with a threefold increased risk of dementia. During early stages of Alzheimer's disease, depression and apathy are common, while agitation, aggression, combativeness, irritability, wandering, and psychotic symptoms emerge as the disease progresses. (Lopez et al., 2003). In later stages of the disease, incontinence, seizures, muscle rigidity and spasms, and disturbances in gait are often observed (APA, 2013).

In addition to comorbid psychiatric symptoms, Marder et al. (1999) found that siblings of individuals who had Parkinson's disease and dementia were three times more likely to develop Alzheimer's disease than controls. Perl, Olanow, and Calne (1998) noted that many patients with Parkinson's disease develop Alzheimer's disease and, conversely, many patients with Alzheimer's disease develop extrapyramidal symptoms characteristic of Parkinson's disease. Patients with Alzheimer's disease are also at increased risk for a number of comorbid chronic health conditions, including thyroid disorders, sleep apnea, osteoporosis, glaucoma, and vascular diseases (Duthie, Chew, & Soiza, 2011).

Etiology

The etiology and physiological underpinnings of Alzheimer's disease are complex and not well understood. The most important known risk factor for the most common form of the disease, later onset, is increasing age. In general, the number of people with the Alzheimer's disease doubles every 5 years after age 65. Research supports that a combination of genetic, lifestyle, and environmental factors increase or decrease the risk of development Alzheimer's disease, and these risks differ from person to person (Graves et al., 1998). From a physiological standpoint, research has focused on genetic, anatomical, molecular, and functional abnormalities of the disorder.

Overview of Genetics

Before discussing genetic findings pertaining to Alzheimer's disease, a brief overview of genetic principles follows. Humans have 23 pairs of chromosomes (one of each is inherited from each parent) and approximately 24,000 genes (Ast, 2005). Chromosomes are located inside the nucleus of a cell. A gene is a segment of DNA (deoxyribonucleic acid) located on specific locations (loci) on the chromosomes, and DNA consists of a sequence of molecules—i.e., nucleotides. DNA provides the coded instructions for synthesis of messenger RNA (ribonucleic acid). Messenger RNA leaves the nucleus, attaches to ribosomes where it is translated into proteins, carries out the genetic code, and leads to the expression of characteristics that are inherited.

Accidental alterations in individual genes can occur and are known as mutations. These different versions of DNA due to mutations are referred to as alleles. Mutations of genes can occur at several levels and can contribute to inherited risk for a disease or disorder depending on whether the mutations are passed on by one or both parents. For example, changes in the sequence of nucleotide bases in DNA (such as substitutions, insertions, or deletions), or large-scale mutations such as duplications of genes, large chunks of DNA repeated or inappropriately inserted, extra copies of a chromosome, deletions of sections of the chromosome, can all be inherited. These inherited mutations can be frequent or rare, and can have a range of effects from small to large depending on a number of factors. The definitions of mutations versus polymorphisms vary widely (Karki et al., 2015). In simple terms, mutations and polymorphisms differ in that a mutation involves an event that results in a change in a DNA sequence and causes the sequence to differ from normal, i.e., a normal allele is present in a population and a mutation changes this to a rare and abnormal variant. A polymorphism is a DNA sequence variation that is common in the population.

The degree of heritability of a construct (e.g., intelligence) or disease/disorder can be estimated and are referred to as heritability estimates. By definition, heritability refers to the proportion of phenotypic variation between individuals in a population due to genetic variation between individuals in that population. It is important to note that heritability refers to a population and *not* to an individual. Heritability estimates are numerical estimates that vary from zero to 1 (i.e., none to 100%) and represent the fraction of phenotype variability (e.g., bipolar disorder) that can be attributed to genetic variation, but they do *not* provide any information about an individual or about specific genes that contribute to a disorder. For example, Type II diabetes is the result of environmental and genetic (heritability) factors and heritability estimates for this disease range from 20% to 80%, depending on the participants included in the studies samples. The concordance rate of Type II diabetes is substantially higher (0.70) in identical twins versus fraternal twins (0.20), hence these data suggest that Type II diabetes has a strong heritability component, but the heritability estimate reveals nothing about particular individuals or specific genes that may underlie the disease (O. Ali, 2013). With respect to clinical disorders such as Alzheimer's disease, Parkinson's disease, major depressive disorder, and bipolar disorder, research has explored heritability estimates via family, twin, and adoption studies, and the role of genetic factors underlying the pathophysiology of these disorders has been explored through linkage, genome-wide association, candidate genes, and molecular studies.

Genetic *linkage studies* search for chromosomal locations ("marker loci") where disease genes may be found. Linkage studies are based on the observation that genes that are located in close proximity on the same chromosome tend to be inherited together more often than expected by chance; hence, these loci are referred to as linked. With regard to Alzheimer's disease, linkage studies seek to determine whether specific chromosomal regions in individuals with the disease have specific DNA markers relative to those without the disorder. Candidate gene studies then explore how specific genes and mutation(s) may be involved in the etiology of Alzheimer's disease. In contrast to candidate gene studies that investigate pre-identified genes of interest, genome-wide association studies (GWAS) use a specific statistical approach to scan complete sets of DNA (i.e., genomes) of thousands of people across all chromosomes simultaneously in an effort to find genetic variations associated with Alzheimer's disease. To date, numerous chromosomal regions have been identified as locations of interest for susceptibility genes, and several genes have been identified for the disease. Specifically, genetic studies have yielded separate findings for early onset versus late onset Alzheimer's disease.

Genetic Findings: Family and Twin Studies

Genetic contributions to the development of Alzheimer's disease have been based on family, twin, and candidate gene studies. Family studies consistently indicate that Alzheimer's disease aggregates in families (e.g., Farrer et al., 1990; Klünemann et al., 2002). For example, Devi et al. (2000) compared the familial aggregation and lifetime risk of Alzheimer's disease in first-degree relatives of 435 individuals with the disease and unrelated controls among whites, African Americans, and Caribbean Hispanics. Results indicated the lifetime risk for Alzheimer's disease was 25.9% in relatives of individuals with the disease compared to 19.1% in control relatives, and the risk was higher than controls in all three ethnic groups. In addition, risk of Alzheimer's disease was greater among relatives of women than men.

Twin studies also support a genetic basis for Alzheimer's disease. For example, Bergem, Engedal, and Kringlen (1997) reported a concordance rate of 78% among monozytotic twins and 39% for dizygotic twin pairs for Alzheimer's disease in Gatz et al. (1997) reported Alzheimer disease concordance rates of 67% and 22% for monozygotic and dizygotic twins in Sweden. In a Finnish study, Raiha and colleagues also reported that the incidence of Alzheimer's disease was significantly higher in monozygotic twins than dizygotic twins. Rapoport, Pettigrew, and Schapiro (1991) reported that monozygotic twins concordant for Alzheimer's disease were significantly more likely to have a family history for the disease than discordant monozygotic twins, further supporting a heritability component of the disease. Recently, Pedersen et al. (2004) examined 662 Swedish twins ages 52–98 and followed them up at two- to three-year intervals. Results revealed that 5.8% of the sample was diagnosed with Alzheimer's disease and the average onset was late in life (83.9 years). In 26 monozygotic pairs, the concordance rate was 32.2%, while the concordance rate was 8.7% for dizygotic twins. Overall, twin studies clearly indicate that Alzheimer's disease is more common in monozygotic than dizygotic twins, but questions remain about the mode of inheritance (Gatz et al., 1997; Rossi et al., 2016).

Genetic Findings: Early Versus Late Onset

There are two main types of Alzheimer's disease: early and late onset. Early onset Alzheimer's disease occurs before age 65 and represents approximately 10% of all people with Alzheimer's. Silverman and colleagues (2003) reported relatives of individuals who develop Alzheimer's disease very late in life (i.e., age 85 or older) had a substantially lower risk for the disease than relatives of early onset Alzheimer's disease. Based on these results, they speculated that early onset Alzheimer's disease has a more prominent genetic basis while very late onset Alzheimer's is likely influenced more by environmental factors.

Early Onset

Early onset is a rare form of Alzheimer's disease, affecting approximately 10% of cases. Relative to late on set, early onset is typically more aggressive and associated with a shorter survival rate (Seltzer & Sherwin, 1983). To date, studies have identified three autosomal dominant genes that are reliably associated with early onset cases: *presenilin 1 (PSEN1)*, *presenilin 2 (PSEN2)*, and *amyloid precursor protein (APP)*. Mutations of these genes are associated with variable ages of onset. For example, with PSEN1 mutations the age of onset of Alzheimer's disease typically falls within the range 35–55 years, while age of onset for APP mutations is between 40 and 65 years, and between 40 and 70 years for PSEN2 mutations (Petok et al., 2018; Ryan & Rossor, 2010).

The PSEN1 gene provides instructions for making a protein called presenilin 1. This protein helps to cut apart (cleave) other proteins into smaller pieces, and this cleavage process is an important step in several chemical signaling pathways that transmit signals from outside the cell into the nucleus. One protein that presenilin 1 helps to cleavage is the amyloid precursor protein (APP). APP is cleaved into soluble amyloid precursor protein (sAPP) and several versions of amyloid-beta (β) peptide. Mutations of the presenilin-1 gene, located on chromosome 14 (14q24.3), are estimated to be responsible for 70% to 80% of all cases of early onset cases (Janssen et al., 2003). Exactly how mutations of this gene lead to Alzheimer's disease is unclear, but some have hypothesized that the mutation leads to faulty functioning of the presenilin 1 protein, while others have suggested that the mutation leads to increased production of amyloid beta peptide—i.e., the main component of amyloid plaques characteristically found in Alzheimer's disease (Bird, 2018). Cai, An, and Kim (2015) reported that over 200 mutations of the PSEN1 gene have been identified in early onset Alzheimer's disease.

Mutations of the presenilin 2 gene located on chromosome 1 (1q31-q42) have also been associated with early onset Alzheimer's disease, although according to Ryan and Rossor (2010) fewer mutations have been identified (14) relative to the PSEN 1 gene. Similar to PSEN 1 gene, the PSEN 2 gene provides instructions for the protein presenilin 2 that plays an important role in cleavage of amyloid beta peptides and (Cai et al., 2015). Mutations of this gene are associated with faulty calcium signaling, aggregation of amyloid beta plaques, and neuronal death (Leissring et al., 2001). It is important to note that mutations of this gene are not unique to early onset Alzheimer's disease and are associated with different types of dementia, breast cancer, heart disease, and Parkinson's disease (Cai et al., 2015).

The third genetic mutation reliably associated with early onset Alzheimer's disease involves the amyloid precursor protein gene (APP) located on chromosome 21(21q21). The APP gene provides instructions for making amyloid precursor protein. This protein is thought to play an important role in neural growth and repair, helps direct the migration of neurons during early brain development, and mutations are hypothesized to lead to overproduction of the amyloid protein. One of the first genetic breakthroughs concerning Alzheimer's disease was the recognition that individuals with Down syndrome inevitably develop neuropathological changes that are also characteristic of Alzheimer's disease— namely, the accumulation of amyloid plaques and neurofibrillary tangles in the brain. Given that Down syndrome is due to trisomy 21, scientists focused on chromosome 21 and specifically the amyloid precursor protein gene (APP) to study Alzheimer's disease. Currently, over 32 mutations of the APP gene have been linked to early onset Alzheimer's disease (Kowalska, 2003; Lanoiselée et al., 2017).

In summary, early onset Alzheimer's disease is a rare form of the disease, affecting approximately 10% of Alzheimer's cases. To date, studies have identified three autosomal dominant genes that are reliably associated with early onset cases: presenilin 1 (PSEN1), presenilin 2 (PSEN2), and amyloid precursor protein (APP). Mutations of these genes plays a role in the breakdown of APP, a protein whose precise function is not yet fully understood, yet is believed to play a critical role in the formation of amyloid plaques in the brain. Beta-Amyloid plaques (Aβ) deposits are a hallmark of Alzheimer's disease. Collectively, mutations of these three genes are estimated to account for approximately 50% of early onset cases; however, they only account for 0.5% of all Alzheimer's disease cases, indicating that the majority of Alzheimer's disease cases, particularly late onset cases, are due to other factors (Bekris, Yu, Bird, & Tsuang, 2010).

Late Onset

Late onset Alzheimer's disease is defined as an onset of the disease after 65 years of age. This form of Alzheimer's disease is more prevalent than early onset, and most cases are believed to be sporadic, with no family history of the disease. Late onset Alzheimer's disease typically progresses more slowly, although there is substantial variability in rates of decline among individuals with the disease (Penegyres & Chen, 2013). Some studies suggest that a more rapid decline in functioning in patients with late onset Alzheimer's disease is linked to comorbid conditions as well as stress, poor sleep quality, and use of multiple medications (Haaksma et al., 2017). The current view in the literature is that late onset Alzheimer's is a multifactorial disease affected by lifestyle and environmental factors as well as genetics.

Although a number of candidate genes have been linked to late onset Alzheimer's disease, the most common gene associated with the disease is apolipoprotein E (APOE). The APOE gene, located on chromosome 19, provides instructions for making a protein called apolipoprotein E (APOE). This protein combines with fats (lipids) in the body and forms lipoprotein molecules that are responsible for packaging cholesterol and other fats and carrying them through the bloodstream. In the brain, APOE is important in synaptogenesis and neuronal plasticity, and is produced by mainly by glial cells but also by neurons (Mahley, 2016). The APOE gene is also associated with increased risk of Alzheimer's disease because of its effect on the production of apolipoprotein, which binds with tau protein. The tau protein is found in the neurofibrillary tangles of individuals with Alzheimer's disease. There are three slightly different versions (alleles) of the APOE gene and the major alleles are called e2, e3, and e4. Hence the APOE gene has three common forms: APOE e2, which is the least common form and appears to reduce the risk of Alzheimer's disease; APOE e3, which is the most common and does not appear to affect the risk of the disease; and, lastly, APOE e4, which *is* associated with increased the risk of Alzheimer's disease. Research consistently indicates that the APOE e4 gene is found more frequently than APOE e2 or APOE e3 in late onset cases of Alzheimer's disease, and the risk of the disease is significantly increased in individuals with one or two copies of the e4 allele (Panegyres & Chen, 2013). Graves et al. (1999) found that presence of the APOE-E4 allele in conjunction with impaired olfaction was associated with a 4.9 times increased risk of cognitive decline compared to individuals without the E4 allele and without olfactory impairment. They noted that since plaques and tangles are commonly found throughout the olfactory pathways in patients with Alzheimer's disease, measures of olfaction could serve as preclinical markers of the disease, especially in individuals with the APOE-E4 allele. Indeed, recent studies advocate for the use of odor identification as a practical and affordable biomarker of Alzheimer's disease (Lafaille-Magnan et al., 2017).

APOE-E4 and Ethnicity

The relationship of the APOE-E4 allele to Alzheimer's disease varies by ethnic group. For example, Tang et al. (1998) found when the APOE-E4 allele was present, the risks for Alzheimer's disease were similar for whites, African Americans, and Hispanics, but in the absence of the APOE e4 allele, the cumulative risks for Alzheimer's were four times higher for African Americans and two times higher for Hispanics compared to whites. Tang et al. suggested that other genes may contribute to the increased risk of Alzheimer's disease in Hispanics and African Americans. Among Koreans, Kim et al. (1999) found the APOE e4 allele was more prevalent in patients with Alzheimer's disease than controls and that the presence of this allele was associated with both early onset and late onset Alzheimer's. Ganguli et al. (2000) studied the prevalence of Alzheimer's disease in Ballabgarh, India, and the United States (specifically, southwestern Pennsylvania). The prevalence was significantly lower in India, but the association of the disease with the APOE e4 allele in the Indian sample was similar to that found in the US sample. Senanarong et al. (2001) found that 59% of individuals with Alzheimer's disease in a sample from Thailand carried the APOE e4 allele. Lastly, Weiner et al. (2009) and others have reported significantly more American Indians with Alzheimer's disease carried the APOE e4 allele compared to controls (63% versus10%).

It is important to note, however, that the APOE e4 allele is neither necessary nor sufficient for the development of Alzheimer's disease. In other words, not everyone who carries the APOE e4 version of the gene develops Alzheimer's, and some individuals who develop the disease do not have the APOE e4 allele (Liu, Kanekiyo, et al., 2013). These findings therefore suggest that the APOE gene does not independently cause Alzheimer's disease and additional genetic or environmental factors likely play a role in the etiology of the disease.

Additional Genes

Indeed, genome-wide association studies implicate several chromosomes in the development of late onset Alzheimer's disease, including 1, 12, 10, 9, and 6. Studies have varied, however, with respect to specific loci on these chromosomes that may harbor susceptibility genes (see Kamboh, 2004 for an extensive review). Nevertheless, several candidate genes have emerged from literature as possibly playing a role in late onset Alzheimer's disease. For example, the ABCA7 gene encodes a protein involved in transportation of substances across the cell membrane and is hypothesized to play a role in amyloid plaque deposits. Recent research reported that two variants of the ABCA7 gene were associated with increased risk of late onset in African Americans (N'Songo et al., 2017).

Three genes that encode proteins hypothesized to play a role in brain inflammation have also been linked to late onset Alzheimer's disease—namely, the clusterin gene (CLU), TREM2, and CR1 gene (Patel et al., 2017; Ulrich et al., 2017). These findings are interesting, as previous research has implicated inflammatory factors in Alzheimer's disease (Dik et al., 2005). Relative to research concerning the APOE gene, however, little empirical information is available concerning the manner in which variants of these genes may confer risk for Alzheimer's disease. Genome-wide association and candidate gene studies have identified additional genes that may play a role in late onset Alzheimer's disease (see Giri et al., 2017) for a review). Given the number of chromosomal regions and genes that have been linked to Alzheimer's disease thus far, it appears that multiple genes are likely involved in the disorder, and it is highly probable that additional genes and gene variants will be identified in the future.

Structural Findings

Beta-Amyloid

Alzheimer's disease is characterized by two pathological hallmarks: the presence of extracellular beta-amyloid (Aβ) plaques and intracellular neurofibrillary tangles that consist of tau protein. The Amyloid Beta Precursor Protein Gene (APP) provides instructions for the production of a protein known as amyloid precursor protein. Amyloid precursor protein is processed by the endoplasmic reticulum and then transported to various parts of the cell, including the cell membrane. Beta-amyloid is a protein fragment derived (cleaved) from the amyloid precursor protein. This process involves an enzyme, β-secretase, first removing part of the amyloid precursor protein that extends from the cell membrane and into the extracellular space. A second enzyme, γ-secretase, then cleaves the remaining fragment of the amyloid precursor protein's transmembrane forming amyloid beta protein. Amyloid beta is then liberated from the cellular membrane to the extracellular space. Normally, these protein fragments are broken down and eliminated; however, in Alzheimer's disease, these fragments accumulate and form plaques (Chow et al., 2010). Although these plaques are found primarily in the extracellular space—i.e., between neurons—they can also accumulate inside the cell in vesicular components, such as lysomes or other vesicles, although the process is believed to differ from the formation of extracellular beta-amyloid (Friedrich et al., 2010; Oakley et al., 2006).

Accumulation of beta-amyloid is believed to accelerate neuronal death and progression of Alzheimer's disease by interfering with neuronal communication and promoting neurofibrillary tangles (Seino et al., 2010; Chintamaneni & Bhaskar, 2012). Tau neurofibrillary tangles and plaques are also associated with neuron and glial cell degeneration and death, loss of synaptic connections inflammatory reactions, oxidative stress, and the development of cerebral vascular disease (R. Bhat et al., 2012).

Whether beta-amyloid plaques are a cause or consequence of Alzheimer's disease remains unclear. For example, Wang, Mims, et al. (2016) noted that amyloid deposits also form in the walls of the blood vessels in the brain, and these deposits promote cerebral vascular disease. Indeed, research has found that amyloid deposits are found in the walls of blood vessels of approximately 90% of the brains of Alzheimer's patients compared to 30% in controls (Love et al., 2014). Furthermore, cerebral vascular disease is believed to promote beta-amyloid deposits by interfering with production, cleavage, and elimination of beta-amyloid fragments, resulting in a chicken or egg question. Strubble and colleagues (2010) argue that amyloid plaques serve as biomarkers rather than causal agents and instead argue that a decline in brain metabolic activity is the underlying cause of cognitive decline characteristic of Alzheimer's disease. Decreased metabolic brain activity in turn increases beta secretase activity that ultimately results in increased production and deposits of amyloid-beta plaques between neurons. Recent studies suggest that amyloid levels in the brain as measured by neuroimaging techniques in healthy middle-age adults are associated with increased risk of mild cognitive impairment and greater rates of cognitive decline (Petersen et al., 2016).

Although associated with Alzheimer's disease, beta-amyloid deposits alone do not result in Alzheimer's disease, and the way in which beta-amyloid becomes toxic is not fully understood. In general, plaque formation is associated with severity of dementia; however, studies have reported evidence of plaque formation in elderly subjects without dementia. Specifically, Iacono and colleagues (2008) established that many individuals with documented normal clinical status have substantial beta-amyloid plaques and neurofibrillary tangles to the same degree as individuals with mild cognitive impairment and in some cases Alzheimer's disease. Iacona et al. termed this status as "asymptomatic Alzheimer's disease". In 2009, Iacono and colleagues studied a subset of participants (38 postmortem brains) from a larger data set from the Nun Study, a longitudinal study of 678 Catholic sisters from the School Sisters of Notre Dame. Specifically, Iacono studied four groups: (a) participants with normal cognitive functioning and no significant Alzheimer's pathology at autopsy, (b) participants with normal cognitive functioning and Alzheimer's pathology, (c) participants with a diagnosis of mild cognitive impairment and Alzheimer's pathology, and (d) participants with dementia and definite Alzheimer's pathology at autopsy. Similar to previous research with males with "asymptomatic Alzheimer's disease", results revealed significant Alzheimer's pathology in cognitive asymptomatic participants compared with controls and mild cognitive impairment. These findings support that the presence of significant plaques and tangles alone does not define Alzheimer's disease since some individuals remain relatively unscathed. The explanation for this perseveration of cognitive functions is unclear, although some have hypothesized innate intelligence, educational or occupational attainments, or lifestyle may supply a cognitive reserve in the form cognitive skills, or processing that enables some individuals to fair better than others with progressing plaques, tangles and neuronal degeneration (Scarmeas & Stern, 2003).

Tau Protein

Tau proteins are encoded by the MAPT gene located on chromosome 17. In healthy neurons, tau binds to tubulin, the main constituent of microtubules, and provides stabilization. But when tau is defective (e.g., hyperphosphorylated, misfolded), it forms neurofibrillary tangles that inhibit the normal functioning and assembly of microtubules, including transportation of substances to and from the cell body to the terminal button (Kahle et al., 2000; Martin et al., 2013). Overexpression of tau is toxic to healthy neurons, as it retards cell growth, causes changes in the shape of cells, leads to the disappearance of mitochondria, and results in the collapse of microtubules (Ebneth et al., 1998).

The formation and pattern of these tangles increase rapidly with increasing age and severity of Alzheimer's disease (Uboga and Price, 2000). Neurons that are in the process of neurofibrillary degeneration release the tau protein, which can be detected in the cerebral spinal fluid (CSF), and these levels are often elevated in individuals with Alzheimer's disease (Kahle et al., 2000). Studies have also found higher levels of tau protein in patients with a family history of Alzheimer's disease and carries of the APOE geneotype compared to patients without a family history of Alzheimer's disease (Thaker et al., 2003). Several studies have also reported a relationship between polymorphisms of the tau gene and Alzheimer's disease (e.g., Bullido et al., 2000; Deming et al., 2017; Miron et al., 2018; Tanahashi, Asada, & Tabira, 2004).

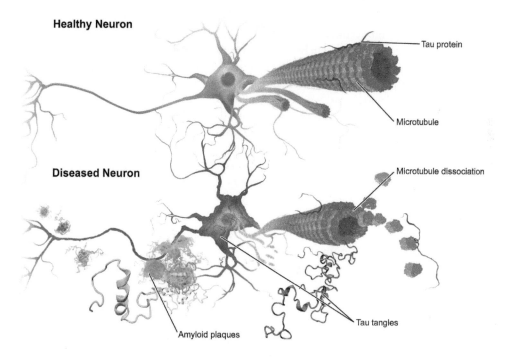

FIGURE 4.1.   Neurons Depicting Plaques and Neurofibrillary Tangles Commonly Found in Individuals With Alzheimer's Disease

Lewy Bodies

In addition to plaques and tangles, individuals with dementia of Alzheimer's type often have additional neuritic pathology, including Lewy bodies. Lewy bodies are inclusions that consist of the synaptic protein alpha-synuclein, which characterize a specific type of dementia—Dementia with Lewy Bodies (DLD) (Kane et al., 2018). A number of studies have reported that between 40% and 60% of patients with Alzheimer's disease had Lewy bodies in addition to plaques and tangles distributed throughout the brain (Arai et al., 2001; Chung et al., 2015; Kotzbauer, Trojanowsk, & Lee, 2001). Dementia with Lewy Bodies (DLB) differs from Alzheimer's disease in a number of ways, such as persistent visual hallucinations, movement difficulties, and REM sleep disorders; however, clinical symptoms prior to death are often similar in Alzheimer's and Dementia with Lewy Bodies patients (Ballard et al., 2004). Collectively, these studies suggest that although Lewy bodies may be present in some cases of Alzheimer's disease, these two types of dementia can be differentiated based on anatomical, physiological, and clinical pathology (Iseki, 2004). In addition to Lewy bodies, the presence of "cotton wool" plaques, consisting of two subtypes of amyloid-beta proteins (Abeta42 and Abeta40), have been documented in some cases of Alzheimer's disease and are associated with specific mutations of the presenilin1 gene (e.g., Mann et al., 2001; Kelleher & Shen, 2017).

Biomarkers

The diagnosis of Alzheimer's disease is based on *DSM-V* diagnostic criteria in conjunction with a neurological examination and additional neuropsychological testing of cognitive functioning. Neuroimaging (MRI, PET, SPECT) can also be used to help examine brain structure and the accumulation of beta-amyloid (β-amyloid) in the brain. In the early stages of the disease, diagnosis can be challenging, particularly with asymptomatic patients. Scientists have therefore, explored whether substances in the blood or cerebral spinal fluid can reliably detect the presence of Alzheimer's disease—i.e., biomarkers. Strimbu and Tavel (2010) defined biomarkers as "a broad subcategory of medical signs—that is, objective indications of medical state observed from outside the patient—which can be measured accurately and reproducibly" (p. 463). To date, three biomarkers, with an estimated 95% sensitivity and 85% specificity, have been established for Alzheimer's including levels of amyloid beta protein, tau protein, and phospho-tau (Blennow et al., 2010; Chintamaneni & Bhaskar, 2012). Unfortunately, the method used to detect these levels requires that cerebral spinal fluid be extracted via painful lumbar punctures. This process is less than ideal, and studies have attempted to identify new biological biomarkers that are less intrusive using blood and urine. For example, studies have explored whether various forms of beta-amyloid can be detected in blood serum as well as indices of neuronal injury (neurofilament light), inflammation (e.g., cytokines), microRNA, and oxidative stress (e.g., protein glutathionylation) can be used to diagnose Alzheimer's disease (Mattsson et al., 2017). To date, however, none of these measures have been established as acceptable biomarkers for Alzheimer's disease (Sharma & Singh, 2016), and as O'Bryant et al. (2017) noted, a collaborative effort between research and clinical application is needed to further advance the biomarker field.

Brain Volume and Specific Structures

Brain volume changes are associated with Alzheimer's disease pathology, and longitudinal studies have found that MRI measurements taken over time can predict the extent of disease progression. For example, Silbert et al. (2003) followed 24 patients with cognitive impairment and 15 patients without dementia until their deaths and at regular intervals measured brain volume and ventricular CSF volume. These findings were compared to postmortem measurements of plaques and neurofibrillary tangles, and revealed that the accumulation of cortical tangles was strongly associated with total brain volume loss, and the rate of increase of ventricular CSF volume was related to both plaques and tangles. Chan and colleagues (2003) followed 12 patients who were pre-symptomatic for Alzheimer's disease through moderate and severe stages of the disease using MRI. Results revealed a 2.8% mean yearly loss of brain volume during the mild stage, figure that increased by 0.32% each year thereafter. Others have reported that the severity of Alzheimer's disease was associated with a progressive deterioration of frontal-temporal structures, evidenced by psychiatric symptoms, such as uncooperativeness, wandering, emotional lability, and psychotic symptoms (Lopez et al., 2003).

Specific structures have also been found to decrease in volume as Alzheimer's disease progresses. For example, Järvenpää et al. (2004) used MRI to compare hippocampal volume in seven pairs of monozygotic twins discordant for Alzheimer's disease compared to control twins and found that the hippocampus was significantly smaller in twins with Alzheimer's disease compared to controls. Earlier MRI studies substantiated that atrophy of the hippocampal formation was associated with mild to severe Alzheimer's disease; with more severe dementia, neuronal atrophy was observed in the parahippocampal gyrus and the cortex of the temporal lobe (Detoledo-Morrell et al., 1997). Numerous studies have found a relationship between hippocampal volume reduction and memory loss on behavioral measures (e.g., Convit et al., 2000; Peterson et al., 2000), and Killiany et al. (2000) reported that MRI scans of structures of the medial temporal lobe (entorhinal cortex, temporal sulcus, anterior cingulate) could differentiate patients with mild Alzheimer's disease from control subjects with 100% accuracy. Laakso et al. (2000) reported that atrophy of the hippocampus was diffuse in patients with Alzheimer's disease compared to other types of dementia (frontotemporal dementia) in which hippocampal atrophy tended to be more localized to the anterior portion of the hippocampus. Studies have also found that changes in the shape of the hippocampus over time as well as the rate of change can distinguish even very mild dementia of Alzheimer's type from the normal aging process in healthy individuals (Wang et al., 2003). Numerous studies have found differential age effects in the white matter of the corpus callosum, frontal, temporal, parietal, and occipital lobes in patients with Alzheimer's disease relative to healthy aging control subjects (Head et al., 2004; Joki et al., 2018). Recent studies emphasize, however, that patterns of brain atrophy differ substantially among individuals, and these patterns of atrophy have an impact on how patients with Alzheimer's disease function over time (Poulakis et al., 2018).

BOX 4.1   Scratch and Sniff Test for Alzheimer's Disease?

Researchers at the Centre for Studies on Prevention of Alzheimer's Disease at the Douglas Mental Health Research Centre of McGill University in Montreal, Canada studied 274 participants deemed at high risk for Alzheimer's disease (Lafaille-Magnan et al., 2017). The average age of the participants was 64 years and genetic analyses were performed in with all participants. In addition, 101 of the participants also underwent lumbar punctures to extract cerebrospinal fluid to measure various protein levels related to Alzheimer's pathology (tau, beta-amyloid). Because brain regions devoted to detecting odors are particularly vulnerable to beta-amyloid deposits, participants were also given a multiple-choice, scratch-and-sniff test (the University of Pennsylvania Smell Identification Test, UPSIT) to measure their ability to identify a varied range of scents. The UPSIT is a commercially available, psychometrically sound, 40-item smell identification test developed by Richard Doty at the University of Pennsylvania. Results revealed that participants who performed most poorly on the scratch and sniff test were also more likely to exhibit other physiological markers of Alzheimer's disease (APOE E4, beta-amyloid) but not cognitive deficits. These findings suggest that the loss of ability to correctly identify odors emerges before cognitive symptoms emerge and may serve as a useful biomarker for Alzheimer's disease.

Functional Findings

Glucose Metabolism

In additional to structural findings, neuroimaging techniques, including single photon emission computed tomography, and ^{18}F-fluorodeoxyglucose-positron emission tomography have been used to investigate the accumulation of the β-amyloid peptide in the brain, as well as glucose metabolism and regional cerebral blood flow (rCBF). The result of functional imaging studies has consistently found reductions in rCBF and glucose metabolism in brains of patients with Alzheimer's disease relative to control participants. For example, when Friedland et al. (1989) examined glucose metabolism in individuals with probable Alzheimer's disease and healthy age-matched controls, despite normal blood-brain-barrier transport of glucose, reduced metabolism in the temporal and parietal cortices was found in individuals with Alzheimer's disease. Rapoport, Horwitz, et al. (1991) and Ogawa et al. (1996) reported that resting rates of global glucose metabolism were lower in participants with Alzheimer's disorder relative to control participants, even early in the disease. Other studies have found early and widespread metabolic disturbances in participants with Alzheimer's disease and reported that these disturbances increase as the disease progresses (Kumar et al., 1991; Sugimoto et al., 2017).

Rapoport (2003) suggested that the early reductions in glucose metabolism observed in Alzheimer's disease are due to changes in gray matter, particularly synaptic structure and cellular function, such as changes in mitochondria functioning that eventually lead to cellular death. Indeed, glucose metabolism studies that have statistically controlled for degree of brain atrophy in participants with Alzheimer's disease have found that reductions in glucose metabolism persist, indicating that abnormalities in cellular function are genuine and not simply an artifact of brain atrophy. Recent studies have found that glucose metabolism was significantly *increased* in white matter (myelinated axons, glial cells) regions of participants with Alzheimer's disease relative to controls. Specifically Jeong, Yoon, and Kang (2017) reported that overall brain glucose metabolism of white matter was 15.3% higher in those with Alzheimer's than in healthy participants, particularly in the frontal, parietal, and temporal lobes. In addition, amyloid accumulation in the whole white matter was 13.7% higher in participants with Alzheimer's disease. Jeong and colleagues interpreted this increased glucose metabolism as a result of neuroinflammatory activity of glial cells located in the white matter in response to beta-amyloid deposits.

A number of studies have found associations between reduced glucose metabolism, severity of dementia, and APOE genotype in participants with Alzheimer's disease, as well as impaired performance on neuropsychological tasks (Mielke et al., 1998; Chen & Zhong, 2013; Kessler et al., 2000; Eustache et al., 2004). Others have reported a relationship between delusional thoughts and glucose metabolism in the frontal lobe regions of participants with Alzheimer's disease (Sultzer et al., 2003). Collectively, these studies indicate that Alzheimer's disease is characterized by widespread reductions in glucose metabolism in gray matter, particularly in the right frontal, temporal, and parietal regions, and is also associated with increased metabolism in white matter regions.

Regional Cerebral Blood Flow

Studies that have investigated rCBF have also found functional differences between participants with and without Alzheimer's disease. For example, Warkentin and colleagues (2004) reported reduced blood flow in the temporal-parietal regions of both hemispheres in patients with Alzheimer's relative to controls and Rodriguez et al. (1998) reported that rCBF measures of the temporal-parietal regions identified participants with Alzheimer's disease with 75% accuracy. Other studies have found a longitudinal pattern of decline with respect to rCBF in participants with mild cognitive impairment who developed Alzheimer's within a subsequent two-year period, specifically in the posterior cingulate gyri, left hippocampus, and parahippocampal gyrus (Huang et al., 2018; Kogure et al., 2000; Kanetaka et al., 2004; Tonini, Shanks, & Venneri, 2003). These studies clearly indicate that Alzheimer's disease is characterized by functional blood flow changes that progressively worsen over time and support a functional disconnection between prefrontal regions and subcortical structures important in memory.

Several rCBF studies suggest that PET and rCBF measures can be used to discriminate Alzheimer's patients who respond favorably to medication from non-responders. For example, given the evidence that Alzheimer's disease is associated with a loss of presynaptic cholinergic functioning, donepezil (a cholinergic inhibitor) is used to treat some of the symptoms of the disease. Hanyu et al. (2003) was among the first to compare rCBF in the lateral and medial frontal lobes in responders and non-responders to donepezil, and discovered significantly lower rCBF in the lateral and medial frontal lobes of non-responders. Interestingly, Staff and colleagues (2000) found that donepezil treatment increased global as well as regional blood flow to the frontal lobes in patients with Alzheimer's disease who showed symptomatic improvement after taking the medication. Several studies investigating the potential long-term effects of donepezil on rCBF in patients with Alzheimer's disease, revealed that after a year or more of treatment, rCBF did not decline in several regions of the brain (e.g., anterior cingulate, temporal gyrus, prefrontal cortex, temporal lobes) (e.g., Nakano et al., 2001; Nobili et al., 2002). Shimizu et al. 2015 compared three types of acetylcholinesterase inhibitors (AchEIs, i.e. donepezil, rivastigmine, and galantamine) and found that all three increased rCBF to the frontal lobes in patients with Alzheimer's disease. These studies support that acetylcholinesterase inhibitors help to maintain functional brain activity in patients with Alzheimer's disease.

In summary, glucose metabolism and rCBF studies have found global and regional reductions in functional activity in patients with Alzheimer's disease relative to control participants, and these functional abnormalities worsen with time. While many early onset cases of Alzheimer's disease are associated with specific genotypes, late onset cases are often of unknown etiology. Collectively, findings suggest that the underlying physiology of normal aging and that of Alzheimer's disease likely involve distinctly different mechanisms.

Table 4.1 FDA-Approved Medications Used in the Treatment of Alzheimer's Disease

Medication	Mode of Action	Agonist/Antagonist
Donepezil (Aricept)	Acetylcholinesterase inhibitor	Ach Agonist
Galantamine (Razadyne)	Acetylcholinesterase inhibitor	Ach Agonist
Memantine (Namenda)	Attaches to NMDA receptor	Glutamate antagonist
Rivastigmine (Exelon)	Acetylcholinesterase inhibitor	Ach Agonist

Pharmacological Treatment

As previously discussed, Alzheimer's disease is characterized by death of neurons as well as glial cells throughout the brain, but particularly in hippocampal and cortical regions. Neurons that synthesize and release acetylcholine (Ach) are of particular interest given their major role learning and memory. It has been well documented that Alzheimer's disease is characterized by degeneration of acetylcholine-releasing neurons, and this process is accompanied by cognitive decline (Arendt et al., 2015). Other neurotransmitter systems (e.g., serotonin, glutamate, and dopamine) have also been implicated in Alzheimer's disease; however, for decades, the Ach system has been the primary target of FDA approved drugs for the treatment of the disease. The FDA has approved several types of medications to treat the symptoms of Alzheimer's disease: acetylcholine esterase inhibitors, memantine (namenda), and a combination of memantine and donepezil (namzaric) (Cherian & Gohil, 2015).

The acetylcholine esterase inhibitors include donepezil (aricept) rivastigmine (exelon), galantamine (reminyl), and cognex (tacrine). All these drugs prevent the enzyme acetylcholinesterase from breaking down acetylcholine; thus, more of the neurotransmitter is available at the level of the synapse. As noted previously, Alzheimer's disease is characterized by degeneration of the cholinergic system, which projects from nuclei in the basal forebrain to areas of the limbic system as well as the cortex. Degeneration of these neurons is associated with the disturbance of attention processes and gradual cognitive decline. Although cholinesterase inhibitors improve memory and cognitive abilities in many, but not all, patients with Alzheimer's disease, they do not slow the progression of the disease at a physiological level. In contrast, memantine (namenda) is prescribed for moderate to severe stages of Alzheimer's disease and targets the glutamate system by blocking NMDA receptors. Namzaric, however, combines memantine and donepezil and is therefore both a glutamate antagonist and an acetylcholinesterase inhibitor (Johnson & Kotermanski, 2006).

All of these drugs temporarily slow memory loss and improve quality of life for Alzheimer's patients. As the disease progresses, however, the effectiveness of these medications appears to wane as the disease progresses (Lopez et al., 2002). A number of short-term side effects are associated with cholinesterase inhibitors, including nausea, diarrhea, vomiting, supression of appetite, weight loss, and indigestion. Cognex has been associated with liver toxicity and is therefore rarely used in the treatment of Alzheimer's disease (Ibach & Haen, 2004; Watkins et al., 1994). Side effects of memantine and namzaric are similar to cholinesterase inhibitors and include diarrhea, insomnia, dizziness, headache, and, less commonly, hallucinations (Jarvis & Figgitt, 2003).

A drug approved for the treatment of Parkinson's disease is also being used to treat Alzheimer's: selegiline (deprenyl), a MAO-B inhibitor. Studies have produced mixed findings concerning the drug's effectiveness with Alzheimer's patients with some reporting that the medication slows the progression of the disease, while other studies have not supported these findings (Sano et al., 1997; Knoll, 1992; Birks & Flicker, 2003). In a recent review of the literature, selegiline was also found to have a small, statistically significant effect on Alzheimer's disease function at 8–17-week follow-up (Laver et al., 2016).

Others have advocated for the use of thrombin inhibitors in the treatment of Alzheimer's disease. For example, Grammas and Martinez (2014) noted that cerebrovascular dysfunction precedes cognitive decline and onset of neurodegenerative changes in Alzheimer's disease and thrombin, an enzyme in the blood that causes clotting, is often elevated in the brain in patients with the disease. Elevated thrombin levels can be toxic, producing inflammatory effects in endothelial cells, microglia, and astrocytes. Thrombin inhibitors, however, block the neurotoxic effects in mice models and furthermore, reduction of inflammatory proteins in Alzheimer's disease mice is associated with improved cognition.

Antioxidants such as vitamin E are recommended by some scientists in the treatment of Alzheimer's disease as a means to help reduce oxidative stress. Studies have been conflicting, however, with some suggesting that antioxidants such as vitamin E may reduce the risk of Alzheimer's disease and decrease mild symptoms, while others do not support these findings (e.g., Gugliandolo, Bramanti, & Mazzon, 2017; Laurin et al., 2004; Tabet, Birks, & Evans, 2000; Zandi et al., 2004). Anti-inflammatory medications have also been investigated in the treatment of Alzheimer's disease based on evidence that a chronic inflammatory response may contribute to the disease's pathology, although findings from meta-analyses have not been encouraging (Hoozemans et al., 2001; Fink et al., 2018; Wang, Wang, & Zhu, 2016). For a review of current and potentially future pharmacological agents for the treatment of Alzheimer's disease, see Kumar et al. 2018.

Psychotropic Medications

In addition to medications designed to treat cognitive functioning, patients with Alzheimer's disease are sometimes prescribed antipsychotic (e.g., seroquel, zyprexa) and anticonvulsant (e.g., tegretol, depakene) medications to help improve behavioral symptoms, such as hallucinations, agitation, and violent outbursts. De Deyn et al. (2004), for example, reported that the antipsychotic medication olanzapine significantly decreased psychosis and behavioral disturbances in Alzheimer's patients. Recent population-based studies have found that approximately 25% of patients with dementia were prescribed two or greater psychotropic drugs other studies have found 20% of Alzheimer's patients had been prescribed antianxiety medications within a three-month period (Lagnaoui et al., 2003; Norgaard et al., 2017). Many have questioned the concomitant use of these medications with medications specifically approved for treatment of Alzheimer's symptoms due to the increased risk of adverse side effects (e.g., increased confusion, dependency).

Risk and Protective Factors Implicated in Dementia of Alzheimer's Type

In addition to gene variants, a variety of factors have been associated with increased risk of Alzheimer's disease. For example, Moceri et al. (2000) predicted that early childhood environment is associated with risk of Alzheimer's disease. Their study of 393 patients with the disease and 377 control families indicated that growing up in a family of five or more siblings increased the risk of developing Alzheimer's by 39%; the risk increased by 8% with each additional family member. Growing up in an urban area (versus a suburb) was also associated with increased risk. Hall and colleagues (2000) also found that growing up in a rural residence combined with less than six years of schooling was associated with increased risk of Alzheimer's disease in a sample of 2,212 African Americans. Moceri et al. (2000) suggested that the number of siblings and area of residence are related to socioeconomic level and may reflect a poorer quality of living environment. In turn, a poor-quality environment may interfere with normal brain development and maturation, and therefore increase the risk of Alzheimer's disease later in life. A number of studies have reported that fewer years of education are associated with greater Alzheimer's risk, while others have suggested that having a college degree has a protective effect on the risk of developing the disease (e.g., Garre-Olmo et al., 2004; Tyas et al., 2001; Ravaglia et al., 2002; Harmanci et al., 2003; Robitaille et al., 2018).

Whether a history of head injury, including TBI, increases risk of Alzheimer's disease is equivocal (e.g., Plassman et al., 2000; Julien et al., 2017; Weiner et al., 2017). Findings have also been mixed as to whether the magnitude of Alzheimer's risk is greater among persons with carriers of a certain APOE genotype (APOE-E4) who sustain head injury relative to those head injury victims who are non-carriers (e.g., Guo et al., 2000). Others have reported increased risk of Alzheimer's disease in those who are prone to psychological distress, have a chronic history of migraines, cigarette smoking, exposed to industrial solvents and/or electromagnetic fields (Kukull et al., 1995; Wilson et al., 2003; Tyas, et al., 2001; Juan et al., 2004; Feychting et al., 1998; Graves et al., 1999; Li, Sung, & Wu, 2002). Luchsinger et al. (2002) reported individuals with a high caloric and fat intake were at greater risk for Alzheimer's disease (compared to those in the lowest quartiles of caloric intake); carriers of the APOE-E4 allele in conjunction with high caloric and fat intake were at greatest risk for the disease. Several studies have found a relationship between cholesterol levels and Alzheimer's disease, although other studies have not substantiated these findings (e.g., Austen, Christodoulou, & Terry, 2002; Evans et al., 2000; Zaldy et al., 2003). Petanceska et al. (2003) noted that the APOE gene mediates cholesterol levels in the brain via the APOE-E4 allele and apolipoprotein, which transports cholesterol in the brain. According to their work, disruptions in cholesterol metabolism may lead to increased production of apolipoprotein and ultimately the plaques and tangles characteristic of Alzheimer's disease.

Dietary factors have also been associated with Alzheimer's disease. For example, decades ago, Butterfield and colleagues (1999) proposed that free radicals are associated with increased production of beta-amyloid, and these free radicals alter cell membrane structure and function, and ultimately result in cellular death. Others reported that diets rich in antioxidants, such as those found in fresh fruits and vegetables, improved learning and memory performance in aged rats (Bickford et al., 2000). In the past 20 years, numerous human studies have reported that diets rich in antioxidants (e.g., vitamins C and E) and flavonoids are associated with a lower risk of Alzheimer's disease (e.g., Airoldi et al., 2018; Vassalle et al., 2017). In a recent systematic review of the literature, Yusufov, Weyandt, and Piryatinsky (2017) reported that 50 of the 64 reviewed studies revealed an association between diet and the incidence of Alzheimer's disease. These studies, although inclusive, offer promising implications for diet as a modifiable risk factor for Alzheimer's disease.

Lastly, in terms of preventative factors, participation in leisure activities and intellectually stimulating activities is negatively correlated with risk of Alzheimer's disease (Crowe et al., 2003). Wilson and colleagues (2002) conducted a 7-year longitudinal study of nearly 800 catholic nuns, priests, and brothers from 40 Catholic organizations across the United States. The researchers measured degree of participation in cognitively stimulating activities (e.g., reading books, magazines, or newspapers; doing crossword puzzles; playing cards or checkers) and incidences of Alzheimer's disease. Results indicated that frequent participation in cognitively stimulating activities was associated with a reduced risk of Alzheimer's disease in both males and females. In contrast, commercial brain training programs that claim to improve a broad range of mental processes in healthy individuals have produced mixed findings. Specifically, well-designed experimental studies have not found evidence that supports benefits of brain training (Lumosity) with regard to changes in (a) decision-making behavior, (b) brain response, or (c) cognitive task performance beyond those cognitive processes specifically trained for the brain training tasks (Kable et al., 2017).

Other studies have found that regular exercise also decreases risk of Alzheimer's disease and improves the physical health, as well as depression levels, of patients with the disease (Mahendra & Arkin, 2003; Halloway et al., 2018; Pedrinolla et al., 2018; Teri et al., 2003). In a recent review of the literature, Livingston and colleagues (2017) concluded that in many cases, dementia is preventable. Specifically, Livingston et al. identified nine risk factors that contribute to approximately 35% of dementia cases: education to a maximum of age 11–12 years, mid-life hypertension, mid-life obesity, hearing loss, late-life depression, diabetes, physical inactivity, smoking, and social isolation. The researchers advocated for early interventions to address each of these modifiable risk factors.

Brain Stimulation

Recent studies have begun to explore the effectiveness of brain stimulation techniques at improving cognitive impairments characteristic of Alzheimer's disease. For example, preliminary findings support that repetitive transcranial magnetic stimulation (rTMS) of the precuneus (PC) induced improvement in episodic memory, but not in other cognitive domains (Koch et al., 2018). Deep brain stimulation in the ventral capsule/ventral striatum (VC/VS) region has also been explored as a method to help decrease decline of cognitive functioning in Alzheimer's disease patients relative to control participants. According to Scharre et al. (2018), DBS was well tolerated and was associated with less cognitive decline. Lastly, Isserles et al. (2017) studied the use of ECT in patients with dementia who had severe neuropsychiatric symptoms. Results revealed a clinically meaningful response in 72% of acute ECT cases and adverse effects affecting cognitive functioning were reported in 7% of the cases. Use of antipsychotic or antidepressant medications, preexisting psychiatric disorder, or gender were not associated with ECT response. These studies are preliminary, however, and additional studies with larger samples are needed to further explore the clinical utility of brain stimulation techniques in the treatment of Alzheimer's disease.

Summary of Alzheimer's Disease

- Alzheimer's type is the most common type of dementia with 7% of diagnosed cases affecting those between 65 and 74 years of age while 53% of diagnosed cases involved individuals between the ages of 74 and 84 years of age.
- It is estimated that a new case of Alzheimer's disease develops every 33 seconds with nearly 13.8 million people worldwide living with the disease.
- Alzheimer's disease is characterized by multiple cognitive impairments, including memory loss and additional cognitive disturbances that interfere with social and occupational functioning.
- Familial and twin studies support a genetic component of Alzheimer's disease in early onset cases and to a lesser extent late onset cases.

■ Although no specific gene has been identified for late onset Alzheimer's disease, cases of early onset Alzheimer's disease (< 65 years) are associated with a variety of genetic mutations, most frequently involving the APP gene.

■ A number of risk and protective factors are associated with the disease.

■ Alzheimer's disease is characterized by extracellular beta-amyloid plaques and intracellular tau protein tangles, although whether these deposits are a cause or consequence of the disease remains equivocal.

■ The disease is primarily associated with degeneration of acetylcholine-releasing neurons and subsequent cognitive decline, although other neurotransmitter systems are also involved in the disease.

■ The etiologic mechanisms that contribute to the development of Alzheimer's disease and the ways in which these mechanisms contribute to the progression of the disease are not yet understood.

■ Acetylcholinesterase inhibitors and glutamate antagonists are the most effective pharmacological treatments to date, but these medications treat only the symptoms and do not cure or substantially slow the progression of the disease.

■ Preliminary studies potentially support an adjunctive role for brain stimulation techniques in the treatment of Alzheimer's disease, although future studies are needed to further explore the effectiveness and safety of these methods.

BOX 4.2   Hoarding Behavior in Parkinson's Disease Patients

The pathological acquisition of and failure to discard large numbers of possessions in living areas to the extent that they preclude activities for which these areas were designed area characteristics of hoarding disorder (APA, 2013). Research has found that a significant percentage of patients with Parkinson's disease who are prescribed dopamine replacement therapy (e.g., dopamine agonists such as pramipexole, levodopa) develop impulsive or compulsive behaviors, including hypersexuality, compulsive shopping and gambling, excessive grooming, and complex stereotyped behaviors known as "punding". In a recent study, O'Sullivan and colleagues (2010) found that approximately 28% of participants with Parkinson's disease in their study were categorized as excessive hoarders compared to 6% of healthy controls. Although the precise cause of hoarding and other compulsive behaviors observed following medication treatment is known, brain regions involved in self-control and decision making have been implicated, as well as dopamine pathways that govern pleasure, addictive behaviors, and reward behavior (i.e., ventromedial prefrontal cortex; Weiss & Marsh, 2012).

Parkinson's Disease

Prevalence and Comorbidity Findings

James Parkinson first described Parkinson's disease symptoms in 1817 and referred to the disease as "shaking palsy" (Parkinson, 1817). William Rutherford Sanders reportedly coined the name "Parkinson's disease" in 1865 (Goedert & Compston, 2018). Parkinson's disease is a progressive neurological disorder characterized by resting tremor, rigidity, postural instability, and slowed ability to start and continue movements (*bradykinesia*) (Guttman, Kish, & Furukawa, 2003). It is the second most common neurodegenerative disease after Alzheimer's disease. Age is the greatest risk factor for the development of Parkinson's disease. There are two main types of Parkinson's disease: familial early onset (< 50 years) and later onset (sporadic). Different subtypes of the disease have also been identified, including the tremor-dominant and postural instability gait difficulty (PIGD) forms. Some research suggests that the PIGD forms are associated with a more rapid progression of motor symptoms as well as cognitive decline (De Virgilio et al., 2016).

The prevalence of the disease increases steadily with age. In the United States, it is estimated that approximately 0.5% of the population between 65 and 69 has the disease while 3% of those 85 and older have Parkinson's disease (APA, 2013). Although the majority of cases emerge later in adulthood, approximately 4% of cases are diagnosed before the age of 50—i.e., early onset (Deng, Wang, & Jankovic, 2017). The worldwide prevalence of Parkinson's disease varies greatly (Muangpaisan et al., 2011; Strickland and Bertoni, 2004). For example, Sanchez and colleagues (2004) reported a prevalence rate of 176 cases per 100,000 in people over age 50 in Antioquia, Columbia; Caradoc-Davies and colleagues (1992) reported a prevalence rate of 76 per 100,000 in New Zealand; while Woo et al. (2004) reported a 0.5% prevalence among those age 55 and older in Hong Kong. Claveria et al. (2002) found 9 cases per 1,000 in individuals age 40 and over in Cantalejo, Spain, a figure that is substantially higher than other studies. A recent meta-analysis of 47 studies assessing the prevalence of Parkinson's disease in Asia, Africa, South America, and Europe/North America/Australia reported significant higher rates of the disease in North America, Europe, and Australia compared to Asia. Higher rates were also found among males compared to females, particularly between the ages of 50–59 (Pringsheim et al., 2014). The reasons for the geographic differences are unknown; however, differences in survival rates have been hypothesized as well as environmental factors.

Schrag, Ben-Shlomo, and Quinn (2002) assessed the prevalence of Parkinson's disease in London and found that 20% of patients who had received medical attention had not been diagnosed with the disease when the diagnosis was warranted, and approximately 15% had been inaccurately diagnosed with the disease. Recent research suggests that prodromal symptoms emerge before significant motor symptoms and include impaired olfaction, depression, excessive daytime sleepiness, rapid eye movement sleep behavior disorder, and gastrointestinal problems (Noyce et al., 2012). Twelves, Perkins, and Counsell (2003) noted that the methods used in epidemiological studies vary considerably and recommended that minimal scientific criteria be developed to help establish more accurate prevalence rates for Parkinson's disease. Interestingly, Ebersbach and colleagues (2000) found sociocultural differences in gait among patients with Parkinson's disease in Berlin, Germany, and Innsbruck, Austria. Specifically, patients with Parkinson's disease from Berlin had significantly faster walking speeds than patients and control subjects from Austria.

Comorbidity

Individuals with Parkinson's disease often have neuropsychological deficits, such as impairments in executive functioning and language processing (Dirnberger & Jahanshahi, 2013; Grossman, 1999). Major or mild neurocognitive disorder commonly occurs in 75% of individuals with Parkinson's disease (APA, 2013). Studies also suggest that patients' awareness of their bodies in space may diminish with the progression of the disease (Maschke et al., 2003). Individuals with Parkinson's disease are at high risk for psychiatric problems: studies indicate

Table 4.2 Parkinson's Disease Symptoms

Core Symptoms

Bradykinesia (slowness of movement)

Rigidity (stiffness of trunk and limbs)

Tremor (involuntary trembling of hands, legs, face, and jaw)

Postural instability (tendency to lose balance)

Secondary Symptoms

Sleep problems

Fatigue

Mood changes

Loss of facial expression

Sexual dysfunction

Constipation

Orthostatic

Loss of sense of smell

Speech problems

Drooling

Cognitive impairment

that at least one psychiatric symptom is reported by most Parkinson's patients, including anxiety, depression, somatization, psychosis, and obsessive compulsive symptoms (Carrozzino et al., 2018; Yapici et al., 2017). Kurlan (2004) reported on six patients with Parkinson's disease who developed pathological gambling as well as cleaning, rearranging, and ordering rituals. Sleep problems, such as difficulty falling asleep, frequent waking, and excessive daytime fatigue and sleepiness, are also common with the disease (Lai & Siegel, 2003; Pal et al., 2004). According to Schrag, Jahanshahi, and Quinn (2001) depression, occurrence of falls, and patient's negative perceptions of the disease are associated with advancing severity and disease deterioration. Glosser (2001) suggested that depression in patients with Parkinson's disease results from multiple factors, including reduced levels of serotonin as well as disruptions in dopamine rich reward pathways extending to and from the midbrain to the frontal regions. Changes in dopamine pathways are also associated with deficits in processing emotionally laden facial expressions in Parkinson's patients (Dujardin et al., 2004).

Approximately 30% of Parkinson's patients develop psychotic symptoms, most frequently visual hallucinations (D'Souza et al., 2003; Holroyd, Currie, & Wooten, 2001). Patients who take antipsychotic medications have a better prognosis compared to patients with Parkinson's disease with untreated psychotic symptoms (Factor et al., 2003). Later-stage Parkinson's disease is associated with loss of autonomy and self-esteem, social isolation, vocal and speech impairments, gait impairment, frequent choking, and substantial deterioration in both physical and mental health (Calne, 2003; Mahler et al., 2012). Studies have also found that vascular disease, such as hypertension and stroke, tends to aggravate the severity of Parkinson's disease (Papapetropoulos et al., 2004). Recently, Ma and colleagues (2018) reported that patients with Parkinson's disease are at increased risk for weight loss and malnutrition, which in turn impacts the progression of the disease and exacerbates dyskinesia symptoms and further contributes to cognitive decline.

Genetic Findings

Family and Twin Studies

Family and twin studies support the existence of genetic risk factors in the development of Parkinson's disease, particularly in early onset cases. Although approximately 15% of patients with the disease have a family history, most cases are idiopathic (Kalinderi, Bostantjopoulou, & Fidani, 2016; Tivota, et al., 2017). Twin studies have produced mixed findings, with some cross-sectional studies reporting higher concordance rates of Parkinson's disease in monozygotic than dizygotic twins while others have not. A longitudinal study conducted with 542 Swedish twins with Parkinson's disease reported an 11% concordance rate for monozygotic twins and a 4% rate for same-sexed dizygotic twin pairs, with a modest heritability estimate of 34% for the disease (Wirdefeldt et al., 2011). Neuroimaging research with monozygotic and dizygotic twins suggests that both twins symptomatic and asymptomatic for Parkinson's disease display reduced activity in the putamen relative to control participants. These findings support that a prodromal stage of Parkinson's disease may exist even when individuals are symptom-free (Laihinen et al., 2000).

As discussed previously, linkage and genome-wide association studies are two main approaches to studying the genetic contributions to disease, and these methods have identified several chromosomal locations and specific genes linked to Parkinson's disease. Deng, Wang, and Jankovic (2018) recently reported that over 23 locations on various chromosomes and 19 genes (10 autosomal dominant genes and 9 autosomal recessive genes) have been implicated in Parkinson's disease. Numerous additional loci and susceptibility genes are currently under investigation for the development of early and later onset Parkinson's disease.

Candidate Genes

With respect to early onset Parkinson's disease, mutations of three genes, PRKN, PINK1, and PARK7 are particularly problematic. In these cases, individuals with Parkinson disease have *two copies* of the mutated gene—one from each parent (autosomal recessive inheritance). Because each parent only carried one copy of the altered gene, they most likely did not show signs and symptoms of the disease, but when both altered genes are inherited, the individual has a high probability of developing Parkinson's disease (Bekris, Mata, & Zabetian, 2010).

The PRKN gene, located on chromosome 6, provides instructions for making a protein called parkin. Parkin plays an important role in the degradation of other proteins that are no longer needed by the cell. A large variety of mutations (i.e., over 200) in the PRKN gene have been found worldwide in families with early onset Parkinson's disease, and it is estimated that 50% of early onset cases are due to PRKN mutations (Deng et al., 2018; Mata et al., 2004). Exactly how the parkin protein leads to the manifestation of Parkinson's disease is unknown; however, the loss or reduction of this protein is believed to interfere with mitochondria function, cell growth, and vesicle formation and release (Mizuno et al., 2001). Ultimately, mutations of the PRKN gene are believed to result in the death of dopamine-releasing neurons in the substantia nigra.

The PINK1 gene, located on chromosome 1, provides instructions for making a protein called PTEN induced putative kinase 1. Within cells, this protein is located inside the mitochondria and is thought to help protect mitochondria during periods of cellular stress, such as unusually high-energy demands. Scientists have linked more than 70 mutations of this gene to Parkinson disease, particularly early onset cases. Mutations in the PINK1 are believed to interfere with the normal delivery of the PTEN protein to the mitochondria. The absence (or reduction) of this protein is thought to cause neurons to die, thereby weakening muscle movements (Bekris et al., 2010).

The PARK7 gene located on chromosome 1 provides instructions for making the DJ-1 protein, a protein whose functions are not well understood, but it is believed to help neurons in several ways, protect neurons from oxidative stress, help fold newly produced proteins and refold damaged proteins, and, lastly, produce RNA (Klein & Westenberg, 2012). Scientists have identified more than 25 mutations of the PARK7 gene that result in small or large changes to portions of the DJ1 protein. These changes interfere with normal functioning of the protein that leads to destructive oxidative stress and a buildup of misfolded or damaged proteins that are toxic to cells, particularly dopamine-releasing neurons, eventually resulting in cell death. As mentioned previously, death of dopamine neurons leads to disrupted motor movements characteristic of Parkinson's disease (Klein & Westenberger, 2012).

In addition to autosomal recessive inheritance, early onset Parkinson's disease is associated with two genes that can be inherited *from only one parent*—i.e., autosomal dominance. Specifically, one copy of the LRRK2 or SNCA gene if altered can be sufficient to cause Parkinson's disease. Research indicates that mutations in the LRRK2 gene is the most common cause of dominant inheritance and mutations in the PRKN gene are the most common causes of recessively inherited Parkinson's disease (Corti, Lesage, & Brice, 2011).

The LRRK2 gene located on chromosome 12 provides instructions for the protein dardarin. Dardarin is important in enzymatic activities that help turn on and off various cell actions. Exactly how dardardin is involved in Parkinson's disease remains unclear. However, more than 100 different mutations of the LRRK2 gene have been linked to late onset Parkinson's disease, and the most prevalent mutation (G2019S) reportedly occurs in 40% of North African Arabs with Parkinson's disease, 15% to 20% of Ashkenazi Jewish patients, and 1% to 2% of patients of European origin with the disease (Goldwurm et al., 2005; Orr-Utreger et al., 2007). Some scientists hypothesize that dysfunction of LRRK2 gene may result in the accumulation of a protein known as alpha synuclein, the protein found in Lewy body deposits found in Parkinson's disease patients. Alpha synuclein is also thought to trigger inflammatory responses by glial cells (Rui et al., 2018). Indeed, the SNCA gene, located on chromosome 4, has also been implicated in late onset Parkinson's disease, and this gene encodes the protein alpha synuclein. This protein is located in the presynaptic terminals and is believed to help maintain an adequate supply of synaptic vesicles in presynaptic terminals and regulate the release of dopamine (Schulte & Gasser, 2011). Greater than 30 mutations (e.g., multiplications, substitutions) of the SCNA gene have been linked to familial Parkinson's disease and are thought to increase the risk of late onset. Although the precise way in which mutations of the SCNA gene lead to Parkinson's disease are unclear, scientists have suggested that excess alpha synuclein proteins interfere with dopaminergic transmission by impairing normal cellular functions and eventually leading to cellular death (Deng et al., 2018).

Recent research has identified additional genes thought to play a critical role in the development of both early and later onset Parkinson's disease, including the GBA gene. The GBA gene is located on chromosome 1 and provides instructions for creation of an enzyme found in lysosomes (beta-glucocerebrosidase) that breaks down waste products and unneeded proteins. It is estimated that approximately 5% and 10% of individuals with Parkinson's disease carry a mutation of the GBA gene, and these individuals tend to have an early onset of the disease and are more likely have a positive family history compared to those without the disease (Markovic et al., 2016). The way in which a GBA mutation leads to Parkinson's is unknown, but mutations appear to impair the proper functioning of lysosomes leading to abnormal protein deposits.

Additional Genes

Mutations in additional genes (e.g., ATP13A2, VPS35) have been linked to familial Parkinson's disease and numerous susceptibility genes have been identified by linkage and genome-wide association studies (e.g., MAPT) (see Deng et al., 2018, for a review). As future studies unfold, undoubtedly more genes will be identified that play a critical role in the development of early and later onset Parkinson's disease. It is important to note, however, that genetic mutations that result in Parkinson's disease exist in only a small number of individuals: in the majority of cases, there is no family history, and genetic causes have not been identified. The current etiologic view in the literature is that the underlying cause of Parkinson's disease appears to be multifactorial involving genetic factors, environmental factors, gene-environment interactions, and unknown influences. As noted by Kalia and Lange (2015),

> Parkinson's disease is now viewed as a slowly progressive neurodegenerative disorder that begins years before diagnosis can be made, implicates multiple neuroanatomical areas, results from a combination of genetic and environmental factors, and manifests with a broad range of symptoms.

> (p. 896)

In additional to genetic factors, scientists have identified structural and functional brain characteristics of individuals with Parkinson's disease.

Structural Findings

Substantia Nigra

As noted previously, Parkinson's disease is a progressive neurological disorder characterized by resting tremor, rigidity, postural instability, and slowed ability to start and continue movements, although the symptoms are often heterogeneous among patients. It is important to note that movement is a highly complex process that involves coordination among numerous brain regions and motor pathways. For example, several descending pathways, including the ventromedial pathway originate at the level of the midbrain or motor cortex and traverse through the brain and brain stem to innervate specific body parts. The lateral corticospinal tract, for example, begins at the motor cortex and terminates in the spinal cord, and is responsible for movement of fingers, hands, and arms (Figure 4.3). Other ascending and descending pathways are involved in movement of the face and tongue (Figure 4.4). Anatomically, Parkinson's disease is characterized by degeneration of dopaminergic neurons in the substantia nigra and to some degree in the ventral tegmental area (Figure 4.5), although it is important to note that various neurotransmitters are currently believed to be involved in the disease.

Depending on the severity of the disease, most motor pathways are affected. The cause of the degeneration of neurons is not completely understood but is believed to be due to

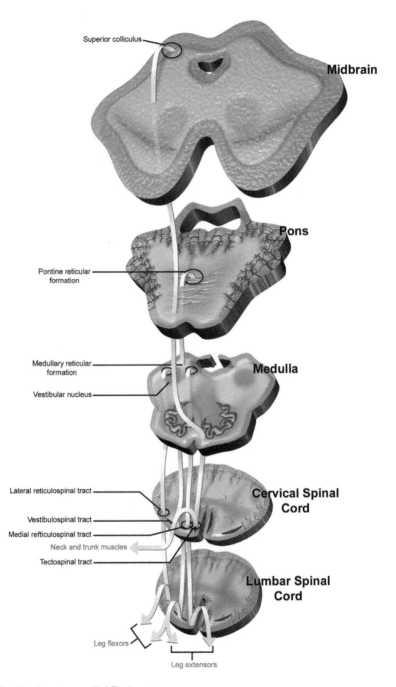

Superior colliculus

Midbrain

Pons

Pontine reticular
formation

Medullary reticular
formation

Vestibular nucleus

Medulla

Lateral reticulospinal tract

**Cervical Spinal
Cord**

Vestibulospinal tract

Medial refticulospinal tract

Neck and trunk muscles

Tectospinal tract

**Lumbar Spinal
Cord**

Leg flexors

Leg extensors

FIGURE 4.2. Ventromedial Pathway

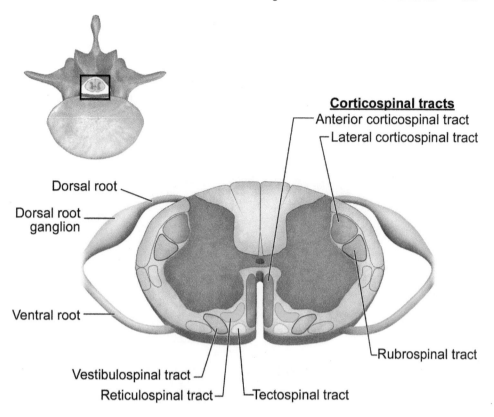

Corticospinal tracts
Anterior corticospinal tract
Lateral corticospinal tract

Dorsal root

Dorsal root ganglion

Ventral root

Rubrospinal tract

Vestibulospinal tract
Reticulospinal tract   Tectospinal tract

Descending *(Motor)* Tracts in the Spinal Cord

FIGURE 4.3.   Descending Motor Pathways

Copyright Blausen Medical Communications. Reproduced by permission.

several interacting factors, including genetic and environmental. The degeneration and death of dopaminergic neurons lead to dopamine reductions in the striatum (putamen, caudate nucleus, and nucleus accumbens) and projecting pathways to the frontal lobes that form parallel loops or circuits. As discussed in Chapter 1, the basal ganglia are a complex group of subcortical cell bodies that play a critical role in movement. The basal ganglia consist of the caudate nucleus, putamen, and the globus pallidus. The caudate nucleus and putamen together are known as the striatum. The striatum receives input from the cortex and other structures (e.g., thalamus and amygdala) and projects information to widespread regions, such as the brain stem and the prefrontal cortex. The nucleus accumbens is a group of cell bodies located adjacent to the striatum. The nigrostriatal system extends from the substantia nigra to the striatum. Parkinson's disease is associated with degeneration of dopaminergic cell bodies of the substantia nigra that affects functioning of the nigrostriatal

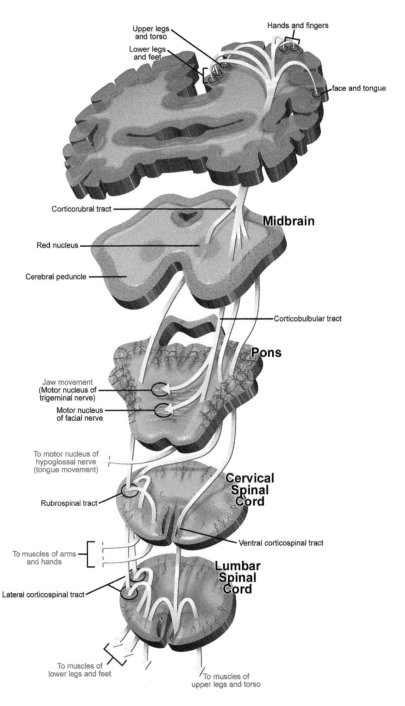

FIGURE 4.4. Corticobulbar Motor Pathway

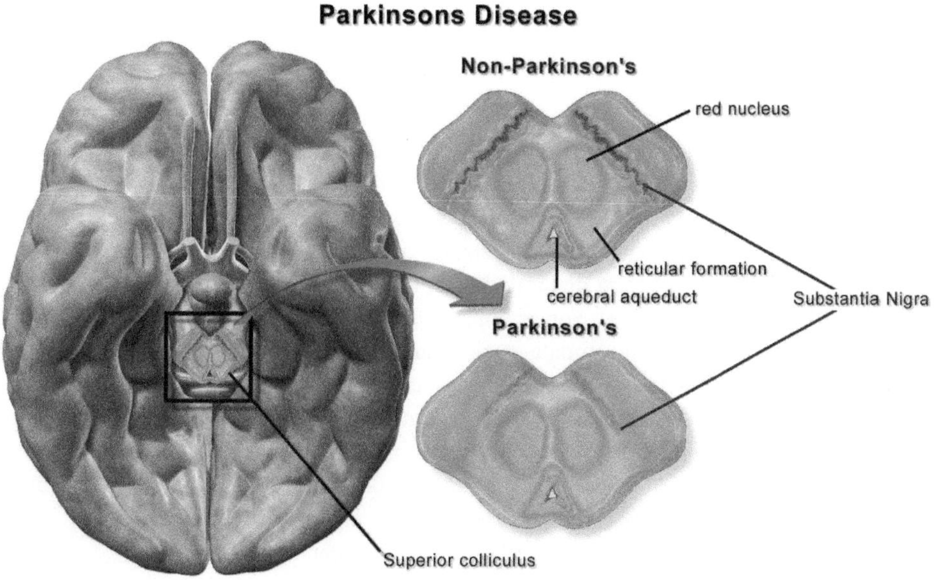

FIGURE 4.5. Location of Substantia Nigra and Degeneration of Cells Characteristic of Parkinson's Disease

Copyright Blausen Medical Communications. Reproduced by permission.

system. Specifically, loss of dopaminergic neurons is hypothesized to result in decreased excitatory activity of the nigrostriatal pathway, resulting in decreased motor response and symptoms of bradykinesia and rigidity (Niccolini, Su, & Politis, 2014). Medication and surgical procedures for Parkinson's disease typically target the nigrostriatal region (Kultas-Ilinsky & Ilinsky, 2001).

Lewy Bodies

In addition to death of dopamine-releasing neurons of the substantia nigra, Parkinson's disease is characterized by Lewy bodies—i.e., aggregates of abnormally folded proteins found primarily inside the cell. Lewy bodies are composed of various proteins (e.g., tau, ubiquitin) and the most prominent constituent is alpha synuclein. Lewy bodies are spherical in shape and insoluable and interfere with internal cellular functioning. Although the precise cause of Lewy bodies is unclear, mutations of the gene (SNCA) that encodes the expression of alpha synuclein is thought to lead to their formation. Over the course of Parkinson's disease, Lewy body aggregates have been hypothesized to progress from specific regions of the brain and impacting motor and non-motor systems characteristic of the disorder (Braak & Del Tredici, 2017; Lozano, Tam, & Lozano, 2017).

Glial Cells

Similar to Alzheimer's disease glial cells are hypothesized to play a role in Parkinson's desease by triggering inflammatory responses in the brain. The mechanisms by which astrocytes become activated is unclear, but scientists have hypothesized that the presence of excessive levels of alpha synuclein and Lewy body deposits may induce astrocytes to release of pro-inflammatory cytokines (Booth, Hirst, & Wade-Martins, 2017). A number of studies have reported reduced risk of Parkinson's disease with the use of anti-inflammatory medications (Gagne & Power, 2010).

Dopamine Receptors

Mandel et al. (2003) noted that approximately 70–75% of dopamine neurons have died by the time Parkinson's disease symptoms are typically diagnosed nevertheless scientists have explored density of remaining dopamine receptors. Postmortem studies have produced contradictory results with respect to dopamine receptors and Parkinson's disease: increased, decreased, and no differences in dopamine receptors in individuals with and without the disease (e.g., Pierot et al., 1988). For example, Rinne et al. (1991) measured the number of dopamine receptors in the caudate nucleus and putamen in postmortem samples of patients with Parkinson's disease relative to age-matched controls. Results revealed a significant decrease in D1 and D2 receptors in the caudate nucleus but not the putamen, and age was not related to receptor densities. Some studies have also reported decreased dopamine receptors in the cerebellum of patients with Parkinson's disease (Hurley, Mash, & Jenner, 2003). Other studies have reported decreased number of dendritic spines in patients with Parkinson's disease and changes in dendritic spines have been observed following treatment with dopamine agonists (Nishijima et al., 2017).

Patterns of Atrophy

Neuroimaging studies have supported atrophy of various brain structures in patients with Parkinson's disease. Furthermore, different patterns of atrophy appear to vary depending on whether the disease is accompanied by dementia. For example, Burton and colleagues (2004) found reduced gray matter volume in the frontal lobes of patients with Parkinson's disease and no dementia relative to control subjects. Parkinson's patients with dementia, however, had significantly greater regions of atrophy, including the occipital lobes. Other MRI studies have found cortical, hippocampal, and cerebellar atrophy in patients with Parkinson's disease compared to controls (e.g., Camicioli et al., 2003; Laakso et al., 1996; Peran et al., 2018; Uribe et al., 2018). Collectively, these findings suggest that structural changes associated with Parkinson's disease are more specific to subcortical structures, but as the disease progresses and is accompanied by dementia and increased motor and non-motor symptoms, widespread brain atrophy is observed.

Autophagy

Autophagy is a process whereby misfolded proteins and debris, such as damaged cellular components are delivered to lysosomes for degradation. Defects in this process can result in an accumulation of protein aggregates, such as Lewy bodies. Recent research has begun to focus on various autophagy delivery pathways as well as the lysosome degradation process to determine the role of these processes in the development of Parkinson's disease. Although preliminary, studies support involvement of autophagy delivery pathways and lysosomes in the development of the disease (Cerri & Blandini, 2018).

Functional Findings

Positron Emission Tomography (PET) and fMRI studies have explored functional differences between patients with and without Parkinson's disease. For example, studies have found that individuals with Parkinson's disease, as well as relatives of patients with Parkinson's disease (who are greater risk of the disorder), show decreased striatal uptake compared to controls in early stages of the disease, even when they are symptom-free (e.g., Fazio et al., 2018; Maraganore et al., 1999). Similarly, a number of studies have reported decreased density of dopamine transporters in individuals with Parkinson's disease, and this reduction is often correlated with severity of symptoms (e.g., Davis, Chen, & Glick, 2003; Seibyl et al., 1995). Recent neuroimaging studies have found that Parkinson's disease often leads to impaired learning from reward and punishment; however, dopamine agonists increase neuronal activity in the putamen and appear to improve learning and prefrontal cortex, and these changes are associated with cognitive improvements in learning (Argyelan et al., 2018).

Regional cerebral blood flow studies have found both reductions and increased activity in patients with Parkinson's disease in various regions relative to controls (Abe et al., 2003; Firbank et al., 2003). For example, Turner and colleagues (2003) found increased blood flow and involvement of more cortical regions in patients with Parkinson's disease while performing eye tracking or limb movement tasks. The authors speculated that patients may recruit more cortical regions as a compensatory response to the degeneration of motor systems that accompany the disease. Playford et al. (1992) also found differential activation of brain regions in subjects with and without Parkinson's disease during motor tasks, and reported that those with the disease had impaired activation of subcortical as well as prefrontal and motor cortices. In contrast, Lozza, Marie, and Baron (2002) used PET to measure glucose metabolism in patients with Parkinson's disease and found that a tremor was negatively correlated with activity in the putamen and cerebellum, while rigidity was positively correlated with activity in the putamen. Kassubek and colleagues (2001) reported increased glucose metabolism in the ventrolateral region of the thalamus of patients with Parkinson's disease; this finding was positively correlated with degree of resting tremor. Recently, Pilotto et al. (2018) suggested that PET patterns could be used as a biomarker for identifying patients with Parkinson's disease who are at risk for developing dementia. Collectively, these findings support differential patterns of brain activity in patients with Parkinson's disease and indicate that as the disease progresses more brain regions are recruited to perform cognitive and motor tasks compared to those without the disease.

Neurotransmitter Findings

In addition to disturbances in the dopaminergic system, other neurotransmitter systems are believed to play a role in the pathophysiology of Parkinson's disease due to the complex interaction between neurotransmitter systems in the substantia nigra. For example, dopamine activity in this region is reportedly modulated by serotonergic, glutamatergic, and GABAergic neurons (Barone, 2010). Serotonin has been implicated in Parkinson's due to the high comorbidity with depression, reward related behavior, and more, recently, in medication-induced dyskinesia commonly found in patients with Parkinson's disease (Carta & Björklund, 2018). Interestingly, Kerenyi et al. (2003) found reduced density of serotonin transporters in the caudate, putamen, and striatum of patients with Parkinson's disease using PET. Scientists have also implicated epinephrine in Parkinson's disease, although to date, findings have been less convincing for the role of epinephrine in the disease.

Lastly, as mentioned previously, Parkinson's disease is often accompanied by dementia and psychosis, and the loss of cholinergic neurons in the nucleus basalis of Meynert is believed to play a critical role in the emergence of these cognitive impairments (Bosboom, Stoffers, & Wolters, 2003). For example, many studies have found a relationship between greater severity of cognitive impairment and degree of reduction in acetylcholine-related activity in patients with Parkinson's disease as well as in postmortem samples (e.g., Kuhl et al., 1996; Mattila et al., 2001; Whitehouse et al., 1988). Given the herterogeneity of motor and non-motor symptoms that typically characterize Parkinson's disease, the underlying neuropathology of the disease is likely mediated by complex, interconnected neurotransmitter systems. Indeed, treatments that focus exclusively on the dopamine system do not effectively treat either motor or non-motor symptoms. Several pharmacological and non-pharmacological interventions are currently available, however, that improve, albeit temporarily, the motoric symptoms that first emerge and become progressively worse with time.

Interventions for Parkinson's Disease

Pharmacological Interventions

Currently, empirically established disease-altering treatments for Parkinson's disease do not exist, partly because the underlying cause of the disease remains a mystery in the majority of cases. Olson (2000) noted that there are three main approaches to treating Parkinson's disease: replacing dopamine, replacing dopamine-releasing neurons via transplantations, and halting neuronal loss. Today, the main form of treatment is pharmacological aimed at increasing (a) dopamine production (levodopa), (b) mimicking the effects of dopamine at the level of the receptor (dopamine agonists), or (c) targeting other neurotransmitter systems.

During the 1950s, Carlsson, Lindqvist, and Magnusson (1957) demonstrated that treatment with levodopa (L-Dopa) improved Parkinson-like symptoms induced in other animals. Today, levodopa is the most frequently used medication for later-stage Parkinson's disease and is converted by cells to dopamine. Approximately 95% of patients show a moderate to very good response to levodopa, but given that dopamine is increased throughout the brain and not only the striatum, it is associated with a number of unpleasant side effects (e.g., involuntary movements, psychosis, nausea; Webster, 2001). Alternatively, dopamine agonists, such as pramipexole (mirapex), pergolide (permax), and ropinirole (requip), that attach to postsynaptic receptors are also used to treat the symptoms of disease, but are most effective in earlier stages of the disease and when used in combination with drugs that promote the synthesis and release of dopamine (Connolly & Lang, 2014). These medications

Table 4.3 FDA-Approved Medications Used in the Treatment of Parkinson's Disease

Medication	Mode of Action	Agonist/Antagonist
Amantadine (Symmetrel)	Blocks dopamine transporter protein, blocks NMDA receptor	Dopamine agonist and glutamate antagonist
Levodopa (Sinemet)	Converted to dopamine	Dopamine agonist
Entacapone (Comtan)	Catechol-o-methyl transferase (COMT) inhibitors	Dopamine agonist
Xadago (Safinamide)	Monoamine oxidase B (MAO-B) inhibitor	Dopamine agonist
Mirapex (Pramipexole)	Attaches to dopamine postsynaptic receptors	Dopamine agonist
Apokyn (Apomorphine)	Attaches to dopamine postsynaptic receptors, blocks serotonin receptors	Dopamine agonist Serotonin Antagonist

have been found to reduce the degree of dyskinesia; however, they are associated with increased impulsive behavior, freezing, sleep problems, and hallucinations, as well as additional side including headache, gastrointestinal problems, and hypotension.

Other drugs that prevent the breakdown of dopamine such as monoamine oxidase inhibitors (MAO inhibitors, e.g., selegiline/eldepryl) and catechol-o-methyl transferase (COMT) inhibitors (e.g., entacapone/comtan) are also used to treat Parkinson's disease symptoms (Tiexeira et al., 2018). A serious side effect associated with MAOIs is hypertension; users of COMT inhibitors may experience nausea, headaches, confusion, gastrointestinal problems, and involuntary muscle movements. For mild Parkinson's symptoms, amantadine (symmetrel), a glutamate receptor antagonist, is sometimes used as well as anticholinergic medications (Weintraub & Claassen, 2017). Side effects of these medications include dizziness, insomnia, nausea, sleep disturbances, dry mouth, and gastrointestinal problems (Physicians' Desk Reference, 2017). Antipsychotic medications (e.g., clozapine) are sometimes used to help decrease psychotic symptoms that often emerge in later stages of Parkinson's disease. In 2017, the FDA approved a new a new drug called Xadago (safinamide) as an adjunctive medication for times when Parkinson's symptoms, such as tremor or difficulty walking, return despite medication. Xadago is a monoamine oxidase (MAO)-B inhibitor and prevents the breakdown of dopamine.

Non-pharmacological, Physiologically Based Interventions

Surgical Procedures   Eskandar and colleagues (2003) reported a shift from ablative procedures (e.g., pallidotomy) to deep brain stimulation in the surgical treatment of Parkinson's disease. In 1996, for example, 0% of surgical procedures involved placement of brain stimulators, a figure that rose to 88% in 2000. In terms of ablative procedures, a pallidotomy involves destruction of part of the globus pallidus and can be performed unilaterally or bilaterally to improve unwanted muscular contractions as well as rigidity. Skalabrin, Laws, and Bennett (1998) found that patients who received a pallidotomy responded more favorably to levodopa after the surgery, based on their performance on timed motor tasks and additional forms of evaluation. An uncommon side effect associated with levodopa treatment as well as pallidotomy surgery for Parkinson's disease is impulse control disorders, including hypersexuality, presumably due to increased dopaminergic functioning (Mendez, O'Connor, & Lim, 2004; Zhang et al., 2014). A thalamotomy involves destruction of part of the thalamus and has been found to improve tremor and, to a lesser extent, rigidity and unwanted excessive motor movements (Krack et al., 2000). Gamma knife radiosurgery has also been used to treat Parkinson's symptoms and is reportedly similarly effective and safer than other thalamotomy methods (Ohyeet al., 2002; Young et al., 2000).

In contrast to ablative surgery, deep brain stimulation does not involve destruction of tissue. Recent research indicates that deep brain stimulation is by far the dominant surgical procedure for Parkinson's disease (Lozano, Tam, & Lozano, 2018). As discussed in Chapter 3, a small lead with an electrode is inserted in specific target areas of the brain (i.e., globus pallidus, subthalamic nucleus). The procedure can be performed under general or local anesthesia (Maltête et al., 2004), and the frequencies at which the stimulation is delivered can vary (Foffani et al., 2003). The lead and electrode remain in the brain and are connected to a programmed, battery-operated pulse generator implanted in the chest. The generator sends impulses directly to the target region of the brain. Many studies have substantiated that DBS improve tremors characteristic of movement disorders, such as

Parkinson's disease, and increase cerebral blood flow to various regions of the brain (Obeso et al., 2001; Vingerhoets et al., 2002; Pinto et al., 2004). Long-term follow-up studies of deep brain stimulation have found sustained improvement in motor functions up to five years after the stimulation (Jiang et al., 2015).

ECT and TMS   Electroconvulsive therapy has also been found to improve motor and depression symptoms of Parkinson's disease (Kennedy et al., 2003; Williams et al., 2017). Other studies have found that ECT was associated with improvement of psychotic symptoms as well as motor symptoms in patients with Parkinson's disease (Shulman, 2003). Transcranial magnetic stimulation TMS has also been explored in the treatment of Parkinson's disease; however, studies have produced mixed findings concerning the effectiveness of this technique at improving motor symptoms, and more research is needed to explore the potential use of TMS in the treatment of Parkinson's disease (Cantello, Tarletti, & Civardi, 2002).

Lifestyle Changes   Exercise has been associated with a lower risk of developing neurodegenerative disease, including Parkinson's disease. In a recent review of the literature, Grazzino and Massano (2013) found that exercise was associated with a lower risk of developing the disease, improved disease symptoms, including mobility, balance, gait, and quality of life, and at a molecular level, the authors suggested that exercise likely increased neurotrophic substances. Others have suggested that dietary habits may interact with the disease process and influence the risk of Parkinson's disease (nutritional genomics), although empirical findings have not supported a strong relationship between diet and Parkinson's (Erro et al., 2018). Studies, have, however, found a relationship between the gastrointestinal system, inflammation, and the disease. For example, Noyce et al. (2012) reported that prodromal symptoms, including chronic constipation, doubles an individual's risk of developing Parkinson's disease.

Neurotrophins and Transplantations   Numerous studies have discovered a reduction of neurotrophic factors (BDNF, NGF) in several brain regions (e.g., substantia nigra, caudate, putamen, frontal cortex, cerebellum) of individuals with Parkinson's disease (e.g., Murer, Yan, & Raiman-Vozari, 2001; Parain et al., 1999). As discussed in Chapter 1, neurotrophins are substances released by glial cells and neurons that promote the survival of neurons in the brain. Reductions of neurotrophins in Parkinson's disease is hypothesized to be due to loss of dopamine neurons that produce the neurotrophin and because surviving dopaminergic neurons produce less BDNF than other types of neurons (Howells et al., 2000). The precise reasons for these reductions is unknown; however, polymorphisms of specific neurotrophin genes occur more frequently in patients with Parkinson's disease than controls, which supports a causal role for abnormalities of BDNF in the pathogenesis of the disease (Momose et al., 2002; Palasz et al., 2017).

Scientists have explored whether delivery of neurotrophins to degenerating nigrostriatal neurons can influence cellular function. Scientists have injected a neurotrophins (e.g., glial cell line derived neurotrophic factor) into the substantia nigra and striatum of other animals who had Parkinson-like symptoms, and discovered regeneration of neurons in these regions (Georgievska et al., 2002; Kordower et al., 2000). Clinical trials have also been performed with humans using a variety of neurotrophins, and unfortunately, to date, the studies have not been successful (Sullivan & O'Keeffe, 2016).

Transplantation

For several decades, studies have been conducted on the efficacy of transplantation of human embryonic or fetal dopamine cells into the brains of individuals suffering from Parkinson's disease (Clarkson & Freed, 1999). Lindvall and colleagues (1990) at the University of Lund, Sweden, were among the first to transplant dopamine neurons from human fetuses (8–9 weeks gestational age) into the putamen of patients with severe Parkinson's disease and document behavioral improvement that correlated with increased dopamine synthesis in the transplanted area. Lindvall et al. (1994) followed up two patients with Parkinson's disease three years after the transplantation and reported that the dopaminergic neurons continued to survive and a continued reduction of clinical symptoms was observed. Sawle et al. (1992) also reported successful outcomes with two patients with Parkinson's disease who had received fetal tissue implants in the putamen. In 2001, Freed and colleagues randomly assigned 40 patients with severe Parkinson's disease to a transplant or sham-surgery group. Results revealed a significant difference in standardized tests of clinical improvement, with the transplant group performing significantly higher than the sham-surgery group. Results also indicated that younger, but not older, patients who had received the transplant demonstrated significant improvement relative to the sham-surgery group.

Despite these encouraging findings, other studies have not supported the efficacy of fetal transplants in the treatment of Parkinson's disease. Olanow et al. (2003), for example, recently conducted a 24-month double-blind, placebo-controlled trial of fetal bilateral transplantation. Findings revealed that 56% of the transplanted patients developed dyskinesia that persisted when dopamine-related medications were ceased. In addition, patients who received the transplant did not differ from patients who did not receive the transplant in scores on the Unified Parkinson's Disease Rating Scale. Freed et al. (2001) also reported that a significant percentage (15%) of transplant patients had developed persistent dyskinesias following the surgery. Ma et al. (2002) suggested that dyskinesias following transplantation surgery results from increased dopaminergic functioning in some, but not all, regions of the striatum. Research also indicates that cognitive performance does not appear to improve during the first year following bilateral fetal transplants (Trott et al., 2003) and that factors such as age of the fetal tissue and patient age may affect the clinical outcome (Freed et al., 2001). Recently, Kefalopoulou et al. (2014) followed up two patients who received fetal grafts in the striatal region 18 years earlier and found motor improvements were sustained and both patients remained free of any, pharmacological dopaminergic therapy. In general, fetal transplantation studies support that the procedure is generally safe with low morbidity, but a significant percentage of patients may experience dyskinesias. Although the results vary among patients, findings indicate that patients often experience short- and long-term clinical benefits of fetal transplant surgery. Despite the benefits of fetal tissue transplantations, experts in this area of research predict a decline in use of this procedure worldwide due to lasting ethical controversies (Ishii & Eto, 2014).

Environmental Factors

Although it has been established that loss of dopaminergic neurons of the substantia nigra lead to Parkinson's disease symptoms, the cause of neuronal death remains speculative. As reviewed earlier, studies clearly support a role for genetic factors in early onset cases of Parkinson's disease, but most cases of the disease appear late in life and are not associated with known genetic factors. This finding has led researchers to identify environmental factors that might contribute to the disease. An unlikely source of discovery occurred in the late

1970s and early 1980s when drug abusers in California, Maryland, and Vancouver, British Columbia, required medical attention due to symptoms that closely resembled Parkinson's disease: generalized slowing and difficulty moving, rigidity, resting tremor, flexed posture, and loss of postural reflexes. The cause of their symptoms was identified as a synthetic street-drug contaminant, N-methyl-4-phenyl-1, 2, 3, 6-tetrahydropyridine (MPTP) and was distributed on the streets as synthetic heroin (Langston et al., 1983). It was soon revealed that MPTP was severely toxic to brain cells and specifically destroyed nerve cells in the substantia nigra. The Parkinson's-like symptoms subsided temporarily after treatment with L-dopa, the medication used to treat Parkinson's disease. This finding, in conjunction with genetic findings that failed to account for most Parkinson's cases, fueled research investigating environmental factors as potential causal agents in the disease.

Further support for the involvement of environment factors soon came from research in Japan as Imaizumi (1995) reported the age-adjusted death rate for Parkinson's disease was higher in urban than rural areas in Japan during the years 1979–1985. In addition, the death rate was higher in the southwest than the northeast regions of the country, and Imaizumi speculated that environmental factors might differ regionally and contribute to the development of Parkinson's disease. Meta-analytic studies in the United States also concluded that living in rural areas increased the risk of Parkinson's disease (Priyadarshi et al., 2001). Later, epidemiological studies of risk factors associated with Parkinson's disease concluded that long-term exposure to lead, copper, and insecticide were significantly associated with development of Parkinson's disease (Gorell et al., 2004). In 2007, a cross-cultural study involving over 700 patients with Parkinson's disease in Scotland, Italy, Sweden, Romania, and Malta concluded that pesticide exposure played a causal role in the development of the disease (Dick et al., 2007). Other studies have also suggested that exposure to herbicides, heavy metals, drinking well water, agent orange, and repeated head injuries resulting in the loss of consciousness increased the risk of Parkinson's disease (e.g., Priyadarshi et al., 2000; Tan, Tan, et al., 2003; Narayan et al., 2017). Exposure to factors such as pesticides, herbicides, metals, and solvents is hypothesized to result in oxidative stress and possibly modification in gene expression (DNA methylation) thereby increasing the likelihood of neurotoxicity and cellular death, leading to further neurodegeneration as observed in Parkinson's disease.

Lifestyle Factors

In addition to chemical exposure, lifestyle factors have been associated with increased risk of developing Parkinson's disease, including obesity and a sedentary lifestyle (Z. F. Bhat et al., 2017; Macpherson et al., 2017). Indeed, exercise and a healthy diet have been found to decrease inflammatory responses and to have neuroprotective effects on the brain (Jang et al., 2017). Interestingly, a large number of studies have reported that moderate to high caffeine consumption is associated with a significantly lower incidence of the disease (e.g., R. D. Abbott et al., 2003; Ascherio et al., 2001; Ross et al., 2000). Moderate alcohol consumption has also been associated with a lower risk of Parkinson's, although recent studies have criticized this body of literature for methodological weaknesses, including low statistical power and selection and recall bias (Checkoway et al., 2002; Bettiol et al., 2015). Additional studies are needed to address whether alcohol has a neuroprotective effect against Parkinson's disease.

Tea consumption, specifically green and black teas are hypothesized to reduce the risk of Parkinson's disease due to the abundant polyphenols found in tea. Specifically, tea polyphenols have been found to possess anti-oxidant and anti-chelating properties, and possibly decrease aggregation of alpha-synuclein proteins in the brain (Ragonese et al., 2003; Tan, Tan et al., 2003; Caruana & Vassallo, 2015). Pets may also play a role in decreasing risk of Parkinson's disease according to Kuopio and colleagues who studied environmental risk factors for the disease in Finland. The authors concluded that living with domestic animals (or something that is connected with domestic animals), may have a neuroprotective effect against Parkinson's disease (Kuopio et al., 1999). A robust finding in the literature is that cigarette smoking is inversely associated with the risk of Parkinson's disease (R. D. Abbott et al., 2003; Ma et al., 2017; Hernan et al., 2002; Preux et al., 2000; Sanyal, 2010). Rybicki and colleagues (1999), however, found this finding held true only in subjects without a family history of the disease; it was *positively* associated with Parkinson's disease in those with a family history of Parkinson's disease. Of course, deleterious health effects of cigarette smoking, including cancer and emphysema cannot be ignored! A history of repeated or TBI particularly when accompanied by the loss of consciousness has also been associated with increased risk of Parkinson's disease (Camacho-Soto et al., 2017; Gardner et al., 2017). Some scientists have attempted to identify "at-risk" populations for developing Parkinson's disease and Schirinzi et al. (2016) based on a large Italian population recently described "a positive family history, toxicants exposure, non-current-smoker, and alcohol non-consumer" as the most robust significant risk factors for the development of Parkinson's disease. Overall, environmental factors have been linked to both increased and decreased risk of developing Parkinson's disease and current research indicates that genetic and environmental factors interact in a complex fashion to ultimately increase or decrease susceptibility to the disease.

Summary of Parkinson's disease

- Parkinson's disease is a progressive neurological disorder characterized by resting tremor, rigidity, postural instability, and slowed ability to start and continue movements.
- Research indicates that men are at greater risk for Parkinson's disease than women.
- It is estimated that approximately 0.5% of the population between 65 and 69 has Parkinson's disease, while 3% of those 85 and older have the disease, although cross-cultural studies have reported differences in prevalence rates.
- Genetic factors have been implicated in early onset cases of the disease, although most cases have no known genetic basis.
- Environmental factors such as long-term exposure to heavy metals, herbicides, pesticides, and solvents are associated with increased risk of the disease.
- Protective factors may include caffeine, cigarette smoking, and alcohol consumption, although the later two factors are associated with increased risk of other health conditions, including cancer.
- An interaction between biological and environmental factors likely contributes to the development of Parkinson's disease.
- Levodopa is the primary medication used to treat the Parkinson's symptoms in later stages of the disease, while other drugs such as dopamine agonists, MAO inhibitors, a glutamate receptor antagonists, and anticholinergic medications are also used to treat symptoms.
- The manner in which biological and environmental factors lead to increased vulnerability to Parkinson's disease is poorly understood.
- Deep brain stimulation and, less commonly, ablative procedures are often effective at decreasing severe symptoms.
- Controversial treatments for Parkinson's disease include ECT, TMS, and fetal tissue transplantations.

Review Questions

1. Compare and contrast structural research findings of Alzheimer's disease and Parkinson's disease.
2. Compare and contrast functional research findings of Alzheimer's disease and Parkinson's disease.
3. Describe the various types of medications are used to treat Alzheimer's disease and Parkinson's disease.
4. Do environmental factors appear to play a role in the development of Alzheimer's disease and Parkinson's disease? Explain.
5. Imagine you were to create a research-based preventative program for current youth to ascribe to in order to reduce the likelihood of developing Alzheimer's disease and Parkinson's disease in the future. Describe the components of this program.
6. Identify the types of brain stimulation techniques that are used in the treatment of Alzheimer's disease and Parkinson's disease.

five
Schizophrenia

The World Health Organization classifies diseases and disorders based on the International Classification of Diseases ICD-10, while the American Psychiatric Association classifies disorders based on the *DSM-V* (APA, 2013). Globally, more psychologists reported using the ICD (51%) than the DSM (44%); however, differences in use are found across regions. For example, respondents in most European countries and in India report using the ICD most often, while others, including psychologists in the USA, reportedly used the *DSM-V* more often (Evans et al., 2013). Therefore, the current and subsequent chapters will refer to *DSM-V* criteria when discussing disorders.

Schizophrenia is included in the *DSM-V* under "schizophrenia spectrum and other psychotic disorders", which includes schizophrenia, schizotypical (personality) disorder, and other psychotic disorders (APA, 2013). These disorders are defined by abnormalities in one or more domains, including hallucinations, delusions, disorganized thinking, grossly disorganized or abnormal motor behavior, and negative symptoms. Given the large body of research that is available concerning schizophrenia, this chapter focuses on the pathophysiology and pharmacological treatment of the disorder.

Chapter 5 Learning Objectives

- Describe the essential features of schizophrenia.
- Describe demographic findings associated with the disorder.
- Describe multicultural findings associated with the disorder.
- Describe genetic findings associated with the disorder.
- Describe findings concerning dopamine-related research and schizophrenia.
- Describe major structural findings.
- Describe major functional findings.
- Identify types of medications used to treat schizophrenia.
- Identify non-pharmacological, physiologically based treatments for the disorder.
- Describe unanswered questions about the underlying pathology of schizophrenia.
- Identify recommendations for future research.

Background, Prevalence, and Developmental Course

The essential features of schizophrenia include delusions, hallucinations, disorganized speech, grossly disorganized or catatonic behavior, or negative symptoms. In order to meet diagnostic criteria, delusions, hallucinations, or disorganized speech must be present during a one-month period and signs of the disorder (whether positive or negative) must persist for at least six months' duration. In addition, symptoms must not be due to another psychological or medical condition and result in impairment in occupational, interpersonal, or adaptive functioning or failure to achieve normal functioning as seen in children and adolescents (APA, 2013).

Schizophrenia is found worldwide, and the lifetime prevalence rate is reportedly 0.3% to 0.7%, although differences exist across countries, sex, race, and ethnicity (APA, 2013; Jablensky, 1997; Luhrmann et al., 2015a, 2015b). For example, the ratio of male to female cases is approximately 1.4:1 with some, but not all studies indicating that males are diagnosed with the disorder at a slightly higher rate than females (McGrath et al., 2008). Males are more likely to experience their first episode of schizophrenia in their early 20s, and women typically experience their first episode in their late 20s or early 30s. The World Health Organization reported that the prevalence of schizophrenia is similar around the world; however, review studies have reported variation in prevalence rates from 0.4% to 0.7% (Saha, Chant, & Mcgrath, 2008). For example, Kebede et al. (2003) reported the prevalence of schizophrenia as 0.47% in Ethiopia, 0.17% in Norway (Evensen et al., 2016), and lower estimates have been reported in Iran (Mohammadi et al., 2005). A recent systematic review reported that one in every 200 persons (i.e., 0.5%) will be diagnosed with schizophrenia in their lifetime (Simeone et al., 2015).

Multicultural Findings

In addition to variation across countries, a recent study suggests expression of symptoms of schizophrenia vary cross culturally. For example, Laroi and colleagues (2014) argued that culture strongly influences the content and expression of hallucinations, and Luhrmann et al. (2015) found participants with schizophrenia in the United States were more likely to report violent auditory hallucinations compared to those in Ghana and in India. Race and ethnicity differences have also emerged among patients with schizophrenia. For example, research has found that rates of schizophrenia are higher among immigrants than native born and among minorities living in urban areas (McGrath et al., 2008; Saha et al., 2008; van Os et al., 2001). In addition, African Americans compared to non-Hispanic white patients are more likely to receive a diagnosis of schizophrenia, are less likely receive an affective disorder diagnosis during inpatient psychiatric hospitalization, and are less likely to receive mental health services for schizophrenia and other disorders (Hamilton et al., 2015). Perlman and colleagues (2016) found that endorsement of hallucinations and delusions symptoms was higher among African Americans compared to Caucasians, and African Americans with mild psychosis over-endorsed "hallucinations in any modality" and under-endorsed "widespread delusions" relative to Caucasians. Bae and Brekke (2002) reported that Korean Americans with schizophrenia were the least acculturated when compared to Euro-Americans, African Americans, and Latino Americans with schizophrenia; however, their level of symptom severity and clinical status were highly comparable with those of the other ethnic groups in the study.

Individuals with schizophrenia (probands) are at higher risk for comorbid psychiatric and medical problems, sexual dysfunction, and illicit substance use and abuse compared to the general population (Duke et al., 2001). Mortality rates are also higher among patients with schizophrenia with a two to threefold increased risk of dying (Gatov et al., 2017; McGrath et al., 2008). Approximately 20% of individuals with schizophrenia attempt suicide, and 5–6% die by suicide. Many individuals schizophrenia in the United States and other countries do not receive proper and adequate treatment, particularly those with severe and comorbid symptoms (Dickey et al., 2003). For example, it has been estimated that 90% of individuals with the schizophrenia in rural Ethiopia do not receive professional care and the practice of restraint (with ropes, chains) is reportedly common in these communities (Asher, Patel, & De Silva, 2017). Millier and colleagues (2017) that prolonged hospitalization was needed in 11–35% of patients (depending on symptom severity) in the United Kingdom, France, and Germany. According to Wimberley, approximately 30% of patients with schizophrenia are treatment resistant (2017). Contrary to popular belief, most individuals with schizophrenia do not commit violent crimes; however, recent findings indicated that individuals with the disorder are more likely to be violent than the general population (Fleischman et al., 2014; Kuroki et al., 2017). Studies also indicate that those who do commit violent acts are more likely to abuse substances and suffer from acute psychotic symptoms (Buckley et al., 2004; Fleischman et al., 2014; Walsh, Buchanan, & Fahy, 2001).

Developmental Course

The onset of schizophrenia typically occurs during late adolescence or young adulthood, and may be either abrupt or gradual. According to the *DSM-V* (APA, 2013), the peak age of onset is early to mid-20s for men and late 20s for women, and most individuals display a slow and gradual progression of negative symptoms prior to the first psychotic episode (prodromal symptoms). In rare cases, schizophrenia emerges in childhood and is characterized by delays and aberrations in cognitive, language motor, and social skills (Nicolson & Rapport, 2000). The course of schizophrenia is variable: some individuals remain chronically ill, while others experience periods of exacerbation or remission. Males are more likely to develop schizophrenia in late adolescence and females in young adulthood. Prior to menopause, women with schizophrenia tend to have less severe symptoms and respond better to pharmacological treatment than males, and late onset cases (after age 40) are more likely to be females (APA, 2013; Gur et al., 1996). Several studies support that a longer duration of untreated psychosis is predictive of a poorer outcome in terms of rate of remission and level of positive and negative symptoms (e.g., Malla et al., 2002). In other words, early intervention is associated with a better prognosis and lower rates of remission for patients with schizophrenia.

BOX 5.1   Are Hallucinations Normal?

Hallucinations in healthy individuals may be more common than previously believed and are not necessarily indicative of a psychotic disorder, nor are they necessarily predictive of schizophrenia in later life. A recent meta-analysis of nearly 85,000 participants from the general population across six continents, including children and adults, revealed approximately one in ten individuals reported auditory hallucinations in their lifetime. Auditory hallucinations were more common in children and adolescents (12.7% and 12.4%), followed by adults (5.8%), and the elderly (4.5%). Other studies have found that hallucinations remitted before adulthood in 75% of child and adolescent cases, suggesting that hallucinations are common prior to adulthood, and they tend to be transient in nature (Rubio et al., 2012). Factors that are associated with persistence of hallucinations include severity and frequency of hallucinations, hostile, conversing voices, multiple voices, and comorbid symptomatology (Askenazy et al., 2007; Escher et al., 2002). Overall, findings suggest that psychotic experiences may exist on a continuum ranging from benign transient experiences to psychotic, clinical symptoms (Dhossche et al., 2002; Johns and van Os, 2001).

Etiologic Theories

Currently, there is no known cause of schizophrenia. Research investigating the pathophysiology of schizophrenia has involved heritability, genetic, neuroanatomical, neurotransmitter, neurodevelopmental, and functional neuroimaging studies.

Genetics Overview

As discussed in Chapter 4, humans have 23 pairs of chromosomes and approximately 24,000 genes (Ast, 2005). Chromosomes are located inside the nucleus of a cell, and each chromosome has two "arms"; the short arm is referred to as p and the long arm is referred to as q. A gene is a segment of DNA located on specific locations on the chromosomes, and genes have a specific function, such as the creation of proteins that serve critical cellular functions. DNA consists of a sequence of molecules—i.e., nucleotides—and consists of four bases: adenine (A), guanine (G), cytosine (C), and thymine (T). These bases are connected systematically with A paired with T and G paired with C. When the sequence of one of these single nucleotides differs between paired chromosomes in an individual, this is known as a single-nucleotide polymorphism (SNP, pronounced "snip") and can influence an individual's susceptibility to disease and disorders. Welter et al. (2014) in a systematic review of the literature reported a total of 4,261 schizophrenia-associated SNPs.

The degree of *heritability* of a disease/disorder or a construct (e.g., intelligence) can be estimated and are referred to as heritability estimates. By definition, heritability refers to the proportion of phenotypic variation between individuals in a population due to genetic variation between individuals in that population. It is important to note that heritability refers to a population and *not* to an individual. Heritability estimates are numerical estimates that vary from zero to 1 (i.e., none to 100%) and represent the fraction of phenotype variability (e.g., schizophrenia) that can be attributed to genetic variation, but they do *not* provide any information about an individual or about specific genes that contribute to a disorder. With respect to clinical disorders such as schizophrenia, research has explored heritability estimates via family, twin, and adoption studies, and the role of genetic factors underlying the pathophysiology of these disorders has been explored through linkage, candidate genes and genome wide association studies.

Genetic Findings

Heritability Studies: Family and Twin Findings

Research concerning the heritability of schizophrenia has investigated the occurrence of schizophrenia in monozygotic and dizygotic twins, biological relatives, unrelated individuals, and adoption cases. The consensus across twin studies is that schizophrenia occurs in monozygotic twins more often than dizygotic pairs. Monozygotic twins are genetically identical, while dizygotic twins share on average 50% of their genes. Twins that are reared together typically experience similar environments, therefore any difference in concordance rates between monozyotic and dizygotic twins is indicative of genetic influence for schizophrenia.

Specific concordance rates vary across studies, ranging from 41% to 87% in monozygotic twins and 10% to 17% for dizygotic twins (Cardno et al., 1999; Holzman & Matthysse, 1990; Gottesman, 1991). A recent nationwide study in Denmark involving 31,524 twin pairs born between 1951 and 2000 reported lower concordance rates (33% in monozygotic twins and 7% in dizygotic twins) but a heritability risk of 79% for schizophrenia (Hilker et al., 2018).

Evidence from adoption studies also supports a heritability factor in schizophrenia. For example, Kety et al. (1994) studied the occurrence of schizophrenia in children who were adopted as well as their biological parents and siblings, and found that 12.5% of the biological relatives developed schizophrenia, while none of the adoptive relatives developed the disorder. Gottesman and Bertelsen (1989) examined the rates of schizophrenia in children whose parent was either a monozygotic or dizygotic twin with schizophrenia (or without) and found the risk the for schizophrenia in offspring of identical twins with schizophrenia was 16.8% and 17.4% in their normal co-twins' offspring.

Family studies have supported that first-degree relatives of individuals with schizophrenia are at higher risk for developing the disorder than second-degree relatives, who in turn are at higher risk compared to controls (Helenius, Munk-Jørgensen, & Steinhausen, 2012). If both parents have schizophrenia, then the risk has been reported to be approximately 40% that they will have a child with schizophrenia (McDonald & Murphy, 2003); however, recent research has reported that children of a parent with schizophrenia are at tenfold risk for developing the disorder (Gejman et al., 2010; Velthorst et al., 2016). Collectively, results from twin, family, and adoption studies suggest that genes are important but not determinant in the development of schizophrenia. As Hyman (2003) stated, "Our brains, not our genes regulate our behavior, and our brains are the product of genes, environment and chance operating over a lifetime" (p. 99). These findings raise important questions: Are particular genes involved in schizophrenia, and if so, in what capacity? And what factors determine whether a person with this genetic vulnerability develops the disorder? Scientists have attempted to identify specific genes and gene variants associated with the development of depression by using linkage, candidate gene, and genome-wide association studies (GWAS). Linkage and GWAS studies complement one another as linkage studies can be useful for the identification of rare variants with larger effect sizes, while GWAS can be useful for identification of common variants with relatively small effect sizes.

Genetic Linkage Findings

Genetic linkage studies search for chromosomal locations ("marker loci") where disease genes may be found. Linkage studies are based on the observation that genes that are located in close proximity on the same chromosome tend to be inherited together more often than expected by chance; hence, these loci are referred to as linked. These studies attempt to identify rare gene variants (e.g., mutations) that confer a high degree of risk of disease (e.g., cystic fibrosis, diabetes etc.). With regard to schizophrenia, linkage studies seek to determine whether specific chromosomal regions in individuals with schizophrenia have specific DNA markers relative to those without the disorder. Molecular genetic studies then explore how specific genes and mutation(s) may be involved in the etiology of schizophrenia (Basset et al., 2001; J. Chen et al., 2015).

Several chromosomal regions have been identified as locations of interest that might harbor susceptibility genes for schizophrenia, including different sites on chromosomes 1p, 1q, 2p, 2q, 4q, 6q, 7q, 9p, 10p, 11q, 13q, 18q, 22q, and others (Bassett et al., 2001; Mimmack et al., 2002; Paunio et al., 2004; Pulver, 2000). In general, findings have been inconsistent across linkage studies; however, chromosomes 6 and 22 have received considerable attention in recent years. Chromosome 6 harbors a gene known as "C4" and alterations of this gene, based on an analysis of 65,000 people and 700 postmortem brains, are associated with a higher risk of developing schizophrenia (Sekar et al., 2016). The C4 gene is believed to play a critical role in synaptic pruning during brain development and is thought to contribute to abnormal pruning in individuals with schizophrenia. A particular deletion on part of chromosome 22 (22q11.2DS) has been associated with a more than 20-fold increased risk for schizophrenia—i.e., schizophrenia occurs in approximately one in four individuals with 22q11.2DS (Karaviorgou et al., 2010). This deletion occurs near the middle of the chromosome and results in a variety of effects, including heart abnormalities, autoimmune disorders, developmental delays, and learning problems. Later-in-life individuals with 22q11 deletion syndrome are at increased risk for schizophrenia; however, research suggests that they are also at increased risk for other types of psychiatric disorders, including bipolar disorder, autistic spectrum disorder, and ADHD (Schneider et al., 2014). It is important to note that this deletion is associated with only a small percentage of individuals with schizophrenia (Bassett et al., 2003). Inconsistencies are likely to occur across linkage studies due to differences in sample size, comorbidity, severity of symptoms, heterogeneity of symptoms, low statistical power, and other demographic and methodological factors.

Candidate Gene Studies

In contrast to linkage studies that search for susceptibility genes, *candidate gene studies* attempt to reveal genetic contributions to schizophrenia by identifying specific susceptibility genes prior to the onset of the study (i.e., a priori). The genes selected are based on theory and previous research, and comparisons are then made between research participants with schizophrenia and those without the disorder in terms of presence of genetic variants (mutations). For example, amphetamines are known to increase extracellular levels of dopamine and in excessive doses can induce psychotic symptoms. The gene, therefore, for a specific type of dopamine receptor has been studied based on the theory that schizophrenia involves dysfunction of the dopaminergic system. Genetic mutations are defined as any permanent change in the DNA sequence of a gene that can be caused during development or by environmental toxins and can lead to changes in proteins that may result in disease (Faraone, Tsuang, & Tsuang, 1999). Examples of genetic mutations include deletions (a DNA segment is missing), translocation mutations (a DNA segment from one chromosome is tacked onto another), duplication mutations (a DNA segment is inserted twice into a chromosome), trinucleotide repeat mutations (a triplet sequence of base pairs is repeated within a gene), and others (see Mundo & Kennedy, 2002, for a review).

It is important to note that genetic mutations can alter proteins but perhaps not enough to cause disease. For example, Egan, Weinberger, and Lu (2003) hypothesized that a variant on the gene for brain-derived neurotroic factor (BDNF) would be associated with increased risk for schizophrenia given that BDNF is important in hippocampal functioning. Three groups were included in their study: individuals with schizophrenia, siblings of these individuals, and healthy comparison subjects. Contrary to expectations, they found that although the presence of the gene variant had deleterious effects on cognitive performance and was associated with abnormal blood flow in the hippocampus during neuroimaging; it did *not* predict risk for schizophrenia. These findings demonstrate that it is critical for scientists to not only identify candidate genes but also to discover *the process by which genes cause symptoms characteristic of disorders*, such as schizophrenia.

According to Allen et al., nearly 800 candidate genes have been investigated in schizophrenia research and results across studies have been contradictory. Although twin, adoption, and family studies support that genetic factors contribute to the development of schizophrenia, to date no single gene or collection of genes has been found to cause the disorder. A number of studies, however, have reported significant associations between particular genes and schizophrenia, especially genes involved in the process of neurotransmission. Of specific interest are genes that play a role in the (a) production and regulation of transporter proteins involved in reuptake of neurotransmitters, (b) production of enzymes that breakdown neurotransmitters, (c) synthesis of monoamine neurotransmitters previously implicated in schizophrenia (e.g., serotonin, norepinephrine, dopamine), and (d) production and functioning of neurotransmitters receptors, all of which have been the target of candidate gene studies. Given the plethora of information available concerning candidate genes and schizophrenia, the following discussion will highlight only a few of these findings (see Mistry et al., 2017, for a review).

Specific Candidate Genes

Dopamine Genes

The hypothesis that dopaminergic systems underlie the etiology of schizophrenia originated from two observations: (a) amphetamines (i.e., dopamine agonists) can induce psychotic symptoms (e.g., Angrist & Gershon, 1970) and (b) dopamine antagonists—i.e., antipsychotic medication that blocks dopamine receptors—often improve schizophrenia symptoms. Given these findings, genes involved in dopamine production, release, reuptake, and in regulating dopamine receptors have been of particular interest in schizophrenia.

Although several dopamine-related genes (e.g., DISC1, DRD1, DRD2, DRD3, DRD4) have been explored with respect to schizophrenia, one of the most frequently studied genes is the dopamine D4 receptor gene (DRD4). This gene specifies the genetic code for a specific dopamine receptor (the D4 receptor) and mutations (e.g., single nucleotide polymorphisms and variable tandem repeat polymorphisms) of this gene have been associated with schizophrenia in a number of studies (e.g., Lung, Chen, & Shu, 2006). However, mutations of the D4 receptor gene are not unique to schizophrenia and have also been associated with other clinical disorders, and with risk taking and criminal behavior (e.g., Cherepkova et al., 2017). These findings suggest that mutations of the D4 receptor gene may increase susceptibility to psychopathology and other, possibly environmental, factors influence the specific phenotype expressed—i.e., schizophrenia or another disorder.

Other dopamine-related genes have been implicated in schizophrenia, including the dopamine transporter gene (DAT). As mentioned in Chapter 2, the dopamine transporter protein is involved in reuptake of dopamine from the synaptic cleft following exocytosis thereby influencing the availability of dopamine in the synaptic cleft and in the terminal button. Studies exploring mutations of the DAT gene have produced conflicting results with some studies reporting greater frequency of DAT gene mutations in patients with schizophrenia, while other studies have not found an association (e.g., Bilic et al., 2014; Zheng, Shen, & Xu, 2012).

Variants of the gene (VMAT1) that encode the vesicular monoamine transporter (VMAT) have also been implicated in schizophrenia. As discussed in Chapter 2, vesicular transporters are involved in the packaging of dopamine and other monoamines into vesicles that are released during exocytosis. Abnormalities of VMAT function can result in excessive or insufficient release of dopamine. Studies have produced conflicting findings with some, but not all studies reporting an association between VMAT gene mutations and schizophrenia. These same polymorphisms have, however, been found in other clinical disorders (e.g., bipolar disorder) and are not unique to schizophrenia (Lohoff, Dahl, et al., 2006).

Meta-analyses exploring dopamine gene variants and schizophrenia have also produced conflicting results. For example, Shi, Gershon, and Liu (2008) conducted population-based analyses and reported a significant association for eight susceptibility genes and schizophrenia, two of which were the DAT gene and the DRD4 gene (Shi et al., 2008); however, Sanders et al. (2008) failed to find an associated between dopamine gene mutations and schizophrenia. More recently, Edward and colleagues (2016) focused on 11 genes directly related to the production and release of dopamine and did *not* find evidence supporting variation in genes that critically impact dopaminergic functioning and increased risk for schizophrenia.

COMT Gene

The catechol O-methyltransferase COMT gene that encodes an enzyme (COMT) that metabolizes dopamine has also been explored in schizophrenia. Mutations in the COMT gene (e.g., ValMet) can cause a decrease in the abundance of COMT in the human brain, thereby altering the enzyme's ability to break down dopamine and resulting in reduced clearance of dopamine from the synaptic cleft. Similar to dopamine gene variant findings, COMT gene results have been conflicting across studies, with some reporting an association with schizophrenia risk and others not (Glatt, Faraone, & Tsuang, 2003; Maria et al., 2012; Williams, Owen, & O'donovan, 2007). Recently, Hirasawa-Fujita and colleagues (2018) reported a significant association between salivary cortisol levels and a COMT gene variant (rs4680) in individuals with schizophrenia and suggested that this particular polymorphism might alter the hypothalamus pituitary axis in these individuals, increasing their susceptibility to environmental stressors. In a recent meta-analysis, Misiak and colleagues (2017) reported that polymorphisms in COMT genes might interact with other genes (e.g., those that regulate neurotrophins) as well as environmental factors, such as stress and substance use/abuse, and lead to the development of schizophrenia (or other disorders). Support for this theory is found in studies that have demonstrated that response to antipsychotic medication in individuals with treatment resistant schizophrenia is modulated by polymorphisms of the COMT and DRD4 gene in combination, but neither polymorphism was independently associated with medication response (Rajagopal et al., 2018).

Serotonin and Glutamate Candidate Genes

The role of gene variants affecting neurotransmitters serotonin and glutamate has also been investigated in schizophrenia. For example, polymorphisms of the serotonin transporter gene (SLC6A4) have been associated with the susceptibility to schizophrenia in some but not all studies (Li et al., 2013; Shi et al., 2008; Zilles et al., 2012). Similar to other studies that have found associations between schizophrenia drug response and interactions among genes, Bilic et al. (2014) found that patients with schizophrenia who had a combination of serotonin and dopamine gene variants were more likely to have treatment resistant schizophrenia relative to controls and patients with one of the gene variants. A meta-analysis by de Medeiros Alves and colleagues (2015) reported that individuals with schizophrenia with a polymorphism of the serotonin transporter gene were significantly more likely to attempt suicide. These findings suggest that gene variants affecting the serotonergic system may be play a role in the etiology of schizophrenia, but additional studies are needed to address the specificities of this relationship.

Concerning glutamate candidate genes, results suggest complex interactions among genes although results have also been conflicting across studies. For example, the DAO (D-amino acid oxidase) gene activates the DAO enzyme that degrades the amino acid, D-Serine. This amino acid facilitates functioning of the glutamate postsynaptic NMDA receptor (N-methyl-D-aspartic acid). Faulty functioning of the NMDA receptor has been implicated in the etiology of schizophrenia, and some have suggested that interactions between the DAO gene and the NMDA receptor gene contribute to the etiology of schizophrenia (Yang et al., 2013). Indeed, Yang et al. referred to the DAO gene as "the master gene of the genetic associations and interactions underlying schizophrenia" (Yang et al., 2013, p. e60099), while others have focused on gene variants that affect other aspects of the NMDA receptor (e.g., Van der Auwera et al., 2016).

Genome-Wide Association Studies

In contrast to candidate gene studies that investigate pre-identified genes of interest, genome wide-association studies (GWAS) use a specific statistical approach to scan complete sets of DNA (i.e., genomes) of thousands of people across all chromosomes simultaneously in an effort to find genetic variations associated with a particular disease or disorder. GWASs typically focus on associations between single-nucleotide polymporphisms (SNPs) in a disorder such as schizophrenia. The first GWAS concerning schizophrenia was published in 2006 (Mah et al., 2006) and since that time numerous GWAS have been published and vary in their approach. For example, some genome-wide association studies focus on several single nucleotide polymorphisms covering one gene, others focus on numerous single nucleotide polymorphisms and numerous genes, and still others focus on major gene mutations and their impact on schizophrenia. Projects have also varied from single studies to large multi-site studies (Bergen & Petryshen, 2012; Sebat, Levy, & McCarthy, 2009).

In general, GWAS results have led to identification of numerous risk loci for susceptibility genes, although findings have been inconsistent across studies. For example, some have supported strong associations between susceptibility genes and the development of schizophrenia, while other studies have failed to replicate these associations (e.g., Liu, Cheng, Wang, et al., 2016). Recently, Fatima and colleagues (2017) conducted a genome-wide study in Pakistan with patients with schizophrenia and concluded that evidence supported three susceptibility genes (CACNA1C, GRM3 and DRD2) for schizophrenia. However, Gejman, Sanders, and Duan (2010) reviewed 14 genes and a total of 789 single nucleotide polymorphisms previously reported as associated with schizophrenia and did not find a strong association with any of the 14 genes. Further, a genome-wide association study by Lencz et al. (2013) revealed that a single nucleotide polymorphism (rs11098403) located on chromosome 4 (4q26), and in the vicinity of the NDST3 gene, was reported to confer risk of schizophrenia in the Ashkenazi Jewish population. However, a 2017 study conducted with the Han Chinese population did not find an association between this polymorphism and risk for schizophrenia, nor was an association found for seven additional polymorphisms in the vicinity of gene NDST3 (Wang & Zhang, 2017). It is possible that subgroups of individuals with schizophrenia are more susceptible to specific polymorphisms (e.g., Jewish, Chinese), and replication studies are needed to address this empirical question.

Contrary to recent media headlines that read "Schizophrenia Gene" discovery sheds light on a possible cause (Scientific American, January 28, 2016); a gene was *not* discovered that caused schizophrenia. The study conducted by Sekar and colleagues (2016), however, did discover that polymorphisms of a gene (C4) that promote synaptic pruning in the brain were more strongly associated in patients with schizophrenia. The authors speculated that these findings might help to explain morphological findings, such as reduced gray matter and cortical thinning frequently observed in individuals with schizophrenia.

Why the inconsistencies across studies? Methodological factors are thought to play a major role as studies differ substantially in terms of participant characteristics, medication usage and history, heterogeneity, comorbidity of symptoms, and so on. Earlier studies, in particular, have been criticized for having small sample sizes, low statistical power, and unacceptably high Type I error rates.

It is also important to note that polymorphisms linked to schizophrenia via GWAS are not unique to the disorder and are often linked to other disorders such as bipolar disorder, ADHD, major depressive disorder, and ASD (Zhao & Nyholt, 2017). Gejman et al. (2010) concluded that schizophrenia is a complex, genetic disorder, involving perhaps hundreds of genes (polygenetic), with each gene conferring only a small effect on the expression on schizophrenia. Clearly, additional research is needed to investigate the genetic complexities involved in conferring risk of developing schizophrenia, the role environmental factors, and the gene-environment interactions (epigenetics) of the disorder. Collaboration among scientists will certainly assist in unraveling the etiologic mystery of schizophrenia. To help foster communication and discovery, Jia, Han, Zhao, Lu, and Zhao (2016) recently established a schizophrenia resource base that serves as a central repository for thousands of genetic studies concerning schizophrenia and includes information concerning hundreds of candidate genes, gene variants, and their function and regulation.

Structural Findings

A large body of research exists concerning neuroanatomical brain differences of individuals with schizophrenia relative to individuals without the disorder. These studies have focused on anatomical size (whole brain and specific structures) and molecular morphological differences. In general, studies have found anatomical differences between individuals with schizophrenia relative to controls; however, the findings have varied among individuals with schizophrenia *and* across studies. In 1913, Emil Kraepelin was among the first to propose that individuals with schizophrenia follow a progressively deteriorating course in symptomatology. Current research suggests that the course can be highly variable, with some individuals showing chronic symptoms and others showing fewer symptoms that appear to remit. Whether these differences in symptomology are related to distinct brain differences is unclear; however, hundreds of studies have explored anatomical and molecular differences between patients with and without schizophrenia. The following discussion summarizes these results in terms of postmortem, brain imaging, and molecular findings.

Postmortem and Imaging Findings

Prior to the advancement of technology and neuroimaging techniques, researchers relied primarily on postmortem samples to investigate the brains of individuals with schizophrenia. Research with postmortem samples and brain imaging findings using computed tomography (CT) and magnetic resonance imaging (MRI) has found anatomical differences between individuals with and without schizophrenia. Although many studies have found anatomical differences in individuals with schizophrenia relative to controls, to date there are no specific structural findings that are diagnostic of, or unique to, schizophrenia.

Ventricular Size

Perhaps the most common structural finding associated with schizophrenia is enlargement of the cerebral ventricles. Haug (1962) was the first to describe enlargement of cerebral ventricles in individuals with schizophrenia and hypothesized cell loss in adjacent and distant regions of the brain contributed to ventricular enlargement (Figure 5.1). The first brain imaging study using computerized axial tomography (CAT scan) to report enlarged ventricles in patients with schizophrenia relative to healthy controls was published by Johnstone et al. in 1976. Since that time, studies regarding ventricular size in schizophrenia have produced conflicting results with some studies finding differences while others have not. Meta-analytic studies, however, have estimated the increase in ventricle sized in patients with schizophrenia compared to controls to be about 26% and the reduction level is similar in males and females with schizophrenia (Harrison, Freemantle, & Geddes, 2003).

To date, the precise cause of ventricular enlargement observed in many individuals with schizophrenia is largely speculative. It is also important to note that the extent of ventricular enlargement varies among individuals with schizophrenia, *and* ventricular size varies among *healthy* individuals. Weinberger (1995) reported that some patients with schizophrenia showed abnormally large ventricles while others showed ventricles resembling those of individuals without schizophrenia. Ventricular size difference has also been explored in monozygotic twins and Suddath et al. (1990) found enlarged ventricles (lateral and third ventricle) in 14 out of 15 twins affected with schizophrenia relative to their non-affected twin pair.

To further investigate the relationship between cell loss and ventricular enlargement, researchers have studied ventricular size in healthy relatives of individuals with schizophrenia and have conducted longitudinal MRI studies with individuals at risk for developing the disorder. For example, Seidman et al. (1997) found enlarged ventricular size in healthy relatives of individuals with schizophrenia, and interpreted the findings as supporting a genetic and physiological predisposition for the disorder, triggered by either environmental events or other genes. More recently, Berger et al. (2017) using MRI compared ventricular size in individuals with schizophrenia to those with first-episode psychosis, high risk for schizophrenia, and healthy controls. Results revealed, relative to controls, ventricular enlargement was observed in only 36% of individuals with schizophrenia and was not found in the other groups, suggesting that ventricular enlargement is not present in at-risk or early stages of the disorder. In contrast, Chung and colleagues (2017) studied youth at risk for schizophrenia and followed them longitudinally using MRI. Results revealed that differences were not found between youth at risk for schizophrenia and controls in ventricular enlargement or cortical thickness at the onset of the study. Longitudinally, however, youth who developed psychosis showed accelerate gray matter reductions in widespread regions of the cortex that corresponded with ventricular enlargement. These changes were not observed in healthy controls and therefore suggest that ventricular enlargement occurs in tandem with loss of cortical gray matter and these changes begin to occur before the onset of psychosis (prodromal). These findings, do not, however, address underlying etiologic cause(s) of the observed cell loss and concomitant expansion of the ventricles (additional information regarding cell loss is discussed in the molecular section that appears later in this chapter). A critical point to remember, however, is that ventricular enlargement is not unique to schizophrenia and is found in other disorders, particularly neurodegenerative disorders such as Alzheimer's disease and Parkinson's disease (Mak et al., 2017).

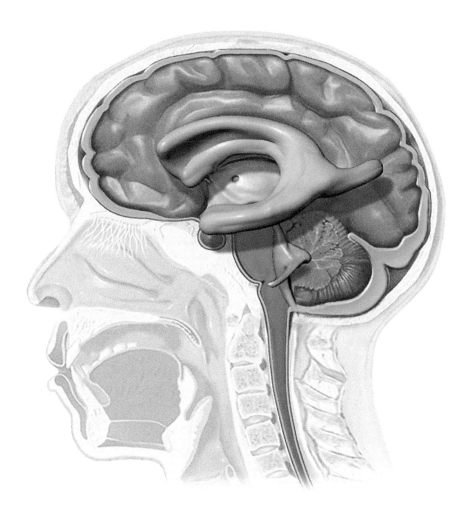

FIGURE 5.1.   Enlarged Ventricles Sometimes Found in Individuals With Schizophrenia

Copyright Blausen Medical Communications. Reproduced by permission.

Structural Differences

Anatomical differences have also been reported between participants with and without schizophrenia with respect to overall brain volume and specific structures. For example, studies have reported a 3% or more decrease in total brain volume in patients with schizophrenia relative to healthy controls (Wright et al., 2000). This loss of brain tissue reportedly continues at twice the rate for individuals with the disorder relative to controls for 20 years or longer after initial symptoms (Hulsoff & Kahn, 2008). Several studies have found that the frontal and temporal lobes are most highly susceptible to volume loss. Based on recent meta-analytic findings, loss of brain tissue has been found to correlate with symptom severity and impaired neuropsychological functioning, with more severe symptoms associated with greater tissue loss, in some but not all studies (Hulsoff & Kahn, 2008; Kwon et al., 1999; Mathalon et al., 2001; Veijola et al., 2014). Dose and years of antipsychotic usage have been found to be predictive of brain volume loss across several studies (Ho et al., 2011; Veijola et al., 2014). Collectively, research supports a pattern of total brain volume loss in individuals with schizophrenia relative to healthy controls and long-term use of antipsychotic medication is association with this volume reduction. However, it is important to note that studies have also reported *increased* volume in some structures (basal ganglia) following antipsychotic treatment that corresponded with symptom improvement, and therefore it would be erroneous to conclude that antipsychotic medication only has deleterious effects on brain morphology (Huhtaniska et al., 2017; Li et al., 2012).

Volume loss of specific regions and structures are also implicated in schizophrenia. For example studies, albeit inconsistently, have reported volume reductions in the frontal and temporal lobes, and diverse structures, including the amygdala, corpus callosum, thalamus, hippocampus, caudate nucleus, cerebellum, and putamen (e.g., Del Bene et al., 2016; Hulsoff & Kahn, 2008; Keller et al., 2003; Koshiyama et al., 2018; Kuroki et al., 2017; McCarley et al., 1999; Okugawa et al., 2002; Okugawa, Sedvall, & Agartz, 2003; Panizzon et al., 2003; Seidman et al., 2002; Woodruff, McManus, & David, 1995; Wright et al., 2000; Xu et al., 2017).

A number of studies have reported asymmetry of specific structures in patients with schizophrenia, although findings across studies have been inconsistent. For example, Petty et al. (1995) examined a particular region of the temporal lobe—the planum temporale—that lies on the superior surface of the temporal lobe. The planum temporale is involved in the production and comprehension of language, and in right-handed people, the surface area of the left planum temporale is typically larger than the right. Petty et al. compared the right and left surface areas of the planum temporale in 14 right-handed individuals with schizophrenia relative to control participants. Results indicated that in all but one of the individuals with schizophrenia, a reversal of the expected asymmetry was found (i.e., the right was larger than the left). Other studies have reported asymmetrical differences in subcortical structures. For example, Haukvik et al. (2018) and others have reported that compared to control participants, participants with schizophrenia demonstrated smaller bilateral hippocampus, amygdala, thalamus and accumbens volumes but larger bilateral caudate, putamen, pallidum, and lateral ventricle volumes. The origin of these differences, whether prenatal or postnatal, is unclear but may support neurodevelopmental disturbances in schizophrenia that occurs as a result of genetic or environmental factors or the interaction of the two.

Molecular Findings

In addition to differences in size and volume of anatomical structures, researchers have investigated molecular differences between patients with schizophrenia relative to healthy controls in terms of cytoarchitecture, reduction and density of white and gray matter, white matter connectivity, and receptor availability.

Cytoarchitecture refers to the arrangement of cells, particularly neurons. A number of studies have reported cytoarchitectural differences in participants with schizophrenia, including disorganized arrangements of neurons, misplacement of neurons, fewer dendritic branches and dendritic spines, and reduction in neuronal size and number in cortical and subcortical regions (e.g., Benes, Davidson, & Bird, 1986; Kovelman & Scheibel, 1984; Lewis et al., 2008; Rioux et al., 2003; Selemon, Rajkowska, & Goldman-Rakic, 1995). Interestingly, neurodegenerative features, such as neurofibrillary tangles and plaques, have not been found to occur at the higher rate in schizophrenia, while levels of tau protein have been found to be significantly lower in patients with schizophrenia relative to healthy controls (Arnold et al., 1998; Demirel et al., 2017).

Review studies have estimated a 15% reduction in neuronal number in individuals with schizophrenia compared to healthy controls (Schmitt et al., 2009). In addition to neuronal number, Glantz and Lewis (2000) reported that synaptic connections are significantly altered in individuals with schizophrenia due to substantial dendritic spine reductions in the prefrontal cortex that directly compromises the number of excitatory inputs to neurons in this area. Interestingly, the prefrontal cortex does not fully mature until late adolescence or early adulthood, which is the period of onset for most individuals with schizophrenia. Therefore, it is plausible that problems that occur early in brain development (cell migration, proliferation, pruning) are cumulative and not observed until later late adolescence or young adulthood.

Studies have also explored the density of neurons and glial cells, and have reported both increased *and* decreased density of neurons and glia depending on the locations examined. Increased density of neurons is thought represent areas where neurons have atrophied, have fewer dendritic branches, and fewer synaptic connections rather than reductions in numbers (Selemon and Goldman-Rakic, 1999). At the level of the cortex, studies have reported decreased and increased neuronal density, while others have reported increased and decreased neuronal density in subcortical structures (Chana et al., 2003; Kreczmanski et al., 2007; Rajkowska et al., 2001; Smiley et al., 2011). It is important to note that some studies have reported no differences in cell density in patients with schizophrenia compared to healthy controls. It is also possible that cell density may change over time and vary with age, medication usage, and other variables.

Gray and White Matter Findings

More recently studies have explored relationships between white and gray matter in participants with schizophrenia relative to healthy controls. A plethora of studies have explored gray matter volume in participants with schizophrenia and many have reported gray matter loss in cortical and subcortical regions, especially the frontal and temporal regions (see Torres et al., 2016, for a review). Specifically, meta-analytic studies have reported gray matter loss in participants with schizophrenia in the insula, thalamus, dorsolateral prefrontal cortex, medial frontal gyrus and posterior cingulate gyrus, superior temporal cortex, bilateral hippocampus, and bilateral amygdala.

Some studies have found a significant relationship between reduced gray matter of the left temporal gyrus and severity of hallucinations (Dietsche, Kircher, & Falkenberg, 2017; Onitsuka et al., 2004).

Zhang et al. (2017) recently found reduced gray matter volume in regions of the left frontal cortex, and the right temporal, occipital, and cerebellar regions in adolescents with schizophrenia compared to controls and participants with adult onset schizophrenia. These findings were consistent with Dietsche (2017) who, in a systematic review, investigated gray matter in participants (a) at risk of developing psychosis, (b) patients with a first episode psychosis, and (c) participants with schizophrenia who were chronically ill. Results revealed that participants at risk who later developed psychosis had more pronounced cortical gray matter loss in the temporal and frontal regions, participants with a first episode psychosis showed decline in multiple gray matter regions over time, and they showed progressive cortical thinning in the frontal cortex. Findings also indicated that participants with chronic schizophrenia showed the most pronounced gray matter loss. Collectively, current findings suggest that gray matter loss is commonly found in patients with schizophrenia, and the loss tends to be greater and more widespread in individuals with chronic schizophrenia compared to first episode patients. In addition, gray matter loss appears to be more severe in early versus later onset cases, and loss is typically progressive. Antipsychotic medications are associated with global gray matter loss, although some subcortical structures appear to increase in volume with medication treatment.

White matter (myelinated axons) findings appear to be less robust than gray matter findings in individuals with schizophrenia (Krakauer et al., 2017). For example, Selemon, Kleinman, Herman, and Goldman-Rakic (2002) compared the postmortem brains of 14 individuals with schizophrenia to 19 brains of healthy individuals. When total gray and white matter volumes of the cortex were measured, only the gray matter of the frontal lobes was found to differ between groups (12% smaller). Samartzis et al. (2014), however, conducted as systematic review of 44 studies all of which used a modified MRI technique (diffusion tensor imaging) to explore white matter connectivity (e.g., integrity and diameter of axons, thickness of myelin) in participants in early stages of schizophrenia. Results were indicative of white matter integrity deficits in frontal, fronto-temporal, fronto-limbic connections, and the corpus callosom in individuals with schizophrenia, although questions remain regarding the effect of age, demographic and environmental variables, and antipsychotic medication on white matter integrity.

Receptor Availability

Stemming from the dopaminergic theory of schizophrenia research has sought to determine whether presynaptic and postsynaptic receptor availability may differ in individuals with schizophrenia relative to controls, using postmortem samples and neuroimaging techniques. Overall, findings are variable across studies with some reporting decreased availability of postsynaptic dopamine receptors, while others report increased availability (Farde et al., 1990; Schmauss et al., 1993; Seeman et al., 1995; Wong et al., 1986).

To investigate whether dopamine synapses were influenced by medication treatment, Roberts et al. (2009) used postmortem tissue to explore density of dopamine synapses in the caudate nucleus in treatment responders, and those who were treatment resistant. Findings revealed dopamine synaptic density was 43% greater in participants with schizophrenia deemed treatment responders compared to controls, and 62% greater in treatment responders compared to treatment resistant cases. Meta-analytic studies, however, have reported discrepant findings with some reporting no postsynaptic receptor differences (e.g., D1, D2) in the striatum in drug-naïve participants with schizophrenia compared to controls (Howes et al., 2012; Yang et al., 2004), while others report increased receptor density in patients with schizophrenia (Kestler, Walker, & Vega, 2001). However, studies have also found that participants with schizophrenia who have used antipsychotic medication over time show increased number of receptors relative to control participants, supporting Roberts et al.'s (2009) earlier work and suggesting that medication and age alters dopamine receptor availability (Abi-Dargham et al., 2000; Howes et al., 2012; Kestler et al., 2001). In summary, studies have produced conflicting results regarding availability of postsynaptic dopamine receptors in participants with schizophrenia relative to controls.

Dopamine Transporters

Research has also investigated density of presynaptic dopamine transporters in the striatum in patients with schizophrenia and results have been more consistent. For example, Joyce et al. (1988) and Lavalaye et al. (2001) did not find increased density of dopamine transporter proteins in participants with schizophrenia relative to control subjects, nor were significant differences found between medicated and non-medicated individuals with schizophrenia. A recent meta-analysis of 13 studies found DAT density was not significantly different between patients and controls in the striatum, putamen, and caudate nucleus, nor was DAT density influenced by duration of schizophrenia or treatment with antipsychotic medication (Fusar-Poli & Meyer-Lindenberg, 2012; Fusar-Poli et al., 2013). DAT density has been found in the amygdala of patients with schizophrenia relative to controls, and some studies have found a positive correlation between hallucinations and delusion symptoms and DAT density (Artiges et al., 2017; Markota et al., 2014).

Structural Findings: Schizophrenia Versus Other Disorders

As noted throughout this textbook, structural and functional findings in isolation are correlational and do not reveal directionality or causality. Furthermore, although it is meaningful to establish that individuals with a particular disorder show structural (and/or functional) brain differences relative to healthy individuals, it is equally if not more important to demonstrate that structural and functional findings are uniquely characteristic of a particular disorder (or symptom). To that end, a substantial number of studies are available that have explored structural and functional differences between individuals with schizophrenia compared to other disorders (e.g., bipolar disorder, ASD) (Lewine et al., 1995). For example, researchers have compared participants with schizophrenia to bipolar disorder and findings have been variable across studies. Benes, Vincent, and Todtenkopf (2001) investigated whether the density of neurons in the anterior cingulate cortex differed between the postmortem brains of individuals with schizophrenia and those with bipolar disorder and controls. Results revealed that glia cell density did not differ across groups; however, the clinical groups both showed decreased density of neurons but in different locations. In 2015, Goodkind and colleagues conducted a meta-analysis of 193 studies comprising 15,892 individuals across six diagnostic groups: schizophrenia, bipolar disorder, depression, addiction, obsessive-compulsive disorder, and anxiety disorder. Results revealed that gray matter loss was observed across all disorders compared to controls and increased gray matter volume in the striatum was only found in participants with schizophrenia. Similarly, Chang, Womer, et al. (2017) examined gray matter volume and white matter integrity in 485 individuals (135 with schizophrenia, 86 with bipolar disorder, 108 with major depressive disorder, and 156 healthy controls) and found that all three groups share significant gray matter loss.

With regard to white matter, a recent systematic review of 50 structural studies published between January 2005 and December 2016 reported that white matter integrity deficits that are similar in patients with schizophrenia and bipolar disorder, while gray matter reductions appear more widespread in those with schizophrenia (Birur et al., 2017). Collectively, these findings support that gray matter loss and compromised white matter integrity is characteristic of schizophrenia, but it is also characteristic of other clinical disorders. Additional studies are needed to investigate the specifics of gray and white matter differences (e.g., location, degree, onset, influencing factors) in individuals with schizophrenia relative to those with different disorders and healthy control participants.

Functional Findings

Neuroimaging techniques such as fMRI, PET, and SPECT have been used to investigate functional brain differences in patients with schizophrenia compared to healthy controls and, due to previous structural and molecular findings, have often focused on the frontal and temporal regions and the striatum. As discussed in Chapter 3, fMRI measures the level of oxygenated to deoxygenated blood near the brain area of increased neuronal activity, while PET and SPECT measure blood flow and/or glucose metabolism depending on the technique employed.

Differences in glucose utilization in the striatum, frontal, temporal, and other brain regions have been reported in neuroimaging and postmortem studies of patients with schizophrenia (e.g., Buchsbaum and Hazlet, 1998; Dean et al., 2016; Horga et al., 2011). There is considerable variability, however, in findings across studies. For example, some studies have reported decreased levels of regional cerebral blood blow (rCBF) (hypoperfusion) in a variety of brain regions and structures, including the frontal and temporal lobes, thalamus, amygdala, striatum, and cerebellum glucose metabolism in participants with schizophrenia relative to healthy controls (Buchsbaum & Hazlett, 1998; Cui et al., 2017; Mitelman et al., 2017; Weinberger & Lipska, 1995). In contrast, others have reported increased levels of glucose metabolism in the striatum, frontal, and temporal regions of participants with schizophrenia relative to controls, particularly in participants with schizophrenia who report auditory hallucinations (Allen, Larøi, McGuire, & Aleman, 2008). Horga et al. (2011) suggested that spontaneous increased neuronal activity in the temporal region may generate auditory perceptions without external stimuli (i.e., hallucinations) and likened these perceptions to those reported by some patients with epilepsy during a seizure. Wake et al. (2016) recently suggested differences may exist in rCBF patterns in patients with early onset versus late onset schizophrenia, and Kawakami and colleagues (2014) reported that reductions in blood flow to the frontal and temporal lobes worsened with increasing age in patients with schizophrenia relative to healthy controls.

Numerous studies have reported reduced neuronal activity in the prefrontal regions in participants with schizophrenia while performing neuropsychological tasks designed to involve frontal lobe involvement (e.g., Bertolino et al., 2000; Curtis et al., 1998; Pickar et al., 1990). To investigate the relationship between prefrontal lobe activity and subcortical structures, Meyer-Lindenberg et al. (2002) used positron emission tomography (PET) to measure both regional cerebral blood flow (rCBF) and presynaptic dopaminergic function using the a radioactive tracer in the same session, while participants with schizophrenia completed the Wisconsin Card Sorting Task (WCST). Results were supportive of previous studies finding decreased cerebral blood flow to the prefrontal regions in participants with schizophrenia relative to healthy controls during the WCST, *and* findings revealed that participants with schizophrenia showed significantly higher dopamine uptake in the striatum compared to controls. Interestingly, Daniel et al. (1991) found that blood flow increased in the prefrontal cortex of individuals with schizophrenia following the administration of amphetamines, and cognitive improvement was noted on the WCST. Laruelle et al. (1996) also administered amphetamines to individuals with schizophrenia and measured dopamine release in the striatum using PET. Results revealed a worsening of psychotic symptoms in participants with schizophrenia that correlated with increased occupancy of dopamine receptors (D2). Collectively, these findings support that the dopaminergic system and pathways extending to the prefrontal regions are involved in the underlying pathophysiology of schizophrenia; however, the specificities of these processes are poorly understood.

It is also important to note that some studies have not found evidence of reduced blood flow or glucose metabolism in individuals with schizophrenia. In a review of the literature, Berman and Weinberger (1991) found that only 60% of the 39 studies reviewed could be interpreted as showing hypofrontality in individuals with schizophrenia. In a recent systematic review of neuroimaging studies, Penades et al. (2017) concluded that findings supported reduced hypofrontality in patients with schizophrenia but emphasized the heterogeneity across studies is problematic for interpretation. Indeed, functional neuroimaging studies investigating schizophrenia differ vastly in terms of participant characteristics (age, sex, medication history, comorbidity, severity of symptoms, diagnostic classification system, etc.); methodological design and rigor, testing, and instrumentation (psychometrics, at rest versus task completion); and statistical procedures and power. It is also important to note that hypofrontality is not unique to schizophrenia and has been found in other disorders, such as ADHD and neurodegenerative disorders.

In summary, functional neuroimaging studies have produced inconsistent findings with regard to rCBF and glucose metabolism in participants with schizophrenia relative to healthy controls. In general, systematic review studies support individuals with schizophrenia tend to display decreased levels of activation in the frontal and temporal regions, and increased activity in subcortical structures relative to controls. These findings are inconclusive, however, and are not unique to schizophrenia. In addition, patterns of blood flow and glucose metabolism only indirectly reflect cellular function and do not reveal etiologic information. It is indeed plausible that changes in biochemistry result in cognitive and behavioral changes, and it is also possible that environmental factors elicit behavioral changes that in turn result in changes in biochemistry. Additional, methodologically well-designed studies are needed to tease apart the complexity of factors that likely influence disparate functional findings, including inclusion criteria, age of onset, comorbidity, sex, ethnicity, treatment history, sample size, statistical power, and so on.

Beyond Dopamine

Additional neurotransmitter systems have been investigated in their role in schizophrenia including GABA, acetylcholine, serotonin, and glutamate (Akbarian et al., 1995; Carlsson et al., 2001; R. C. Cloninger, 2003; Lewis, 2000; Raedler et al., 2003; Soares & Innis, 1999). Two neurotransmitters that have received the most attention other than dopamine include serotonin and glutamate. The serotonergic system is closely linked anatomically with both the dopaminergic and glutamate system, and all three neurotransmitters are thought to function interactively.

Support for a role for serotonin and glutamate in the pathophysiology of schizophrenia stems from several sources, including the drugs lysergic acid diethylamide (LSD) and phencyclidine (PCP). LSD has been found to activate serotonin receptors (5-HT2A) and produce hallucination-type sensations and sensory experiences of bliss and disembodiment (Kraehenmann et al., 2017), while PCP stimulates release of dopamine and occupies and blocks the glutamate NMDA receptor. PCP also induces a number of symptoms that resemble those in schizophrenia, including hallucinations, and worsens psychotic symptoms in individuals with schizophrenia (Javitt and Zukin, 1991). Currently, use of PCP is viewed as the gold standard rodent model for schizophrenia (Ma & Guest, 2017).

Research investigating the density and functioning of serotonin and NMDA receptors, serotonin and glutamate metabolite levels, and precursor levels of these neurotransmitters in humans, however, has produced contradictory results (Cruz et al., 2004; Sumiyoshi, Stockmeier, Overholser, Dilley, & Meltzer; Tauscher et al., 2002). In addition, although studies have reported decreased density and/or altered functioning of NMDA receptors individuals with schizophrenia, studies have also reported these same findings in participants with depression, bipolar disorder, ASD, Down syndrome, and Rett syndrome (Law & Deakin 2001; Manchia et al., 2017; Moretto et al., 2017; Benes et al., 2001). More research is needed to better understand the role of serotonin and glutamate in schizophrenia.

BOX 5.2   Does the Flu Virus Cause Schizophrenia?

Schizophrenia does not typically occur in both monozygotic twin pairs, and these findings suggest that environmental factors play an important role in the development of the disorder. Scientists have discovered that, in the Northern Hemisphere, people born between January and April are more likely to be diagnosed with schizophrenia compared to people born during the other months of the year (Davies, Welham, Chant, Torrey, & McGrath, 2003). Although the reason for this pattern of findings is unclear, some have speculated that the peak season for the influenza virus corresponds with gestational months when mothers of individuals who develop schizophrenia were likely to be exposed to the influenza virus—i.e., viral infections are most common during the fall. Barr, Mednick, and Munk-Jorgensen (1990) explored this hypothesis by studying the number of live births, births of individuals who later developed schizophrenia, and of cases of influenza reported to the Ministry of Health in Denmark across a 40-year period. Results indicated that influenza rates higher than seasonally expected and occurring in the sixth month of gestation, were associated with significantly higher rates of births of individuals later diagnosed with schizophrenia. These findings have been replicated in other studies (Mednick, Machon, and Huttunen, 1990; Torrey et al., 1997) and in other countries, such as China, Korea, and Taiwan (e.g., Wang & Zhang, 2017; Tam & Sewell, 1995).

Although the influence virus rarely crosses the placenta, women who contract a viral infection during pregnancy may suffer from a fever, which can slow the division of fetal neurons and development and may affect cellular processes, such as migration, differentiation, cell death, synaptic connections, and establishment of neural networks (Jung et al., 2016; Laburn, 1996; Weinberger, 1987, 1996). It is important to note that these findings are only correlational—i.e., many individuals whose mothers were exposed to the flu virus during pregnancy do not develop the disorder, and, similarly, individuals develop the disorder whose mothers did not contract the flu virus. In addition, not all studies have found a relationship between season of birth and incidence of schizophrenia (Battle et al., 1999; McGrath & Welham, 1999) and a recent meta-analysis (Selten & Termorshuizen, 2017) concluded that the evidence for exposure to influenza during gestation is insufficient. Lastly, maternal exposure, including influenza, is also associated with increased risk of other disorders in offspring, such as bipolar disorder and depression (Parboosing et al., 2013; Torrey et al., 1997).

Pharmacological Interventions for Schizophrenia

Although a variety of therapies have been found to improve the cognitive and behavioral functioning of individuals with schizophrenia (e.g., Hogarty et al., 2004; Penn et al., 2004), the focus of this text is on physiological based substrates and treatment methods; therefore, the remaining sections of the chapter reviews pharmacological- and physiologically based interventions for the treatment of schizophrenia.

One of the first medications used to treat psychosis was insulin. In 1933, at a meeting of the Medical Society of Vienna, Manfred Sakel announced the discovery of insulin-induced comas as an effective treatment for reducing psychotic symptoms in patients with schizophrenia (Shorter, 2009). Insulin comas continued to be used in the treatment of schizophrenia until the discovery of chlorpromazine (Thorazine) in the early 1950s (López-Muñoz et al., 2005). Today, medications used to treat schizophrenia include *typical* (first-generation antipsychotic medications) and *atypical* neuroleptics (second-generation antipsychotic medication) (see Table 5.1) (P. Li, Snyder, & Vanover, 2016; Lohr & Braff, 2003). The use of antipsychotic medications to treat schizophrenia symptoms is based on the theory that schizophrenia involves a dysregulation of dopaminergic functioning in the brain, with excess dopaminergic activity occurring in the mesolimbic pathway (positive symptoms) and reduced dopaminergic signaling occurring in the mescortical pathway (negative symptoms) (Davis et al., 1991; Patel et al., 2014). By blocking dopamine postsynaptic receptors, dopamine signaling decreases and is correlated with a reduction of psychotic symptoms but relatively little improvement in negative symptoms (Miyamoto et al., 2012; Salokangas et al., 2002).

Typical refers to neuroleptics that (a) are dopamine antagonists, (b) produce extrapyramidal side effects, and (c) improve positive symptoms. *Atypical* neuroleptics (a) have an affinity for several types of neurotransmitter receptors (dopamine, serotonin), (b) produce fewer extrapyramidal side effects, and (c) improve positive symptoms and to a lesser extent negative symptoms characteristic of schizophrenia. Research also suggests that different types of atypical antipsychotic medications may bind more tightly (or loosely) to dopamine receptors than dopamine itself and may disengage from the receptor more quickly (or slowly) than typical antipsychotics (Miyamoto et al., 2012).

Typical and atypical neuroleptics are similar in that both are effective at improving psychotic symptoms due to their affinity for D2 receptors. The affinity for other dopamine subtypes (e.g., D1, D3) varies widely among neuroleptics. An affinity for D2 receptors is positively correlated with the potency of neuroleptics, while an affinity for D4 receptors is associated with fewer extrapyramidal side effects and improvement in negative symptoms (Carvey, 1998).

Typical and atypical neuroleptics differ in a number of ways. Typical neuroleptics tend to produce greater extrapyramidal side effects due to their widespread blockage of dopamine in the subcortical structures that are important in movement including the basal ganglia and nigrostriatal pathway (Grace et al., 1997). These effects include slowed movements, decreased facial expression, resting tremor, muscle spasms of the neck and shoulder, and restlessness. Over time, *tardive dyskinesia* may develop, and more severe tardive dyskinesia effects are associated with typical neuroleptics. Jest et al. (1999) and Mamo et al. (2002) found that the risk of tardive dyskinesia was higher in older patients with schizophrenia even with low doses and short-term treatment. Neuroleptics also differ in their affinity for other types of neurotransmitter receptors such as serotonergic, muscarinic, noradrenergic, and histaminergic. An affinity for these receptors is associated with various side effects, such as sedation, dry mouth, blurred vision, intestinal slowing, sexual dysfunction, and weight gain. Lastly, research suggests that atypical antipsychotic medications, particularly when prescribed in the early stages of schizophrenia, may have neuroprotective effects due to increased neuroplasticity—i.e., production of neurotrophic factors, decreased glutamate excitotoxicity, decreased oxidative stress and apoptosis and increased neurogenesis (van Haren et al., 2007). In contrast, typical antipsychotic medications have been reported to have neurotoxic effects, including increased apoptosis and reductions in neurotrophic factors (Nandra & Agius, 2012).

Not all individuals with schizophrenia respond favorably to antipsychotic medication and approximately 20–30% are considered treatment resistant (Hálfdánarson, 2017; Meltzer & Kostakoglu, 2001). Treatment resistant refers to patients that have tried several medications, lasting for at least 4–6 weeks using adequate doses, but have not found sufficient reductions in positive symptoms (Suzuki et al., 2012). Kapur (2003) suggested that antipsychotic medications do not cure psychotic symptoms but instead decrease the salience of the distressing ideas and perceptions. In other words, during treatment with neuroleptics, a patient's hallucinations and delusions do not disappear but instead are dampened or in remission. During relapse, these delusions and hallucinations become more salient and return to their previously distressing state. Kapur also suggested that dopamine dysregulation underlies psychosis but "a subject's own cognitive, psychodynamic, and cultural context gives form to the experience" (p. 17).

Table 5.1 Antipsychotic Medications

Typical Neuroleptics

Thioridazine (Mellaril)

Acetophenazine (Tindal)

Thiothixene (Navane)

Chlorpromazine (Chlorpromazine hydrochloride)

Perphenazine (Trilafon)

Pimozide (Orap)

Loxapine (Loxitane)

Trifluoperazine (Stelazine)

Chlorprothixene (Truxal)

Mesoridazine (Serentil)

Fluphenazine (Prolixin)

Haldol (Haloperidol)

Atypical Neuroleptics

Aripiprazole (Abilify)

Ziprasidone (Geodon)

Clozapine (Clozaril)

Latuda (Lurasidone)

Molindone (Moban)

Rexulti (Brexpiprazole)

Quetiapine (Seroquel)

Risperidone (Risperdal)

Saphris (Asenapine)

Zyprexa (Olanzapine)

Note: The Physicians' Desk Reference (PDR) (2018) provides additional information concerning these and other drugs.

Mode of Action of Typical and Atypical Antipsychotic Medication

Typical and atypical neuroleptic medications differ in their level of effectiveness at improving positive and negative symptoms of schizophrenia, degree of side effects, and in their mode of action. Although the precise mode of action of antipsychotic medications is not completely understood, all antipsychotics—whether typical or atypical—have a greater or lesser affinity for D2 receptors and fully or partially block the receptor (Kapur and Seeman, 2001). Typical antipsychotics have a greater affinity for D2 receptors over other types of dopamine receptors and fully block the receptor (e.g., Haldol). The extent of receptor occupancy needed for improvement of symptoms appears to vary among individuals and within the same individual depending on the stage and phase of the illness. Some studies have reported dopamine receptor occupancy of 65–80% is needed for improvement of positive symptoms; however, this level of occupancy substantially increases the risk of tardive dyskinesia symptoms (Haan et al., 2003; Remington & Kapur, 1999). Tauscher and colleagues (2004) used PET to investigate D1 and D2 receptor occupancy in 25 patients with schizophrenia who were receiving one of four atypical antipsychotic medications: clozapine, risperidone, olanzapine, or quetiapine. Results revealed that clozapine had the highest rate of D1 occupancy in the striatum (55%) and quetiapine the lowest (12%). Risperidone had the highest D2 occupancy (81%) and quetiapine the lowest (30%); clozapine, however, had the highest ratio of striatal D1/D2 occupancy of the four medications. These findings may help to explain why many patients who are treatment resistant to other antipsychotic medications respond favorably to clozapine.

Unlike typical neuroleptics, most atypical antipsychotic medications (e.g., risperidone, olanzapine, clozapine, quetiapine, ziprasidone) show a greater affinity and occupancy for other types of dopamine receptors *and* serotonin receptors, although affinity/occupancy differences exist even among the atypical medications (Kapur et al., 2000). For example, aripiprazole (Abilify) has a higher affinity for D2 receptors than serotonin receptors and is a partial dopamine agonist, while amisulpride (Solian) has minimal affinity for serotonin receptors (Tyson, Roberts, & Mortimer, 2004); however, both atypical medications are often effective at improving positive symptoms in many patients with schizophrenia. With respect to negative symptoms, meta-analyses indicate that atypical antipsychotics are not significantly more effective at improving negative symptoms than typical antipsychotics (Harvey, James, & Shields, 2016).

Atypical antipsychotic medications also differ from typical neuroleptics with respect to the extent and rapidity at which they bind and disengage from the receptor (Pilowsky, Costa, & Eli, 1992). Typical neuroleptics in general bind more tightly and dissociate from the receptor more slowly than atypical neuroleptics. Atypical antipsychotics bind more loosely or partially and release rapidly from the postsynaptic receptors, resulting in fewer extrapyramidal side effects (Meltzer, 2017; Seeman & Tallerico, 1999). Findings have been equivocal with respect to efficacy of typical versus atypical neuroleptics, and a large number of studies are available comparing the efficacy of specific medications. In general, meta-analytic findings have reported that some, but not all, atypical antipsychotic medications are more efficacious than typical antipsychotics at alleviating a greater variety of symptoms and significant differences exist with regard to side effects, such as weight gain, sedation, increases in prolactin, restlessness, fatigue, and cognitive impairment (e.g., Asmal et al., 2013; Conley & Mahmoud, 2001; Davis et al., 2003; Lieberman et al., 2003; Marder et al., 2003; Nemani et al., 2017; Samara et al., 2014).

Augmentation and Experimental Interventions

Augmentation of antipsychotic medications with other medications or brain stimulation techniques is sometimes used to treat the negative symptoms of schizophrenia and/or to enhance the effectiveness of antipsychotic medication. For example, antidepressants, anti-seizure medications, glutamate antagonists, ECT, and TMS, have been used to treat negative symptoms, and/or to enhance the effectiveness of antipsychotic medication (Andrade, 2017; Pompili et al., 2017; Silver, 2003; Vuksan et al., 2017). A number of experimental interventions (e.g., variety of neurotransmitter agonists and antagonists) have also been explored in the treatment of schizophrenia (wee Miyamoto et al., 2012 for a review).

No "ideal" medication or physiologically based intervention for the treatment of schizophrenia is currently available. Webster (2001) suggested that the ideal neuroleptic would (a) reduce dopamine activity in the mesolimbic system to reduce positive symptoms, (b) increase dopamine activity in the prefrontal cortex to improve negative symptoms, and (c) have no effect on the striatum to avoid inducing extrapyramidal symptoms. Perhaps, in addition to Webster's criteria, drugs should (d) have minimal affinity for other neurotransmitter receptors so as to minimize non-extrapyramidal side effects and (e) achieve a balance between neurotransmitter systems that produces optimal behavioral effects. Undoubtedly, newer drugs will be developed for the treatment of schizophrenia. A greater understanding of the mode of action of all antipsychotic medications may help to elucidate the pathophysiology of schizophrenia. Although medications can certainly improve behavioral and cognitive symptoms characteristic of schizophrenia, they are not without side effects nor are they curative in nature.

Chapter Summary

The essential features of schizophrenia include delusions, hallucinations, disorganized speech, grossly disorganized or catatonic behavior, or negative symptoms. The disorder is found worldwide, and the lifetime prevalence rate is reportedly 0.3% to 0.7%, although differences exist across countries, sex, race, and ethnicity. The ratio of male to female cases is approximately 1.4:1 with some, but not all studies indicating that males are diagnosed with the disorder at a slightly higher rate than females. This chapter reviewed research findings concerning the role of genetic factors in the etiology of schizophrenia, as well as a variety of structural and functional findings. Information was also reviewed concerning neurotransmitter findings and current pharmacological treatment approaches. Experimental, physiologically based interventions for schizophrenia were also discussed.

Chapter Summary: Main Points

- Schizophrenia is characterized by changes in behavior and cognition, and the essential features reflect a distortion or excess of perceptions and a restriction in the change and intensity of emotion, thought and behavior.
- Schizophrenia is found worldwide, and the lifetime prevalence rate is reportedly 0.3% to 0.7%, although differences exist across sex, race, and cultures.
- Onset of schizophrenia typically occurs during late adolescence or young adulthood and the course is variable over time.
- Despite decades of research, the cause of schizophrenia remains unknown.

- Evidence from family, twins, and adoption studies supports a heritability factor in schizophrenia.
- Numerous chromosomal regions have been identified as locations of interest that might harbor susceptibility genes for schizophrenia.
- Hundreds of candidate genes have been investigated in schizophrenia, and results across studies have been inconsistent.
- No single gene or group of genes has been identified as causing schizophrenia.
- Methodological factors across studies contribute to conflicting findings, including participant characteristics, medication usage and history, heterogeneity and comorbidity of symptoms, sample size, statistical analyses, and statistical power.
- Research has found a number of structural and molecular differences in individuals with schizophrenia relative to healthy controls, including enlarged ventricles; reduced gray and white matter; reduced brain, frontal, and temporal volume; and reduced size of the amygdala, corpus callosum, thalamus, hippocampus, caudate nucleus, cerebellum, and putamen, as well as cytoarchitectural differences, including disorganized arrangements of neurons, misplacement of neurons, reduced receptors, fewer dendritic branches and dendritic spines, and reduction in neuronal size and number in cortical and subcortical regions; however, these findings are inconsistent across studies and are not unique to schizophrenia.
- Differences in glucose metabolism and BOLD signals in the striatum, frontal, temporal, and other brain regions have been reported in neuroimaging studies of patients with schizophrenia, although there is considerable variability of findings across studies.
- Although dopamine has been the primary focus of studies, additional neurotransmitter systems have been investigated in their role in schizophrenia, including GABA, acetylcholine, serotonin, and glutamate.
- Treatment of schizophrenia typically involves the use of antipsychotic medication although the mode of action of these drugs is not completely understood and not all individuals with schizophrenia respond favorably to antipsychotic medication.
- To date, no distinctive pattern of structural or functional abnormalities has been identified as reliably or uniquely characteristic of schizophrenia.

Review Questions

1. Does research support that individuals with schizophrenia have a higher propensity for violence?
2. If you were to describe the "cause" of schizophrenia, how would you respond and why?
3. What does twin research suggest about the etiology of schizophrenia?
4. Summarize research concerning the role of dopamine genes in the development of schizophrenia.
5. Describe methodological issues associated with the study of schizophrenia.
6. Enlarged ventricles are often associated with schizophrenia. Is this an appropriate association? Why or why not?
7. Compare and contrast DAT and postsynaptic receptor findings with regard to schizophrenia.
8. Compare and contrast typical versus atypical antipsychotic medications.

six
Major Depressive Disorder and Bipolar Disorder

Understanding the neurobiological basis of major depressive disorder remains one of the foremost challenges for clinical neuroscience. The current version of the *Diagnostic and Statistical Manual of Mental Disorders* (*DSM-V*, APA, 2013) no longer classifies mood disorders into depressive disorders and bipolar disorders; instead, these disorders are classified separately; "depressive disorders" and "bipolar and related disorders". The depressive disorders include disruptive mood dysregulation disorder, major depressive disorder, persistent depressive disorder, premenstrual dysphoric disorder, substance/medication-induced depressive disorder, depressive disorder due to another medical condition, other specified depressive disorder, and unspecified depressive disorder. The bipolar and related disorders include bipolar I, bipolar II, cyclothymic disorder, substance/medication-induced bipolar and related disorder, bipolar and related disorder due to another medical condition, other specified bipolar and related disorder, and unspecified bipolar and related disorder.

The distinguishing feature between major depressive disorder and bipolar disorder is the lack of a manic episode. Given that the majority of studies have investigated major depressive disorder and bipolar disorders, these disorders are the focus of this chapter, particularly major depressive disorder, as it affects a larger segment of the population than bipolar disorders. Specifically, this chapter reviews information concerning, prevalence, demographic factors, and other relevant findings pertaining to major depression and bipolar I disorder, and discusses the genetic, anatomical, neurochemical, and neuroimaging findings associated with these disorders. An overview is also provided concerning medication and other physiologically based treatment approaches for major depressive and bipolar I disorders.

Chapter 6 Learning Objectives

- Distinguish between major depressive disorder and bipolar disorder.
- Describe demographic findings associated with each disorder.
- Describe multicultural findings associated with each disorder.
- Describe genetic findings associated with each disorder.
- Describe findings concerning neurotransmitter research.

- Describe major neuroanatomical findings.
- Describe major functional findings.
- Describe limitations of genetic, neuroanatomical, neurotransmitter, and functional studies.
- Identify types of medications used to treat major depressive and bipolar disorders.
- Describe molecular effects of antidepressants.
- Describe research findings concerning suicidality and antidepressants.
- Identify brain stimulation techniques used to treat both disorders.
- Describe unanswered questions about the physiological bases of both disorders.
- Identify recommendations for future research.

Major Depressive Disorder

Prevalence and Demographic Information

Major depressive disorder is characterized by a change in mood and previous functioning that is enduring and results in functional impairment. The *Diagnostic and Statistical Manual of Mental Disorders, 5th edition*'s (*DSM-V*, APA, 2013) criteria for major depressive disorder requires a 2-week period where five of the following symptoms are present most of the day, nearly every day: depressed mood (may be an irritable mood in children), loss of interest or pleasure, increased or decreased appetite, insomnia or hypersomnia, psychomotor agitation or retardation, loss of energy, excessive guilt, decreased concentration, and suicidal thoughts. At least one of the symptoms must be either depressed/irritable mood or loss of interest and the symptoms must cause significant distress or impairment in functioning.

Findings from the 2015 National Survey on Drug Use and Health (NSDUH) revealed 16.1 million adults aged 18 or older in the United States had at least one episode of major depressive disorder in the past year. This figure represented 6.7% of all US adults and is consistent with prevalence estimates published in the *DSM-V* (APA, 2013). Although depression affects all ages, prevalence rates among individuals between 18 and 29 years of age are three times higher than those 60 years and older. Females experience a 1.5–3 times higher rate of major depressive disorder compared to males, and the onset increases markedly during puberty (APA, 2013; Steiner, Dunn & Born, 2003). Comorbid conditions such as anxiety and substance use disorders are commonly reported in patients with major depressive disorder (Kessler et al., 2003; Zimmerman, Chelminski, & McDermut, 2002; Torvik et al., 2017).

Multicultural Findings

A number of studies have reported cultural differences in the clinical presentation of depression. Among Latinos, for example, depression has been experienced as physical complaints (somatization) such as stomachaches, headaches, and back pain rather than emotions (Alarcón et al., 2014). African Americans have a lower lifetime prevalence of depressive disorders than do non-Hispanic Whites based on epidemiological studies in the United States; however, depression appears to be more persistent in African Americans relative to non-Hispanic Whites (Gibbs et al., 2013). Recent findings suggest that rates of depression have increased among whites relative to other ethnic groups (Weinberger et al., 2017), and Oquendo et al. (2001) reported that the highest one-year prevalence rates for major depression were among whites, followed by African Americans, Mexican Americans, and lowest rates were among Cuban Americans. Recent meta-analytic studies have found rates of depressive disorder elevated in sexual minority youth in comparison to heterosexual young people (Lucassen et al., 2017). Kirmayer (2001) expressed that culture-specific symptoms may lead to under or misdiagnosis of depression. Racial and ethnic minorities in the United States experiencing depression are also less likely to receive appropriate intervention and care (Han, Olfson, & Mojtabai, 2017). Depression rates have been examined in other countries, and according to Bhugra and Mastrogianni (2004), measuring depression across cultures is controversial largely due to reliance on quantitative methods that have "proved to be of limited value". Bhugra and Mastrogianni recommended more flexible approaches be developed using qualitative research techniques and focus group methods deemed more appropriate for minority populations. As Bhugra and Mastrogianni stated,

> The challenge for cultural psychiatry is to identify genuine differences between populations, without being misled by ethnic stereotyping. Individual differences are as great as ethnic ones, and the clinician treats the individual within the larger socioeconomic context, not the ethnic group.
>
> (p. 18)

Identifying genuine differences between populations is also important for delivering effective interventions. For example, genetic research suggests that differences exist among ethnic populations with respect to genes that encode enzymes that are involved in the metabolism of psychotropic medications, and this information plays a role in the selection of appropriate medications for the treatment of major depressive disorder as well as other clinical disorders (Karlovic & Karlovic, 2013; Lin, 2001; M. llic et al., 2013).

The economic burden of major depressive disorder is also increasing as reflected in costs associated with depression in the workplace, mortality costs from depression-related suicides, and direct costs. According to the World Health Organization, depression is the leading cause of disability among adults under the age of 45. In the workplace, research has found the highest rates of depression among workers who require frequent or difficult interactions with the public or clients, and have high levels of stress and low levels of physical activity (Wulsin et al., 2014). A number of studies have reported that individuals suffering from major depression are more likely to report a poorer quality of life during early, middle, and later adulthood (Papakostas et al., 2004; Renn & Arean, 2017). Individuals with major depression are at greater risk for attempting suicide, with the rate of suicide twice as high in families of suicide victims compared to families without this history (Runeson and Åsberg, 2003). Brent et al. (2003) also reported that suicidal behavior is mediated by familial transmission but noted that impulsive, aggressive tendencies are the most powerful predictors of suicide attempts, particularly at an early age.

Developmental Findings

Developmentally, the incidence of depression is similar among boys and girls prior to puberty, after which depression rates are higher in females (Kazdin & Marciano, 1998; Merikangas et al., 2010). Goodyer, Park, and Herbert (2001) suggested that endocrine processes, such as higher cortisol levels, are associated with depression in adolescents but not younger children. They also found that personal disappointments were associated with persistent depression in adolescents and argued that adverse life events may result in a hypersecretion of cortisol, which may lead to memory distortions and cognitive rumination. These cognitive processes may in turn amplify the negative feelings and contribute to the progression of depression during adolescence. Adolescents with depression often experience periods of remission; however, Melvin and colleagues (2013) found that 53% experienced a recurrence of depressive disorder and 79% had a comorbid diagnosis.

A number of studies have reported that childhood depression is associated with poor psychosocial and academic outcome and increased risk for self-harm, bipolar disorder, suicide, and substance abuse in adolescence (Birmaher et al., 1996; Morgan et al., 2017). Recent studies also suggest that children suffering from depression are more likely to be bullied, and bullying can induce depression in children without a prior history of depression (Singham et al., 2017). Juvenile offenders in the USA, particularly female juvenile offenders, are at elevated risk for depression, and according to Holzer and colleagues (2017), rates of depression are increasing among this population. Specifically, these researchers found that between 2005 and 2014, the prevalence of depression episodes among female offenders increased from 24.4% to 33.0% and from 12.4% to 16.7% in the non-offenders. Collectively, these findings suggest that the nature of depression differs in children and adults, and more research is needed to better understand these differences.

Researchers have also studied later-onset of major depressive disorder with prevalence estimates ranging from 2% to 5% of community-dwelling adults age 60 and older to 50% of those living in long-term care facilities (Fountoulakis et al., 2003; Mottram et al., 2006; Park & Unützer, 2011). Ulbricht and colleagues (2017) reported that 26% of adults 65 and older recently admitted to nursing home facilities in the United States had an active diagnosis of major depressive disorder and the majority were non-Hispanic white women.

Similar to the childhood literature, research suggests that depression differs in many aspects in older individuals than young and middle-aged adults. For example, physiological and neuropsychological studies have found an increased severity of subcortical vascular disease and greater cognitive impairment in those over 65 who suffer from depression (R. Baldwin et al., 2004; Salloway et al., 1996; Ulbricht et al., 2017). Ballmaier et al. (2004) suggested that depression in elderly patients is characterized by specific brain changes, such as reductions in gray matter, white matter, and cerebral spinal fluid, although it is important to note that late onset depression is associated with a number of neurologic conditions, such as Alzheimer's disease and Parkinson's disease (Reynolds, 1992), HIV infection (Elliott & Roy-Byrne, 1998), diabetes (Lustman, Clouse, & Freedland, 1998), multiple sclerosis (Feinstein et al., 2004), and stroke (Narushima, Kosier, & Robinson, 2003; Omura et al., 2018), all of which can result in morphological brain changes. Overall, research has found an association between depression and increased mortality risk in children, adolescents, and adults in both males and females (Gilman et al., 2017; Morgan et al., 2017).

Etiologic Theories

Genetic Findings

The level of heritability of depression has been explored through three main approaches twin, adoption, and family studies, and results of these studies implicate genetic factors in childhood and adult depression (Kendler, Prescott, et al., 2003; van Hecke et al., 2017). In twin studies, for example, Glowinski et al. (2003) studied a sample of 3,416 female adolescent twins and reported a genetic risk of 40.4% for major depression. A meta-analysis of twin studies by Sullivan, Neale, and Kendler (2000) reported an overall heritability of 37% for major depression. Other studies have reported much higher heritability estimates (i.e., 78% for females, 57% for males; Kendler et al., 1995).

With respect to family studies, two main approaches are to study (a) relatives of individuals with depression and (b) offspring of parents with depression. For example, Maher et al. (2002) reported that first-degree relatives of a family member with depression are two times more likely to suffer from major depression. Lieb and colleagues (2002) followed up 2,427 adolescents and young adults for whom diagnostic information was available for both parents and calculated the risk of depression in their offspring. Results indicated that major depression in parents significantly increased the risk for depression as well as other psychiatric disorders. Specifically, offspring of depressed parents reported higher persistence of depression, more depressive episodes, higher social impairment, and increased rates of seeking treatment. Surprisingly, having either or both parents with depression influenced equally the offspring's risk for depression. Guffanti and colleagues (2016) studied the heritability of major depression and comorbid anxiety disorders in a multigenerational study of family members at high risk for depression and reported a heritability estimate of 67%. In a large generational study in Scotland, researchers reported the heritability for depression was between 28% and 44%, and was greater for recurrent depression (Fernandez-Pujals et al., 2015). Adoption study findings have been less robust, particularly with respect to childhood depression, although as Rice, Harold, and Thapar (2002) noted, measurement and environmental factors in adoption studies likely contribute to these inconsistent findings. Collectively family, twin, and, to a lesser extent, adoption studies indicate that genetic factors mediate part of the vulnerability and susceptibility to depression. Because of the epidemiologic evidence supporting a genetic component to depression, scientists have attempted to identify specific genes and gene variants associated with the development of depression by using linkage, candidate gene, and genome wide association studies.

As discussed in previous chapters, *genetic linkage studies* search for chromosomal locations ("marker loci") where disease genes are found. Linkage studies are based on the observation that genes that are located in close proximity on the same chromosome tend to be inherited together more often than expected by chance; hence, these loci are referred to as linked. These studies attempt to identify rare gene variants (e.g., mutations) that confer a high degree of risk of the disease. For example, the gene for cystic fibrosis (CF), located on a specific locus of chromosome 7 (7q31.2), was discovered by linkage analysis. Mutations in this gene cause the body to make thick sticky mucus in the lungs instead of thin, free-flowing mucus, leading to the respiratory symptoms of CF, including thick sputum, wheezing, and breathlessness.

With respect to major depressive disorder, linkage studies are based on the premise that chromosomal segments might harbor vulnerability genes for depression and that these segments are inherited within families more often than expected by chance. For example, linkage research often studies siblings who experience episodes of depression and genetic analyses are performed to determine whether a segment of a chromosome is shared between affected siblings more often than by chance. In other words, by chance, siblings are likely to share both copies of any chromosome about 25% of the time and one copy of a chromosome about 50% of the time. Genetic linkage is supported when deviations from these expectations are statistically significant, and these deviations can be represented in a logarithm of odds score.

A number of linkage studies have been conducted with major depressive disorder and several chromosomal regions have been identified as locations of interest that might harbor susceptibility genes for depression, including chromosomes 3p, 12q, 15q, 18q, 1p, 17p, and 8p (Abkevich et al., 2003; Cohen-Woods, Craig, & McGuffin, 2013; Holmans et al., 2007; McGuffin et al., 2005; McMahon et al., 2010). Although some studies have reported linkage between specific loci and major depression, findings have been inconsistent across studies, and those employing larger sample sizes frequently do not report significant findings. As Hamilton (2011, p. 784) noted, "An important requirement for genetic studies is the replicability of findings, which has been a particular problem for linkage-based studies, where it is rare to see replication across samples for complex traits like major depression". To date, linkage studies have not supported main effects of genes on the development of depression. Given that heritability data do suggest that genetic factors are involved in depression, however, it is likely that genetic contributions to major depressive disorder are complex, and it is also likely that methodological variables contribute to the inconsistent findings across studies. For example, linkage studies differ substantially with respect to sample size, comorbidity, severity of symptoms, heterogeneity of symptoms, low statistical power, and other demographic and methodological factors.

In contrast to linkage studies that search for susceptibility genes, *candidate gene studies* attempt to reveal genetic contributions to depression by identifying specific susceptibility genes prior to the onset of the study (i.e., a priori). The genes selected are based on theory and previous research and comparisons are then made between research participants with depression, and those without the disorder in terms of presence of genetic variants (mutations). A large number of candidate genes have been investigated in the study of depression and those that are involved in the process of neurotransmission have been of particular interest. For example, genes that play a role in the (a) production and regulation of transporter proteins involved in reuptake of neurotransmitters, (b) production of enzymes that breakdown neurotransmitters, (c) synthesis of monoamine neurotransmitters previously implicated in depression (e.g., serotonin, norepinephrine, dopamine), and (d) production and functioning of neurotransmitters receptors, all have been the target of candidate gene studies. Rao and colleagues (2017) recently reported that nearly 200 genes have been found to be associated with depression. Given the plethora of information available concerning candidate genes and depression, the following discussion will highlight only a few of these findings (see Tsang et al., 2017; McEvoy et al., 2017, for a review).

Serotonin Transporter Gene

A number of studies have suggested that the serotonin transporter is implicated in depression. As discussed in Chapter 1, the serotonin transporter protein (SERT) plays a key role in reuptake of serotonin from the synaptic cleft. The gene for SERT is known as the SLC6A4 gene, and it encodes a protein integral to the normal functioning of the transporter protein. Several variants of this gene (e.g., insertions, deletions, repeats) have been found to affect availability of the serotonin transporter protein (e.g., Murthy et al., 2010; Karlović & Serretti (2013); Rao et al., 2017). Variations in SERT availability affect levels of serotonin available in the extracellular fluid. To explore whether SERT availability is lower in individuals with depression and whether the severity of depression correlated with SERT availability Ho et al. (2013) used neuroimaging (SPECT) to measure SERT availability in the thalamus of individuals with and without depression. The researchers also investigated whether brain SERT availability was affected by different variants of the SLC6A4 gene. As predicted, SERT availability was reduced in those with depression relative to those without the disorder. Interestingly, genetic variants of SLC6A4, age, gender, and severity of depression were *not* related to SERT availability. It is important to note that other studies investigating SERT availability and depression have been inconsistent with some studies reporting a relationship and others not replicating these findings (e.g., Herold et al., 2006; Joensuu et al., 2007). Studies have also explored variants of the SLC6A4 gene in other areas, such as predicting antidepressant effectiveness and findings have been mixed (Perlis et al., 2003; Ito et al., 2002; Peterson et al., 2017; Zhu, Klein-Fedyshin, & Stevenson, 2017). Researchers have also investigated the role of SLC6A4 in late-life depression, stress, and suicidality (Caspi et al., 2003; Mirkovic et al., 2017; Tsang et al., 2017), and no consistent findings have emerged among these studies.

In summary, although preliminary findings suggest a role for the SERT gene in major depressive disorder, findings across studies have been inconsistent, and future studies are warranted. It is also important to note that the SLC6A4 gene has been implicated in other psychiatric disorders, including anxiety, autistic spectrum disorder, post-traumatic stress disorder, obsessive compulsive disorder, and schizophrenia (Mushtaq & Mushtaq, 2011); hence, findings related to SERT are not unique to depression.

COMT Gene

As discussed in Chapter 1, enzymes are important in the breakdown of specific neurotransmitters and alterations in the activity of these enzymes can increase or decrease neurotransmitter availability. For example, the COMT (catechol-O-methyltransferasae) is an extracellular enzyme that breaks down dopamine, epinephrine, and norepinephrine into inactive metabolites, and is encoded by the COMT gene. The COMT gene has been studied as a susceptibility gene for depression for decades (e.g., Li, Vallada, et al., 1997; Ohara, Nagai, Suzuki, & Ohara, 1998; Gong, He, et al., 2017). One of the most studied variants of the COMT genes is the Val158Met polymorphism (rs4680). Some studies have reported that individuals with the COMT Val-allele have higher COMT activity and lower levels of dopamine compared to individuals without this polymorphism; however, other studies have not supported this finding (Antypa, Drago, & Serretti, 2013; Gong, He, et al., 2017; Lachman, Papolos et al., 1996; Opmeer, Kortekaas, & Aleman, 2010). These findings suggest that similar to the SERT gene, questions remain about the role of COMT in depression. A recent systematic review study investigating a number of genes implicated in depression, including the COMT gene concluded,

> Despite the significant amount of work and the sophisticated technology, it is not fully elucidated which genes or regions of nuclear or mitochondrial DNA, or else, which types of genetic changes, alone or in combination, can represent reliable genetic markers of anxiety and/or depression.
>
> (Lacerda-Pinheiro et al., 2014, p. 396)

TPH Gene and 5-HT Receptor Gene

The role of candidate genes in depression has also been studied with respect to the biosynthesis of neurotransmitters such as serotonin. As discussed in Chapter 1, serotonin and other neurotransmitters are biosynthesized in the cell via a complex, dynamic process that involves a number of enzymatic changes. Given that level of availability of neurotransmitters are partially determined by their biosynthesis, researchers have explored whether genes that encode specific enzymes might play a role in depression. Serotonin is synthesized from tryptophan by 5HTP (5-hydroxytryptophan) and the rate-limiting enzyme TPH (tryptophan hydroxylase) plays a critical role in determining the amount of serotonin that is synthesized. Several studies have explored whether variants of the TPH gene (located on chromosome 11) are related to depression and findings across studies have been conflicting (Arango et al., 2003; Haavik et al., 2008; Porter et al., 2008). Some researchers have suggested that stress may affect TPH gene functioning (Gitzatullin et al., 2008), and recently, Chen, Xu, et al. (2017) found that rats exposed to high levels of stress had lower levels of serotonin as well as less TPH expression. The implications of these finding for humans warrant further investigation however to date research concerning the role of candidate genes and biosynthesis of serotonin and other neurotransmitters is inconclusive.

Neurotransmitter Receptor Genes

Candidate genes involved in serotonin receptors (e.g., 5-HT2a, 5-HT1b) have also been investigated in depression, including presynaptic and postsynaptic serotonin receptors, and similar to transporter protein, degradation, and biosynthesis studies, results have been inconsistent and inconclusive across studies (Arango et al., 2003; Chang, Fang, et al., 2017).

In addition to serotonin genes, other genes associated with the GABA, acetylcholine, and glutamate neurotransmitter systems have been implicated in major depressive disorder (Oswald, Souery, & Mendlewicz, 2003). For example, Merali et al. (2004) compared postmortem brains of depressed suicide victims to non-depressed, non-suicide individuals and discovered lower density and structural abnormalities of the GABA receptor in the brains of suicide victims. They speculated that these differences were due to GABA genes that affect receptor formation and functionality. Kosel and colleagues (2004) also reported reduced GABA receptor binding and altered GABA receptor functioning in a case study of a severely treatment-resistant, 42-year-old male with major depression and GAD. This patient received electroconvulsive therapy (ECT) and relative to a control individual who also received ECT, the patient demonstrated an insensitivity to anesthesia. Genetic analyses revealed the presence of a gene variant that contributed to the altered GABA receptor functioning and was associated with the patient's insensitivity to anesthesia. The authors speculated that the gene variant and altered GABA receptor functioning may help to explain depression cases who do not respond to traditional pharmacological treatments. Similarly, Yamada et al. (2003) reported polymorphisms of two GABA receptor genes were associated with depression in females and suggested that GABA receptor genes play an important, albeit unknown, role in females higher susceptibility to develop major depressive disorder.

Nicotinic Receptor Genes

Given findings that indicate that individuals with depression are more likely to smoke cigarettes than the general population, Lai, Hong, and Tsai (2001) explored whether a specific gene variant for the nicotinic acetylcholine receptors (alpha7 nAChR) was associated with major depression. Results revealed a modest difference between subjects with major depression and controls, and the authors suggested that variation in the acetylcholine receptor gene may influence the risk of major depression. Gene variants that encode glutamate receptors have also been investigated and Ren and colleagues (2017) found greater frequency of a specific polymorphism (rs56275759) of the GRIK4 glutamate receptor gene in individuals with depression compared to controls. Recently, Bountress and colleagues (2017) reported that a specific gene variant of the GABA transporter protein, GAT1, was associated with individuals with depression and PTSD relative to controls. The authors recommended that prevention and intervention efforts be aimed at individuals who are at high risk based for these disorders based on presence of GAT1 polymorphisms. Collectively, these findings suggest that variants in glutamate and GABA genes may increase the risk of developing depression; however, additional research is needed to tease apart the role of these genetic variants (and others) in depression as well as other disorders (Yu, Baune et al., 2018).

Linkage Studies, Candidate Genes, and Genome-Wide Association Studies

In contrast to candidate gene studies that investigate pre-identified genes of interest, genome-wide association studies (GWAS) use a specific approach to scan complete sets of DNA (i.e., genomes) of thousands of people across all chromosomes simultaneously in an effort to find genetic variations associated with a particular disease or disorder. GWAS typically focus on associations between single-nucleotide polymporphisms (SNPs) in a disorder such as depression. Several genome wide association studies have not found an association between specific genetic polymorphisms and depression (e.g., Lewis et al., 2010; Ripke et al., 2013; Wray et al., 2012); however, more recent studies using larger samples and different methodology have reported a relationship between genetic invariants and depression. For example, the CONVERGE Consortium (China, Oxford and Virginia Commonwealth University Experimental Research on Genetic Epidemiology) studied over 10,000 Chinese women with and without severe recurrent major depressive disorder and found two genome wide associations involving the SIRT1 gene and the LHPP gene (CONVERGE, 2015). SIRT1 is involved in the biogenesis of mitochondria and the LHPP gene encodes an enzyme known as phospholysine phosphohistidine inorganic pyrophosphate phosphatase (LHPP). LHPP is found throughout the brain and is involved in cell metabolism. Cui et al. (2016) recently reported that a polymorphism of the LHPP gene was associated with differences in resting brain activity in patients with major depressive disorder compared to those without the disorder; however, the specifics of this relationship are not understood. Direk et al. (2017) studied over 70,000 participants with and without major depressive disorder and found genome-wide significance associated with the FHIT gene. The FHIT gene is expressed in multiple regions throughout the brain and plays a role in regulating circadian rhythms as well as oxidative stress that can lead to DNA damage (Byrne et al., 2014). The specific ways in which polymorphisms of the FHIT gene may lead to major depressive disorder are unknown. It is also important to note that variations in the FHIT gene have been linked to other disorders, including anxiety and ASD (Tsang et al., 2013). In a recent genome-wide study involving over 300,000 participants, the genetic testing company 23andMe identified 17 variants in 15 regions of DNA associated with an increased risk of major depressive disorder in people of European descent (Hyde et al., 2016). These recent studies have attempted to address methodological weaknesses of previous genome wide studies and by increasing sample sizes have increased statistical power, enabling the identification of otherwise obfuscated associations. Although these findings are an important step in unraveling the moderating effects of genetic factors in the vulnerability of major depressive disorder, they do not reveal the molecular mechanisms by which these variants translate into depressive symptoms. As Mullins and Lewis (2017) aptly noted, "The next challenge is to establish the molecular mechanisms by which GWAS loci mediate their effects and translate these into much-needed new biomarkers and therapeutic targets" (p. 6).

Summary Genetics and Depression

In summary, although a number of genes and gene variants have been associated with major depression, linkage, association, and candidate gene studies have not found evidence of a "depression gene". In fact, genetic studies have produced conflicting results, and most of the studies have *not* found a significant association between gene variants and depression (Anguelova, Benkelfat, & Turecki, 2003). Instead, results suggest that depression is likely the result of combined risk factors that may interact with multiple genes. In addition, environmental factors have been found to affect gene functioning by inducing molecular and physiologic changes that increase the risk of developing depression (epigenetics). Relatively little is known, however, about the interaction between genetic and environmental factors and the ways in which these factors might be modified to promote adaptive changes at the cellular level. As Lohoff (2010b, p. 2) noted,

> The major impediments to mood disorder gene localization and identification are as follows: 1) no single gene is necessary and sufficient for major depressive disorder; 2) each susceptibility gene contributes a small fraction of the total genetic risk; and 3) complex genetic heterogeneity, meaning that multiple partially overlapping sets of susceptibility genes (which interact with the environment) can predispose individuals to similar syndromes that are indistinguishable on clinical grounds.

As technology advances and additional methodologically sound, theory-driven studies are conducted, research will likely elucidate the roe of genetics in the development of major depressive disorder.

Neurotransmitter Levels: Monoamine Theory and Depletion Studies

In 1954, physician Edward Freis published an article in the *New England Journal of Medicine* describing cases in which patients with hypertension had developed depression after being treated with the drug reserpine (Serpasil). Reserpine blocks the vesicular monoamine transporter (VMAT) and prevents vesicular storage of neurotransmitters (dopamine, norepinephrine, serotonin); consequently, less neurotransmitter is available for release during exocytosis. As discussed in Chapter 1, monoamines play an important role in a wide variety of functions physiological functions, such as appetite, sleep, motivation, libido, immune and endocrine system functioning, and mood, most of which are compromised in major depression (Cowen & Browning, 2015; Nemeroff, 1998). Studies in the 1960s supported Freis' hypothesis as an increase in monoamine metabolites was found following antidepressant treatment (e.g., Schildkaut, 1965). In the 1980s and 1990s, decreased levels of serotonin metabolites were reported in the cerebral spinal fluid of individuals with depression (particularly those with a history of suicide attempts) in several studies, further implicating monoamines in depression (Coccaro et al., 1989; Rao et al., 1998). Collectively, these findings lead to the *monoamine theory of depression*, which predicts that depression is due to reduced levels of monoamines—i.e., "a chemical imbalance", involving serotonin, dopamine, and norepinephrine (Delgado, 2000).

Catecholamine Depletion Studies

The monoamine theory of depression has been challenged on a number of grounds and current perspectives reject the simplicity of the theory. For example, if monoamine levels are directly related to depression, then altering levels should reliably affect mood—i.e., lowering levels would be expected to induce depression. Contrary to these expectations, pharmacological agents that deplete serotonin and norepinephrine levels do not induce depression in healthy individuals (Duman, Heninger, & Nestler, 1997; Stimpson, Agrawal, & Lewis, 2002). Depletion studies with depressed patients or patients in remission have produced mixed findings. For example, when Delgado et al. (1991) investigated the effects of depletion of the serotonin precursor tryptophan in 43 depressed patients, they found that tryptophan depletion did not rapidly worsen patients' symptoms. However, as Delgado et al. (1991) and Bell, Abrams, and Nutt (2001) reported, in most patients who had previously responded favorably to antidepressants, tryptophan depletion caused a rapid relapse of depression. Johnson and colleagues (2001) reported that mood was unaffected by tryptophan depletion in patients with major depression or bipolar disorder, all of whom had been taking lithium for at least a year. Interestingly, Miller et al. (1996) found a relapse of depression in participants who responded to norepinephrine reuptake inhibitors (but not SSRIs) following treatment with agents that blocked norepinephrine and dopamine synthesis. Given that depression occurs more often in females, it is interesting that tryptophan depletion studies have found that women are more likely to experience "mood lowering" (but not depression) than men (Nishizawa et al., 1997).

Some, but not all, studies have reported an increased vulnerability to mood lowering in participants who have a family history of mood disorders (e.g., Klaassen et al., 1998). Others have used brain imaging to investigate tryptophan depletion in depressed individuals and have reported decreased brain metabolism in several regions: dorsolateral prefrontal cortex, orbitofrontal cortex, thalamus, and amygdala (Morris et al., 1999). Hassler and colleagues (2008) found that individuals with a history of major depressive disorder and in remission reported greater depression symptoms relative to controls when treated with a medication to induce catecholamine depletion. Hassler et al. interpreted their findings as "direct evidence for catecholaminergic dysfunction as a trait abnormality in major depressive disorder" (p. 2).

What can be concluded from the monoamine depletion studies? Given that depression is not induced in healthy individuals following depletion, monoamines may play a modulatory role in depression rather than a primary role. Although findings are mixed, some studies have found a worsening of depression symptoms in those with active depression or with a history of depression. Based on studies that indicate some depressed individuals respond to different types of antidepressants that target different neurotransmitter systems (e.g., serotonin versus norepinephrine), depression may have multiple origins or at least multiple mechanisms for attenuating symptoms. In other words, since severity of symptoms is associated with the effects of monoamine depletion, perhaps a threshold of neurotransmitter depletion is needed to induce symptoms and such a threshold may be individually dependent. It is also possible that the effects of neurotransmitter reductions are offset by other neurotransmitter or intracellular systems.

Structural Findings

Researchers have explored whether anatomical brain differences exist between individuals with and without major depressive disorder with a focus on brain structure and receptor density. With respect to anatomical structure, some have proposed that depression may result in part from death of hippocampal cells given that these cells are thought to be particularly vulnerable to glucocorticoid levels in response to stress and repeated episodes of depression (Stahl, 2000b). Indeed, decreased hippocampal volumes have been found in those with depression relative to control subjects and meta-analytic findings exploring hippocampal volume in patients with depression, and have concluded that the hippocampus does tend to be smaller in those with depression compared to controls (Campbellet al., 2004; Sheline et al., 1996; Videbech & Ravnkilde, 2004).

Other studies have reported smaller amygdala volumes in individuals with depression relative to controls, and a number of depressive episodes has been negatively correlated with gray-matter volume in the right hippocampus and right amygdala (e.g., Bremner et al., 2000; Frodl et al., 2002a; Stratmann et al., 2014). Sheline, Mokhtar, and Price (1998) used MRI to compare amygdala volumes in 40 adults with and without depression between the ages of 23–86 years. No differences were found between the groups with respect to whole-brain volume or total amygdala volume, but those with depression did show a bilaterally reduced core volume of the amygdala. The core volume of the amygdala consists of nuclei that are highly connected with subcortical and cortical structures. The authors speculated that a reduced core volume of the amygdala may have widespread implications for emotional aspects of memory, attention, and perception, which may in turn be related to the pathogenesis of depression. Contrary to expectations, Frodl et al. (2002b) and Frodl et al. (2003) found *enlarged* amygdala volumes in patients with major depression relative to controls. The authors speculated that increased blood flow in this region, as found by neuroimaging studies, may have contributed to the enlarged size of the amygdala. It is important to note that not all studies have found volume differences in the hippocampus and amygdala between individuals with and without depression (e.g., Posener et al., 2003; Vakili et al., 2000).

Differences have also been reported in other brain structures, including the hypothalamus (Schindler et al., 2012). Structural differences of the cerebellum have also been reported in individuals with depression relative to controls (Schutter, 2016), and a meta-analysis of 64 studies (nearly 4,500 participants) reported large volume reductions in the frontal regions, especially (anterior cingulate and orbitofrontal cortex) in participants with depression and moderate volume reductions in the hippocampus, the putamen, and the caudate nucleus relative to controls (Koolschijn et al., 2009). Global brain size has also been measured in depressed individuals, resulting in inconsistent findings. For example, Vythilingam et al. (2003) did not find global brain size differences in adults with major depression. Although these findings are only correlational in nature, it is possible that volume reductions may have widespread effects on neural projections and circuits that stem from these structures. Pigoni and colleagues (2017) recently conducted a systematic review of monzygotic and dizygotic twin studies using MRI (and FMRI), and although not all of the studies included in the review found significant differences in all brain regions and some studies did not report any significant differences (e.g., Munn et al., 2007), most of the studies did report significant anatomical differences between participants with depression compared to controls. Pigoni et al., therefore concluded that major depressive disorder was associated with "significant alterations in brain regions within a brain network presiding over emotion recognition and evaluation, including amygdala, hippocampus, insula and prefrontal cortex" (pp. 2 and 4).

A number of factors may account for the anatomical size differences found in brain structures of individuals with major depressive disorder relative to controls, including cell death. For example, reductions in gray matter volume (i.e., cell bodies) have been observed in individuals with depression and have been corroborated by meta-analyses (van Tol et al., 2010; Wise et al., 2017). Loss of gray matter contributes to the observed atrophy in various brain structures and is also hypothesized to lead to a reduction of neurotrophins and neurogenesis in the hippocampus. These processes are important in brain plasticity—i.e., ability of the brain to adapt and change morphologically and neurochemically throughout life, and studies suggest that dysfunction of synaptic plasticity along with cell death and atrophy of brain structures contributes to the pathophysiology of depression (i.e., neuroplasticity theory of depression) (Liu, Liu, et al., 2017). Support for the neuroplasticity theory of depression stems not only from studies supporting a reduction in neuroplastic responses in patients with depression but also from findings that indicated that antidepressants increase synthesis of neurotrophins and promote neurogenesis in the hippocampus (Duman & Voleti, 2012; Smith et al., 2013). Also lending support to the neuroplasticity theory of depression is that other drugs, including the anesthetics ketamine and dextromethorphan, have been found to induce neuroplastic changes in the brain (e.g., synaptogenesis), and they produce rapid antidepressant effects within 48 hours, which last for 7 days or longer (Lauterbach, 2016; Li et al., 2010).

Structural Findings Across Clinical Groups

In order for structural findings to have clinical relevance it is important to explore whether structural differences are unique to depression or whether they are present in other clinical disorders. Reduced volume of the hypothalamus although found in individuals with depression have also been found in individuals with bipolar disorder, schizophrenia, and autism, as well as other disorders (Schindler et al., 2012; Wolfe et al., 2015). Studies have also compared postmortem hippocampal samples from individuals with major depression, bipolar disorder, and schizophrenia, as well as normal control participants and contrary to expectations, anatomical differences were not found between these groups (Damadzic et al., 2001; Muller et al., 2001). Reduced volume of the hippocampus is commonly found in Alzheimer's disease, as well as other disorders (Josephs et al., 2017). Lastly, Elkis et al. (1995) conducted a meta-analysis of structural findings in mood disorders and reported that 97% of the studies found evidence of ventricular and sulci enlargement in participants with depression relative to controls. However, ventricular and sulci enlargement are not unique to depression and have been reported in schizophrenia (Elkis et al., 1995), Alzheimer's disease (Fazekas et al., 1989), anorexia nervosa (Krieg et al., 1988), alcoholism (Lishman, 1990), autism (Wolfe et al., 2015), and other disorders.

What can be concluded from these structural findings? In general, participants with depression have been found to have volumetric differences in several brain structures relative to participants without the disorder. These structural differences are not found consistently, however, and are also found in other clinical disorders. Therefore, the meaning and clinical significance of these structural findings remains inconclusive.

Transporter Proteins and Receptors

Serotonin reuptake inhibitors (SSRIs) are one of the most commonly prescribed and effective antidepressant drugs in the United States and have been found to increase serotonin levels in the synaptic cleft by inhibiting the action of SERT (Fournier et al., 2010). Because major depressive disorder can often be successfully treated with antidepressants that block SERT, studies have explored the density of the transporters in postmortem tissue and in living participants. Results of postmortem studies that have measured serotonin transporter binding sites in individuals with depression have been mixed, with some studies reporting reductions in the transporter (e.g., Malison et al., 1998) and other studies no differences between serotonin binding sites in those with and without depression (e.g., Klimek et al., 2003; Little et al., 1997). Dahlstrom et al. (2000) measured serotonin transporter availability in children and adolescents with depression who were not treated with antidepressants using SPECT. Results revealed that children and adolescents with depression had significantly *higher* serotonin transporter availability in the midbrain region than children without the disorder. No differences were found with respect to dopamine transporter availability in the striatum. Bligh-Glover et al. (2000) measured density of the serotonin transporter in the midbrain region of suicide victims with major depression and age-matched controls and found no differences between the groups. Arango et al. (2001) also examined postmortem tissue of suicide victims and reported that, in general, the concentration of serotonin transporter binding sites did not differ between control subjects and suicide victims. A recent meta-analysis of SERT density in postmortem and living individuals with depression found reduced SERT availability in limbic regions of the brain (amygdala, striatum) and no significant differences in the hypothalamus, hippocampus, or frontal structures. In no regions were elevated levels of SERT found across the 50 studies (Kambeitz & Howes, 2015). The authors interpreted their findings as supporting brain serotonin dysregulation in depression; however, it is important to note that the findings are only correlational and do address underlying mechanisms that may contribute to reduced SERT in areas identified.

It is also interesting to note that factors other than depression have been associated with reduced availability of SERT. For example, age-related declines in the availability of serotonin transporters have been reported as van Dyck et al. (2000) found that the binding potential of serotonin transporter declined 4.2% per decade in a sample of healthy subjects (18–88 years). Jacobsen and colleagues (2000) suggested that age-related declines in serotonin transporter binding might explain the poor response to SSRIs observed in some adult and elderly patients with depression. In addition to age-related changes in serotonin transporters, Tafet et al. (2001) suggested that chronic stress that often accompanies depression may further reduce the density of serotonin transporters. In addition to serotonin, dopamine transporters have also been investigated in depression. Therefore, the question of whether serotonin transporters play a role in major depression remains equivocal and additional, well-designed studies are warranted.

Receptors and Depression

In addition to SERT, studies have explored the role of autoreceptors and postsynaptic receptors in the physiological basis of depression. Postmortem and brain imaging studies regarding postsynaptic serotonin receptors have been inconsistent with some reporting an increase, decrease, and other no difference compared with controls (e.g., Larisch et al., 2001; Meyer et al., 1999; Yatham, Clark, & Zis, 2000). Autoreceptor studies have produced more consistent findings. For example, Drevets et al. (2000, 2007) used brain imaging to study serotonin autoreceptor (5-HT1A) binding in individuals with major depression relative to controls and reported a 42% binding reduction in the midbrain raphe and 25–33% reduction in limbic and cortical regions in those with depression. Other studies have corroborated these findings and results suggest that major depressive disorder might be characterized by abnormal functioning (and reduction) of serotonin autoreceptors (Hjorth, 2016). As discussed in Chapter 1, autoreceptors play a critical role in detecting the presence of serotonin in the extracellular fluid and triggering the presynaptic neuron to alter release of the neurotransmitter. Findings have been mixed with regard to the effects on antidepressants on receptor density and binding (e.g., Celada, Bortolozzi, & Artigas, 2013; Drevets et al., 2007; Massou et al., 1997; Sargent et al., 2000). It is important to note that reduced serotonin receptor density and binding is not unique to depression but is characteristic of other clinical disorders such as schizophrenia (Ngan et al., 2000).

Summary: Structural Findings

In summary, research findings suggest that individuals with major depressive disorder are more likely to have reduced density of SERT and serotonin autoreceptors relative to individuals without the disorder. These findings are not unique to depression, however, and are only correlational in nature. Additional studies are needed to investigate etiologic factors that may contribute to receptor density findings and to explore the role of pharmacological and non-pharmacological treatment on receptor density and functioning. Research is also needed to investigate whether molecular morphological changes are associated with symptom improvement and if so the direction of this relationship. It is important to note that neurotransmitter receptors other than serotonin have also been implicated in depression, particularly glutamate receptors (Abdallah et al., 2017). Future studies are warranted and will likely reveal complex interactions between neurotransmitter systems that contribute to the underlying pathophysiology of major depressive disorder.

Functional Findings

As discussed in Chapter 3, functional neuroimaging studies explore brain activation patterns based on glucose metabolism and cerebral blood flow, depending on the specific technique employed (e.g., fMRI, MEG, PET, SPECT). In general, results have been conflicting with some studies finding increased metabolism in various brain regions of individuals with depression relative to controls, especially prefrontal and limbic regions (Scheinost et al., 2017), while most studies have found decreased metabolism rates (Bonne, Louzoun, et al., 2003; Drevets, Ongur, & Price, 1998; Kimbrell et al., 2002; Soares & Mann, 1997; Drevets, 2000; Kennedy, Javanmard, & Vaccarino, 1997; Biver et al., 1994; Kimbrell et al. 2002). A 2015 meta-analyis by Kaiser and colleagues analyzed 27 data sets from published studies of participants with depression relative to controls in an effort to identify hyperconnectivity (increased positive, or reduced negative, connectivity) or hypoconnectivity (increased negative, or reduced positive, connectivity) in various brain regions during a resting state (i.e., no tasks). Results supported hypoconnectivity between frontal and parietal regions of the brain in participants with major depressive disorder and hyperconnectivity between regions of the brain implicated in affective decision-making and self-referential thinking. The authors interpreted the findings as indicative of dysfunction of network systems critical for regulating mood and attention. These findings, however, do not speak to the directionality of the findings—i.e., do "dysfunctional networks" result in depression symptoms or do depression symptoms result in observed differences in connectivity?

Cerebral blood flow studies have also revealed inconsistent findings pertaining to major depressive disorder. Murata et al. (2000), for example, reported regional cerebral blood flow was significantly lower in patients with major depression relative to controls in the right anterior frontal cortex, temporal cortex, thalamus, and putamen. Silfverskiold and Risberg (1989), however, reported a positive relationship between global cerebral blood flow and symptoms of depression. Orosz et al. (2012) initially found reduced blood flow in the default mode network of individuals with major depressive disorder compared to controls; however, this difference was no longer significant after controlling for whole brain gray matter. Recently, Yin and colleagues (2018) explored patterns of cerebral blood flow in patients with major depressive disorder who displayed psychomotor retardation and reported substantial reduction of blood flow in the primary motor cortex relative to control participants. In addition, Yin et al., found a negative correlation between blood flow perfusion and symptomatology, and a significant increase in blood flow to this region following antidepressant treatment. The authors suggested that cerebral blood flow of the right primary motor cortex is a potential biomarker of psychomotor retardation in major depressive disorder.

In addition to comparing neuroimaging scans of depressed individuals with non-depressed individuals, studies have examined scans of individuals with various clinical disorders relative to major depressive disorder. For example, Sackeim et al. (1993) compared global and regional areas of cerebral blood flow in 30 adults with major depression, 30 patients with Alzheimer's disease, and 30 normal controls. Results indicated that the two clinical groups both showed reduced global blood flow but distinct regions were associated with depression (prefrontal) versus Alzheimer's (parieto-temporal). Saxena et al. (2003) used PET to measure glucose metabolism in individuals with major depression or OCD and a group of individuals who had both disorders. All participants were treated with a serotonin reuptake inhibitor (paroxetine) and pre- and post-antidepressant scans were compared. Results indicated that individuals with OCD who showed *increased* activity in the right caudate responded better to antidepressants, while those with major depression who showed *reduced* activity in the right amygdala and increased activity in the prefrontal region responded better to antidepressants. Overall, these findings suggest that although patients with OCD and with major depressive disorder tend to respond well to the same antidepressant, the neurophysiological substrates that predict drug response appear to be different.

Other studies have explored brain changes observed during provocation of sadness, or during the presentation of affective and neutral visual stimuli in individuals with and without depression, and results have suggested that those with depression respond differently with respect to blood flow and neural activation than those without the disorder (e.g., Liotti et al., 2002; Davidson et al., 2003). Specifically, individuals with depression as well as controls showed bilateral activation in the visual cortex, prefrontal cortex, and amygdala. Relative to healthy control subjects, the group with major depression showed greater activation in the visual cortex and less activation in the left prefrontal cortex in response to negative versus neutral stimuli. In addition, participants with depression who were treated with antidepressants showed significant increases in various brain regions after two weeks, similar to the level of activity observed in control subjects, and increased activity was correlated with symptom improvement. According to Davidson and colleagues (2003), these findings implicate a neural circuit that underlies emotional responses to visual stimuli, and alterations of this circuitry may be characteristic of major depression. A number of studies suggest that antidepressants and/or psychotherapy, such as cognitive behavior therapy, that invokes cognitive control training may "normalize" faulty neural activity and lead to symptom improvement (Siegle et al., 2002; Sosic-Vasic et al., 2017).

Summary Functional Findings

Given the lack of consistency among functional neuroimaging studies, it is difficult to draw firm conclusions concerning brain regions involved in the pathophysiology of major depression. It is important to keep in mind that results of neuroimaging studies can be influenced by a variety of factors, including technical issues specific to the neuroimaging methods used (e.g., PET, fMRI, SPECT), statistical power and analyses, and sample size, effect size, gender, age, and comorbidity. In addition, given the heterogeneity of symptoms associated with major depressive disorder, more refined subtyping of depression may help to uncover neural correlates associated with the disorder (Pizzagalli et al., 2003). To date, the current view based on functional neuroimaging studies is that no single brain region is solely implicated in major depressive disorder; rather, the disorder appears to involve multiple large scan networks distributed throughout the brain (Scheinost et al., 2017). Specifics regarding these networks and how differences in these networks manifest as depression symptoms, however, are lacking.

BOX 6.1   Depression and Cerebrovascular Functioning

According to the World Health Organization, cerebrovascular diseases (CVDs) are the leading cause of death worldwide. CVD is often accompanied by major depressive disorder in later life, and current ultrasound technology allows the detection of subtle cerebrovascular disease in mid-life depression (Desmidt et al., 2017). CVD is associated with increased risk of stroke, and many patients who suffer a stroke develop major depressive disorder (Ayerbe et al., 2013). Research has established that integrated vascular prevention programs reduce cardiovascular risk in patients with established CVD and in those at high multifactorial risk for developing CVD (Connolly et al., 2017). Behavioral lifestyle interventions targeting exercise, nutrition, psychological coping strategies, and improving attitudes toward health have been found to help reduce the risk of CVD and comorbid depression.

Additional Etiologic Areas of Research: Major Depressive Disorder

In addition to genetic, molecular, anatomical, and neurotransmitter theories of depression, researchers have explored the role of the endocrine system, immune system, neurotrophins, omega 3 fatty acids, diet, and lifestyle behaviors in major depressive disorder. For example, some studies have reported that major depression is accompanied by activation of the immune system that leads to autoimmune abnormalities affecting neurotransmitter receptors and functioning of the hypothalamic-pituitary-adrenal (HPA) axis (Tanaka et al., 2003; Tiemeier, 2003). In this model, stress is hypothesized to activate an inflammatory response in the brain that results in activation of microglia and release of cytokines and nitric oxide. Cytokines and nitric oxide result in the breakdown of neurotransmistter precursors such as tryptophan. Reduced levels of precursors result in reduced production of neurotransmitters (serotonin), which in turn is associated with major depressive disorder symptoms (Miller et al., 2009; Yrondi et al., 2018).

Others such as Leonard (2000) have suggested that depression is caused by an interaction of immune, endocrine, and neurotransmitter systems that results in inflammatory response in the brain. In a recent systematic review of the literature, Rosenblat (2017) reported that minocycline, an antibiotic with anti-inflammatory effects, is effective at reducing depression symptoms. Steiner et al. (2003) noted that the lifetime prevalence of depression in women is twice that of men and argued that fluctuating levels of estrogen and other sex steroids may underlie the development of mood disorders in some women. Still others such as Logan (2003) suggested that omega-3 fatty acids may increase cAMP, CREB, and BDNF and thereby improve depression symptoms, although studies exploring these areas have been conflicting (Wani, Bhat, & Ara, 2015). More recently, Phillips (2017) reported that mechanisms involving BDNF are deleteriously altered in major depressive disorder (MDD) leading to disruptions in neuroplasticity at the regional and circuit level.

Phillips suggested that exercise and antidepressants increase production of BDNF in key brain regions thereby promoting neuronal health and recovery of function in individuals with major depressive disorder. Clearly, more research is needed to investigate the physiological bases of major depressive disorder in order that empirically based and efficacious treatments can be developed.

Physiologically Based Treatment Methods for Major Depressive Disorder

Table 6.1 Examples of Medications Used to Treat Major Depressive Disorder

SSRIs

Sertraline (Zoloft)

Fluoxetine (Prozac)

Citalopram (Celexa)

Escitalopram (Lexapro)

Paroxetine (Paxil)

Fluvoxamine (Luvox)

SNRIs

Effexor (Venlafaxine)

Desvenlafaxine (Pristiq)

Duloxetine (Cymbalta)

Levomilnacipran (Fetzima)

Venlafaxine (Effexor XR)

MAO Inhibitors

Isocarboxazid (Marplan)

Phenelzine (Nardil)

Selegiline (Emsam)

Tranylcypromine (Parnate)

Tricyclics

Anafranil (Clomipramine)

Amitriptyline:

Desipramine (Norpramin)

Doxepin (Sinequan)

Imipramine (Tofranil)

Nortriptyline (Pamelor)

Protriptyline (Vivactil)

Trimipramine (Surmontil)

Note: The Physicians' Desk Reference (PDR) (2018) provides additional information concerning these and other drugs.

Antidepressants: Demographic Information and Efficacy

According to the American Psychiatric Association, the majority of patients respond to antidepressant treatment and many show improvement with combinations of antidepressants (Safer, 2017; Stahl, 2000a, 2000b) (Table 6.1). Numerous studies are available attesting to the effectiveness of antidepressants at improving depression symptomatology, particularly among patients with severe symptoms, and these findings are corroborated by meta-analyses (e.g., Cipriani et al., 2018; Fournier et al., 2010; Li et al., 2017). Recently, however, the effectiveness of antidepressants relative to placebo in cases of mild depression has recently come under question. For example, Jakobsen and colleagues (2017) conducted a systematic review of clinical trials and assessed the effectiveness of SSRIs versus a placebo in terms of symptom reduction, adverse events, and remission. Results revealed minimal benefits in patients with mild or moderate symptoms and substantial benefits for patients with severe depression. Studies have documented that some of the improvement in behavioral symptoms can be attributed to a *placebo effect*. A placebo is a treatment that is devoid of specific actions on the individual's symptoms yet somehow causes a beneficial effect. Mayberg and colleagues (2002) were the first to use neuroimaging techniques to investigate areas of brain activation in depressed patients who took a placebo or an antidepressant. Results revealed that a similar pattern of brain activation occurred in both those taking the drug and those taking a placebo. Additional areas were activated in those taking the antidepressant, however, and the authors speculated that these regions might be particularly important in the therapeutic effects of antidepressant medications. Recent studies with children and adolescents comparing placebo effects with SSRIs and SNRIs reported that the antidepressants were significantly more beneficial than placebo (Locher et al., 2017).

These findings are interesting given that antidepressant use has increased in globally (Poluzzi et al., 2004; Gusmão et al., 2013) and recent findings in the United States indicate that one in eight individuals age 12 and older reported taking antidepressants in the past month, and one in four indicated they have taken antidepressants for 10 or more years (Pratt et al., 2011). Pratt et al., also found a 64% increase in the percentage of people using antidepressants between 1999 and 2014. In terms of demographics, females are twice as likely as males to take antidepressants in all age groups, the highest percentage (16.6%) are used by people age 40–59 and non-Hispanic white Americans take depressants three times as much as any other race or ethnic group.

Research also indicates that antidepressant use has increased among children (Chon et al., 2017). El-Mallakh, Peters, and Waltrip (2000) have raised concerns over the use of antidepressants with this population given the unknown long-term structural and cellular side effects of antidepressants. As discussed in Chapter 1, the brain is still developing in children and adolescents, and it is unknown whether antidepressants alter normal developmental processes, such as neurogenesis, synaptogenesis, dendritic expansion, and synaptic pruning. Clearly, individuals of all ages are seeking treatment and are being prescribed antidepressants; however, questions remain regarding the potential deleterious effects in children, the efficacy of antidepressants in mild cases of depression, and whether alterative interventions might be warranted in some cases given the potential and unknown side effects associated with antidepressants on the developing brain.

BOX 6.2   Can Exercise Help Alleviate Depression Symptoms?

Physical exercise has been found to increase serotonin levels in the brain (Lan et al., 2014), and a large body of literature supports that exercise is effective at improving depression symptoms even in adults without major depressive disorder (Conn, 2010; Seo & Chao, 2017). In some cases, exercise has also been found to effectively augment antidepressant treatment (Trivedi et al., 2011) and can be equally effective as SSRIs in treating depression in patients with congestive heart failure (Samartzis et al., 2013). Research does not support, however, that exercise is more effective than psychotherapy or pharmacological interventions at improving symptoms of major depressive disorder (Cooney et al., 2013).

As addressed in Chapter 2, five broad categories of antidepressants are used to treat depression: monoamine oxidase inhibitors, tricyclic antidepressants, selective serotonin reuptake inhibitors (SSRIs), serotonin and norepinephrine reuptake inhibitors (SNRIs), and atypical antidepressants. The mode of action differs with each type of antidepressant and is discussed in Chapter 2. SSRIs are the most frequently prescribed medication for major depressive disorder. One of the first meta-analyses exploring the effectiveness of five SSRIs (citalopram, fluoxetine, fluvoxamine, paroxetine, and sertraline) was completed by Edwards and Anderson (1999). Results indicated that fluoxetine had a slower onset of symptom improvement but there was no difference in the clinical efficacy of the drugs. Research has found that the onset of symptom improvement varies among individuals and ranges from one to eight weeks (Quitkin et al., 2003; Taylor et al., 2017). Contrary to popular belief, however, improvement of symptoms is not substantially delayed as meta-analytic findings support a 50% reduction in depression symptoms *within the first week*, with continued improvement for at least six weeks. The pharmacological and molecular reasons for continued symptom improvement over time is poorly understood. Rasenick and colleagues (2016), however, recently suggested that the delay may be due to faulty second-messenger systems in patients with depression. Specifically, Rasenick et al. found that part of the cell membrane known as "lipid rafts" inappropriately sequester a particular protein important in cellular functioning ($G\alpha_s$), thus preventing it from carrying out its duties. When treated with SSRIs, however, SSRIs first collected in the rafts, and the protein was released subsequently from the lipid rafts (Erb, Schappi, & Rasenick, 2016). It is plausible that the lipid raft segment of the cell is, for an unknown reason, faulty in patients with depression and SSRIs correct this dysfunction.

Meta-analytic findings also support that higher doses of SSRIs are associated with better symptom improvement but also with an increased likelihood of cessation of medication due to side effects (Jakubovski et al., 2015; Rosenblat & McIntyre, 2018). Some studies suggest males and females respond differently to SSRIs and that drug response may also differ with ethnicity and during pregnancy (Avram et al., 2016; Keers et al., 2010; Friedman et al., 2009; Lesser et al., 2010). These studies suggest that efficacy of antidepressants is likely influenced by a number of factors and therefore their selection, dose, and use should be individually determined.

BOX 6.3   Ecstasy: 'Molly' used in therapy?

In August 2017, the US Food and Drug Administration (FDA) granted the drug MDMA (3,4-methylenedioxymethamphetamine) a "Breakthrough Therapy Designation", ensuring close collaboration between the FDA and the Multidisciplinary Association for Psychedelic Studies to empirically and expeditiously study the use of MDMA in the treatment of mental health disorders. MDMA, also known as "Molly", is a synthetic drug that alters mood and perception. MDMA is chemically similar to stimulants and hallucinogens, and produces feelings of pleasure, increased energy, emotional connectedness, and distorted sensory and time perception. MDMA is believed to increase the release of monoamines (particularly serotonin) by reversing the action of transporter proteins and inhibiting reuptake. Preliminary studies have supported the effectiveness of MDMA-assisted therapy at improving the symptoms of post-traumatic stress disorder (PTSD), and researchers are exploring the use of MDMA-assisted therapy in the treatment of other disorders including anxiety and major depressive disorders (Yazar-Klosinski & Mithoefer, 2017).

Antidepressants: Neuroimaging Studies

Research investigating brain metabolic responses to SSRIs suggest that they have differential effects depending on the disorder and the symptomatic response to the medication. For example, Saxena and colleagues (2002) administered paroxetine (paxil) to individuals with depression, individuals with OCD, and individuals with comorbid depression and OCD, and compared their response to controls. Results indicated that participants with OCD alone showed significant metabolic decreases in the right caudate nucleus, right ventrolateral prefrontal cortex (VLPFC), bilateral orbitofrontal cortex, and thalamus that were unique to their group. Both the major depressive disorder and concurrent OCD + depression groups showed metabolic decreases in the left VLPFC and increases in the right striatum. Treatment response was associated with a decrease in striatal metabolism in non-depressed OCD patients but with an increase in striatal activity in patients with OCD + depression. Other studies have reported that blood flow is reduced in prefrontal brain regions, and in the left occipital lobe, right cerebellum, bilateral temporal cortex, and bilateral thalamus following antidepressant treatment, and these changes in blood flow correspond with improvement of depressive symptoms. (Nobler, Olvet, and Sackeim, 2002; Davies, Lloyd, et al., 2003).

Little et al. (1996) were among the first to demonstrate that decreased glucose metabolism (hypoperfusion) in frontal regions was associated with a favorable response to antidepressants (venlafaxine or bupropion) compared to non-responders who did not display this pattern of glucose metabolism. Mayberg et al. (2000) used PET to measure glucose metabolism changes with fluoxetine treatment in patients with major depression over a 6-week period. Results indicated that improvement of symptoms over time was associated with a decrease in glucose metabolism in the striatum and limbic regions and increases in glucose metabolism in the prefrontal, parietal, anterior, and posterior cingulate regions. Individuals who did not improve with fluoxetine showed an inverse pattern of glucose response, leading the researchers to speculate that failure to increase and decrease glucose metabolism in specific brain regions might underlie non-treatment response. In contrast, Daou et al. (2017) recently reported that increased blood flow (hyperperfusion) in the orbital frontal cortex, and the anterior cingulate cortex was associated with a poor response to an SSRI (sertraline) in patients with major depressive disorder. Collectively, these studies suggest that response to antidepressants might depend on underlying patterns of brain metabolism, although future studies are needed to determine whether these patterns are characteristic of depression in general or whether they vary among individuals depending on their specific type of clinical symptoms.

BOX 6.4   What Happens to the Brain of A Healthy, Non-depressed Person if They Take an Antidepressant?

To explore whether antidepressants affect the brain of individuals without depression differently, Bonne et al. (1999) administered fluoxetine (Prozac) to 15 healthy volunteers using brain imaging (SPECT). Results revealed that compared to baseline and placebo conditions, contrary to what tends to occur with those with depression, no significant changes in cerebral blood flow emerged following 6 weeks of treatment. Gelfin, Gorfine, and Lerer (1998) also investigated the effects of fluoxetine in normal volunteers over a 7-week, placebo-controlled trial and found no significant changes in mood or other psychological variables. Others, however, have found that after a single dose of fluoxetine, healthy volunteers showed decreased binding and desensitization of serotonin autoreceptors compared to placebo, and participants were less accurate at identifying anger and sadness based on visual images (Capitão et al., 2015; Sibon et al., 2008). In contrast, Harmer and colleagues (2003) found that healthy volunteers were more efficient at identifying positive emotions after administration of a single dose of an antidepressant (reboxetine) compared to the placebo but no differences were found with respect to anger, disgust, fear, or sadness. These findings suggest that in healthy individuals, molecular and psychological changes occur immediately in response to fluoxetine and support differential effects in individuals with and without depression.

BOX 6.5   Do Antidepressants Affect Relapse Rates?

Depression is associated with a greater risk of heart disease, diabetes, eating disorders, suicide, decreased physical, cognitive, and social functioning, self-neglect, and shorter life span (Goldschmidt et al., 2017; Kessler, 2009). Follow-up studies indicate that depression has a recurring course but use of antidepressants may reduce relapse rates. According to Hirschfeld and Schatzberg (1994), approximately 30% of adults with depression will relapse within a year; for adults who have experienced at least two episodes of depression, the relapse rate is 70–80%. According to Stahl (2000a, p. 8), five factors increase the risk of relapse: (a) multiple prior episodes, (b) severe episodes, (c) long-lasting episodes, (d) episodes with bipolar disorder or psychotic features, and (e) incomplete recovery between two consecutive episodes. Studies indicate that antidepressants significantly reduce relapse rates by as much as 50%, particularly if the medication is taken for one year (Reimherr et al., 1998). Frank et al. (1990) found that relapse rates were also reduced over a 3-year period, as only 15% of adults taking an antidepressant (imipramine) had a reoccurrence of depression compared to 90% who took a placebo. Nelson and colleagues (2004) reported that combining SSRIs (e.g., fluoxetine) and norepinephrine reuptake inhibitors (e.g., desipramine) significantly increases remission rates than either antidepressant used alone during a six-week study. However, research also suggests that although depressive symptoms may improve, 50% or more of patients who respond to antidepressants fail to reach remission (nonsymptomatic) and even fewer attain recovery—that is, remission lasting for 6–12 months (Warden et al., 2007). Stahl (2000b) noted that, when left untreated, depression may "have a long-lasting or even irreversible neuropathological effect on the brain, rendering treatment less effective if symptoms are allowed to progress than if they are removed by appropriate treatment early in the course of the illness" (p. 18).

Antidepressants and Suicidal Behavior

Individuals with major depressive disorder, particularly those with severe symptoms have been found to be at increased risk for suicidal behavior and antidepressants are often effective at improving symptoms in these patients. Teicher, Glod, and Cole (1993), however, were among the first to suggest that antidepressant treatment may actually increase suicidality in patients treated with antidepressants and proposed nine clinical mechanisms that may underlie this effect. As discussed in Chapter 2, in 2004, the US Food and Drug Administration (FDA) reviewed 24 trials involving over 4,400 children and adolescents treated with nine antidepressant drugs (or placebo) for OCD, major depression, or other psychiatric disorders. Results revealed an average suicide risk of 4% compared to 2% for placebo (no suicides actually occurred during the trials). As a result of these findings, the FDA directed manufacturers of all antidepressant drugs to include a boxed warning statement about the increased risk of suicidal thinking or behavior among children and adolescents treated with these medications. In December 2006, the Psychopharmacologic Drugs Advisory Committee of the US Food and Drug Administration (FDA) conducted its own meta-analyses on 77,382 adults from 295 randomized controlled clinical trials that evaluated treatments for major depressive disorder and other psychiatric disorders. The FDA defined suicidality as suicidal ideation, preparatory acts, attempts, or completions, and findings revealed that approximately 70% of the suicidality reported was suicidal thoughts; however, there were eight suicide deaths in the adult trials (five in participants randomized to the investigational agent, one to an active comparator, and two to placebo). Additionally, findings supported a protective effect of antidepressants for ages ≥ 65 years and a statistically nonsignificant elevation in risk of suicidality for ages 18–25 years. On the basis of these findings, the FDA issued a revised blackbox warning for *all antidepressants* in May 2007, thereby extending the coverage of the 2004 warning that applied to children and adolescents to include patients under 25 years of age. The warning label currently reads, "Antidepressants increased the risk compared to placebo of suicidal thinking and behavior (suicidality) in children, adolescents, and young adults in short-term studies of major depressive disorder (MDD) and other psychiatric disorders" (FDA, revisions to product labeling).

In addition to the FDA analyses, a number of studies have explored the relationship between antidepressants and suicidality and the data have been conflicting. For example, studies support that, although a rare occurrence, antidepressants can increase the risk of suicide ideation and suicide attempts, particularly in children and adolescents (Oberlander & Miller, 2011; Schneeweiss et al., 2010) and to a lesser extent in adults (e.g., Moller, 2006). Other studies have found that antidepressants *decrease* the risk of suicidal behavior in adults, especially adults with severe depression and those with worsening of symptoms (Leon et al., 2011; Nischal et al., 2012). Studies investigating whether some antidepressant drugs may be safer than others with respect to suicidality have produced conflicting results: some report no or limited differences in suicide risk between different types of antidepressants (Miller et al., 2014; Khan et al., 2003; Rossi, Barraco, & Donda, 2004), others have reported that SNRIs carry a higher risk than SSRIs (Rubino et al., 2007), and still others have reported that SSRIs carry a higher risk for suicidality than other antidepressants (Emslie et al., 2015; Healy, 2003). Interestingly, Bielefeldt, Danborg, and Gøtzsche (2016) recently conducted a systematic review of studies that have administered antidepressants to healthy volunteers and assessed the risk of suicidality and violence. Results revealed that administration antidepressants in adult healthy volunteers doubled their risk of suicidality and violence. Given the lack of consistency across studies and the potentially lethal outcome of suicidality, additional research is needed to better understand variables that may predict drug and psychological response to antidepressants.

Brain Stimulation and Non-Pharmacological Interventions

A number of non-pharmacological, physiologically based interventions are available for the treatment of major depressive disorder, particularly for those who are treatment resistant to antidepressants. The degree of empirical support for these methods varies and questions remain about the mode of action of these interventions at the level of the brain. Examples of non-pharmacological, physiologically based interventions include electroconvulsive therapy (ECT), deep brain stimulation, repetitive transmagnetic stimulation (rTMS), and vagus nerve stimulation (VNS).

Electroconvulsive Therapy (ECT)

Electroconvulsive therapy (ECT) is a procedure that involves the administration of controlled electrical currents to the brain while the individual is sedated, and results in a brief seizure. According to the National Institutes of Mental Health, given that ECT is delivered while the patient is under sedation and a muscle relaxant, the procedure is painless. A typical course of treatment occurs two to three times weekly for 6–12 sessions, followed by individually determined maintenance sessions. The FDA recommends the use of ECT with adult patients who have treatment-resistant depression or who require a rapid response due to the severity of their symptoms (McDonald et al., 2016). Although ECT has been found to improve symptoms of severe major depressive disorder the mechanism by which this occurs is uncertain (Kellner et al., 2006; UK ECT Review Group, 2003).

In an effort to understand the effects of ECT on the brain Nobler and colleagues (1994) used PET to measure global and regional cerebral blood flow and glucose metabolism in patients with major depression and patients with bipolar disorder 30 minutes before, 50 minutes after, and a week after ECT. Results indicated larger blood flow reductions were associated with a better outcome for both groups of patients. Nobler et al. (2001) also studied glucose patterns in patients with major depression before and 5 days after bilateral treatment with ECT. Results indicated that following ECT, widespread decreases in cerebral glucose metabolism were found. The researchers suggested that ECT reduces neuronal activity in subcortical and cortical regions, which potentially explains its antidepressant effects. A study by Milo et al. (2001) reported that prior to ECT, patients with depression had reduced blood flow of the frontal regions relative to controls. Following ECT, those who showed improvement in depressive symptoms had significant increases (toward normal) in blood flow and those who showed minimal response no significant change in rCBF. Blumenfeld et al. (2003) measured rCBF *during* bilateral ECT (bifrontal or bitemporal) in patients with major depression. Results indicated blood flow increased in the prefrontal and anterior cingulate regions with bifrontal ECT, with the greatest increase in the prefrontal regions.

At the molecular level, research with other animals suggests that ECT increases sensitivity of serotonin postsynaptic receptors in the hippocampus and increases release of neurotransmitters such as GABA and glutamate (Ishihara et al., 1999; Ishihara & Sasa, 2001). ECT may also decrease the sensitivity of serotonin autoreceptors resulting in an increased release of neurotransmitters (Gur, Lerer, & Newman, 1997; Gur et al., 2002), and research with other animals suggests that ECT increases dopamine receptor availability in the striatum thereby facilitating dopamine transmission and contributing to therapeutic effects (Landau et al., 2017). Recently, Wilkinson, Sanacora, and Bloch (2017) conducted a meta-analysis and found significant increases in hippocampal volume of patients with depression following ECT treatment. Collectively, these findings suggest that ECT may promote neuroplastic changes in the brain, although the underlying mechanisms that lead to symptom improvement are not fully understood. Importantly, Euba (2012) noted that ECT is used primarily with whites and emphasized the need offer ECT to individuals from diverse backgrounds.

Vagus Nerve Stimulation

As reviewed in Chapter 3, VNS was approved by the FDA for treatment of epilepsy given its effectiveness at attenuating seizures. VNS is also approved for treatment of resistant major depressive disorder and bipolar disorder in Europe and Canada, where several studies have shown improvement in 30% or more of patients who received such treatment (Goodnick et al., 2001; Sackeim et al., 2001). Sackeim and colleagues (2001) studied 60 individuals with treatment-resistant major depression for 12 weeks (2 weeks baseline, 10 weeks post-VNS implantation) and concluded that VNS was most effective with patients with low to moderate antidepressant resistance. In addition, patients who had never received ECT were nearly four times more likely to respond favorably to VNS. Marangell et al. (2002) followed 30 patients with major depression for a year to explore the long-term effectiveness of VNS. Results indicated that VNS was associated with a sustained response and increased rates of remission in patients with major depression. Muller et al. (2017) also reported long-term effectiveness of VNS and found stimulation tunings between 0.5 and 2.0 mA and 20–25 Hz were the best dosages for achieving remittance in long-term treatment of major depressive disorder. Similar to ECT, the mechanisms responsible for therapeutic improvement following VNS are poorly understood. Preliminary research, however, suggests that VNS increases afferent inputs to limbic and higher cortical brain regions and that ECT results in neuroplastic changes in the hippocampus including neurogenesis and these changes likely contribute to symptom improvement (Carpenter, Friehs, & Price, 2003; Perini et al., 2017).

rTMS

Repetitive transcranial magnetic stimulation (rTMS) as described in Chapter 2 involves the placement of an electromagnetic coil on an individual's scalp and short repetitive magnetic pulses are delivered to different areas of the brain. The FDA approved rTMS for treatment resistant mild depression in 2008. rTMS sessions typically last 20–40 minutes, several days a week, for approximately 6 weeks. Efficacy results have been variable across studies. For example, Padberg et al. (1999) compared the effectiveness of fast rTMS to slow rTMS in 18 patients with treatment-resistant major depression. Results revealed a 19% reduction of depression scores after slow rTMS but only a 6% reduction after fast rTMS. These results suggest that slow rTMS may be more effective than fast rTMS and, as noted by the researchers slow rTMS can be safely applied at higher intensities. More current studies have also supported the effectiveness of rTMS in improving depression symptoms (e.g., Benadhira et al., 2017; George et al., 2010; Nahas et al., 1998); however, when Garcia-Toro and colleagues (2001) examined the effectiveness of rTMS compared to antidepressants and when used in conjunction with antidepressants, they found that rTMS was no more efficacious than standard antidepressant medication and appeared to have no additive effects. Other studies, however, have reported that rTMS significantly augmented antidepressant treatment in patients with major depressive disorder (Wang, Li, et al., 2017). Studies have also compared rTMS to ECT (Janicak et al., 2002) compared rTMS to ECT and results indicated that rTMS and ECT produced similar therapeutic effects. Loo et al. (2001) and Martis et al. (2003) did not find evidence of side effects after a 2- to 4-week course of rTMS in individuals with major depressive disorder supporting that rTMS is safe, at least over a 3- to 4-week period.

Not all studies have supported the use of rTMS in the treatment of depression, however. For example, Martin et al. (2003) conducted a meta-analysis of the effectiveness of rTMS for the treatment of depression and concluded, "There is currently insufficient evidence to suggest that rTMS is effective in the treatment of depression" (p. 483). Indeed, Razza and colleagues (2018) recently conducted a meta-analyses of rTMS compared to sham intervention and reported a large placebo response in rTMS depression trials, suggesting that placebo response likely contributed to improvement in depression symptoms. Given the conflicting findings across studies additional research is warranted to further explore the effectiveness of rTMS at improving depression symptoms either as a sole form of treatment or in the augmentation of pharmacological treatment.

Deep Brain Stimulation

Deep brain stimulation (DBS), as discussed in Chapter 2, involves the implantation of electrodes directly into the brain and the placement of a pulse generator in the chest. DBS is regarded by the FDA as an experimental method for the treatment of major depressive disorder, although a significant number of studies have examined its effectiveness at improving depression symptoms. Similar to rTMS and VNS results have been inconsistent with some studies supporting the efficacy of DBS at improving depression symptoms while others have not (e.g., Barrett, 2017; Cleary et al., 2015; Holtzheimer et al., 2017). Eggers (2014) reported about 50% of patients with treatment resistant depression improve with DBS. Other research has explored whether symptom improvement varies depending on location of electrodes in patients with treatment resistant depression and results suggest that various locations are efficacious at improving symptoms, although the underlying physiological mechanisms contributing to symptom improvement are poorly understood (Beeker et al., 2017). Physiologic theories have suggested that DBS targets dysfunctional networks involving the nucleus accumbens, subgenual cingulate, limbic cortical pathways, facilitates GABA neurotransmission, and/or alters conscious perceptions of emotions (Eggers, 2014; Mayberg et al., 2005). Similar to other brain stimulation interventions for major depressive disorder, additional research is needed to better understand the effects of DBS at the behavioral and physiological levels.

Additional Physiologically Based Interventions

Although empirical studies are more numerous concerning the effectiveness of pharmacological treatments for depression, a number of alternative approaches have also been studied. For example, many studies have reported benefits of the medicinal plant St. John's wort in the treatment of mild to moderate depression comparable to the efficacy and safety of SSRIs (e.g., Kirsch, 2003; Ng XQ et al., 2017). Numerous studies have also attested to the effectiveness of bright-light exposure as well as aerobic exercise in improving depressed mood (e.g., Henderson & Morries, 2017; Leppamaki, Partonen, & Lonnqvist, 2002). Nutritional therapies are more controversial, but some studies have found increased mood stabilization with minerals and other supplements (e.g., Kaplan et al., 2001; Schefft et al., 2017). Use of biofeedback in the treatment of depression has received substantial attention and studies have produced mixed findings (e.g., Hartogs et al., 2017; Marzbani, Marateb, & Mansourian, 2016). Additional, well-designed studies are needed to further explore the effectiveness of physiologically based interventions for the treatment of mild, moderate, and severe forms of major depressive disorder.

Summary of Major Depressive Disorder: Main Points

- The pathophysiology of major depressive disorder remains largely obscure.
- The monoamine theory of major depressive disorder postulates that low levels of serotonin, dopamine, and norepinephrine contribute to a chemical imbalance in the brain that leads to depression symptoms; however, research findings contradict the theory and instead support complex interactions among neurotransmitters systems, receptors, and intracellular changes in the pathophysiology of major depressive disorder.
- Structural neuroimaging studies have produced mixed findings with some studies reporting anatomical differences between participants with and without bipolar disorder in the hippocampus, amygdala, hypothalamus, cerebellum, and other structures, while other studies have not replicated these findings,
- Functional neuroimaging studies have also produced mixed findings with some studies reporting reduced blood flow and glucose metabolism in frontal and limbic regions of participants with bipolar disorder while other studies have not found these differences.
- Antidepressants often improve symptoms of major depressive disorder particularly in those with severe symptoms.
- Some studies have reported that antidepressants are not more effective than placebo in individuals with mild depression although other studies have not replicated these findings.
- Some studies have reported that antidepressants are associated with increased risk of suicide ideation in children and adolescents, although other studies have not replicated these findings.
- Heritability studies suggest that genes likely play a role in the susceptibility of major depression although no single gene has been found to confer a high degree of risk for the disorder.
- The neuroplasticity theory of major depressive disorder proposes that the disorder is due in part to stress induced death of neurons and glial cells followed by decreased neurogenesis, synaptogenesis, and production of neurotrophic factors.
- Environmental factors are hypothesized to contribute to the risk of major depressive disorder by altering functioning of the HPA axis and triggering an inflammatory immune response.

- Brain stimulation methods including ECT, rTMS, and DBS have been found to improve symptoms in individuals with treatment resistant major depressive disorder.
- The pathophysiology of major depressive disorder appears to be complex and likely involves interactions among genetic, cellular, morphological, neurochemical, psychological, and environmental factors.

Bipolar Disorder

Prevalence and Demographic Information

The American Psychiatric Association separates bipolar and related disorders from depressive disorders in the *DSM-V* and places them between schizophrenia and psychotic disorders. Although a number of bipolar and related disorders are identified in the *DSM-V*, the following section focuses on bipolar I disorder. The distinguishing feature between major depressive disorder and bipolar disorder I is the presence of mania. A manic episode is characterized by an abnormally and persistently elevated, expansive, or irritable mood, along with increased energy or activity present daily for at least one week. These symptoms cause impairment and may be preceded or followed by major depressive episodes (see *DSM-V* for additional diagnostic information).

According to the American Psychiatric Association (APA, 2013) less than 1% (0.6) of people in the United States experience bipolar disorder (during a 12-month period). The ratio of males to females is 1.1:1, and the mean onset is 18 years of age, although the disorder does occur in children and in later life. Individuals with bipolar disorder are 15 times at greater risk for suicide than the general population (Pandey, 2013). Families of individuals with bipolar disorder compared to those without the disorder tend to have greater family conflict, less expressiveness of emotions, and less cohesiveness (Reinares et al., 2016). Information concerning cultural differences in the occurrence and expression of bipolar disorder are limited; however, recent findings have revealed marked disparities in treatment of Hispanic and non-Hispanic whites. Specifically, Salcedo, McMaster, and Johnson (2017) found Hispanics were less likely to receive medications for emotional problems, receive professional treatment for manic episodes, or participate in psychotherapy, and 0% compared to 21% of non-Hispanic whites were taking mood stabilizers at the time of the study. Similar inadequate treatment findings have been reported for African Americans compared to whites with bipolar disorder (Johnson & Johnson, 2014). Other studies have compared offspring of patients with bipolar disorder living in the United States relative to the Netherlands and found higher levels of psychopathology and medical problems in US offspring (Mesman et al., 2016; Post et al., 2014). Quality of life studies in Iran have found lower quality among individuals with bipolar disorder relative to controls and relative to those with bipolar II disorder (Modabbernia et al., 2016). Studies have also reported higher levels of stigmatizing experiences of individuals with bipolar disorder living in Canada and South Korea (Lee, Milev, & Paik, 2015)

The disorder is often accompanied by associated problems, such as occupational failure, marital difficulties, school failure, neuropsychological impairment, substance use and abuse, anxiety disorders (e.g., panic disorder, social phobia), ADHD, and eating disorders (e.g., bulimia nervosa, binge eating) (e.g., Basso et al., 2002; Boulanger et al., 2018; Freeman, Freeman, & McElroy, 2002; MacKinnon et al., 2002; Sharma et al., 2017). For example, MacKinnon et al.

(2002) reported that more than a third of individuals with bipolar disorder or major depression had experienced at least one panic attack, and panic disorder was diagnosed more frequently in families of individuals with bipolar disorder relative to a control group. According to Yildiz and Sachs (2003), psychotic symptoms are also common in bipolar disorder.

With respect to education, family, and occupational status, Kupfer and colleagues (2002) studied 2,839 patients with bipolar disorder and found that 85% were hospitalized at least once (43% for mania episodes and 69% for depressive episodes). Greater than 50% had attempted suicide and most attempts occurred during a depressed episode. One-third of the sample was married; one-third were never married; the remaining participants were divorced, widowed, or separated. Approximately 45% had children under the age of 18. More than 90% of the group had completed high school, and 11% had earned a graduate or professional degree. Nearly 65%, however, were unemployed at the time of the study and 40% were receiving public assistance or disability support. Over 17% of the sample had received ECT and 75% were taking one to three medications (40% were taking anticonvulsants, one-third lithium, and 25% benzodiazepine). According to Kupfer et al., over 50% of the participants reported having at least one family member with bipolar disorder and/or depression. The mean age of onset of bipolar disorder was 19.8 years, with the majority reporting depression as the first episode experienced. Over 50% of the sample reported that they did not receive any treatment during their first episode of depression or mania. Of those who did receive treatment, 28.2% were hospitalized, one-third received medication, and one-third received psychotherapy. Collectively, these findings are consistent with other studies that indicate that bipolar disorder has a relatively early onset and tends to run in families. Findings also suggest that most individuals with the disorder attain a high school education or above but do not maintain employment in adulthood and that bipolar disorder is a chronic condition characterized by social, interpersonal, and occupational struggles.

Genetic Findings

Family and Twin Studies

Bipolar disorder tends to run in families and genetic studies have consistently reported a high heritability estimate for bipolar disorder. According to Smoller and Fin (2003), first-degree relatives of an individual with bipolar disorder have a tenfold risk of developing bipolar disorder compared to relatives of control participants. Heritability estimates vary slightly across studies and range from 85% to 93% (Craddock et al., 2013; McGuffin et al., 2003). Further support for a heritability component of bipolar disorder comes from twin studies; twin studies have reported consistently higher concordance rates for monozygotic twins with bipolar relative to dizygotic twin pairs (e.g., 0.79 for monozygotic and 0.19 for dizygotic twin pairs) (Bertelsen, Harvald, & Hauge, 1977; Kendler et al., 1995; McGuffin et al., 2003). Further, Bootsman and colleagues (2015) and Squarcina et al. (2016) studied over 200 twin pairs and found a higher heritability of size of brain structures in identical versus fraternal twins. Adoption studies also support a heritability component for bipolar disorder; the incidence of the disorder is higher in biological parents compared to adoptive parents of children who later develop bipolar disorder (Smoller & Fin, 2003).

Linkage and Association Studies

Similar to major depressive disorder, linkage studies have focused on families with members with bipolar disorder in order to attempt to identify gene variants that confer a high degree of risk of developing bipolar disorder. Genome wide association studies have scanned complete sets of DNA seeking genetic variations associated with bipolar disorder in hundreds of thousands of individuals. Results from linkage studies have produced a number of chromosomal regions of interest and meta-analyses have linked bipolar disorder in non-Hispanic whites and individuals of Latino ancestry to regions on several chromosomes including 1, 4, 8, 10, 11, 12, 13, 14, 16, 17, 18, and 22 (e.g., Badner & Gershon, 2002; Berrettini et al., 1994; Blackwood et al., 1996; Buttenschøn et al., 2010; Detera-Wadleigh et al., 1999; Egeland et al., 1987; Ewald et al., 1995; Foroud et al., 2000; Gonzalez et al., 2014; McMahon et al., 2001; Ophoff et al., 2002; Potash et al., 2003; Rajkumar et al., 2015). However, none of the linkage studies have identified a region or loci that confers a high degree of risk for developing bipolar disorder. Genome wide scans have also identified a number of susceptibility alleles (e.g., CACNA1C, GRIN2D, NCAN, SYNE1) but none have been identified as causal or warrant genetic testing for the disorder (Gasso et al., 2016; Sharp et al., 2017). These findings support that the etiology of the disorder is currently poorly understood and likely genetically complex.

Candidate Genes

A large number have candidate genes have been identified a priori and studied for their potential role in the heritability of bipolar disorder. For example, due to pharmacological agents that target specific neurotransmitter systems and produce symptom improvement in patients with bipolar disorder, many studies have focused on genes that are specifically involved in neurotransmitter functioning. For example, as discussed previously in this chapter the enzyme catechol-O-methyltransferase (COMT) deactivates monoamines (e.g., dopamine and norepinephrine), and the gene that encodes this enzyme has received considerable attention over the years. Polymorphisms of this gene (e.g., Val158Met) have been associated with reduced dopamine in the prefrontal cortex of individuals with bipolar disorder, rapid-cycling episodes, and cognitive impairments (e.g., Lachman, Morrow, et al., 1996a; Tunbridge et al., 2004; Kirov et al., 1998; Lachman, Papolos, et al., 1996b; Miskowiak et al., 2017; Taylor, 2018). Although these findings are encouraging, it is important to note that these same polymorphisms have been implicated in other psychiatric disorders (e.g., schizophrenia, autism) and hence are not unique to bipolar disorder.

BDNF has also been implicated in bipolar disorder and a polymorphism (Val66MET) of the BDNF gene has been associated with increased susceptibility to bipolar disorder in children and adolescents (Geller et al., 2004). Recently, Pereira et al. (2017) conducted a systematic review of 26 gene variants in bipolar disorder studies and concluded that individuals with bipolar disorder who carried a particular gene variant related to BDNF (BDNF Val66Met) were more likely to have smaller hippocampal volumes compared to non-carriers. Similar to other candidate genes, this particular polymorphism has been associated with other disorders such as obsessive-compulsive disorder (Geller et al., 2004; Reshma Jabeen Taj et al., 2017).

Genes that regulate the neurotransmitter serotonin have also been investigated in bipolar disorder, largely due to findings that suggest antidepressants can induce mania in 20% or more of individuals with bipolar disorder (e.g. Angst, 1985; Karlović & Serretti, 2013; Kwok & Lim, 2017; Solomon, Rich, & Darko, 1990). Given that most antidepressants affect the serotonin system, researchers have speculated that abnormal serotonergic functioning may increase vulnerability to bipolar disorder. Mundo et al. (2001) investigated the prevalence of a polymorphism of the serotonin transporter gene (SLC6A4) in 27 patients with bipolar disorder who experienced antidepressant-induced mania relative to 29 bipolar patients who had been treated with antidepressants but did not experience mania. Results indicated that 63% of patients with induced mania showed a particular polymorphism (5HTTLPR) compared to 29% of the bipolar patients who did not experience antidepressant-induced mania. Additional studies have supported a link between the 5HTTLPR polymorphism and bipolar disorder including the age of onset of the disorder (Buoli, Serati, & Cahn, 2016; Etain et al., 2015). As with other polymorphisms discussed, 5HTTLPR is not unique to bipolar disorder.

The gene that regulates the somatostatin receptor has also been explored in bipolar disorder for over a decade. Somatostatin functions as a neuropeptide in the brain and helps to modulate the release of neurotransmitters and other neuropeptides. Nyegaard et al. (2002) considered whether polymorphisms of the gene that regulates the somatostatin receptor were associated with bipolar disorder given that somatostatin receptors interact with dopamine receptors and enhance binding of neurotransmitters to the receptors (and dopamine antagonists are sometimes used to treat bipolar disorder). Results supported a linkage between the somatostatin gene variant and bipolar disorder, and recently, Pantazopoulos et al. (2017) found decreased numbers of somatostatin expressing neurons in the amygdala of participants with bipolar disorder. Studies have also explored the role of the gene that regulates a glutamate receptor (N-methyl-D-aspartate receptor, NDMAR) in bipolar disorder largely due to the fact that mood stabilizers, such as lithium and valproate, are often used to treat bipolar disorder and these drugs affect glutamate transmission (Mundo et al., 2003; Surget et al., 2006).

Additional candidate genes have been investigated, and although several chromosomal regions and candidate genes have generated intense interest and have been linked to bipolar disorder, to date, no robust, conclusive findings have yet emerged from the literature (Amare et al., 2017). For example, Bigdeli and colleagues (2013) studied 83 candidate genes and reported that no one gene was statistically associated with bipolar disorder. These findings are somewhat perplexing given that familial studies clearly support a strong heritability component for bipolar disorder. It is plausible that bipolar disorder involves multiple genes working singly or in combination, or that two or more gene variants (e.g., serotonin transporters and COMT) may result in physiological conditions that increase vulnerability to bipolar disorder. It is also possible that a single gene variant may play a role in multiple psychiatric disorders depending on environmental and physiologic factors. As Craddock and Sklar (2013) stated,

> The association between genotype and phenotype for psychiatric disorders is clearly complex. Reductionist thinking has no place and to think of any case as being either genetic or environmental, or to talk about a gene for bipolar disorder, makes no sense.
> (Craddock & Sklar, 2013, p. 1655)

Structural Findings

Similar to major depressive disorder, structural imaging studies regarding anatomical differences between patients with and without bipolar disorder have produced mixed results. Bipolar studies have explored a number of anatomical structures, including the hippocampus, thalamus, basal ganglia, amygdala, whole brain volume, and size of the ventricles.

With respect to ventricular size, many studies, including meta-analyses, have found increased ventricular size in the right, left, or both right/left lateral ventricles, and in the third ventricle in participants with bipolar disorder relative to control participants (e.g., Lim et al., 1999; Kempton et al., 2008; Wise et al., 2017; Zipursky et al., 1997), but other studies have not found evidence of ventricular size difference in those with bipolar disorder compared to control participants (e.g., Brambilla et al., 2001). Andreasen et al. (1990) found increased ventricular size in male patients with bipolar disorder relative to those with depression and healthy controls, and this difference was unrelated to previous ECT or medication history. A meta-analysis conducted by Arnone et al. (2009) found the lateral ventricles were smaller in participants with bipolar disorder compared to those with schizophrenia. In contrast, Lewine and colleagues found evidence of ventricular abnormalities only in males with schizophrenia relative to participants with depression, bipolar disorder, and controls. Collectively, these findings suggest that individuals with bipolar disorder are more likely to have enlarged cerebral ventricles compared to control participants and smaller ventricular size relative to individuals with schizophrenia; however, enlarged cerebral ventricles are characteristic of other psychiatric and medical disorders.

Studies exploring other brain structures including whole brain, prefrontal regions, globus pallidus, amygdala, thalamus, and postmortem cellular morphology have also produced conflicting results (Z. Peng et al., 2012). For example, meta-analytic findings by McDonald et al. (2004) did not find significant differences in total brain volume, whole brain gray or white matter, or for the volume of any of the cortical, subcortical, or limbic structures between participants with bipolar disorder relative to and healthy comparison participants. Similarly, Kempton et al. (2008) analyzed 98 structural imaging studies of participants with bipolar disorder and found across the studies, 377 different regions or abnormalities were measured, but only 47 of these were analyzed by 3 or more studies. Findings revealed very few structural differences between participants with bipolar disorder other than the lateral ventricles and increased lesions of the frontal and parietal lobes. In contrast, Arnone et al. (2009) reported global and prefrontal volumetric brain reductions, enlarged lateral ventricles, and an enlarged globus pallidus in individuals with bipolar disorder compared to controls. Arnone and colleagues also noted that whole gray matter volume correlated with duration of bipolar disorder with and use of antipsychotic medication. These findings suggest that individuals with longer durations of bipolar disorder, particularly those who use antipsychotic medication, are more likely to have distinct anatomical brain differences compared to those without the disorder. However, Kempton et al., emphasized that their meta-analytic findings did not support that age at onset, use of medication, or duration of illness was associated with increased ventricular enlargement. In fact, Ali et al. (2001) explored the severity of symptoms of bipolar disorder with the size of the hippocampus, temporal lobes, third ventricles, and lateral ventricles using MRI and found that greater duration of the disorder and severity of symptoms were associated with a significantly *larger*—rather than smaller—left temporal lobe. Similar to structural findings in living individuals with bipolar disorder, postmortem studies have produced conflicting results with some studies reporting a decrease in neuronal and/or glial cell density in specific regions (e.g., prefrontal) and structures (e.g., amygdala, hippocampus), while other studies have not reported these differences (e.g., Benes et al., 2001; Cotter et al., 2001, Keshavarz, 2017; Ongur, Drevets, & Price, 1998).

In summary, a number of structural differences have been found in living and postmortem brains of individuals with bipolar disorder relative to those without the disorder. These findings have been inconsistent, however, and are likely influenced by a number of methodological and statistical factors. It is important to emphasize that when anatomical differences are found between participants with bipolar disorder relative to controls; it is unclear whether these differences occur before, during, or after onset of the disorder. Further, none of the structural abnormalities found in individuals with bipolar disorder are unique to the disorder and are sometimes found in other psychiatric disorders and medical conditions. A crucial point is that current findings are inconclusive and are only correlational in nature—i.e., they do not reflect underlying etiology nor are they necessarily directly related to clinical symptomatology. The etiology of structural abnormalities sometimes found in bipolar disorder is unknown but may reflect neurodevelopmental abnormalities or cellular degeneration over the course of the disorder due to environmental or physiologic factors. Most past and current studies employ a cross-sectional design and longitudinal studies are needed to clarify the emergence of structural differences.

Neurotransmitter Studies

Nearly every major neurotransmitter system has been implicated in bipolar disorder, including serotonin, dopamine, norepinephrine, GABA, and glutamate (Shi et al., 2008). For example, postmortem studies have found reductions in serotonin metabolites in the frontal and parietal regions (e.g., Young et al., 1994), and cerebral spinal fluid studies of living individuals with bipolar disorder have also reported significantly lower levels of serotonin metabolites (e.g., Asberg et al., 1984; Polettiet al., 2016). With respect to serotonin transporters, Leake and colleagues (1991) reported fewer serotonin reuptake sites in postmortem samples of bipolar patients. Several studies have reported increased glutamate levels in the frontal regions of the brain and in the cerebral spinal fluid relative to control participants (Ehrlich et al., 2015; Palsson, et al., 2015). GABA has also been implicated in bipolar disorder. For example, Petty et al. (1993) reported that GABA plasma levels were significantly reduced in patients with bipolar disorder (mania and depression) and in patients with major depression. However, similar research by Roy, Dejong, and Ferraro (1991) did not find differences in cerebral spinal fluid GABA metabolites. Recently researchers have reported on metabolome analysis—a method used to measure small molecules in blood plasma of patients with bipolar disorder. For example, Kageyama and colleagues (2017) found that levels of the amino acid citrulline were lower in participants with bipolar disorder relative to controls. Citrulline is purported to be a biomarker of mitochondria dysfunction, and molecular anomaly theories, including mitrochondria dysfunction, have recently proposed for bipolar disorder (Kim, Santos, et al., 2017).

Other monoamines have also been implicated in bipolar disorder. Ali and Milev (2003), for example, reported that abrupt antidepressant withdrawal, along with drugs that result in excessive levels of monoamines, are associated with the induction of manic symptoms. Bhanji et al. (2002) reported that the antidepressant mirtazapine, which blocks serotonin and norepinephrine autoreceptors, induces mania in some individuals. Bunney and Garland (1982) proposed that dopamine abnormalities may be implicated in bipolar disorder, given that dopamine agonists can induce manic like symptoms and antagonists can reduce mania and sometimes improve symptoms of depression (Goldberg, Burdick, & Endick, 2004). Overall, however, metabolite studies of patients with bipolar disorder have been inconsistent (Yildiz et al., 2001).

Functional Studies

With respect to functional neuroimaging studies, a plethora of studies have been conducted in an attempt to understand the underlying neurophysiological processes involved in bipolar disorder. Numerous glucose metabolism and blood flow studies are available concerning the performance of individuals with bipolar disorder relative to those with other disorders and control groups during cognitive tasks or at rest. Similar to the neuroimaging findings with major depressive disorder, glucose metabolism and blood flow differences have been found between those with and without bipolar disorder—but the findings have been inconsistent (e.g., Gonul, Coburn, & Kula, 2009; Ketter et al., 2001; Nobler et al., 1994; Rubin et al., 1995; Tutus et al., 1998).

An early study by O'Connell et al. (1995) used brain imaging (SPECT) with 11 individuals with bipolar disorder and found significantly higher levels of serotonin reuptake in these individuals relative to control participants. Later review studies (e.g., Mahmood & Silverstone, 2001) concluded that serotonin activity was frequently reduced during the depression state of bipolar disorder, but findings were inconsistent concerning serotonin and periods of mania. Similarly, elevated dopamine receptor binding (DAT and postsynaptic receptors) has been reported in individuals with bipolar disorder (Pearlson et al., 1995; Savits & Drevets, 2013). In addition, several studies have also reported blood flow and glucose abnormalities in the basal ganglia (an area rich in dopamine) of individuals with bipolar disorder (Caliguri et al., 2003; Loonen et al., 2017). Given these findings, Ashok, Marques, et al. (2017) recently proposed that a failure of dopamine receptor and transporter homoeostasis might underlie the pathophysiology of bipolar disorder.

Aside from receptor binding studies, neuroimaging studies using PET, SPECT, fMRI, and other technologies have studied level of activity in various regions of the brain of participants with bipolar disorder. Given that bipolar disorder is characterized by episodes of major depression as well as mania, researchers have focused on regions and structures believed to underlie cognitive and emotional processes problematic in patients with bipolar disorder, including prefrontal regions and subcortical pathways involved in decision-making, planning, and emotional regulation (Smucny et al., 2017). Although findings are inconsistent across studies, some studies have reported increased activity (blood flow, glucose metabolism) in the left ventrolateral prefrontal cortex and orbitofrontal cortex during anticipation of rewards in patients with bipolar disorder, relative to control participants (Dutra et al., 2017). These findings suggest that individuals with bipolar disorder may have heightened reward sensitivity that may in turn predispose them to mania (Phillips & Swartz, 2014).

Other studies have found increased activity in the amygdala and medial prefrontal cortex activity and decreased activity in frontal regions, as well as the amygdala during emotional recognition tasks (happy, sad, angry, etc., faces) and during resting states relative to control participants further supporting dysfunctional frontal-limbic connectivity (Surguladze et al., 2010; Wang, Wang, et al., 2017). Phillips and Swartz (2014) interpreted the neuroimaging data as indicative of neural circuitry pathology in patients with bipolar disorder stating,

> Bipolar disorder can thus be conceptualized in neural circuitry terms as parallel dysfunction in bilateral prefrontal cortical (especially ventrolateral prefrontal cortex and orbitofrontal cortex)—hippocampal-amygdala emotion processing and emotion regulation neural circuitries, together with an "overactive" left-sided ventral striatal-ventrolateral prefrontal cortex reward processing circuitry, that may, together, result in the characteristic behavioral abnormalities associated with bipolar disorder: emotional lability, emotional dysregulation and reward sensitivity.
>
> (Phillips & Swartz, 2014, p. 7)

This conclusion seems premature, however, given that other researchers have not found reliable functional differences in brain activation patterns between patients with bipolar disorder relative to healthy control participants (Birur et al., 2017).

Future research is clearly warranted to better understand potential functional brain differences between individuals with and without bipolar disorder. Ideally, future studies will involve well-designed, longitudinal studies with large sample sizes and control over demographic variables, such as age of onset, severity of symptoms, sex, ethnicity, and medication usage. In addition, corroboration across different types of neuroimaging techniques and cognitive tasks would help to establish the validity and reliability of neuroimaging findings.

Molecular Processes

As discussed in Chapter 2, a variety of intracellular processes are involved in a neuron's ability to receive, process, and respond to information, including complex signaling pathways of second-messenger systems. Abnormalities in signaling pathways have received considerable attention in bipolar disorder. For example, Bezchlibnyk and Young (2002) reviewed studies that used either blood samples or postmortem brain tissue of individuals with bipolar disorder and concluded that the disorder is likely due, at least in part, to abnormalities in signal transduction pathways. Specifically, altered levels of functioning of intracellular G-proteins, protein kinase A, and protein kinase C have been associated with bipolar disorder (e.g., A. Chang, Li, & Warsh, 2003) and lithium and anticonvulsants used to treat bipolar disorder are believed to target second-messenger systems (Stewart et al., 2001; Young, 1993, 2001).

As mentioned previously in this chapter, a current pathophysiologic theory of bipolar disorder relates to mitochondria, organelles that are critical for energy production and, consequently, normal cellular functioning (Iwamoto et al., 2004; Kim, Santos, et al., 2017). Molecular studies have found reduced levels of substances necessary for ATP synthesis and mitochondria functioning (e.g., phosphocreatine, citrulline), particularly in the frontal cortex of individuals with bipolar disorder relative to controls (Frey et al., 2007; Kageyama et al., 2017). Other researchers have focused on the role of autophagy in bipolar disorder, dysregulation of circadian rhythms, and density of neurons and glial cells in individuals with bipolar disorder. For example, in 2004 Uranova and colleagues found a 29% reduction of glial cells (oligodendroglia) in the prefrontal cortex of individuals with bipolar disorder relative to controls. Others have explored whether the normal process of autophagy (self-digestion of old or damaged parts of the cell including organelles) is dysfunctional in bipolar disorder. Interestingly, lithium, the most established long-term treatment for bipolar disorder, is thought to help enhance or regulate autophagy (Motoi et al., 2014). Although the role of molecular processes in bipolar disorder is inconclusive, in recent years, there has been a substantial shift in the literature from investigating levels of monoamines to exploring the molecular mechanisms of bipolar disorder (Kim, Santos, et al., 2017).

Pharmacological Treatment of Bipolar Disorder

Medications used in the treatment of bipolar disorder include (a) mood stabilizers (e.g., lithium, carbamazepine), (b) antipsychotic medications (e.g., quetiapine), (c) antidepressants (e.g., fluoxetine), and (d) antianxiety medications (e.g., Xanax). These classifications are based on the chemical structure of the drug as well as the effect of the drug. For example, anticonvulsants differ in their chemical structure from lithium, but they have mood-stabilizing properties. Based on meta-analytic studies, lithium is considered the most effective long-term pharmacological treatment of bipolar disorder and is often prescribed in conjunction with antipsychotic medications (Bauer & Mitchner, 2004; Connolly & Thase, 2011; Goodwin et al., 2016).

As discussed in Chapter 2, the precise mode of action of lithium is unknown but research suggests that it affects multiple signaling pathways and cellular processes and promotes neuroplasticity (e.g., increases neurotrophic factors, synaptogenesis, regulates autophagy) (Alda, 2015). The mode of action of anticonvulsants (e.g., carbamazepine, divalproex) is also unclear, but research suggests they inhibit norepinephrine reuptake and block sodium channels (Heinze & Grunz, 2010). The effectiveness of lithium and anticonvulsants varies among individuals depending on a number of factors including severity of symptoms, comorbidity, sex, and ethnicity (Connolly & Thase, 2011; Goodwin et al., 2016; Sit, 2004).

Antipsychotic medications are recommended when symptoms persist despite treatment with a mood stabilizer. Research supports the effectiveness of antipsychotic medication used in combination with mood stabilizers at improving bipolar symptoms and regulating mood (Connolly & Thase, 2011; Poon et al., 2015). Antipsychotic and other medications frequently used in the treatment of bipolar disorder are presented in Table 6.2. Extensive empirically supported treatment guidelines for use of antipsychotic medications (and others) in the treatment of bipolar disorder are recommended by Goodwin and colleagues (2016).

Antidepressant medications are used judiciously as adjuncts to mood stabilizers due to their potential to exacerbate or induce mania symptoms and precipitate rapid cycling in individuals with bipolar disorder (Salvadore et al., 2010). For example, Ghaemi and colleagues (2004) compared outcomes of a wide range of antidepressant trials with 41 patients with bipolar disorder and 37 patients with major depression and reported that mania was induced in 48.8% of patients with bipolar disorder, and rapid cycling was accelerated in 25.6% of the bipolar patients (neither of these symptoms occurred in any of the patients

Table 6.2 Examples of Medications Used to Treat Bipolar Disorder

Mood Stabilizers

Lithium (Lithobid)

Valproic acid (Depakene)

Divalproex sodium (Depakote)

Carbamazepine (Tegretol)

Lamotrigine (Lamictal)

Antipsychotics

Olanzapine (Zyprexa)

Risperidone (Risperdal)

Quetiapine (Seroquel)

Aripiprazole (Abilify)

Ziprasidone (Geodon)

Lurasidone (Latuda)

Asenapine (Saphris)

with major depression). In addition, tolerance (i.e., loss of favorable response) was 3.4 times as frequent in patients with bipolar disorder compared to those with major depression. As Goodwin et al. and others have stated, use of antidepressants in the treatment of bipolar disorder should be individually determined.

It has been estimated that 20% or more of individuals with bipolar disorder have comorbid panic disorder (MacKinnon et al., 2002), and many are prescribed benzodiazepines in addition to mood stabilizers. Long-term use of benzodiazepines can lead to tolerance, addiction, withdrawal, and possibly neurotoxicity, and short-term use is typically recommended (Goodwin et al., 2016; Michelini et al., 1996).

Brain Stimulation

Brain stimulation techniques, such as ECT, DBS, and rTMS discussed previously in this chapter are studied less often with bipolar disorder relative to major depressive disorder. However, recent research found ECT was effective in patients with treatment resistant bipolar disorder, with nearly 69% responding favorably to the treatment (Perugi et al., 2017). ECT has also been found to decrease remission rates in patients with bipolar disorder based on meta-analytic findings (Dierckx et al., 2012). Rostami and colleagues (2017) found that rTMS improved bipolar symptoms in 41% of participants and that younger participants with bipolar disorder showed the most improvement. Other studies have also supported the use of rTMS with patients with bipolar disorder. Only a few studies have explored the effectiveness of DBS in the treatment of bipolar disorder, and Gippert and colleagues (2017) recently conducted a systematic review of these studies and reported that DBS was effective at improving symptoms in 100% of patients with treatment resistant bipolar disorder. Lastly, preliminary studies have supported the effectiveness of transcranial direct current stimulation (tDCS) in the treatment of bipolar disorders. tDCS is a noninvasive technique in which a weak electrical current is applied on the scalp and is believed to hyperpolarize and depolarize neurons, leading to increased (or decreased) neuronal activity. Like rTMS, the specific mode of action of tDS is unknown but is hypothesized to affect neurotransmitter systems. Brunoni et al. (2011) were the first to study the effectiveness of tDS in 14 patients with bipolar disorder who received five stimulation sessions, 20 minutes each, twice per day for 5 days. Participants were evaluated at baseline and followed up for a period of one month after treatment onset. Results revealed that the treatment was immediately effective at improving symptoms, the improvement was sustained at follow-up, and no adverse side effects were reported. Additional studies using more diverse and larger sample sizes are needed to further explore the effectiveness of brain stimulation techniques in the treatment of bipolar disorder.

Summary of Bipolar Disorder: Main Points

■ Bipolar disorder occurs more often in first-degree relatives with a heritability estimate of approximately 85%.

■ A number of susceptibility genes have been identified for bipolar disorder, but to date none have been identified that confer a high degree of risk.

■ Several neurotransmitter systems have been implicated in bipolar disorder, and given the effectiveness of mood stabilizers and anticonvulsant medications at reducing manic symptoms, these systems likely play a role in the pathophysiology of bipolar disorder.

- Both structural and functional neuroimaging studies have reported differences in brain anatomy and function in individuals with bipolar disorder relative to control participants, but these findings have been inconsistent across studies.
- It is critical to note that structural and functional findings are based on correlational studies and therefore do not reveal causation.
- Preliminary molecular studies implicate a variety of intracellular processes in the pathophysiology of bipolar disorder.
- Additional genetic, neuroanatomical, neurochemical, functional, and molecular studies are needed to better understand the pathophysiological substrates of bipolar disorder as well as the effect of environmental factors on the expression of the disorder.
- Methodological differences in sample size, participant selection, imaging protocol, statistical analyses, and demographic characteristics of participants, including age, sex, ethnicity, severity of illness, medication usage and history, and comorbid disorders likely contribute to inconsistent findings across studies.

Review Questions

1. What can be concluded at this time about the etiology of major depressive disorder? Bipolar disorder?
2. Which neurotransmitter systems appear to be implicated the most in major depressive disorder and bipolar disorder? Explain based on genetic, neurotransmitter, and pharmacological treatments.
3. Consider the information covered in Chapter 5 regarding schizophrenia. How do those genetic, structural, and functional findings compare to bipolar research findings?
4. Compare and contrast non-pharmacological, physiologically based treatments for major depressive disorder and bipolar disorder. What is your perspective on the use of each of these techniques?

seven

Anxiety Disorder and Obsessive-Compulsive Disorder

Anxiety disorders share symptoms of feelings of excessive fear, anxiety, and changes in behavior. The American Psychiatric Association defines fear as "the emotional response to real or perceived imminent threat" while anxiety involves the "anticipation of future threat" (APA *DSM-V*, 2013 p. 189). As noted by Crocq (2015), the nosology of anxiety has a long history extending back to Greek and Latin physicians and philosophers who identified anxiety as a medical disorder. Modern psychiatry also views anxiety disorders largely from a medical perspective. Anxiety disorders identified by the American Psychiatric Association (APA *DSM-V*, 2013) include separation anxiety disorder, selective mutism, specific phobia, social anxiety disorder, panic disorder, agoraphobia, GAD, substance/medication-induced anxiety disorder, and other and unspecified anxiety disorder. Anxiety disorders are distinguished by developmental factors as well as the situations that induce fear, anxiety, and avoidant behaviors. Obsessive compulsive disorder is no longer classified as an anxiety disorder and instead appears under obsessive-compulsive and related disorders. Given the voluminous amount of research findings available regarding anxiety disorders and OCD, this chapter focuses on two disorders: panic disorder and obsessive-compulsive disorder (OCD).

Like previous chapters, this chapter presents background, genetic, structural, and functional findings associated with each disorder. Although a plethora of information is available concerning therapy approaches for these disorders, this information is beyond the scope of this text and will not be presented. In keeping with the nature of the text, the primary focus will be on physiologically based treatment approaches for panic disorder and OCD.

Chapter 7 Learning Objectives

- Describe demographic findings concerning panic disorder and OCD.
- Describe multicultural findings for both disorders.
- Describe genetic findings for panic disorder and OCD, including research concerning heritability and candidate genes.
- Describe pharmacological treatment of both disorders.

BOX 7.1   Does Worrying Affect Mortality Risk?

Catherine Gale, a psychology professor at the University of Edinburgh, and colleagues explored the association between "neuroticism" and mortality and the influence of self-rated health on this relationship in a sample of 321,456 people from the United Kingdom. Neuroticism refers to the tendency to experience negative emotions and in this study was measured by the Neuroticism Scale of the Eysenck Personality Questionnaire—Revised. Participants also rated their overall level of health. Results revealed a number of interesting findings: (a) higher neuroticism was associated with a 6% increase in mortality risk, (b) neuroticism scores tended to be lower with increasing age, (c) neuroticism scores were positively correlated with smoking and drinking alcohol daily or nearly daily, and (d) among people who rated their health as poor or fair, higher neuroticism was associated with a reduced mortality from all causes, but such an effect was not observed in participants with excellent self-rated health. What is the take away from this study? Overall people who rate themselves as experiencing higher levels of negative emotions appear to have a greater risk of dying at an earlier age. However, people who rate their health as fair or poor and report worrying about their health have a reduced rate of mortality. Therefore, certain personality facets of neuroticism may actually serve as a protective factor against death (Gale et al., 2017).

Panic Disorder

Background Information

The distinguishing feature of panic disorder is the presence of recurrent, unexpected panic attacks. A panic attack is characterized by "an abrupt surge of intense fear or intense discomfort that reaches a peak within minutes and during which time four or more additional symptoms occur" (*DSM-V*, p. 208). Additional symptoms include physiological changes, such as increased heart rate or palpitations, sweating, trembling, chest discomfort, dizziness, fear of losing control, and fear of dying. Furthermore, individuals with the disorder worry about additional panic attacks occurring and substantially alter their behavior to try to avoid experiencing another panic attack. According to the American Psychiatric Association (2013), the lifetime prevalence rate of panic disorder (PD) in the United States in the general population is between 2% and 3%, and higher in clinical samples. The disorder occurs more often in females than males with a ratio of approximately 2:1 (APA, 2013; Carlbring et al., 2002) and even higher rates are found among postmenopausal women (Colenda et al., 2010; Smoller et al., 2003). The frequency and severity of panic attacks vary widely among individuals, with the age of onset typically between adolescence and adulthood, with a median age of onset between 20 and 24 years.

Comorbidity and Multicultural Findings

African Americans, Latinos, and Asian Americans have reported lower rates of panic disorder compared to non-Latino whites (APA, 2013; Levine et al., 2013). Some studies have found slightly higher rates of panic disorder among American Indians while others have not (APA, 2013; Neligh et al., 1990; Sawchuk et al., 2016). Studies have also reported higher rates of panic disorder among gay, lesbian, and bisexual adults in the United States (Cochran, Sullivan, & Mays, 2003). Panic disorder occurs throughout the world, and European countries report similar prevalence rates as the USA, while lower rates have been reported in Latin America, Asia, Africa, and India (Gater et al., 1998; Carlbring et al., 2002; Hollifield, Finley, & Skipper, 2003; Neerakal & Srinivasan, 2003).

Panic disorder is often comorbid with other anxiety disorders (e.g., GAD, simple phobias, social phobia) as well as other clinical disorders, such as substance abuse, major depressive disorder, and bipolar disorder (Ahmad, Mufti, & Farooq, 2001; Freeman et al., 2002; Pary et al., 2003; Goodwin, Fergusson, & Horwood, 2004). Panic disorder also commonly occurs with chronic medical conditions such as cardiovascular disease, hypertension, pulmonary disease, lipid disorders, and asthma (Machado et al., 2017; McLaughlin, Geissler, & Wan, 2003; Karajgi et al., 1990).

Genetic Findings

Heritability: Family and Twin Findings

Family and twin studies support a genetic influence in the development of panic disorder. Kendler et al. (1993), for example, reported a heritability estimate of 30% to 40% for panic disorder in a population-based twin registry of 2,163 women. Skre and colleagues (1993) examined the prevalence of anxiety disorders in a sample of 20 monozygotic and 29 dizygotic twins and found the concordance ratio for panic disorder in monozygotic twins relative to dizygotic twins was greater than 2:1. Weissman (1993) reported population-based lifetime rates of panic disorder range from 1.2/100 to 2.4/100, while the lifetime rates for first-degree relatives of those with panic disorder was substantially higher (7.7/100–20.5/100). A meta-analysis of family and twin studies conducted by Hettema, Neale, and Kendler (2001) concluded that panic disorder has a significant heritability component (0.48). Collectively, these studies support that genetic factors likely contribute to the development of panic disorder and linkage studies have explored chromosomal regions that might harbor susceptibility genes for panic disorder.

Linkage Studies and Candidate Genes

A number of linkage studies have been conducted with panic disorder and several chromosomal regions have been identified as locations of interest that might harbor susceptibility genes involving chromosomes 2, 4, 7, 10, 13, 15, 17, and 18 (Gratacòs et al., 2001; Fyer et al., 2012; Hamilton, Fyer, et al., 2003; Hamilton et al., 2004). Similar to other disorders discussed in this text, some studies have reported linkage between specific loci and panic disorder; however, findings have been equivocal. For example, Hamilton and colleagues found evidence linking panic disorder to chromosome 13q; however, Hodges et al. (2009) explored 21 single nucleotide polymorphisms (SNPs) and did not find evidence of linkage of these SNPs with panic disorder. Hodges noted that very small genetic effects may underlie complex disorders such as panic disorder and linkage analysis simply cannot detect these small effects.

To date, linkage studies have not supported main effects of and particular gene or combination of genes on the development of panic disorder. However, given that heritability data do suggest that genetic factors are involved in panic disorder, it is likely that genetic contributions to the disorder are complex. In an effort to understand the genetic factors involved in panic disorder, researchers have focused on specific candidate genes. As discussed in previous chapters, candidate genes are often selected based on linkage studies and/or their putative role in cellular or neurotransmitter functioning.

Candidate Genes and Genome-Wide Association Studies

As discussed in previous chapters, in contrast to linkage studies that search for susceptibility genes, *candidate gene studies* attempt to reveal genetic contributions to panic disorder by identifying specific susceptibility genes a priori. The genes selected are based on theory and previous research and comparisons are then made between research participants with panic disorder and those without the disorder in terms of presence of genetic variants (mutations) or polymorphisms. A number of candidate genes have been investigated in the study of panic disorder and those that are involved in the process of neurotransmission have been of particular interest. For example, genes that play a role in the (a) production of enzymes that breakdown neurotransmitters, particularly catecholamines; (b) functioning of pre- and postsynaptic neurotransmitter receptors (e.g., serotonin, norepinephrine, dopamine); and (c) production and functioning of neuromodulators, all have been the target of candidate gene studies.

COMT Gene

Genes that are involved in regulating the catecholaminergic system have been investigated in the pathogenesis of panic disorder, given that the somatic symptoms of anxiety (e.g., increased heart rate) are closely linked to the activation of the sympathetic nervous system and release of catecholamines. For example, Domschke et al. (2004) and others have explored whether polymorphisms of the catechol-O-methyl-transferase (COMT) gene are associated with panic disorder. As discussed in the previous chapter, catechol-O-methyl-transferase is an enzyme that breaks down catecholamines and, if over or underactive, can lead to dysfunction of neurotransmitter systems such as dopamine, norepinephrine, and serotonin. Domschke et al. studied 115 men and women with panic disorder and measured the presence of a single polymorphism of the COMT gene (Val158Met). Results revealed an association with panic disorder in women but not men. Hamilton et al. (2002) also studied polymorphisms of the COMT gene and suggested that a susceptibility locus for panic disorder involved the COMT gene or a nearby region of chromosome 22. Woo, Yoon, and Yu (2002) concurred with Domschke et al. and Hamilton et al. Based on a study of 51 patients with panic disorder and 45 controls, they reported that 19.6% of those with panic disorder versus 2.2% of controls had a specific COMT polymorphism (Val158Met). Other studies have not supported these findings, however, and a meta-analysis of six studies revealed there was no significant association between the Val158Met polymorphism of the COMT gene and panic disorder in the total sample of participants (Domschke et al., 2007; Henderson et al., 2000). However, when data were analyzed based on gender and ethnicity, a significant association was found between the polymorphism and female Caucasian participants only. These findings suggest that the COMT Val158Met polymorphism may be a vulnerability factor in panic disorder *in select populations only*. The way in which this genetic mutation affects the development and expression of panic disorder, at least in some individuals, is unclear, but Domschke et al. (2008) and others have postulated that it affects dopaminergic functioning in the limbic and prefrontal regions resulting in increased activation in response to unpleasant stimuli (Kang et al., 2016). A critical point, however, is that the COMT Val158Met polymorphism has been implicated in numerous clinical disorders including ADHD, OCD, schizophrenia, bipolar disorder, and substance use disorder, and differences have been found based on sex and ethnicity in several studies (Ohara et al., 1998;

Park et al., 2002; Rotondo et al., 2002; Taylor, 2016). Given the inconsistencies in the literature, the role of the COMT gene in panic disorder remains uncertain.

Serotonin Transporter Gene and Serotonin Receptor Gene

The serotonin transporter (5-HTT) is encoded by the SLC6A4 gene and several variants of this gene (e.g., insertions, deletions, repeats) have been found to affect availability of the serotonin transporter protein (e.g., Murthy et al., 2010; Rao et al., 2017). Genetic variations of the serotonin transporter affects levels of serotonin available in the extracellular fluid. A number of studies have explored whether polymorphisms of the SLC6A4 gene are present in individuals with panic disorder compared to healthy controls. Based on systematic reviews and meta-analyses, most studies have not reported a significant difference in polymorphism frequencies of the SLC6A4 gene and participants with PD compared to healthy controls (e.g., Blaya et al., 2007; Hamilton et al., 1999).

Although current evidence does not support a role for the SLC6A4 gene in panic disorder, knockout mice bred without a specific type of serotonin *receptor* (5-HT1A), located abundantly in the cerebral cortex and limbic system, demonstrated increased anxiety behaviors suggesting a key role for the receptor in panic disorder (Lesch et al., 1992; Oleskevich et al., 2005). Indeed, human studies have found decreased 5-HT1A binding in patients with untreated panic disorder (Neumeister et al., 2004) and associations between polymorphisms of the 5-HT1A gene (HTR1A rs6295) and panic disorder (Straube et al., 2014; Watanabe et al., 2017). This same polymorphism, however, has been implicated in other psychiatric disorders and questions remain regarding the specific contributions of genetic polymorphisms to panic disorder (Gatt et al., 2015).

ADORA2A Gene

Adenosine is released by neurons and glial cells and serves as a neuromodulator in the brain by activating second-messenger systems, increasing neuronal inhibition, and activating neurons in pathways involved in anxiety reactions. Consequently, variants of the adenosine 2A receptor gene (ADORA2A) (located on chromosome 22) have been explored in panic disorder. Indeed, preliminary studies have found an overrepresentation of a particular polymorphism (rs5751876) of the ADORA2A gene in patients with panic disorder relative to healthy controls (e.g., Deckert et al., 1998; Hamilton et al., 2004; Hohoff et al., 2010). Studies have also found a relationship between polymorphisms of the ADORA2A gene and personality traits such as harm avoidance in patients with panic disorder compared to controls (Hohoff et al., 2010). Adenosine gene variants, however, have also been associated with ASD and are not unique to panic disorder (Freitag et al., 2010).

Additional Candidate Genes

In addition to COMT, serotonin, and adenosine genes, numerous additional candidate genes have been investigated in panic disorder, including those that affect BDNF, dopamine transporters, dopamine receptors, cholecystokinin receptors, and norepinephrine transporters and receptors (e.g., Han et al., 2015; Park et al., 2016; Sand et al., 2002). Recently, Gregerson and colleagues (2016) studied three candidate genes SNAPC2 (small-nuclear RNA activating complex, polypeptide 2), MAP2K7 (mitogen-activated protein kinase kinase 7), LRRC8E (leucine-rich repeat containing 8 family, member E), and 8 polymorphisms on a specific region of chromosome 19 (19p13.2) in 511 patients with PD and 1029 healthy controls. Findings revealed that *only one* of the polymorphisms (of the SNAPC2 gene) was associated with panic disorder and only in a subset of the total sample. Similarly, Howe et al. (2016) conducted a meta-analysis involving 20 candidate genes and 23 gene variants in participants with panic disorder and concluded that only three variants were significant associated with panic disorder, and noted that panic disorder "likely involves genetic variation in a multitude of biological pathways that is diverse among populations" (p. 665).

Further support for the complexity of genetic factors in panic disorder comes from genome-wide association studies. For example, in an effort to increase sample size and statistical power, Otowa et al. (2012) conducted a genome-wide association study of 12 single nucleotide polymorphisms in 329 participants with panic disorder compared to controls and no significant relationship emerged. Collectively, these findings suggest that despite the apparently strong familial component of panic disorder, the contributions of genetic factors in the development of the disorder remain obscure. In addition to the complexity of genetic variables at play, methodological variables, including sample size, comorbidity, severity of symptoms, heterogeneity of symptoms, low statistical power, and other demographic and methodological factors, likely contribute to the inconsistent findings across studies as well as the contribution of environmental factors. Shimada-Sugmoto and colleagues (2015) noted that although environmental factors make a substantial contribution to the cause of anxiety disorders to date, no genome-wide search for gene by environmental (G × E) interactions have been conducted. To help address the complex contribution of genetic factors to the development of panic disorder, genome-wide association studies conducted by large consortia are needed.

BOX 7.2   Can Panic Attacks Be Provoked?

Given their random nature, it is difficult to study panic attacks, as they occur spontaneously. It has been well documented, however, that several substances can induce panic-like symptoms, including recreational drugs such as cocaine and ecstasy and medications such as asthma medications and prescription stimulants (Dager et al., 1997; Louie et al., 1996; Pallanti & Mazzi, 1992). In addition, the synthetic neuropeptide cholecystokinintetrapeptide (CCK-4) and CCK receptor agonists (e.g., pentagastrin) can provoke anxiety symptoms in humans that closely resemble spontaneously occurring panic attacks experienced by those with panic disorder (Bradwejn & Koszycki, 1994; Ruland et al., 2015). Cholecystokinin (CCK) is a neuropeptide secreted abundantly in the brain that appears to play a critical role in anxiety-related behaviors in patients with panic disorder. Plag and colleagues (2012), for example, administered CCK-4 to participants with panic disorder and healthy controls, and found that CCK-4 induced panic in the majority of participants of panic disorder but not in healthy controls. Panic attacks have also been observed during fMRI, and findings revealed increased activation in the amygdala and left temporal gyrus (Pfleiderer et al., 2007; Spiegelhalder et al., 2009). A number of studies have explored changes in rCBF following injections of pharmacologically induced panic with CCK-4 in healthy volunteers. Using fMRI or PET, results indicated that CCK-4 quickly induced increases in rCBF in the limbic region, anterior cingulate gyrus, the claustrum-insular-amygdala region, and the cerebellar vermis with concomitant reductions in blood flow in the frontal regions (Benkelfat et al., 1995; Eser et al., 2009; Javanmard et al., 1999). Collectively, these findings support that distinct physiologic changes occur during panic episodes and support involvement of limbic and prefrontal regions.

Structural Findings

A variety of brain structures have been implicated in panic disorder, including the hippocampus, amygdala, temporal gyrus, anterior cingulate, cerebellum, and frontal and temporal lobes. Specifically, anatomical studies have explored whether morphological differences exist in volume, size, and shape of brain structures as well as molecular features, such as size and density of cells including gray and white matter. Studies have also explored ventricular size and several, but not all, studies have reported enlarged ventricles in participants with panic disorder relative to controls (e.g., Wurthmann et al., 1997; Uhde et al., 1987). As discussed in previous chapters, however, enlarged ventricles are also found in other clinical disorders.

One of the most frequent anatomical findings in the literature involves reduced volume (e.g., 9% or greater) of the temporal lobes in participants with panic disorder relative to controls (e.g., Brambilla et al., 2002; Fontaine et al., 1990; Ontiveros et al., 1989; Sobanski et al., 2016; Uchida et al., 2003; Vythilingam et al., 2000). Findings regarding structures located within the temporal lobes, however, have varied greatly with some studies finding bilateral reduction of the temporal lobes, temporal gyrus, hippocampus, and amygdala, while others have reported unilateral reduction of the temporal lobes and normal hippocampal and amygdala volume. Given the inconsistencies across studies, specific structural differences of the temporal lobes between participants with and without panic disorder remains unclear.

Given the amygdala's involvement with processing of emotion, the size and shape of the amygdala has received particular attention in panic disorder. For example, Fontaine, Massana et al. (2003a) found smaller left and right hemisphere amygdalar volume differences in medication-free patients with panic disorder compared to controls; however, no size differences were found in temporal lobe or hippocampi volumes. Recently, Yoon et al. (2016) reported shape alterations in the right amygdala in patients with panic disorder, although no differences were found in overall volume of the amygdala.

Additionally, volume reductions have been found in the insula and basal ganglia in patients with panic disorder (Asami et al., 2008; Lai et al., 2010), while *increased* volume has of the temporal lobe, insula, and brain stem have also been reported by some studies (e.g., Fujiwara et al., 2011; Protopopescu et al., 2006; Uchida et al., 2003). In summary, structural studies have found reduced and increased size of a number of brain structures; however, these findings are inconsistent across studies and additional research is needed to explore whether anatomical differences are associated with functional differences and whether these differences are specific to panic disorder (Del Casale et al., 2013).

Gray and White Matter Findings

A substantial number of studies have investigated gray and white matter differences between participants with and without panic disorder. Overall, studies tend to find differences in gray matter volume in limbic structures including the amygdala, hippocampus, basal ganglia, pituitary, frontal, cingulate and temporal cortical areas, and in the midbrain and pons (Dresler et al., 2013).

To determine whether *gray matter* volumes differed by disorder, Lai and Wu (2015) compared gray matter volume of patients with panic disorder to those with major depressive disorder and healthy controls. Lai et al. discovered gray matter reductions in the right inferior frontal gyrus and right insula in participants with panic disorder, while participants with major depressive disorder had gray matter reductions in bilateral medial frontal cortex, right superior frontal gyrus, right superior temporal gyrus and bilateral cerebellums relative to participants with panic disorder and controls. These findings suggest that differences in gray matter volume in the frontal-temporal regions may differentiate patients with panic disorder from depression; however, additional studies with larger sample sizes are needed to explore this hypothesis. Similarly, Na et al. (2013) compare gray matter volume of the orbital frontal region in patients with panic disorder with and without agoraphobia compared to healthy controls and found that those with panic disorder with agoraphobia had decreased gray matter volume in the orbital frontal gyrus; however, no differences were found between participants with panic disorder only and controls. A recent meta-analysis by Shang et al. (2014) compared gray matter volumes in participants with panic disorder, social anxiety disorder, GAD, and specific phobia, and controlled for comorbid major depressive disorder, age, and medication use. Findings revealed reduced volume of the right anterior cingulate and left frontal gyrus in participants with anxiety disorders, consistent with neuroanatomical models of physiological fear responses. These findings support a role for the anterior cingulate and prefrontal cortex in mediating anxiety symptoms, although the manner in which these pathways may be differentially involved in anxiety is unclear. In addition, it is important to note that similar gray matter volume reductions have been found in other disorders (e.g., autism, conduct disorder) and additional studies are needed to determine whether specific types of gray matter differences are characteristic of panic disorder compared to other disorders, including other types of anxiety disorders (Rogers & De Brito, 2016; Yang, Si, et al., 2016).

White Matter Findings

Compared to gray matter studies, relatively few *white matter* studies are available concerning panic disorder; however, preliminary studies support differences in white matter integrity in these patients. For example, Lai & Wu (2013) showed reduced integrity in WM tracts of the right inferior fronto-occipital fasciculus, left body of corpus callosum and left superior longitudinal fasciculus, in participants with panic disorder relative to 21 control participants. Similarly, Kim et al. (2014) reported bilateral decreases in white matter in the frontal regions as well as the corpus callosum in participants with panic disorder relative to controls. Recently, Kim, Kim, Choi, and Lee (2017) found that degree of white matter alterations were significantly correlated with self-reported anxiety sensitivity and avoidance behaviors in participants with panic disorder compared to healthy controls.

Given that numerous brain regions have been implicated in panic disorder, including fronto-limbic regions, thalamus, brain stem, and the cerebellum, Konishi et al. (2014) evaluated volumetric white matter changes in the fiber bundles *connecting these regions* in 40 participants with panic disorder and 40 healthy control participants. Results were supportive of previous white matter studies and found significant volumetric reductions in widespread white matter regions including fronto-limbic, thalamo-cortical, and cerebellar pathways. At least one study, however, has not reported white matter volume differences in participants with panic disorder relative to controls (Kim, Oh, et al., 2015) and the studies that have been conducted often employ small sample sizes (e.g., 20–40). Additional white matter studies of panic disorder are needed using larger samples and inclusion of healthy controls, as well as clinical comparison groups.

It is important to note that factors unrelated to panic are also associated with anatomical changes in the brain. For example, Convit et al. (1995) found reductions in medial and lateral temporal lobe volumes as well as the hippocampus corresponding with increasing age in *healthy* individuals. In addition, reduced hippocampal and amygdala volumes have been found in other disorders, including bipolar disorder and PTSD (Anand & Shekhar, 2003;

Nutt & Malizia, 2004; Rauch, Shin, & Wright, 2003; Schmahl, Vermetten, Elzinga, & Bremner, 2003). Collectively, current research concerning structural differences between patients with and without panic disorder appears most often to implicate the temporal lobes and reduced gray and white matter; however, results are inconsistent across studies.

Functional Findings

In contrast to structural studies that focus on morphological differences between participants with and without panic disorder, functional studies explore activation differences inferred from blood flow, glucose metabolism, and effects of medication on brain functioning. Functional studies differ in terms of technology used (fMRI, PET, etc.), task parameters (at rest or activity), methodological approach (e.g., design, statistics, power), and demographic variables (e.g., inclusion criteria, comorbidity). Functional studies of panic disorder can be particularly challenging as noted by Gorman et al. (2000). For example, deep cortical structures are more difficult to image than cortical regions, unprovoked panic attacks often occur at random and are therefore difficult to capture, provocation of panic attacks often leads to hyperventilation and vasoconstriction, which may obfuscate blood flow changes in the brain, and patients with panic disorder may be more sensitive to substances that induce panic. Also, it is possible that the experience of being inside a scanner influences glucose metabolism, blood flow, and medication effects in the brain (Nazemi & Dager, 2003). Thus, functional neuroimaging studies of panic disorder should be interpreted with these methodological issues in mind.

Resting States

Functional neuroimaging studies can measure regional cerebral blood flow (rCRF) or glucose metabolism of participants with panic disorder and controls while at rest or during an activity (e.g., finger pressing, processing of visual stimuli). A number of studies have compared rCBF and glucose metabolism in participants with panic disorder relative to healthy controls while at rest, during anticipation of an infusion of a drug that triggers panic symptoms (e.g., lactate challenge), and following the drug challenge (Boshuisen et al., 2002; Reiman et al., 1989). Findings have been fairly consistent across studies suggesting that, at rest, those with panic disorder tend to display increased activation in the hippocampal and frontal regions relative to control participants and decreased activation in the anterior cingulate gyrus, amygdala, parietal, and temporal lobe regions (Bisaga et al., 1998; Boshuisen et al; Nordahl et al., 1990). Lee and colleagues (2006) found decreased cerebral blood flow in the temporal regions in participants with panic disorder compared to controls and blood flow to this region was negatively correlated with severity of panic symptoms and duration of illness. Others have found rCBF differences between participants with panic disorder compared to other clinical disorders, such as OCD, with OCD participants displaying reduced blood flow in the caudate relative to participants with panic disorder. Interestingly participants with panic disorder did not show rCBF differences the caudate relative to healthy controls (Lucey et al., 1997). Collectively, these findings suggest differential patterns of brain activation may exist patients with panic disorder compared to healthy controls and possibly compared to other clinical disorders; however, additional methodologically sound research is needed to further investigate brain activation patterns.

Activity States During Cognitive Tasks

Research has also explored functional differences in patients with panic disorder relative to controls while exposed to visual images and during cognitive, motor, and sensory tasks. Imagery studies, for example, have involved presentation of neutral images versus panic-related themes, and emotionally neutral versus threatening images, to participants with and without panic disorder. Cognitive tasks have included sensory discrimination tasks, motor tasks, and emotional processing tasks as well as others (see Sobanski and Wagner, 2017, for a review).

One of the most studied areas involves activations patterns of patients with and without panic disorder in response to neutral and disorder-related (i.e., threatening) visual images. Many studies have found participants with panic disorder display greater activation to disorder-related images compared to neutral scenes in several brain regions, including the brain stem, insula, thalamus amygdala, and cingulate cortex; however, most studies report activation differences in some but not all of these brain structures (Anders et al., 2004; Bystritsky et al., 2001; Demenescu et al., 2013; Feldker et al., 2016; Holtz et al., 2012; Kim, Dager, & Lyoo, 2012; Wiedemann et al., 1999). Collectively, these studies suggest that patients with panic disorder have a heightened sensitivity to anxiety-provoking stimuli that is characterized by increased neuronal activity in subcortical, limbic, and frontal regions, as measured by techniques such as fMRI, PET, or SPECT. Feldker et al. (2016) suggested that patients with panic disorder have a heightened awareness of emotion-specific stimuli *as well as* an increased awareness of interoceptive stimuli (i.e., internal body sensations) compared to healthy controls.

Exposure to varying facial expressions is another task frequently employed in the panic disorder literature. For example, Whalen et al. (2001) found increased activity occurred in the amygdala when healthy volunteers were shown pictures of fearful facial expressions compared to neutral or angry facial expressions; however, patients with panic disorder tend to show an exaggerated amygdala and/or insula response (i.e., increased activity) to fearful faces compared to healthy controls (Fonzo et al., 2015; Thomas et al., 2001). Killgore and colleagues (2014) using fMRI investigated whether participants with different disorders (specific phobia and PTSD) compared to controls showed a similar activation pattern of the amygdala and prefrontal regions when shown fearful, happy, and neutral faces. Contrary to expectations, results revealed that participants with panic disorder, specific phobia, and PTSD displayed a very similar activation response to the fearful versus neutral faces with *all three groups* showing greater activation within the left amygdala and reduced activation within the ventromedial prefrontal cortex compared to the healthy control group. Collectively, these findings suggest that participants with panic disorder have a heightened sensitivity to anxiety-provoking stimuli that is often characterized by increased activity in the amygdala and decreased activity in frontal regions; however, these findings appear to be characteristic of several anxiety disorders and not solely panic disorder.

Motor and Sensory Tasks

Motor and sensory tasks have also been used in functional neuroimaging studies of panic disorder. The basal ganglia have been explored in panic disorder based on the observation of increased bilateral putamen activation and decreased cortical activation in healthy participants in response to a fearful situation (Butler et al., 2007). In contrast, research with participants with panic disorder demonstrated *reduced* activation of the putamen during motor tasks (Marchand et al., 2009) and deep brain stimulation of the basal ganglia has reportedly triggered panic attacks in patients without panic disorder (Sousa et al., 2015).

Nordahl et al. (1990) used PET to measure glucose metabolism rates in participants with panic disorder while they performed an auditory task. Results indicated that participants with panic disorder showed glucose metabolism decreases in the left parietal lobe and an increase in the orbital frontal cortex. In cognitive tasks such as word fluency production, participants with panic disorder have shown reduced activation of the prefrontal cortex compared to healthy controls in some but not all studies (Helmes & Hall, 2016; Ohta et al., 2008). Participants with panic disorder have also shown different activation patterns in the amygdala, thalamus, prefrontal regions, and anterior cingulate during olfaction tasks compared to healthy controls (Wintermann et al., 2013). Collectively, findings from motor and sensory tasks support differences in activation responses in participants with panic disorder relative to controls, particularly in subcortical and prefrontal cortical regions.

Summary

Functional neuroimaging studies are useful in helping to identify brain regions of increased or decreased glucose metabolism or blood flow in panic disorder, but it is important to keep in mind that findings do not reveal the cause of the functional differences between those with and without panic disorder (e.g., Bonne, Gilboa et al., 2003). Nevertheless, a general theme emerges from functional neuroimaging (e.g., fMRI, DTI, and PET) studies to date: participants with panic disorder often show differential activation patterns relative to healthy control participants at rest and during a variety of cognitive, sensory, and motor tasks. Although findings differ across studies, in general, functional studies in conjunction with structural studies implicate reduced gray matter, altered white matter connectivity, and decreased and increased neuronal activation in pathways extending from the amygdala and hippocampal regions to the frontal cortex in the underlying pathophysiology of panic disorder. These findings compliment current theoretical models of anxiety and panic disorder.

Anxiety Models

A single, universally accepted structural and functional theory explaining panic disorder does not currently exist, although several models have been proposed. One of the most widely cited models was advanced by Gorman and colleagues (1989, 2000) who emphasized the role of multiple structures and pathways, including the prefrontal cortex, brain stem, amygdala, hippocampus, thalamus, and hypothalamus, the periaqueductal gray, and locus ceruleus (i.e., "fear network"). With regard to panic, Gorman and colleagues suggested that a deficit exists in "relay and coordination of upstream (cortical) and downstream (brain stem) sensory information, which results in heightened amygdalar activity with resultant behavioral, autonomic, and neuroendocrine activation" (p. 495). Gorman et al. suggested that individuals with panic disorder have a lower threshold for activating the "fear network", and this hyperactive activation in turn leads to stimulation of the autonomic and neuroendocrine systems (via projections from the amygdala to the brain stem and hypothalamus). Stimulation of the autonomic sympathetic nervous system and neuroendocrine systems results in physiological symptoms of accelerated heart rate, release of norepinephrine and stress hormones, increased blood pressure, and so on. Meanwhile, prefrontal regions of the brain receive input from limbic systems and are involved in processing and evaluating sensory information. According to Gorman et al., faulty processing at the level of the cortex can lead to misinterpretation of interoceptive (body sensations), leading to excitatory projections to the amygdala and other limbic structures hence further stimulating the fear network. In other words, individuals with panic disorder may process sensory information in a faulty manner, and these cognitive misperceptions trigger physiological changes resulting in an extreme anxiety response: panic.

Research from a variety of perspectives has provided support for elements of Gorman et al.'s model. As discussed previously in this chapter, many studies have found participants with panic disorder display greater activation to disorder-related images compared to neutral scenes in several brain regions including the brain stem, prefrontal cortex, insula, thalamus amygdala, and cingulate cortex. Studies also support that patients with panic disorder have a heightened awareness of emotion-specific stimuli as well as an increased awareness of interoceptive stimuli (i.e., internal body sensations) compared to healthy controls (Felder et al., 2016). Shinoura et al. (2011) reported that damage to the anterior cingulate cortex during surgery induced panic disorder in two patients. Research concerning hyperactivity of the amygdala, however, has been less robust (Sobinski et al., 2017). Work by Brambilla et al. (2003) also supports the neuroendocrine component of Gorman et al.'s model as they found elevated plasma concentrations of neurosteroids (e.g., progesterone, dehydroepiandrosterone) in individuals with panic disorder relative to controls and other studies have found elevated plasma levels of norepinephrine in patients with panic disorder. Gorman et al. acknowledged that in addition to autonomic and neuroendocrine factors, panic disorder is also highly familial and that environmental factors, such as early childhood trauma and disruptions in infant-parent attachment, increase the risk of developing the disorder. Specifically, Gorman and colleagues proposed that individuals with panic disorder inherit a central nervous system that is overly sensitive to fear, and structures such as the amygdala, hypothalamus, thalamus, and locus coeruleus, as well as environmental factors play a critical role in the development of panic disorder. The degree of hyperactivity of the "fear network" and pattern of autonomic and neuroendocrine responses is thought to vary among individuals with panic disorder.

Gorman et al.'s model does not address the role of the hypo-thalamic-pituitary-adrenal axis (HPA) directly; however, other scientists have emphasized the HPA in panic disorder (Charney, 2003). The HPA axis is involved in the stress response and the release of stress-related hormones such as corticotropin-releasing factor (CRF). CRF, in turn, increases the release of norepinephrine as well as other peptides and steroids (Arborelius et al., 1999). Antidepressants are hypothesized to normalize functioning of a hyperactive hypothalamic-pituitary-adrenal system in panic disorder (Ströhle & Holsboer, 2003). The hypothalamic-pituitary-thyroid-axis (HPT) has also been implicated in panic disorder given that many of the symptoms of panic are similar to those in hyperthyroidism. In a recent review of the literature, Fischer and Ehlert (2017) found a high rate of comorbidity between thyroid disorder and anxiety disorder, and Helmreich et al. (2005) emphasized the interactive relationship between the two systems. Others have emphasized that pathways extending from the prefrontal cortex to limbic structures are likely involved in most forms of anxiety and are not uniquely implicated in panic disorder (Coplan & Lydiard, 1998; Quirk & Gehlert, 2003; Shekhar et al., 2003).

In summary, a number of brain structures and regions have been implicated in panic disorder and theoretical models emphasize the role of the brain stem, cortex, and subcortical structures in the pathophysiology of the disorder. At the level of the brain stem and subcortical structures, physiologic alterations are proposed to result in a hyperactive "fear network" that triggers stimulation of sympathetic nervous system and neuroendocrine systems. At the level of the cortex, misinterpretation of interoceptive signals leads to misperceptions of danger that further stimulates the "fear network" leading to physiologic symptoms of panic. Partial support exists for elements of this model although additional research is warranted to further explore the relationship among structures and systems implicated in panic disorder (Feldker et al., 2018). As discussed in Chapter 2, communication between neurons and pathways projecting to and from subcortical and cortical structures and brain regions occurs via neurotransmission.

Neurotransmitter Findings

Most major neurotransmitter systems have been implicated in panic disorder to a greater or lesser extent including, serotonin, GABA, dopamine, norepinephrine, and glutamate. The following section will provide an overview of the putative role of these neurotransmitters, and the reader is referred to Santos, D'Amico, and Dierssen (2015) and Sobinski et al. (2017) for more detailed information.

Serotonin

Serotonin has also been implicated in panic disorder largely due to the efficacy of antidepressants, including tricyclics, monoamine oxidase inhibitors, selective serotonin reuptake inhibitors (SSRIs), and serotonin-norepinephrine reuptake inhibitors (SNRIs) in reducing anxiety symptoms (e.g., Asnis et al., 2001). Pollack and colleagues (2003) noted that SSRIs are the most desirable treatment for panic disorder given their effectiveness at decreasing anxiety symptoms, limited side effects, and lack of physical dependency, and they are now generally accepted as the first-line of pharmacological treatment for panic disorder (D. S. Baldwin et al., 2014).

Although levels of neurotransmitters cannot be directly measured in the brain, Esler et al. (2007) measured serotonin metabolites (5-hydroxyindole acetic acid) in medication-naïve participants with panic disorder compared to healthy controls using internal jugular venous sampling. Results revealed that brain serotonin turnover was increased approximately fourfold in subcortical brain regions and in the cerebral cortex in participants with panic disorder. Serotonin turnover was highest in participants with the most severe symptoms was unrelated and was significantly reduced following treatment with an SSRI (citalopram). Lower rCBF has been found in women with panic disorder in the temporal cortex, and following treatment with a serotonin agonist, significantly higher blood flow was observed in this region compared to control participants (Meyer et al., 2000). These findings further support that serotonin increases may modulate an underlying functional pathology of the serotonergic system in patients with panic disorder.

A study by Den Boer and Westenberg (1990) further implicates serotonin in panic disorder as patients treated with an SSRI (fluvoxamine) showed a dramatic reduction in frequency of panic attacks, but treatment with a serotonin antagonist was ineffective at improving symptoms. The specific role that serotonin plays in panic disorder is unclear, but a few studies have implicated serotonin pre and postsynaptic receptors (5-HT1A) and some studies (not all) have found lower density of these serotonin receptors in several brain regions relative to controls including the anterior and posterior cingulate cortex, orbitofrontal cortex, temporal cortex, amygdala, and in the raphe nuclei (e.g., Martini et al., 2004; Nash & Nutt, 2005; Neumeister et al., 2004). Similarly, at least one study has reported decreased binding of the serotonin transporter in the thalamus and hippocampus in participants with panic disorder and increased serotonin transporter (SERT) binding in numerous brain regions, including the raphe nuclei and several areas of the cortex (Maron et al., 2011). Gender differences have also emerged in SERT binding in healthy individuals and panic disorder with females having higher levels of SERT binding than males in several brain regions, including the hippocampus (Jovanovic et al., 2008; Maron et al., 2011). These findings suggest that differences in serotonin receptor expression and functioning exists between healthy males and females, and may also be implicated in the higher rate of panic disorder among females than males.

Dopamine and Norepinephrine

The potential role of dopamine in panic disorder has been explored for a number of reasons: (a) norepinephrine is biosynthesized from dopamine; (b) dopamine agonists have been found to produce panic symptoms (Alonso-Navarro et al., 2009; Hebert, Blanchard, & Blanchard, 1999; Louie et al. (1996); (c) dopamine antagonists have been found to extinguish conditioned fear responses in mice (Ponnusamy, Nissim, & Barad, 2005), but their effectiveness in humans is questionable (Anfinson, 2002); and (d) plasma dopamine levels tend to be higher in patients prior to antidepressant treatment and may normalize following treatment (Oh, Yu, Heo, et al., 2015). Norepinephrine, however, is the primary focus in panic disorder studies.

The role of norepinephrine in panic disorder has also been investigated largely due to its known sympathetic effects on the nervous system "fight or flight" response to stress resulting in increased arousal, vigilance, heart rate, and blood pressure. Coplan and Lydiard (1998) noted that serotonin and norepinephrine systems function interactively and thus an abnormality in this interactive system may manifest as pathological anxiety. For example, serotonergic neurons project from raphe nuclei to the locus coeruleus and have an inhibitory effect on neurons in this area. The locus coeruleus is rich in norepinephrine-releasing neurons that project to midbrain and forebrain regions that play an important role in modulating fear and anxiety responses. Norepinephrine-releasing neurons also project from the locus coeruleus to neurons in the median raphe and can have an excitatory effect, resulting in changes such as increased heart rate and blood pressure (Gorman et al., 2000). Consequently, factors that disrupt the homeostasis of the serotonin system can affect other neurotransmitter systems, such as norepinephrine, and result in symptomatic behavior such as panic (Graeff, 2017).

Treatment of panic disorder with SSRIs has been found to alter both serotonin and norepinephrine cerebral spinal fluid metabolite levels and lead to symptom improvement (De Bellis et al., 1993; Lucki & O'Leary, 2004; Sheline, Bardgett, & Csernansky, 1997). For example, when serotonin activity and availability is increased by SSRIs, norepinephrine receptors have been found to respond by decreasing norepinephrine activity (Lucki & O'Leary, 2004). By decreasing norepinephrine activity, somatic symptoms of panic disorder are thought to decrease although the specifics of this process are not well understood (Aston-Jones et al., 1991). SSRIs also appear to decrease the release of stress-related hormones (e.g., cortisol) from the hypothalamus and adrenal gland, thereby decreasing firing rate in the locus coeruleus (which leads to increased heart rate, blood pressure, and so on) (Ruhe et al., 2015). Lastly, SSRIs appear to modulate the effects of glutamate and decrease excitatory glutamate projections from the amygdala to the hypothalamus and brain stem, consequently mitigating the anxiety response (Frizzo, 2017; Gorman et al., 2000).

GABA

In addition to being rich in norepinephrine-releasing neurons, the locus coeruleus contains cells that release neuropeptides and other neurotransmitters, such as GABA. Benzodiazepines, which act on GABA receptors, also improve anxiety symptoms and are used in the treatment of panic disorder. Cox et al. (1989) found that over 83% of individuals who experienced panic attacks and were being treated for alcohol or drug abuse, used alcohol—a GABA agonist—to self-medicate their attacks, and 72% described this method as effective at reducing or preventing panic attacks. Benzodiazepines are also effective at reducing panic symptoms by enhancing GABA transmission. As Ströhle et al. (2002) demonstrated, however, GABA receptors and the effects of GABA are modulated by other factors such as peptides and neurosteroids. In addition, recent research indicates that chronic antidepressant treatment (SSRI) affects functioning of GABA receptors (Asaoka et al., 2017); hence, the way in which neurotransmitters interact and contribute to panic symptoms is complex and poorly understood. Given the apparent interactive effects of neurotransmitters and the fact that pharmacological agents that target vastly different neurotransmitter systems can improve symptoms of anxiety, these studies suggest that parallel and interactive changes in neurotransmitter systems may underlie pathological states, such as panic disorder.

Pharmacological Intervention and Brain Stimulation Techniques

According to Pary, Matuschka, Lewis, Caso, and Lippmann (2003), the primary treatment approach for anxiety disorders is pharmacological. The main classes of medications used in the treatment of panic disorder are SSRIs (e.g., Prozac, Paxil, Zoloft), tricyclic antidepressants (e.g., anafranil, tofranil), SNRIs (e.g., venlafaxine, Effexor), MAOIs (e.g., marplan, nardil), and benzodiazepines (e.g., Valium, Xanax, klonopin). Busiprone (BuSpar) is a non-sedating anxiolytic serotonin agonist that is also used to treat panic disorder, as are beta-blockers. Beta-blockers are prescribed to enhance heart rhythm are also used off label in the treatment of panic disorder (Lambert, 2012). The current first line of treatment for panic disorder is SSRIs due to their efficacy in reducing symptoms as well as their relative safety (Batelaan, Van Balkom, & Stein, 2012). A number of SSRIs are used to treat panic disorder, and most are equally effective in reducing panic symptoms, although differences exist with respect to side effects (Bandelow et al., 2004; Vermeulen, 1998). SSRIs are most often prescribed in the treatment of panic disorder compared to other medications, such as beta-blockers and benzodiazepines (Lambert, 2012).

Benzodiazepines are also used in the treatment of panic disorder, although short-term use is preferred due to their high risk of dependence (Fujii et al., 2015). Temporary use of benzodiazepines in conjunction with SSRIs is recommended in more severe cases (Batelaan et al., 2012). Research suggests these recommendations are often not followed in clinical practice among primary care physicians and psychiatrists. For example, Bruce et al. (2003) examined 443 patients who were followed as part of a longitudinal study and found that approximately two-thirds of the patients studied were taking benzodiazepines in combination with SSRIs. In addition, Batelaan et al. (2012) found benzodiazepines and beta-blockers were prescribed more often than tricyclic antidepressants against current clinical guidelines.

The mode of action of two of the most widely prescribed medications for panic disorder—benzodiazepines and SSRIs—is substantially different. As discussed in Chapter 2, SSRIs are serotonin agonists, while benzodiazepines are GABA agonists. Although both SSRIs and benzodiazepines are effective at treating panic disorder, benzodiazepines carry a high risk for tolerance and withdrawal. Benzodiazepines bind to part of the GABA receptor and modulate the effects of GABA by allowing lower concentrations of the neurotransmitter to open the Cl- channel, hence facilitating neuronal inhibition. Several studies have found lower GABA receptor binding in patients with panic disorder compared to controls in the hippocampus (Bremmer et al., 2000), left temporal lobes (Kaschka, Feistel, and Ebert, 1995), prefrontal cortex (Bremmer et al., 2000), and global reduction in benzodiazepine binding throughout the brain (Malizia et al., 1998). Other studies, however, have reported increased receptor density in the prefrontal cortex in patients with panic disorder (Brandt et al., 1998) and greater right versus left hemisphere receptor binding in the prefrontal cortex (Kuikka et al., 1995). Importantly, decreased levels of benzodiazepine receptor binding have also been found in other disorders, such as PTSD (Bremmer et al., 2000), and in participants with alcoholism (Abi-Dargham et al., 1998). Given the effectiveness of SSRIs at improving panic symptoms and their selectivity for the serotonin and not GABA receptor, as well as the inconsistencies among studies concerning density of benzodiazepine binding receptors, the role of GABA transmission in panic disorder remains unclear.

Long-term treatment of panic disorder typically involves medication in conjunction with cognitive-behavioral therapy to improve treatment response (Doyle & Pollack, 2004). Many studies, including meta-analyses, have found that a combination of pharmacological intervention and cognitive-behavioral therapy is effective at improving panic symptoms, but given methodological limitations of studies, it is often difficult to determine whether the effects are additive (Bandelow et al., 2015; Gelder, 1998; Spiegel & Bruce, 1997). In addition, some researchers have argued that cognitive-behavioral therapy is preferable to pharmacological interventions (e.g., Rayburn & Otto, 2003), while others advocate for the management of panic disorder with short-term use of benzodiazepines and long-term use of SSRIs (Sheehan, 2002). Bandelow, Michaelis, and Wedekind (2017) recommend that after remission, medications should be continued for 6–12 months.

Alternative Interventions

Neurosurgical Techniques and Brain Stimulation

Although pharmacological interventions are the most well-studied physiologically based intervention for panic disorder, a number of other physiologically based techniques have also received attention. Transcranial magnetic stimulation (TMS), for example, has been studied in the treatment of panic disorder, although the FDA has not yet approved the use of TMS in anxiety disorders. Pallanti and Bernardi (2009) published a systematic review of the use of TMS in the treatment of anxiety disorders and concluded that TMS has a significant effect, but in some studies, the effect is small and short lived.

Neurosurgery has been used in rare cases of treatment-resistant anxiety disorders. Rück et al. (2003) followed up 26 individuals who had not responded to pharmacological or behavioral interventions and had undergone neurosurgery for anxiety disorders (5 with social phobia, 13 with GAD, and 8 with panic disorder). All of the patients had undergone capsulotomy, which involves bilateral lesioning of an area deep in the brain (internal capsule). Results indicated that 67% of the patients responded favorably to the procedure and displayed a significant reduction in anxiety symptoms. Seven of the 26 subjects, however, demonstrated adverse symptoms following the procedure such as neuropsychological impairment on executive function tasks and emotional apathy. The authors suggested that capsulotomy is an effective treatment for severe cases of anxiety disorder, including panic disorder but noted the significant risk of adverse symptoms associated with the procedure.

A less invasive intervention that has received empirical attention is exercise. Several studies have reported that regular, high intensity exercise is associated with significant improvement in symptoms of panic disorder but appears to be less effective than treatment with an antidepressant (Broocks et al., 1998; Broman-Fulks, et al., 2018; Broman-Fulks & Dratcu, 2018). A recent systematic review of the effects of exercise on decreasing anxiety symptoms, including pain disorder concluded that exercise is effective at improving symptoms although questions remain regarding its effectiveness compared to medication as well the correct intensity of aerobic exercise needed to achieve the best results (Marcos de Souza Moura et al., 2015; Hovland et al., 2013).

Alternative interventions such as acupuncture, autogenic training, and biofeedback are often recommended for the treatment of panic disorder, however, only a few methodologically sound studies are currently available. Additional information regarding the empirical effectiveness of these interventions is warranted (Bandelow et al., 2017; Domschke et al., 2010; Spence et al., 2004; Meuret, Wilhelm, and Roth, 2004).

Summary of Panic Disorder

The lifetime prevalence rate of panic disorder in the United States in the general population is between 2% and 3%, and African Americans, Latinos, and Asian Americans have reported lower rates compared to non-Latino whites. Panic disorder occurs worldwide and is more common in females than males at all ages. Familial and twin studies support a heritability component of the disorder. Genetic studies have identified a number of candidate genes although no single or group of genes has been conclusively linked to panic disorder. Structural and functional neuroimaging studies implicate subcortical limbic structures and pathways extending to and from the frontal cortex in the pathophysiology of panic disorder. A number of neurotransmitter and neuroendocrine systems have been implicated in the disorder, particularly serotonin, norepinephrine, and GABA. Acute treatment of panic disorder typically involves use of benzodiazepines, and a combination of SSRIs or SNRIs, and cognitive behavioral therapy is often recommended for long-term management.

Table 7.1 Common Obsessions and Compulsions: Developmental Factors

Childhood	
Obsessions	**Compulsions**
Catastrophic events	Verbal checking
Contamination	Seeking reassurance
Aggressive/harm	Hand washing
Illness and death	
Adolescence	
Obsessions	**Compulsions**
Sexual	Mental rituals
Religious	Ordering/arranging
Symmetry	Checking
Aggressive/harm	
Adulthood	
Obsessions	**Compulsions**
Contamination	Cleaning
Sexual	Checking
Superstitious	Ordering
Fear of losing things	

Note: Research findings indicate that although developmental differences are sometimes found, obsessions and compulsions are not unique to a particular age group.

Source: Boileau (2011) and Mancebo et al. (2008).

Obsessive-Compulsive Disorder (OCD)

The American Psychiatric Association (*DSM-V*, 2013) no longer classifies OCD as an anxiety disorder; rather, it is classified under "OCD and related disorders". Recurrent obsessions and/or compulsions that are time consuming or cause significant distress and impairment in daily living characterize OCD. *Obsessions* are persistent ideas, impulses, thoughts, or images that experiences as intrusive and unwanted, while *compulsions* are repetitive overt or mental acts that an individual feels compelled to perform. Common obsessions include contamination, doubts, symmetry or exactness, somatic fears, sexual thoughts, and thoughts of harm. The most common obsession is contamination as approximately 45–60% of OCD patients suffer from this obsession (Matsunaga et al., 2010). Common compulsions include cleaning, checking, counting, and ordering (Gonçalves et al., 2017; Shafran, Ralph, & Tallis, 1995) (Table 7.1). According to Okasha et al. (1994), most patients with OCD have both obsessions and compulsions. Empirical evidence suggests that OCD symptoms fall into distinct subtypes, including (a) symmetry/repeating/ordering/counting, (b) forbidden thoughts/checking, (c) contamination/washing, and (d) hoarding (Bloch et al., 2008). It is important to note that obsessions tend to be highly idiosyncratic and are often connected with "magical" or implausible beliefs (Rozin et al., 1986).

Prevalence, Cross-Cultural, Diversity, and Developmental Findings

The 12-month prevalence of OCD in the United States is approximately 1.2% with a lifetime prevalence of 2.3% (APA, 2013; Ruscio et al., 2010). Similar rates have been reported in other countries although slightly higher rates have been reported in some countries, including India and Norway (APA, 2013; Jaisoorya et al., 2017; Mojsa-Kaja, Golonka, & Gawlowska, 2016). Maggini et al. (2001) reported that 3% of nearly 3,000 Italian adolescents reported significant OCD symptoms, whereas Heyman et al. (2001) found only 0.25% of British children aged 5–15 reported significant OCD symptoms. With regard to ethnicity findings, Guerrero et al. (2003) reported that Native Hawaiians have a twofold higher risk for OCD than other ethnicities, while Karno et al. (1988) reported OCD is less common among black than non-Hispanic white respondents.

Religiosity and OCD

Although similar rates of OCD are often found around the world, according to Matsunaga and Seedat (2007) and Lemelson (2003), OCD symptoms and the course of the disorder can be shaped by cultural, ethnic, and religious experiences. For example, the most common obsessions in a sample of OCD patients from Bali, Indonesia, included the need to know information about passersby, somatic obsessions, and obsessions concerning witchcraft and spirits. Several studies have reported a relationship between religiosity and OCD. For example, Okasha et al. (1994) found that the most common obsessions in 90 patients with OCD attending an outpatient clinic in Cairo, Egypt, were religious and contamination obsessions and the most common compulsion repeating rituals. Tek and Ulug (2001) reported that 42% of a sample of 45 patients with OCD had religious obsessions. Abramowitz and colleagues (2002) used a self-report scale designed to measure religious obsessive compulsive symptoms—the PIOS (Penn Inventory of Scrupulosity)—with a group of college students and found that self-reported highly devout participants (i.e., Catholics, Protestants) evidenced higher scores on the PIOS than less religious participants. Greenberg and Witztum (1994) reported that religious symptoms were found in 13 of 19 ultraorthodox Jewish patients with OCD but only 1 of 15 non-ultraorthodox Jewish patients with OCD. Huppert, Siev, and Kushner (2007) emphasized the importance of considering faith beliefs and customs when treating religious patients with OCD. Collectively, these studies suggest that OCD may be expressed in religious practices but is not a determinant of the disorder.

Developmentally, OCD is equally common in adults of both sexes but more common in boys during childhood. OCD typically begins in adolescence or adulthood with a gradual onset. Bogetto and colleagues (1999) found that males tend to have an earlier onset of OCD, and the disorder is more likely to occur in males with tic or other anxiety disorders, such as phobias. Females are more likely to have an acute onset of OCD symptoms (Heyman et al., 2001). In the majority of cases, OCD is chronic with periods of waxing and waning, and childhood onset is associated with continuation of symptoms into adulthood in the majority of cases (APA, 2013).

Comorbidity

OCD is associated with a number of psychiatric disorders, including depression, eating psychotic, and tic disorders, and Tourette's disorder. A large intercontinental study involving seven countries found major depressive disorder was the most common comorbid condition with OCD (Brakoulias, Perkes, & Tsalamanios, 2017). Several studies have found differences in OCD symptoms between clinical groups. For example, George and colleagues (1993) compared obsessions and compulsions in a group of individuals with OCD only and a group with OCD and comorbid Tourette's disorder. Results indicated that participants with comorbid OCD and Tourette's disorder reported significantly more sexual, violent, and symmetrical obsessions and counting, blinking, and touching compulsions. Those with OCD reported significantly more contamination obsessions and cleaning compulsions. Similarly, Holzer et al. (1994) reported that patients with OCD and comorbid tic disorder compared to those with OCD only, had significantly more rubbing, touching, tapping, blinking, and staring compulsions—but the two groups did not differ with respect to obsessions. Perugi et al. (2002) found that OCD patients with comorbid bipolar disorder had a significantly higher rate of sexual obsessions and significantly fewer ordering compulsions than those with OCD alone. McDougle and colleagues (1995) compared the obsessions and compulsions of adults with autistic disorder and adults with OCD and found that the latter group was more likely to experience contamination, sexual, aggressive, and religious obsessions. Results also revealed that touching, tapping, rubbing, hoarding, ordering, and self-mutilating behaviors were more common in the group with autistic disorder. Matsunaga et al. (1999) compared the obsessions and compulsions of patients with OCD and patients with anorexia nervosa and comorbid OCD and found patients with anorexia and OCD had a higher need for symmetry and ordering than those with OCD alone. Finally, a number of studies have reported that patients with schizophrenia and comorbid OCD have a poorer prognosis and treatment outcome and perhaps poorer neuropsychological functioning (Kazhungil et al., 2017). Collectively, these studies suggest that the obsessions and compulsions of patients with comorbid OCD differ from those with OCD alone. These behavioral differences may reflect differential neurophysiological underpinnings of the disorders.

Genetic Findings

Heritability: Family and Twin Findings

Family studies support a heritability component to OCD, although it is important to understand that increased rates of transmission within families can be due to either shared genetic or shared environmental factors. However, Brander et al. (2016) in a systematic review of the literature concerning environment factors and OCD concluded that no environmental risk factors have convincingly been associated with OCD. More empirical support is found for familial factors in OCD. For example, Okasha et al. (1994) reported that 20% of patients with OCD in their cross-cultural study had a family history of OCD, and a number of studies have found OCD occurs significantly more often in relatives of patients with OCD than control subjects (Mataix-Cols et al., 2017; Nestadt et al., 2001). Meta-analyses of family studies and OCD have reported a fourfold increase in the likelihood of developing OCD in first-degree relatives of adult patients with the disorder, while relatives of patients with early onset OCD have a tenfold increase of developing the disorder (do Rosario-Campos et al., 2005; Hettema et al., 2001). Collectively, familial studies support a heritability component to OCD (Hettema et al., 2001).

Twin studies also support a role for genetics in the pathophysiology of OCD. Jonnal et al. (2000) investigated a sample of 1,054 female twins and reported a heritability estimate of 33% for obsessions and 26% for compulsions, while Taylor (2011) reported a heritability estimate of 40% based on a meta-analysis of twin studies. Additional twin studies with substantially smaller samples have also reported a high degree of concordance for OCD ranging between 0.63 to 0.87 (e.g., McGuffin & Mawson, 1980; Menzies et al., 2008; Rasmussen & Tsuang, 1984). Hoaken and Schnurr (1980) noted, however, that for every ten monozygotic twin pairs that are concordant for OCD, four or so are discordant, and thus non-genetic factors clearly also play a role in the development of the disorder.

Linkage, Candidate Gene, and Genome-Wide Association Studies

As discussed in previous chapters, linkage studies identify loci on chromosomes that may harbor susceptibility genes for disorders of interest and numerous chromosomal regions have been identified for OCD, including 1q, 1p21, 1p36, 1p36, 2p14, 3q27–28, 5q13, 6p25, 6q, 9p24, 10p13, 15q11–13, 15q14, 16q24, 17p12, and 22q11 (e.g., Delorme et al., 2010; Hanna et al., 2002; Mathews et al., 2012; Ross et al., 2011; Shugart et al., 2006). It is important to note, however, that inconsistencies exist across the studies and many studies fail to replicate findings of previous studies. Therefore, to date, no firm conclusions can be drawn from linkage studies with respect to chromosomal loci unequivocally implicated in OCD. Follow-up candidate gene studies, however, have explored variants of a number of susceptibility genes particularly those involved in the serotonergic and dopaminergic neurotransmitter systems.

Serotonin Candidate Genes

Serotonin genes have been the focus of OCD genetic studies for several reasons: (a) serotonin agonists including antidepressants such as SSRIs (e.g., Prozac) and tricyclics (e.g., clomipramine) are often highly effective at reducing OCD symptoms, (b) serotonin antagonists can trigger or worsen OCD symptoms in patients being treated with serotonin antagonists (e.g., clozapine), and (c) some recreational drugs that are serotonin agonists (e.g, LSD, ecstacy, psilocybin) have been found to improve OCD symptoms while other studies suggest they worsen OCD symptoms (Baker et al., 1992; Grover et al., 2015; Kyzar, Stewart, & Kalueff, 2016; Leonard et al., 1987; Marchesi, Tonna, & Maggini, 2009; Wilcox, 2014).

For example, the *serotonin transporter gene* (SLC6A4) that encodes for the serotonin transporter has been extensively investigated in OCD given that serotonin reuptake inhibitors block the serotonin transporter and are effective at reducing OCD symptoms. Meta-analyses have found that a specific polymorphism in the SLC6A4 gene (serotonin transporter-linked polymorphic region, 5-HTTLPR) is significantly associated with OCD (Grünblatt et al., 2018; Taylor, 2016), although it is important to note that several studies have failed to replicate this finding (e.g., Atmaca et al., 2011; Bloch, Landeros-Weisenberger, et al., 2008). Other polymorphisms and gene variants of the SLC6A4 gene (e.g., Ile-425Val, rs25532, and rs16965628) have also been investigated in OCD, and findings have been conflicting across studies with some reporting an association with OCD while others have not (Billett et al., 1997; Grünblatt et al., 2018; Ozaki et al., 2003; Voyiaziakis et al., 2011).

Serotonin receptor genes have also been investigated in OCD. For example, a recent meta-analysis conducted by Taylor (2013) explored 230 polymorphisms from 113 genetic association studies and found that polymorphisms of the serotonin receptor gene HTR2A was significantly associated with OCD. The HTR2A gene, located on chromosome 13, encodes the serotonin receptor 5-HT2A that is important in normal functioning of the serotonergic system. Interestingly, this receptor has been found to down-regulate with the chronic administration of SSRIs (Muguruza et al., 2014). The 5-HT3A receptor has also been implicated in OCD as several polymorphisms and variants of the 5-HT3A receptor gene (HTR3) have been associated with OCD (Kim, Kang, et al., 2016). Kim et al. noted that activation of 5-HT3A receptors in the insular cortex enhance disgust sensitivity in rats and faulty functioning of these receptors in humans may contribute contamination concerns and compulsive hand washing commonly observed in OCD.

Additional serotonin genes have been studied in OCD (e.g., HTR1B, and HTR2C) with mixed results. In a recent systematic review of the role of serotonin genes in OCD, Sinopoli et al. (2017) concluded that the serotonin transporter polymorphism 5-HTTLPR and receptor HTR2A polymorphisms (rs6311, rs6313) are most consistently associated with OCD. As noted with other disorders discussed in this text, mixed findings across studies are likely the result of methodological factors as well as the genetic complexity and heterogeneity of OCD symptoms across participants.

Dopamine Candidate Genes

Dopamine genes have also been the focus of OCD genetic studies for several reasons: (a) dopamine agonists such as amphetamine have been found to induce or worsen OCD symptoms, (b) dopamine antagonists such as antipsychotic medications have been found to improve OCD symptoms, and (c) neuroimaging and brain stimulation studies support involvement of the dopaminergic system in OCD (Figee et al., 2014; Pignon et al., 2017; Shakeri et al., 2016).

Similar to the serotonin transporter gene, the *dopamine transporter gene* (SLC6A3, DAT1) located on chromosome 5 has been studied as a candidate gene in OCD. This gene is of particular interest given the importance of the dopamine transporter protein in retrieving dopamine from the synaptic cleft. A specific polymorphism (VNTR) of the dopamine transporter gene is believed to affect the expression and functioning of the dopamine transporter gene and has been found to increase susceptibility to Tourette's disorder that is often comorbid with OCD. Several studies, however, have failed to find an association between VNTR and OCD (e.g., Zhang et al., 2014). A recent meta-analysis by Taylor (2016) did not find an association between polymorphisms or gene variants of the SLC6A3, DAT1 gene, and OCD.

In contrast to lack of support for polymorphisms of the dopamine transporter gene, a number of studies have found an association between polymorphisms of *dopamine receptor genes* and OCD. For example, Millet et al. (2003) compared polymorphisms of a dopamine postsynaptic receptor gene (DRD4) in patients with OCD relative to matched controls and found a significantly lower frequency of a gene variant in patients with OCD. The DRD4 gene encodes a particular dopamine receptor (D4) and antipsychotic medications such as clozapine have a high affinity for the D4 receptor. A later study by Camarena et al. (2007) using a larger sample, replicated the findings of Millet et al., further supporting a possible role for the DRD4 gene in OCD.

Additional dopamine genes (e.g., D2, D3 receptors) have also been investigated in OCD and in general, these studies have not found an association between polymorphisms or gene variants and OCD (Billett et al., 1998; Hemmings and Stein, 2006; Taylor, 2013).

Glutamate Genes

Glutamate is the principle excitatory neurotransmitter in the brain and in the past decade has received significant attention with respect to OCD. For example, studies have found that mice genetically engineered to lack a gene (SAPAP3 also known as DLGAP3) that encodes proteins highly expressed in the striatum and important in glutamate signaling, groomed themselves compulsively and exhibited additional anxiety behaviors. When the mice were treated with an SSRI the OCD-like behaviors improved, and when the gene was reinserted, the behaviors were prevented (Welch et al., 2007). More recent studies have found that glutamate antagonists improve OCD-like behaviors in SAPAP3 knockout mice (Ade et al., 2016). In humans, some glutamate antagonists (memantine and riluzole) have been effective at improving OCD symptoms in preliminary studies (Pittenger, 2015). Given the apparent, although poorly understood role of glutamate in OCD, geneticists have studied gene variants and polymorphisms of the glutamate transporter and receptor genes.

The glutamate transporter gene, SLC1A1, located on chromosome 9, encodes *glutamate transporters*, and findings across studies consistently implicate polymorphisms of this gene with OCD. Hanna and colleagues (2002) were the first to conduct a genome-wide association study and identify a specific region of chromosome 9 (9p24) as likely to harbor susceptibility genes for OCD. Since that time a number of studies have reported associations between polymorphisms and variants of the SLC1A1 gene and OCD (see Rajendram et al., 2017, for a review). These gene variants are believed to alter the normal functioning of the glutamate transporter that is essential for retrieving glutamate from the synaptic cleft and transporting it across the plasma membrane.

Genes that encode *glutamate receptors* (NMDA) have also been studied in OCD, although less extensively than transporter genes. Research has found, for example, that glutamate receptors are widely distributed in structures and regions implicated in OCD via neuroimaging including the fronto-parieto-temporal cortex, amygdala, and the basal ganglia. Polymorphisms (e.g., rs1019385) and variants of NMDA receptor genes (e.g., GRIN2A GRIN2B) have been consistently linked to OCD (Bozorgmehr, Ghadirivasfi, & Shahsavand Ananloo, 2017; Kohlrausch et al., 2016). Additional studies are needed to continue to unravel the complex contributions of glutamate genes in the pathophysiology of OCD.

Additional Candidate Genes

A number of additional candidate genes have been and continue to be explored in OCD including those that encode for monoamine oxidase, catechol-o-methyltransferace, BDNF, and others. Findings across these studies have been variable with some reporting genetic associations while others have failed to replicate previous findings (see Bloch & Pittenger, 2010, and Taylor, 2016, for a review). A potentially important finding from several of these studies is that polymorphisms of several different types of genes occurred significantly more frequently in females than males, suggesting that gender differences may exist in genetic susceptibility to the disorder (e.g., Camarena et al., 2001a; Lochner et al., 2004; Taylor et al., 2016).

Genetic Summary

Collectively, family and twin studies support a heritability component to OCD. To date, over 100 genetic association studies involving over 200 polymorphisms and gene variants have been studied in the disorder (Taylor, 2016). The results of these linkage, genome-wide association, and candidate gene studies suggest that OCD is likely associated with multiple genes with most having a small to modest effects, and the specific nature of these effects remains largely unknown. The heterogeneity of OCD, as well as methodological challenges, increases the difficulty of elucidating the complex relationships among genetic and other factors. Future studies, with sufficient power to detect small, additive, and interactive effects, are needed to investigate the genetic contributions to OCD.

Structural Findings

Numerous studies have found structural differences in participants with OCD, most often involving the subcortial and cortical regions; however, inconsistencies exist across studies. To address these inconsistencies and increase statistical power, several meta-analyses have been conducted regarding structural findings in OCD, including a worldwide meta and mega-analysis (Boedhoe et al., 2016). In this study, MRI scans from over 1,800 participants with OCD and over 1,700 controls were compared. Results revealed that adults with OCD had significantly smaller hippocampal volumes and larger pallidum volumes compared with adult controls. Both effects were larger in medicated adults with OCD. In contrast, medication-naïve children with OCD had significantly larger thalamic volumes compared to controls. Other studies have also reported reduced hippocampal volumes in adult participants with OCD (Hong et al., 2007; Kwon et al., 2003a; Reess et al., 2017) and severity of OCD symptoms tends to be negatively correlated with hippocampal size (Kang et al., 2004; Reess et al., 2017).

Cortical Thickness

A number of studies including meta-analyses have reported decreased cortical thickness in participants with OCD group compared with controls in several regions, including the superior and inferior frontal regions, posterior cingulate, temporal lobe, inferior parietal lobe, and precuneus gyri (e.g., Fouche et al., 2017; Hoexter et al., 2015; Rus et al., 2017). Investigations have also found increased thinning of the cortex with increasing age in the participants OCD group relative to controls and an association between cortical thickness and medication response (Fouche et al., 2017; Hoexter et al., 2015). Other studies, however, have reported increased cortical thickness in some regions and decreased thickness in other regions participants with OCD relative to controls (Fan et al., 2013; Piras et al., 2015). Piras et al. have suggested that widespread structural abnormalities contribute to neurobiological vulnerability to OCD and not simply those involving cortices.

Gray Matter

Many studies have reported reduced gray matter in participants with OCD. For example, a meta-analysis by Eng, Sim, and Chen (2015) found widespread reductions in gray matter in the frontal, striatal, thalamus, and parietal and cerebellar regions of participants with OCD relative to controls, suggesting that OCD involves many more pathways than the traditional orbitofrontal region typically implicated in OCD pathophysiology. Similarly, Peng et al. (2015) found OCD participants had smaller gray matter volume than healthy controls in the frontal eye fields, medial frontal gyrus and anterior cingulate cortex and similar findings were reported by Gilbert et al. (2009). It is important to note that not all studies report reduced gray matter in participants with OCD, and specific gray matter findings are highly variable across studies (e.g., Rus et al., 2017).

Functional neuroimaging studies typically implicate the basal ganglia (e.g., caudate, globus pallidus, putamen, nucleus accumbens) in OCD, and, interestingly, structural studies have reported increased, reduced, or no difference in gray matter of the basal ganglia between participants with and without OCD (Bartha et al., 1998; Robinson et al., 1995; Rosenberg et al., 1997). For example, Peng et al. (2015) reported a reduction of gray matter in several brain regions in participants with OCD relative to controls but a significant increase in gray matter volume of the lenticular nucleus, caudate nucleus, and a small region in the right superior parietal lobule. Similarly, Hu, Du et al. (2017) recently found both adults and adolescents with OCD had smaller gray matter volume of the prefrontal cortex but greater caudate and putamen volume.

Meta-analytic studies have also, although not always, reported larger gray matter volumes in the lenticular nucleus caudate, and other basal ganglia related structures (e.g., Hu et al., 2017; Pujol et al., 2004; Radua et al., 2009; Narayanaswamy et al., 2012). Interestingly, Fouche et al. (2017) reported a negative correlation between hand washing severity and gray matter volume in the right thalamus. Some have speculated that increased basal ganglia volume resulted from chronic compulsive behavior, resulting in neuroplastic changes due to chronic compulsivity (Gilbert et al., 2009).

White Matter

As described previously in this text, white matter refers to areas of myelinated axons and tracts of axona. Studies have found white matter differences in patients with OCD, and depending on the study and the specific brain regions examined, both reduced and increased density of white matter has been reported (e.g., Hu et al., 2016; Fouche et al., 2017; Nakamae et al., 2008). For example, Jenike and colleagues (1996) reported significantly less white matter in three posterior regions of the brain in participants with OCD than controls but no differences were found in siix other widespread regions examined in the study. In contrast, Szesko et al. (2005) and Glahn et al. (2015) reported reduced white matter in widespread regions of the brain of participants with OCD, including the posterior cingulate gyrus, occipital lobe, and parietal lobe. The sample size in these studies, however, was very small (< 20 participants with OCD), and given the large number of dependent variables and statistical analyses in conjunction with low statistical power, the findings are equivocal.

White Matter, Corpus Callosum

Several studies have focused on the *corpus callosum* in participants with and without OCD and findings have been inconsistent across studies. For example, Di Paola et al. (2013) compared thickness and white matter density of the corpus callosum in participants with OCD relative to controls. Findings revealed smaller anterior and posterior regions of the corpus callosum in participants with OCD, and white matter density was positively correlated with performance on verbal memory, visuo-spatial memory, verbal fluency, and visuo-spatial reasoning tasks. Contradicting this perspective are findings by Mac Master et al. (1999) and Rosenberg et al. (1997), who reported increased volumes of portions of the corpus callosum as well as increased myelination in participants with OCD compared to healthy controls.

Additional white matter differences have been found in participants with OCD in some studies. Piras et al. (2013) conducted a review of the OCD white matter literature and concluded that findings supported altered white matter connectivity between lateral frontal and parietal regions and pathways linking areas of the prefrontal cortex to posterior parietal and occipital association cortices. Piras et al. also concluded that evidence supported the existence of microstructural alterations in white matter in various locations in the brains of participants with OCD including the corpus callosum. Lastly, this review reported decreased white matter connectivity in the rostrum region of the corpus callosum and hyperconnectivity in the genu region of the corpus callosum in participants with OCD compared to healthy controls.

A systematic review by Koch et al. (2014) also reported decreased white matter integrity of the corpus callosum is commonly found adult participants with OCD. Koch et al. also noted, however, that results support *increased* white matter connectivity in several brain regions pediatric and adolescent participants with OCD. These white matter alterations are hypothesized to vary as a function of clinical characteristics, and some have suggested that myelination may occur prematurely in the brain of patients with OCD, especially those with an early onset of symptoms (Gruner et al., 2012). It is important to keep in mind, however, that white matter density findings are heterogeneous across studies and additional research is needed to further explore white matter density in participants with OCD relative to healthy controls and other clinical groups.

Amygdala

Variable findings have been reported in terms of amygdala volume and OCD. Szeszko and colleagues (1999) and Atmaca et al. (2008) reported that the amygdala volume was significantly smaller in participants with OCD than healthy control subjects; however, other studies have not replicated this difference. For example, Rus, Reess, Wagner, et al. (2016) explored amygdala structural differences between participants with and without OCD, and reported an absence of structural connectivity differences between the two groups. Similarly, Kwon, Shin, et al. (2003) used MRI to compare volumes of the hippocampus, amygdala, and thalamus in patients with OCD to patients with schizophrenia and healthy controls, and reported that the left amygdala was significantly *larger* in patients with OCD compared to the other two groups.

Summary

In summary, structural differences are often reported in subcortical and cortical regions in participants with OCD relative to healthy controls. These findings are not consistent among studies, however, and morphological differences of cortical and subcortical structures have also been found in children and adults with other disorders. The heterogeneity of structural findings in OCD likely reflects differences among participants with OCD, such as age of onset, comorbid disorders, ethnicity, family history of OCD, medication history, as well as methodological characteristics of the studies. Additional studies are warranted that explore the integrity of brain structures in patients with OCD as well as the relevance of these findings with respect to OCD symptomatology. Structural findings in conjunction with functional studies are needed to unravel the physiological underpinnings of OCD.

Functional Findings

In the last decade, a plethora of functional neuroimaging studies have been conducted with participants with OCD. Although the techniques used across studies differ (e.g., fMRI, rtfMRI, PET, SPECT, MEG) the common goal is to elucidate regions, pathways, and functional patterns that may underlie the pathophysiology of OCD. Differences in brain functioning patterns are typically inferred from glucose metabolism, blood flow, signaling, or receptor density and receptor responsivity in participants with OCD compared to healthy controls (and in some studies other clinical groups). These studies have been performed during varying parameters—e.g., while participants are at rest, during various activities (e.g., contamination challenges)—and before, during, and after administration of medication(s).

Historically the most common regions implicated in OCD involved pathways extending from subcortical structures to the prefrontal cortex and back again—i.e., the *cortico-striatal-thalamic loop* (Fettes, Schulze, & Downar, 2017; Saxena et al., 1998). In 1987, Baxter et al. were among the first to explore functional differences between patients with and without OCD using PET. Findings revealed glucose metabolic rates were significantly increased in the cortico-striatal-thalamic loop—namely, in the left orbital gyrus and bilaterally in the caudate nuclei of participants with OCD compared to controls. Since that time, a wealth of studies has compared functional findings of the cortico-striatal-thalamic loop in participants with OCD and healthy controls. Although inconsistencies have been found across studies, meta-analyses have supported different patterns of activation in participants with OCD relative to control subjects during rest conditions as well as during cognitive, memory, executive function, and emotional tasks that illicit emotions of fear, disgust, guilt, and shame (e.g., Busatto et al., 2000; Castillo et al., 2005; Kwon, Kim et al., 2003; Brem et al., 2012; Gonçalves et al., 2016; Moon & Jeong, 2017).

Beyond the Cortico-Striatal-Thalamic Loop

In recent years, research has substantiated that regions other than the cortico-striatal-thalamic loop appear to be involved in OCD. For example, studies now implicate limbic structures, temporal cortex, parietal cortex, pallidum, anterior cingulate cortex, angular gyrus, and cerebellum in OCD (Carlisi et al., 2016; Posner et al., 2014; Rasgon et al., 2017; Gonçalves, 2016). For example, Nakao, Okada, and Kanba (2014) found increased activation in cortico-cerebellar regions of participants with OCD with hand-washing rituals compared to healthy controls, while participants with checking rituals showed decreased activation in the left caudate and left anterior cingulate cortex compared to healthy controls. Based on these results and further review of the literature, Nakao et al. advocated for a revised model of OCD extending beyond the cortico-striatal-thalamic loop.

A recent meta-analysis by Rasgon et al. (2017) also advanced a more extensive neurobiological model of OCD. Specifically, Rasgon and colleagues interpreted meta-analytic findings in terms of neurobiological processes underlying affective, cognitive, and behavioral symptoms of OCD. Rasgon et al. concluded that meta-analytic evidence supports increased activation in the anterior cingulate cortex, insula, caudate head, and putamen during affective tasks in participants with OCD. These structures have been shown to be involved in salience, arousal, and habitual responding; cognitive processes problematic in patients with OCD. Rasgon et al. also found support for decreased activity in regions implicated in cognitive and behavioral control (medial prefrontal cortex, posterior caudate) in participants with OCD relative to controls. During non-affective cognitive tasks, participants with OCD displayed a pattern of increased activation in structures linked to self-referential processing (precuneus, posterior cingulate cortex) and decreased activation in subcortical regions that are involved in goal-directed behavior and motor control (pallidum, ventral anterior thalamus, posterior caudate). Rasgon et al. interpreted the overall pattern of findings as indicative of increased affective and self-referential processing, habitual responding, and blunted cognitive control in participants with OCD relative to adults without the disorder.

BOX 7.3   What Happens in the Brain When OCD Symptoms Are Provoked?

While placed in an fRMI scanner, participants with OCD have been shown individually tailored visual images of scenes that trigger their OCD symptoms (e.g., dirty door knobs, food crusted dishes, messy clothing, crooked paintings, pet hair). While viewing the images, participants with OCD compared to healthy controls have consistently shown increased activation of the cortico-striatal-thalamic loop as well as temporal and parietal cortices and subcortical structures (anterior cingulate cortex, globus pallidus, hippocampus, uncus). These same structures and regions have been identified in previous neuroimaging studies and provide support for an extended model of OCD. It is been hypothesized that the increased activity of the orbitofrontal regions contributes to evaluation of the occurrence of negative consequences following an action, which in turn leads to the generation of obsessive thoughts. In order to prevent the imagined negative consequences and/or alleviate anxiety triggered by the obsessive thoughts, repetitive or ritualistic behaviors are performed. These obsessive thoughts and compulsive behaviors are purportedly mediated by complex pathways within the cortico-striatal-thalamic loop, temporal and parietal cortices, cerebellum, and subcortical structures, including the anterior cingulate cortex, amygdala, basal ganglia and limbic structures (Adler et al., 2000; Breiter et al., 1996; Rotge et al., 2008; Takagi et al., 2017). This explanation is inherently circular because neuroimaging data is only correlational in nature.

Functional Findings and Medication

Further support for involvement of the cortico-striatal-thalamic loop in OCD stems from studies that have found higher rCBF in the caudate, cingulate, and dorsolateral prefrontal region of medication-naïve participants with OCD relative to healthy controls. Following treatment with an SSRI, these regions have showed significant reductions in rCBF (Diler, Kibar, and Avci, 2004). Additionally, increased activation in the cortico-striatal-thalamic loop has been associated with increased severity of OCD symptoms and following SSRI treatment glucose metabolism changes of the putamen, cerebellum, and hippocampus have been significantly associated with improved performance on neuropsychological tasks. (Lacerda et al., 2003b; Kang et al., 2003; Hansen et al., 2002; Saxena et al., 2001, 2002; Hoehn-Saric et al., 2001; Rauch et al., 2002).

Additionally, studies suggest that the underlying pathophysiology of OCD may differ depending on the age at which OCD symptoms begin. For example, Busatto et al. (2001) compared rCBF in two groups of adults with OCD: those who developed the disorder prior to age 10 (early onset) and those who developed OCD after age 12 (late onset). Based on SPECT scans, both groups showed decreased rCBF in the right orbitofrontal regions. Participants with early onset OCD, however, had reduced rCBF in the left anterior cingulate and increased rCBF in the right cerebellum compared to controls. In addition, compared to late onset OCD cases, participants with early onset OCD showed reduced rCBF in the right thalamus. Other studies have reported structural and functional differences of the thalamus in patients with OCD. Gilbert et al. (2000), for example, investigated the volume of the thalamus of 21 children and adolescents (8–17 years) with OCD who had never taken medication for the disorder. Compared to control children, those with OCD had significantly larger thalamic volumes. However, following 12 weeks of treatment with an SSRI, the size of the thalamus decreased substantially, comparable in size to controls, and thalamic reduction was associated with symptom reduction. Rosenberg et al. (2000) assessed whether cognitive behavior therapy would also result in thalamic volume changes in children of the same age as those in Gilbert's study and contrary to expectations, cognitive behavior therapy was not associated with changes in thalamic volume. These findings are intriguing as they suggest that pharmacological intervention can uniquely foster brain plasticity that corresponds with improvement in OCD symptoms.

Summary

Overall, functional studies conducted for approximately two decades implicate cortico-striatal-thalamic pathways in OCD. These pathways extend from the subcortical structures to and from the prefrontal cortex and have been associated with increased (cortical) and decreased (subcortical) activity inferred from rCBF and glucose metabolism studies. Treatment with SSRIs has been found to decrease activity within these regions and to result in neuroplastic changes. Inconsistencies do exist across studies, however, and likely reflect participant characteristics as well as methodological factors and measurement differences stemming from imaging techniques (Reba, 1993). In addition, it is critical to keep in mind that the cortico-striatal-thalamic pathways are implicated in other disorders (e.g., ADHD, Tourette's disorder). Furthermore, neuroimaging findings are correlational in nature and structural and functional differences are not necessarily related to or responsible for OCD symptoms. It is plausible, for example, that neural functioning may be influenced by cognitive, affective, and behavioral symptoms associated with OCD rather than causative. As aptly noted by McKay et al. (2017),

> It appears that a disorder-specific structural pathophysiology of OCD is far from identified, and the few brain areas identified as different from control subjects have very weak and nonspecific association with the condition. At present, there is a poverty of research that evaluates brain structural and functional indices between OCD and clinically relevant controls, and there is no experimental or longitudinal research that identifies causal biological mechanisms of the disorder. Until such evidence is presented, conclusions regarding disorder-specific pathophysiology of brain areas in association with OCD—especially causal conclusions—are unfounded.

In the meantime, future research is warranted to continue to try to identify and understand structural and functional differences between patients with OCD relative to healthy controls and clinical comparison groups.

BOX 7.4   Does Strep Throat Cause OCD?

Pediatric autoimmune neuropsychiatric disorders associated with streptococcal infections (PANDAS) has been used to describe children and in some cases adults who have abrupt onset of OCD or tics (see Chapter 9) following documented group-A beta-hemolytic streptococcal infections (Bodner, Morshed, & Peterson, 2001; Orvidas & Slattery, 2001; Swedo et al., 1998). A number of earlier studies reported an association between exposure to streptococcal infections and subsequent development of OCD or tics (Kiessling, 1989; Arnold and Richter, 2001). Neuroimaging studies also reported increased basal ganglia volumes that corresponded with severity of abrupt OCD or tic symptoms, presumably due to increased antibodies within the basal ganglia in reaction to the streptococcal infection (Peterson et al., 2000). Murphy and Pichichero (2002) reported treatment with antibiotics eradicated a group-A beta-hemolytic streptococcal infection as well as associated OCD symptoms in 12 school-aged children. Other studies, however, have not found antibiotics helpful in either preventing or decreasing PANDAS-related OCD symptoms (Arnold & Richter, 2001; Macerollo & Martino, 2013). It is important to note that most cases of OCD are not linked to streptococcal infections and, as Snider and Swedo (2003) pointed out, it may be that individuals who develop OCD in reaction to streptococcal infections are genetically susceptible to the illness. Presently, the clinical definition and prevalence of PANDAS are still hotly debated. According to Macerollo and Martino (2013), reliable diagnostic biomarkers are not available, and the pathogenesis of PANDAS remains undefined. Hence Macerollo and Martino recommend that treatment of OCD follow empirically supported approaches, including pharmacological and cognitive behavior therapy.

Neurotransmitter Findings

Serotonin

As mentioned in the previous genetics section, serotonin been studied in OCD largely due to (a) serotonin agonists, including antidepressants such as SSRIs (e.g., Prozac) and tricyclics (e.g., clomipramine), are often highly effective at reducing OCD symptoms; 9b) serotonin antagonists can trigger or worsen OCD symptoms in patients being treated with serotonin antagonists (e.g., clozapine); and (c) some recreational drugs that are serotonin agonists (e.g, LSD, ecstacy, psilocybin) have been found to improve OCD symptoms, while other studies suggest they worsen OCD symptoms (Baker et al., 1992; Grover et al., 2015; Kyzar et al., 2016; Leonard et al., 1987; Marchesi et al., 2009; Wilcox, 2014).

Serotonin Transporter Availability   With regard to serotonin and antidepressants, molecular studies have explored whether differences exist in serotonin transporter availability in participants with OCD relative to healthy controls. For example, Pogarell et al. (2003) used SPECT to assess serotonin transporter availability in unmedicated individuals with OCD and healthy volunteers. Results indicated that individuals with OCD had 25% *higher* serotonin transporter binding in the midbrain and pons regions relative to controls, and binding was highest in individuals with early onset OCD. There was no significant binding difference between groups with respect to striatal regions. Other studies, however, have reported no difference in serotonin transporter binding or *lower* availability relative to controls in the midbrain, insular cortex, thalamus, and orbitofrontal cortex (Matsumoto et al., 2010; Reimold et al., 2007; Simpson et al., 2003). Two confounding factors in these studies, however, is age of onset of symptoms (i.e., early versus later) and medication history. For example, Hesse et al. (2011) reported higher serotonin transporter availability in drug-naïve early onset cases compared to later onset, and antidepressants appear to affect the availability of serotonin transporters (Descarries & Raid, 2012).

To address the confounds of onset and medication, Lee, Kim, et al. (2018) recently studied six patients with early onset OCD and six with later onset OCD and measured availability of serotonin transporters at baseline and while taking an SSRI using PET. The primary region of interest was the cortico-striato-thalamo-cortical loop including the putamen, caudate nucleus, thalamus, and the dorsal raphe nucleus. Results revealed that serotonin transporter availability was significantly *higher* in the putamen of early onset participants during baseline and while they were medicated, but no difference was found between groups in the other structures. In addition, results indicated that serotonin transporter availability was not correlated with severity of symptoms. These findings suggest that structural binding differences may exist in early versus later onset OCD cases in at least one structure (putamen) and that this difference persists with SSRI treatment. It is important to note that sample sizes in these studies were quite small, and statistical power was compromised. Also, whether elevated binding reflects a higher density of serotonin transporters in participants with OCD resulting in an increased capacity of serotonin reuptake or higher density of serotonin transporters is a compensatory response to low serotonin levels remains indeterminate. Additional studies are needed to further understand the role of age of onset, medication, and other factors that may be related to serotonin transporters in OCD.

Serotonin Receptors   A few studies have examined serotonin receptor binding in OCD. Simpso, Slifstein, et al. (2011), for example, using PET explored serotonin receptor binding in widespread regions, including cortical (orbitofrontal, dorsolateral prefrontal, medial prefrontal, anterior cingulate, temporal, parietal, occipital, and insular cortex) and limbic regions (entorhinal cortex, parahippocampal gyrus, and medial temporal lobe) in 19 participants with OCD and 19 healthy controls. Contrary to expectations results did not reveal binding differences in any of the regions measured. Perani et al. (2008), however, reported a significant reduction of serotonin receptor (5-HT2A) availability in frontal, dorsolateral, and medial frontal cortices, as well as parietal and temporal associative cortices of participants (9) with OCD compared to controls. Perani et al. also found a significant correlation between receptor availability in orbitofrontal and dorsolateral frontal cortex and severity of OCD symptoms. Lastly, preliminary findings suggest availability of 5-HT1B receptors (that serve as autoreceptor and heteroreceptors) do not differ in participants with OCD compared to controls (Clark & Neumaier, 2001; Pittenger et al., 2016). Given the inconsistencies across studies, findings regarding availability of serotonin receptors and OCD are inconclusive.

Dopamine   Several lines of research implicate dopamine in the mediation of OCD symptoms: (a) other animal studies have demonstrated that dopamine agonists can induce behavior that resembles OCD behavior in humans, (b) dopamine antagonists can improve OCD symptoms, and (c) dopamine agonists can trigger or worsen OCD symptoms.

To explore the role of dopamine in OCD, scientists have studied compulsive behavior in other animals, including mice, rats, and dogs. These studies have revealed that rats and mice treated with the dopamine receptor agonists (e.g., quinpirole) have developed checking behavior and excessive lever pressing (Joel, Avisar, & Doljansky, 2001; Tizabi et al., 2002). Dogs, cats, and rabbits often spontaneously display compulsive behaviors (e.g., licking, tail chasing, circling behavior) and have been successfully treated with antidepressants, such as clomipramine and, in some cases, dopamine antagonists (Overall & Dunham, 2002). Dopamine antagonists have also been used in the treatment of OCD in humans who do not respond to SSRIs or to augment SSRIs, although they can also induce or worsen OCD symptoms (Alevizos et al., 2002). For example, Metin et al. (2003) reported that amisulpiride, an antipsychotic dopamine antagonist, was associated with significant reductions in OCD behavior in patients when used in conjunction with SSRIs. Meta-analytic studies have reported that some dopamine antagonists are useful for short-term treatment of OCD (e.g., aripiprazole, risperidone) while others are not more effective than placebo (quetiapine or olanzapine) (Fountoulakis et al., 2004; Veale et al., 2014).

The *dopamine transporter protein* (DAT) has also been investigated preliminarily in humans and other animals in OCD. For example, Vermeire et al. (2012) studied DAT density in dogs with compulsive behaviors relative to healthy dogs and reported that 78% of the compulsive dogs had either abnormally high *or* abnormally low DAT binding in the left and right striatum. In humans, findings have been highly inconsistent with some studies reported reduced DAT binding in the striatum while others increased or no difference relative to healthy controls (Hesse et al., 2005; van der Wee et al., 2004).

Preliminary studies support reduced availability of *dopamine receptors* in participants with OCD compared to healthy control participants. In a review of the literature, Nikolaus et al. (2010) reported an 18% decrease in striatal dopamine receptors (D2) in participants with OCD. Other studies have reported decreased availability of D2 and D3 receptors in the striatum of patients with OCD, and an association between effectiveness of antipsychotic medication (dopamine antagonists) and D2 and D3 receptor affinity (Denys et al., 2013; Ducasse et al., 2014).

Additional evidence of dopaminergic involvement in OCD stems from research involving Parkinson's disease, Tourette's disorder, and ADHD. Genetic, structural, and functional studies have implicated dopamine in all three of these disorders, and OCD is often comorbid with these disorders (Geller, 2004; Hirschtritt et al., 2017; Segawa, 2003; Weyandt, 2001, 2006). Interestingly, amphetamines that primarily affect the dopaminergic system and are used to treat ADHD, have been found to sometimes induce OCD symptoms in children and adults (Borcherding et al., 1990; Serby, 2003; Shakeri et al., 2016). Similarly, a side effect of dopamine agonists used to treat Parkinson's disease is compulsive, repetitive behaviors (Raja & Bentivoglio, 2012). Research has also found a relationship between use of cocaine, a dopamine agonist, and increased risk of OCD in adults and in other animals (Crum & Anthony, 1993; Metaxas et al., 2012). Collectively, these studies suggest that dopamine plays a role in OCD symptomology, however, the intricacies of this relationship are poorly understood. As Micallef and Blin (2001) noted, the serotonergic and dopaminergic neurotransmitter systems function interactively, and it is possible that decreased inhibitory influences of serotonin on dopaminergic neurons results in hyperactivity of dopaminergic neurons within the basal ganglia. OCD may be the consequence of dysfunctional interactive neurotransmitter systems within the basal ganglia and associated circuitry, and highly comorbid syndromes, such as Tourette's disorder and ADHD may represent derivations of this faulty system.

Glutamate, GABA, Opioid Receptors   Given that 40–60% of patients with OCD do not respond to antidepressants yet often respond to other types of medications suggests involvement of additional neurotransmitter systems in the disorder (Marazziti et al., 2017; Pallanti et al., 2006). Glutamate, GABA, and opioid receptors, for example, have been implicated in OCD to varying levels. For example, recent research suggests that the glutamate system directly affects dopamine-releasing neurons in the striatum, and glutamate antagonists have been found to improve OCD symptoms in treatment resistant cases (Bellini et al., 2017; Vicek et al., 2017). In addition, Rosenberg and colleagues (2000) measured glutamate concentrations in the caudate nucleus in children and adolescents with OCD before and after antidepressant (paroxetine) treatment. Results revealed glutamate concentrations were significantly higher in patients with OCD than control subjects at baseline, and after 12 weeks of antidepressant treatment, glutamate concentrations were reduced to a level similar to control participants. Bolton et al. (2001) suggested that dysfunction of the glutamate system within the caudate nucleus may be reversible with antidepressant treatment.

GABA appears to play a role in OCD given the adjunctive effectiveness of benzodiazepines in reducing OCD symptoms in treatment-resistant adults and children (Francobandiera, 2001; Leonard et al., 1994; Hollander, Kaplan, & Stahl, 2003; D'Amico et al., 2003). With respect to the role of opioid receptors in OCD, several studies have found that the rate of OCD was four times higher in individuals addicted to opioids, and oral weekly doses of morphine reduced OCD symptoms in OCD treatment-resistant patients (Friedman, Dar, & Shilony, 2000; Fals-Stewart & Angarano, 1994; Koran et al., 2005). Findings have been mixed, however, regarding the effectiveness of the opioid antagonist, naltrexone, at reducing OCD symptoms (Amiaz et al., 2008; Grant & Kim, 2001).

Physiologically Based Interventions for OCD
Pharmacological

Numerous reviews are available concerning the pharmacological treatment of OCD in children, adolescents, and adults (e.g., Geller et al., 2003; Hollander et al., 2002; Bloch et al., 2014). As reviewed previously in this chapter, antidepressants are the most commonly used medications for treating OCD, particularly SSRIs and the tricyclic antidepressant clomipramine. Meta-analyses indicate that SSRIs and cognitive behavior therapy are the most effective form of treatment currently available for OCD in both children and adults (Albert et al., 2017; Hirschtritt et al., 2017).

Research suggests that different SSRIs (e.g., paroxetine, fluoxetine, fluvoxamine, sertraline) are equally effective in the treatment of OCD with higher doses typically more effective than lower doses (Bloch et al., 2010; Soomro et al., 2008). On average, the greatest benefits are found after 6 weeks of initiating SSRIs, although 12 weeks or longer may be required to determine efficacy of SSRIs (Issaria et al., 2016). Studies suggest that even among patients whose symptoms reduce and are considered to be "responders" to SSRIs, most continue to experience significant OCD symptoms (Pallanti et al., 2006).

Clomipramine (tricyclic) is highly effective at reducing OCD symptomatology, although it is associated with more side effects (e.g., dry mouth, blurred vision, constipation, fatigue, tremor, cardiac arrhythmia) than SSRIs and consequently tends to have a lower compliance rate (Pigott & Seay, 1999). Findings are mixed in terms of comparative efficacy of clomipramine and SSRIs with some studies reporting that clomipramine is more effective at reducing OCD symptoms while others report similar effect sizes (Geller et al., 2003; Skapinakis et al., 2016).

Augmentation   Hollander et al. (2002) noted that it is not uncommon for patients with OCD to not respond to treatment with SSRIs and recommended that other medications (or cognitive-behavioral therapy) be tried such as another SSRI or a serotonin-norepinephrenine reuptake inhibitor. Augmentation with neuroleptics (haloperidol, olanzapine, and risperidone) is also recommended treatment-resistant OCD (Bloch et al., 2006). McDougle et al. (2000) examined the effectiveness of the antipsychotic medication risperidone in treating OCD and found that 50% of patients with OCD showed a favorable response to the medication. Figueroa and colleagues (1998) reported that a combination of SSRI and clomipramine was more effective at decreasing OCD symptoms than either drug used alone in children and adolescents with OCD. As noted previously in this chapter, preliminary studies suggest that glutamate antagonists (e.g., memantine, riluzole) may have beneficial effects in some individuals with OCD (Ghaleiha et al., 2013; Pittenger et al., 2015).

Neuorosurgery

There is considerable interest in the use and further development of physiologically based treatments for OCD due to the fact that 40%–60% of patients do not respond to pharmacological or cognitive behavioral interventions (Greenberg & Rezai, 2003; Pallanti et al., 2006). In the early 1930s, Egas Moniz coined the phrase "psychosurgery" to describe brain operations he performed to treat institutionalized patients with severe mental illness (Moniz, 1937). Today, neurosurgery is reserved for patients with chronically severe and treatment-refractory mental illness, including mood, anxiety disorders, and OCD (Cosgrove & Rauch, 1995; Shah et al., 2008). Given structural and functional findings that implicated pathways projecting to and from subcortical to cortical regions (orbitofrontal cortex, thalamus, anterior cingulate, and striatum), surgical procedures typically target regions within this circuitry. Examples of five surgical procedures used in patients with severe treatment-resistant OCD include (a) subcaudate tractotomy, (b) anterior capsulotomy, (c) anterior cingulotomy, (d) limbic leucotomy (a combination of anterior cingulotomy and capsulotomy), and (e) gamma ventral capsulotomy. *Subcaudate tractotomy* involves lesioning an area under the head of the caudate nucleus to interrupt connections between subcortical and orbitofrontal regions, while an *anterior capsulotomy* targets pathways connecting the thalamus and the frontal lobes. An *anterior cingulotomy* involves lesioning an area of the cortex of the anterior cingulate, and a *limbic leucotomy* involves lesioning the anterior cingulate as well as an area of the caudate nucleus. Lastly, gamma ventral capsulotomy, unlike the other four craniotomy procedures, does not require opening of the skull but instead involves the delivery of gamma rays through the skull. These gamma rays are concentrated on the pathways connecting the dorsomedial thalamus *and* ventral prefrontal cortex and destroy cells therein (Spofford et al., 2014).

Research indicates that these neurosurgical procedures are effective at reducing intractable OCD symptoms in 35–75% of cases, with benefits extending 6–24 months after surgery in the majority of patients (Baer et al., 1995; Dougherty et al. 2002; Gouvea et al., 2010;

Greenberg, Rauch, & Haber, 2010; Jenike et al., 1991). Potential and commonly reported negative side effects associated with these procedures include memory deficits, apathy, urinary incontinence, and seizures (e.g., Montoya et al., 2002).

To explore potential functional effects of neurosurgical procedures, Sachdev and colleagues (2001) used PET to measure glucose metabolism in a 37-year-old female 18 days and again at 3 years following a bilateral orbitomedial leucotomy for severe OCD. Results revealed a significant reduction of activity in the head of the caudate, anterior cingulate, thalamus, and several frontal regions 18 days following the procedure, and a sustained reduction in glucose metabolism in many of these regions after 3 years. These reductions in activity were associated with improvement of symptoms and support involvement of subcortical-cortical pathways in OCD. Similarly, Kim et al. (2001) measured rCBF in patients who had undergone a limbic leukotomy for intractable OCD and found significant decreases in the medial frontal cortex, cingulate, and striatum.

On a positive note, recent findings suggest that neurosurgical treatment of OCD does not have deleterious effects on personality, and in fact, patients who showed OCD symptom reduction also reported a reduction in neuroticism and an increase in extraversion, novelty seeking, and self-directedness. Interestingly, no significant changes were found in patients deemed non-responders to surgery (Paiva et al. 2018). Collectively, these studies suggest that a significant percentage of individuals who do not respond to traditional treatment methods for OCD may respond to neurosurgery. Given the risks associated with brain surgery and the potential side effects, psychosurgery is obviously reserved for severe, intractable cases of OCD.

Brain Stimulation Techniques

Several brain stimulation techniques have been used with treatment resistant OCD cases including deep brain stimulation (DBS), repetitive Transcranial magnetic stimulation (rTMS), transcranial direct current stimulation (tDCS), and electroconvulsive therapy (ECT). As discussed in Chapter 3, DBS requires neurosurgery with associated risks, while ECT, rTMS, and tDCS are noninvasive forms of treatment that pose minimal known risks (Zaman & Robbins, 2017).

The effectiveness of DBS at improving treatment resistant OCD has been explored by a number of studies although sample sizes tend to be small. Nuttin and colleagues (1999), for example, studied the effectiveness of DBS in four patients with chronic treatment-resistant OCD and reported that three of the four showed significant improvement of symptoms. Gabriëls et al. (2003) reported that two of three patients treated for OCD with DBS showed sustained improvement of symptoms over time (33 months) with no harmful side effects. In a recent systematic review, Vázquez-Bourgon and colleagues (2017) concluded that empirical evidence supports the efficacy of DBS in treatment-resistant OCD with assumable side effects.

Location of DBS has been reported to affect efficacy outcome as small deviations in the placement of the DBS electrode, as well as unilateral or bilateral placement, can substantially alter the degree of activation of structures involved (McIntyre et al., 2004; Sturm et al., 2003).

When used for OCD, DBS placement typically involves the anterior limb of the internal capsule/nucleus accumbens or thalamus/subthalamic nucleus. For example, Anderson and Ahmed (2003) described the case of a female patient who was treated with bilateral electrical stimulators that were placed in the interior limbs of the internal capsules (between the thalamus and caudate nucleus). Placement of the stimulators resulted in chronic electrical stimulation, and findings revealed shorter- and longer-term improvement in the patients' OCD symptoms and general functioning. Nuttin et al. (2003) reported that during stimulation (compared to stimulation-off periods) bilateral stimulators led to decreased metabolism in the frontal regions of six patients with treatment-refractory OCD. Other studies, however, have relied on unilateral placement of electrodes with varying results. In a recent meta-analysis sponsored by the American Society for Stereotactic and Functional Neurosurgery and the Congress of Neurological Surgeons, and endorsed by the American Association of Neurological Surgeons, Hamini and colleagues (2014) recommended use of bilateral nucleus accumbens DBS and did not endorse use of unilateral DBS for treatment resistant OCD.

A few studies have found that adult patients treated with ECT have shown short- and longer-term reduction in OCD symptoms (Mellman & Gorman, 1984; Thomas and Kellner 2003). Maletzky et al. (1994) reported that nearly all of the 32 patients with intractable OCD benefited from ECT and that improvement in their symptoms was sustained over a 1-year period. A number of side effects are associated with ECT including headaches, memory impairment, nausea, and muscle aches, although most of these symptoms are thought to be transitory (Datto, 2000). A recent study involving over 1,000 participants with OCD reported that only 13 (1.3% of the sample) reported having been treated with ECT in their lifetime. Compared to other participants in the study, these participants were treated more often with antipsychotics and reported higher suicidality and psychotic symptoms (Dos Santos-Ribeiro et al., 2016). According to Russell et al. (2002), there is reluctance among psychiatrists to use ECT with children and adolescents with any psychiatric illness, including OCD, and its use with this population is even more controversial than adult patients.

Finally, rapid transcranial magnetic stimulation (rTMS) and transcranial direct current stimulation (tDCS) appear promising as adjunctive treatments for OCD, as preliminary studies support their effectiveness in reducing OCD symptomatology (Trevizol et al., 2016; Tendler et al., 2016). As discussed previously in this text, rTMS involves the rapid delivery of brief magnetic pulses directly to the scalp that induce neuronal depolarization (increased excitation) while low frequency pulses are thought to increase neuronal inhibition (Voineskos et al., 2013). In contrast, tDCS passes small *electrical* currents through the skull and purportedly has a modulatory effect on neurotransmission by either increasing or decreasing neural firing at the level of the cortex (Elder & Taylor, 2014). To date, compared to pharmacological interventions, relatively few studies have investigated the efficacy of these techniques at improving OCD symptoms but preliminary findings are encouraging (Najafi et al., 2017).

Summary of Obsessive-Compulsive Disorder

- The 12-month prevalence of OCD in the United States is approximately 1.2% with a lifetime prevalence of 2.3%.
- *Obsessions* are persistent ideas, impulses, thoughts, or images that experiences as intrusive and unwanted while *compulsions* are repetitive overt or mental acts that an individual feels compelled to perform.
- Common obsessions include contamination, doubts, symmetry or exactness, somatic fears, sexual thoughts, or thoughts of harm.
- Common compulsions include cleaning, checking, counting, and ordering.
- Although similar rates of OCD are often found around the world, OCD symptoms and the course of illness can be shaped by cultural, ethnic, and religious experiences.

- Developmentally, OCD is equally common in adults of both sexes but more common in boys in childhood.
- OCD typically begins in adolescence or adulthood with a gradual onset.
- OCD is associated with a number of psychiatric disorders, including depression, eating psychotic, and tic disorders, and Tourette's disorder.
- Based on familial and twin studies, OCD appears to have a heritability component.
- Genetic studies have not identified a gene or group of genes that cause OCD.
- Structural studies have found morphological differences in a variety of subcortical structures and regions in participants with OCD relative to healthy controls.
- Structural findings are not consistent among studies, however, and similar morphological differences of cortical and subcortical structures have also been found in children and adults with other disorders.
- The heterogeneity of structural findings in OCD likely reflects differences among participants with OCD participants, such as age of onset, comorbid disorders, ethnicity, family history of OCD, medication history, as well as methodological characteristics of the studies.
- Functional studies implicate cortico-striatal-thalamic pathways in OCD, and more recently, additional regions, including temporal and parietal regions, as well as the cerebellum, have been implicated in OCD.
- Treatment with SSRIs has been found to decrease activity within cortico-striatal-thalamic pathways and lead to neuroplastic changes.
- Functional differences are not necessarily related to or responsible for OCD symptoms. It is plausible, for example, that neural functioning may be influenced by cognitive, affective, and behavioral symptoms associated with OCD rather than causative.
- Several neurotransmitter systems have been implicated in OCD particularly serotonin, dopamine, and glutamate.
- It is important to note that structural and functional studies are correlational in nature and not reveal the underlying cause(s) of the disorder.
- Pharmacological treatment of OCD typically involves antidepressants (SSRIs and clomipramine).
- For severe, refractory OCD, neurosurgery and brain stimulation techniques have been found to reduce OCD symptoms.

Review Questions

1. Compare and contrast genetic structural and functional findings of panic disorder and OCD. What can be concluded from these findings?
2. What type of pharmacological treatment is most effective for panic disorder? OCD? What is the mode of action of these drugs and how does this relate to neurotransmitter findings?
3. What do panic disorder and OCD have in common?
4. What do developmental findings pertaining to OCD suggest about the etiology of the disorder?
5. What can be concluded about the cause of panic disorder and OCD at this time?

eight
Addiction and Substance Use Disorders

This chapter reviews theories of drug addiction and research findings concerning substance use disorders. Information concerning prevalence, developmental and multicultural factors, and reward pathways is reviewed and particular attention is given to molecular, structural, and genetic findings. Lastly, neurotransmitter and neuroimaging findings pertaining to alcohol, stimulants, opioids, and cannabis are reviewed and pharmacological treatment approaches to substance use disorders are discussed.

Chapter 8 Learning Objectives

■ Define addiction and substance use disorder.
■ Describe demographic information pertaining to substance use disorders.
■ Describe multicultural findings pertaining to addiction.
■ Explain reinforcement theories of addiction.
■ Explain the role of dopamine and the mesolimbic pathway in addiction.
■ Describe molecular and anatomical brain changes that occur with addiction.
■ Describe functional brain changes associated with addiction.
■ Summarize current genetic findings pertaining to addiction.
■ Describe pharmacological approaches to treating substance use disorder.

Drug Addiction

There is no single, universally accepted definition of addiction (NIDA, 2016; Wise & Gardner, 2004). Nestler (2004) defined drug addiction as "the compulsive seeking (drug craving) and administration of a drug despite grave adverse consequences or as a loss of control over drug intake" (p. 698), while Volkow, Koob, and McLellan (2016) described addiction as "a term used to indicate the most severe, chronic stage of substance-use disorder, in which there is a substantial loss of self-control, as indicated by compulsive drug-taking despite the desire to stop taking the drug" (Volkow, Koob, et al., 2001, p. 364). The National Institute for Drug Abuse (NIDA) defines addiction as "a chronic, relapsing brain disease that is characterized by compulsive drug seeking and use, despite harmful consequences" (NIDA,

2016). The perspective that addiction is a brain disease was promoted by Alan Leshner in 1997 when he served as the director of NIDA and reported that "addiction is, at its core, a consequence of fundamental changes in brain function means that a major goal of treatment must be to either reverse or compensate for those brain changes" (Leshner, 1997, p. 46). Others, however, have criticized and challenged this brain-based view arguing that the disease model disregards human decision making and choice (Satel & Lilienfeld, 2014).

In contrast, the American Psychiatric Association (*DSM-V*, APA, 2013) categorizes addiction under "substance-related and addictive disorders" (p. 481) and Volkow et al. (2016) noted that the *DSM-V* uses addiction and substance use disorder synonymously. Substance-related disorders are classified into two groups: substance use disorders and substance induced disorders. Substance induced disorders include substance intoxication, substance withdrawal, and other substance/medication-induced mental disorders. Substance use disorders involve a cluster of cognitive, behavioral, and physiological symptoms as well as continued use of the substance despite significant substance-related problems. Substance abuse disorder may involve nine separate classes of drugs including alcohol, cannabis, hallucinogens, PCP, opioids, inhalants, sedatives, stimulants, or tobacco.

In order to be classified as a substance use disorder, various criteria must be met, and the criteria differ depending on the specific substance use disorder (e.g., alcohol versus opioids). However, general criteria that must be met for a diagnosis include increasing larger amounts of use of the substance, unsuccessful efforts to decrease use, drug craving, impairment in occupational, home, social, and/or academic functioning, substantial time spent procuring or recovering from use of the substance, risky use of the substance, and persistent use of the substance despite negative consequences. Tolerance and withdrawal symptoms may also characterize substance use disorders, although neither is required for the diagnosis (*DSM-V*, p. 484). *Tolerance* refers to the need for increased amounts of the substance to achieve the desired effect or substantial reduced effect when the usual amount is consumed, and the degree varies across substances and among individuals. *Withdrawal* refers to the aversive physiological effects that ensue when the addictive substance is removed or reduced and may include insomnia, anxiety, agitation, and digestive problems. However, withdrawal symptoms vary substantially across drugs and some drugs (e.g., hallucinogens and inhalants) are not characterized by withdrawal symptoms.

Background, Prevalence, Multicultural, and Developmental Findings

According to the National Substance Use and Services Administration (2013), approximately 10% of individuals 12 years of age or older (i.e., 20–22 million people) are addicted to alcohol or other drugs. The NIDA identifies cannabinoids, depressants, hallucinogens, opioids, stimulants, alcohol, PCP, benzodiazepines, and nicotine as commonly abused drugs. Craving and withdrawal symptoms are not associated with some types of hallucinogens (e.g., LSD, mescaline, and psilocybin) and are typically considered non-addictive (Hyman & Malenka, 2001; NIDA, 2016). In contrast, alcohol, benzodiazepines, nicotine, and opioids are highly addictive. Cigarette smoking (nicotine) is the most prevalent addiction worldwide with an estimated 22.5% of all adults smoking regularly (Gowing et al., 2015). Alcohol use disorder is estimated to affect 7.8% of men and 1.5% of women worldwide, and 8.5% of adults and 4.6% of adolescents in the United States (APA, 2013). Recent research indicates that opioid addiction rates have increased nearly 500% in the past seven years, with approximately two million (0.8%) of the US population addicted to prescription

Table 8.1 Five Substances With the Highest Potential for Addiction Worldwide

Criteria

- The extent to which the drug activates the brain's dopamine system
- Degree of pleasure experienced from the drug
- The degree to which the drug causes withdrawal symptoms
- The degree of physical and cognitive harm caused by the drug
- How quickly the drug results in addiction

Substances

- Heroin
- Alcohol
- Nicotine
- Cocaine
- Sedatives

Source: Nutt, King, Saulsbury, and Blakemore (2007).

opioids (Kanouse & Compton, 2015). In 2015, one in three Americans were prescribed opioids (Blue Cross and Blue Shield, 2017; Kanouse & Compton, 2015).

Research also indicates that substance use disorders often co-occur with psychiatric disorders and increase the complexity of providing effective treatment interventions. For example, Havassy, Alvidrez, and Owen (2004) studied over 400 patients from the public mental health system and a substance abuse treatment system, and found that 54% had comorbid psychiatric and substance use disorders. A significantly larger percentage of public health patients met the criteria for comorbidity than those from the substance abuse settings (65% and 49%, respectively). The presence of co-occurring psychiatric disorders (e.g., bipolar disorder, major depressive disorder) increases the risk of a poor prognosis.

Epidemiological studies indicate that males are more likely than females to suffer from substance-related disorders; however, the prevalence gap appears to be narrowing as substance use disorders are increasing among females (McHugh et al., 2017). Research also indicates that the initiation of the substance use is occurring at younger ages, females appear to have an accelerated progression to dependence, adverse medical, psychiatric, and functional consequences associated with substance use disorders are often more severe in females. With respect to treatment outcomes, however, substantive differences have not been found between males and females (McHugh et al., 2017; Zilberman, Tavares, & el-Guebaly, 2003).

Greenfield, Manwani, and Nargiso (2003) noted that, among boys and girls aged 12–17 years, there is a comparable rate of use and initiation for alcohol, cocaine, heroin, and tobacco. The researchers also reported that women are particularly vulnerable to the medical, physical, mental, and social consequences of substance use and dependence, and have the added potential risk of drug-induced complications during pregnancy. Howell, Heiser, and Harrington (1999) reported that approximately 5% of pregnant women abuse illicit drugs during their pregnancy, but recent statistics indicate higher rates, particularly with respect to opioid drug use and women from low-socioeconomic status (Metz et al., 2017).

It is important to note that the majority of individuals who use drugs do not become addicted suggesting that some individuals are more susceptible to addiction than others. Specifically, it has been estimated that approximately 10% of individuals are highly susceptible to addiction, although rates vary depending on the particular drug involved (Substance Abuse and Mental Health Services Administration, 2013; Warner et al., 1995). For example, approximately 23% of individuals who try heroin become addicted, and 80% of individuals using heroin reported using prescription opioids first (NIDA, 2018). In contrast, some studies suggest that less than 1% of individuals prescribed benzodiazepines become addicted (Hidalgo & Sheehan, 2009). A number of factors have been found to increase susceptibility to addiction including genetic, environmental, and social, although the way in which these variables interact are not fully understood (Demers, Bogdan, & Agrawal, 2014). For example, exposure to child maltreatment is associated with increased risk of lifetime substance use disorders, and Forster et al. (2018) reported that 50% to 75% of college students with substance use problems had a history of adverse childhood experiences. Preliminary studies suggest that associations between physical abuse, sexual abuse, and witnessing parental violence and substance use disorder are similar across race and ethnicities (Meyers et al., 2018). Andrews and colleagues (2003) investigated the prevalence of substance use and future intentions among elementary school children and found that with most substances, prevalence, and intention to use substances increased with grade level. For cigarettes and alcohol, intention to use at younger grades was related to subsequent use of the substance, suggesting that intention may be an early warning sign of substance use among children and adolescents. Adolescents are particularly vulnerable to addiction due a combination of environmental, psychosocial, and brain development factors (Burnett-Zeigler et al., 2012). Research with college students suggest that this population is at high risk for use of alcohol and illicit drugs, with greater than 98% of drug users using more than one substance (Forster et al., 2018; Mohler-Kuo, Lee, & Wechsler, 2003). College students are also at risk for using prescription stimulants without a valid prescription, particularly those with lower grade point averages and psychological difficulties (Dussault & Weyandt, 2013; Gudmundsdottir, Weyandt, & Ernudottir, 2016; Weyandt, et al., 2009, 2013, 2016; Janusis & Weyandt, 2010; Marraccini et al., 2016; Munro, Weyandt, Marraccini & Oster, 2017; Verdi, Weyandt, & Zavras, 2016).

Multicultural Findings

Wide cultural variations exist in attitudes toward substance use as shown by patterns of use both within and between countries. According to the American Psychiatric Association (APA, 2013) alcohol is the most frequently used intoxicating substance with 3.6% of the world population between the ages of 15–64 years having a current alcohol use disorder. Prevalence rates are highest (10.9%) in the Eastern European region of the world, slightly lower in the Americas (5.2%), and lower still (1.1%) in the African region. In the United States, the 12-month prevalence rates of alcohol use disorder vary substantially across race/ethnic groups with highest rates among adults for Native Americans and Alaska Natives (12.1%) followed by whites (8.9%), Hispanics (7.9%), African Americans (6.9%), and, lastly, Asian Americans and Pacific Islanders (4.5%). Ethnic and racial differences are also found among adult cannabis users with the highest rates among Native Americans and Alaska Natives (3.4%), followed by African Americans (1.8%), whites (1.4%), Hispanics (1.2%), and Asian Americans and Pacific Islanders (1.2%) (APA, 2013). Recently, Mulia et al. (2017) conducted a 30-year longitudinal study of heavy drinking and found a steady and steep reduction in white men and women's heavy drinking frequency throughout their 20s. Black men and women, however, increased their frequency of heavy drinking during their early and mid-20s. Results also indicated that Blacks and Hispanics, compared to Whites, showed a slower decline in heavy drinking over time. With respect to prescription medications such as stimulants and opioids, research indicates that rates of prescription stimulant misuse and prescription opioid misuse are higher among whites (Netherland & Hansen, 2017; Weyandt et al., 2016). Additional information concerning race/ethnicity findings will be discussed in subsequent sections.

Research has clearly established a strong relationship between substance use disorder and comorbid mental health disorders and in some cases race and ethnicity. However, less empirical information is available concerning substance use disorder among individuals with disabilities such as learning and physical disabilities. Preliminary findings have produced mixed results with some studies suggesting higher rates of alcohol and drug use among this population, while other studies have suggested slightly lower rates compared to individuals without disabilities (e.g., Elmquist, Morgan, & Bolds, 1992; Janusis & Weyandt, 2010; West, Graham, & Temple, 2017).

Onset of Substance Use Disorders and Addiction

The development and course of substance use disorders varies among individuals and by the particular substance used. For example, research indicates that the age of onset for alcohol use disorder typically occurs in the early or mid-20s but can also occur in the late teens. The majority of individuals develop alcohol use disorder by their late 30s, while the onset for most drugs of abuse and dependence occurs during their 20s to 40s (APA, 2013; Cleland et al., 2011; del Mar Capella & Adan, 2017). The course of substance use disorder (i.e., addiction) is usually chronic with periods of exacerbation and remission. Psychosocial factors have been associated with the clinical course and outcome of substance use disorder with depression and drug craving serving as major triggers for relapse in both men and women (Chung et al., 2003; Coelho et al., 2000; Sinha, 2011; Snow & Anderson, 2000; Wu, Kouzis, & Schlenger, 2003). Age is also an important predictive factor as numerous studies have found that the early the onset of use, the higher the likelihood of relapse and physical and psychiatric comorbidity (e.g., del Mar Capella & Adan 2017; Naji et al., 2017; Shah et al., 2017). Although psychosocial factors are crucial in the onset, development, and prognosis of substance use disorders, this chapter focuses on the pathophysiology of substance use disorders—i.e., addiction.

BOX 8.1   Inebriated Mice Chow Down

Inebriated mice eat far more than sober mice. How do we know this? Researchers Sarah Cains and colleagues at the Francis Crick Institute Mill Hill Laboratory in London decided to mimic a weekend of heavy drinking in humans by injecting mice with the equivalent of two bottles of wine per day for three consecutive days (the amount reported to be consumed by 27% of young people in the United Kingdom at least once per week). Control mice were injected with saline only. The eating behavior of the mice was subsequently observed, and their standard mice chow was conveniently placed close to the floor for easy access to compensate for potential ethanol-induced motor coordination difficulties. Results revealed that the intoxicated mice consumed far more mice chow than the control mice, and the magnitude of this difference was similar in male and female mice. At the end of the experiment the mice were sacrificed, and slices of their brains revealed that alcohol (ethanol) induced activation of specialized neurons known as agouti-related protein (AgRP) neurons. These neurons normally become activated following fasting or release of hunger hormones in the brain. The researchers concluded that increased activity of AgRP neurons by exposure to alcohol plays a critical role in alcohol-induced binge eating (Cains et al., 2017).

Initiation and Maintenance of Addiction: Reinforcement Theories

There is no single cause of substance use disorders and addictive behaviors. Like many other psychiatric disorders, addiction is thought to be a product of environmental and physiological factors (Bevilacqua & Goldman, 2009; Crabbe, 2002). Research into the physiological basis of substance use disorders and addictive behaviors is conducted via genetic and heritability studies, neurotransmitter and molecular studies, and neuroimaging studies. Much of the knowledge of the neurobiology of addiction is based on animal models; however, as Wise and Gardner (2004) noted, currently, there is no universally accepted animal model of addiction. Furthermore, animal models are severely limited by the fact that animals become addicted to a substance only when a human creates the addiction condition. As Wise and Gardner stated, "Addiction is a uniquely human phenomenon . . . each animal model is an approximation that captures some but not all of the characteristics of the human condition" (p. 683). Others, however, argue that animal models are highly informative in identification of pathophysiological mechanisms involved in of voluntary drug intake and addiction, and in drug development (e.g., Spanagel, 2017).

How does the addiction cycle begin? Positive reinforcement models suggest pleasurable effects of using a drug reinforce initial drug use; however, negative reinforcement may also explain initial drug use in those who use drugs to escape emotional distress, including negative affect or stress (Eissenberg, 2004). Over time, however, the rewarding effects of drug use are reduced and compulsive drug-taking behavior results from a need to achieve a state of homeostasis—i.e., for the individual to feel normal, or to alleviate pain, discomfort, and withdrawal symptoms (negative reinforcement). The rewarding properties of drugs do not justify the negative consequences that accompany their repeated use, however, and current theories emphasize conditioned stimuli as triggers and incentives of drug-taking behavior (Di Chiara, 1999; Di Chiara & Bassareo, 2007). Current theories also emphasize that individuals struggling with addition exhibit impaired cognitive processes, including salience attribution and response inhibition known as the I-RISA Model (impaired response inhibition and salience attribution) (Goldstein & Volkow, 2002). Research supports that processes such as response inhibition, salience attribution, drug reward, and drug craving are mediated by the mesocorticolimbic pathway including structures that comprise the striatum, midbrain, limbic system, and prefrontal regions (Feil et al., 2010; Volkow, Koob, et al., 2016).

Mesocorticolimbic Pathways

Although the neurobiological underpinnings of addiction are not fully understood, a common feature of all addictive drugs is that they activate "reward pathways" in the brain by triggering the release of the neurotransmitter dopamine (Volkow et al., 2016). Reward pathways refer to complex connections between striatal, midbrain, limbic, and prefrontal regions of the brain, known as mesocorticolimbic pathways, and a plethora of research has supported activation of these pathways during activities associated with pleasure or reward. However, despite being under investigation for over 60 years, details concerning the specific functioning of these pathways remain poorly understood. As discussed in Chapter 2, the mesocorticolimbic system comprises several interconnected brain regions, including the ventral tegmental area (VTA) substantia nigra, caudate nucleus and putamen (striatum), nucleus accumbens, amygdala, and frontal cortical regions that correspond to rat prefrontal cortex or human anterior cingulate (Goldstein & Volhow, 2002). These pathways contain highly complex neural networks that are rich in dopamine, arising from cell bodies in the VTA of the midbrain, and other neurotransmitters, such as serotonin, glutamate, and GABA are also found within these regions.

A large body of research with other animals and with humans has implicated the meso-corticolimbic pathways in addiction. Olds and Miller (1954) were the first to discover that rats would repeatedly self-administer brief bursts of electrical stimulation to brain sites that mediate pleasurable effects of natural rewards, such as food, water, and sex (i.e., *intracra-nial self stimulation*). Later studies demonstrated that rats quickly learned to press a lever to self-administer intravenous injections of cocaine and other addictive drugs, and would do so despite adverse consequences—e.g., rats would lever press in lieu of drink or food, and mothers would abandon their newborn pups in order to self-administer drugs (e.g., Mattson & Morrell, 2005). Wise et al. (1995) observed that dopamine levels in the nucleus accumbens increased during self-administered intravenous cocaine administration in rats. Remarkably, dopamine antagonists decreased lever-pressing behavior and lesioning of the nucleus accumbens drastically reduced the rate of drug self-administration, strongly supporting a role for dopamine and the mesolimbiccortico pathways in drug addiction (Stein, 1962; Zito, Vickers, & Roberts, 1985).

Research with humans has corroborated involvement of "reward" pathways in substance use disorders and that dopamine plays an integral role in the rewarding effects of different types of drug addiction. For example, neuroimaging studies using PET and fMRI have found significant increases in dopamine levels in the nucleus accumbens, caudate, and putamen in healthy men during placebo and amphetamine administration (Boileau et al., 2003; Leyton et al., 2002). Other studies have demonstrated dopamine release is increased in the nucleus accumbens and striatum of humans in anticipation of drug administration and drug cues (de la Fuente-Fernandez et al., 2002; Hu et al., 2015; Risinger et al., 2005; Volkow, Wang, et al., 2002; Volkow et al., 2006). Recent studies have also found differences in brain activation patterns in mesocorticolimbic pathways using fMRI in participants with cocaine use disorder while at rest, compared to participants without cocaine addiction (Gawrysiak et al., 2017). Collectively, these studies support involvement of the mesocorticolimbic pathways in substance use disorders and addiction.

Orbitofrontal Pathways   Frontal regions have also been implicated in substance use disorders, and these areas are important for higher-order cognitive functions such as the ability to monitor one's own behavior and inhibit impulsive responding (i.e., executive functions). The orbitofrontal cortex—i.e., prefrontal cortex—has been particularly implicated in substance use disorders and addiction. The orbitofrontal cortex has extensive connections with midbrain, limbic, and subcortical structures and is believed to a play critical role in regulating complex cognitive functioning, such as response inhibition, decision making, and working memory (Bolla et al., 3003; Goldstein & Volkow, 2002). A number of studies have found that individuals with substance abuse disorder (e.g., cocaine, heroin, methamphetamine) show increased activation in the prefrontal cortex relative to controls during brain imaging studies when they are at rest and when they are exposed to drug related cues (Bolla et al., 2002; Goldstein &; Nestler, 2002; Moorman, 2018; Volkow, 2002; Yamamoto et al., 2017). Furthermore, individuals suffering from addiction have repeatedly been found to exhibit executive function deficits, which are mediated by frontal regions (Matochik et al., 2003). The frontal regions also have been implicated in motivation, craving, and withdrawal symptoms characteristic of addiction (Goldstein & Volkow, 2002). Interestingly, Small et al. (2001) reported that blood flow increased significantly in the orbitofrontal cortex and striatum in healthy volunteers while they ate chocolate and rated eating the chocolate as "very pleasant". These regions were not associated with increased activity, however, when the participants ate chocolate but were satiated and indicated that they did not find the experience pleasurable. Collectively, these findings support that pleasure and reward involve regions extending from the midbrain to the frontal cortex and specifically implicate the mesolimbic and orbitofrontal pathways.

Stage Theory of Addiction   Volkow and colleagues (2016) recently proposed an integrative step-by-step theory of addiction and posited that addiction occurs in three stages: (a) binge and intoxication, (b) withdrawal and negative affect, and (c) preoccupation and anticipation (or craving). Volkow et al. theorized that each stage is associated with "the activation of specific neurobiologic circuits and the consequential clinical and behavioral characteristics" (p. 363). Specifically, Volkow et al. suggested that *all* addictive drugs trigger the release of dopamine and with repeated use environmental stimuli elicit conditioned surges of dopamine in anticipation of the drug. This repetitive surge in dopamine in anticipation of the drug results in a physiological desire for fulfillment—i.e., "drug craving". Over time, continued use of drugs results in reduced dopamine release and less pleasurable effects leading to negative affect, increased reactivity to stress, and withdrawal symptoms when the drug is not available. Consistent with learning theories of drug addiction, Volkow et al. argued the process of addiction progresses from using drugs to get high to using drugs to escape dysphoria and withdrawal symptoms. As drug addiction continues, dopamine down-regulation continues resulting in impaired functioning of the orbitofrontal pathways leading to deficits in executive functions, including diminished capacity for decision making, self-regulation, and inhibition of impulsive responding. Consequently, individuals suffering from addiction often succumb to desire and, craving and continue to use drugs despite their intentions to stop and the negative consequences of their actions.

It is important to note, however, that a unitary theory of addiction has been challenged by those who argue that addiction to a drug such as cocaine has different neurobiological effects than addiction to another drug such as opioids (Badiani et al., 2011). Indeed, there may be a high degree of overlap regarding cellular adaptations with the use of these drugs. Although different drugs may produce different behavioral and psychological effects, they may share core underlying neurobiological substrates of addiction. Future research will undoubtedly continue to explore and unravel the neurobiological effects of different classes of addictive substances.

Dopamine and Beyond   Research findings unequivocally implicate dopamine and the mesocorticolimbic pathways in addiction. As Gardner (2002) noted, addictive drugs commonly influence these pathways as they do the following: (a) activate the neurons in the mesolimbic and projecting systems; (b) result in an increase in firing of dopamine-releasing neurons; (c) are associated with increased dopamine levels in the extracellular space; (d) are self-administered; and (e) often result in relapse after detoxification. Further substantiating dopamine's involvement in addiction is the fact that dopamine antagonists often block the rewarding effects of drugs (e.g., cocaine, amphetamines) (e.g., Ritz et al., 1987). Humans diagnosed with Parkinson's Disease are known to have a compromised level of dopamine in the nucleus accumbens and mesolimbic pathways, and research has found that these patients report blunted effects of stimulants, further supporting the role of dopamine in the rewarding effects of drugs of abuse (Persico et al., 1998).

Although the cellular and molecular events that trigger dopamine release are not fully understood, research suggests a complex relationship between dopamine and other neurotransmitter systems. For example, drug addiction is often characterized by anhedonia (failure to experience rewarding stimuli), and Kranz, Kasper, and Lanzenberger (2010) argue that the serotonergic system plays a critical in mediating the experience of pleasure as evidenced by a voluminous body of depression-related research. Others have suggested that GABA plays a role in addiction. For example, Leite-Morris and colleagues (2004) reported that when opioid receptors located on GABA neurons in the ventral tegmental area are activated, dopamine cell activity is enhanced and dopamine is subsequently released in the nucleus accumbens. Self (2004) reported that opiates increase dopamine in part by removing the inhibitory influence of GABA neurons on dopamine-releasing cells. Recently, studies suggest that gabapentin, a GABA agonist, has been found to reduce drinking, decrease craving, and improve sleep and affect in participants with alcohol use disorder (Mason, Quello, & Shadan, 2018). More recent studies implicate glutamate in the addiction process. For example, Cheng et al. (2018) recently found that significantly lower glutamate levels in the forebrain (dorsal anterior cingulate region) in participants with alcohol use disorder compared to healthy controls. Glutamate signaling in the prefrontal regions has also been implicated in nicotine addiction, amphetamine, cocaine, opioids, and other drugs (Hearing et al., 2018; Pena-Bravo, Reichel, & Lavin, 2017; White et al., 2018).

Given that the mesocortiocolimbic dopaminergic system has implicated in the rewarding effects of all drugs including nicotine, alcohol, barbituates, benzodiazepines, and cannabis, a variety of pharmacological and brain stimulation methods that interfere with dopamine release and/or cellular functioning of the mesocorticolimbic pathways have been investigated. For example, research with other animals has discovered that opiate antagonists injected into the nucleus accumbens can block the rewarding effects of opiates (Vaccarino, Bloom, & Koob, 1985), and a popular pharmacological treatment for human alcohol and opiate addiction is the daily administration of naltrexone—an opioid, mu receptor antagonist (Mason et al., 2002; Kelly et al., 2017). In addition, Di Ciano and Everitt (2003) found that a GABA receptor agonist, baclofen, reduced the propensity of conditioned stimuli to induce drug-seeking behavior in rats however baclofen trials with humans have produced mixed findings, with some studies supporting the efficacy of baclofen in reducing cocaine use and alcohol craving and consumption while other studies do not (Addolorato et al., 2002; Lile et al., 2004; Pujol et al., 2018; Shoptaw et al., 2003).

Collectively, neuroimaging and pharmacological studies support that mesocorticolimbic dopamine activation plays a critical role in the rewarding effects of drugs and, over time, chronic drug use leads to cellular adaptations. Additional neurotransmitter systems also appear to play a role in the rewarding effects of drugs. Although the changes are complex, researchers are beginning to unravel the morphological and molecular effects of chronic drug use at the molecular and structural levels.

Cellular Adaptation

Molecular research regarding addiction supports that chronic drug use leads to changes in internal processing of cells as well as morphological changes. Many questions remain about the nature of these changes and whether distinct differences exist across classes of drugs. To date, however, research supports that addiction leads to enduring changes in

(a) synaptic plasticity, (b) dendritic size and spines, (c) changes in white and gray matter, (d) up/down-regulation of receptors, and (e) changes in internal cellular processing.

Synaptic Plasticity   Synaptic plasticity refers to the ability of synaptic connections to strengthen or weaken as a result of increased or decreased activity (Hebb, 1949). Typically, synapses are strengthened or weakened by an increase or decrease in receptors that respond to neurotransmitters (i.e., up or down-regulation). In addition to changes in receptor quantity, receptors change in quality—i.e., increased or decreased sensitivity or responsivity to neurotransmitter substances. At the molecular level, two receptors have received particular attention in synaptic plasticity: the NMDA and AMPA glutamate receptors (N-methyl-D-aspartate [NMDA] and α-amino-3-hydroxy-5-methyl-4-isoxazolepropionic acid [AMPA]). When the NMDA receptors are occupied by glutamate, the NMDA channels open slightly resulting in entry of calcium into the cell, but a section of the channel is blocked by magnesium preventing an influx of calcium (Dongen, 2009). When magnesium is removed as a result of stimulation of neighboring AMPA receptors, this triggers a cascade of events that induces a process known as long-term potentiation (LTP). Long-term potentiation results in excitatory synapses, increased efficiency of neurotransmission and plays a critical role in learning and memory (Nicoll & Malenka, 1999). Notably, NMDA antagonists have been found to block the rewarding or reinforcing effects of drugs of abuse such as morphine and cocaine and are believed to play an integral role in addiction. Cocaine abuse has been found to result in LTP in the ventral tegmental area lasting for days to months after cessation of the drug (Chen, Hopf, & Bonci, 2010). Opioids, Cannabis, and alcohol have all been found to elicit LTP in mesocorticolimbic structures, such as the nucleus accumbens, hippocampus, amygdala, and prefrontal cortex (e.g., Stuber et al., 2010).

The second type of glutamate receptor implicated in addiction is the AMPA receptor. The AMPA receptor, like the NMDA receptor, responds to glutamate, but unlike the NMDA receptor when occupied it allows sodium ions to enter the cell, resulting in depolarization of the membrane. As the membrane depolarizes, magnesium is dislodged from the neighboring NMDA receptor occupied by glutamate, thereby allowing an influx of calcium through the NMDA channel resulting in LTP. This process results in a neuroplastic change—i.e., up-regulation of AMPA receptors that results in strengthening of the synapse (M. S. Bowers, Chen, & Bonci, 2010; Kemp & McKernan, 2002). Drugs of abuse result in up-regulation of AMAPA receptors, and interestingly activation of AMPA receptors in the nucleus accumbens is required for drug-seeking behavior in other animals (Ferrario, Li, & Wolf, 2011; Hopf, 2017). Studies also suggest that after cessation of an abused drug, AMPA transmission remains enhanced, resulting in stronger responding to environmental drug cues (Wolf & Ferrario, 2010). Interestingly, lamotrigine, an antiseizure medication, exhibits antagonistic effects on AMPA, reduces glutamate release, and has been found to reduce cocaine craving and use (Brown et al., 2012).

Dendritic Plasticity   Numerous other animal studies have explored the effects of various drugs on dendritic plasticity. For example, repeated cocaine administration has been found to produce structural changes in the dendritic spines of neurons, such as an increase in dendritic spine density in the nucleus accumbens (Dos Santos et al., 2018). In contrast, alcohol is associated with decreased dendritic spine density as well as altered size and shape (Romero et al., 2013). Opioid administration and withdrawal is also associated with smaller dendrites, decreased density of dendritic spines, and reduced size of neurons and cell bodies of dopaminergic neurons in the ventral tegmental area (Spiga et al., 2005; Sklair-Tavron et al., 1996). Robinson et al. (2001) found structural changes in neurons located in the prefrontal cortex of rats that self-administered cocaine using lever pressing. Specifically, they reported that the dendrites of cells of the rats that self-administered cocaine were misshapen, with large, bulbous structures at their tips. The authors speculated that these morphological changes affect the compromised decision making and judgment typical of human cocaine abusers. Current technology does not enable dendritic density and size measurements in humans; however, neuroimaging studies allow for estimates of gray and white matter in humans with substance use disorders.

Gray Matter As discussed in previous chapters, gray matter refers to brain tissue containing cell bodies with unmyelinated axons. Gray matter volume and density has been explored in a many substance use disorders including alcohol, nicotine, methamphetamine, and cocaine. Meta-analytic studies have consistently reported gray matter volume reductions in the prefrontal regions and additional mesocorticolimbic structures (Bullock, Cservenka, & Ray, 2017; Hall et al., 2015; Morales et al., 2015; Yip et al., 2018). Studies have also revealed that drug craving was negatively associated with gray-matter volume in the insula, prefrontal cortex, amygdala, temporal cortex, occipital cortex, cerebellum, and thalamus (Morales et al., 2015). With regard to daily and chronic marijuana use and gray matter, studies have produced inconsistent findings with some reporting that, when alcohol use, gender, age, and other variables are controlled for, there is no association between marijuana use and standard volumetric or shape measurements of subcortical or cortical structures including gray matter, while others report greater and/or reduced gray matter density in adult and adolescent marijuana users than in control participants in the left nucleus accumbens hypothalamus, and left amygdala, even after controlling for age, sex, alcohol use, and cigarette smoking (Filbey et al., 2014; Lorenzetti, Alonso-Lana, et al., 2016; Weiland et al., 2015; Gilman et al., 2017). Given the inconsistencies in the literature, longitudinal studies are needed to determine whether marijuana exposure is associated with alterations of mesocorticolimbic structures and, if so, to identify mitigating factors.

White Matter White matter refers to tracks of myelinated axons and reduced white matter has been found in participants with substance use disorders. With respect to alcohol, a large number of studies have reported a significant loss of cerebral white matter found in postmortem and living individuals with alcohol use disorder (e.g., Harper et al., 2003; Pfefferbaum, Sullivan, Mathalon, & Lim, 1997; Monnig et al., 2014). Similarly, Fein et al. (2002) measured total brain volume and cortical gray and white matter volumes in alcohol-dependent males who had not received treatment. Relative to control participants, those with alcohol use disorder showed reduced total brain volume (and reduced prefrontal and parietal cortical gray matter) based on MRI scans. Adolescents with alcohol use disorders compared to controls have also been found to have reduced white matter, particularly in the hippocampus (De Bellis et al., 2001; Thayer et al., 2017). Cannabis use among adolescents is also associated with white matter reduction in some but not all studies (e.g., Meruelo et al., 2017; Thayer et al., 2017). Notably, Rivkin et al. (2008) reported that children exposed to cocaine, tobacco, marijuana, or alcohol in utero had smaller head circumference and white and gray matter relative to children not exposed to these substances. Studies also indicated that opioid use disorder is associated with white matter (and gray matter) changes in brain regions implicated in addiction including those involved in the regulation of affect and impulse control, as well as in reward and motivational functions (Upadhyay et al., 2010). Collectively, these findings suggest that addiction is associated with significant reductions in white matter and future research is needed to better understand the molecular changes that lead to these reductions.

Receptors and Transporters In addition to changes synaptic plasticity, dendritic morphology, and gray and white matter, addiction and substance use disorder is associated with changes in presynaptic transporters and postsynaptic receptors. For example, several studies have found decreased density of postsynaptic dopamine receptors (D2) in participants with substance use disorder relative to controls, however, studies have been mixed with respect to density of dopamine transporter proteins. One of the first neuroimaging studies to explore density of dopamine receptors and transporters was conducted by Volkow and colleagues (1996) using PET. Results revealed decreased levels of D2 receptors in individuals with alcohol use disorder relative to controls; however, no differences were found in the density of dopamine transporters. Other neuroimaging and postmortem studies have reported mean density of the dopamine transporters naturally decline with age in control participants relative to those with alcohol use disorder (Tupala et al., 2003a, 2003b). Still other studies have reported lower dopamine transporter density in participants with substance use disorder relative to controls (Tiihonen et al., 1995, 1998; Volkow, Fowler, & Wang, 2002). Collectively, these studies implicate the D2 receptor in the pathophysiology of alcohol use disorder; however, questions remain regarding the role of dopamine transporter proteins.

With regard to other substance use disorders, including cocaine and opioids, studies have been mixed with some reporting reduced dopamine receptor and transporter density in the striatum of participants addicted to opioids or stimulants while others have not (Cosgrove et al., 2010; Kreek et al., 2012; Liang et al., 2016). Recently, Dubol and colleagues (2017) explored the relationship between dopamine function and DAT availability during reward anticipation in participants with cocaine addiction, schizophrenia, or depression using fMRI and PET, and found that dopamine transporter availability in the mesolimbic system correlated positively with response to anticipation of reward in all groups regardless of diagnostic categories. The authors interpreted the findings as supporting that dysfunction of the dopaminergic system is a common mechanism underlying the alterations of reward processing observed in patients with mental health disorders. In a review of the literature concerning dopamine receptors and transporters, L. Chang, Alicata, and Volkow (2007) concluded that the majority of studies found reduced dopamine transporter density and reduced dopamine D2 receptors in the striatum of participants addicted to methamphetamine. Collectively, current findings support involvement of the dopamine transporter and postsynaptic receptors in addiction; however, questions remain regarding the extent of their involvement across addictive substances. In addition, it is important to note that other neurotransmitter receptors and transporters (e.g., serotonin, glutamate) also have been studied with respect to substance use disorders; however, the primary emphasis has been on the dopaminergic system (Bellini, Fleming, et al., 2018; Berrettini et al., 2017).

Glial Cells As discussed in previous chapters, astrocytes are the most abundant glial cell type in the central nervous system and administration of cocaine, amphetamines, and psychostimulants has been found to induce activation of astrocytes. For example, stimulants, opioids, and alcohol have been found to increase the expression of glial fibrillary acidic protein (GFAP), a protein found in the cytoskeleton of astrocytes, in multiple brain regions (e.g., striatum, ventral tegmentum, hippocampus, and frontal cortex) (Marie-Claire et al.,

2004; Pubill et al., 2003). Morphological changes in the end feet of astrocytes that connect with blood vessels have also been found with drug administration, leading to reductions in fluids and other substances passing from the blood supply to the astrocytes (Fan et al., 2005). In addition, astrocytes release neurotrophins (e.g, BDNF), and these substances decrease in production and release with the use of various drugs (Zhang, Jiang, et al., 2016). Functional changes in other types of glial cells have more recently been implicated in addition, including microglia and oligodendrocytes (McCarthy et al., 2018).

Internal Changes (CREb)   Although substance abuse initially induces changes at the level of the synapse—such as increased levels of dopamine in the intracellular fluid—continued use is associated with complex intracellular changes. Specifically, with repeated drug exposure, neurons adapt over time, and these cellular changes are believed to be responsible for tolerance, addiction, and withdrawal (Volkow, et al. 2016). A number of studies have reported that substance disorder is associated with a number of internal structural changes including a significant decrease in the amount of neurofilament proteins (Garcia-Sevilla et al., 1997; Salery et al., 2017). Neurofilament proteins are the major components of the neuronal cytoskelton and are important in maintaining the structure of the cell and the transport of substances from the soma to the terminal button. Additional intracellular changes associated with drug addiction include up-regulation of the cyclic adenosine monophosphate (cAMP) pathway, supersensitization of adenylyl cyclase, coupling of opioid receptors to second and perhaps third-messenger systems, and activation and interactions of various intracellular proteins. These same intracellular changes are associated with other drugs of abuse such as cocaine, methamphetamine, and alcohol (Wille-Bille et al., 2017; Zhang, Liu, et al., 2016).

The cAMP pathway is part of a complex second-messenger system that is activated when addictive drugs are administered. For example, when the mu receptor is occupied by opiates, the conductance of the K+ channels is increased, and second-messenger systems are activated. When the second-messenger system is activated, a cascade of events occurs, the details of which are not fully understood. Research with other animals suggests that K+ channels are coupled to intracellular G-proteins that inhibit the enzyme adenylyl cyclase, which in turn reduces cAMP levels (Smart, Smith, & Lambert, 1994). Reduction in these enzymes results in a series of intracellular changes. One such change is the reduced phosphorylation of the protein CREB (cyclic adenosine monophosphate response element binding protein), thought to initiate additional intracellular events, such as altered gene expression that lead to long-term changes in cellular function (Figure 8.1).

One example is the increased production of the transcription factors dynorphin and delta FosB. Dynorphin levels have been found to increase with chronic drug use and are associated with the decreased rewarding effects of drugs and tolerance (Kreek et al., 2012). Another intracellular protein, delta FosB, also increases with chronic drug use and levels remain elevated after prolonged abstinence. These prolonged changes in delta FosB activity are associated with increased sensitivity to environmental cues and the rewarding effects of drugs and likely contribute to drug craving and relapse (Nestler, Barrot, & Self, 2001). Interestingly, research has also found that cAMP levels change over time. For example, initially exposure to opiates decreases cAMP levels and cellular inhibition is increased, but chronic exposure results in increased levels of cAMP (Nestler, 2002). This up-regulation of cAMP is thought to increase the firing of neurons in certain regions of the brain (i.e., locus coeruleus) to the previously normal level, and according to Monteggia and Nestler (2003), it can be viewed as the brain's effort to establish homeostasis in response to the increased opiate induced cellular inhibition.

An additional effect of chronic exposure to drugs is a decreased sensitivity of neuron receptors to the drug, which means larger amounts of the drug are required to achieve a desired effect (tolerance). Although the physiological basis of tolerance is not well understood, long-lasting intracellular, enzymatic, and genetic changes modulated by CREB and other transcription factors, such as delta FosB may account for drug tolerance (Nestler, 2002; Hasbi et al., 2018). In summary, addictive drugs are believed to produce complex, long-lasting intracellular changes that are associated with drug tolerance, dependence, and withdrawal. It is important to note, however, that the majority of molecular and intracellular studies concerning addiction are based on other animal models and questions arise concerning the generalization and application of these findings to humans.

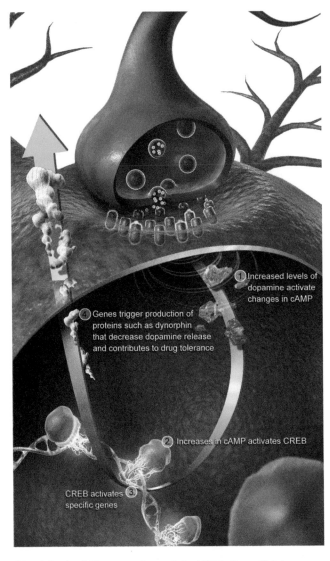

FIGURE 8.1.   Physiological Changes Associated With Drug Tolerance

Copyright Blausen Medical Communications. Reproduced by permission.

BOX 8.2 Rapid Detox

Chronic use of opiates results in cellular adaptation and as the opiate receptors become less sensitive to the drug tolerance occurs, followed by withdrawal symptoms in the absence of the drug. Withdrawal symptoms from opioids are usually severe and long lasting (e.g., nausea, vomiting, chills, insomnia, depression), and, consequently, are highly problematic to successful detoxification treatment. Detoxification options include abrupt cessation of the opiate ("cold turkey"), tapering with other drugs used to minimize withdrawal symptoms, pharmacological substitution (e.g., methadone), or a procedure known as rapid detox (McCabe, 2000). Rapid detox involves a medical procedure designed to avoid the physiological discomfort associated with withdrawal. Specifically, rapid detox requires hospitalization and the administration of general anesthesia. An opioid antagonist (e.g., naltrexone, naloxone) is then administered to the patient who reportedly undergoes rapid and painless withdrawal. Rapid detox programs vary with respect to length of hospital stay, safety, cost, pre-evaluation measures, follow-up interventions, and the actual detox method. According to McCabe (2000), a typical detox procedure lasts from 4 to 6 hours and following the procedure patients are technically detoxified from the opiate. To reduce cravings and the likelihood of relapse, an opiate antagonist is generally prescribed for several weeks to a year post-detox. Although rapid detox is a method that avoids the distressing effects of withdrawal, it is an invasive procedure that carries all the risks associated with general anesthesia. In addition, rapid detox is a medical procedure and psychological treatment is often needed to address the emotional and behavioral aspects of addiction. Unfortunately, little empirical information is available concerning the long-term safety and efficacy of rapid detox relative to other treatment methods for opioid addiction and studies that are available or not encouraging. Rabinowitz, Cohen, and Atias (2002), for example, compared the relapse rates of 30 opiate-dependent individuals who underwent rapid detox and a 9-month, follow-up course of naltrexone and a similar group of opiate-dependent individuals who detoxified in a 30-day inpatient program and did not receive naltrexone. Result indicated that 34% of the subjects overall relapsed within 13 months of detox and there was no significant difference in relapse rates between the two groups. More research is needed to understand the benefits and limitations of rapid detoxification as a treatment approach to opioid use disorder (Praveen et al., 2011).

Genetic Findings

Family and Twin Findings

Research supports that the development of substance use disorders is influenced by both genetic and environmental factors. Genetic factors, for example, can influence the metabolism, sensitivity, and effects of drugs while environmental factors such as age of exposure, route of administration, stress, family, peers, and community factors also contribute to addiction (NIDA, 2018). Methods used to identify the role of genetics in addition have included family, twin, linkage, candidate gene, and genome-wide association studies.

Family, adoption, and twin studies have been instrumental in helping to tease apart the contribution of genetic and environmental factors in the development of addiction. Family studies clearly indicate that relatives of individuals with substance use disorder have increased risk of substance use disorder including alcohol, cannabis, cocaine, hallucinogens, sedatives, stimulants, and opiates. For example, studies indicate that the siblings of individuals meeting criteria for alcohol dependence had elevated rates of alcohol dependence (50% for men and 25% for women), and first-degree relatives of those with opioid, cannabis, or cocaine use disorders have an eightfold increased risk of developing a substance use disorder (Bierut et al., 1998; Merikangas et al., 1998). Environmental experiences, however, appear to determine the specific type of substance an individual who is at increased risk will use or misuse (e.g., Agrawal & Lynskey, 2008; Kendler et al., 2000; Kendler, Jacobson, et al., 2003). Monozygotic and dizygotic twin studies vary in terms of concordance rates for addiction although NIDA reports that genetic factors account for 40% to 60% of a person's vulnerability to addiction (NIDA, 2018; Enoch & Goldman, 2001; Ystrom et al., 2014).

Twin studies also find that substance use disorders typically involve misuse of more than one substance, although the specific heritability estimates vary across studies and across substances. For example, Tsuang and colleagues (1996) studied 3,372 twin pairs and found that 10.1% of the sample had been addicted to at least one illicit drug. The concordance rate for monozygotic twins was 26.2% as compared to 16.5% of dizygotic twins, supporting a genetic influence in addiction. The heritability estimates for specific drugs were 0.33 for marijuana, 0.43 for opiates, 0.44 for stimulants, and 0.34 for general drug use. Fu and colleagues (2002) interviewed 3,360 pairs of twins and reported slightly higher heritability estimates—i.e., 0.56 and 0.50 for alcohol and marijuana respectively.

Family, adoption, and twin studies such as the Harvard Twin Study of Substance Abuse (Tsuang et al., 2001) also support a high degree of comorbidity between substance use disorders and psychological disorders including depression, anxiety, PTSD, and personality disorders (Fu et al., 2002; Gillespie et al., 2018; Jacob et al., 2003; Long et al., 2017). Recent studies further indicate that personality traits such as novelty seeking, harm-avoidance, low cooperation, and impulsivity are predictive of substance use disorders in adults (Maremmani et al., 2018; Pino-Gutiérrez et al., 2017). In childhood, externalizing disorders such as conduct disorder and antisocial behaviors are associated with early use of drugs and alcohol.

Collectively, findings from family, adoption, and twin studies indicate that genetic factors contribute to the development of addiction, although their interplay with environmental factors is not fully understood. Furthermore, it is important to note that neither family history nor use of drugs or a combination of genetic risk and exposure necessarily lead to addiction as the majority of individuals who use drugs do not develop substance use disorders. Current theories emphasize that genetic factors likely alter the brain's sensitivity to drugs and alcohol, making an individual more prone to addiction. Individuals with this family/genetic history who are depressed or possess certain personality traits are at even higher risk for substance abuse disorders, particularly when onset of use occurs during adolescence or childhood (Bellón et al., 2017; C. R. Cloninger, 1999; Rhew et al., 2017). Family, adoption, and twin studies can provide degree of concordance among family members and heritability estimates of substance use disorders however they do not provide information about specific chromosomes or genes that may be involved in addition. To address this aspect of genetics, linkage, candidate genes, and genome-wide association studies are conducted. A plethora of genetic studies have been conducted with other animals using knockout methodology and other techniques discussed previously in this text; however, the focus of the following section is on reviewing human studies.

Linkage Studies

As discussed in previous chapters, linkage studies attempt to identify specific chromosomes and chromosomal locations that may harbor susceptibility genes involved in substance use disorders. Linkage studies use samples of related individuals and look for specific segments of chromosomes that are associated with a particular disorder in these related individuals. Hundreds of linkage studies have been conducted and many have found associations between substance use disorders and specific chromosomes. For example, chromosome 4 has been linked to alcohol use disorder and different loci (4q, 4p) have been investigated in the disorder (van Beek et al., 2010). A different locus on chromosome 4 has been linked to opioid use disorder, and segments of chromosomes 6, 7, 11, and 17 (Yang et al., 2017) have also been linked to opioid use disorders. Additional chromosomes have been linked to other types of substance use disorders, and the reader is referred to Yang and Li (2016) for further information concerning linkage studies and substance use disorders. It is important to note that conflicting results have been found across linkage studies and furthermore, linkage studies do *not* reveal causal relationships between genetic findings and substance use disorders. Nevertheless, linkage studies do provide clues for chromosomal regions and nearby susceptibility genes potentially involved in addiction and these results in turn lead to candidate gene studies.

Candidate Gene Studies

Based on theory, other animal studies, and linkage studies, scientists have attempted to uncover specific genes that play a role in substance use disorders and addiction. Candidate gene studies have taken several approaches and two main approaches include (a) exploring the role of genes that regulate neurotransmitter systems and (b) exploring specific genes associated with specific drugs and their potential role in substance use disorders.

Genes involved in regulating monoamine neurotransmitters (dopamine, serotonin, norepinephrine) that are commonly studied in the addiction literature include COMT, SLC6A, and MAO-A genes. A large number of studies have examined the presence of polymorphisms or gene variants of these genes in individuals with substance use disorders compared to controls. For example, COMT is an enzyme that breaks down dopamine and the Val158Met polymorphism of the COMT gene is associated with lower dopamine levels in mesocorticolimbic regions of the brain. Furthermore, presence of this polymorphism has been found to occur more often in participants with substance use disorder relative to controls in some, but not all studies (Goldman et al., 2005). Zhang, Lee, et al. (2013) reported that individuals with substance use disorders who had the Val158Met polymorphism also had increased white matter alterations in the prefrontal regions of the brain that may have increased their susceptibility to addiction.

The SLC6A4 gene regulates serotonin levels and the reuptake process by encoding a membrane protein involved in the serotonin transporter. Polymorphisms of this gene have been associated with increased risk of substance use disorders in several studies (Ducci & Goldman, 2012). Variants of the MAO-A gene that encodes an enzyme that breaks down monoamines have also been implicated in substance use disorders, including nicotine, opioids, and other substances (Tiili et al., 2017; Saify et al., 2015).

Additional candidate genes have been studied that are specific to substances such as alcohol, opioids, nicotine, and stimulants. For example, polymorphisms in genes that encode for the alcohol-metabolizing enzymes such as the alcohol dehydrogenase IB (ADH1B) and aldehyde dehydrogenase 2 (ALDH2) have been found to influence alcohol consumption and risk of alcohol use disorders. Interestingly, a polymorphism of the ALDH2 gene results in acetaldehyde not being broken down in about 10% of the Asian population, leading to an aversive response to alcohol consumption. When carriers of this gene variant drink alcohol, the buildup of acetaldehyde causes unpleasant effects, such as nausea, dizziness, and skin flushing, and therefore the likelihood of using alcohol is greatly diminished. Although the ALDH2 gene may serve protective effects against alcohol use disorder, it does not appear to affect the risk for dependence on other drugs (Chen, Lu, et al., 1999; Peng et al., 2017).

Similarly, candidate genes have been studied with opioid use disorder. Because the dopaminergic system plays an integral role in rewarding effects of addictive drugs, dopamine genes have also been a focus of etiologic studies of opioid addiction For example, Li, Xu, et al. (1997) reported that two variants of a dopamine receptor gene (DRD4) occurred more frequently in 121 heroin-dependent subjects than controls; however, in a later studies, Li et al. (2000) and Li, Zhu, et al. (2002) did not find a significant difference between heroin users and controls with respect to polymorphisms of the DRD4 gene. Meta-analyses have concluded variants of the D2 receptor gene are associated with a number of addiction disorders, including alcoholism and cocaine, nicotine, and opioid dependence (Noble, 2003). More recently, Yang et al. (2017) and Berretti (2017) identified additional candidate genes linked to opioid addiction including VEGFR, CLOCK, PDCL2, NMU, NRSF, IGFBP7, KCNC1, and KCNG2 genes.

With regard to stimulants, a number of candidate genes have been investigated, including those that regulate the dopamine transporter protein (DAT1). Recent research reports that polymorphisms of this gene are associated with crack-cocaine addiction (Stolf et al., 2017). Additional candidate genes have been studied for these and additional addictive substances and the reader is referred to Lebowitz et al. (2017) for detailed information. It is important to note, however, that inconsistencies exist across candidate gene studies with some studies failing to find significant associations between gene variants/polymorphisms and substance use disorders. Furthermore, although the familiarity and heritability of substance use disorders is well documented, to date, no single gene or group of candidate genes have been identified that confer strong and reliable risk for *any* substance use disorder (Ducci & Goldman, 2012; Stickel et al., 2017; van Beek et al., 2010).

Genome-Wide Association Studies

Linkage studies and candidate gene studies produce information concerning genes that may play a role in the development of substance use disorders. Genome-wide association studies, in contrast to linkage studies, are then used to observe the entire genome of different populations to determine whether specific gene variants are associated with a particular substance use disorder. In other words, linkage studies address whether there is an association between segments of DNA and a particular substance use disorder while genome-wide studies address or differences exist among individuals with respect to DNA sequence variations and a particular substance use disorder. In general, genome-wide studies have greater power to detect smaller effects and chromosome regions. Numerous genome-wide studies have been conducted with respect to substance use disorders, including alcohol, nicotine, opioids, and others. These studies vary with respect to populations investigated (e.g., opioid dependent versus alcohol) and polymorphisms or gene variants used as markers to rapidly scan the complete sets of DNA (Hall et al., 2013). What can be deduced from these various genome wide studies is that *no particular marker is causally related to "addiction" or to all substance use disorders*. In fact, genes expected to be related to substance use disorders based on theory and linkage studies often are not identified in genome-wide studies. For example, Liu et al. (2006) analyzed 96 genes and contrary to expectations, genes involved in regulating monoamines (dopamine, serotonin) were not associated with substance use disorder (those that were related to cell adhesion molecules were significant). Also, it is important to note that relative to the substantial literature available for alcohol and nicotine use disorders, comparatively less information is available concerning opioid, cannabis, stimulants, and other addictive substances (Prom-Wormley et al., 2017). In a recent review of genome-wide association studies of stimulant and opioid use disorders, Jensen (2017) stressed the importance of replication of genome wide studies using independent samples.

Summary of Genetic Studies

Several conclusions can be deduced from linkage, candidate genes, and genome-wide association studies with respect to substance use disorders and addiction. First, research does not support that the development of substance use disorders is influenced by a single gene, rather, multiple genes likely interact with constitutional (e.g., personality traits) and environmental factors. Second, to date, no single gene or group of genes has been identified as causing a particular substance use disorder and the amount of genetic variance accounted for by genetic factors appears to be relatively small. Indeed, Ducci and Goldman (2012, p. 19) stated, "More than 95% of the genetic variance remains unaccounted for, indicating that most of the genetic risk factors for addictions have not been discovered". Future research will likely continue to unravel the complex relationships between genetic and environment factors and ideally lead to preventative and intervention efforts to curtail the increasing prevalence of substance use disorders.

Neurotransmitter Findings   As discussed in Chapter 2, drugs exert their effects by enhancing (agonist) or interfering with (antagonist) the brain's neurotransmitter systems. These effects occur at the level of the synapse and, depending on the drug, the mode of action varies. For example, opiates attach to opioid receptors and mimic the effects of naturally occurring opioids. Nicotine is an agonist at the level of the nicotonic receptor (acetylcholine). Alcohol is a GABA agonist and attaches to a portion of the benzodiazepine receptor and enhances the effects of GABA. Alcohol also has antagonisitic effects as it inhibits functioning of the NMDA glutamate receptor, which is associated with the intoxicating effects of alcohol (Nestler, 2004). Stimulants such as cocaine prevent reuptake of dopamine and, to a lesser extent, serotonin and norepinephrine (Cami & Farre, 2003), whereas barbituates and benzodiazepines are GABA agonists. Cannabinoids attach to cannabinoid CB1 receptors that activate second-messenger systems and enhance the release of dopamine in the midbrain and forebrain (Gardner, 2002). The receptors for various neurotransmitters are differentially distributed throughout the brain, and thus the behavioral effects of drugs differ depending on the targeted brain regions. For example, opioid receptors are located in various regions throughout the brain and include different subtypes: mu, delta, and kappa receptors. These receptors are located throughout the central nervous system but are heavily concentrated in the locus coeruleus, brain stem, and spinal cord, which explains why opiates such as morphine and oxycotin can have profound effects on respiration (Leino et al., 1999). Differences also exist among humans with regard to the quantity and distribution pattern of other types of receptors, such as dopamine and serotonin (Cravchik & Goldman, 2000), which may in part account for inter-individual drug effects.

It is important to note that other neurotransmitters can have modulating effects on the dopaminergic system and appear to play an important role in drug addiction, but these effects are not well understood. For example, Vollenweider et al. (1999) studied the effects of a serotonin receptor agonist (psilocybin) on dopamine receptor (D2) binding and found that serotonin receptor activation helped to modulate (increase) dopamine release in the striatum. Studies have also found that in addition to affecting the dopaminergic system, cocaine is associated with alterations in serotonergic function (Buydens-Branchey et al., 1999; Wolfe et al., 2000). More recent findings suggest that cocaine affects hippocampal GABA and glutamate synapses by directly modulating production and degradation of enzymes that are important for normal functioning of the dopaminergic system (Rivera et al., 2013). In addition to dopaminergic activation, opioids modulate glutamate-releasing neurons in the mesolimbic system and increase inhibition of GABAergic synapses (Hearing et al., 2018; Margolis et al., 2014). Multiple neurotransmitter systems also appear to be involved in chronic use of ecstasy as well as alcohol use disorders (Bogen et al., 2003; Kashem et al., 2016). Collectively, these findings suggest that multiple neurotransmitter systems are involved in different types of substance use disorders however the complex modulatory and interactive relationships among these systems is poorly understood.

Functional Findings   A plethora of neuroimaging studies have been conducted in the past decade concerning substance use disorders and a comprehensive review of these studies is beyond the scope of this chapter. The following section therefore summarizes major findings with respect to alcohol, stimulants, opioids, and cannabis and neuroimaging studies.

Alcohol

Children from families in which one or both parents are alcohol-dependent are at heightened risk for substance use disorders during adolescence and adulthood and neuroimaging studies suggest this risk may be related to early childhood brain differences. Specifically, several neuroimaging studies conducted longitudinally have found that smaller volumes of the orbitofrontal cortex during childhood and adolescence are predictive of onset of alcohol (and cannabis) use disorder in adolescence and adulthood (Cheetham et al., 2017). Neuroimaging studies have also found that adolescents and adults with alcohol use disorder have thinner and lower volume in prefrontal cortex and cerebellar regions, decreased white matter development, and elevated brain activity in fronto-parietal regions during working memory, inhibitory control, and verbal learning tasks (Cservenka & Brumback, 2017). Heinz et al. (2004) used fMRI and PET to compare dopamine receptor binding in the striatum of detoxified males with alcohol use disorder and healthy men during the presentation of alcohol cues. Results indicated that males with a history of alcoholism had fewer dopamine receptors in the striatum, which significantly correlated with alcohol craving severity.

A number of studies have found increased activation in mesocorticolimbic regions (striatum, anterior cingulate cortex, hippocampus, amygdala) in individuals with alcohol use disorder in response to alcohol related cues compared to those without the disorder. Studies have also found that increased activation in mesolimbic regions in college students predicted subsequent transition into heavy drinking (Dager et al., 2014). Interestingly, Eiler et al. (2017) using fMRI found that individuals with a family history of alcoholism showed increased brain activation in "reward pathways" in response to sugar (oral sucrose) compared to individuals without a family history of alcoholism. The authors suggested that oral sucrose response might be an endophenotypic marker of alcoholism risk. In summary, neuroimaging studies of participants at risk of developing alcohol use disorder and those with alcohol use disorder have found both morphological and functional brain differences compared to control participants.

Pharmacological Treatment

Medications such as naltrexone, bupropion hydrochloride, baclofen, methadone, and varenicline that block dopamine release have been found to decrease neural activity in mesolimbic regions and alcohol and drug craving (Courtney et al., 2016). Other medications such as modafinil have been used to improve cognitive and impulse control. Naltrexone is approved by the FDA to treat alcohol and opioid use disorders. Naltrexone, an opioid receptor antagonist, also blocks the release of dopamine in the nucleus accumbens in response to alcohol. Neuroimaging research with adults with alcohol use disorder has found that naltrexone blocks opioid mu and to a lesser extent delta receptors. Blockage of these receptors is correlated with self-reported reduced craving (Weerts et al., 2008). These results compliment those of Bencherif et al. (2004) who found that participants with alcohol use disorder showed lower levels of mu receptor binding in several brain regions (right frontal, parietal, and dorsal lateral precortex), and this reduced level of binding was correlated with higher levels of craving. Disulfiram (antabuse) is used to deter alcohol use by inhibiting the enzyme aldehyde dehydrogenase from clearing acetaldehyde from the body, resulting in highly unpleasant physiological reactions (nausea, vomiting) if alcohol is consumed. Collectively, pharmacological interventions further implicate mesolimbic pathways in alcohol use disorder. Questions remain, however, regarding the temporal relationship between alcohol use disorder and morphological and functional brain changes.

BOX 8.3   Is Tylenol Just as Effective as Oxycodone?

Despite the opioid crisis in the United States prescription opioids remain the first line of treatment for moderate to severe acute pain in emergency rooms. In July of 2015 through August 2016, a study was conducted in two emergency rooms in the Bronx, New York, to explore whether non-opioid medications might be as effective as opioids in managing acute pain. Specifically, adult patients (ages 21–64) who presented with acute extremity pain were randomly assigned to receive one of four oral analgesics: one was opioid free (400 mg ibuprofen and 1000 mg acetaminophen) and three contained an opioid combined with acetaminophen (5 mg of oxycodone and 325 mg of acetaminophen; 5 mg of hydrocodone and 300 mg of acetaminophen; or 30 mg of codeine and 300 mg of acetaminophen). The degree of pain reduction was measured in emergency room patients 2 hours after ingesting the medication. Results revealed there was no difference in pain reduction based on medication, in other words, the ibuprofen + acetaminophen combination was just as effective at reducing pain within the 2-hour period as the opioid medications. These findings suggest therefore, that a combination of ibuprofen and acetaminophen represents a viable alternative to prescription opioids for the treatment of acute extremity pain in hospital emergency rooms (Chang, Bijur, et al., 2017). Findings from this study were corroborated by Krebs and colleagues (2018), who also found that treatment with opioids was not superior to acetaminophen (paracetamol) or a nonsteroidal anti-inflammatory drug for treating moderate to severe chronic back pain or hip or knee osteoarthritis pain. It is important to note that Krebs et al. compared the effects of opioids and non-opioid medications for improving pain-related function over a 12-month period compared to Chang et al., whose study was over the course of a 2-hour period. Collectively, these studies support that different types of pain can be effectively managed with non-addictive medications rather than prescription opioids that have a high propensity for addiction.

Opioids Opium extracted from poppy seeds is a highly effective but addictive pain reliever. Opioids include endogenous opioids (enkephalins and endorphins), morphine, and synthetic opioids such as heroin, Darvon (propoxyphene), Demerol (meperidine), Sublimaze (fentanyl), Talwin (pentazocine), Dilaudid (hydromorphone), Oxycontin (oxycodone), and Vicodin (hydrocodone). Oxycodone has become one of the most frequently prescribed opioids in the United States, and the overdose death rate in the United States in 2008 due to opioids was nearly four times the 1999 (NIDA, 2015). Research indicates that there are large individual differences in clinical response to opiates and not everyone who uses opiates becomes addicted (Lotsch et al., 2002). For example, Robbins (1993) reported that 35–38% of US soldiers used heroin during the Vietnam War; however, only 5% remained addicted in the first year after returning to the United States (Robins & Slobodyan, 2003). Currently, the National Institute of Drug Abuse estimates that 8–12% of those who misuse prescription opiates become addicted.

The endogenous opioid system consists of several complex pathways that are distributed throughout the central nervous system. Opioids occupy and activate opioid receptors (mu, delta, kappa), particularly mu receptors, that in turn stimulate a number of interacting neurotransmitter pathways, including the mesolimbic pathway (Inturrisi, 2002) (Figure 8.2). Kieffer and Simonin (2003) referred to the mu receptor as the "molecular gate for opioid addiction" (p. 12). Margolis et al. (2003) recently reported that activation of the mu-opioid receptor in the ventral tegmental area of the brain stimulates dopaminergic neurons while activation of the kappa opioid receptor inhibits dopaminergic neurons in this same region. Additional research is needed to understand the role of these different types of opioid receptors in addiction.

As with all drugs prone to abuse, the mesolimbic pathway plays a critical role in the rewarding effects of opioids. Neuroimaging findings have revealed visual cues, such as videos and pictures of opioids activated regions rich in dopamine and opiate receptors (ventral

Opioid Overdose

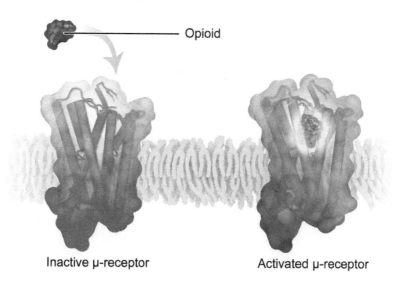

Inactive μ-receptor

Activated μ-receptor

Reversing Opioid Overdose

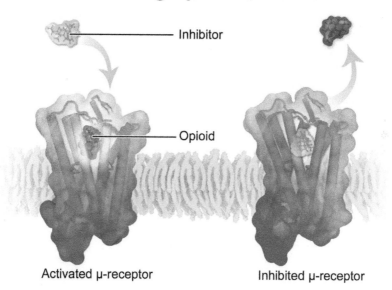

Activated μ-receptor

Inhibited μ-receptor

FIGURE 8.2. Opioid Receptor With Oxycontin Attached

Reproduced by permission.

tegmental area, mesolimbic system) in participants with opioid use disorders and these findings correlated with drug craving (Daglish et al., 2003; Sell et al., 1999; Zubieta et al., 2000). Daglish and colleagues suggested that craving and addiction are "normal" brain circuits but are activated to a significantly greater degree in those with substance use disorders. H. Chang et al. (2016) using fMRI recently suggested that increased activation in the right caudate while at rest may serve as a biomarker for opioid relapse. Collectively, these studies provide evidence that particular brain regions become more activated during opioid drug use and that salient environmental cues also activate these same regions. These neuroimaging findings help to explain how cues can elicit cravings and conditioned emotional reactions that increase the risk of relapse.

Pharmacological Treatment

Pharmacological treatments are also used to help manage opioid use disorders (Table 8.2). Medications such as methadone, for example, have been used to treat heroin addiction and naltrexone and suboxone have been used to treat other types of opioid use disorders. In 2002, the FDA approved an opioid agonist, buprenorphine, for the treatment of opioid dependence, and since that time, studies support its effectiveness in reducing opiate craving and use. For example, Greenwald et al. (2002) studied whether high versus low doses of buprenorphine influenced opiate craving and use and reported that high-dose buprenorphine was associated with opioid drug seeking and craving. Other studies have compared monthly injections of vivitrol (extended release naltrexone) versus daily suboxone (a combination of buprenorphine and naltrexone) in participants with opioid use disorder. Lee et al. (2017) recently reported that after 6-month's treatment, 65% of the vivitrol group had relapsed compared to 57% of suboxone group. Of the patients who started treatment about half of both groups dropped out and fatal overdoses were not statistically different. In 2013, the FDA approved another maintenance drug, Zubsolv for the treatment of opioid use disorder.

Neuroimaging studies have explored brain regions targeted by these medications. For example, long-term use of methadone has been found to reduce activation in the bilateral dorsal striatum in adults addicted to heroin in response to heroin related cues, and this reduction in activity is associated with reduced drug craving (Wang et al., 2014). Other studies have reported reduced perfusion in the left anterior cingulate cortex, the left medial prefrontal cortex, and in the insula (both hemispheres) in heroin addicted individuals immediately following an injection of heroin relative to placebo in both males and females. In a recent review of the neuroimaging literature concerning opioid dependent individuals who abstain from using opioids, Ieong and colleagues (2017) concluded that differences in mesolimbic functioning persist during abstinence including reduced brain connectivity within the mesolimbic pathways.

Table 8.2 FDA-Approved Medications for the Treatment of Opioid Addiction

Medication	Purpose	Mode of Action
Methadone	Detoxification and maintenance	Opioid receptor agonist
Buprenorphine	Detoxification and maintenance	Partial opioid receptor agonist
Zubsolv	Maintenance	Partial opioid agonist and antagonist
Naltrexone	Detoxification and maintenance	Opioid receptor antagonist
Naloxone	Opioid overdose reversal	Opioid receptor antagonist

BOX 8.4   Safe Injection Sites—What Is Your Opinion?

According to the CDC and the Philadelphia Department of Public Health, Philadelphia, Pennsylvania, has the highest fatal opioid overdose rate in the United States among large cities. In January 2018, city officials announced that Philadelphia would allow "supervised injection sites" to operate in the city which would provide a safe place and clean needles to inject illicit drugs such as heroin and other opioids. The sites will also provide trained staff to administer naloxone (narcan), a drug that reverses overdose, should overdose occur. Seattle, Washington, is the second city in the United States to offer supervised injection sites and, unlike Philadelphia, Seattle city government will reportedly provide funds to financially support the sites. Proponents of supervised injection sites argue that there are currently over 100 such sites successfully operating around the world, and they drastically reduce rates of death, the spread of disease, and refer individuals for substance abuse treatment. Opponents argue that cities that provide supervised injection sites are facilitating illegal activity and are simply allowing people to inject drugs and break the law in a safe, comfortable public place. Governments and law-abiding citizens, they argue, should not be facilitating illegal, dangerous activities, and instead funding should be directed toward programs that promote prevention as well as treatment and recovery. What is your opinion?

(Hedegaard et al., 2017; Philadelphia Department of Public Health, 2016)

Stimulants

Stimulants increase arousal of the central nervous system and the most well-studied stimulants are cocaine and amphetamines. Although both drugs increase extracellular dopamine concentrations, cocaine does so by binding to the dopamine transporter and thereby inhibiting dopamine reuptake. Amphetamines cause a reversal of the transporter so that substantially more dopamine is released into the extracellular fluid (White & Kalivas, 1998).

Similar to other drugs of abuse, neuroimaging studies have suggested that cocaine dependence is associated with structural and functional brain changes. For example, Matochik et al. (2003) compared MRI scans of cocaine abusers abstinent for 20 days and a control group in terms of gray and white matter tissue volumes. Results revealed that cocaine abusers had significantly lower gray matter tissue in several brain regions, particularly frontal areas, relative to controls; however, no differences were found with respect to white matter. Other studies, however, have found chronic cocaine use is associated with reduced white matter (Narayana et al., 2014). Studies also suggest that cocaine dependence alters the functioning of the connections between the frontal lobes and other brain regions, and this altered connectivity may underlie the decision-making deficits often observed in cocaine abusers (Kelly et al., 2011; Lim et al., 2002). Similar to other drugs of abuse, a number of studies have found environmental cues produced less activation in several brain regions (e.g., orbitofrontal cortex, amygdala, cingulate cortex) in individuals addicted to cocaine (Kilts et al., 2004). Even after periods of abstinence, chronic cocaine use is associated with widespread reductions in cerebral glucose metabolism in various brain regions, particularly in the prefrontal regions (Ernst et al., 2000; Paulus et al., 2002).

The director of NIDA, Nora Volkow and colleagues has studied the effects of stimulants (cocaine, methamphetamine, methylphenidate) on the brain using neuroimaging techniques for several decades. In 1997, Volkow et al., using neuroimaging, were the first to report at least 50% occupancy of the dopamine transporter was required to induce a "high", and subsequent studies consistently reported increased dopamine in the striatum following cocaine administration (Schlaepfer et al., 1997; Laruelle et al., 1995; Leyton et al., 2002; Volkow et al., 2016). Volkow, Fowler, and Wang (2002) and Volkow, Wang, et al. (2002) also discovered a 50% increase in glucose metabolism in mesolimbic regions of the brain of cocaine abusers when methylphenidate was expected compared to when it was unexpected. Later, Volkow and colleagues found that chronic cocaine use was associated with lower functional activity in the midbrain, cingulate, and cerebellum, and this reduced activity predicted poor performance on attention tasks (Tomasi et al., 2010). Recently, Volkow's team reported that both drugs and food increase activity of dopamine neurons in the mesolimbic pathway, including the ventral tegmental area, nucleus accumbens, and frontal regions of the brain (Lingren et al., 2018). Over time, however, as the addiction process becomes more chronic, Volkow and others have demonstrated a blunting of dopamine release in the mesolimbic regions leading to compulsive drug-seeking behavior (van de Giessen et al., 2017). Collectively, neuroimaging studies support that stimulant use is initially associated with increased release and availability of dopamine in the extracellular fluid leading to rewarding effects of the drug. With chronic use, however, dopamine release is diminished.

Pharmacological Treatment

Despite the prevalence of cocaine and amphetamine addiction, no pharmacological treatment is currently approved by the FDA to treat this type of substance use disorder. Several studies, however, have reported that naltrexone reduces craving in adults addicted to cocaine (Comer et al., 2013; Grosshans, Mutschler, & Kiefer, 2015). Other drugs that facilitate GABA transmission, such as anticonvulsants (e.g., baclofen), have also been used to treat stimulant addiction; however, empirical findings are equivocal regarding the effectiveness of these medications at reducing craving and relapse rates (Minozzi et al., 2015).

Cannabis

Although numerous cannabinoids are found in cannabis, the psychoactive effects are mainly attributed to THC (delta-9-tetrahydrocannbinol). Cannabinoids are generally inhaled by smoking but can also enter the body through edibles (e.g., brownies, cookies, candies). Cannabinoids—i.e., THC attaches to CB1 endogenous receptors that are widely distributed throughout the brain including regions involved in memory, perception, appetite, and motor control (Ameri, 1999). For example, neuroimaging findings have found high to moderate concentrations of CB1 receptors in the hippocampus, amygdala, cerebral cortex, stratium, globus pallidus, cerebellum, and brain stem (Bhattacharyya et al., 2012). It has been estimated that approximately 5–10% of the population, worldwide, who regularly use cannabis will develop cannabis use disorder and display tolerance, craving, and withdrawal symptoms (Ramesh et al., 2015). Research concerning whether cannabis use results in structural and functional brain changes has been conflicting. Some studies, for example, report significant effects of cannabis on brain structure particularly in regions that have an abundance of CB1 receptors (prefrontal cortex, amygdala, hippocampus, striatum, and cerebellum), while other studies have not replicated these findings (Hill, Sharma, & Jones, 2016; Koenders et al., 2017). Longitudinal studies, however, suggest that regular use of cannabis during adolescence and adulthood is associated with abnormal activity in frontal-parietal regions in cannabis users, particularly in heavier users, and in some cases, this pattern of activity corresponds with reduced performance on memory and inhibition tasks (Lorenzetti, Alonso-Lana, et al., 2016; Lorenzetti, Solowij, & Yücel, 2016).

Research has found that individuals with substance use disorders often display poor decision making, such as continuing to use addictive substances despite negative consequences (Stewart et al., 2013). Interestingly, neuroimaging studies have discovered that participants who decided to use cannabis during a decision-making task while undergoing an fMRI scan exhibited significantly higher activation in several brain regions, including the dorsal striatum, insula, posterior parietal regions, anterior and posterior cingulate, and dorsolateral prefrontal cortex compared to those who choose not to use. In contrast, participants who declined cannabis use exhibited activation in different brain regions leading to a 100% accuracy classification rate that the researchers referred to as a "neural signature of decisions to smoke cannabis" (Bedi et al., 2015, p. 2259).

Medicinal Cannabis

It is important to note that cannabis users are not homogeneous in their motives for using cannabis as some use for recreational purposes while others use for medicinal purposes. Furthermore, recent research suggests that those who use for medicinal purposes may respond differently to cannabis in terms of brain function. For example, Gruber and colleagues (2018) recently examined brain activation patterns of patients prior to medicinal marijuana treatment and after 3 months of treatment as part of a larger longitudinal study. Participants completed the Multi-Source Interference Test (MSIT) while undergoing fMRI at the beginning of the study, and after 3 months, data were also collected regarding conventional medication use, clinical state, and health-related measures at each visit. Comparisons of fMRI scans revealed that patients demonstrated improved task performance that was accompanied by changes in brain activation patterns within the cingulate cortex and frontal regions. In contrast, non-medicinal cannabis users have been shown to exhibit decrements in task performance accompanied by altered brain activation. Surprisingly, brain activation patterns of medicinal cannabis users appeared more similar to those of healthy controls, leading the researchers to suggest that cannabis used for medicinal purposes may normalize brain function relative to baseline. More research is needed, however, to explore brain activation and cognitive and behavioral effects of cannabis with different types and severity of medical conditions.

Pharmacological Treatment

Research indicates a relapse rate of approximately 70% for cannabis use disorders and on average, adults seeking treatment have used cannabis nearly every day for more than 10 years and have attempted to quit six or more times (Budney, Roffman, Stephens, & Walker, 2007). Currently, however, the FDA has not approved any medications for the treatment of cannabis use disorder. During chronic cannabis use, down-regulation and desensitization of the CB_1 receptors is thought to occur, and these neuroplastic changes are hypothesized to lead to cannabis dependence (Breivogel et al., 2003). Given the clear role of CB1 receptors in cannabis use disorders, scientists are exploring the use of CB1 antagonists that block the effects of THC as well as CB1 agonists that compete with cannabis for occupation of the receptors. For example, dronabinol and nabilone are synthetic forms of THC and CB1 receptor agonists that have been found to reduce cannabis withdrawal symptoms in some studies (Budney, Vandrey, Hughes, Moore, & Bahrenburg, 2007; Haney et al., 2013). Additional drugs have been studied with other animals and humans, although most have been found to be ineffective at treating cannabis use disorders (see Copeland & Pokorski, 2016, for a review). Currently, NIDA is investigating the efficacy, safety, and tolerability of the fatty acid amide hydrolase (FAAH) inhibitor in adult cannabis use disorder with an expected completion date of 2022. In the meantime, the main form of treatment for cannabis use disorders is psychosocial interventions.

Chapter Summary

■ Substance use disorders are a major health problem in the United States and around the world.

■ Research with other animals, genetic studies, neurotransmitter, and neuroimaging studies with humans implicate several brain regions and systems in substance use disorders.

■ Prominently involved in addiction is the dopaminergic system, including the mesolimbic system and associated ascending and descending pathways and connecting prefrontal and subcortical regions.

■ Dopamine and other neurotransmitter systems, such as endogenous opioids, GABA, serotonin, and glutamate systems, appear to play a modulating, albeit poorly understood, role in addiction.

■ Intracellular transcription factors, such as CREB and delta FosB, appear to play an integral role in altering gene expression that appears to contribute to several facets of drug addiction.

■ Molecular and neuroplastic changes including alterations in synaptic plasticity, dendritic size and density of spines, white and gray matter, and up and down-regulation of receptors are thought to contribute to drug craving, withdrawal, and relapse.

■ Heritability studies implicate genetic and environmental factors in the risk of addiction; however, the specific genes involved in addiction as well as the complex relationship between biological and environmental factors in the development and maintenance of substance use disorders are poorly understood.

Review Questions

1. What can be concluded about the contribution of genetic factors to substance use disorder and addiction?
2. Does research support the existence of a "reward pathway"? Explain.
3. In what way(s) has dopamine been implicated in addiction?
4. Why is it important to study neurotransmitters other than dopamine in substance use disorders?
5. What would be required for you to conclude that addiction is genetically determined or "brain based"?
6. In your opinion, is addiction a "disease"? Why or why not?

nine

Disorders of Childhood Origin

Attention Deficit Hyperactivity Disorder, Autism Spectrum Disorder, and Tourette's Disorder

This chapter focuses on three disorders commonly diagnosed in childhood: attention deficit hyperactivity disorder (ADHD), autism spectrum disorder (ASD), and Tourette's disorder (TD). An overview of research regarding genetic, structural, and functional findings is presented for each disorder as well as information concerning physiologically based treatments, including pharmacological and physiologically based interventions.

Chapter 9 Learning Objectives

- Describe demographic information pertaining to ADHD, ASD, and TD.
- Describe research findings concerning the heritability of ADHD, ASD, and TD.
- Describe genetic findings concerning ADHD, ASD, and TD.
- Describe structural findings ADHD, ASD, and TD.
- Describe functional findings ADHD, ASD, and TD.
- Identify types of medication used in the treatment of ADHD, ASD, and TD.
- Identify non-pharmacological-, physiologically based treatments for ADHD, ASD, and TD.

Background Information

Prevalence

The American Psychiatric Association identifies disorders that originate during the developmental period as neurodevelopmental disorders (APA, 2013). Neurodevelopmental disorders include intellectual disabilities, communication disorders, ASD, ADHD, specific learning disorders, motor disorders, and tic disorders. Children also experience adult-associated disorders, such as major depressive disorder, bipolar disorder, schizophrenia, anxiety disorders, and others, but the onset of these disorders does not necessarily occur during the developmental period.

Table 9.1 Disorders of Childhood Onset

Disorder	Core Features	Pharmacological Agents
ADHD	Deficits in attention, impulse control, and/or hyperactivity	Stimulants, pro-stimulants, non-stimulants
Tourette's disorder	Presence of both vocal and motor tics	Antipsychotic and adrenergic alpha-2 medications
ASD	Persistent deficits in social communication and social interactions, and a pattern of restricted and repetitive behaviors	Antipsychotic medication

Prevalence estimates of neurodevelopmental disorders vary depending on the specific disorder and a variety of factors, including diagnostic methods (e.g., criteria, number of informants), as well as sampling differences. Overall, however, studies indicate that a significant percentage of children and adolescents in the United States and throughout the world have clinical disorders that cause impairment in daily living. For example, Merikangas and colleagues (2009) reported that approximately one-fourth of children and adolescents worldwide had experienced a mental disorder in the past year and one-third in their lifetimes. Anxiety disorders were the most frequent disorder among youth followed by behavior, mood, and substance use disorders. Recently, a large, nationwide population-based study in the United States reported ASD prevalence was 2.47% among children and adolescents in 2014–2016 (Xu et al., 2018). Others have reported that nearly one child or adolescent of every two children in the child welfare system was identified as meeting criteria for a current mental disorder, particularly neurodevelopmental behavior disorders (e.g., conduct and oppositional defiant disorder, ADHD) followed by anxiety and depressive disorders (Bronsard et al., 2016). Cross-cultural studies (e.g., Australia, China, Israel, Jamaica, Netherlands, Turkey, and United States) have consistently found higher rates of internalizing disorders (e.g., anxiety) among girls and higher rates of externalizing disorders among boys (e.g., behavior disorders) (Verhulst et al., 2003). Others have reported that among the neurodevelopmental disorders, ADHD, ASD, and TD most commonly occur and are often comorbid (Hansen et al., 2018).

Attention Deficit Hyperactivity Disorder (ADHD)

ADHD is characterized by a persistent pattern of inattention and/or hyperactivity and impulsivity that causes impairment in multiple settings such as school and work. Onset of symptoms typically occurs in childhood, although current diagnostic criteria require only that several inattentive or hyperactive-impulsive symptoms were present prior to age 12. The American Psychiatric Association distinguishes between three subtypes of ADHD: combined presentation, predominately inattentive presentation, and predominately hyperactive-impulsive presentation (APA, 2013).

ADHD occurs worldwide and is estimated to affect 5% children and approximately 2.5% of adults, although estimates vary considerably in different regions of the United States and in different countries (Polanczyk et al., 2007). For example, Wolraich et al. (2014) reported significantly higher prevalence rates for children 5–13 years of age living in South Carolina and Oklahoma—i.e., 8.7% and 10.6%. The disorder is diagnosed more frequently in males than females, with a male to female ratio ranging from 2:1 to 9:1 depending on subtype and evaluation setting. In Uganda, recent studies report that 11% of children attending neurology and psychiatry clinics met criteria for ADHD (Wamuluga et al., 2017). According to Rowland, Lesesne, and Abramowitz (2002), not only is ADHD the most common neurodevelopmental disorder of childhood, it is the most commonly studied neurodevelopmental disorder. Research has found that the prevalence of ADHD increased by an average of 5% annually, with approximately 6.4 million children and adolescents in the United States diagnosed with ADHD (Visser et al., 2014).

Comorbidity

Disorders such as conduct disorder, oppositional defiant disorder, Tourette's disorder, mood disorders, and learning disabilities often co-occur with ADHD. Developmentally, children and adolescents with ADHD are at greater risk for academic deficits, school-related problems, social skill deficits, and peer rejection (Fischer et al., 1990; Barkley, 2016). Adolescents with ADHD are at greater risk for antisocial behavior and school dropout, although a small percentage pursues higher education (Heiligensteinet al., 1999; Weyandt & DuPaul, 2012). Preliminary studies suggest that college students with ADHD do not differ with respect to intelligence compared to control subjects (Weyandt, 2007; Weyandt, Mitzlaff, & Thomas, 2002), but are more likely to have a lower GPA and report greater difficulty paying attention in lectures compared to college students without ADHD (Weyandt & DuPaul, 2012). College students with ADHD are also likely to struggle with depression and/or anxiety disorders and report an overall lower quality of life (Anastopoulos et al., 2018; Pinho et al., 2017). As young adults, individuals with ADHD are more likely to suffer from depression or a personality disorder compared to control subjects (Fischer et al., 2002), and many experience problems with employment, sexual relationships, driving, and illegal activities (Barkley, 2002; Barkley et al., 2004). Rasmussen, Almvik, and Levander (2001) reported that ADHD is common among Norwegian prison inmates. According to Wilens (2004), ADHD is a risk factor for substance abuse in adults, and individuals with ADHD tend to become addicted more rapidly and severely than individuals without the disorder. Kodl and Wakschlag (2004) reported that persistent cigarette smokers are more likely to have a history of ADHD than spontaneous quitters or nonsmokers. Cognitively, young adults with ADHD have reported greater degrees of internal restlessness compared to controls (Weyandt et al., 2003), and both children and adults with ADHD are more likely to have executive function deficits (Weyandt, 2005). It is important to note, however, that executive function deficits are not unique to ADHD (Weyandt, 2005; Weyandt, Oster, et al., 2017). Despite the popularized myth that it is advantageous to have ADHD, preliminary studies do not support that young adults with ADHD have superior divided attention skills relative to young adults without the disorder (Linterman & Weyandt, 2001). Collectively, these studies indicate that ADHD is a chronic disorder that causes impairment in social, occupational, and academic functioning, and as the following sections attest, neurobiological studies strongly support a physiological basis for ADHD.

Genetic Findings

Family and Twin Studies

Extensive research into the genetic etiology of ADHD has been conducted for decades and collectively family, twin, and candidate gene studies support a genetic component to the disorder. For example, family studies have found that ADHD is more common in first- and second-degree relatives as mothers, fathers, and biological relatives of individuals with ADHD are five to ten times more likely than control families to have a history of ADHD (Faraone et al., 2015; Frick et al., 1991; Roizen et al., 1996). Safer (1973) was among the first to report that ADHD occurred more frequently among siblings who shared the same mother and father than those who shared only one parent (i.e., half brothers and sisters). Later, Biederman and colleagues (1986, 1995) reported that individuals with ADHD are more likely to have siblings with ADHD relative to controls, and if one biological parent had ADHD the likelihood that a child had ADHD was 57%. Studies also indicate that adoptive relatives of children with ADHD are less likely to have ADHD than biological relatives of children with the disorder (e.g., Alberts-Corush, Firestone, & Goodman, 1986; Morrison & Stewart, 1973).

Twin studies indicate that ADHD occurs significantly more often in identical than fraternal twins. For example, Gjone, Stevenson, and Sundet (1996) reported a correlation of 0.78 between adolescent male monozygotic twins and 0.45 for dizygotic twins with respect to attention problems and others have reported similar concordance rates (e.g., Burt, Krueger, McGue, & Iacono, 2001; Larsson, Larsson, & Lichtenstein, 2004; Willcutt, Pennington, & DeFries, 2000; Rydell et al., 2017). Twin studies also suggest that although girls tend to display fewer behavioral problems than boys, heritability estimates for ADHD are similar for both (Rietveld et al., 2003). Overall, twin studies indicate that the heritability component of ADHD is 0.70 to 0.80, which is substantially higher than many psychiatric illnesses (Faraone et al., 2015).

Candidate Genes

Given the nature of ADHD symptomatology involving inattention, hyperactivity, and/or impulsivity, and the involvement of subcortical and prefrontal regions in these symptoms, scientists have largely focused primarily on the role of dopamine genes in the etiology of ADHD. To date multiple candidate genes involving several types of polymorphisms of dopamine genes (and other neurotransmitter genes) are associated with ADHD, although it is important to note that effect sizes have been small, and results have often not been replicated across studies (Hawi et al., 2015). Specifically, numerous studies have investigated genes that govern postsynaptic dopamine receptors (e.g., DRD4, DRD5) and presynaptic dopamine transporter proteins (DAT1). For example, the DRD4 gene, located on chromosome 11 encodes the D4 subtype of the dopamine receptor and is activated by dopamine (as well as epinephrine and norepinephrine). The D4 receptor is found in various locations in the brain, particularly the mesolimbic and prefrontal regions. Mutations and polymorphisms of this gene (e.g., 120bp repeat) have been associated with ADHD, although the mechanisms for this involvement are not understood (McCracken et al., 2000). Recently, Chang and colleagues (2018) reported that children with a specific type of DRD4 gene (e.g., rs752306) and who also had been exposed to pesticides had an increased risk of ADHD relative to children without the disorder. The DRD5 gene has also been implicated in ADHD. The DRD5 gene is located on chromosome 4 and widely distributed throughout the brain. Several polymorphisms (repeats) have been found to occur more frequently in individuals with ADHD relative to controls in some studies but recent meta-analyses have not replicated these findings (Klein et al., 2016).

In addition to postsynaptic D4 and D5 receptor genes, the presynaptic dopamine transporter gene, DAT1 also known as SLC6A3 gene, has been implicated in ADHD. The

SLC6A3 gene is located on chromosome 5 and encodes the transporter protein for dopamine. This transporter protein is embedded in the presynaptic membrane and is responsible for reuptake of dopamine from the synaptic cleft following exocytosis. Polymorphisms of the SLC6A3 gene have been found more often in individuals with ADHD compared to controls; however, it remains unknown how these genetic variations translate into the cognitive and behavioral symptoms of ADHD (Faraone & Mick, 2010). Kirley et al. (2003) studied a sample of Irish children with ADHD and found a relationship between a polymorphism of this gene (10-repeat VNTR) and a positive response methylphenidate. The authors speculated that this polymorphism may lead to overactivity of dopamine transporters in children with ADHD and helps to explain the effectiveness of methylphenidate in treating ADHD since methylphenidate is known to block the transporter protein. A meta-analysis by Zhang and colleagues (2011) reported that nearly 50% of the studies reviewed found a significant relationship between variations of the SLC6A3 gene and ADHD, while 70% reported a significant relationship between variations of the DRD4 gene and ADHD.

In addition to dopamine genes, linkage and genome-wide association studies have implicated serotonin genes in ADHD. Specifically, some studies have reported variations of the SLC6A4 gene are associated with increased risk of ADHD (Gomez-Sanchez et al., 2016). The SLC6A4 gene located on chromosome 17 encodes the serotonin transporter protein that removes serotonin from the synaptic cleft following release from the presynaptic neuron. Although prescription stimulants that target the dopamine system are the first line of treatment for ADHD, studies have found the drugs that target and block the serotonin transporter (SSRIs) are sometimes effective at treating ADHD symptomatology (Buoli et al., 2016). Additional candidate genes (e.g., COMT, SNAP25, ADRA2) are also under investigation in ADHD more genes are likely to be explored in the future (Middeldorp et al., 2016; Roman et al., 2003).

To date, the literature suggests that dopamine and serotonin genes may be involved in the etiology of ADHD by altering neurotransmitter systems (e.g., dopamine, serotonin) and functional connectivity in individuals with ADHD (Castellanos et al., 2017; Swanson et al., 2000). However, it is important to note that genetic studies do not produce highly replicable findings, and some studies have not reported significant associations between genetic variations and ADHD (Fonseca et al., 2015). As noted by Thapar and colleagues (2013) "the genetic risks implicated in ADHD generally tend to have small effect sizes or be rare and often increase risk of many other types of psychopathology. Thus, they cannot be used for prediction, genetic testing or diagnostic purposes beyond what is predicted by a family history" (p. 3). To date, research indicates that ADHD is likely caused by complex interactions of numerous genetic and environmental risk factors. Future studies employing larger sample sizes enabling greater statistical power are needed to further explore the potential role of genetic factors in the etiology of ADHD. Studies are also needed to elucidate the specific ways in which genetic alterations may manifest as ADHD symptomatology.

Structural Findings

Numerous structural studies using MRI and other techniques have been conducted with children and adults with ADHD and many, but not all, have found structural differences between individuals with and without ADHD. These studies have examined total brain volume, volume of specific structures, gray and white matter, cortical thickness/thinning, and, more recently, white matter connectivity between structures.

With regard to total brain volume, Castellanos and colleagues (1994) were among the first to report that total brain volume was 5% smaller in boys with ADHD relative to children without the disorder, and the caudate nucleus was significantly larger in children with ADHD. Castellanos et al. (2002) later found smaller total brain volumes, cerebral volumes, white matter volumes, and cerebellar volumes in 152 children and adolescents with ADHD relative to controls. Group differences were not found with respect to the caudate nucleus however when examining identical twins, Castellanos et al. (2003) found twins with ADHD had significantly smaller caudate volumes than their unaffected co-twins. The caudate nucleus is rich in dopamine neurons, and stimulant medication used to treat ADHD, such as methylphenidate, has been found to increase activity in the caudate nucleus and is concomitantly associated with improvement in behavioral symptoms (Clauseen & Dafny, 2012). Unlike Castellanos et al., who found volume reductions in affected twins only, Durston et al. (2004) reported that participants with ADHD and their unaffected siblings *both* had volume reductions in right prefrontal and left occipital regions and that the right cerebellar volume was significantly smaller in those with ADHD. These findings suggest a biological vulnerability to ADHD but do not explain why some siblings develop ADHD and others do not. Collectively, these morphological findings support genetic studies that implicate the dopaminergic system in ADHD.

Volume reductions have also been found in other structures in individuals with ADHD including the globus pallidus, striatum, cerebellum, prefrontal cortex, and corpus callosum (Aylward et al., 1996; Berquin et al., 1998; Castellanos et al., 2001; Mostofsky et al., 1998; Giedd et al., 1994; Hill et al., 2003; Hynd et al., 1991; Semrud-Clikeman et al., 1994). One of the first longitudinal studies to investigate brain morphology in ADHD relative to controls was conducted by Shaw et al. (2007). Results revealed significant differences in the rate at which children with ADHD reached peak levels of cortical thickness—approximately 3 years later than children without the disorder, particularly in regions associated with motor and executive functions. Other studies have found asymmetry of the basal ganglia, reduced gray matter, cortical thinning, and white matter connectivity (i.e., myelinated pathways) (Bos et al., 2017; Hynd et al., 1993; Marcos-Vidal et al., 2018; Ouhaz, Fleming, & Mitchell, 2018). Collectively, these studies suggest that multiple brain regions and structures may be altered in individuals with ADHD. It is also critical to note that research has produced conflicting findings between and within studies—i.e., smaller volumes of some structures (e.g., corpus callosum) but no differences in other structures (e.g., cerebellum). Furthermore, some studies have not found volume, gray, or white matter differences between individuals with and without ADHD (e.g., Friedman & Rapoport, 2015; Overmeyer et al., 2000). Lastly, it is important to emphasize that when structural differences are found, the source of these differences is speculative, and these structural differences are not necessarily directly related to ADHD symptomology. In conclusion, to date, no alterations of any single brain structure have been found to be reliably diagnostic of ADHD.

Functional Findings

In contrast to studies that examine morphological differences, functional studies explore differences in brain activity in participants with ADHD relative to those without the disorder. In general, functional MRI, SPECT, and PET studies implicated frontal-striatal structures and pathways in ADHD. For example, Lou, Henriksen, and Bruhn (1984, 1989) were among the first to use PET to measure rCBF in children with ADHD and found reduced blood flow in the frontal lobes and basal ganglia, and these findings have been replicated in other studies

(Lorberboym et al., 2004). Lou et al. (1984) also noted that following administration of methylphenidate, blood flow increased in the frontal lobes as well as the basal ganglia. Research has also found that methylphenidate has different physiological effects in children with ADHD compared to healthy controls. Vaidya et al. (1998), for example, found that based on fMRI scans both children with and without ADHD showed increased activation in the frontal lobes following methylphenidate treatment, but methylphenidate increased activity in the striatum with children with ADHD and decreased activity in this region in healthy control children. Teicher et al. (2000) reported increased blood flow in the striatum (caudate and putamen) of boys with ADHD, and subsequent administration of methylphenidate reduced the activity within these regions. Studies with adults with ADHD also support that methylphenidate modulates basal ganglia and frontal lobe activity and increased rCBF in these brain regions are associated a reduction in ADHD symptoms including inattention and hyperactivity (Kim et al., 2001; Schweitzer et al., 2003). These results compliment structural findings and further support abnormal striatal-frontal circuitry in children with ADHD.

Studies have been mixed with regard to glucose metabolism and ADHD. Zametkin et al. (1990) was among the first to explore glucose metabolism using PET in adults with ADHD relative to controls. Results revealed overall brain glucose metabolism was reduced by 8.1% compared to controls, particularly in the prefrontal and premotor cortices. Zametkin et al. (1993), however, did not find global glucose metabolism differences in adolescents with and without ADHD, although lower metabolism in the left frontal lobe was inversely correlated with ADHD symptom severity. Some studies have found reductions in glucose metabolism in specific areas of the brain including the striatum in adults with ADHD, particularly females (e.g., Ernst et al., 1998; Zametkin et al., 1990). Studies also suggest that the neural substrates involved in cognitive processes (e.g., decision making) may differ in adults with and without ADHD. A number of studies have found reduced glucose activity in the prefrontal regions in child and adult participants with ADHD while performing neuropsychological tasks that require planning, working memory, and decision making (Ernst et al., 2003; Spalletta et al., 2001). The findings have been replicated with fMRI studies as well (Durston et al., 2003; Rubia et al., 1999; Schulz et al., 2004; Munro et al., 2017).

In addition to activation studies, research has examined dopamine receptor density in participants with ADHD relative to controls. For example, Lou and colleagues (2004) found increased dopamine receptor (D2, D3) availability in adolescents with ADHD who had low cerebral blood flow as neonates. They speculated that low blood flow (cerebral ischemia) during infancy may increase susceptibility to ADHD later in life. Recently, Cherkasova et al. (2017) found decreased D2 and D3 receptor availability in drug-naïve adults with ADHD, and this finding correlated with a thinner cortex compared to healthy controls.

In addition to postsynaptic dopamine receptors, some studies have reported decreased density of dopamine transporters in the striatum of individuals with ADHD, while others have found increased density, or no difference compared to health controls (Cheon et al. 2003; Chu et al., 2017; Van Dyck et al., 2002). Studies have found that treatment with methylphenidate over time (e.g., 4 to 6 weeks) is associated with decreased DAT binding in the striatum but not with changes in global glucose metabolism (Krause et al., 2000; Matochik et al., 1994). Vles et al. (2003) studied the effects of chronic (three months) methylphenidate administration in male children with ADHD and found a 20% down-regulation of postsynaptic dopamine receptors and a 74% reduction of the dopamine transporter in the striatal system. These reductions in receptors were associated with improved neuropsychological test performance and ADHD symptoms.

Rohde and colleagues (2003) suggested that faulty frontal-striatal circuitry observed in ADHD may be modulated by gene variants of the dopaminergic system. Specifically, the researchers found significantly higher rCBF in the medial frontal and left basal ganglia following administration of methylphenidate in children with ADHD who had a specific polymorphism of the DAT1 gene compared to children with ADHD without the polymorphism. Interestingly, studies with other animals have found that methylphenidate is associated with neuroplasticity including increased dendritic length and branching of neurons in the frontal cortex, (Diaz-Heijtz, Kolb, & Forssberg, 2003; Simchon et al., 2015; Quansah et al., 2017). These findings suggest that stimulants, like antidepressants, may promote growth and expansion of neurons in certain regions of the brain. Wu and colleagues (2015) reported that methylphenidate resulted in changes in gene expression in the prefrontal cortex of rats that was associated with neuroplastic changes (neurite growth and axon regeneration) as well as changes in attention and locomotion. A dearth of information is available concerning the neuroplasticity effects of prescription stimulants in humans although scientists have speculated that faulty mechanisms of neuroplasticity may contribute to the development of ADHD and that prescription stimulants may promote neuroplasticity (Kasparek et al., 2014; Nyberg, 2014). Studies are sorely needed to further investigate the potential role of stimulant medication in neuroplasticity in children, adolescents, and adults with ADHD.

Summary

In summary, structural and functional neuroimaging studies support that frontal-striatal regions of the brain are implicated in ADHD; however, the pathogenesis of the disorder is likely the result of complex structural and functional abnormalities involving catecholaminergic deficiency as well as a number of brain regions and connections therein (Castellanos et al., 2005). Genetic factors also appear to contribute to the development of the disorder and a wealth of information also exists regarding the role of environmental factors (i.e., prenatal) that increase the risk of ADHD (Pohlabeln et al., 2017). Indeed, recent epigenetic research suggests that environmental risk factors for ADHD (prenatal, nutritional factors, stressful life events) can lead to changes in DNA (methylation and in histone modification levels) that in turn can affect gene expression and increased vulnerability to ADHD (Hamza et al., 2017).

Pharmacological Interventions

Psychostimulants are the most widely used and effective medications for the treatment of ADHD (Brown et al., 2018). In the United States, approximately two-thirds (3.5 million) of children and adolescents with ADHD were prescribed psychostimulants (Visser et al., 2014). Effectiveness of psychostimulants depends on several factors including age, severity of symptoms, and duration of symptoms (Chan et al., 2016). Currently, the FDA has approved stimulants, nonstimulants, and one prostimulant medication for the treatment of the disorder (Table 9.2). Approximately 20–30% of children who are prescribed stimulants do not show improvement in their ADHD symptoms and, as a result, alternative medications such as antidepressants or anticonvulsants are sometimes used (Chon et al., 2017; Ullman & Sleator, 1986).

Currently, there are no reliable biomarkers to determine who will and will not respond favorably to stimulant medications. A number of pharmacogenetic studies, however, have reported that polymorphisms of dopamine, norepinephrine, and noradrenaline genes are associated with a poor response to stimulant medication (methylphenidate) (Hong et al., 2012; Yu-Feng et al., 2004; Myer et al., 2017). Meanwhile, Kim and colleagues (2015) reported a classification accuracy rate of 84.6% for methylphenidate response in children and adolescents

Table 9.2 Examples of FDA Approved Medications for the Treatment of ADHD

Medication	Trade Name
Stimulants	
Methylphenidate	Ritalin, Metadate, Methylin, Concerta
Dexmethylphenidate	Focalin
Dextroamphetamine	Dexedrine, Zenzedi, Procentra
Pemoline	Cylert
Amphetamine	Evekeo, Adzenys XR
Amphetamine salts	Adderall
Prostimulant	
Lisdexamfetamine dimesylate	Vyvanse
Nonstimulants	
Atomoxetine	Strattera

Note: Medications come in short, intermediate, and sustained release forms.

using a combination of genetic polymorphisms, neuropsychological performance, age, weight, and rating scale data. Recently, Schulz (2017) reported that the degree of activation in the caudate nucleus as determined by fMRI while participants with ADHD performed an executive function task was predictive of a superior response to methylphenidate over atomoxetine. Although these approaches are not yet recommended for clinical practice, they do have major implications for future approaches to ADHD treatment. It is also important to note that the American Academy of Pediatrics recommends non-pharmacological behavioral interventions for children under the age of six prior to medication trials (Subcommittee on ADHD, AAP, 2011). Non-pharmacological approaches include behavioral support programs, educational interventions, and counseling (see Weyandt, 2007). Interestingly, results from the National Survey of Children's Health revealed that in 2016 nearly two-thirds (62%) of children with ADHD were taking medication and slightly less than half (46.7%) had received behavioral treatment for ADHD within the past year. The study also reported that nearly one-fourth (23%) had received neither treatment (Danielson et al., 2018).

Safety of Prescription Stimulants

A plethora of studies have supported the efficacy and safety of stimulants with preschoolers, children, adolescents, and adults with ADHD (Charach, Ickowicz, & Schachar, 2004; Short et al., 2004; Spencer, 2004). Fischer and Barkley (2003) found that stimulant therapy for ADHD in childhood is *not* associated with increased risk of adolescent experimentation with substance use, frequency of such use, or the risk of developing psychoactive substance use disorders by young adulthood. As discussed in Chapter 2, stimulants such as methylphenidate (Ritalin) increase arousal level of the CNS primarily by blocking the dopamine transporter (DAT), thereby increasing the availability of dopamine in the extracellular fluid (Volkow, Wang, et al., 2005). Although stimulants are considered a safe and effective treatment for ADHD, Schwartz and colleagues (2004) noted that stimulants can induce slight, but significant, sleep disturbances in children and adolescents treated with these medications. A common misconception is that stimulants produce a paradoxical effect—that is, calm a hyperactive system—but research indicates that the CNS of individuals with ADHD is actually under-aroused (Anderson et al., 2000; Hastings & Barkley, 1978). Stimulants, therefore, increase arousal and help to regulate frontal-striatal pathways believed to be dysfunctional in ADHD (Volkow, Wang et al., 2002, 2005, Volkow, Fowler, et al., 2002).

Antidepressants or other medications such as anticonvulsants or antidepressants are sometimes used to treat ADHD when individuals fail to respond to stimulants or when comorbid disorders are present such as depression and OCD. For example, research by Biederman et al. (1989) found that 68% of children who failed to show improvement with stimulants demonstrated significant improvement in ADHD symptoms while taking tricyclic antidepressants. Selective serotonin reuptake inhibitors are most effective for obsessive compulsive disorder and depression, and may be effective in children and adolescents with ADHD who also have coexisting mood problems (Spencer & Biederman, 2002). Delate et al. (2004) reported that 2.4% of children were prescribed antidepressants in 2002, and a 2004 annual report by Medco Health Solutions, Inc. indicated that 3.4% of children were prescribed antidepressant medications specifically for ADHD. Several studies have also found bupropion, an SNRI, to be effective at improving ADHD symptoms in children (Spencer, 2004). A recent meta-analysis of 48 studies examining efficacy and safety of medications used to treat ADHD in children, and young adults reported that methylphenidate was more effective than atomoxetine and guanfacine at reducing symptoms (Padilha et al., 2018). With regard to safety, lisdexamfetamine was more likely to cause sleep disorders (39%) as well as loss of appetite (65%) and behavior problems, such as irritability (60%). The fewest adverse events were associated with reboxetine. As noted previously, antidepressants are also used in the treatment of ADHD; however, most research indicates that stimulants are superior to antidepressants at improving ADHD symptoms. In addition, the FDA has *not* approved the use of antidepressants for the specific treatment of ADHD.

Non-Pharmacological Interventions

In addition to medication, research has found that a variety of behavioral and psychosocial interventions, as well can be effective at reducing the symptoms of ADHD (DuPaul & Weyandt, 2006; Weyandt, 2007). Several types of non-pharmacological, physiologically based interventions marketed for the treatment of ADHD have produced highly conflicting results. Moreover, because these interventions have not received the same level of scientific scrutiny as medication and behavioral interventions, numerous questions remain about their effectiveness and safety. Examples of these alternative interventions include dietary modifications, nutritional supplements, biofeedback, caffeine, and homeopathy (Brue & Oakland, 2002). Based on a survey of parents of 381 children with ADHD, Stubberfield and Parry (1999) found that 69% were using medication, but almost as many (64% of the sample) were using alternative therapies for ADHD. The most commonly used alternative method was dietary changes (60%), and there was no difference in the prevalence of the use of alternative interventions among families whose children were medicated or non-medicated. Chan, Rappaport, and Kemper (2003) found that 54% of 114 parents of children with ADHD reported using alternative interventions with their children, with vitamins and dietary manipulations the most common. Interestingly, only 11% of the parents had discussed using these methods with their child's physician.

The effects of nutritional supplements and dietary restrictions on ADHD symptoms have been explored by a substantial number of studies, with several reporting a reduction in ADHD symptoms (e.g., Dykman and Dykman, 1998; Harding, Judah, and Grant, 2003; Kaplan et al., 1989; Richardson & Puri, 2002) and others no change (Adams, 1981;

Mattes & Gittelman, 1981; Voigt et al., 2001; Wender, 1986). Recent research with children and college students with ADHD concluded that results failed to support the hypothesis that ADHD is driven by dietary micronutrient inadequacy (Holton et al., 2018). Caffeine studies have also produced mixed findings (e.g., Garfinkel, Webster, & Sloman, 1981; Huestis, Arnold, & Smeltzer, 1975). Comparison studies of the effectiveness of caffeine versus stimulants have generally found that stimulants are significantly more effective at reducing ADHD symptoms (Garfinkel, Webster, and Sloman, 1975; Leon, 2000), although Ioannidis et al. (2014) recommended the use of caffeine as an adjunctive treatment for ADHD. A few studies have reported that anthroposophic treatments including massage therapy and acupuncture were effective at reducing ADHD symptoms, although more well-designed studies are needed to empirically investigate these methods in the treatment of ADHD (e.g., Arnold, 2001; Khilnani et al., 2003; Hamre et al., 2010).

Neurofeedback (or biofeedback) has also been reported to effectively reduce ADHD symptomology in some studies (e.g., Fuchs et al., 2003; Monastra, Monastra, & George, 2002), whereas other studies have failed to support its efficacy (e.g., Heywood & Beale, 2003). In general, neurofeedback studies have been criticized for a lack of methodological rigor and potentially misleading findings (e.g., Loo, 2003; Willis et al., 2011). Even recent meta-analyses have produced conflicting findings (Cortese et al., 2016; Van Doren et al., 2018). Given research that indicates many adults and parents are already using these approaches with their children, well-designed, double-blind studies are needed to explore the potential effectiveness or lack of effectiveness of alternative interventions for ADHD.

Summary of Attention Deficit Hyperactivity Disorder

- Family and twin studies strongly support the heritability of ADHD.
- Molecular genetic studies have focused on polymorphisms of dopaminergic genes and more recently serotonergic genes.
- To date, a specific gene or group of genes has not been determined to cause ADHD, and it is likely that several interactive genes increase the susceptibility to ADHD.
- Structural, functional, and medication studies implicate dysfunctional frontal-striatal circuitry in ADHD.
- Pharmacological interventions are the most effective method for acutely treating ADHD symptoms.
- Reliable biomarkers for predicting medication response are not currently available; however, preliminary studies support genetic markers and brain activation patterns.
- Many behavioral interventions have also been shown to reduce ADHD symptoms in children and adolescents with the disorder while alternative interventions have produced mixed findings.

Autism Spectrum Disorder

Prevalence

Autism spectrum disorder (ASD) a neurodevelopmental syndrome representing a spectrum of impairments rather than discrete disorders. ASD is characterized by persistent deficits in social communication and social interactions, and a pattern of restricted and repetitive behaviors. These impairments are present in multiple contexts and settings and cause impairment in social, education, occupational, or other areas of functioning. The onset of ASD typically manifests in early childhood and level of severity varies significantly among individuals (APA, 2013). Studies have reported a mean age at diagnosis of 66.36 months, with a range of 19–207 months (Cop et al., 2015). The disorder occurs four to five times more often in boys than girls, and according to the CDC, 1 in 68 children in the United States are estimated to have the disorder (Ferri et al., 2018; www.cdc.gov). Prevalence of ASD varies cross culturally. For example, a recent study in Shanghai, China, reported the prevalence of ASD was 8.3 per 10,000 and 6.1% in Nordic countries (Hansen et al., 2018; Jin et al., 2018).

Comorbidity

Research has found that many individuals with ASD also have intellectual impairment, language impairment, motor deficits, poor adaptive behavior, and medical problems (APA, 2013). Behavioral problems are also common in ASD and may include aggressiveness, hyperactivity, impulsivity, attention problems, and self-injurious behavior (Lyall et al., 2017). In general, ASD follows a continuous course, but, depending on intelligence level and language skills, developmental gains are possible during the school-age years and beyond (Pallathra et al., 2018). Outcome studies have revealed that only a minority of individuals with ASD live and work independently. A number of studies have reported that early intervention and structured education and behavioral support programs can enhance the functioning of children in later life, and those with higher intellectual and language abilities have a greater likelihood of living independently (Andersen et al., 2017; APA, 2013).

Savants

Although most individuals with ASD also have varying degrees of intellectual impairment, in rare cases, they may have exceptional skills known as savant talents. Savant talents typically include music, memory, mathematics, specific knowledge, and art. Estimates vary but Treffert (2017) recently reported that savant abilities occur in approximately one in ten individuals with ASD. In 1999, Miller reviewed the savant literature and concluded that (a) the skills displayed by savants share many characteristics with the same skills displayed by people without a disability such as autism and (b) savant talents are usually accompanied by at least an average level of intelligence. Currently, there is no physiological explanation that adequately addresses the rare but documented exceptional skills of a minority of individuals with ASD (Wallace et al., 2009).

Genetic Findings

Family and Twin Studies

In 1976, Hanson and Gottesman reported that genetic factors contributed very little, if at all, to childhood autism and schizophrenia. In contrast, over 40 years later, based on family, twin, and candidate gene studies, experts often purport that genetic factors play a major role in the development of ASD. Family studies, for example, have found having at least one older sibling with ASD increases the risk of the disorder in younger siblings by 18.7%, a risk that is considerably higher than previous estimates of 3% to 10%, and younger boys of a sibling with ASD are at even greater risk than girls (26.2% versus 9.1%)(Ozonoff, et al., 2011). Simonoff (1998) reported that the risk of ASD 33% to 50% if two or more siblings have the disorder.

First-degree relatives of individuals with ASD have also been found to have an increase in behavioral or cognitive symptoms associated with ASD, such as social or communication problems when compared with the general population (Pisula et al., 2015). The heritability of ASD based on family studies is estimated to be 50% to (Sandin et al., 2014). Twin studies investigating the concordance rate of ASD in monozygotic versus dizygotic twins, however, suggest a higher heritability estimate of 0.64 to 0.91 for monozygotic twins and 0.18 to 0.34 for dizygotic twins (Hallmayer et al., 2011; Tick et al., 2016).

Linkage Studies and Candidate Genes

A number of chromosomes, chromosomal regions, and candidate genes have been linked to ASD, and although the majority of cases of ASD are idiopathic, approximately 10% have an identifiable genetic condition, such as fragile X syndrome, tuberous sclerosis, and Prader Willi syndrome (Carter & Scherer, 2013; Ferri et al., 2018).

Yuen and colleagues (2015) reported that substantial genetic heterogeneity exists in ASD and may be different for almost every individual. Given the phenotypic variability of ASD scientists have suggested that ASD has a complex inheritance and may involve anywhere from 10 to 100s of genes, and these genes may interact with environmental factors, increasing the risk of the disorder (e.g., Bespalova and Buxbaum, 2003; Forsberg et al., 2018).

Linkage and genome-wide analyses have identified numerous chromosomal regions as likely to harbor susceptibility genes for ASD, and a variety of gene variants and candidate genes have also been identified. Indeed, a variety of structural chromosomal abnormalities involving *nearly every chromosome* have been linked to ASD and including chromosomal duplications, inversions, terminal and interstitial deletions, and translocations (Chen, Chen, et al., 2017; Gillberg, 1998).

According to NIH, over 1,000 genes have been linked to ASD and researchers recently identified 18 additional genes linked to ASD (Yuen et al., 2017). Alterations of the GABA system have been linked to ASD for a number of years, particularly variants of the GABRA4 gene located on chromosome 4 and the GABRB3 gene located on chromosome 15 (Griswold et al., 2018). These genes encode a protein that is part of the GABA receptor, a receptor that plays a critical role in neuronal inhibition. The GABRB3 gene became a major focus of ASD research because individuals with Prader-Willi syndrome and Angelman's syndrome, genetic conditions due to chromosomal 15 abnormalities, often have co-existing ASD (Dykens et al., 2011).

The oxytocin receptor gene OXTR, located on chromosome 20, has been investigated in ASD due to the involvement of the hormone oxytocin in social bonding and affiliative behavior. ASD is characterized by social communication and affiliation deficits. Meta-analyses have reported that at least four polymorphisms of the OXTR gene are significantly associated with differences in amygdala volume and white matter connectivity is ASD (LoParo & Waldman, 2015).

The RELN gene located on chromosome 7 provides instructions for producing the protein reelin. During brain development, reelin is thought to play a critical role in cell migration and in neural plasticity. A recent meta-analysis supported that polymorphisms (e.g., rs362691) of the RELN gene was significantly associated with an increased risk of ASD (Wang et al., 2014), although the way in which this gene variant influences the development of ASD is unknown. Fatemi et al. (2001) reported greater than 40% reductions of the protein reelin in postmortem samples of the cerebellum of individuals with autistic disorder. Lammert and Howell (2016) noted that the RELN gene is particularly susceptible to epigenetic changes and suggested that a single mutation could possibly result in decreased RELN expression and consequently reduced reelin production. Reduced reelin levels could result in compromised cellular function, including neuroplasticity. Interestingly, RELN mutations occur in approximately four times as many males as females with ASD (Lammert & Howell, 2016).

A third gene frequently studied in ASD is the SHANK3 gene. This gene is located on chromosome 22 and provides instructions for making a protein (proline-rich synapse-associated protein) that plays a critical role in formation of dendritic spines and in synaptic connections. Mutations of the SHANK3 gene have been linked to ASD in several but not all studies (Uchino & Waga, 2015) (Uchino & Waga, 2015). Additional genes commonly linked to ASD include the serotonin transporter gene (SLC6A4); N-methyl-D-aspartate receptor gene (NMDA; GRIN2B); arginine vasopressin receptor 1A gene (AVPR1A); engrailed homeobox 2 (EN2); integrin, beta 3 (platelet glycoprotein IIIa, antigen CD61; ITGB3); met proto-oncogene (hepatocyte growth factor receptor; MET); and contactin-associated protein-like 2 (CNTCAP2) genes (Cop et al., 2015; Yoo et al., 2015). Although linkage, candidate gene, and genome-wide association studies provide valuable information in helping to unravel the complexity of ASD, it is critical to note that the specific ways in which gene variants are linked to ASD symptoms is largely unknown. In addition, the way in which environmental factors may impact gene expression (epigenetics) is ASD is speculative although preliminary studies support that stress and other factors can influence cellular functioning (Crider et al., 2017).

Structural Findings

A voluminous body of literature is available concerning structural brain findings in children and adults with ASD relative to controls and in some cases, other clinical groups. Many, but not all studies, have found structural differences between individuals with and without ASD with respect to total brain volume, volume of specific structures, gray and white matter, cortical thickness/thinning, and more connectivity between structures and brain regions.

For example, numerous MRI studies have reported enlarged brain volume (i.e., macroencephaly) in individuals with ASD relative to those without the disorder (e.g., Gillberg & de Souza, 2002; Piven et al., 1996). In 1999, Fombonne et al. reported that approximately 20% of individuals with ASD had unusually large head circumference (> 97th percentile); however, nearly 15% of individuals with ASD in their sample had unusually small head circumference (< third percentile). In a landmark study, Courchesne et al. (2001) studied 60 boys ages 2–16 with ASD and found that overall brain volume was normal at birth; however, by ages 2–4 years, 90% of boys with the disorder had greater than average brain size and 37% were macroencephalic relative to control children (Courchesne, 2002; Sacco et al., 2015). This macrocephaly finding is particularly associated with lower functioning ASD but is not typically found in older children or in adolescents with ASD compared to controls (Courchesne et al., 2011).

During childhood and adolescence, however, a number of studies have reported regional brain volume differences in the frontal and temporal lobes of individuals with ASD (Brun et al., 2009). Concomitant with regional volume increases, reductions in cortical thickness in the temporal cortex, and increased cortical thickness in the frontal cortex have been reported in individuals with ASD ranging in age from 2 to 64 years (van Rooij et al., 2017). At the molecular level, postmortem studies have reported a few but unreliable structural abnormalities in individuals with ASD relative to controls (Williams et al., 1980; Coleman et al., 1985). Several postmortem studies, however, have reported significantly fewer neurons (Purkinje cells), smaller neurons, and receptor densities in the cerebellum and in the frontal and temporal cortex compared to controls (Ritvo et al., 1986; Lee et al., 2002; Fatemi et al., 2002; Casanova, Buxhoeveden, & Gomez, 2003; Stoner et al., 2014). The reason for these structural cellular differences is unclear, but some researchers have suggested early problems with neural migration and connectivity characterize individuals with ASD (Chih et al., 2004).

Cross-sectional studies have also reported smaller subcortical volumes of the pallidum, putamen, amygdala, nucleus accumbens, and corpus callosum in children, adolescents, and adults with ADHD (e.g., Giuliano et al., 2018; van Rooij et al., 2017). Enlargement of the caudate nucleus has also been reported in ASD, and the degree of enlargement has been found to correlate with severity of symptoms as well as restricted and repetitive behaviors (Yu, Qiu, & Zhang, 2017). These findings appear to support an altered trajectory of brain development in ASD with frontal, parietal, and subcortical structures implicated most often. Interestingly, these structures and regions are involved with language, social perception, language, self-referential, and self-regulation: processes that are characteristically impaired in ASD (Yang et al., 2017).

White Matter and Support Vector Machine Technology

In addition to total brain and volume and morphological differences in specific structures of the brain, ASD is associated with gray matter reductions, excess white matter, and widespread compromised integrity of white matter tracts throughout the brain (Im et al., 2018; McFadden & Minshew, 2013). For example, Gibbard et al. (2018) recently reported that abnormalities of white matter tracts connecting the right amygdala to the right cortex, and this finding correlated with the severity of emotion recognition deficits in participants with ASD compared to controls. Additional brain regions and structures have been studied in ASD and the reader is referred to Li et al. (2017) for a review of these morphological findings.

It is critical to note that (a) not all studies have reported morphological differences between research participants with and without ASD and (b) many of the morphological findings reported are not unique to ASD. For example, Piven et al. (1998) studied MRI scans of 35 individuals with ASD relative to 36 controls and found that the volume of the hippocampus did not differ between these groups. In a recent meta-analytic study, Lefebrve et al. (2015) did not find evidence of total brain volume or corpus callosum differences in ASD despite achieving 99% statistical power. Lefebrve has expressed concerns with the use of multivariate analyses with small sample sizes and designs with low statistical power and have advocated for additional methodologically sound studies. Additionally, cortical thinning, reduced gray/white matter, compromised white matter integrity, enlarged caudate, and so on have been observed in other psychiatric conditions, including schizophrenia, anxiety disorders, OCD, ADHD, bipolar disorder, and Tourettes's disorder (e.g., Blumberg et al., 2003; Bloch et al., 2005). More recently, studies have begun to compare morphological differences between participants with ASD relative to controls and preliminary findings suggest shared and disorder-specific differences between groups (e.g., Carlisi, Norman, Lukito, et al., 2017). Additional studies, of course, are needed to replicate these findings. Lastly, others have encouraged the use of Support Vector Machine (SVM) technology, a type of supervised machine learning that aims to develop optimal algorithms able to discriminate between groups previously defined (e.g., ASD versus controls). SVM uses multivariate statistics that and takes into account inter-regional correlations, and it is reportedly well suited to assess subtle differences in brain metabolism, function, and anatomy (Retico et al., 2016). Indeed, some scientists have suggested that brain imaging studies can be useful at identifying brain volume changes in infants deemed at risk for ASD (Hazlett et al., 2017). Although these brain imaging techniques and analytic methods are considered preliminary they hold substantial promise for early identification of ASD in the not too distant future.

BOX 9.1   ASD Brain Bank

While neuroimaging technology is useful in exploring structural and functional brain findings of individuals with ASD, these techniques lack the quality of resolution necessary for investigating cellular and molecular characteristics of the disorder. Postmortem studies of high quality human brain tissue are ideally suited to study these molecular characteristics; however, samples of brain tissue from deceased individuals with ASD are extremely limited. Recently, Amaral and colleagues (2018) described the establishment of a privately funded network of brain tissue collection sites that collectively form a brain tissue bank, known as Autism Brain Net (autismbrainnet.org). The National Institutes of Health recently aligned with Autism Brain Net and together they established strict procedures for collecting, preparing, and preserving human brain donations, and for procedures for scientists to obtain brain tissue from the brain banks for research purposes. Collaborative efforts like these between individuals with ASD, their families, and scientists will certainly help propel discovery of the underlying causes of the disorder and lead to preventative efforts and future treatments for ASD.

In summary, structural differences have been found between individuals with and without ASD with respect to total brain volume, volume of specific structures, gray and white matter, cortical thickness/thinning, and more connectivity between structures and brain regions.

Macrocephaly is particularly associated with lower functioning ASD but is not typically found in older children or in adolescents with ASD compared to controls. Concomitant with regional volume increases, reductions in cortical thickness in the temporal cortex and increased cortical thickness in the frontal cortex have been reported in individuals with ASD. Cross-sectional studies have also reported smaller subcortical volumes of the pallidum, putamen, amygdala, nucleus accumbens, and corpus callosum, as well as enlargement of the caudate nucleus. These findings support an altered trajectory of brain development in ASD with frontal, parietal, and subcortical structures implicated most often. Interestingly, these structures and regions are involved with language, social perception, language, self-referential, and self-regulation: processes that are characteristically impaired in ASD.

In addition, research with ASD supports gray matter reductions, excess white matter, and widespread compromised integrity of white matter tracts throughout the brain. It is critical to note that (a) not all studies have reported morphological differences between research participants with and without ASD, (b) many of the morphological findings reported are not unique to ASD, and (c) anatomical studies are correlational in nature and do not reveal whether the anatomical differences are related to the expression of the disorder or whether the symptoms of ASD influence the development of anatomical structures. Of course, it is also possible that the anatomical findings are unrelated to the behavioral symptoms and reflect disturbances elsewhere in the brain.

Functional Findings

rCBF Findings

A substantial number of functional neuroimaging studies have been conducted with individuals with ASD, and although many studies have reported decreased activation in various brain regions, other studies have produced conflicting findings. Functional findings have largely been based on rCBF and glucose metabolism studies (PET) and fMRI studies.

Early PET studies reported that overall blood perfusion was significantly decreased in participants with ASD relative to controls (George et al., 1992). Later Zilbovicius et al. (1995, 2000) measured rCBF in a group of children with ASD when they were between 3 and 4 years of age and 3 years later. Results revealed that children with the disorder initially had decreased rCBF in the frontal regions and 76% showed increased rCBF in the temporal lobes relative to control children. Normal blood flow values were reportedly attainted by ages 6–7, however, compared to control children.

Other studies have reported significantly reduced blood flow in the prefrontal areas of children and adults with ASD compared to controls. Wilcox et al. (2002) hypothesized that these findings support that prefrontal and language-related regions are dysfunctional in individuals with ASD at an early age, and this early dysfunction interferes with the subsequent normal development of language. Social communication deficits characteristic of ASD have also been linked to differential brain activation patterns observed when is individuals with ASD are presented with facial stimuli depicting emotions. For example, Hall, Szechtman, and Nahmias (2003) compared rCBF in eight high-functioning males with ASD and eight controls during an emotion recognition task. Results indicated individuals with ASD had lower rCBF in the inferior frontal regions and higher rCBF in the anterior cingulate and thalamus relative to those without the disorder. Additional and more recent PET studies have also reported rCBF differences between participants with and without ASD, and these findings have correlated with poor neuropsychological task performance (Horwitz et al., 1988; Hashimoto et al., 2000; Haznedar et al., 2000; Ohnishi et al., 2000; Kumar et al., 2017; Mitelman et al., 2017). Overall, rCBF findings support functional brain differences individuals with ASD. However, it is important to note (a) the regions in which these differences have emerged varied substantially across studies, (b) many of the studies included small samples and were underpowered, and (c) some studies reported no rCBF differences across clinical groups (e.g., Heh et al., 1989; Mana et al., 2010).

Glucose Metabolism Findings

Glucose metabolism brain activation patterns have also been investigated in ASD. For example, Rumsey et al. (1985) were among the first to report that participants with autistic disorder had significantly elevated glucose metabolism in widespread regions of the brain and no specific brain region showed reduced glucose metabolism in individuals with the disorder. Other studies, however, have reported significantly lower glucose metabolism in the medial frontal lobes (but not the lateral regions) and significantly higher metabolism in occipital and parietal regions in individuals with ASD relative to controls while at rest and during attention related tasks (Hazlett et al., 2004; Siegel, Nuechterlein, Abel,

Wu, & Buchsbaum, 1995). More recent findings have also reported inconsistent glucose patterns among participants with ASD, including reduced activity in the cerebellum, temporal, and frontal regions, as well as the occipital cortices (Kumar et al., 2017). These findings support altered glucose metabolism in ASD but also support variable findings among participants consistent with the heterogeneity of ASD symptoms.

Activation patterns in participants with ASD have also been explored using fMRI (BOLD) while at rest and during various tasks. For example, Allen and Courchesne (2003) used fMRI to study activation patterns of the cerebellum while eight participants with ASD and eight without performed a visual attention task and a motor function (pressing a button). Results revealed that those with ASD showed significantly greater activation of the cerebellum during the motor task than controls and significantly less cerebellar activation than controls during the attention task. These differential findings supported earlier structural studies reported decreased cerebellum volume in participants with ASD.

Given the social communication deficits characteristic of ASD, numerous fMRI studies have explored the performance of individuals with ASD while performing a variety of tasks including attention, eye gazing, emotional processing, and so on. In general, these studies have found both decreased and increased activation in regions involved in emotional face processing and social cognition, including the frontal cortex, amygdala, insula, and additional limbic structures (Aoki et al., 2015; Philip et al., 2012; Sommer et al., 2018). Likewise, studies have revealed differences in brain activation patterns elicited during cognitive control tasks, repetitive behaviors, and during language tasks in individuals with ASD relative to controls (Carlisi, Norman, Murphy, et al., 2017; Herringshaw et al., 2016; Kohls et al., 2018).

In recent years, functional studies have focused on white matter connectivity among brain regions implicated in ASD including limbic, frontal, and temporal regions while participants are at rest and/or during various tasks. These studies have yielded inconsistent findings with some reporting overactivity, while others report under-activity or a combination of both (Di Martino et al., 2014). Recent studies have reported that severity of repetitive and restrictive behaviors in participants with ASD were correlated with white matter connectivity patterns (Wei et al., 2018).

In summary, functional neuroimaging studies have found evidence of both decreased and increased glucose metabolism and blood flow in individuals with ASD relative to controls. Similar to structural findings, functional disturbances of limbic regions and projecting cortical pathways to frontal and temporal regions are most often implicated in ASD. Although overall functional findings support brain differences in individuals with ASD relative to those without the disorder, there are significant discrepancies and conflicting findings across studies. Differences among these functional neuroimaging studies may reflect the heterogeneity of ASD and/or methodological and procedural differences between studies (specific tasks, design variables, age, sex). It is also critical to note that to date, the brain differences found are not necessarily unique to ASD (e.g., Paradiso et al., 2003; Pelphrey et al., 2017). Lastly, and perhaps more importantly, although genetic and environmental theories exist regarding the etiology of ASD, the underlying cause of observed brain differences remains unknown.

Additional Theories

Prenatal Factors, Viruses, Vaccines, Dietary Deficiencies

In addition to genetic, structural, and functional studies of ASD, researchers have explored other factors that potentially increase the risk of ASD. Although a review of these studies is beyond the scope of this chapter, areas of current research include prenatal factors, such as pregnancy complications such as maternal melatonin levels, vaginal infection, and uterine bleeding (Braam et al., 2018; Juul-Dam, Townsend, & Courchesne, 2001). Other studies have investigated the relationship between exposure to viruses (cytomegalovirus, viral encephalitis, viral meningitis) during pregnancy and ASD (Yamashita et al., 2003). Postnatal factors such as vaccinations (e.g., measles mumps rubella, or MMR) have also been investigated and according to numerous studies, however, epidemiological evidence does *not* support an association between MMR vaccination and autistic disorder (e.g., Hviid et al., 2003; Kuppili et al., 2018; Miller, 2003; Phelan, 2002; Takahashi, 2003). Others have suggested that immunological abnormalities such as decreased T and B cells, macrophages, and natural killer cells are implicated in the pathogenesis of ASD, while others have implicated gut microbiota and inflammation in the development of ASD (e.g., Doenyas, 2018; Gupta, 2000). Still others have hypothesized a role for medications used to control infectious fevers (e.g., acetaminophen) in pregnant women or in young children may interfere with normal immunological development and lead to neurodevelopmental disorders including ASD (Good, 2018; Torres, 2003). Lastly, dietary factors such as metabolic and nutritional deficiencies, phenylketonuria, choline, and creatine have also been explored in ASD and some have suggested that metabolic indices may serve as biomarkers for ASD (Adams et al., 2011; Baieli et al., 2003; Khemakhem et al., 2017; Sokol et al., 2002; Zaffanello et al., 2003). Overall, evidence suggests that a variety of prenatal and postnatal factors have been implicated in some individuals with ASD, but none of these factors are regarded as causal agents or diagnostic biomarkers. Empirical studies are needed to further explore these and other etiologic hypotheses of ASD.

Pharmacological and Additional Interventions

Currently, the US Food and Drug Administration (FDA) have not approved a pharmacological treatment for the core symptoms of ASD. The FDA has, however, approved two antipsychotic medications (aripiprazole and risperidone) for the treatment of non-core symptoms of ASD such as irritability and aggressive behavior. Additional antipsychotic medications have also been used as adjunctive treatments for ASD to reduce behavioral problems associated with the disorder such as agitation, hyperactivity, stereotypies (repetitive behavior), and self-injurious behavior, although their effectiveness varies (Minshawi et al., 2014). Other medications have also been investigated in ASD with varying effectiveness including anticonvulsants, α-agonists, norepinephrine reuptake inhibitors, lithium, GABA agonists, buspirone, and oxytocin (see Stepanova, Dowling, Phelps, & Findling, 2017, for a review).

Children with ASD often display significant attention, impulsivity, and hyperactivity symptoms, and prescription stimulants such as methylphenidate have been found to improve attention skills in some children with ASD (Handen, Johnson, & Lubetsky, 2000). Sturman and colleagues (2017) recently conducted a systematic review concerning the use of methylphenidate in children and adolescents with ASD and concluded that short-term use of methylphenidate was associated with improved symptoms of hyperactivity and inattention in children with ASD who are tolerant of the medication. Improvement was not found in social interaction, repetitive behaviors, or overall ASD. The authors expressed concern, however, with the quality of the studies and recommended more rigorous inclusion criteria and longer duration of studies. In light of recent research that reported that among 33,565 children with ASD, 64% had a filled prescription for at least one psychotropic medication, 35% had been prescribed two or more, and 15% concurrently used medications from more than three classes of psychotropic medications, additional studies are sorely needed to understand the safety and effectiveness of these medications with individuals with ASD (Spencer et al., 2013). Common combinations of medications included antidepressants and stimulants (38% of subjects), antipsychotic and stimulants (28%), antipsychotics and antidepressants (20%), and antipsychotic, antidepressant, and stimulants (18%). Interestingly, antidepressants are commonly used in the treatment of ASD however empirical studies do not support their effectiveness with this population (Stepanova et al., 2017).

Alternative Approaches

Despite only two medications approved by the FDA, research has found that nearly 50% of insured children with ASD are treated with stimulants, α-agonists, antipsychotics, and antidepressants (Madden et al., 2017). In additional, it's been estimated that 30% of more of individuals with ASD are treated with alternative remedies such as nutritional supplements, chelating agents, hormone therapy, and restrictive diets despite their potential adverse effects and lack of empirical data supporting their effectiveness (Owley et al., 2001; Levy et al., 2003, 2015). Lastly, although not the focus of this chapter, a variety of non-pharmacological behavioral interventions that target communication and social behaviors while reducing problem behavior have strong empirical support and are considered primary and effective forms of intervention for ASD symptoms. Excellent reviews of this literature are available elsewhere (Campbell, 2003; Kuder & Accaro, 2018; Hong et al., 2018; Billeci et al., 2016).

Summary of Autism Spectrum Disorder

- ASD is characterized by significant impairments in communication and social relationships, as well as a restricted repertoire of interests and activities.
- Research supports a role for genetic factors in the development of ASD, although other variables such as prenatal factors may also play a role in its development.
- Postmortem and structural studies have produced conflicting results but generally indicate morphological differences in the cerebellum, subcortical, temporal, and frontal regions; however, these differences found are not necessarily unique to ASD.
- Functional studies also implicate glucose and blood flow differences in individuals with ASD, as well as compromised white matter connectivity, although findings are highly variable across studies.
- Differences among functional neuroimaging studies may reflect the heterogeneity of ASD and/or methodological and procedural differences between studies.
- Pharmacological interventions play a secondary role to behavioral interventions in the treatment of ASD.
- Additional research is needed to better understand the effects and safety of medications used to treat the aggressive, repetitive, and self-injurious behaviors characteristic of some individuals with ASD.
- Although genetic and environmental theories exist regarding the etiology of ASD, the underlying cause of the disorder remains unknown.

Tourette's Disorder

Prevalence

Gilles de la Tourette syndrome is named after Gilles de la Tourette who, in 1885, described patients who suffered from a disorder characterized by involuntary movements, echolalia, coprolalia, and unusual, uncontrollable sounds (Lajonchere, Nortz, & Finger, 1996). The American Psychiatric Association currently refers to Gilles de la Tourette syndrome as Tourette's disorder (APA, 2013). The disorder is characterized by multiple motor tics and one or more vocal tics that have persisted for more than one year (APA, 2013). A *tic* is a sudden, recurrent, rapid, and stereotyped vocalization or movement that may be either simple or complex. Eye blinking, nose wrinkling, and shoulder shrugging are examples of *simple motor tics*, while jumping, pressing, stomping, squatting, twirling, and hand gestures are examples of *complex motor tics*. Throat clearing, sniffing, chirping, and snorting are examples of *simple vocal tics* and sudden expression of a single word or phrase or echolalia are examples of *complex vocal tics*. Contrary to popular perception, coprolalia (sudden and inappropriate expression of obscenities, racial or religious slurs) is not a diagnostic criterion for Tourette's disorder, as it is seen in only 10% to 25% of individuals with the disorder (Kobierska et al., 2014). The prevalence of Tourette's disorder in school-age children in the United States is estimated to be 3–8 per 1,000 and 0.05% in adults (Robertson & Eapen, 2014). Tourette's disorder is found throughout the world, but the prevalence appears to vary among countries and race with a lower rate reported in African Americans, sub-Saharan Africans, and in Japan and Taiwan (Robertson et al., 2009; Freeman et al., 2000; Wang & Kuo, 2003).

The disorder occurs more frequently in males than females with a ratio of 4:1 to 9:2 (Freeman et al., 2000; Want & Kuo, 2003). The age of onset is typically during childhood with a mean age of onset of tics is 6.4 years (Freeman et al., 2000). The course of Tourette's disorder is variable with waxing and waning and changes in vocalizations, as well as muscle groups over time. Follow-up studies indicate that tics often decline during adolescence, but many individuals continue to struggle with tics into adulthood. Groth et al. (2017), for example, reported that 17.7% of their sample of 227 participants above age 16 years had no tics, 59.5% had minimal or mild tics, and 22.8% had moderate or severe tics. Premonitory urges—i.e., uncomfortable sensations—typically precede tics and a feeling of release following the expression of the tic typically emerge in childhood and have been linked to increased neural activity in the insula and pathways extending from the basal ganglia to the frontal cortex (Conceição et al., 2017; Robertson, 2015). Comorbid conditions also arise in childhood and are associated with a poorer quality of life in patients with Tourette's disorder (Eapen et al., 2016).

Comorbidity

Tourette's disorder is frequently accompanied by sleep disturbances, inappropriate sexual behavior, social, academic, neuropsychological, and occupational impairment, and occasionally self-injurious behavior (Robertson, 2015; Sukhodolsky et al., 2003). Studies have also found that children and adolescents with Tourette's disorder are at greater risk for being bullied by their peers, and for low self-esteem, anxiety, and depression (Muller-Vahl et al., 2010). The lifetime prevalence of psychiatric comorbidity in individuals with Tourette's disorder is approximately 86% and approximately 58% of individuals with Tourette's have two or more psychiatric disorders (Hirschtritt et al., 2015). Studies around the world consistently find that the two most commonly co-occurring disorders are ADHD (35–90%) and OCD (35–50%) (Freeman et al., 2000; Roessner et al., 2007; Storch et al., 2007). Explosive rage (25–75%), depression (13–76%), learning disabilities (23%), and migraine headaches (25%) also commonly occur with Tourette's disorder (Hirschtritt et al., 2018; Kumar et al., 2016).

Hirschtritt and colleagues found that the greatest risk for the onset of most comorbid disorders was between 4 and 10 years of age; however, the onset of eating and substance use problems was typically during adolescence. The impact of Tourette's disorder on the individual and the family is significantly greater when comorbidities are present and when the symptoms of Tourette's disorder are severe (Spencer et al., 1998; Wilkinson et al., 2002).

Genetic Findings

Family and Twin Findings

For decades, family, twin, and candidate gene studies have explored genetic factors involved in the development of Tourette's disorder. Family studies, for example, have reported that the disorder is more common in first and second-degree relatives, although the level of reported risk varies across studies. For example, Pauls et al. (2014) reported that Tourette's disorder is 10 to 100 times higher in first-degree relatives than in the general population, while McMahon and colleagues (2003) reported that the rates of Tourette's disorder in children were three times higher if both parents rather than one parent had the disorder. Twin studies have also shed light on the heritability of the disorder as the concordance rate in twins ranges from 53% to 63% for monozygotic twins and 8% to 33% for dizygotic twins (Price, Kidd, Cohen, Pauls, & Leckman, 1985; Bolton et al., 2007; Zilhão et al., 2017). Collectively, family and twin studies support a heritability component of Tourette's disorder; however, the rates are lower than those reported for ASD, ADHD, bipolar disorder, and schizophrenia.

Linkage Studies and Candidate Genes

Early linkage studies examining families in which Tourette's disorder was present in two or more members sought to identify chromosomal regions that harbored susceptibility genes for the disorder. No single locus or gene was identified as causing Tourette's disorder, and findings supported that the disorder was unlikely to be due to a specific genetic mutation and instead suggested that Tourette's is a genetically complex disorder (Walkup et al., 1996). Multiple chromosomes and chromosomal regions have been the focus of genetic studies of Tourette's disorder, including chromosomes 1, 3, 4, 5, 6, 9, 11, 13, 17, 22, among others (see Qi et al., 2017, for a review). Attention to these loci is based on neurobiological theories of Tourette's disorder involving frontal-striatal pathways and the genes that govern neurotransmitter systems found within these pathways (dopamine, serotonin, glutamate) and histamine genes.

With regard to dopamine, Price and colleagues (1986) were among the first to report that stimulants worsened tics in 24% of individuals with Tourette's disorder, thereby implicating the dopaminergic system in the disorder. Nomura and Segawa (2003) as well as others hypothesized that Tourette's disorder is a disorder of the dopaminergic system, and many studies have attempted to link single nucleotide polymorphisms or other mutations of dopamine genes to Tourette's disorder. Dopamine genes that have been investigated include D1 through D5 as well as the dopamine transporter gene (DAT1). Variants of these genes have been explored in a large number of studies and results have been inconsistent (see Qi et al., 2017, for a review).

The D2 receptor has frequently been implicated in Tourette's disorder. A recent meta-analysis investigating a restriction fragment length polymorphism (rs1800497) of the dopamine receptor gene (DRD2) concluded that this variant was indeed associated with increased risk of Tourette's disorder, particularly in Caucasians (Yuan et al., 2015). The DRD2 gene is located on chromosome 11 and encodes the D2 subtype of the dopamine receptor. The way in which the rs1800497 polymorphism contributes to Tourette's disorder is unknown; however, studies have found increased density of the D2 receptor in the frontal cortex and striatum in participants with Tourette's disorder when compared to the controls (Yoon et al., 2007). It is important to note that only a minority of individuals with Tourette's disorder have this variant and the DRD2 gene is also linked to schizophrenia and substance use disorders.

The dopamine transporter gene (DAT1/SLC6A3) located on chromosome 5 encodes for the dopamine transporter protein located on the presynaptic membrane. As stated previously in this chapter, this transporter protein retrieves dopamine from the synaptic cleft following exocytosis. This protein has also been linked to Tourette's disorder over the years with some studies reporting increased density in the striatum (e.g., 37% to 50%), while others have not replicated this finding (Minzer et al., 2004; Singer, Hahn, and Moran 1991). Despite the inconsistent findings across studies, some hypothesized that genetic mutations or other variants affecting the dopamine system lead to symptoms characteristic of Tourette's disorder. Overall some studies have reported a linkage between variants of the DAT1 gene and Tourette's disorder although other studies have produced conflicting findings (Wong et al., 2007; Qi et al., 2017).

More recently, additional genes governing serotonin, glutamate, and other neurotransmitters, as well as histamine, have been investigated in Tourette's disorder (e.g., IMMP2L, CNTNAP2, NLGN4X, DPP6, SLITRK1, COL27A1, NTN4, MRPL3, DNAJC13, OFCC1, GPR64, NDUFA4, and KLHL32 genes) (see Qi et al., 2017, and Richer & Fernandez, 2015, for a review). Similar to dopamine studies, results have been inconsistent and inclusive regarding the role that these genes and variants of these genes might play in the development of Tourette's disorder. Richer and Fernandez (2015) noted that candidate gene studies have largely produced nonsignificant or non-reproducible findings most likely due to small sample sizes and inadequate statistical power. He further noted, "Although the low cost of examining only a few specific variants is appealing, the a priori probability that these variants will play a role in conferring risk for the disease is low" (p. 158). What can be concluded to date is that no gene(s) or gene variants have been found to reliably confer risk for the disorder. What also remains unclear and for future research to address is the degree to which genetic findings are unique to Tourette's disorder or overlap with other psychiatric conditions (e.g., ADHD, OCD). Future research will also need to address epigenetic factors and disentangle the ways in which environmental factors may affect genetic expression and how this process relates to the development of Tourette's disorder.

Structural Findings

Gray and White Matter

Numerous studies have been conducted exploring structural brain differences between children and adults with Tourette's disorder relative to healthy controls. These studies have examined a number of differences including gray and white matter volume, ventricular enlargement, cortical thickness/thinning, specific structural differences, and, more recently, white matter connectivity between structures and regions.

With respect to gray and white volume, studies have reported disproportionate white matter increases in participants with Tourette's disorder compared to controls in the frontal regions (Peterson et al., 2001; Wittfoth, 2012). Studies have also reported increased white matter in parietal regions and smaller occipital volumes, a finding that significantly correlates with severity of symptoms (Peterson et al., 2001). More recent studies have applied newer MRI methods (voxel-based morphometry) to measure white and gray matter volume differences between participants with Tourette's disorder and healthy controls, and findings have revealed lower white matter volume bilaterally in the prefrontal cortex and greater gray volume in the thalamus, hypothalamus, and midbrain (Greene et al., 2017; Liu et al., 2013). These studies also reported that lower white matter volume was positively correlated with tic severity and duration. Some scientists have questioned whether the reduced white matter findings in Tourette's disorder are due to true morphological differences or are the result of medication. Specifically, Jeppesen et al. (2014) investigated gray and white matter in children with Tourette's who had not been treated with medication and did not find differences between controls and participants with Tourette's in gray or white matter.

With respect to gray matter, studies have also reported reduced gray matter thickness in participants with Tourette's disorder the insula and sensorimotor cortex, and this finding was inversely correlated with tic severity and premonitory urges (Draper et al., 2016). Participants with Tourette's disorder have also been found to have abnormal structural patterns of cortical sulci, specifically lower depth, and reduced thickness of gray matter in the sulci relative to controls and to participants with OCD (Muellner et al., 2015).

Ventricular Enlargement and Basal Ganglia

With regard to ventricular enlargement, studies have produced conflicting findings with some reporting enlarged ventricles, smaller ventricles, and no ventricular size difference between participants with and without Tourette's disorder (Harcherik et al., 1985; Singer et al., 1993; Zimmerman, Abrams, Giuliano, Denckla, & Singer, 2000). It is also important to note that ventricular enlargement is sometimes found in neurodegenerative disorders as well as schizophrenia and chronic substance use disorders.

Peterson et al. (1993, 2003) were among the first to report basal ganglia differences (smaller in size) in children and adult participants with Tourette's disorder relative to controls. Peterson and colleagues also reported that children with Tourette's disorder lacked the normal symmetry (left larger than right) of the basal ganglia. These findings, however, have not been corroborated by other investigations involving both children and adults (Debes et al., 2015). Interestingly, research has documented that cerebral strokes that affect the basal ganglia often result in subsequent tics and other symptoms of Tourette's (Kwak & Jankovic, 2002). It is important to note, however, that structural differences involving the basal ganglia are not unique to Tourette's disorder and have been reported in ASD, ADHD, and OCD (Riva et al., 2018 Robertson).

Several studies have reported size differences (both larger and smaller) of the corpus callosum in participants with Tourette's disorder (Peterson et al., 1994; Baumgardner et al., 1996; Wolff et al., 2016). Kim and Peterson (2003) reported that the cavum septum pellucidum (CSP), an area near the corpus callosum that fuses early in development, was significantly smaller in children with Tourette's compared controls, supporting early disturbances in brain development in individuals with Tourette's disorder. However, Mostofsky and colleagues (1999) studied girls with Tourette's disorder and found no differences in the size of the corpus callosum compared to control subjects and girls with ADHD.

It is important to note that structural findings, although informative descriptively, are useful in generating hypotheses, are purely correlational in nature, and do not reveal whether the morphological differences lead to Tourette's disorder symptoms or whether the verbal and motor tics contribute to observed morphological differences. Furthermore, as is true of all structural findings, morphological results may reflect secondary effects of disturbances (e.g., neurochemical or genetic) elsewhere in the brain. In contrast to structural studies, functional studies enable scientists to examine brain activation patterns that may be associated with symptoms as well as structural findings.

Functional Findings

Given the core symptoms of Tourette's disorder—i.e., motor and vocal tics, as well as results of structural studies, functional studies have focused on subcortical regions of the brain implicated in movement (basal ganglia) and the pathways extending from these areas to the frontal cortex (cortico-basal ganglia circuits) (Dale, 2017). For example, Wolf et al. (1996) were among the first to use PET to study monozygotic twins discordant for Tourette's and found increased binding to postsynaptic dopamine receptors (D2) in the caudate nucleus in all five twins affected with Tourette's relative to twins without the disorder (no differences were found with respect to the putamen). Minzer and colleagues (2004) examined postmortem tissue of three individuals with Tourette's disorder and found an approximate 140% increase in prefrontal D2 receptors in individuals with the disorder relative to controls. Increases were also found with respect to dopamine transporters and metabolite concentration of dopamine and norepinephrine in prefrontal and striatum regions of individuals with Tourette's disorder.

Basal Ganglia

Additionally, studies have reported functional differences in specific basal ganglia structures of participants with Tourette's disorder relative to controls, although not all studies find the same differences in all basal ganglia structures. Singer and colleagues (2002), for example, compared dopamine release in participants with and without Tourette's disorder following an intravenous injection of amphetamine. Results revealed that those with Tourette's disorder had significant increased dopamine release (21%) in the putamen compared to controls; however, dopamine release was not significantly different between groups in the caudate. Additional studies have also reported activity in the caudate did not differ between participants with Tourette's disorder and controls (e.g., Meyer et al., 1999; Stamenkovic et al., 2001; Turjanski et al., 1994). Based on the putamen findings, Singer et al. speculated that and overactive dopamine transporter system, particularly in the region of the basal ganglia, may underlie Tourette's disorder. Indeed, dopamine agonists (stimulants) have been found to exacerbate Tourette symptoms in some, but not all individuals. Other studies, however, using fMRI, SPECT, and PET *have* reported increased presynaptic dopamine activity in the caudate and/or putamen in both child and adult participants with Tourette's disorder relative to controls (e.g., Albin et al., 2003; Ernst et al., 1999; Cheon et al., 2004; Malison et al., 1995). Interestingly, Gates et al. (2004) used fMRI to study a patient with Tourette's disorder during coprolalia and found increased activity in the caudate nucleus, cingulate gyrus, occipital, and frontal regions relative to a healthy control. Recent studies using fMRI have also reported increased activity in the striatum (caudate and putamen) and the frontal cortex in participants with Tourette's disorder during eye-blink inhibition compared to controls (Mazzone et al., 2010). Others have suggested that the increased activity in the basal ganglia support brain maturation defects in Tourette's disorder.

Suppression of Tics

A number of studies have attempted to address the physiological underpinnings of suppression of tics. For example, Peterson et al. (1998) used fMRI to study voluntary suppression of tics compared to expression of tics in 22 adults with Tourette's disorder. Findings revealed increased activation in the frontal cortex and right caudate nucleus, and decreased activation in the globus pallidus during tic expression compared to suppression. More recently, Worbe et al. (2015) suggested that frontal regions appear to fail to exert control over motor pathways in individuals with Tourette's disorder resulting in tic expression and emphasized that Tourette's is not simply a disorder affecting the basal ganglia.

Glucose Metabolism and rCBF

With regard to glucose metabolism and rCBF, studies have reported differences between individuals with Tourette's disorder relative to controls; however, conflicting findings have been reported. Braun et al. (1993), for example, reported decreased glucose metabolism in prefrontal cortices, orbitofrontal regions, and hippocampal regions and striatum in 16 medication-free subjects with Tourette's disorder relative to controls. Stern and colleagues (2000) reported increased activity in the premotor cortices, anterior cingulate cortex, putamen, caudate, and primary motor cortex that was significantly correlated with the presence of tics as determined by PET and synchronized audio and videotaping of participants. Other studies have reported increased glucose metabolism in the premotor and motor cortex and decreased activity in the caudate, thalamus, and hippocampal regions in subjects with Tourette's disorder (Eidelberg et al., 1997), while other reported no differences with respect to global glucose metabolism (Jeffries et al., 2002). With respect to rCBF, studies have also been inconsistent, with some reporting elevated rCBF in the frontal regions (George et al., 1992; de Vries et al., 2013) and others reduced rCBF in frontal and striatal regions (e.g., Moriarty et al., 1997).

The current consensus in the scientific literature appears to be that the basal ganglia, including the putamen, caudate, and globus pallidus, are indisputably involved in movement and abnormalities affecting the basal ganglia can result in several movement disorders including Tourette's disorder. It is possible that different parts of the basal ganglia are functionally segregated and form separate circuits that likely influence the motor and cognitive symptoms of Tourette's disorder (Gillman & Sandyk, 1986; Groenewegen et al., 2003). The cause of alterations of the basal ganglia in Tourette's disorder are unknown but are hypothesized to be the result of genetic and structural differences and possibly epigenetic factors (Pagliaroli et la., 2016). In addition, functional findings also implicate the frontal and limbic regions of the cortex in Tourette's disorder as conscious suppression of tics is possible and tics often remit completely or reduce in frequency during high-attention demanding tasks such a musical performance, listening to music, and even mental imagery of a musical performance (Bodeck et al., 2015; Robertson et al., 2017). Stress and emotionally charged situations have also been found to exacerbate tics, implicating the limbic region as well in the pathogenesis of Tourette's disorder (Godar et al., 2017). Lastly, as noted previously in this chapter, it is important to keep in mind that the basal ganglia as well as pathways extending to and from the frontal cortex have been implicated in disorders other than Tourette's disorder such as OCD and ADHD.

Pharmacological Interventions

Several types of medication are available to treat Tourette's disorder and degree of effectiveness varies depending on severity of symptoms as well as medication type. In general, however, medications are estimated to reduce symptoms of Tourette's disorder by 25% to 70% (Huys et al., 2012; Roessner et al., 2013). Use of medication is recommended when symptoms cause social-emotional problems, physical discomfort, and/or impairment in daily living. Although not the focus of this chapter, it is important to note that cognitive behavioral approaches have been found to be highly effective at helping to manage symptoms of Tourette's disorder and are often recommended prior to trying medication (Piacentini et al., 2010). Medications commonly used in the treatment of Tourette's disorder include antipsychotic and adrenergic alpha-2 medications.

Antipsychotic Medication

Typical antipsychotic medications that block postsynaptic dopamine receptors (e.g., haloperidol/haldol, thioridazine/mellaril, thiothixene/navane, pimozide/orap) are often highly effective at reducing symptoms (43% to 70%) (Huys et al., 2012). Haloperidol was the first medication shown to be effective at reducing tics haloperidol and has been commonly for treating Tourette's disorder in children (Sallee et al., 1997). Other typical antipsychotic medications also block dopamine postsynaptic receptors with varying degrees of affinity for D1-D4 receptors. There are multiple double-blind, placebo-controlled trials investigating the effectiveness of these medications in reducing symptoms of Tourette's disorder (see Quezada & Coffman, 2018, for a review). The down side of typical antipsychotic medications is the negative side effects including tardive dyskinesia, weight gain, drowsiness, and sedation.

In contrast to typical antipsychotic medications, atypical antipsychotic medications have fewer side effects. Their mode of action is slightly different from typical antipsychotics, as they partially block dopamine receptors and serotonin receptors, and in some cases, they serve as dopamine and serotonin agonists. Currently, the FDA has approved ten atypical antipsychotics including risperidone, paliperidone, clozapine, olanzapine, ziprasidone, quetiapine, aripiprazole, asenapine, iloperidone, and lurasidone. The most frequently studied atypical antipsychotic, risperidone, reportedly reduces symptoms by 21 to 61% (Dion et al., 2002; Scahill et al., 2003). Several studies have reported that risperidone, pimozide, and clonidine are equally effective at reducing tic symptoms in children and adolescents with Tourette's disorder but that fewer side effects were associated with risperidone (Bruggeman et al., 2001; Gaffney et al., 2002).

Adrenergic Alpha-2 Medications

According to Kossoff and Singer (2001), adrenergic alpha-2 agonists, such as clonidine (catapres) and guanfacine (tenex) that decrease the release of norpeinphrine as well as dopamine and glutamate, are often effective at treating Tourette's disorder. Leckman and colleagues (1991) reported that approximately 50% of individuals with Tourette's disorder experience substantial improvement with clonidine, but common side effects, such as fatigue and sedation, are reported by nearly 90% of patients. Other studies also attest to the efficacy of clonidine in treating Tourette's disorder (Pringsheim et al., 2012). Guanfacine reportedly has a less sedating effect than clonidine, but some studies have reported it has a propensity to induce mania in individuals with a family history of mania (Horrigan & Barnhill, 1999). A study by Cummings and colleagues (2002) reported that guanfacine was not more effective than placebo at reducing tic severity and parental ratings of the tics of children with Tourette's disorder. Chappell et al. (1995), however, found that guanfacine was effective at decreasing motor and vocal tics, and improving neuropsychological performance of children with Tourette's disorder and comorbid ADHD.

Research has also explored the use of dopamine agonists, antidepressants, vesicular monoamine transporter-2 inhibitors, benzodiazepines, and other medications in the treatment of Tourette's disorder. Results have varied tremendously across studies and the FDA has not approved any of these medications for the treatment of Tourette's disorder (see Quezada & Coffman, 2018, for a review).

Alternative Interventions

In addition to medications, preliminary studies suggest that marijuana, nicotine, and botulinum toxin injections may improve symptoms of Tourette's disorder (Kossoff & Singer, 2001; Mihailescu & Drucker-Colin, 2000; McConville et al., 1991; Mueller-Vahl et al., 2002; Termine et al., 2013). For example, Mueller-Vahl et al. (2003) conducted a 6-week study of 24 patients with Tourette's who were treated with 10 mg per day of delta-9-tetrahydrocannabinol marijuana (THC). Results revealed a significant decline in symptoms relative to placebo and no serious side effects. Other studies have produced similar results, suggesting that THC may be a safe and effective treatment for tics. With respect to nicotine, a few studies have reported that transdermal nicotine patch application reduces tics in patients with Tourette's disorder both short and long term (e.g., Dursun & Reveley, 1997; Dursun et al., 1994; Sanberg et al., 1997; Silver et al., 2001). According to Zhou, Wilson, and Dani (2003), the striatum contains a dense mingling of dopamine receptors as well as other types of receptors, including nicotinic receptors. Research indicates that these diverse neurotransmitter systems work together to coordinate functioning of the striatum and hence may help to explain the improvement of tics following application of the nicotine patch. Because botulinum toxin A injections have proven to be an effective treatment for several disorders characterized by abnormal muscle contractions, Kwak, Hanna, and Jankovic (2000) assessed whether these injections would improve motor tics in patients with Tourette's disorder. Thirty-five individuals with the disorder participated in the study and received botulinum toxin injections in the areas of their most severe tics (most frequently, the upper thoracic region and the upper face). Results indicated that 84% of the subjects experienced a reduction in premonitary sensations (i.e., urges to tic), and the majority showed a substantial improvement in tics within 3.8 days. Porta and colleagues (2004) reported that botulinum toxin injections in both vocal cords of 30 patients with Tourette's disorder resulted in improvement in 93% of patients; 50% became completely tic-free. The researchers also noted a significant reduction in premonitary experiences. Recently, however, Pandey and colleagues (2018) argued that the quality of research investigating botulinum toxin in the treatment of Tourette's disorder was very low and advocated for additional randomized controlled studies.

Neurosurgery and Brain Stimulation Techniques

According to Temel and Visser-Vandewalle (2004), the first ablative procedure for intractable Tourette's disorder was performed in 1962. Since that time, the target sites for psychosurgery for the disorder have been diverse and have included such areas as the frontal lobes, limbic system, thalamus, and cerebellum. For example, Kurlan and colleagues (1990) described the outcome of an anterior cingulotomy performed on two individuals with Tourette's disorder and comorbid OCD. Results indicated short- and long-term improvement in tics. In 2001, Babel, Warnke, and Ostertag followed up 11 patients with Tourette's disorder who underwent surgical treatment in Germany (lesioning of the thalamus) between 1970 and 1998. Results revealed that motor and vocal tics were substantially reduced, as were premonitary urges. Nearly 68% of the patients, however, experienced transient side effects of the surgery such as confusion, attention problems, numbness, and loss of muscle control.

Deep brain stimulation has emerged as a promising alternative to lesioning surgery (Martinez-Ramirez et al., 2018). For example, approximately 15 years ago, Visser-Vandewalle and colleagues (2003) implanted chronic pulse generators in the region of the thalamus in three male patients who had manifested symptoms of intractable Tourette's disorder since childhood. Follow-up assessments (8 months to 5 years) indicated that major vocal and motor tics had disappeared, and only minor serious side effects were observed (fatigue and changes in sexual behavior). Since that time additional studies have supported the use of DBS as an effective and relatively safe treatment for severe, intractable Tourette's disorder (Dowd et al., 2018). Lastly, preliminary studies support that repetitive TMS applied to the supplemental motor cortex of participants with Tourette's disorder has shown promising therapeutic results at reducing symptoms (Bloch et al., 2016; Termine et al., 2013).

BOX 9.2   Does Strep Throat Cause Tourette's Disorder?

Several studies have linked the development of Tourette's disorder in some children to an autoimmune response to streptococcal infections, known as PANDAS (Pediatric Autoimmune Neuropsychiatric Disorder Associated with Streptococcal Infections) (Hoekstra et al., 2002; Loisell et al., 2003). Specifically, children who have had streptococcal infections and subsequently developed Tourette's syndrome often have increased basal ganglia volumes, presumably due to increased antibodies within the basal ganglia. For example, Mueller and colleagues (2000) examined titers of two different antistreptococcal antibodies (antistreptolysin and antiDNase B) in 13 children with Tourette's disorder, 23 adults with Tourette's disorder, 17 adults with schizophrenia, and healthy controls. Results revealed that the titers were significantly higher in participants with Tourette's disorder compared to participants with schizophrenia and healthy controls. These findings suggest that streptococcal infections can sometimes play a critical role in the development of Tourette's disorder, but specifically how this occurs is unclear. Hallett et al. (2000) suggested that antineuronal bodies may bind to neurons in the striatum of children and induce functional changes in cells within this region, leading to Tourette's. Not everyone who is exposed to the streptococcal virus develops Tourette's disorder, however, and not everyone with the disorder had necessarily developed a strep infection. Recent studies, including neuroimaging studies continue to support a role for PANDAS in the development of Tourette's disorder although numerous questions remain regarding the details of this process (Kumar et al., 2015). For example, Spinello and colleagues (2016) emphasized a need to investigate prenatal and postnatal factors and the role they might play in increasing individual vulnerability to PANDAS.

(Kumar et al., 2015; Spinello et al., 2016)

Summary of Tourette's Disorder

■ The cause of Tourette's disorder is unknown.

■ Family, twin, and candidate gene studies support a genetic component to the development of Tourette's disorder.

■ Although numerous genes have been investigated to date no gene or gene variants has been found to reliably confer risk in most cases of the disorder.

■ Structural and functional studies support involvement of the basal ganglia, limbic, and frontal regions in the underlying pathophysiology of Tourette's disorder.

■ The dopaminergic system is most often implicated in Tourette's disorder; however, given the involvement of other neurotransmitters in the cortico-ganglia pathways as well as the effectiveness of non-dopaminergic medications in reducing symptoms, additional neurotransmitters are likely involved in the pathophysiology of the disorder.

■ Non-pharmacological approaches, including cognitive behavioral therapy and deep brain stimulation, are effective at reducing symptoms of the disorder.

■ Preliminary findings support adjunctive interventions, including botulinum toxin and THC, in the treatment of Tourette's disorder.

Review Questions

1. Does research support a genetic basis for ADHD, ASD, and TD? Why or why not?

2. Summarize the structural and functional findings associated with all three disorders. Are the findings consistent or do the findings diverge?

3. What can be concluded about the etiology of ADHD, ASD, and TD disorders at this time? What questions remain unanswered?

4. How does the mode of action of medications used to treat the symptoms of these disorders relate to functional findings of each disorder?

References

Aarsland, D., Bronnick, K., Williams-Gray, C., Weintraub, D., Marder, K., Kulisevsky, J., . . . & Santangelo, G. (2010). Mild cognitive impairment in Parkinson disease: A multicenter pooled analysis. *Neurology*, *75*(12), 1062–1069.

Abbott, A. (2003). British panel bans use of antidepressant to treat children. *Nature*, *423*, 792.

Abbott, R. D., Ross, G. W., White, L. R., Sanderson, W. T., Burchfiel, C. M., Kashon, M., et al. (2003). Environmental, life-style, and physical precursors of clinical Parkinson's disease: Recent findings from the Honolulu—Asia Aging Study. *Journal of Neurology*, *250*, 30–39.

Abdallah, C. G., Hannestad, J., Mason, G. F., Holmes, S. E., DellaGioia, N., Sanacora, G., et al. (2017). Metabotropic glutamate receptor 5 and glutamate involvement in major depressive disorder: A multimodal imaging study. *Biological Psychiatry: Cognitive Neuroscience and Neuroimaging*, *2*, 449–456.

Abe, Y., Kachi, T., Kato, T., Arahata, Y., Yamada, T., Washimi, Y., et al. (2003). Occipital hypoperfusion in Parkinson's disease without dementia: Correlation to impaired cortical visual processing. *Journal of Neurology, Neurosurgery, and Psychiatry*, *74*, 419–422.

Abi-Dargham, A., Krystal, J. H., Anjilvel, S., Scanley, B. E., Zoghbi, S., Baldwin, R. M., et al. (1998). Alterations of benzodiazepine receptors in type II alcoholic subjects measured with SPECT and [123I]iomazenil. *American Journal of Psychiatry*, *155*, 1550–1555.

Abi-Dargham, A., Rodenhiser, J., Printz, D., Zea-Ponce, Y., Gil, R., Kegeles, L. S., et al. (2000). Increased baseline occupancy of D2 receptors by dopamine in schizophrenia. *Proceedings of the National Academy of Sciences*, *97*, 8104–8109.

Abkevich, V., Camp, N. J., Hensel, C. H., Neff, C. D., Russell, D. L., Hughes, D. C., et al. (2003). Predisposition locus for major depression at chromosome 12q22–12q23. 2. *The American Journal of Human Genetics*, *73*(6), 1271–1281.

Abramowitz, J. S., Huppert, J. D., Cohen, A. B., Tolin, D. F., & Cahill, S. P. (2002). Religious obsessions and compulsions in a non-clinical sample: The Penn Inventory of Scrupulosity (PIOS). *Behaviour Research and Therapy*, *40*, 825–838.

Abrams, R. (2000). Electroconvulsive therapy requires higher dosage levels: Food and Drug Administration action is required. *Archives of General Psychiatry, 57,* 445–446.

Adams, J. B., Audhya, T., McDonough-Means, S., Rubin, R. A., Quig, D., Geis, E., et al. (2011). Nutritional and metabolic status of children with autism vs. neurotypical children, and the association with autism severity. *Nutrition & Metabolism, 8*(1), 34.

Adams, W. (1981). Lack of behavioral effects from Feingold diet violations. *Perception and Motor Skills, 52,* 307–313.

Addolorato, G., Caputo, F., Capristo, E., Domenicali, M., Bernardi, M., Janiri, L., et al. (2002). Baclofen efficacy in reducing alcohol craving and intake: A preliminary double-blind randomized controlled study. *Alcohol and Alcoholism, 37,* 504–508.

Ade, K. K., Wan, Y., Hamann, H. C., O'Hare, J. K., Guo, W., Quian, A., et al. (2016). Increased metabotropic glutamate receptor 5 signaling underlies obsessive-compulsive disorder-like behavioral and striatal circuit abnormalities in mice. *Biological Psychiatry, 80*(7), 522–533.

Adler, C. M., McDonough-Ryan, P., Sax, K. W., Holland, S. K., Arndt, S., & Strakowski, S. M. (2000). fMRI of neuronal activation with symptom provocation in unmedicated patients with obsessive compulsive disorder. *Journal of Psychiatric Research, 34,* 317–324.

Adnan, A., Chen, A. J., Novakovic-Agopian, T., D'Esposito, M., & Turner, G. R. (2017). Brain changes following executive control training in older adults. *Neurorehabilitation and Neural Repair, 31*(10–11), 910–922.

Agid, O., Seeman, P., & Kapur, S. (2006). The "delayed onset" of antipsychotic action: An idea whose time has come and gone. *Journal of Psychiatry & Neuroscience, 31*(2), 93.

Agnesi, F., Johnson, M. D., & Vitek, J. L. (2013). Deep brain stimulation: How does it work? In *Handbook of clinical neurology* (Vol. 116, pp. 39–54). Amsterdam: Elsevier.

Agrawal, A., & Lynskey, M. T. (2008). Are there genetic influences on addiction: Evidence from family, adoption and twin studies. *Addiction, 103*(7), 1069–1081.

Ahmad, B., Mufti, K. A., & Farooq, S. (2001). Psychiatric comorbidity in substance abuse (opioids). *JPMA. The Journal of the Pakistan Medical Association, 51*(5), 183–186.

Airoldi, C., La, B. F., D'Orazio, G., Ciaramelli, C., & Palmioli, A. (2018). Flavonoids in the treatment of Alzheimer's and other neurodegenerative diseases. *Current Medicinal Chemistry* Vol. 25 Issue 27, 2018.

Akbarian, S., Huntsman, M. M., Kim, J. J., Tafazzoli, A., Potkin, S. G., Bunney, W. E., Jr., et al. (1995). GABAA receptor subunit gene expression in human prefrontal cortex: Comparison of schizophrenics and controls. *Cerebral Cortex, 5,* 550–560.

Alarcón, R. D., Oquendo, M. A., & Wainberg, M. L. (2014). Depression in a Latino Man in New York. *American Journal of Psychiatry, 171*(5), 506–508.

Albert, P. R. (2014). Light up your life: Optogenetics for depression? *Journal of Psychiatry & Neuroscience: JPN, 39*(1), 3–5.

Albert, U., Marazziti, D., Di, G. S., Solia, F., Rosso, G., & Maina, G. (2017). A systematic review of evidence-based treatment strategies for obsessive-compulsive disorder resistant to first-line pharmacotherapy. *Current Medicinal Chemistry, 25*(1).

Albrecht, J., & Zielińska, M. (2017). Mechanisms of excessive extracellular glutamate accumulation in temporal lobe epilepsy. *Neurochemical Research, 42*(6), 1724–1734.

Alberts-Corush, J., Firestone, P., & Goodman, J. T. (1986). Attention and impulsivity characteristics of the biological and adoptive parents of hyperactive and normal control children. *American Journal of Orthopsychiatry, 56,* 413–423.

Albin, R. L., Koeppe, R. A., Bohnen, N. I., Nichols, T. E., Meyer, P., Wernette, K., et al. (2003). Increased ventral striatal monoaminergic innervation in Tourette syndrome. *Neurology, 61,* 310–315.

Alda, M. (2015). Lithium in the treatment of bipolar disorder: Pharmacology and pharmacogenetics. *Molecular Psychiatry, 20*(6), 661–670.

Alegria, A. A., Wulff, M., Brinson, H., Barker, G. J., Norman, L. J., Brandeis, D., et al. (2017). Real-time fMRI neurofeedback in adolescents with attention deficit hyperactivity disorder. *Human Brain Mapping, 38*(6), 3190–3209.

Alevizos, B., Lykouras, L., Zervas, I. M., & Christodoulou, G. N. (2002). Risperidone-induced obsessive-compulsive symptoms: A series of six cases. *Journal of Clinical Psychopharmacology, 22,* 461–467.

Alexander, A. L., Lee, J. E., Lazar, M., & Field, A. S. (2007). Diffusion tensor imaging of the brain. *Neurotherapeutics, 4*(3), 316–329.

Alfaro, A., Bernabeu, Á., Badesa, F. J., García, N., & Fernández, E. (2017). When playing is a problem: An atypical case of Alien Hand syndrome in a professional pianist. *Frontiers in Human Neuroscience, 11,* 198.

Ali, O. (2013). Genetics of type 2 diabetes. *World Journal of Diabetes, 4*(4), 114.

Ali, S. O., Denicoff, K. D., Altshuler, L. L., Hauser, P., Li, X., Conrad, A. J., et al. (2001). Relationship between prior course of illness and neuroanatomic structures in bipolar disorder. *Neuropsychiatry, Neuropsychology, and Behavioral Neurology, 14,* 227–232.

Ali, S., & Milev, R. (2003). Switch to mania upon discontinuation of antidepressants in patients with mood disorders: A review of the literature. *Canadian Journal of Psychiatry, 48,* 258–264.

Allen, G., & Courchesne, E. (2003). Differential effects of developmental cerebellar abnormality on cognitive and motor functions in the cerebellum: An fMRI study of autism. *American Journal of Psychiatry, 160,* 262–273.

Allen, N. C., Bagade, S., McQueen, M. B., Ioannidis, J. P., Kavvoura, F. K., Khoury, M. J., et al. (2008). Systematic meta-analyses and field synopsis of genetic association studies in schizophrenia: The SzGene database. *Nature genetics, 40*(7), 827.

Allen, P., Larøi, F., McGuire, P. K., & Aleman, A. (2008). The hallucinating brain: A review of structural and functional neuroimaging studies of hallucinations. *Neuroscience & Biobehavioral Reviews, 32*(1), 175–191.

Alonso-Navarro, H., Jiménez-Jiménez, F. J., Pilo-de-la-Fuente, B., & Plaza-Nieto, J. F. (2009). Panic attack-like episodes possibly associated with ropinirole. *Clinical Neuropharmacology, 32*(4), 237–238.

Altar, C. A., Cai, N., Bliven, T., Juhasz, M., Conner, J. M., Acheson, A. L., et al. (1997). Anterograde transport of brain-derived neurotrophic factor and its role in the brain. *Nature, 389,* 85–860.

Alzheimer, A. (1907). Uber eine eigenartige Erkrankung der Hirnrinde. *Allgemeine Zeitschrift für Psychiatrie und psychisch-gerichtliche Medizin, 64,* 146–148.

Alzheimers Dement. 2016. Alzheimer's disease facts and figures. *Alzheimer's Association, 12*(4), 459–509.

Amaral, D. G., Anderson, M. P., Ansorge, O., Chance, S., Hare, C., Hof, P. R., . . . Tamminga, C. (2018). Autism BrainNet: A network of postmortem brain banks established to facilitate autism research. *Handbook of Clinical Neurology, 150,* 31–39.

Amare, A. T., Schubert, K. O., & Baune, B. T. (2017). Pharmacogenomics in the treatment of mood disorders: Strategies and Opportunities for personalized psychiatry. *EPMA Journal, 8*(3), 211–227.

Amato, D., Vernon, A. C., & Papaleo, F. (2017). Dopamine, the antipsychotic molecule: A perspective on mechanisms underlying antipsychotic response variability. *Neuroscience & Biobehavioral Reviews 85*(2), 146–159.

Ameri, A. (1999). The effects of cannabinoids on the brain. *Progress in Neurobiology, 58*(4), 315–348.

American Psychiatric Association. (2001). *The practice of electroconvulsive therapy: Recommendationsfor treatment, training, and privileging, 2nd ed. A task force report of the American Psychiatric Association.* Washington, DC: American Psychiatric Association.

American Psychiatric Association. (2013). *Diagnostic and statistical manual of mental disorders (DSM-5®). American Psychiatric Pub.*

Amiaz, R., Fostick, L., Gershon, A., & Zohar, J. (2008). Naltrexone augmentation in OCD: A double-blind placebo-controlled cross-over study. *European Neuropsychopharmacology, 18*(6), 455–461.

Anand, A., & Shekhar, A. (2003). Brain imaging studies in mood and anxiety disorders: Special emphasis on the amygdala. *Annals of the New York Academy of Sciences, 985,* 370–388.

Anastopoulos, A. D., King, K. A., Besecker, L. H., O'Rourke, S. R., Bray, A. C., & Supple, A. J. (2018). Cognitive-behavioral therapy for college students with ADHD: Temporal stability of improvements in functioning following active treatment. *Journal of Attention Disorders*, 1–12. https://doi.org/10.1177/1087054717749932.

Anders, S., Lotze, M., Erb, M., Grodd, W., & Birbaumer, N. (2004). Brain activity underlying emotional valence and arousal: A response-related fMRI study. *Human Brain Mapping*, *23*(4), 200–209.

Andersen, P. N., Hovik, K. T., Skogli, E. W., & Øie, M. G. (2017). Severity of autism symptoms and degree of attentional difficulties predicts emotional and behavioral problems in children with high-functioning autism: A two-year follow-up study. *Frontiers in Psychology*, *8*, 2004.

Anderson, D., & Ahmed, A. (2003). Treatment of patients with intractable obsessive-compulsive disorder with anterior capsular stimulation: Case report. *Journal of Neurosurgery*, *98*(5), 1104–1108.

Anderson, G. M., Dover, M. A., Yang, B. P., Holahan, J. M., Shaywitz, S. E., Marchione, K. E., et al. (2000). Adrenomedullary function during cognitive testing in attention-deficit/hyperactivity disorder. *Journal of the American Academy of Child and Adolescent Psychiatry*, *39*, 635–643.

Andoh, J., Diers, M., Milde, C., Frobel, C., Kleinböhl, D., & Flor, H. (2017). Neural correlates of evoked phantom limb sensations. *Journal of Biological Psychology*, *126*, 89–97.

Andrade, C. (2017). Memantine as an augmentation treatment for schizophrenia: Limitations of meta-analysis for evidence-based evaluation of research. *The Journal of Clinical Psychiatry*.

Andrade, C., Srinivasamurthy, G. M., Vishwasenani, A., Prakash, G. S., Srihari, B. S., & Chandra, J. S. (2002). High but not low ECS stimulus intensity augments apomorphine-stimulated dopamine postsynaptic receptor functioning in rats. *Journal of ECT*, *18*, 80–83.

Andreasen, N. C., Swayze, V., II, Flaum, M., Alliger, R., & Cohen, G. (1990). Ventricular abnormalities in affective disorder: Clinical and demographic correlates. *American Journal of Psychiatry*, *147*, 893–900.

Andrews, J. A., Tildesley, E., Hops, H., Duncan, S. C., & Severson, H. H. (2003). Elementary school age children's future intentions and use of substances. *Journal of Clinical Child and Adolescent Psychology*, *32*, 556–567.

Anfinson, T. J. (2002). Akathisia, panic, agoraphobia, and major depression following brief exposure to metoclopramide. *Psychopharmacology Bulletin*, *36*, 82–93.

Angelova, A., Tiveron, M. C., Cremer, H., & Beclin, C. (2018). Neuronal subtype generation during postnatal olfactory bulb neurogenesis. *Journal of Experimental Neuroscience*, *12*, 1179069518755670.

Angrist, B. M., & Gershon, S. (1970). The phenomenology of experimentally induced amphetamine psychosis: Preliminary observations. *Biological Psychiatry*, *2*(2), 95–107.

Angst, J. (1985). Switch from depression to mania: A record survey over decades between 1920 and 1982. *Psychopathology*, *18*, 140–154.

Anguelova, M., Benkelfat, C., & Turecki, G. (2003). A systematic review of association studies investigating genes coding for serotonin receptors and the serotonin transporter: I. Affective disorders. *Molecular Psychiatry*, *8*, 574–591.

Antal, A., Alekseichuk, I., Bikson, M., Brockmöller, J., Brunoni, A. R., Chen, R., et al. (2017). Low intensity transcranial electric stimulation: Safety, ethical, legal regulatory and application guidelines. *Clinical Neurophysiology*, *128*(9), 1774–1809.

Antypa, N., Drago, A., & Serretti, A. (2013). The role of COMT gene variants in depression: Bridging neuropsychological, behavioral and clinical phenotypes. *Neuroscience & Biobehavioral Reviews*, *37*(8), 1597–1610.

Aoki, Y., Cortese, S., & Tansella, M. (2015). Neural bases of atypical emotional face processing in autism: A meta-analysis of fMRI studies. *The World Journal of Biological Psychiatry*, *16*(5), 291–300.

Arai, Y., Yamazaki, M., Mori, O., Muramatsu, H., Asano, G., & Katayama, Y. (2001). Alpha-synuclein-positive structures in cases with sporadic Alzheimer's disease: Morphology and its relationship to tau aggregation. *Brain Research*, *888*, 287–296.

Arango, V., Huang, Y. Y., Underwood, M. D., & Mann, J. J. (2003). Genetics of the serotonergic system in suicidal behavior. *Journal of Psychiatric Research*, *37*(5), 375–386.

Arango, V., Underwood, M. D., Boldrini, M., Tamir, H., Kassir, S. A., Hsiung, S., et al. (2001). Serotonin 1A receptors, serotonin transporter binding and serotonin transporter mRNA expression in the brainstem of depressed suicide victims. *Neuropsychopharmacology*, *25*, 892–903.

Arborelius, L., Owens, M. J., Plotsky, P. M., & Nemeroff, C. B. (1999). The role of corticotropin-releasing factor in depression and anxiety disorders. *Journal of Endocrinology*, *160*, 1–12.

Archer, H. A., Smailagic, N., John, C., Holmes, R. B., Takwoingi, Y., Coulthard, E. J., & Cullum, S. (2015). Regional cerebral blood flow single photon emission computed tomography for detection of frontotemporal dementia in people with suspected dementia. *Cochrane Systematic Review*, 6.

Arciniegas, D. B., Harris, S. N., & Brousseau, K. M. (2003). Psychosis following traumatic brain injury. *International Review of Psychiatry*, *15*(4), 328–340.

Ardila, A., Bernal, B., & Rosselli, M. (2017). Executive functions brain system: An activation likelihood estimation meta-analytic study. *Archives of Clinical Neuropsychology*, 1–27.

Arendt, T., Brückner, M. K., Morawski, M., Jäger, C., & Gertz, H. J. (2015). Early neurone loss in Alzheimer's disease: Cortical or subcortical? *Acta neuropathologica Communications*, *3*(1), 10.

Argyelan, M., Herzallah, M., Sako, W., DeLucia, I., Sarpal, D., Vo, A., et al. (2018). Dopamine modulates striatal response to reward and punishment in patients with Parkinson's disease: A pharmacological challenge fMRI study. *NeuroReport*, *29*(7), 532–540.

Armistead-Jehle, P., Soble, J. R., Cooper, D. B., & Belanger, H. G. (2017). Unique aspects of traumatic brain injury in military and veteran populations. *Physical Medicine and Rehabilitation Clinics*, *28*(2), 323–337.

Armstrong, D., Dunn, J. K., Antalffi, B., & Trivetti, R. (1995). Selective dendritic alterations in the cortex of Rett syndrome. *Journal of Neuropathology and Experimental Neurology*, *54*, 195–201.

Arnold, P. D., & Richter, M. A. (2001). Is obsessive-compulsive disorder an autoimmune disease? *Canadian Medical Association Journal*, *165*, 1353–1358.

Arnold, S. E., Trojanowski, J. Q., Gur, R. E., Blackwell, P., Han, L. Y., & Choi, C. (1998). Absence of neurodegeneration and neural injury in the cerebral cortex in a sample of elderly patients with schizophrenia. *Archives of General Psychiatry*, *55*(3), 225–232.

Arnone, D., Cavanagh, J., Gerber, D., Lawrie, S. M., Ebmeier, K. P., & McIntosh, A. M. (2009). Magnetic resonance imaging studies in bipolar disorder and schizophrenia: Meta-analysis. *The British Journal of Psychiatry*, *195*(3), 194–201.

Artiges, E., Leroy, C., Dubol, M., Prat, M., Pepin, A., Mabondo, A., et al. (2017). Striatal and extrastriatal dopamine transporter availability in schizophrenia and its clinical correlates: A voxel-based and high-resolution PET study. *Schizophrenia Bulletin*, *43*(5), 1134–1142.

Asami, T., Hayano, F., Nakamura, M., Yamasue, H., Uehara, K., Otsuka, T., et al. (2008). Anterior cingulate cortex volume reduction in patients with panic disorder. *Psychiatry and Clinical Neurosciences*, *62*(3), 322–330.

Asaoka, N., Nishitani, N., Kinoshita, H., Kawai, H., Shibui, N., Nagayasu, K., . . . & Kaneko, S. (2017). Chronic antidepressant potentiates spontaneous activity of dorsal raphe serotonergic neurons by decreasing GABA B receptor-mediated inhibition of L-type calcium channels. *Scientific Reports*, *7*(1), 13609.

Åsberg, M., Bertilsson, L., Mårtensson, B., Scalia-Tomba, G. P., Thoren, P., & Träskman-Bendz, L. (1984). CSF monoamine metabolites in melancholia. *Acta Psychiatrica Scandinavica*, *69*(3), 201–219.

Ascherio, A., Zhang, S. M., Hernan, M. A., Kawachi, I., Colditz, G. A., Speizer, F. E., et al. (2001). Prospective study of caffeine consumption and risk of Parkinson's disease in men and women. *Annals of Neurology*, *50*, 56–63.

Asher, L., Patel, V., & De Silva, M. J. (2017). Community-based psychosocial interventions for people with schizophrenia in low and middle-income countries: Systematic review and meta-analysis. *BMC Psychiatry*, *17*(1), 355.

Ashok, A. H., Marques, T. R., Jauhar, S., Nour, M. M., Goodwin, G. M., Young, A. H., & Howes, O. D. (2017). The dopamine hypothesis of bipolar affective disorder: The state of the art and implications for treatment. *Molecular Psychiatry 22*(5), 666.

Ashok, A. H., Mizuno, Y., Volkow, N. D., & Howes, O. D. (2017). Association of stimulant use with dopaminergic alterations in users of cocaine, amphetamine, or methamphetamine. *JAMA Psychiatry, 74*(5), 511–519.

Ashwell, K., Tancred, E., & Paxinos, G. (2000). The brain's anatomy. In E. Gordon (Ed.), *Integrative neuroscience: Bringing together biological, psychological, and clinical models of the human brain* (pp. 88–108). Amsterdam, Netherlands: Overseas Publishers Association.

Askenazy, F. L., Lestideau, K., Meynadier, A., Dor, E., Myquel, M., & Lecrubier, Y. (2007). Auditory hallucinations in pre-pubertal children. *European Child & Adolescent Psychiatry, 16*(6), 411–415.

Asmal, L., Flegar, S. J., Wang, J., Rummel-Kluge, C., Komossa, K., & Leucht, S. (2013). Quetiapine versus other atypical antipsychotics for schizophrenia. *Cochrane Database of Systematic Reviews*, (11).

Asnis, G. M., Hameedi, F. A., Goddard, A. W., Potkin, S. G., Black, D., Jameel, M., et al. (2001). Fluvoxamine in the treatment of panic disorder: A multi-center, double-blind, placebo-controlled study in outpatients. *Psychiatry Research, 103*, 1–14.

Ast, G. (2005). The alternative genome. *Scientific American, 292*(4), 58–65.

Aston-Jones, G., Akaoka, H., Charlety, P., & Chouvet, G. (1991). Serotonin selectively attenuates glutamate-evoked activation of noradrenergic locus coeruleus neurons. *Journal of Neuroscience, 11*(3), 760–769.

Atmaca, M., Onalan, E., Yildirim, H., Yuce, H., Koc, M., Korkmaz, S., & Mermi, O. (2011). Serotonin transporter gene polymorphism implicates reduced orbito-frontal cortex in obsessive—compulsive disorder. *Journal of Anxiety Disorders, 25*(5), 680–685.

Atmaca, M., Yildirim, H., Ozdemir, H., Ozler, S., Kara, B., Ozler, Z., et al. (2008). Hippocampus and amygdalar volumes in patients with refractory obsessive-compulsive disorder. *Progress in Neuro-psychopharmacology and Biological Psychiatry, 32*(5), 1283–1286.

Aum, D. J., & Tierney, T. S. (2018). Deep brain stimulation: Foundations and future trends. *Frontiers in Bioscience (Landmark Edition), 23*, 162–182.

Austen, B., Christodoulou, G., & Terry, J. E. (2002). Relation between cholesterol levels, statins and Alzheimer's disease in the human population. *Journal of Nutrition, Health & Aging, 6*, 377–382.

Avram, M. J., Stika, C. S., Rasmussen-Torvik, L. J., Ciolino, J. D., Pinheiro, E., George, A. L., & Wisner, K. L. (2016). Rationale and design for an investigation to optimize selective serotonin reuptake inhibitor treatment for pregnant women with depression. *Clinical Pharmacology & Therapeutics, 100*(1), 31–33.

Ayerbe, L., Ayis, S., Crichton, S., Wolfe, C. D., & Rudd, A. G. (2013). The natural history of depression up to 15 years after stroke. *Stroke, 44*(4), 1105–1110.

Aylward, E. H., Reiss, A. L., Reader, M. J., Singer, H. S., Brown, J. E., & Denckla, M. B. (1996). Basal ganglia volumes in children with attention-deficit hyperactivity disorder. *Journal of Child Neurology, 11*(2), 112–115.

Azari, N. P., & Seitz, R. J. (2000). Brain plasticity and recovery from stroke. *American Scientist, 88*, 426–431.

Baba, M., Jakajo, S., Tu, P., Tomita, T., Nakaya, K., Lee, V. M. Y., et al. (1998). Aggregation of alpha-synuclein in bodies of sporadic Parkinson's disease and dementia with Lewy bodies. *American Journal of Pathology, 152*, 879–884.

Bachmann, C. J., Aagaard, L., Burcu, M., Glaeske, G., Kalverdijk, L. J., Petersen, I., & Hoffmann, F. (2016). Trends and patterns of antidepressant use in children and adolescents from five western countries, 2005–2012. *European Neuropsychopharmacology, 26*(3), 411–419.

Badiani, A., Belin, D., Epstein, D., Calu, D., & Shaham, Y. (2011). Opiate versus psychostimulant addiction: The differences do matter. *Nature Reviews Neuroscience, 12*(11), 685–700.

Badner, J. A., & Gershon, E. S. (2002). Meta-analysis of whole-genome linkage scans of bipolar disorder and schizophrenia. *Molecular Psychiatry, 7*, 405–411.

Bae, S. W., & Brekke, J. S. (2002). Characteristics of Korean-Americans with schizophrenia: A cross-ethnic comparison with African-Americans, Latinos, and Euro-Americans. *Schizophrenia Bulletin, 28*(4), 703–717.

Baeken, C., Raedt, R. D., Schuerbeek, P. V., Vanderhasselt, M., Mey, J. D., Bossuyt, A., & Luypaert, R. (2010). Right prefrontal HF-rTMS attenuates right amygdala processing of negatively valenced emotional stimuli in healthy females. *Journal of Behavioural Brain Research, 214*(2), 450–455.

Baer, L., Rauch, S. L., Ballantine, H. T. Jr., Martuza, R., Cosgrove, R., Cassem, E., et al. (1995). Cingulotomy for intractable obsessive-compulsive disorder. Prospective long-term follow-up of 18 patients. *Archives of General Psychiatry, 52*, 384–392.

Baieli, S., Pavone, L., Meli, C., Fiumara, A., & Coleman, M. (2003). Autism and phenylketonuria. *Journal of Autism and Developmetal Disorders, 33*, 201–204.

Baiyewu, O., Adeyemi, J. D., & Ogunniyi, A. (1997). Psychiatric disorders in Nigerian nursing home residents. *International Journal of Geriatric Psychiatry, 12*, 1146–1150.

Baker, R. W., Chengappa, K. R., Baird, J. W., Steingard, S., Christ, M. A., & Schooler, N. R. (1992). Emergence of obsessive compulsive symptoms during treatment with clozapine. *The Journal of Clinical Psychiatry, 53*(12), 439–442.

Balbernie, R. (2001). Circuits and circumstances: The neurobiological consequences of early relationship experiences and how they shape later behaviour. *Journal of Child Psychotherapy, 27*, 237–255.

Baldinger, P., Lotan, A., Frey, R., Kasper, S., Lerer, B., & Lanzenberger, R. (2014). Neurotransmitters and electroconvulsive therapy. *The Journal of ECT, 30*(2), 116–121.

Baldwin, D. S., Anderson, I. M., Nutt, D. J., Allgulander, C., Bandelow, B., den Boer, J. A., et al. (2014). Evidence-based pharmacological treatment of anxiety disorders, post-traumatic stress disorder and obsessive-compulsive disorder: A revision of the 2005 guidelines from the British Association for Psychopharmacology. *Journal of Psychopharmacology, 28*(5), 403–439.

Baldwin, R., Jeffries, S., Jackson, A., Sutcliffe, C., Thacker, N., Scott, M., et al. (2004). Treatment response in late-onset depression: Relationship to neuropsychological, neuroradiological and vascular risk factors. *Psychological Medicine, 34*, 125–136.

Ballard, C. G., Jacoby, R., Del Ser, T., Khan, M. N., Munoz, D. G., Holmes, C., et al. (2004). Neuropathological substrates of psychiatric symptoms in prospectively studied patients with autopsy-confirmed dementia with Lewy bodies. *American Journal of Psychiatry, 161*, 843–849.

Balldin, J., Granerus, A. K., Lindstedt, G., Modigh, K., & Walinder, J. (1982). Neuroendocrine evidence for increased responsiveness of dopamine receptors in humans following electroconvulsive therapy. *Psychopharmacology, 76*, 371–376.

Ballmaier, M., Toga, A. W., Blanton, R. E., Sowell, E. R., Lavretsky, H., Peterson, J., et al. (2004). Anterior cingulated, gyrus rectus, and orbitofrontal abnormalities in elderly depressed patients: An MRI-based parcellation of the prefrontal cortex. *American Journal of Psychiatry, 161*, 99–108.

Bandelow, B., Behnke, K., Lenoir, S., Hendriks, G. J., Alkin, T., Goebel, C., et al. (2004). Sertraline versus paroxetine in the treatment of panic disorder: An acute, double-blind noninferiority comparison. *Journal of Clinical Psychiatry, 65*, 405–413.

Bandelow, B., Michaelis, S., & Wedekind, D. (2017). Treatment of anxiety disorders. *Dialogues in Clinical Neuroscience, 19*(2), 93–107.

Bandelow, B., Reitt, M., Röver, C., Michaelis, S., Görlich, Y., & Wedekind, D. (2015). Efficacy of treatments for anxiety disorders: A meta-analysis. *International Clinical Psychopharmacology, 30*(4), 183–192.

Barkley, R. A. (2002). Major life activity and health outcomes associated with attention-deficit/hyperactivity disorder. *The Journal of Clinical Psychiatry*.

Barkley, R. A. (2016). Opinion: A Response to the CDC Press Conference on Behavioral Parent Training and Treating ADHD in Young Children. *The ADHD Report*, *24*(4), 11.

Barkley, R. A., Fischer, M., Smallish, L., & Fletcher, K. (2004). Young adult follow-up of hyperactive children: Antisocial activities and drug use. *Journal of Child Psychology and Psychiatry*, *45*(2), 195–211.

Barnes, L. L., Wilson, R. S., Schneider, J. A., Bienias, J. L., Evans, D. A., & Bennett, D. A. (2003). Gender, cognitive decline, and risk of AD in older persons. *Neurology*, *60*, 1777–1781.

Barnes, N. M., & Sharp, T. (1999). A review of central 5-HT receptors and their function. *Neuropharmacology*, *38*(8), 1083–1152.

Barone, P. (2010). Neurotransmission in Parkinson's disease: Beyond dopamine. *European Journal of Neurology*, *17*(3), 364–376.

Barr, C. E., Mednick, S. A., & Munk-Jorgensen, P. (1990). Exposure to influenza epidemics during gestation and adult schizophrenia: A 40-year study. *Archives of General Psychiatry*, *47*(9), 869–874.

Barrett, K. (2017). Psychiatric neurosurgery in the 21st century: Overview and the growth of deep brain stimulation. *BJPsych Bull*, *41*(5), 281–286.

Bartha, R., Stein, M. B., Williamson, P. C., Drost, D. J., Neufeld, R. W., Carr, T. J., et al. (1998). A short echo 1H spectroscopy and volumetric MRI study of the corpus striatum in patients with obsessive-compulsive disorder and comparison subjects. *American Journal of Psychiatry*, *155*, 1584–1591.

von Bartheld, C. S., Bahney, J., & Herculano-Houzel, S. (2016). The search for true numbers of neurons and glial cells in the human brain: A review of 150 years of cell counting. *Journal of Comparative Neurology*, *524*(18), 3865–3895.

Bartolo, M., Zucchella, C., Pichiecchio, A., Pucci, E., Sandrini, G., & Sinforiani, E. (2011). Alien hand syndrome in left posterior stroke. *Journal of Neurological Sciences*, *32*(3), 483–486.

Bassett, A. S., Chow, E. W. C., AbdelMalik, P., Gheorghiu, M., Husten, J., & Weksberg, R. (2003). The schizophrenia phenotype in 22q11 deletion syndrome. *American Journal of Psychiatry*, *160*, 1580–1586.

Bassett, A. S., Chow, E. W. C., Waterworth, D. M., & Brzustowica, L. (2001). Genetic insights into schizophrenia. *Canadian Journal of Psychiatry*, *46*, 131–137.

Basso, M. R., Lowery, N., Neel, J., Purdie, R., & Bornstein, R. A. (2002). Neuropsychological impairment among manic, depressed, and mixed-episode inpatients with bipolar disorder. *Neuropsychology*, *16*, 84–91.

Batelaan, N. M., Van Balkom, A. J., & Stein, D. J. (2012). Evidence-based pharmacotherapy of panic disorder: An update. *International Journal of Neuropsychopharmacology*, *15*(3), 403–415.

Bates, E. (1999b). Language and the infant brain. *Journal of Communication Disorders*, *32*, 195–205.

Battle, Y. L., Martin, B. C., Dorfman, J. H., & Miller, L. S. (1999). Seasonality and infectious disease in schizophrenia: The birth hypothesis revisited. *Journal of Psychiatric Research*, *33*(6), 501–509.

Bauer, M. S., & Mitchner, L. (2004). What is a "mood stabilizer"? An evidence-based response. *American Journal of Psychiatry*, *161*, 3–18.

Baumgardner, T. L., Dinger, H. S., Denckla, M. B., Rubin, M. A., Abrams, M. T., Colli, M. J., et al. (1996). Corpus callosum morphology in children with Tourette syndrome and attention deficit hyperactivity disorder. *Neurology*, *47*, 477–482.

Baxter, L. R., Phelps, M. E., Mazziotta, J. C., Guze, B. H., Schwartz, J. M., & Selin, C. E. (1987). Local cerebral glucose metabolic rates in obsessive-compulsive disorder: A comparison with rates in unipolar depression and in normal controls. *Archives of General Psychiatry*, *44*(3), 211–218.

Beart, P. M. (2000). The brain's chemistry. In E. Gordon (Ed.), *Integrative neuroscience: Bringing together biological, psychological, and clinical models of the human brain* (pp. 75–85). Amsterdam, Netherlands: Overseas Publishers Association.

Bedi, G., Lindquist, M. A., & Haney, M. (2015). An fMRI-based neural signature of decisions to smoke cannabis. *Neuropsychopharmacology, 40*(12), 2657–2665.

Beeker, T., Schlaepfer, T. E., & Coenen, V. A. (2017). Autonomy in depressive patients undergoing DBS-treatment: Informed consent, freedom of will and DBS' potential to restore it. *Frontiers in Integrative Neuroscience, 11,* 11.

Bekris, L. M., Mata, I. F., & Zabetian, C. P. (2010). The genetics of Parkinson disease. *Journal of Geriatric Psychiatry and Neurology, 23*(4), 228–242.

Bekris, L. M., Yu, C. E., Bird, T. D., & Tsuang, D. W. (2010). Genetics of Alzheimer disease. *Journal of Geriatric Psychiatry and Neurology, 23*(4), 213–227.

Bélanger, M., Allaman, I., & Magistretti, P. J. (2011). Brain energy metabolism: Focus on astrocyte-neuron metabolic cooperation. *Cell Metabolism, 14*(6), 724–738.

Bell, C., Abrams, J., & Nutt, D. (2001). Tryptophan depletion and its implications for psychiatry. *British Journal of Psychiatry, 178,* 399–405.

Belleville, S., Clément, F., Mellah, S., Gilbert, B., Fontaine, F., & Gauthier, S. (2011). Training-related brain plasticity in subjects at risk of developing Alzheimer's disease. *Brain; A Journal of Neurology, 134*(6), 1623–1634.

Bellini, N. K., Santos, T. M., da Silva, M. T. A., & Thiemann, O. H. (2018). The therapeutic strategies against Naegleria fowleri. Experimental Parasitology, *187,* 1–11.

Bellini, S., Fleming, K. E., De, M., McCauley, J. P., Petroccione, M. A., D'Brant, L. Y., . . . & Scimemi, A. (2017). Neuronal glutamate transporters control dopaminergic signaling and compulsive behaviors. *Journal of Neuroscience,* 1906–1017.

Bellón, J. Á., de Dios Luna, J., King, M., Nazareth, I., Motrico, E., GildeGómez-Barragán, M. J., et al. (2017). Predicting the onset of hazardous alcohol drinking in primary care: Development and validation of a simple risk algorithm. *British Journal of General Practise, 67*(657), e280–e292.

Bellot-Saez, A., Kékesi, O., Morley, J. W., & Buskila, Y. (2017). Astrocytic modulation of neuronal excitability through K spatial buffering. *Neuroscience & Biobehavioral Reviews, 77,* 87–97.

Belzung, C., Yalcin, I., Griebel, G., Surget, A., & Leman, S. (2006). Neuropeptides in psychiatric diseases: An overview with a particular focus on depression and anxiety disorders. *CNS & Neurological Disorders-Drug Targets (Formerly Current Drug Targets-CNS & Neurological Disorders), 5*(2), 135–145.

Ben-Menachem, E., Hamberger, A., Hedner, T., Hammond, E. J., Uthman, B. M., Slater, J., et al. (1995). Effects of vagus nerve stimulation on amino acids and other metabolites in the CSF of patients with partial seizures. *Epilepsy Research, 20,* 221–227.

Benadhira, R., Thomas, F., Bouaziz, N., Braha, S., Andrianisaina, P. S. K., Isaac, C., et al. (2017). A randomized, sham-controlled study of maintenance rTMS for treatment-resistant depression (TRD). *Psychiatry Research, 258,* 226–233.

Bencherif, B., Wand, G. S., McCaul, M. E., Kim, Y. K., Ilgin, N., Dannals, R. F., et al. (2004). Mu-opioid receptor binding measured by [11C]carfentanil positron emission tomography is related to craving and mood in alcohol dependence. *Biological Psychiatry, 55,* 255–262.

Benes, F. M., Davidson, J., & Bird, E. D. (1986). Quantitative cytoarchitectural studies of the cerebral cortex of schizophrenics. *Archives of General Psychiatry, 43,* 31–35.

Benes, F. M., Vincent, S. L., & Todtenkopf, M. (2001). The density of pyramidal and nonpyramidal neurons in anterior cingulate cortex of schizophenic and bipolar subjects. *Society of Biological Psychiatry, 50,* 395–406.

Benkelfat, C., Bradwejn, J., Meyer, E., Ellenbogen, M., & Milot, S. (1995). Functional neuroanatomy of CCK4-induced anxiety in normal healthy volunteers. *The American Journal of Psychiatry, 152*(8), 1180–1184.

Bennett, C. M., & Miller, M. B. (2010). How reliable are the results from functional magnetic resonance imaging? *Annals of the New York Academy of Sciences, 1191*(1), 133–155.

Bennett, C. M., Baird, A. A., Miller, M. B., & Wolford, G. L. (2011). Neural correlates of interspecies perspective taking in the post-mortem atlantic salmon: An argument for proper multiple comparisons correction. *Journal of Serendipitous and Unexpected Results, 1,* 1–5.

Bennett, C. M., Baird, A. A., Miller, M. B., & Wolford, G. L. (2012). Journal of serendipitous and unexpected results. *Journal of Serendipitous and Unexpected Results (jsur. org)-Vol, 1*(1), 1–5.

Benton, A. L., Hannay, H. J., & Varney, N. R. (1975). Visual perception of line direction in patients with unilateral brain disease. *Neurology, 25*, 907–910.

Bergem, A. L., & Lannfelt, L. (1997). Apolipoprotein E type epsilon4 allele, heritability and age at onset in twins with Alzheimer disease and vascular dementia. *Clinical Genetics, 52*, 408–413.

Bergem, A. L., Engedal, K., & Kringlen, E. (1997). The role of heredity in late-onset Alzheimer's disease and vascular dementia: A twin study. *Archives of General Psychiatry, 54*, 264–270.

Bergem, A. L., & Lannfelt, L. (1997). Apolipoprotein E type epsilon4 allele, heritability and age at onset in twins with Alzheimer disease and vascular dementia. *Clinical Genetics, 52*, 408–413.

Bergen, S. E., & Petryshen, T. L. (2012). Genome-wide association studies (GWAS) of schizophrenia: Does bigger lead to better results? *Current Opinion in Psychiatry, 25*(2), 76.

Berger, G. E., Bartholomeusz, C. F., Wood, S. J., Ang, A., Phillips, L. J., Proffitt, T., et al. (2017). Ventricular volumes across stages of schizophrenia and other psychoses. *Australian & New Zealand Journal of Psychiatry, 51*(10), 1041–1051.

Berlim, M. T., Van den Eynde, F., & Daskalakis, Z. J. (2013a). A systematic review and meta-analysis on the efficacy and acceptability of bilateral repetitive transcranial magnetic stimulation (rTMS) for treating major depression. *Psychological Medicine, 43*(11), 2245–2254.

Berlim, M. T., Van den Eynde, F., & Daskalakis, Z. J. (2013b). Clinical utility of transcranial direct current stimulation (tDCS) for treating major depression: A systematic review and meta-analysis of randomized, double-blind and sham-controlled trials. *Journal of Psychiatric Research, 47*(1), 1–7.

Berman, K. F., & Weinberger, D. R. (1991). Functional localization in the brain in schizophrenia. In A. Tasman & S. M. Goldfinger (Eds.), *American psychiatric press review of psychiatry* (Vol. 10, pp. 24–59). Washington, DC: American Psychiatric Press.

Berquin, P. C., Giedd, J. N., Jacobsen, L. K., Hamburger, S. D., Krain, A. L., Rapoport, J. L., & Castellanos, F. X. (1998). Cerebellum in attention-deficit hyperactivity disorder a morphometric MRI study. *Neurology, 50*(4), 1087–1093.

Berrettini, W. (2017). A brief review of the genetics and pharmacogenetics of opioid use disorders. *Dialogues in Clinical Neuroscience, 19*(3), 229–236.

Berrettini, W. H., Ferraro, T. N., Goldin, L. R., Weeks, D. E., Detera-Wadleigh, S., Nurnberger, J. I. J., et al. (1994). Chromosome 18 DNA markers and manic-depressive illness: Evidence for a susceptibility gene. *Proclamations of the National Academy of Science, U.S.A., 91*, 5918–5921.

Bertelsen, A., Harvald, B., & Hauge, M. (1977). A Danish twin study of manic-depressive disorders. *British Journal of Psychiatry, 130*, 330–351.

Bertolino, A., Esposito, G., Callicott, J. H., Mattay, V. S., Van Horn, J. D., Frank, J. A., et al. (2000). Specific relationship between prefrontal neuronal N-Acetylaspartate and activation of the working memory cortical network in schizophrenia. *American Journal of Psychiatry, 157*, 26–33.

Bertschy, G., Ragama-Pardos, E., Ait-Ameur, A., Muscionico, M., Favre, S., & Roth, L. (2003). Lithium augmentation in venlafaxine non-responders: An open study. *European Psychiatry, 18*, 314–317.

Besio, W. G., Martínez-Juárez, I. E., Makeyev, O., Gaitanis, J. N., Blum, A. S., Fisher, R. S., & Medvedev, A. V. (2014). High-frequency oscillations recorded on the scalp of patients with epilepsy using tripolar concentric ring electrodes. *IEEE Journal of Translational Engineering in Health and Medicine, 2*.

Bespalova, I. N., & Buxbaum, J. D. (2003). Disease susceptibility genes for autism. *Annals of Medicine, 35*, 274–281.

Bettcher, B. M., Mungas, D., Patel, N., Elofson, J., Dutt, S., Wynn, M., et al. (2016). Neuroanatomical substrates of executive functions: Beyond prefrontal structures. *Journal of Neuropsychologia, 85*, 100–109.

Bettiol, S. S., Rose, T. C., Hughes, C. J., & Smith, L. A. (2015). Alcohol consumption and Parkinson's disease risk: A review of recent findings. *Journal of Parkinson's Disease, 5*(3), 425–442.

Betz, W. J., Bewick, G. S., & Ridge, R. M. (1992). Intracellular movements of the fluorescently lableled synaptic vesicles in frog motor nerve terminals during nerve stimulation. *Neuron, 9*, 805–813.

Bevilacqua, L., & Goldman, D. (2009). Genes and addictions. *Clinical Pharmacology and Therapeutics, 85*(4), 359–361.

Bezchlibnyk, Y., & Young, L. T. (2002). The neurobiology of bipolar disorder: Focus on signal transduction pathways and the regulation of gene expression. *Canadian Journal of Psychiatry, 47*, 135–148.

Bhagvat, K., Blaschko, H., & Richter, D. (1939). Amine oxidase. *Biochemical Journal, 33*(8), 1338.

Bhanji, N. H., Margolese, H. C., Saint-Laurent, M., & Chouinard, G. (2002). Dysphoric mania induced by high-dose mirtazapine: A case for "norepinephrine syndrome"? *International Clinical Psychopharmacology, 17*, 319–322.

Bhat, R., Crowe, E. P., Bitto, A., Moh, M., Katsetos, C. D., Garcia, F. U., et al. (2012). Astrocyte senescence as a component of Alzheimer's disease. *PloS One, 7*(9), e45069.

Bhat, Z. F., Morton, J. D., Mason, S., Bekhit, A. E. D. A., & Bhat, H. F. (2017). Obesity and neurological disorders: Dietary perspective of a global menace. *Critical Reviews in Food Science and Nutrition*, 1–17.

Bhattacharyya, S., Atakan, Z., Martin-Santos, R., A Crippa, J., & McGuire, K. P. (2012). Neural mechanisms for the cannabinoid modulation of cognition and affect in man: A critical review of neuroimaging studies. *Current Pharmaceutical Design, 18*(32), 5045–5054.

Bhugra, D., & Mastrogianni, A. (2004). Globalisation and mental disorders. *The British Journal of Psychiatry, 184*(1), 10–20.

Bickford, P. C., Gould, T., Briederick, L., Chadman, K., Pollock, A., Young, D., et al. (2000). Antioxidant-rich diets improve cerebellar physiology and motor learning in aged rats. *Brain Research, 866*, 211–217.

Biederman, J., Baldessarini, R. J., Wright, V., Knee, D., & Harmatz, J. S. (1989). A double-blind placebo controlled study of desipramine in the treatment of ADD: I. efficacy. *Journal of the American Academy of Child & Adolescent Psychiatry, 28*(5), 777–784.

Biederman, J., & Faraone, S. V. (2002). Current concepts on the neurobiology of attention-deficit/hyperactivity disorder. *Journal of Attention Disorders, 1*, S7–S16.

Biederman, J., Faraone, S. V., Mick, E., Spencer, T., Wilens, T., Kiely, K., et al. (1995). High risk for attention deficit hyperactivity disorder among children of parents with childhood onset of the disorder: A pilot study. *American Journal of Psychiatry, 152*, 431–435.

Biederman, J., Munir, K., Knee, D., Habelow, W., Armentano, M., Autor, S., et al. (1986). A family study of patients with attention deficit disorder and normal controls. *Journal of Psychiatry Research, 20*, 261–274.

Bielefeldt, A. Ø., Danborg, P. B., & Gøtzsche, P. C. (2016). Precursors to suicidality and violence on antidepressants: Systematic review of trials in adult healthy volunteers. *Journal of the Royal Society of Medicine, 109*(10), 381–392.

Bierut, L. J., Dinwiddie, S. H., Begleiter, H., Crowe, R. R., Hesselbrock, V., Nurnberger, J. I., et al. (1998). Familial transmission of substance dependence: Alcohol, marijuana, cocaine, and habitual smoking: A report from the collaborative study on the genetics of alcoholism. *Archives of General Psychiatry, 55*(11), 982–988.

Bigdeli, T. B., Maher, B. S., Zhao, Z., Sun, J., Medeiros, H., Akula, N., et al. (2013). Association study of 83 candidate genes for bipolar disorder in chromosome 6q selected using an evidence-based prioritization algorithm. *American Journal of Medical Genetics Part B: Neuropsychiatric Genetics, 162*(8), 898–906.

Bilic, P., Jukic, V., Vilibic, M., Savic, A., & Bozina, N. (2014). Treatment-resistant schizophrenia and DAT and SERT polymorphisms. *Gene, 543*(1), 125–132.

Billeci, L., Tonacci, A., Tartarisco, G., Narzisi, A., Di Palma, S., Corda, D., . . . Pioggia, G. (2016). An integrated approach for the monitoring of brain and autonomic response of children with autism spectrum disorders during treatment by wearable technologies. *Frontiers in Neuroscience, 10*, 276.

Billett, E. A., Richter, M. A., King, N., Heils, A., Lesch, K. P., & Kennedy, J. L. (1997). Obsessive compulsive disorder, response to serotonin reuptake inhibitors and the serotonin transporter gene. *Molecular Psychiatry, 2*, 403–406.

Billett, E. A., Richter, M. A., Sam, F., Swinson, R. P., Dai, X. Y., King, N., et al. (1998). Investigation of dopamine system genes in obsessive-compulsive disorder. *Psychiatric Genetics, 8*(3), 163–169.

Bird, T. D. (2008). Genetic aspects of Alzheimer disease. *Genetics in Medicine, 10*(4), 231.

Birkenhager, T. K., van den Broek, W. W., Mulder, P. G., Bruijin, J. A., & Moleman, P. (2004). Comparison of two-phase treatment with imipramine or fluvoxamine, both followed by lithiuim addition in inpatients with major depressive disorder. *American Journal of Psychiatry, 161*, 2060–2065.

Birks, J., & Flicker, L. (2003). Selegiline for Alzheimer's disease. *Cochrane Database of Systematic Reviews*, CD000442.

Birmaher, B., Ryan, N. D., Williamson, B. A., Brent, D. A., Kaufman, J., Dahl, R. E., et al. (1996). Childhood and adolescent depression: A review of the past 10 years. Part I. *Journal of the American Academy of Child and Adolescent Psychiatry, 35*, 1427–1437.

Birur, B., Kraguljac, N. V., Shelton, R. C., & Lahti, A. C. (2017). Brain structure, function, and neurochemistry in schizophrenia and bipolar disorder—A systematic review of the magnetic resonance neuroimaging literature. *npj Schizophrenia, 3*.

Bisaga, A., Katz, J. L., Antonini, A., Wright, C. E., Margouleff, C., Gorman. J. M., et al. (1998). Cerebral glucose metabolism in women with panic disorder. *American Journal of Psychiatry, 155*, 1178–1183.

Bitsko, R. H. (2016). Health care, family, and community factors associated with mental, behavioral, and developmental disorders in early childhood: United States, 2011–2012. *MMWR: Morbidity and Mortality Weekly Report, 65*.

Biver, F., Goldman, S., Delvenne, V., Luxen, A., De Maertelaer, V., Hubain, P., et al. (1994). Fontal and parietal metabolic disturbances in unipolar depression. *Biological Psychiatry, 36*, 381–388.

Björkman, B., Lund, I., Arnér, S., & Hydén, L. C. (2017). The meaning and consequences of amputation and mastectomy from the perspective of pain and suffering. *Scandinavian Journal of Pain, 14*, 100–107.

Blackwell, A. D., Sahakian, B. J., Vesey, R., Semple, J. M., Robbins, T. W., & Hodges, J. R. (2004). Detecting dementia: Novel neuropsychological markers of preclinical Alzheimer's disease. *Dementia and Geriatric Cognitive Disorders, 17*, 42–48.

Blackwood, D. H. R., He, L., Morris, S. W., McLean, A., Whitton, C., Thomson, M., et al. (1996). A locus for bipolar affective disorder on chromosome 4p. *Nature Genetics, 4*, 427–430.

Blair, C., & Raver, C. C. (2016). Poverty, stress, and brain development: New directions for prevention and intervention. *Journal of Academic Pediatrics, 16*(3).

Blair Simpson, H., Tenke, C. E., Towey, J. B., Liebowitz, M. R., & Bruder, G. E. (2000). Symptom provocation alters behavioral ratings and brain electrical activity in obsessive-compulsive disorder: A preliminary study. *Psychiatry Research, 95*, 149–155.

Blair, C., & Raver, C. C. (2016). Poverty, stress, and brain development: New directions for prevention and intervention. *Journal of Academic Pediatrics, 16*(3), S30–S36.

Blaschko, H. (1939). The specific action of L-dopa decarboxylase. *The Journal of Physiology, 96*, 50P–51P.

Blasi, V., Young, A. C., Tansy, A. P., Petersen, S. E., Snyder, A. Z., & Corbetta, M. (2002). Word retrieval learning modulates right frontal cortex inpatients with left frontal damage. *Neuron, 36*, 159–170.

Blaya, C., Salum, G. A., Lima, M. S., Leistner-Segal, S., & Manfro, G. G. (2007). Lack of association between the Serotonin Transporter Promoter Polymorphism (5-HTTLPR) and Panic Disorder: A systematic review and meta-analysis. *Behavioral and Brain Functions, 3*(1), 41.

Blennow, K., Hampel, H., Weiner, M., & Zetterberg, H. (2010). Cerebrospinal fluid and plasma biomarkers in Alzheimer disease. *Nature Reviews Neurology, 6*(3), 131–144.

Bligh-Glover, W., Kolli, T. N., Shapiro-Kulnane, L., Dilley, G. E., Friedman, L., Balraj, E., et al. (2000). The serotonin transporter in the midbrain of suicide victims with major depression. *Biological Psychiatry, 47*, 1015–1024.

Bloch, M., Landeros-Weisenberger, A., Kelmendi, B., Coric, V., Bracken, M. B., & Leckman, J. F. (2006). A systematic review: Antipsychotic augmentation with treatment refractory obsessive-compulsive disorder. *Molecular Psychiatry, 11*(7), 622.

Bloch, M. H., Landeros-Weisenberger, A., Sen, S., Dombrowski, P., Kelmendi, B., Coric, V., et al. (2008). Association of the serotonin transporter polymorphism and obsessive-compulsive disorder: Systematic review. *American Journal of Medical Genetics Part B: Neuropsychiatric Genetics, 147*(6), 850–858.

Bloch, M. H., Leckman, J. F., Zhu, H., & Peterson, B. S. (2005). Caudate volumes in childhood predict symptom severity in adults with Tourette syndrome. *Neurology, 65*(8), 1253–1258.

Bloch, M. H., McGuire, J., Landeros-Weisenberger, A., Leckman, J. F., & Pittenger, C. (2010). Meta-analysis of the dose-response relationship of SSRI in obsessive-compulsive disorder. *Molecular Psychiatry, 15*(8), 850.

Bloch, M. H., Panza, K. E., Yaffa, A., Alvarenga, P. G., Jakubovski, E., Mulqueen, J. M., . . . & Leckman, J. F. (2016). N-Acetylcysteine in the treatment of pediatric Tourette syndrome: Randomized, double-blind, placebo-controlled add-on trial. *Journal of Child and Adolescent Psychopharmacology, 26*(4), 327–334.

Bloch, M., & Pittenger, C. (2010). The genetics of obsessive-compulsive disorder. *Current Psychiatry Reviews, 6*(2), 91–103.

Bloch, M. H., & Storch, E. A. (2015). Assessment and management of treatment-refractory obsessive-compulsive disorder in children. *Journal of the American Academy of Child & Adolescent Psychiatry, 54*(4), 251–262.

Bloch, M. H., Bartley, C. A., Zipperer, L., Jakubovski, E., Landeros-Weisenberger, A., Pittenger, C., & Leckman, J. F. (2014). Meta-analysis: Hoarding symptoms associated with poor treatment outcome in obsessive–compulsive disorder. *Molecular Psychiatry, 19*(9), 1025.

Bloom, O., Evergren, E., Tomilin, N., Kjaerulff, O., Low, P., Brodin, L., et al. (2003). Colocalization of synapsin and actin during synaptic vesicle recycling. *Journal of Cell Biology, 161*, 737–747.

Blue Cross and Blue Shield. (2017). America's opioid epidemic and its effect on the nation's commercially insured population, Blue Cross and Blue Shield, 2017.

Blumberg, H. P., Kaufman, J., Martin, A., Whiteman, R., Zhang, J. H., Gore, J. C., et al. (2003). Amygdala and hippocampal volumes in adolescents and adults with bipolar disorder. *Archives of General Psychiatry, 60*, 1201–1208.

Blumenfeld, H., McNally, K. A., Ostroff, R. B., & Zubal, I. G. (2003). Targeted prefrontal cortical activation with bifrontal ECT. *Psychiatry Research, 123*, 165–170.

Boccard, S. G., Prangnell, S. J., Pycroft, L., Cheeran, B., Moir, L., Pereira, E. A., et al. (2017). Long-term results of deep brain stimulation of the anterior cingulate cortex for neuropathic pain. *World Neurosurgery, 106*, 625–637.

Bodea, S. (2017). CNS metabolism in high-risk drug abuse: Insights gained from 1H-, 31P-MRS and PET. *Radiologe*, 443–449.

Bodeck, S., Lappe, C., & Evers, S. (2015). Tic-reducing effects of music in patients with Tourette's syndrome: Self-reported and objective analysis. *Journal of the Neurological Sciences, 352*(1), 41–47.

Bodner, S. M., Morshed, S. A., & Peterson, B. S. (2001). The question of PANDAS in adults. *Biological Psychiatry, 49*, 807–810.

Boedhoe, P. S., Schmaal, L., Abe, Y., Ameis, S. H., Arnold, P. D., Batistuzzo, M. C., et al. (2016). Distinct subcortical volume alterations in pediatric and adult OCD: A worldwide meta- and mega-analysis. *American Journal of Psychiatry, 174*(1), 60–69.

Bogen, I. L., Haug, K. H., Myhre, O., & Fonnum, F. (2003). Short-and long-term effects of MDMA ("ecstasy") on synaptosomal and vesicular uptake of neurotransmitters in vitro and ex vivo. *Neurochemistry International, 43*(4–5), 393–400.

Bogetto, F., Venturello, S., Albert, U., Maina, G., & Ravizza, L. (1999). Gender-related clinical differences in obsessive-compulsive disorder. *European Psychiatry, 14*, 434–441.

Boileau, B. (2011). A review of obsessive-compulsive disorder in children and adolescents. *Dialogues in Clinical Neuroscience, 13*(4), 401.

Boileau, I., Assadd, J. M., Pihl, R. O., Benkelfat, C., Leyton, M., Diksic, M., et al. (2003). Alcohol promotes dopamine release in human nucleus accumbens. *Synapse, 49*, 226–231.

Boll, S., Minas, A. A., Raftogianni, A., Herpertz, S., & Grinevich, V. (2017). Oxytocin and pain perception: From animal models to human research. *Neuroscience, 387*, 149–161.

Bolla, K. I., Brown, K., Eldreth, D., Tate, K., & Cadet, J. L. (2002). Dose-related neurocognitive effects of marijuana use. *Neurology, 59*(9), 1337–1343.

Bolla, K. I., Eldreth, D. A., London, E. D., Kiehl, K. A., Mouratidus, M., Contoreggi, C., et al. (2003). Orbitofrontal cortex dysfunction in abstinent cocaine abusers performing a decision-making task. *Neuroimage, 19*, 1085–1094.

Bolton, D., Rijsdijk, F., O'connor, T. G., Perrin, S., & Eley, T. C. (2007). Obsessive-compulsive disorder, tics and anxiety in 6-year-old twins. *Psychological Medicine, 37*(1), 39–48.

Bolton, J., Moore, G. J., MacMillan, S., Stewart, C. M., & Rosenberg, D. R. (2001). Case study: Caudate glutamatergic changes with paroxetine persist after medication discontinuation in pediatric OCD. *Journal of the American Academy of Child and Adolescent Psychiatry, 40*, 903–906.

Bolwig, T. G. (2003). Putative common pathways in therapeutic brain stimulation for affective disorders. *CNS Spectrums, 8*, 490–495.

Bolwig, T. G. (2014). Neuroimaging and electroconvulsive therapy: A review. *The Journal of ECT, 30*(2), 138–142.

Bonne, O., Gilboa, A., Louzoun, Y., Brandes, D., Yona, I., Lester, H., et al. (2003). Resting regional cerebral perfusion in recent posttraumatic stress disorder. *Biological Psychiatry, 54*, 1077–1086.

Bonne, O., Krausz, Y., Abaron, Y., Gelfin, Y., Chisin, R., & Lerer, B. (1999). Clinical doses offluoxetine and cerebral blood flow in healthy volunteers. *Psychopharmacology, 143*, 24–28.

Bonne, O., Louzoun, Y., Aharon, I., Krausz, Y., Karger, H., Lerer, B., et al. (2003). Cerebral blood flow in depressed patients: A methodological comparison of statistical parametric mapping and region of interest analyses. *Psychiatry Research, 122*, 49–57.

Bookstein, F. L., Sampson, P. D., Connor, P. D., & Streissguth, A. P. (2002). Midline corpus callosum is a neuroanatomical focus of fetal alcohol damage. *Anatomical Record, 269*, 162–174.

Booth, H. D., Hirst, W. D., & Wade-Martins, R. (2017). The role of astrocyte dysfunction in Parkinson's disease pathogenesis. *Trends in Neurosciences, 40*(6), 358–370.

Bootsman, F., Brouwer, R. M., Kemner, S. M., Schnack, H. G., van der Schot, A. C., Vonk, R., et al. (2015). Contribution of genes and unique environment to cross-sectional and longitudinal measures of subcortical volumes in bipolar disorder. *European Neuropsychopharmacology, 25*(12), 2197–2209.

Borcherding, B. G., Keysor, C. S., Rapoport, J. L., Elia, J., & Amass, J. (1990). Motor/vocal tics and compulsive behaviors on stimulant drugs: Is there a common vulnerability? *Psychiatry Research, 33*, 83–94.

Boronat, S., Sánchez-Montañez, A., Gómez-Barros, N., Jacas, C., Martínez-Ribot, L., Vázquez, E., & Del Campo, M. D. (2017). Correlation between morphological MRI findings and specific diagnostic categories in fetal alcohol spectrum disorders. *European Journal of Medical Genetics, 60*(1), 65–71

Bos, D. J., Oranje, B., Achterberg, M., Vlaskamp, C., Ambrosino, S., de Reus, M. A., . . . Durston, S. (2017). Structural and functional connectivity in children and adolescents with and without attention deficit/hyperactivity disorder. *Journal of Child Psychology and Psychiatry, 58*(7), 810–818.

Bosboom, J. L. W., Stoffers, D., & Wolters, E. (2003). The role of acetylcholine and dopamine in dementia and psychosis in Parkinson's disease. *Journal of Neural Transmission, 65*, 185–195.

Bosch-Bayard, J., Baldes-Sosa, P., Virues-Alba, T., Aubert-Vazquez, E., John, E. R., Harmony, T., et al. (2001). 3D statistical parametric mapping of EEG source spectra by means of variable resolution electromagnetic tomographay (VARETA). *Clinical Electroencephalograph, 32*, 47–61.

Boshuisen, M. L., Ter Horst, G. J., Paans, A. M., Reinders, A. A., den Boer, J. A., et al. (2002). rCBF differences between panic disorder patients and control subjects during anticipatory anxiety and rest. *Biological Psychiatry, 52*, 126–135.

Bosworth, A. P., & Allen, N. J. (2017). The diverse actions of astrocytes during synaptic development. *Current Opinion in Neurobiology, 47*, 38–43.

Bouckaert, F., Sienaert, P., Obbels, J., Dols, A., Vandenbulcke, M., Stek, M., & Bolwig, T. (2014). ECT: Its brain enabling effects a review of electroconvulsive therapy-Induced structural brain plasticity. *The Journal of ECT, 30*(2), 143–151.

Boulanger, H., Tebeka, S., Girod, C., Lloret-Linares, C., Meheust, J., Scott, J., et al. (2018). Binge eating behaviours in bipolar disorders. *Journal of Affective Disorders, 225*, 482–488.

Bounds, T. A., Schoop, L., Johnstone, B., Unger, C., & Goldman, H. (2003). Gender differences in a sample of vocational rehabilitation clients with TBI. *NeuroRehabilitation, 18*, 189–196.

Bountress, K. E., Wei, W., Sheerin, C., Chung, D., Amstadter, A. B., Mandel, H., & Wang, Z. (2017). Relationships between GAT1 and PTSD, depression, and substance use disorder. *Brain Sciences, 7*(1), 6.

Bowers, D., Bauer, R. M., Coslett, H. B., & Heilman, K. M. (1985). Processing of faces by patients with unilateral hemispheric lesions. I. Dissociations between judgements of facial affect and identity. *Brain and Cognition, 4*, 258–272.

Bowers, M. S., Chen, B. T., & Bonci, A. (2010). AMPA receptor synaptic plasticity induced by psychostimulants: The past, present, and therapeutic future. *Neuron, 67*(1), 11–24.

Bozorgmehr, A., Ghadirivasfi, M., & Shahsavand Ananloo, E. (2017). Obsessive-compulsive disorder, which genes? Which functions? Which pathways? An integrated holistic view regarding OCD and its complex genetic etiology. *Journal of Neurogenetics, 31*(3), 153–160.

Braak, H., & Del Tredici, K. (2017). Neuropathological staging of brain pathology in sporadic Parkinson's disease: Separating the wheat from the chaff. *Journal of Parkinson's Disease, 7*(s1), S73-S87.

Braam, W., Ehrhart, F., Maas, A., Smits, M. G., & Curfs, L. (2018). Low maternal melatonin level increases autism spectrum disorder risk in children. *Research in Developmental Disabilities, 4222*(18), 30042–30048.

Bradwejn, J., & Koszycki, D. (1994). The cholecystokinin hypothesis of anxiety and panic disorder. *Annals of the New York Academy of Sciences, 713*, 273–282.

Brakoulias, V., Perkes, I. E., & Tsalamanios, E. (2017). A call for prevention and early intervention in obsessive-compulsive disorder. *Early Intervention in Psychiatry, 12*(4), 572–577.

Brambilla, F., Biggio, G., Pisu, M. G., Bellodi, L., Perna, G., Bogdanovich-Djukic, V., et al. (2003). Neurosteroid secretion in panic disorder. *Psychiatry Research, 118*, 107–116.

Brambilla, P., Barale, F., Caverzasi, E., & Soares, J. C. (2002). Anatomical MRI findings in mood and anxiety disorders. *Epidemiologia E Psichiatria Sociale, 11*, 88–99.

Brambilla, P., Harenski, K., Nicoletti, M., Mallinger, A. G., Frank, E., Kupfer, D. J., et al. (2001). MRI study of posterior fossa structure and brain ventricles in bipolar patients. *Journal of Psychiatry Research, 35*, 313–322.

Bramlett, H. M., & Dietrich, W. D. (2015). Long-term consequences of traumatic brain injury: Current status of potential mechanisms of injury and neurological outcomes. *Journal of Neurotrauma, 32*(23), 1834–1848.

Brander, G., Pérez-Vigil, A., Larsson, H., & Mataix-Cols, D. (2016). Systematic review of environmental risk factors for obsessive-compulsive disorder: A proposed roadmap from association to causation. *Neuroscience & Biobehavioral Reviews, 65*, 36–62.

Brandt, C. A., Meller, J., Keweloh, L., Höschel, K., Staedt, J., Munz, D., et al. (1998). Increased benzodiazepine receptor density in the prefrontal cortex in patients with panic disorder. *Journal of Neural Transmission, 105*, 1325–1333.

Braun, A. R., Stoetter, B., Randolph, C., Hsiao, J. K., Vladar, K., Gernert, J., et al. (1993). The functional neuroanatomy of Tourette's syndrome: An FDG-PET study, I: Regional changes in cerebral glucose metabolism differentiating patients and controls. *Neuropsychopharmacology, 9,* 277–291.

Breakey, W. R., & Dunn, G. J. (2004). Racial disparity in the use of ECT for affective disorders. *American Journal of Psychiatry, 161,* 1635–1641.

Breiter, H. C., Rauch, S. L., Kwong, K. K., Baker, J. R., Weisskoff, R. M., Kennedy, D. N., et al. (1996). Functional magnetic resonance imaging of symptom provocation in obsessive-compulsive disorder. *Archives of General Psychiatry, 53,* 595–606.

Breivogel, C. S., Scates, S. M., Beletskaya, I. O., Lowery, O. B., Aceto, M. D., & Martin, B. R. (2003). The effects of Δ9-tetrahydrocannabinol physical dependence on brain cannabinoid receptors. *European Journal of Pharmacology, 459*(2–3), 139–150.

Brem, S., Hauser, T. U., Iannaccone, R., Brandeis, D., Drechsler, R., & Walitza, S. (2012). Neuroimaging of cognitive brain function in paediatric obsessive compulsive disorder: A review of literature and preliminary meta-analysis. *Journal of Neural Transmission, 119*(11), 1425–1448.

Bremmer, J. D., Innis, R. B., Southwick, S. M., Staib, L., Zoghbi, S., & Charney, D. S. (2000). Decreased benzodiazepine receptor binding in prefrontal cortex in combat-related posttraumatic stress disorder. *American Journal of Psychiatry, 157,* 1120–1126.

Bremner, J. D., Narayan, M., Anderson, E. R., Staib, L. H., Miller, H. L., & Charney, D. S. (2000). Hippocampal volume reduction in major depression. *American Journal of Psychiatry, 157,* 115–118.

Brener, S., & Holubowich, C. (2017). Pharmacogenomic testing for psychotropic medication selection: A systematic review of the assurex genesight psychotropic test. *Ontario Health Technology Assessment Series, 17,* 1–39.

Brent, D. A., Oquendo, M., Birmaher, B., Greenhill, L., Kolko, D., Stanley, B., et al. (2003). Peripubetal suicide attempts in offspring of suicide attempters with sibling concordant for suicidal behavior. *American Journal of Psychiatry, 160,* 1486–1493.

Broman-Fulks, J. J., Berman, M. E., Rabian, B. A., & Webster, M. J. (2004). Effects of aerobic exercise on anxiety sensitivity. *Behaviour Research and Therapy, 42*(2), 125–136.

Broman-Fulks, J. J., Abraham, C. M., Thomas, K., Canu, W. H., & Nieman, D. C. (2018). Anxiety sensitivity mediates the relationship between exercise frequency and anxiety and depression symptomology. *Stress and Health.* doi: 10.1002/smi.2810. [Epub ahead of print]

Bronsard, G., Alessandrini, M., Fond, G., Loundou, A., Auquier, P., Tordjman, S., & Boyer, L. (2016). The prevalence of mental disorders among children and adolescents in the child welfare system: A systematic review and meta-analysis. *Medicine, 95*(7).

Broocks, A., Bandelow, B., Pekrun, G., George, A., Meyer, T., Bartmann, U., et al. (1998). Comparison of aerobic exercise, clomipramine, and placebo in the treatment of panic disorder. *American Journal of Psychiatry, 155,* 603–609.

Brookmeyer, R., Abdalla, N., Kawas, C. H., & Corrada, M. M. (2018). Forecasting the prevalence of preclinical and clinical Alzheimer's disease in the United States. *Alzheimer's & Dementia: The Journal of the Alzheimer's Association, 14*(2), 121–129.

Brown, E. S., Sunderajan, P., Hu, L. T., Sowell, S. M., & Carmody, T. J. (2012). A randomized, double-blind, placebo-controlled, trial of lamotrigine therapy in bipolar disorder, depressed or mixed phase and cocaine dependence. *Neuropsychopharmacology, 37*(11), 2347–2354.

Brown, K. A., Samuel, S., & Patel, D. R. (2018). Pharmacologic management of attention deficit hyperactivity disorder in children and adolescents: A review for practitioners. *Translational Pediatrics, 7*(1), 36.

Brozzoli, C., Gentile, G., & Ehrsson, H. H. (2012). Thats near my hand! Parietal and premotor coding of hand-centered space contributes to localization and self-attribution of the hand. *Journal of Neuroscience, 32*(42), 14573–14582.

Bruce, S. E., Vasile, R. G., Goisman, R. M., Salzman, C., Spencer, M., Machan, J. T., et al. (2003). Are benzodiazepines still the medication of choice for patients with panic disorder with or without agoraphobia? *American Journal of Psychiatry, 160*, 1432–1438.

Brue, A. W., & Oakland, T. D. (2002). Alternative treatments for attention-deficit/hyperactivity disorder: Does evidence support their use? *Alternative Therapy in Health and Medicine, 8*, 72–74.

Bruggeman, R., van der Linden, C., Buitelaar, J. K., Gericke, G. S., Hawkridge, S. M., & Temlett, J. A. (2001). Risperidone versus pimozide in Tourette's disorder: A comparative double-blind parallel-group study. *The Journal of Clinical Psychiatry, 62*(1), 50–56.

Brühl, A. B. (2015). Making sense of real-time functional magnetic resonance imaging (rtfMRI) and rtfMRI neurofeedback. *International Journal of Neuropsychopharmacology, 18*(6), pyv020.

Brühl, A. B., Scherpiet, S., Sulzer, J., Stämpfli, P., Seifritz, E., & Herwig, U. (2014). Real-time neu-rofeedback using functional MRI could improve down-regulation of amygdala activity during emotional stimulation: A proof-of-concept study. *Brain Topography, 27*(1), 138–148.

Brummelte, S., Mc Glanaghy, E., Bonnin, A., & Oberlander, T. F. (2017). Developmental changes in serotonin signaling: Implications for early brain function, behavior and adaptation. *Neuroscience, 342*, 212–231.

Brun, C. C., Nicolson, R., Lepore, N., Chou, Y. Y., Vidal, C. N., DeVito, T. J., . . . Thompson, P. M. (2009). Mapping brain abnormalities in boys with autism. *Human Brain Mapping, 30*(12), 3887–3900.

Brunner, H. G., Breakefield, N. X. O., Ropers, H. H., & van Oost, B. A. (1993). Abnormal behavior associated with a point mutation in the structural gene for monoamine oxidase A. *Science, 262*, 578–580.

Brunoni, A. R., Chaimani, A., Moffa, A. H., Razza, L. B., Gattaz, W. F., Daskalakis, Z. J., & Carvalho, A. F. (2017). Repetitive transcranial magnetic stimulation for the acute treatment of major depressive episodes: A systematic review with network meta-analysis. *JAMA Psychiatry, 74*(2), 143–152.

Brunoni, A. R., Ferrucci, R., Bortolomasi, M., Vergari, M., Tadini, L., Boggio, P. S., et al. (2011). Transcranial direct current stimulation (tDCS) in unipolar vs. bipolar depressive disorder. *Progress in Neuro-Psychopharmacology and Biological Psychiatry, 35*(1), 96–101.

Buchsbaum, M. S., & Hazlett, E. A. (1998). Positron emission tomography studies of abnormal glucose metabolism in schizophrenia. *Schizophrenia Bulletin, 24*(3), 343–364.

Buckley, P. F., Hrouda, D. R., Friedman, L., Noffsinger, S. G., Resnick, P. J., & Camlin-Shingler, K. (2004). Insight and its relationship to violent behavior in patients with schizophrenia. *American Journal of Psychiatry, 161*, 1712–1714.

Budney, A. J., Roffman, R., Stephens, R. S., & Walker, D. (2007). Marijuana dependence and its treatment. *Addiction Science & Clinical Practice, 4*(1), 4–16.

Budney, A. J., Vandrey, R. G., Hughes, J. R., Moore, B. A., & Bahrenburg, B. (2007). Oral delta-9-tetrahydrocannabinol suppresses cannabis withdrawal symptoms. *Drug & Alcohol Dependence, 86*(1), 22–29.

Buell, S. J., & Coleman, P. D. (1981). Quantitative evidence for selective dendritic growth in normal aging, but not in senile dementia. *Brain Research, 214*, 23–31.

Bugental, B. D., Martorell, G. A., & Barraza, V. (2003). The hormonal costs of subtle forms of infant maltreatment. *Hormones and Behavior, 43*, 237–244.

Bullido, M. J., Aldudo, J., Frank, A., Coria, F., Avila, J., & Valdivieso, F. (2000). A polymorphism in the tau gene associated with risk for Alzheimer's disease. *Neuroscience Letters, 278*, 49–52.

Bullock, K., Cservenka, A., & Ray, L. A. (2017). Severity of alcohol dependence is negatively related to hypothalamic and prefrontal cortical gray matter density in heavy drinking smokers. *The American Journal of Drug and Alcohol Abuse, 43*(3), 281–290.

Bunney, W. E., & Garland, B. L. (1982). A second generation catecholamine hypothesis. *Pharmacopsychiatry, 15*, 111–115.

Buoli, M., Serati, M., & Cahn, W. (2016). Alternative pharmacological strategies for adult ADHD treatment: A systematic review. *Expert Review of Neurotherapeutics, 16*(2), 131–144.

Burda, J. E., Bernstein, A. M., & Sofroniew, M. V. (2016). Astrocyte roles in traumatic brain injury. *Experimental Neurology, 275*, 305–315.

Burnett-Zeigler, I., Walton, M. A., Ilgen, M., Barry, K. L., Chermack, S. T., Zucker, R. A., et al. (2012). Prevalence and correlates of mental health problems and treatment among adolescents seen in primary care. *Journal of Adolescent Health, 50*(6), 559–564.

Burruss, J. W., Hurley, R. A., Taber, K. H., Rauch, R. A., Norton, R. E., & Hayman, L. A. (2000). Functional neuroanatomy of the frontal lobe circuits. *Radiology, 214*, 227–230.

Burt, S. A., Krueger, R. F., McGue, M., & Iacono, W. G. (2001). Sources of covariation among attention-deficit/hyperactivity disorder, oppositional defiant disorder, and conduct disorder: The importance of shared environment. *Journal of Abnormal Psychology, 110*, 516–525.

Burt, T., Lisanby, S. H., & Sackeim, H. A. (2002). Neuropsychiatric applications of transcranial stimulation: A meta analysis. *International Journal of Neuropsychopharmacology, 5*, 73–103.

Burton, E. J., McKeith, I. G., Burn, D. J., Williams, E. D., & O'Brien, J. T. (2004). Cerebral atrophy in Parkinson's disease with and without dementia: A comparison with Alzheimer's disease, dementia with Lewy bodies and controls. *Brain, 127*, 791–800.

Busatto, G. F., Buchpiguel, C. A., Zamignani, D. R., Garrido, G. E., Glabus, M. F., Rosario-Campos, M. C., et al. (2001). Regional cerebral blood flow abnormalities in early-onset obsessive-compulsive disorder: An exploratory SPECT study. *Journal of the American Academy of Child and Adolescent Psychiatry, 40*, 347–354.

Busatto, G. F., Zamignani, D. R., Buchpiguel, C. A., Garrido, G. E., Glabus, M. F., Rocha, E. T., et al. (2000). A voxel-based investigation of regional cerebral blood flow abnormalities in obsessive-compulsive disorder using single photon emission computed tomography (SPECT). *Psychiatry Research, 99*, 15–27.

Bush, G., Luu, P., & Posner, M. I. (2000). Cognitive and emotional influences in anterior cingulate cortex. *Trends in Cognitive Sciences, 4*, 215–222.

Bushnell, G. A., Stürmer, T., Swanson, S. A., White, A., Azrael, D., Pate, V., & Miller, M. (2016). Dosing of selective serotonin reuptake inhibitors among children and adults before and after the FDA Black-Box warning. *Psychiatric Services, 67*(3), 302–309.

Bütefisch, C. M., Davis, B. C., Sawaki, L., Waldvogel, D., Classen, J., Kopylev, L., & Cohen, L. G. (2002). Modulation of use-dependent plasticity by d-amphetamine. *Annals of Neurology, 51*(1), 59–68.

Butler, A. J., & Wolf, S. L. (2007). Putting the brain on the map: Use of transcranial magnetic stimulation to assess and induce cortical plasticity of upper-extremity movement. *Physical Therapy, 87*(6), 719–736.

Buttenchøn, H. N., Foldager, L., Flint, T. J., Olsen, I. M. L., Deleuran, T., Nyegaard, M., et al. (2010). Support for a bipolar affective disorder susceptibility locus on chromosome 12q24. 3. *Psychiatric Genetics, 20*(3), 93–101.

Butterfield, D. A., Howard, B., Yatin, S., Koppal, T., Drake, J., Hensley, K., et al. (1999). Elevated oxidative stress in models of normal brain aging and Alzheimer's disease. *Life Sciences, 65*, 1883–1892.

Buydens-Branchey, L., Branchey, M., Hudson, J., Rothman, M., Fergeson, P., & McKernin, C. (1999). Serotonerigic function in cocaine addicts: Prolactin responses to sequential D, L-fenfluaramine challenges. *Biological Psychiatry, 45*, 1300–1306.

Byrne, E. M., Heath, A. C., Madden, P. A., Pergadia, M. L., Hickie, I. B., Montgomery, G. W., et al. (2014). Testing the role of circadian genes in conferring risk for psychiatric disorders. *American Journal of Medical Genetics Part B: Neuropsychiatric Genetics, 165*(3), 254–260.

Bystritsky, A., Pontillo, D., Powers, M., Sabb, F. W., Craske, M. G., & Bookheimer, S. Y. (2001). Functional MRI changes during panic anticipation and imagery exposure. *Neuroreport, 12*, 3953–3957.

Caccia, S. (2000a). Biotransformation of post-clozapine antipsychotics: Pharmacological implications. *Clinical Pharmacokinetics, 38*, 393–414.

Cai, L., Dong, Q., & Niu, H. (2018). The development of functional network organization in early childhood and early adolescence: A resting-state fNIRS study. *Developmental Cognitive Neuroscience, 30,* 223–235.

Cai, Y., An, S. S. A., & Kim, S. (2015). Mutations in presenilin 2 and its implications in Alzheimer's disease and other dementia-associated disorders. *Clinical Interventions in Aging, 10,* 1163–1172.

Cains, S., Blomeley, C., Kollo, M., Rácz, R., & Burdakov, D. (2017). Agrp neuron activity is required for alcohol-induced overeating. *Nature Communications, 8,* 14014.

Caliguri, M. P., Brown, G. G., Meloy, M. J., Eberson, S. C., Kindermann, S. S., Frank, L. R., et al. (2003). An fMRI study of affective state and medication on cortical and subcortical brain regions during motor performance in bipolar disorder. *Psychiatry Research, 123,* 171–182.

Calne, S. M. (2003). The psychosocial impact of late-stage Parkinson's disease. *Journal of Neuroscience Nursing, 35,* 306–313.

Camacho-Soto, A., Warden, M. N., Searles Nielsen, S., Salter, A., Brody, D. L., Prather, H., & Racette, B. A. (2017). Traumatic brain injury in the prodromal period of Parkinson's disease: A large epidemiological study using medicare data. *Annals of Neurology, 82*(5), 744–754.

Camarena, B., Loyzaga, C., Aguilar, A., Weissbecker, K., & Nicolini, H. (2007). Association study between the dopamine receptor D4 gene and obsessive-compulsive disorder. *European Neuropsychopharmacology, 17*(6), 406–409.

Camarena, B., Rinetti, G., Cruz, C., Gómez, A., de La Fuente, J. R., & Nicolini, H. (2001a). Additional evidence that genetic variation of MAO-A gene supports a gender subtype in obsessive-compulsive disorder. *American Journal of Medical Genetics, 105,* 279–282.

Cami, J., & Farre, M. (2003). Drug addiction. *New England Journal of Medicine, 349,* 975–986.

Camicioli, R., Moore, M. M., Kinney, A., Corbridge, E., Glassberg, K., & Kaye, J. A. (2003). Parkinson's disease is associated with hippocampal atrophy. *Movement Disorders, 18,* 784–790.

Campbell, F. A., & Ramey, C. T. (1994). Effects of early intervention on intellectual and academic achievement: A follow up study of children from low income families. *Child Development, 65,* 684–698.

Campbell, J. M. (2003). Efficacy of behavioral interventions for reducing problem behavior in persons with autism: A quantitative synthesis of single-subject research. *Research in Developmental Disabilities, 24,* 120–138.

Campbell, S., Marriott, M., Nahamias, C., & MacQueen, G. M. (2004). Lower hippocampal volume in patients suffering from depression: A meta-analysis. *American Journal of Psychiatry, 161,* 598–607.

Cantello, R., Tarletti, R., & Civardi, C. (2002). Transcranial magnetic stimulation and Parkinson's disease. *Brain Research Reviews, 38*(3), 309–327.

Canuto, A., Weber, K., Baertschi, M., Andreas, S., Volkert, J., Dehoust, M. C., . . . Crawford, M. J. (2018). Anxiety disorders in old age: Psychiatric comorbidities, quality of life, and prevalence according to age, gender, and country. *The American Journal of Geriatric Psychiatry, 26*(2), 174–185.

Capitão, L. P., Murphy, S. E., Browning, M., Cowen, P. J., & Harmer, C. J. (2015). Acute fluoxetine modulates emotional processing in young adult volunteers. *Psychological Medicine, 45*(11), 2295–2308.

Caplan, L. R., Gomez Beldarrain, M., Bier, J. C., Vokaer, M., Bartholme, E. J., & Pandolfo, M. (2002). The cerebellum may be directly involved in cognitive functions. *Neurology, 59,* 790–791.

Caradoc-Davies, T. H., Weatherall, M., Dixon, G. S., Caradoc-Davies, G., & Hantz, P. (1992). Is the prevalence of Parkinson's disease in New Zealand really changing? *Acta Neurologica Scandinavica, 86,* 40–44.

Cardno, A. G., Marshall, E. J., Coid, B., Macdonald, A. M., Ribchester, T. R., Davies, M. J., et al. (1999). Herititability estimates for psychotic disorders: The Mudsley twin psychosis series. *Archives of General Psychiatry, 56,* 162–168.

Carlbring, P., Gustafsson, H., Ekselius, L., & Andersson, G. (2002). 12-month prevalence of panic disorder with or without agoraphobia in the Swedish general population. *Social Psychiatry and Psychiatric Epidemiology, 37*, 207–211.

Carlisi, C. O., Chantiluke, K., Norman, L., Christakou, A., Barrett, N., Giampietro, V., . . . & Rubia, K. (2016). The effects of acute fluoxetine administration on temporal discounting in youth with ADHD. *Psychological Medicine, 46*(6), 1197–1209.

Carlisi, C. O., Norman, L. J., Lukito, S. S., Radua, J., Mataix-Cols, D., & Rubia, K. (2017). Comparative multimodal meta-analysis of structural and functional brain abnormalities in autism spectrum disorder and obsessive-compulsive disorder. *Biological Psychiatry, 82*(2), 83–102.

Carlisi, C. O., Norman, L., Murphy, C. M., Christakou, A., Chantiluke, K., Giampietro, V., et al (2017). Disorder-specific and shared brain abnormalities during vigilance in autism and obsessive-compulsive disorder. *Biological Psychiatry: Cognitive Neuroscience and Neuroimaging, 2*(8), 644–654.

Carlson, M., & Earls, F. (1997). Physiological and neuroendocrinological sequelae of early social deprivation in institutionalized children in Romania. *Annals of the New York Academy of the Sciences, 807*, 419–428.

Carlsson, A., Lindqvist, M., & Magnusson, T. (1957). 3, 4-Dihydroxphenylalanine and 5-hydroxytyramine as resperpine antagonists. *Nature, 180*, 1200–1202.

Carlsson, A., Waters, N., Holm-Waters, S., Tedroff, J., Nilsson, M., & Carlsson, M. (2001). Interactions between monoamines, glutamate, and GABA in schizophrenia: New evidence. *Annual Review of Pharmacology and Toxicology, 41*, 237–260.

Carmichael, S. T. (2006). Cellular and molecular mechanisms of neural repair after stroke: Making waves. *Annals of Neurology: Official Journal of the American Neurological Association and the Child Neurology Society, 59*(5), 735–742.

Carney, S., Cowen, P., Geddes, J., Goodwin, G., Rogers, R., Dearness, K., . . . Scott, A. (2003). Efficacy and safety of electroconvulsive therapy in depressive disorders: A systematic review and meta-analysis. *The Lancet, 361*(9360), 799–808.

Carpenter, L. L., Friehs, G. M., & Price, L. H. (2003). Cervical vagus nerve stimulation for treatment-resistant depression. *Neurosurgery Clinics of North America, 14*, 275–282.

Carreno, F. R., & Frazer, A. (2017). Vagal nerve stimulation for treatment-resistant depression. *Neurotherapeutics, 14*(3), 716–727.

Carrozzino, D., Morberg, B. M., Siri, C., Pezzoli, G., & Bech, P. (2018). Evaluating psychiatric symptoms in Parkinson's Disease by a clinimetric analysis of the Hopkins Symptom Checklist (SCL-90-R). *Progress in Neuro-Psychopharmacology and Biological Psychiatry, 81*, 131–137.

Carta, M., & Björklund, A. (2018). The serotonergic system in L-DOPA-induced dyskinesia: Pre-clinical evidence and clinical perspective. *Journal of Neural Transmission,* 1–8.

Carter, M. T., & Scherer, S. W. (2013). Autism spectrum disorder in the genetics clinic: A review. *Clinical Genetics, 83*(5), 399–407.

Caruana, M., & Vassallo, N. (2015). Tea polyphenols in Parkinson's disease. In *Natural compounds as therapeutic agents for amyloidogenic diseases* (pp. 117–137). Cham: Springer.

Carvey, P. M. (1998). *Drug action in the central nervous system.* New York: Oxford University Press.

Casanova, M. F., Buxhoeveden, D., & Gomez, J. (2003). Disruption in the inhibitory architecture of the cell minicolumn: Implications for autisim. *The Neuroscientist, 9*, 496–507.

Case, L. K., Brang, D., Landazuri, R., Viswanathan, P., & Ramachandran, V. S. (2017). Altered white matter and sensory response to bodily sensation in female-to-male transgender individuals. *Archives of Sexual Behavior, 46*(5), 1223–1237.

Caspi, A., Sugden, K., Moffitt, T. E., Taylor, A., Craig, I. W., Harrington, H., et al. (2003). Influence of life stress on depression: Moderation by a polymorphism in the 5-HTT gene. *Science, 301*, 386–389.

Castellanos, F. X., & Elmaghrabi, S. E. (2017). On the road to physiological models of brain function in ADHD. *The American Journal of Psychiatry, 174*(9), 825–826.

Castellanos, F. X., Giedd, J. N., Berquin, P. C., Walter, J. M., Sharp, W., Tran, T., . . . Zijdenbos, A. (2001). Quantitative brain magnetic resonance imaging in girls with attention-deficit/hyperactivity disorder. *Archives of General Psychiatry, 58*(3), 289–295.

Castellanos, F. X., Giedd, J. N., Eckburg, P., & Marsh, W. L. (1994). Quantitative morphology of the caudate nucleus in attention deficit hyperactivity disorder. *The American Journal of Psychiatry, 151*(12), 1791.

Castellanos, F. X., Lee, P. P., Sharp, W., Jeffries, N. O., Greenstein, D. K., Clasen, L. S., . . . Zijdenbos, A. (2002). Developmental trajectories of brain volume abnormalities in children and adolescents with attention-deficit/hyperactivity disorder. *Jama, 288*(14), 1740–1748.

Castellanos, F. X., Sharp, W. S., Gottesman, R. F., Greenstein, D. K., Giedd, J. N., & Rapoport, J. L. (2003). Anatomic brain abnormalities in monozygotic twins discordant for attention deficit hyperactivity disorder. *American Journal of Psychiatry, 160*(9), 1693–1696.

Castellanos, F. X., Sonuga-Barke, E. J., Scheres, A., Di Martino, A., Hyde, C., & Walters, J. R. (2005). Varieties of attention-deficit/hyperactivity disorder-related intra-individual variability. *Biological Psychiatry, 57*(11), 1416–1423.

Castillo, A. R., Buchpiguel, C. A., de Araujo, L. A., Castillo, J. C., Asbahr, F. R., Maia, A. K., et al. (2005). Brain SPECT imaging in children & adolescents with obsessive-compulsive disorder. *Journal of Neural Transmission*, 1435–1463.

Celada, P., Bortolozzi, A., & Artigas, F. (2013). Serotonin 5-HT1A receptors as targets for agents to treat psychiatric disorders: Rationale and current status of research. *CNS Drugs, 27*(9), 703–716.

Centers for Disease Control and Prevention. (2016). *TBI: Get the facts.* Atlanta, GA: Centers for Disease Control and Prevention.

Ceri, V., Özlü-Erkilic, Z., Özer, Ü., Kadak, T., Winkler, D., Dogangün, B., & Akkaya-Kalayci, T. (2017). Mental health problems of second generation children and adolescents with migration background. *International Journal of Psychiatry in Clinical Practice, 21*(2), 142–147.

Cerri, S., & Blandini, F. (2018). Role of autophagy in Parkinson's disease. *Current Medicinal Chemistry, 25*(1).

Chan, D., Janssen, J. C., Whitwell, J. L., Watt, H. C., Jenkins, R., Frost, C., et al. (2003). Change in rates of cerebral atrophy over time in early-onset Alzheimer's disease: Longitudinal MRI study. *Lancet, 362*, 1121–1122.

Chan, E., Fogler, J. M., & Hammerness, P. G. (2016). Treatment of attention-deficit/hyperactivity disorder in adolescents: a systematic review. *Jama, 315*(18), 1997–2008.

Chan, E., Rappaport, L. A., & Kemper, K. J. (2003). Complementary and alternative therapies in childhood attention and hyperactivity problems. *Journal of Development in Behavioral Pediatrics, 24*, 4–8.

Chan, V., Mollayeva, T., Ottenbacher, K. J., & Colantonio, A. (2017). Clinical profile and comorbidity of traumatic brain injury among younger and older men and women: A brief research notes. *BMC Research Notes, 10*(1).

Chana, G., Landau, S., Beasley, C., Everall, I. P., & Cotter, D. (2003). Two-dimensional assessment of cytoarchitecture in the anterior cingulate cortex in major depressive disorder, bipolar disorder, and schizophrenia: Evidence for decreased neuronal somal size and increased neuronal density. *Biological Psychiatry, 53*(12), 1086–1098.

Chanaday, N. L., & Kavalali, E. T. (2017). How do you recognize and reconstitute a synaptic vesicle after fusion? *F1000 Research, 6*, 1734.

Chang, A. K., Bijur, P. E., Esses, D., Barnaby, D. P., & Baer, J. (2017). Effect of a single dose of oral opioid and nonopioid analgesics on acute extremity pain in the emergency department: A randomized clinical trial. *JAMA, 318*(17), 1661–1667.

Chang, A., Li, P. P., & Warsh, J. J. (2003). cAMP-Dependent protein kinase (PKA) subunit mRNA levels in postmortem brain from patients with bipolar affective disorder (BD). *Molecular Brain Research, 116*, 27–37.

Chang, C. C., Fang, W. H., Chang, H. A., Chang, T. C., Shyu, J. F., & Huang, S. Y. (2017). Serotonin 2A receptor (5-HT2A) gene promoter variant interacts with chronic perceived stress to modulate resting parasympathetic activity in humans. *Psychoneuroendocrinology, 76,* 119–126.

Chang, H., Li, W., Li, Q., Chen, J., Zhu, J., Ye, J., et al. (2016). Regional homogeneity changes between heroin relapse and non-relapse patients under methadone maintenance treatment: A resting-state fMRI study. *BMC Neurology, 16*(1), 145.

Chang, L., Alicata, D., Ernst, T., & Volkow, N. (2007). Structural and metabolic brain changes in the striatum associated with methamphetamine abuse. *Addiction, 102*(s1), 16–32.

Chang, M., Womer, F. Y., Edmiston, E. K., Bai, C., Zhou, Q., Jiang, X., et al. (2017). Neurobiological commonalities and distinctions among three major psychiatric diagnostic categories: A structural MRI study. *Schizophrenia Bulletin, 44*(1), 65–74.

Chappell, P. B., Riddle, M. A., Scahill, L., Lynch, K. A., Schultz, R., Arnsten, A., et al. (1995). Guanfacine treatment of comorbid attention-deficit hyperactivity disorder and Tourette's syndrome: Preliminary clinical experience. *Journal of the American Academy of Child and Adolescent Psychiatry, 34,* 1140–1146.

Charach, A., Ickowicz, A., & Schachar, R. (2004). Stimulant treatment over five years: Adherence, effectiveness, and adverse effects. *Journal of the American Academy of Child and Adolescent Psychiatry, 43,* 559–567.

Charnay, Y., Leger, L., Vallet, P. G., Hof, P. R., Jouvet, M., & Bouras, C. (1995). [3H] Nisoxetine binding sites in the cat brain: An autoradiographic study. *Neuroscience, 69,* 259–270.

Charney, D. S. (2003). Neuroanatomical circuits modulating fear and anxiety behaviors. *Acta Psychiatrica Scandinavica, Supplementum,* 38–50.

Checkoway, H., Powers, K., Smith-Weller, T., Franklin, G. M., Longstreth, W. T., Jr., & Swanson, P. D. (2002). Parkinson's disease risks associated with cigarette smoking, alcohol consumption, and caffeine intake. *American Journal of Epidemiology, 155,* 732–738.

Cheetham, A., Allen, N. B., Whittle, S., Simmons, J., Yücel, M., & Lubman, D. I. (2017). Orbitofrontal cortex volume and effortful control as prospective risk factors for substance use disorder in adolescence. *European Addiction Research, 23*(1), 37–44.

Chen, B. T., Hopf, F. W., & Bonci, A. (2010). Synaptic plasticity in the mesolimbic system. *Annals of the New York Academy of Sciences, 1187*(1), 129–139.

Chen, C. C., Lu, R. B., Chen, Y. C., Wang, M. F., Chang, Y. C., Li, T. K., et al. (1999). Interaction between the functional polymorphisms of the alcohol-metabolism genes in protection against alcohol. *American Journal of Human Genetics, 6,* 795–807.

Chen, C. H., Chen, H. I., Liao, H. M., Chen, Y. J., Fang, J. S., Lee, K. F., & Gau, S. S. F. (2017). Clinical and molecular characterization of three genomic rearrangements at chromosome 22q13. 3 associated with autism spectrum disorder. *Psychiatric Genetics, 27*(1), 23–33.

Chen, G., Hasanat, K. A., Bebchuk, J. M., Moore, G. J., Glitz, D., & Manji, H. K. (1999). Regulation of signal transduction pathways and gene expression by mood stabilizers and antidepressants. *Psychosomatic Medicine, 61,* 599–617.

Chen, J., Cao, F., Liu, L., Wang, L., & Chen, X. (2015). Genetic studies of schizophrenia: An update. *Neuroscience Bulletin, 31*(1), 87–98.

Chen, K., Zhang, L., Tan, M., Lai, C. S., Li, A., Ren, C., & So, K. (2017). Treadmill exercise suppressed stress-induced dendritic spine elimination in mouse barrel cortex and improved working memory via BDNF/TrkB pathway. *Translational Psychiatry, 7*(3).

Chen, R. H., Li, Q., Snidal, C. A., Gardezi, S. R., & Stanley, E. F. (2017). The calcium channel C-terminal and synaptic vesicle tethering: Analysis by immuno-nanogold localization. *Frontiers in Cellular Neuroscience, 11.*

Chen, R., Cohen, L. G., & Hallett, M. (2002). Nervous system reorganization following injury. *Neuroscience, 111*(4), 761–773.

Chen, R., Wei, J., Fowler, S. C., & Wu, J. Y. (2003). Demonstration of functional coupling between dopamine synthesis and its packaging into synaptic vesicles. *Journal of Biomedical Science, 10,* 774–781.

Chen, R. H., Li, Q., Snidal, C. A., Gardezi, S. R., & Stanley, E. F. (2017). The calcium channel C-terminal and synaptic vesicle tethering: Analysis by immuno-nanogold localization. *Frontiers in Cellular Neuroscience, 11.*

Chen, S. D., Wu, C. L., Hwang, W. C., & Yang, D. I. (2017). More insight into BDNF against neuro-degeneration: Anti-apoptosis, anti-oxidation, and suppression of autophagy. *International Journal of Molecular Sciences, 18*(3), E545.

Chen, Y., Xu, H., Zhu, M., Liu, K., Lin, B., Luo, R., . . . Li, M. (2017). Stress inhibits tryptophan hydroxylase expression in a rat model of depression. *Oncotarget, 8*(38), 63247.

Chen, Z., & Zhong, C. (2013). Decoding Alzheimer's disease from perturbed cerebral glucose metabolism: Implications for diagnostic and therapeutic strategies. *Progress in Neurobiology, 108*, 21–43.

Cheng, H., Kellar, D., Lake, A., Finn, P., Rebec, G. V., Dharmadhikari, S., . . . Newman, S. (2018). Effects of alcohol cues on MRS glutamate levels in the anterior cingulate. *Alcohol and Alcoholism, 53*(3), 209–215.

Cheng, L., Wang, S., Jia, N., Xie, M., & Liao, X. (2014). Environmental stimulation influence the cognition of developing mice by inducing changes in oxidative and apoptosis status. *Journal of Brain and Development, 36*(1), 51–56.

Cheon, K. A., Ryu, Y. H., Kim, Y. K., Namkoong, K., Kim, C. H., & Lee, J. (2003). Dopamine transporter density in the basal ganglia assessed with [123 I] IPT SPET in children with attention deficit hyperactivity disorder. *European Journal of Nuclear Medicine and Molecular Imaging, 30*(2), 306–311.

Cheon, K. A., Ryu, Y. H., Namkoong, K., Kim, C.-H., Kim, J. J., & Lee, J. D. (2004). Dopamine transporter density of the basal ganglia assessed with [123I]IPT SPECT in drug-naïve children with Tourette's disorder. *Psychiatry Research, 130*, 85–95.

Cherepkova, E. V., Maksimov, V. N., Kushnarev, A. P., Shakhmatov, I. I., & Aftanas, L. I. (2017). The polymorphism of dopamine receptor D4 (DRD4) and dopamine transporter (DAT) genes in the men with antisocial behaviour and mixed martial arts fighters. *The World Journal of Biological Psychiatry*, 1–14.

Cherkasova, M. V., Faridi, N., Casey, K. F., Larcher, K., O'Driscoll, G. A., Hechtman, L., . . . Dagher, A. (2017). Differential associations between cortical thickness and striatal dopamine in treatment-naïve adults with ADHD vs. healthy controls. *Frontiers in Human Neuroscience, 11*, 421.

Cherry, J. D., Olschowka, J. A., & O'Banion, M. (2014). Neuroinflammation and M2 microglia: The good, the bad, and the inflamed. *Journal of Neuroinflammation, 11*(1), 98.

Chih, B., Afridi, S. K., Clark, L., & Scheiffele, P. (2004). Disorder-associated mutations lead to functional inactivation of neuroligins. *Human Molecular Genetics, 13*, 1471–1477.

Chon, M. W., Lee, J., Chung, S., Kim, Y., & Kim, H. W. (2017). Prescription pattern of antidepressants for children and adolescents in Korea based on nationwide data. *Journal of Korean Medical Science, 32*(10), 1694–1701. http://doi.org/10.3346/jkms.2017.32.10.1694

Chintamaneni, M., & Bhaskar, M. (2012). Biomarkers in Alzheimer's disease: A review. *ISRN Pharmacology* (Vol. 2012, 6 pp.). doi:10.5402/2012/984786.

Chow, V. W., Mattson, M. P., Wong, P. C., & Gleichmann, M. (2010). An overview of APP processing enzymes and products. *Neuromolecular Medicine, 12*(1), 1–12.

Chu, R. K., Rosic, T., & Samaan, Z. (2017). Adult ADHD: Questioning diagnosis and treatment in a patient with multiple psychiatric comorbidities. *Case Reports in Psychiatry, 2017*.

Chugani, D. C., Muzik, O., Behen, M., Rothermel, R., Janisse, J. J., Lee, J., et al. (1999). Developmental changes in brain serotonin synthesis capacity in autistic and nonautistic children. *Annals of Neurology, 45*, 287–295.

Chugani, H. T. (1998). Biological basis of emotions: Brain systems and brain development. *Pediatrics, 102*, 1225–1229.

Chugani, H. T., Behen, M. E., Muzik, O., Juhasz, C., Nagy, F., & Chugani, C. D. (2001). Local brain functional activity following early deprivation: A study of postinstitutionalized Romanian orphans. *Neuroimage, 14*, 1290–1301.

Chugani, H., & Phelps, M. (1991). Imaging human brain development with positron emission tomography. *Journal of Nuclear Medicine, 32*, 23–26.

Chung, E. J., Babulal, G. M., Monsell, S. E., Cairns, N. J., Roe, C. M., & Morris, J. C. (2015). Clinical features of Alzheimer disease with and without Lewy bodies. *JAMA Neurology, 72*(7), 789–796.

Chung, T., Martin, C. S., Grella, C. E., Winters, K. C., Abrantes, A. M., & Brown, S. A. (2003). Course of alcohol problems in treated adolescents. *Alcoholism: Clinical and Experimental Research, 27*, 253–261.

Chung, Y., Haut, K. M., He, G., van Erp, T. G., McEwen, S., Addington, J., et al. (2017). Ventricular enlargement and progressive reduction of cortical gray matter are linked in prodromal youth who develop psychosis. *Schizophrenia Research, 189*, 169–174.

Cimpianu, C. L., Strube, W., Falkai, P., Palm, U., & Hasan, A. (2017). Vagus nerve stimulation in psychiatry: A systematic review of the available evidence. *Journal of Neural Transmission, 124*(1), 145–158.

Cipriani, A., Furukawa, T. A., Salanti, G., Chaimani, A., Atkinson, L. Z., Ogawa, Y., et al. (2018). Comparative efficacy and acceptability of 21 antidepressant drugs for the acute treatment of adults with major depressive disorder: A systematic review and network meta-analysis. *The Lancet, 1357–1366.*

Cirmanova, V., Zofkova, I., Kasalicky, P., Lanska, V., Bayer, M., Starka, L., & Kanceva, R. (2017). Hormonal and bone parameters in pubertal girls. *Physiological Research, 66*(4).

Cirstea, C. M., Choi, I. Y., Lee, P., Peng, H., Kaufman, C. L., & Frey, S. H. (2017). Magnetic resonance spectroscopy of current hand amputees reveals evidence for neuronal-level changes in former sensorimotor cortex. *Journal of Neurophysiology, 117*(4), 1821–1830.

Clark, A. B. (2017). Juvenile solitary confinement as a form of child abuse. *The Journal of the American Academy of Psychiatry and the Law, 45*(3), 350–357.

Clark, M. S., & Neumaier, J. F. (2001). The 5-HT1B receptor: Behavioral implications. *Psychopharmacology Bulletin, 35*(4), 170–185.

Clarkson, E. D., & Freed, C. R. (1999). Development of fetal neural transplantation as a treatment for Parkinson's disease. *Life Sciences, 65*, 2427–2437.

Claussen, C., & Dafny, N. (2012). Acute and chronic methylphenidate modulates the neuronal activity of the caudate nucleus recorded from freely behaving rats. *Brain Research Bulletin, 87*(4–5), 387–396.

Claveria, L. E., Duarte, J., Sevillano, M. D., Pérez-Sempere, A., Cabezas, C., Rodriguez, F., et al. (2002). Prevalence of Parkinson's disease in Cantalejo, Spain: A door-to-door survey. *Movement Disorders, 17*, 242–249.

Cleary, D. R., Ozpinar, A., Raslan, A. M., & Ko, A. L. (2015). Deep brain stimulation for psychiatric disorders: Where are we now. *Neurosurgical Focus, 38*(6), e2.

Cleland, C. M., Rosenblum, A., Fong, C., & Maxwell, C. (2011). Age differences in heroin and prescription opioid abuse among enrolees into opioid treatment programs. *Substance Abuse Treatment, Prevention, and Policy, 6*(1), 11.

Cloninger, C. R. (1999). Genetics of substance abuse. In M. Galanter & H. Kleber (Eds.), *Textbook of substance abuse treatment* (2nd ed., pp. 59–66). Washington, DC: American Psychiatric Press, Inc.

Cloninger, R. C. (2003). The discovery of susceptibility genes for mental disorders. *Proceedings of the National Academy of the Sciences, 99*, 13365–13367.

Coccaro, E. F., Siever, L. J., Klar, H. M., Maurer, G., Cochrane, K., Cooper, T. B., et al. (1989). Serotonergic studies in patients with affective and personality disorders: Correlates with suicidal and impulsive aggressive behavior. *Archives of General Psychiatry, 46*, 587–599.

Cochran, S. D., Sullivan, J. G., & Mays, V. M. (2003). Prevalence of mental disorders, psychological distress, and mental health services use among lesbian, gay, and bisexual adults in the United States. *Journal of Consulting and Clinical Psychology, 71*(1), 53–61.

Coelho, R., Rangel, R., Ramos, E., Martins, A., Prata, J., & Barros, H. (2000). Depression and severity of substance abuse. *Psychopathology, 33*, 103–109.

Cohen, D. J., Shaywitz, B. A., Caparulo, B., Young, J. G., & Bowers, M. B. Jr. (1978). Chronic, multiple tics of Gilles de la Tourette's disease. CSF acid monoamine metabolites after probenecid administration. *Archives of General Psychiatry, 35*, 245–250.

Cohen-Woods, S., Craig, I. W., & McGuffin, P. (2013). The current state of play on the molecular genetics of depression. *Psychological Medicine, 43*(4), 673–687.

Coleman, P. D., Romano, J., Lapham, L., & Simon, W. (1985). Cell counts in cerebral cortex of an autistic patient. *Journal of Autism and Developmental Disorders, 15,* 245–255.

Colenda, C. C., Legault, C., Rapp, S. R., DeBon, M. W., Hogan, P., Wallace, R., . . . Sarto, G. E. (2010). Psychiatric disorders and cognitive dysfunction among older, postmenopausal women: Results from the Women's Health Initiative Memory Study. *The American Journal of Geriatric Psychiatry, 18*(2), 177–186.

Colohan, H., O'Callaghan, E., Larkin, C., & Waddington, J. L. (1989). An evaluation of cranial CT scanning in clinical psychiatry. *Irish Journal of Medical Science, 58,* 178–181.

Comer, S. D., Mogali, S., Saccone, P. A., Askalsky, P., Martinez, D., Walker, E. A., et al. (2013). Effects of acute oral naltrexone on the subjective and physiological effects of oral D-amphetamine and smoked cocaine in cocaine abusers. *Neuropsychopharmacology, 38*(12), 2427–2438.

Conceição, V. A., Dias, Â., Farinha, A. C., & Maia, T. V. (2017). Premonitory urges and tics in Tourette syndrome: Computational mechanisms and neural correlates. *Current Opinion in Neurobiology, 46,* 187–199.

Conley, R. R., & Kelly, D. L. (2001). Management of treatment resistance in schizophrenia. *Biological Psychiatry, 50,* 898–911.

Conley, R. R., & Mahmoud, R. (2001). A randomized double-blind study of risperidone and olanzapine in the treatment of schizophenia or schizoaffective disorder. *American Journal of Psychiatry, 158,* 765–774.

Conn, V. S. (2010). Depressive symptom outcomes of physical activity interventions: Meta-analysis findings. *Annals of Behavioral Medicine, 39*(2), 128–138.

Connolly, B. S., & Lang, A. E. (2014). Pharmacological treatment of Parkinson disease: A review. *JAMA, 311*(16), 1670–1683.

Connolly, K. R., & Thase, M. E. (2011). The clinical management of bipolar disorder: A review of evidence-based guidelines. *The Primary Care Companion to CNS Disorders, 13*(4).

Connolly, S. B., Kotseva, K., Jennings, C., Atrey, A., Jones, J., Brown, A., et al. (2017). Outcomes of an integrated community-based nurse-led cardiovascular disease prevention programme. *Heart, 103*(11), 840–847.

Conti, L., Sipione, S., Magrassi, L., Bonfanti, L., Rigamont, D., Pettirossi, V., et al. (2001). Shc signaling in differentiating neural progenitor cells. *Nature Neuroscience, 4,* 579–586.

Converge Consortium. (2015). Sparse whole genome sequencing identifies two loci for major depressive disorder. *Nature, 523*(7562), 588.

Convit, A., de Asis, J., de Leon, M. J., Tarshish, C. Y., De Santi, S., & Rusinek, H. (2000). Atrophy of the medial occipitotemporal, inferior, and middle temporal gyri in non-demented elderly predict decline to Alzheimer's disease. *Neurobiology of Aging, 21,* 19–26.

Convit, A., de Leon, M. J., Hoptman, M. J., Tarshish, C., De Santi, S., & Rusinek, H. (1995). Age-related changes in brain: I. Magnetic resonance imaging measures of temporal lobe volumes in normal subjects. *Psychiatric Quarterly, 66,* 343–355.

Cook, I. A., Leuchter, A. F., Morgan, M., Witte, E., Stubbeman, W. F., Abrams, M., et al. (2002). Early changes in prefrontal activity characterize clinical responders to antidepressants. *Neuropsychopharmacology, 27,* 120–131.

Cooney, G. M., Dwan, K., Greig, C. A., Lawlor, D. A., Waugh, F. R., McMurdo, M., & Mead, G. E. (2013). Exercise for depression. *The Cochrane Database of Systematic Reviews, 12*(9).

Cooper, J. R., Bloom, F. E., & Roth, R. H. (2003). *The biochemical basis of neuropharmacology* (8th ed.). New York: Oxford University Press.

Cop, E., Yurtbasi, P., Oner, O., & Munir, K. M. (2015). Genetic testing in children with autism spectrum disorders. *Anadolu Psikiyatri Dergisi-Anatolian Journal of Psychiatry, 16*(6), 426–432.

Cope, D. N. (1995). The effectiveness of traumatic brain injury rehabilitation: A review. *Brain Injury, 9,* 649–670.

Copeland, J., & Pokorski, I. (2016). Progress toward pharmacotherapies for cannabis-use disorder: An evidence-based review. *Substance Abuse and Rehabilitation, 7,* 41–53.

Coplan, J. D., & Lydiard, R. B. (1998). Brain circuits in panic disorder. *Biological Psychiatry, 44,* 1264–1276.

Cortese, S., Ferrin, M., Brandeis, D., Holtmann, M., Aggensteiner, P., Daley, D., et al. (2016). Neurofeedback for attention-deficit/hyperactivity disorder: Meta-analysis of clinical and neuropsychological outcomes from randomized controlled trials. *Journal of the American Academy of Child & Adolescent Psychiatry, 55*(6), 444–455.

Corti, O., Lesage, S., & Brice, A. (2011). What genetics tells us about the causes and mechanisms of Parkinson's disease. *Physiological Reviews, 91*(4), 1161–1218.

Cosgrove, G. R., & Rauch, S. L. (1995). Psychosurgery. *Neurosurgery Clinics in North America, 6,* 167–176.

Cosgrove, K. P., Tellez-Jacques, K., Pittman, B., Petrakis, I., Baldwin, R. M., Tamagnan, G., et al. (2010). Dopamine and serotonin transporter availability in chronic heroin users: A [123I] β-CIT SPECT imaging study. *Psychiatry Research: Neuroimaging, 184*(3), 192–195.

Cotter, D., Mackay, D., Landau, S., Kerwin, R., & Everall, I. (2001). Reduced glial cell density and neuronal size in the anterior cingulate cortex in major depressive disorder. *Archives of General Psychiatry, 58,* 545–553.

Courchesne, E. (2002). Abnormal early brain development in autism. *Molecular Psychiatry, 7*(S2), S21.

Courchesne, E., Campbell, K., & Solso, S. (2011). Brain growth across the life span in autism: Age-specific changes in anatomical pathology. *Brain Research, 1380,* 138–145.

Courchesne, E., Karns, C. M., Davis, H. R., Ziccardi, R., Carper, R. A., Tigue, Z. D., et al. (2001). Unusual brain growth patterns in early life in patients with autistic disorder: An MRI study. *Neurology, 57,* 245–254.

Courtney, K. E., Schacht, J. P., Hutchison, K., Roche, D. J., & Ray, L. A. (2016). Neural substrates of cue reactivity: Association with treatment outcomes and relapse. *Addiction Biology, 21*(1), 3–22.

Coutin-Churman, P., Anez, Y., Uzcategui, M., Alvarez, L., Vergara, F., Mendez, L., et al. (2003). Quantitative spectral analysis of EEG in psychiatry revisited: Drawing signs out of numbers in a clinical setting. *Clincal Neurophysiology, 114,* 2294–2306.

Cowan, M. W., & Kandel, E. R. (2001). A brief history of synapses and synaptic transmission. In M. W. Cowan, T. C. Sudhof, & C. F. Stevens (Eds.), *Synapses* (pp. 1–88). Baltimore: Johns Hopkins University Press.

Cowan, M. W., Sudhof, T. C., & Stevens, C. F. (2001). *Synapses.* Baltimore: Johns Hopkins University Press.

Cowan, W. M. (1979). The development of the brain. *Scientific American, 241,* 113–133.

Cowen, P. J., & Browning, M. (2015). What has serotonin to do with depression? *World Psychiatry, 14*(2), 158–160.

Cox, B. J., Norton, G. R., Dorward, J., & Fergusson, P. A. (1989). The relationship between panic attacks and chemical dependencies. *Addictive Behaviors, 14,* 53–60.

Coyle, J. T., & Duman, R. S. (2003). Finding the intracellular signaling pathways affected by mood disorder treatments. *Neuron, 38,* 157–160.

Crabbe, J. (2002). Genetic contributions to addiction. *Annual Review of Psychology, 53,* 435–462.

Craddock, N., & Sklar, P. (2013). Genetics of bipolar disorder. *The Lancet, 381*(9878), 1654–1662.

Cragg, B. G. (1975). The density of synapses and neurons in normal, mentally defective and aging human brains. *Brain, 98,* 81–90.

Craig, A. M., & Lichtman, J. W. (2001). Getting a bead on receptor movements. *Nature Neuroscience, 4,* 219–220.

Craig, E. M., Yeung, H. T., Rao, A. N., & Baas, P. W. (2017). Polarity sorting of axonal microtubules: A computational study. *Molecular Biology of the Cell, 28*(23).

Cravchik, A., & Goldman, D. (2000). Neurochemical individuality: Genetic diversity among human dopamine and serotonin receptors and transporters. *Archives of General Psychiatry, 57,* 1105–1114.

Crider, A., Ahmed, A. O., & Pillai, A. (2017). Altered expression of endoplasmic reticulum stress-related genes in the middle frontal cortex of subjects with autism spectrum disorder. *Molecular Neuropsychiatry, 3*(2), 85–91.

Crivelli, D., & Balconi, M. (2017). The agent brain: A review of non-invasive brain stimulation studies on sensing agency. *Frontiers in Behavioral Neuroscience, 11*.

Crocq, M. A. (2015). A history of anxiety: From Hippocrates to DSM. *Dialogues in Clinical Neuroscience, 17*(3), 319–325.

Crowe, M., Andel, R., Pedersen, N. L., Johansson, B., & Gatz, M. (2003). Does participation in leisure activities lead to reduced risk of Alzheimer's disease? A prospective study of Swedish twins. *Journals of Gerontology, 58*, 249–255.

Crum, R. M., & Anthony, J. C. (1993). Cocaine use and other suspected risk factors for obsessive-compulsive disorder: A prospective study with data from the Epidemiologic Catchment Area surveys. *Drug and Alcohol Dependence, 31*, 281–295.

Cruz, D. A., Eggan, S. M., Azmitia, E. C., & Lewis, D. A. (2004). Serotonin1A receptors at the axon segment of prefrontal pyramidal neurons in schizophrenia. *American Journal of Psychiatry, 161*, 739–742.

Cservenka, A., & Brumback, T. (2017). The burden of binge and heavy drinking on the brain: Effects on adolescent and young adult neural structure and function. *Frontiers in Psychology, 8*, 1111.

Cui, L., Gong, X., Tang, Y., Kong, L., Chang, M., Geng, H., et al. (2016). Relationship between the LHPP gene polymorphism and resting-state brain activity in major depressive disorder. *Neural Plasticity* (Vol. 2016, 8 pp), Article ID 9162590.

Cui, L. B., Wang, L. X., Tian, P., Wang, H. N., Cai, M., Guo, F., et al. (2017). Aberrant perfusion and its connectivity within default mode network of first-episode drug-naïve schizophrenia patients and their unaffected first-degree relatives. *Scientific Reports, 7*(1), 16201.

Cummings, D. D., Singer, H. S., Krieger, M., Miller, T. L., & Mahone, E. M. (2002). Neuropsychiatric effects of guanfacine in children with mild Tourette syndrome: A pilot study. *Clinical Neuropharmacology, 25*, 325–332.

Cunningham, C. J., Zaamout, M. E. F., Goodyear, B., & Federico, P. (2008). Simultaneous EEG-fMRI in human epilepsy. *Canadian Journal of Neurological Sciences, 35*(4), 420–435.

Curtis, V. A., Bullmore, E. T., Brammer, M. J., Wright, L. C., Williams, S. C. R., Morris, R. G., et al. (1998). Attenuated frontal activation during verbal fluency in schizophrenia. *American Journal of Psychiatry, 155*, 1056–1063.

Curtiss, S., & Schaeffer, J. (1997). Syntactic development in children with hemispherectomy: The Infl-system. In E. Hughes, M. Hughes, & Greenhill, A. (Eds.), *Proceedings of the 21st Annual Boston University Conference on Language Development* (Vol. 2, pp. 103–114). Somerville, MA: Cascadilla Press.

Cusack, R., McCuaig, O., & Linke, A. C. (2017). Methodological challenges in the comparison of infant fMRI across age groups. *Developmental Cognitive Neuroscience*.

D'Amico, G., Cedro, C., Muscatello, M. R., Pandolfo, G., Di Rosa, A. E., Zoccali, R., et al. (2003). Olanzapine augmentation of paroxetine-refractory obsessive-compulsive disorder. *Progress in Neuro-Psychopharmacology & Biological Psychiatry, 27*, 619–623.

D'Sa, C., & Duman, R. S. (2002). Antidepressants and neuroplasticity. *BiPolar Disorders, 4*, 183–194.

D'Souza, C., Gupta, A., Alldrick, M. D., & Sastry, B. S. (2003). Management of psychosis in Parkinson's disease. *International Journal of Clinical Practice, 57*, 295–300.

Dager, A. D., Anderson, B. M., Rosen, R., Khadka, S., Sawyer, B., Jiantonio-Kelly, R. E., et al. (2014). Functional magnetic resonance imaging (fMRI) response to alcohol pictures predicts subsequent transition to heavy drinking in college students. *Addiction, 109*(4), 585–595.

Dager, S. R., Holland, J. P., Cowley, D. S., & Dunner, D. L. (1997). Panic disorder precipitated by exposure to organic solvents in the work place. *American Journal of Psychiatry, 144*, 1056–1058.

Daglish, M. R., Weinstein, A., Malizia, A. L., Wilson, S., Melichar, J. K., Lingford-Hughes, A., et al. (2003). Functional connectivity analysis of the neural circuits of opiate craving: "More" rather than "different"? *Neuroimage, 20*, 1964–1970.

Dahlstrom, M., Ahonen, A., Ebeling, H., Torniainen, P., Heikkila, J., & Moilanen, I. (2000). Elevated hypothalamic/midbrain serotonin (monoamine) transporter availability in depressive drug-naïve children and adolescents. *Molecular Psychiatry, 5*, 514–522.

Dale, R. C. (2017). Tics and Tourette: A clinical, pathophysiological and etiological review. *Current Opinion in Pediatrics, 29*(6), 665–673.

Damadzic, R., Bigelow, L. B., Krimer, L. S., Goldenson, D. A., Saunders, R. C., Kleinman, J. E., et al. (2001). A quantitative immunohistochemical study of astrocytes in the entorhinal cortex in schizophrenia, bipolar disorder and major depression: Absence of significant astrocytosis. *Brain Research Bulletin, 55*, 611–618.

Damasio, H. C. (1991). Neuroanatomical correlates of the aphasias. In M. T. Sarno (Ed.), *Acquired aphasia* (2nd ed., pp. 45–70). New York: Academic Press.

Danbolt, N., Furness, D., & Zhou, Y. (2016). Neuronal vs glial glutamate uptake: Resolving the conundrum. *Neurochemistry International, 98*, 29–45.

Daniel, D. G., Weinberger, D. R., Jones, D. W., Zigon, J. R., Cippola, R., Handel, S., et al. (1991). The effect of amphetamine on regional cerebral blood flow during cognitive activation in schizophrenia. *Journal of Neuroscience, 11*, 1907–1917.

Danielson, M. L., Visser, S. N., Chronis-Tuscano, A., & DuPaul, G. J. (2018). A national description of treatment among United States children and adolescents with attention-deficit/hyperactivity disorder. *The Journal of Pediatrics, 192*, 240–246.

Daou, M. A. Z., Boyd, B. D., Donahue, M. J., Albert, K., & Taylor, W. D. (2017). Frontocingulate cerebral blood flow and cerebrovascular reactivity associated with antidepressant response in late-life depression. *Journal of Affective Disorders, 215*, 103–110.

Datto, C. J. (2000). Side effects of electroconvulsive therapy. *Depression and Anxiety, 12*, 130–134.

Davidson, R. J., Irwin, W., Anderle, M. J., & Kalin, N. H. (2003). The neural substrates of affective processing in depressed patients treated with venlafaxine. *American Journal of Psychiatry, 160*, 64–75.

Davies, G., Welham, J., Chant, D., Torrey, E. F., & McGrath, J. (2003). A systematic review and meta-analysis of Northern Hemisphere season of birth studies in schizophrenia. *Schizophrenia Bulletin, 29*(3), 587–593.

Davies, J., Lloyd, K. R., Jones, I. K., Barnes, A., & Pilowsky, L. S. (2003). Changes in regional cerebral blood flow with venlafaxine in the treatment of major depression. *American Journal of Psychiatry, 160*, 374–376.

Davies, M. (2002). A few thoughts about the mind, the brain, and a child with early deprivation. *Journal of Analytical Psychology, 47*, 421–435.

Davis, J. M., Chen, N., & Glick, I. D. (2003). A meta-analysis of the efficacy of second-generation antipsychotics. *Archives of General Psychiatry, 60*, 553–564.

Davis, K. L., Kahn, R. S., Ko, G., & Davidson, M. (1991). Dopamine in schizophrenia: A review and reconceptualization. *American Journal of Psychiatry, 148*, 1474–1486.

Dawson, G., Klinger, L. G., Panagiotides, H., Lewy, A., & Castelloe, P. (1995). Subgroups of autistic children based on social behavior display distinct patterns of brain activity. *Journal of Abnormal Child Psychology, 23*, 569–583.

De Bellis, M. D. (2001). Developmental traumatology: The psychobiological development of maltreated children and its implication for research, treatment, and policy. *Development and Psychopathology, 13*, 539–564.

De Bellis, M. D., Clark, D. B., Beers, S. R., Soloff, P. H., Boring, A. M., Hall, J., et al. (2001). Hippocampal volume in adolescent-onset alcohol use disorders. *American Journal of Psychiatry, 157*, 737–744.

De Bellis, M. D., Geracioti, T. D., Altemus, M. Jr., & Kling, M. A. (1993). Cerebrospinal fluid monoamine metabolites in fluoxetine-treated patients with major depression and in healthy volunteers. *Biological Psychiatry, 33*, 636–641.

de Bode, S., & Curtiss, S. (2000). Language after hemispherectomy. *Brain and Cognition, 43*, 135–138.

De Camilli, P., Haucke, V., Takei, K., & Mugnaini, E. (2001). The structure of synapses. In M. W. Cowan, T. C. Sudhof, & C. F. Stevens (Eds.), *Synapses* (pp. 89–133). Baltimore: Johns Hopkins University Press.

De Camilli, P., Slepnev, V. I., Shupliakov, O., & Brodin, L. (2001). Synaptic vesicle endocytosis. In M. W. Cowan, T. C. Sudhof, & C. F. Stevens (Eds.), *Synapses* (pp. 217–274). Baltimore: Johns Hopkins University Press.

De Deyn, P. P., Carrasco, M. M., Deberdt, W., Jeandel, C., Hay, D. P., Feldman, P. D., et al. (2004). Olanzapine versus placebo in the treatment of psychosis with or without associated behavioral disturbances in patients with Alzheimer's disease. *International Journal of Geriatric Psychiatry, 19*, 115–126.

de Faria, Jr., O., Pama, E. A. C., Evans, K., Luzhynskaya, A., & Káradóttir, R. T. (2018). Neuroglial interactions underpinning myelin plasticity. *Developmental Neurobiology, 78*(2), 93–107.

De la Fuente-Fernandez, R., Phillips, A. G., Zamburlini, M., Sossie, V., Calne, D. B., Ruth, T. J., et al. (2002). Dopamine release in human ventral striatum and expectation of reward. *Behavioral Brain Research, 136*, 359–363.

de Medeiros Alves, V., Goncalves Bezerra, D., Gomes de Andrade, T., Leao de Melo Neto, V., & E Nardi, A. (2015). Genetic polymorphisms might predict suicide attempts in mental disorder patients: A systematic review and meta-analysis. *CNS & Neurological Disorders-Drug Targets (Formerly Current Drug Targets-CNS & Neurological Disorders), 14*(7), 820–827.

de San Martin, J. Z., Jalil, A., & Trigo, F. F. (2015). Impact of single-site axonal GABAergic synaptic events on cerebellar interneuron activity. *The Journal of General Physiology, 146*(6), 477–493.

De Virgilio, A., Greco, A., Fabbrini, G., Inghilleri, M., Rizzo, M. I., Gallo, A., et al. (2016). Parkinson's disease: Autoimmunity and neuroinflammation. *Autoimmunity Reviews, 15*(10), 1005–1011.

de Vries, F. E., van den Heuvel, O. A., Cath, D. C., Groenewegen, H. J., van Balkom, A. J., Boellaard, R., et al. (2013). Limbic and motor circuits involved in symmetry behavior in Tourette's syndrome. *CNS Spectrums, 18*(1), 34–42.

Dean, B., Thomas, N., Scarr, E., & Udawela, M. (2016). Evidence for impaired glucose metabolism in the striatum, obtained postmortem, from some subjects with schizophrenia. *Translational Psychiatry, 6*(11), e949.

DeAngelis, T. (2017). Prescription authority: Renewed action in the states. *APA Monitor*, 16–17.

Debes, N., Jeppesen, S., Raghava, J. M., Groth, C., Rostrup, E., & Skov, L. (2015). Longitudinal magnetic resonance imaging (MRI) analysis of the developmental changes of Tourette syndrome reveal reduced diffusion in the cortico-striato-thalamo-cortical pathways. *Journal of Child Neurology, 30*(10), 1315–1326.

Debowska, W., Wolak, T., Nowicka, A., Kozak, A., Szwed, M., & Kossut, M. (2016). Functional and structural neuroplasticity induced by short-term tactile training based on braille reading. *Frontiers in Neuroscience, 10*.

Deckert, J., Nöthen, M. M., Franke, P., Delmo, C., Fritze, J., Knapp, M., . . . Propping, P. (1998). Systematic mutation screening and association study of the A 1 and A 2a adenosine receptor genes in panic disorder suggest a contribution of the A 2a gene to the development of disease. *Molecular Psychiatry, 3*(1), 81.

Dehaene, S. (2013, May). Inside the letterbox: How literacy transforms the human brain. In *Cerebrum: The Dana forum on brain science* (Vol. 2013). New York, NY: Dana Foundation.

Dekaban, A. S. (1978). Changes in brain weights during the span of human life: Relation of brain weights to body heights and body weights. *Annals of Neurology, 4*, 345–356.

Delate, T., Gelenberg, A. J., Simmons, V. A., & Motheral, B. R. (2004). Trends in the use of antidepressants in a national sample of commercially insured pediatric patients, 1998 to 2002. *Psychiatric Services, 55*, 387–391.

Del Bene, V. A., Foxe, J. J., Ross, L. A., Krakowski, M. I., Czobor, P., & De Sanctis, P. (2016). Neuroanatomical abnormalities in violent individuals with and without a diagnosis of schizophrenia. *PLoS One*, *11*(12), e0168100.

Del Casale, A., Serata, D., Rapinesi, C., D Kotzalidis, G., Angeletti, G., Tatarelli, R., et al. (2013). Structural neuroimaging in patients with panic disorder: Findings and limitations of recent studies. *Psychiatria Danubina*, *25*(2), 108–114.

del Mar Capella, M., & Adan, A. (2017). The age of onset of substance use is related to the coping strategies to deal with treatment in men with substance use disorder. *Peer J*, *5*, e3660.

del Pino-Gutiérrez, A., Jiménez-Murcia, S., Fernández-Aranda, F., Agüera, Z., Granero, R., Hakansson, A., et al. (2017). The relevance of personality traits in impulsivity-related disorders: From substance use disorders and gambling disorder to bulimia nervosa. *Journal of Behavioral Addictions*, *6*(3), 396–405.

Delgado, P. L. (2000). Depression: The case for a monoamine deficiency. *Journal of Clinical Psychiatry*, *61*, 7–11.

Delgado, P. L., Price, L. H., Miller, H. L., Salomon, R. M., Aghajanian, G. K., Heninger, G. R., et al. (1991). Serotonin and the neurobiology of depression: Effects of tryptophan depletion in drug-free depressed patients. *Archives of General Psychiatry*, *51*, 865–874.

Delorme, R., Moreno-De-Luca, D., Gennetier, A., Maier, W., Chaste, P., Mössner, R., et al. (2010). Search for copy number variants in chromosomes 15q11-q13 and 22q11. 2 in obsessive compulsive disorder. *BMC Medical Genetics*, *11*(1), 100.

Delsing, B. J., Catsman-Berrevoets, C. E., & Appel, I. M. (2001). Early prognostic indicators of outcome in ischemic childhood stroke. *Pediatric Neurology*, *24*, 283–289.

Demenescu, L. R., Kortekaas, R., Cremers, H. R., Renken, R. J., van Tol, M. J., van der Wee, N. J. A., et al. (2013). Amygdala activation and its functional connectivity during perception of emotional faces in social phobia and panic disorder. *Journal of Psychiatric Research*, *47*(8), 1024–1031.

Demers, C. H., Bogdan, R., & Agrawal, A. (2014). The genetics, neurogenetics and pharmacogenetics of addiction. *Current Behavioral Neuroscience Reports*, *1*(1), 33–44.

Deming, Y., Li, Z., Kapoor, M., Harari, O., Del-Aguila, J. L., Black, K., et al. (2017). Genome-wide association study identifies four novel loci associated with Alzheimer's endophenotypes and disease modifiers. *Acta Neuropathologica*, *133*(5), 839–856.

Demirel, Ö. F., Cetin, I., Turan, Ş., Yıldız, N., Sağlam, T., & Duran, A. (2017). Total tau and phosphorylated tau protein serum levels in patients with schizophrenia compared with controls. *Psychiatric Quarterly*, *88*(4), 921–928.

Den Boer, J. A., & Westenberg, H. G. (1990). Serotonin function in panic disorder: A double blind placebo controlled study with fluvoxamine and ritanserin. *Psychopharmacology*, *102*, 85–94.

Deng, H., Wang, P., & Jankovic, J. (2018). The genetics of Parkinson disease. *Ageing Research Reviews*, *42*, 72–85.

Denys, D., de Vries, F., Cath, D., Figee, M., Vulink, N., Veltman, D. J., et al. (2013). Dopaminergic activity in Tourette syndrome and obsessive-compulsive disorder. *European Neuropsychopharmacology*, *23*(11), 1423–1431.

Derbyshire, S. W., Vogt, B. A., & Jones, A. K. (1998). Pain and stroop intereference tasks activate separate processing modules in anterior cingulate cortex. *Experimental Brain Research*, *118*, 52–60.

Descarries, L., & Riad, M. (2012). Effects of the antidepressant fluoxetine on the subcellular localization of 5-HT1A receptors and SERT. *Philosophical Transactions of the Royal Society of London B: Biological Sciences*, *367*(1601), 2416–2425.

Desmidt, T., Brizard, B., Dujardin, P. A., Ternifi, R., Réméniéras, J. P., Patat, F., et al. (2017). Brain tissue pulsatility is increased in mid-life depression: A comparative study using ultrasound tissue pulsatility imaging. *Neuropsychopharmacology* (Vol. 42, pp. 2575–2582).

Detera-Wadleigh, S. D., Badner, J. A., Berrettini, W. H., Yoshikawa, T., Goldin, L. R., Turner, G., et al. (1999). A high-density genome scan detects evidence for a bipolar-disorder susceptibility locus on 13q32 and other potential loci on 1q32 and 18p11.2. *Proclamations of the National Academy of Science, U.S.A., 96,* 5604–5609.

Detoledo-Morrell, L., Sullivan, M. P., Morrell, F., Wilson, R. S., Bennett, D. A., & Spencer, S. (1997). Alzheimer's disease: In vivo detection of differential vulnerability of brain regions. *Neurobiology of Aging, 18,* 463–468.

Devi, G., Ottman, R., Tang, M. X., Marder, K., Stern, Y., & Mayeux, R. (2000). Familial aggregation of Alzheimer disease among whites, African Americans, and Caribbean Hispanics in northern Manhattan. *Archives of Neurology, 57,* 72–77.

Dhossche, D., Ferdinand, R., van Der Ende, J., Hofstra, M. B., & Verhulst, F. (2002). Diagnostic outcome of self-reported hallucinations in a community sample of adolescents. *Psychological Medicine, 32,* 619–627.

Di Chiara, G. (1999). Drug addiction as dopamine-dependent associative learning disorder. *European Journal of Pharmacology, 375,* 13–30.

Di Chiara, G., & Bassareo, V. (2007). Reward system and addiction: What dopamine does and doesn't do. *Current Opinion in Pharmacology, 7*(1), 69–76.

Di Ciano, P., & Everitt, B. J. (2003). The GABA(B) receptor agonist baclofen attenuates cocaine- and heroin-seeking behavior by rats. *Neuropsychopharmacology, 28,* 510–518.

Di Martino, A., Yan, C. G., Li, Q., Denio, E., Castellanos, F. X., Alaerts, K., et al. (2014). The autism brain imaging data exchange: Towards a large-scale evaluation of the intrinsic brain architecture in autism. *Molecular Psychiatry, 19*(6), 659.

Di Paola, M., Luders, E., Rubino, I. A., Siracusano, A., Manfredi, G., Girardi, P., et al. (2013). The structure of the corpus callosum in obsessive compulsive disorder. *European Psychiatry, 28*(8), 499–506.

Diamond, M. C., & Hopson, J. (1998). *Magic trees of the mind: How to nurture your child's intelligence, creativity, and healthy emotions from birth through adolescence.* New York: Dutton.

Diamond, M. C., Scheibel, A. B., Murphy, J. G. M., & Harvey, T. (1985). On the brain of a scientist: Albert Einstein. *Experimental Neurology, 88,* 198–204.

Dick, F. D., De Palma, G., Ahmadi, A., Scott, N. W., Prescott, G. J., Bennett, J., et al. (2007). Environmental risk factors for Parkinson's disease and parkinsonism: The Geoparkinson study. *Occupational and Environmental Medicine, 64*(10), 666–672.

Diaz Heijtz, R., Kolb, B., & Forssberg, H. (2003). Can a therapeutic dose of amphetamine during pre-adolescence modify the pattern of synaptic organization in the brain? *European Journal of Neuroscience, 18*(12), 3394–3399.

Dickenson, A. H. (2001). Amino acids: Excitatory. In R. A. Webster (Ed.), *Neurotransmitters, drugs, and brain function* (pp. 211–223). New York: Wiley.

Dickey, B., Normand, S. L. T., Hermann, R. C., Eisen, S. V., Cortés, D. E., Cleary, P. D., & Ware, N. (2003). Guideline recommendations for treatment of schizophrenia: The impact of managed care. *Archives of General Psychiatry, 60*(4), 340–348.

Dierckx, B., Heijnen, W. T., van den Broek, W. W., & Birkenhäger, T. K. (2012). Efficacy of electroconvulsive therapy in bipolar versus unipolar major depression: A meta-analysis. *Bipolar Disorders, 14*(2), 146–150.

Dietrich, M. O., Andrews, Z. B., & Horvath, T. L. (2008). Exercise-induced synaptogenesis in the hippocampus is dependent on UCP2-regulated mitochondrial adaptation. *Journal of Neuroscience, 28*(42), 10766–10771.

Dietsche, B., Kircher, T., & Falkenberg, I. (2017). Structural brain changes in schizophrenia at different stages of the illness: A selective review of longitudinal magnetic resonance imaging studies. *Australian & New Zealand Journal of Psychiatry, 51*(5), 500–508.

Dik, M. G., Jonker, C., Hack, C. E., Smit, J. H., Comijs, H. C., & Eikelenboom, P. (2005). Serum inflammatory proteins and cognitive decline in older persons. *Neurology, 64*(8), 1371–1377.

Diler, R. S., Kibar, M., & Avci, A. (2004). Pharmacotherapy and regional cerebral blood flow in children with obsessive compulsive disorder. *Yonsei Medical Journal, 29,* 90–99.

Dion, Y., Annable, L., Sandor, P., & Chouinard, G. (2002). Risperidone in the treatment of tourette syndrome: A double-blind, placebo-controlled trial. *Journal of Clinical Psychopharmacology, 22*, 31–39.

Direk, N., Williams, S., Smith, J. A., Ripke, S., Air, T., Amare, A. T., et al. (2017). An analysis of two genome-wide association meta-analyses identifies a new locus for broad depression phenotype. *Biological Psychiatry, 82*(5), 322–329.

Dirnberger, G., & Jahanshahi, M. (2013). Executive dysfunction in Parkinson's disease: A review. *Journal of Neuropsychology, 7*(2), 193–224.

Di Tommaso, M. C. (2012). A comparative study of bipolar disorder and attention deficit hyperactivity disorder through the measurement of regional cerebral blood flow. *Journal of Biological Regulators and Homeostatic Agents, 26*(1), 1–6.

do Rosario-Campos, M. C., Leckman, J. F., Curi, M., Quatrano, S., Katsovitch, L., Miguel, E. C., & Pauls, D. L. (2005). A family study of early-onset obsessive-compulsive disorder. *American Journal of Medical Genetics Part B: Neuropsychiatric Genetics, 136*(1), 92–97.

Do, K. Q., Benz, B., Binns, K. E., Eaton, S. A., & Salt, T. E. (2004). Release of homocysteic acid from rat thalamus following stimulation of somatosensory afferents in vivo: Feasibilitiy of glial participation in synaptic transmission. *Neuroscience, 124*, 387–393.

Dobkin, B. H. (2003). *The clinical science of neurologic rehabilitation* (2nd ed.). New York: Oxford University Press.

Doenyas, C. (2018). Gut microbiota, inflammation, and probiotics on neural development in autism spectrum disorder. *Neuroscience*, 271–286.

Domschke, K., Deckert, J., O'Donovan, M. C., & Glatt, S. J. (2007). Meta-analysis of COMT val-158met in panic disorder: Ethnic heterogeneity and gender specificity. *American Journal of Medical Genetics Part B: Neuropsychiatric Genetics, 144*(5), 667–673.

Domschke, K., Freitag, C. M., Kuhlenbumer, G., Schirmacher, A., Sand, P., Nyhuis, P., et al. (2004). Association of the functional V158M catechol-O-methyl-transferase polymorphism with panic disorder in women. *International Journal of Neuropsychopharmacology, 7*, 183–188.

Domschke, K., Ohrmann, P., Braun, M., Suslow, T., Bauer, J., Hohoff, C., . . . Deckert, J. (2008). Influence of the catechol-O-methyltransferase val158met genotype on amygdala and prefrontal cortex emotional processing in panic disorder. *Psychiatry Research: Neuroimaging, 163*(1), 13–20.

Domschke, K., Stevens, S., Pfleiderer, B., & Gerlach, A. L. (2010). Interoceptive sensitivity in anxiety and anxiety disorders: An overview and integration of neurobiological findings. *Clinical Psychology Review, 30*(1), 1–11.

Donaldson, L. F., & Lumb, B. M. (2017). Top-down control of pain. *The Journal of Physiology, 595*(13), 4139–4140.

Dondé, C., Amad, A., Nieto, I., Brunoni, A. R., Neufeld, N. H., Bellivier, F., et al. (2017). Transcranial direct-current stimulation (tDCS) for bipolar depression: A systematic review and meta-analysis. *Progress in Neuro-Psychopharmacology and Biological Psychiatry, 78*, 123–131.

Dorpat, T. L. (1971). Phantom sensations of internal organs. *Comprehensive Psychiatry, 12*(1), 27–35.

dos Santos-Ribeiro, S., Lins-Martins, N. M., Frydman, I., do Rosário, M. C., Ferrão, Y. A., Shavitt, R. G., et al. (2016). Prevalence and correlates of electroconvulsive therapy delivery in 1001 obsessive-compulsive disorder outpatients. *Psychiatry Research, 239*, 145–148.

Dos Santos, M., Cahill, E. N., Dal Bo, G., Vanhoutte, P., Caboche, J., Giros, B., & Heck, N. (2018). Cocaine increases dopaminergic connectivity in the nucleus accumbens. *Brain Structure and Function, 223*(2), 913–923.

dos Santos-Ribeiro, S., Lins-Martins, N. M., Frydman, I., do Rosário, M. C., Ferrão, Y. A., Shavitt, R. G., et al. (2016). Prevalence and correlates of electroconvulsive therapy delivery in 1001 obsessive-compulsive disorder outpatients. *Psychiatry Research, 239*, 145–148.

Dostrovsky, J. O., Levy, R., Wu, J. P., Hutchison, W. D., Tasker, R. R., & Lozano, A. M. (2000). Microstimulationinduced inhibition of firing in human globus pallidus. *Journal of Neurophysiology, 84*, 570–574.

Dougherty, D. D., Baer, L., Cosgrove, G. R., Cassem, E. H., Price, B. H., Nierenberg, A. A., et al. (2002). Prospective long-term follow-up of 44 patients who received cingulotomy for treatment-refractory obsessive-compulsive disorder. *American Journal of Psychiatry, 159*, 269–275.

Doussoulin, A., Arancibia, M., Saiz, J., Silva, A., Luengo, M., & Salazar, A. P. (2017). Recovering functional independence after a stroke through Modified Constraint-Induced Therapy. *NeuroRehabilitation, 40*(2), 243–249.

Dowd, R. S., Pourfar, M., & Mogilner, A. Y. (2018). Deep brain stimulation for Tourette syndrome: A single-center series. *Journal of Neurosurgery, 128*(2), 596–604.

Doyle, A., & Pollack, M. H. (2004). Long-term management of panic disorder. *Journal of Clinical Psychiatry, 65, Supplement 5*, 24–28.

Drake, R. G., Davis, L. L., Cates, M. E., Jewell, M. E., Ambrose, S. M., & Lowe, J. S. (2003). Baclofen treatment for chronic posttraumatic stress disorder. *Annals of Pharmacotherapy, 37*, 1177–1181.

Draper, A., Jackson, G. M., Morgan, P. S., & Jackson, S. R. (2016). Premonitory urges are associated with decreased grey matter thickness within the insula and sensorimotor cortex in young people with Tourette syndrome. *Journal of Neuropsychology, 10*(1), 143–153.

Dresler, T., Guhn, A., Tupak, S. V., Ehlis, A. C., Herrmann, M. J., Fallgatter, A. J., Deckert, J., & Domschke, K. (2013). Revise the revised? New dimensions of the neuroanatomical hypothesis of panic disorder. *J Neural Transm (Vienna), 120*, 3–29.

Drevets, W. C., Frank, E., Price, J. C., Kupfer, D. J., Greer, P. J., & Mathis, C. (2000). Serotonin type-1A receptor imaging in depression. *Nuclear Medicine and Biology, 27*, 499–507.

Drevets, W. C., Oengur, D., & Price, J. L. (1998). Reduced glucose metabolism in the subgenual prefrontal cortex in unipolar depression. *Molecular Psychiatry, 3*, 190–191.

Drevets, W. C., Price, J. L., Simpson, J. R., Todd, R. D., Reich, T., Vannier, M., et al. (1997). Subgenual prefrontal cortex abnormalities in mood disorders. *Nature, 386*, 824–827.

Drevets, W. C., Thase, M. E., Moses-Kolko, E. L., Price, J., Frank, E., Kupfer, D. J., & Mathis, C. (2007). Serotonin-1A receptor imaging in recurrent depression: Replication and literature review. *Nuclear Medicine and Biology, 34*(7), 865–877.

Du, X., Wang, X., & Geng, M. (2018). Alzheimer's disease hypothesis and related therapies. *Translational Neurodegeneration, 7*(1), 2.

Dubol, M., Trichard, C., Leroy, C., Sandu, A., Rahim, M., Granger, B., et al. (2017). Dopamine transporter and reward anticipation in a dimensional perspective: A multimodal brain imaging study. *Journal of Neuropsychopharmacology, 43*, 820–827.

Ducasse, D., Boyer, L., Michel, P., Loundou, A., Macgregor, A., Micoulaud-Franchi, J. A., et al. (2014). D2 and D3 dopamine receptor affinity predicts effectiveness of antipsychotic drugs in obsessive-compulsive disorders: A metaregression analysis. *Psychopharmacology, 231*(18), 3765–3770.

Ducci, F., & Goldman, D. (2012). The genetic basis of addictive disorders. *Psychiatric Clinics, 35*(2), 495–519.

Dujardin, K., Blairy, S., Defebvre, L., Duhem, S., Noël, Y., Hess, U., et al. (2004). Deficits in decoding emotional facial expressions in Parkinson's disease. *Neuropsychologia, 42*, 239–250.

Duke, P. J., Pantelis, C., McPhillips, M. A., & Barnes, T. R. E. (2001). Comorbid non-alcohol substance misuse among people with schizophrenia. *British Journal of Psychiatry, 179*, 509–513.

Duman, R. S., Heninger, G. R., & Nestler, E. J. (1997). A molecular and cellular theory of depression. *Archives of General Psychiatry, 54*, 597–606.

Duman, R. S., & Voleti, B. (2012). Signaling pathways underlying the pathophysiology and treatment of depression: Novel mechanisms for rapid-acting agents. *Trends in Neurosciences, 35*(1), 47–56.

DuPaul, G. J., & Weyandt, L. L. (2006). School-based intervention for children with attention deficit hyperactivity disorder: Effects on academic, social, and behavioural functioning. *International Journal of Disability, Development and Education, 53*(2), 161–176.

Dupaul, G. J., Weyandt, L. L., Rossi, J. S., Vilardo, B. A., O'Dell, S. M., Carson, K. M., et al. (2011). Double-blind, placebo-controlled, crossover study of the efficacy and safety of lisdexamfetamine dimesylate in college students with ADHD. *Journal of Attention Disorders, 16*(3), 202–220.

Durston, S., Hulshoff, H. E., Casey, B. J., Gieed, J. N., Buitelaar, J. K., & van Engeland, H. (2001). Anatomical MRI of the developing human brain: What have we learned? *Journal of the American Academy of Child and Adolescent Psychiatry, 40*, 1012–1020.

Durston, S., Pol, H. E. H., Schnack, H. G., Buitelaar, J. K., Steenhuis, M. P., Minderaa, R. B., & Kahn, R. S. (2004). Magnetic resonance imaging of boys with attention-deficit/hyperactivity disorder and their unaffected siblings. *Journal of the American Academy of Child & Adolescent Psychiatry, 43*(3), 332–340.

Durston, S., Tottenham, N. T., Thomas, K. M., Davidson, M. C., Eigsti, I. M., Yang, Y., . . . & Casey, B. J. (2003). Differential patterns of striatal activation in young children with and without ADHD. *Biological Psychiatry, 53*(10), 871–878.

Dursun, S. M., & Reveley, M. A. (1997). Differential effects of transdermal nicotine on microstructured analyses of tics in Tourette's syndrome: An open study. *Psychological Medicine, 27*, 483–487.

Dursun, S., Reveley, M., Bird, R., & Stirton, F. (1994). Longlasting improvement of Tourette's syndrome with transdermal nicotine. *The Lancet, 344*(8936), 1577.

Dussault, C. L., & Weyandt, L. L. (2013). An examination of prescription stimulant misuse and psychological variables among sorority and fraternity college populations. *Journal of Attention Disorders, 17*(2), 87–97.

Duthie, A., Chew, D., & Soiza, R. L. (2011). Non-psychiatric comorbidity associated with Alzheimer's disease. *QJM: An International Journal of Medicine, 104*(11), 913–920.

Dutra, S. J., Man, V., Kober, H., Cunningham, W. A., & Gruber, J. (2017). Disrupted cortico-limbic connectivity during reward processing in remitted bipolar I disorder. *Bipolar Disorders, 19*(8), 661–675.

Dykens, E. M., Lee, E., & Roof, E. (2011). Prader–Willi syndrome and autism spectrum disorders: An evolving story. *Journal of Neurodevelopmental Disorders, 3*(3), 225–237.

Dykman, K. D., & Dykman, R. A. (1998). Effects of nutritional supplements on attention-deficit hyperactivity disorder. *Integration of Physiology and Behavioral Science, 33*, 49–60.

Eapen, V., Snedden, C., Črnčec, R., Pick, A., & Sachdev, P. (2016). Tourette syndrome, comorbidities and quality of life. *Australian & New Zealand Journal of Psychiatry, 50*(1), 82–93.

Ebersbach, G., Sojer, M, Müller, J., Heijmenberg, M., & Poewe, W. (2000). Sociocultural differences in gait. *Movement Disorders, 15*, 1145–1147.

Ebneth, A., Godemann, R., Stamer, K., Illenberger, S., Trinczek, B., Mandelkow, E. M., et al. (1998). Overexpression of tau protein inhibits kinesin-dependent trafficking of vesicles, mitochondria, and endoplasmic reticulum: Implications for Alzheimer's disease. *Journal of Cell Biology, 143*, 777–794.

ECT Review Group. (2003). Efficacy and safety of electroconvulsive therapy in depressive disorders: A systematic review and meta-analysis. (2003). *The Lancet, 361*(9360): 799–808.

Edwards, A. C., Bacanu, S. A., Bigdeli, T. B., Moscati, A., & Kendler, K. S. (2016). Evaluating the dopamine hypothesis of schizophrenia in a large-scale genome-wide association study. *Schizophrenia Research, 176*(2), 136–140.

Edwards, J. G., & Anderson, I. (1999). Systematic review and guide to selection of selective serotonin reuptake inhibitors. *Drugs, 57*, 507–533.

Egan, M. F., Weinberger, D. R., & Lu, B. (2003). Brain-derived neurotropic factor and genetic risk. *American Journal of Psychiatry, 160*, 1242.

Egeland, J. A., Gerhard, D. S., Pauls, D. L., Sussex, J. N., Kidd, K. K., Allen, C. R., et al. (1987). Bipolar affective disorders linked to DNA markers on chromosome 11. *Nature, 325*, 783–787.

Eggers, A. E. (2014). Treatment of depression with deep brain stimulation works by altering in specific ways the conscious perception of the core symptoms of sadness or anhedonia, not by modulating network circuitry. *Medical Hypotheses, 83*(1), 62–64.

Ehrlich, A., Schubert, F., Pehrs, C., & Gallinat, J. (2015). Alterations of cerebral glutamate in the euthymic state of patients with bipolar disorder. *Psychiatry Research: Neuroimaging, 233*(2), 73–80.

Eidelberg, D., Moeller, J. R., Antonini, A., Kazumata, K., Dhawan, V., Budman, C., et al. (1997). The metabolic anatomy of Tourette's syndrome. *Neurology, 48,* 927–934.

Eiler II, W. J., Dzemidzic, M., Soeurt, C. M., Carron, C. R., Oberlin, B. G., Considine, R. V., et al. (2017). Family history of alcoholism and the human brain response to oral sucrose. *NeuroImage: Clinical, 17,* 1036–1046.

Eiler II, W. J., Dzemidzic, M., Soeurt, C. M., Carron, C. R., Oberlin, B. G., Considine, R. V., et al. (2018). Family history of alcoholism and the human brain response to oral sucrose. *NeuroImage: Clinical, 17,* 1036–1046.

Eissenberg, T. (2004). Measuring the emergence of tobacco dependence: The contribution of negative reinforcement models. *Addiction, 99*(s1), 5–29.

Eklund, A., Nichols, T. E., & Knutsson, H. (2016). Cluster failure: Why fMRI inferences for spatial extent have inflated false-positive rates. *Proceedings of the National Academy of Sciences, 113*(28), 7900–7905.

El-Mallakh, R. S., Peters, C., & Waltrip, C. (2000). Antidepressant treatment and neural plasticity. *Journal of Child and Adolescent Psychopharmacology, 10,* 287–294.

Elbert, T., Pantev, C., Wienbruch, C., Rockstroh, B., & Taub, E. (1995). Increased cortical representation of the fingers of the left hand in string players. *Science, 270,* 305–307.

Elder, G. J., & Taylor, J. P. (2014). Transcranial magnetic stimulation and transcranial direct current stimulation: Treatments for cognitive and neuropsychiatric symptoms in the neurodegenerative dementias? *Alzheimer's Research & Therapy, 6*(5), 74.

Eliwa, H., Belzung, C., & Surget, A. (2017). Adult hippocampal neurogenesis: Is it the alpha and omega of antidepressant action? *Biochemical Pharmacology, 141,* 86–99.

Elkis, H., Friedman, L., Wise, A., & Meltzer, H. Y. (1995). Meta-analyses of studies of ventricular enlargement and cortical sulcal prominence in mood disorders: Comparisons with controls or patients with schizophrenia. *Archives of General Psychiatry, 52,* 735–746.

Elliott, A. J., & Roy-Byrne, P. P. (1998). Major depressive disorder and HIV-1 infection: A review of treatment trials. *Seminars in Clinical Neuropsychiatry, 3,* 137–150.

Elmquist, D. L., Morgan, D. P., & Bolds, P. K. (1992). Alcohol and other drug use among adolescents with disabilities. *International Journal of the Addictions, 27*(12), 1475–1483.

Emslie, G. J., Wells, T. G., Prakash, A., Zhang, Q., Pangallo, B. A., Bangs, M. E., & March, J. S. (2015). Acute and longer-term safety results from a pooled analysis of duloxetine studies for the treatment of children and adolescents with major depressive disorder. *Journal of Child and Adolescent Psychopharmacology, 25*(4), 293–305.

Eng, G. K., Sim, K., & Chen, S. H. A. (2015). Meta-analytic investigations of structural grey matter, executive domain-related functional activations, and white matter diffusivity in obsessive compulsive disorder: An integrative review. *Neuroscience & Biobehavioral Reviews, 52,* 233–257.

Engineer, C. T., Hays, S. A., & Kilgard, M. P. (2017). Vagus nerve stimulation as a potential adjuvant to behavioral therapy for autism and other neurodevelopmental disorders. *Journal of Neurodevelopmental Disorders, 9*(1), 20.

Enoch, R. J., & Goldman, D. (2001). The genetics of alcoholism and alcohol abuse. *Current Psychiatric Reports, 3,* 144–151.

Epstein, C. M., Lah, J. J., Meador, K., Weissman, J. D., Gaitan, L. E., & Dihenia, B. (1996). Optimum stimulus parameters for lateralized suppression of speech with magnetic brain stimulation. *Neurology, 47,* 1590–1593.

Erb, S. J., Schappi, J. M., & Rasenick, M. M. (2016). Antidepressants accumulate in lipid rafts independent of monoamine transporters to modulate redistribution of the G protein, Gas. *Journal of Biological Chemistry, 291*(38), 19725–19733.

Erberich, S. G., Friedlich, P., Seri, I., Nelson, M. D., & Bluml, S. (2003). Functional MRI in neonates using neonatal head coil and MR compatible incubator. *Neuroimaging, 20,* 683–692.

Eriksson, P., Perfilieva, E., Bjork-Eriksson, T., Albom, A. M., Nordborg, C., Peterson, D. A., et al. (1998). Neurogenesis in the adult human hippocampus. *Nature Medicine, 4,* 1313–1317.

Ernst, M., Kimes, A. S., London, E. D., Matochik, J. A., Eldreth, D., Tata, S., . . . Bolla, K. (2003). Neural substrates of decision making in adults with attention deficit hyperactivity disorder. *American Journal of Psychiatry, 160*(6), 1061–1070.

Ernst, M., Zametkin, A. J., Matochik, J. A., Jons, P. H., & Cohen, R. M. (1998). DOPA decarboxylase activity in attention deficit hyperactivity disorder adults: A [fluorine-18] fluorodopa positron emission tomographic study. *Journal of Neuroscience, 18*(15), 5901–5907.

Ernst, M., Zmetkin, A. J., Jons, P. H., Matochik, J. A., Pascualvaca, D., & Cohen, R. M. (1999). High presynaptic dopaminergic activity in children with Tourette's disorder. *Journal of the American Academy of Child and Adolescent Psychiatry, 38*, 86–94.

Ernst, T., Chang, L., Oropilla, G., Gustavson, S., & Speck, O. (2000). Cerebral perfusion abnormalities in abstinent cocaine abusers: A perfusion MRI and SPECT study. *Psychiatry Research, 99*, 63–74.

Erro, R., Brigo, F., Tamburin, S., Zamboni, M., Antonini, A., & Tinazzi, M. (2017). Nutritional habits, risk, and progression of Parkinson disease. *Journal of Neurology*, 12–23.

Escher, S., Romme, M., Buiks, A., Delespaul, P., & Van Os, J. I. M. (2002). Independent course of childhood auditory hallucinations: A sequential 3-year follow-up study. *The British Journal of Psychiatry, 181*(43), s10–s18.

Eser, D., Leicht, G., Lutz, J., Wenninger, S., Kirsch, V., Schüle, C., et al. (2009). Functional neuroanatomy of CCK-4-induced panic attacks in healthy volunteers. *Human Brain Mapping, 30*(2), 511–522.

Eskandar, E. N., Flaherty, A., Cosgrove, G. R., Shinobu, L. A., & Barker, F. G. (2003). Surgery for Parkinson's disease in the United States, 1996 to 2000: Practice patterns, short-term outcomes, and hospital charges in a nationwide sample. *Journal of Neurosurgery, 99*, 863–871.

Esler, M., Lambert, E., Alvarenga, M., Socratous, F., Richards, J., Esler, M., et al. (2007). Increased brain serotonin turnover in panic disorder patients in the absence of a panic attack: Reduction by a selective serotonin reuptake inhibitor. *Stress, 10*(3), 295–304.

Etain, B., Lajnef, M., Henrion, A., Dargél, A. A., Stertz, L., Kapczinski, F., et al. (2015). Interaction between SLC6A4 promoter variants and childhood trauma on the age at onset of bipolar disorders. *Scientific Reports, 5*.

Euba, R. (2012). Electroconvulsive therapy and ethnicity. *The Journal of ECT, 28*(1), 24–26.

Eum, S., Lee, A. M., & Bishop, J. R. (2016). Pharmacogenetic tests for antipsychotic medications: Clinical implications and considerations. *Dialogues in Clinical Neuroscience, 18*(3), 323–337.

Eustache, F., Piolino, P., Giffard, B., Viader, F., Sayette Vde, L., Baron, J. C., et al. (2004). "In the course of time": A PET study of the cerebral substrates of autobiographical amnesia in Alzheimer's disease. *Brain, 127*, 1549–1560.

Evans, R. M., Emsley, C. L., Gao, S., Sahota, A., Hall, K. S., Farlow, M. R., et al. (2000). Serum cholesterol, *APOE* genotype, and the risk of Alzheimer's disease: A population-based study of African Americans. *Neurology, 54*, 240–242.

Evans, S. C., Reed, G. M., Roberts, M. C., Esparza, P., Watts, A. D., Correia, J. M., et al S. (2013). Psychologists' perspectives on the diagnostic classification of mental disorders: Results from the WHO-IUPsyS Global Survey. *International Journal of Psychology, 48*(3), 177–193.

Evensen, S., Wisløff, T., Lystad, J. U., Bull, H., Ueland, T., & Falkum, E. (2015). Prevalence, employment rate, and cost of schizophrenia in a high-income welfare society: A population-based study using comprehensive health and welfare registers. *Schizophrenia Bulletin, 42*(2), 476–483.

Evensen, S., Wisløff, T., Lystad, J. U., Bull, H., Ueland, T., & Falkum, E. (2016). Prevalence, employment rate, and cost of schizophrenia in a high-income welfare society: A population-based study using comprehensive health and welfare registers. *Schizophrenia Bulletin, 42*(2), 476–483.

Ewald, H., Mors, O., Flint, T., Koed, K., Eiberg, H., & Kruse, T. A. (1995). A possible locus for manic depressive illness on chromosome 16p13. *Psychiatric Genetics, 5*, 71–81.

Factor, S. A., Feustel, P. J., Friedman, J. H., Comella, C. L., Goetz, C. G., Kurlan, R., et al. (2003). Longitudinal outcome of Parkinson's disease patients with psychosis. *Neurology, 60,* 1756–1761.

Fahnestock, M., Garzon, D., Holsinger, R. M., & Michalski, B. (2002). Neurotrophic factors and Alzheimer's disease: Are we focusing on the wrong molecule? *Journal of Neural Transmission Supplement, 62,* 241–252.

Fair, D. A., Cohen, A. L., Dosenbach, N. U., Church, J. A., Miezin, F. M., Barch, D. M., et al. (2008). The maturing architecture of the brain's default network. *Proceedings of the National Academy of Sciences, 105*(10), 4028–4032.

Fairchild, G. (2011). The developmental psychopathology of motivation in adolescence. *Developmental Cognitive Neuroscience, 1*(4), 414–429.

Fall, P. A., Ekman, R., Granerus, A. K., & Granerus, G. (2000). ECT in Parkinson's disease-dopamine transporter visualised by [123I]-beta-CIT SPECT. *Journal of Neural Transmission, 107,* 997–1008.

Fall, P. A., Ekman, R., Granerus, A. K., Thorell, L. H., & Walinder, J. (1995). ECT in Parkinson's disease. Changes in motor symptoms, monoamine metabolites and neuropeptides. *Journal of Neural Transmission, Parkinson's Disease and Dementia Section, 10,* 129–140.

Fals-Stewart, W., & Angarano, K. (1994). Obsessive-compulsive disorder among patients entering substance abuse treatment. Prevalence and accuracy of diagnosis. *Journal of Nervous and Mental Disease, 182,* 715–719.

Fan, Q., Palaniyappan, L., Tan, L., Wang, J., Wang, X., Li, C., et al. (2013). Surface anatomical profile of the cerebral cortex in obsessive—compulsive disorder: A study of cortical thickness, folding and surface area. *Psychological Medicine, 43*(5), 1081–1091.

Fan, Y., Zhang, J., Sun, X. L., Gao, L., Zeng, X. N., Ding, J. H., et al. (2005). Sex-and region-specific alterations of basal amino acid and monoamine metabolism in the brain of aquaporin-4 knockout mice. *Journal of Neuroscience Research, 82*(4), 458–464.

Fang, Y., Tao, Q., Zhou, X., Chen, S., Huang, J., Jiang, Y., et al. (2017). Patient and family member factors influencing outcomes of poststroke inpatient rehabilitation. *Archives of Physical Medicine and Rehabilitation, 98*(2).

Farah, M. J. (2014). Brain images, babies, and bathwater: Critiquing critiques of functional neuroimaging. *Hastings Center Report, 44*(s2) 19–30.

Faraone, S. V., & Mick, E. (2010). Molecular genetics of attention deficit hyperactivity disorder. *Psychiatric Clinics, 33*(1), 159–180.

Faraone, S. V., Tsuang, M. T., & Tsuang, D. W. (1999). *Genetics of mental disorders.* New York: Guilford.

Farde, L., Wiesel., F. A., Stone-Elander, S., Halldin, C., Nordstrom, A. L., Hall, H., et al. (1990). D2 Dopamine receptors in neuroleptic-naïve schizophrenic patients. *Archives of General Psychiatry, 47,* 213–219.

Fares, R. P., Belmeguenai, A., Sanchez, P. E., Kouchi, H. Y., Bodennec, J., Morales, A., et al. (2013). Standardized environmental enrichment supports enhanced brain plasticity in healthy rats and prevents cognitive impairment in epileptic rats. *PLoS One, 8*(1).

Farrer, L. A., Myers, R. H., Cupples, L. A., St George-Hyslop, P. H., Bird, T. D., Rossor, M. N., et al. (1990). Transmission and age-at-onset patterns in familial Alzheimer's disease: Evidence for heterogeneity. *Neurology, 40,* 395–403.

Fatemi, S. H., Earle, J. A., Stary, J. M., Lee, S., & Sedgewich, J. (2001). Altered levels of the synaptosomal associated protein SNAP-25 in hippocampus of subjects with mood disorders and schizophrenia. *Clinical Neuroscience and Neuropathology, 12,* 3257–3262.

Fatemi, S. H., Halt, A. R., Realmuto, G., Earle, J., Kist, D. A., Thuras, P., et al. (2002). Purkinje cell size is reduced in cerebellum of patients with autism. *Cellular and Molecular Neurobiology, 22,* 171–175.

Fatima, A., Farooq, M., Abdullah, U., Tariq, M., Mustafa, T., Iqbal, M., et al. (2017). Genome-wide supported risk variants in MIR137, CACNA1C, CSMD1, DRD2, and GRM3 contribute to schizophrenia susceptibility in Pakistani population. *Psychiatry Investigation, 14*(5), 687–692.

Fazekas, F., Alavi, A., Chawluk, J. B., Zimmerman, R. A., Hackney, D., Bilaniuk, L., et al. (1989). Comparison of CT, MR and PET in Alzheimer's dementia and normal aging. *Journal of Nuclear Medicine, 30*, 1607–1615.

Fazio, P., Svenningsson, P., Cselényi, Z., Halldin, C., Farde, L., & Varrone, A. (2018). Nigrostriatal dopamine transporter availability in early Parkinson's disease. *Movement Disorders, 33*(4), 592–599.

Feil, J., Sheppard, D., Fitzgerald, P. B., Yücel, M., Lubman, D. I., & Bradshaw, J. L. (2010). Addiction, compulsive drug seeking, and the role of frontostriatal mechanisms in regulating inhibitory control. *Neuroscience & Biobehavioral Reviews, 35*(2), 248–275.

Fein, G., Di Schlafani, V., Cardenas, V. A., Goldmann, H., Tolou-Shams, M., & Meyerhoff, D. J. (2002). Cortical gray matter loss in treatment-naïve alcohol dependent individuals. *Alcoholism: Clinical and Experimental Research, 26*, 558–564.

Feinberg, I. (1982). Schizophrenia: Caused by a fault in programmed synaptic elimination during adolescence. *Journal of Psychiatric Research, 17*, 319–334.

Feinstein, A., Roy, P., Lobaugh, N., Feinstein, K., O'Connor, P., & Black, S. (2004). Structural brain abnormalities in multiple sclerosis patients with major depression. *Neurology, 62*, 586–590.

Feldker, K., Heitmann, C. Y., Neumeister, P., Brinkmann, L., Bruchmann, M., Zwitserlood, P., & Straube, T. (2018). Cardiorespiratory concerns shape brain responses during automatic panic-related scene processing in patients with panic disorder. *Journal of Psychiatry & Neuroscience: JPN, 43*(1), 26.

Feldker, K., Heitmann, C. Y., Neumeister, P., Bruchmann, M., Vibrans, L., Zwitserlood, P., & Straube, T. (2016). Brain responses to disorder-related visual threat in panic disorder. *Human Brain Mapping, 37*(12), 4439–4453.

Felipo, V., Grau, E., Minana, M. D., & Grisolia, S. (1993). Hyperammonemia decreases proteinkinase-C-dependent phosphorylation of microtubule-associated protein 2 and increases its binding to tubulin. *European Journal of Biochemistry, 214*, 243–249.

Felling, R. J., & Song, H. (2015). Epigenetic mechanisms of neuroplasticity and the implications for stroke recovery. *Experimental Neurology, 268*, 37–45.

Feng, C. M., Narayana, S., Lancaster, J. L., Jerabek, P. A., Arnow, T. L., Zhu, F., et al. (2004). CBF changes during brain activation: FMRI vs. PET. *Neuroimage, 22*(1), 443–446.

Ferguson, J. M. (1993). The use of electroconvulsive therapy in patients with intractable anorexia nervosa. *International Journal of Eating Disorders, 13*, 195–201.

Fernandez-Pujals, A. M., Adams, M. J., Thomson, P., McKechanie, A. G., Blackwood, D. H., Smith, B. H., et al. (2015). Epidemiology and heritability of major depressive disorder, stratified by age of onset, sex, and illness course in Generation Scotland: Scottish Family Health Study (GS: SFHS). *PloS One, 10*(11), e0142197.

Ferrario, C. R., Li, X., & Wolf, M. E. (2011). Effects of acute cocaine or dopamine receptor agonists on AMPA receptor distribution in the rat nucleus accumbens. *Synapse, 65*(1), 54–63.

Ferri, S. L., Abel, T., & Brodkin, E. S. (2018). Sex differences in Autism Spectrum Disorder: A review. *Current Psychiatry Reports, 20*(2), 9.

Fettes, P., Schulze, L., & Downar, J. (2017). Cortico-striatal-thalamic loop circuits of the orbitofrontal cortex: Promising therapeutic targets in psychiatric illness. *Frontiers in Systems Neuroscience, 11*, 25.

Feychting, M., Pedersen, N. L., Svedberg, P., Floderus, B., & Gatz, M. (1998). Dementia and occupational exposure to magnetic fields. *Scandinavian Journal of Work, Environment & Health, 24*, 46–53.

Fields, R. D. (2010). Release of neurotransmitters from glia. *Neuron Glia Biology, 6*(03), 137–139.

Figee, M., de Koning, P., Klaassen, S., Vulink, N., Mantione, M., van den Munckhof, P., et al. (2014). Deep brain stimulation induces striatal dopamine release in obsessive- compulsive disorder. *Biological Psychiatry, 75*(8), 647–652.

Figueroa, Y., Rosenberg, D. R., Birmaher, B., & Keshavan, M. S. (1998). Combination treatment with clomipramine and selective serotonin reuptake inhibitors for obsessive-compulsive disorder in children and adolescents. *Journal of Child and Adolescent Psychopharmacology*, *8*, 61–67.

Filbey, F. M., Aslan, S., Calhoun, V. D., Spence, J. S., Damaraju, E., Caprihan, A., & Segall, J. (2014). Long-term effects of marijuana use on the brain. *Proceedings of the National Academy of Sciences*, *111*(47), 16913–16918.

Filkowski, M. M., Olsen, R. M., Duda, B., Wanger, T. J., & Sabatinelli, D. (2017). Sex differences in emotional perception: Meta analysis of divergent activation. *NeuroImage*, *147*, 925–933.

Finberg, J. P., & Rabey, J. M. (2016). Inhibitors of MAO-A and MAO-B in psychiatry and neurology. *Frontiers in Pharmacology*, *7*, 7–340.

Fink, H. A., Jutkowitz, E., McCarten, J. R., Hemmy, L. S., Butler, M., Davila, H., et al. (2018). Pharmacologic interventions to prevent cognitive decline, mild cognitive impairment, and clinical alzheimer-type dementia: A systematic review. *Annals of Internal Medicine*, *168*(1), 39–51.

Fink, M., & Coffey, C. E. (1998). ECT in pediatric neuropsychiatry. In C. E. Coffey & R. Brumback (Eds.), *Textbook of pediatric neuropsychiatry* (pp. 1389–1408). Washington, DC: American Psychiatric Press.

Firbank, M. J., Colloby, S. J., Burn, D. J., McKeith, I. G., & O'Brien, J. T. (2003). Regional cerebral blood flow in Parkinson's disease with and without dementia. *Neuroimage*, *20*, 1309–1319.

Fischer, M., & Barkley, R. A. (2003). Childhood stimulant treatment and risk for later substance abuse. *Journal of Clinical Psychiatry*, *64*, 19–23.

Fischer, M., Barkley, R. A., Edelbrock, C. S., & Smallish, L. (1990). The adolescent outcome of hyperactive children diagnosed by research criteria: II. Academic, attentional, and neuropsychological status. *Journal of Consultation in Clinical Psychology*, *58*, 580–588.

Fischer, M., Barkley, R. A., Smallish, L., & Fletcher, K. (2002). Young adult follow-up of hyperactive children: Self-reported psychiatric disorders, comorbidity, and the role of childhood conduct problems and teen CD. *Journal of Abnormal Child Psychology*, *30*, 463–475.

Fischer, S., & Ehlert, U. (2017). Hypothalamic-pituitary-thyroid (HPT) axis functioning in anxiety disorders. A systematic review. *Depression and Anxiety*, *35*(1), 98–110.

Fleischman, A., Werbeloff, N., Yoffe, R., Davidson, M., & Weiser, M. (2014). Schizophrenia and violent crime: A population-based study. *Psychological Medicine*, *44*(14), 3051–3057.

Fletcher, J. M. (1996). Executive functions in children: Introduction to the special series. *Developmental Neuropsychology*, *12*, 1–3.

Floegel, M., & Kell, C. A. (2017). Function hemispheric asymmetries during the planning and manual control of virtual avatar movements. *Public Library of Science One*, *12*(9), e0185152.

Flores-Cuadrado, A., Ubeda-Bañon, I., Saiz-Sanchez, D., & Martinez-Marcos, A. (2017). α-Synucleinopathy in the human amygdala in Parkinson disease: Differential vulnerability of somatostatin- and parvalbumin-expressing neurons. *Journal of Neuropathology & Experimental Neurology*, *76*(9), 754–758.

Foffani, G., Priori, A., Egidi, M., Rampini, P., Tamma, F., Caputo, E., et al. (2003). 300-Hz subthalamic oscillations in Parkinson's disease. *Brain*, *126*, 2153–2163.

Foged, M. T., Lindberg, U., Vakamudi, K., Larsson, H. B., Pinborg, L. H., Kjær, T. W., et al. (2017). Safety and EEG data quality of concurrent high-density EEG and high-speed fMRI at 3 Tesla. *PloS One*, *12*(5), e0178409.

Fonseca, D. J., Mateus, H. E., Gálvez, J. M., Forero, D. A., Talero-Gutierrez, C., & Velez-van-Meerbeke, A. (2015). Lack of association of polymorphisms in six candidate genes in colombian adhd patients. *Annals of Neurosciences*, *22*(4), 217.

Fontaine, R., Breton, G., Déry, R., Fontaine, S., & Elie, R. (1990). Temporal lobe abnormalities in panic disorder: An MRI study. *Biological Psychiatry*, *27*, 304–310.

Fonzo, G. A., Ramsawh, H. J., Flagan, T. M., Sullivan, S. G., Letamendi, A., Simmons, A. N., et al. (2015). Common and disorder-specific neural responses to emotional faces in generalised anxiety, social anxiety and panic disorders. *The British Journal of Psychiatry*, *206*(3), 206–215.

Foroud, T., Castelluccio, P. F., Koller, D. L., Edenberg, H. J., Miller, M., Bowman, E., et al. (2000). Suggestive evidence of a locus on chromosome 10p using the NIMH genetics initiative bipolar affective disorder pedigrees. *American Journal of Medical Genetics, 96*, 18–23.

Forsberg, S. L., Ilieva, M., & Michel, T. M. (2018). Epigenetics and cerebral organoids: Promising directions in autism spectrum disorders. *Translational Psychiatry, 8*(1), 14.

Forster, M., Grigsby, T. J., Rogers, C. J., & Benjamin, S. M. (2018). The relationship between family-based adverse childhood experiences and substance use behaviors among a diverse sample of college students. *Addictive Behaviors, 76*, 298–304.

Fouche, J. P., du Plessis, S., Hattingh, C., Roos, A., Lochner, C., Soriano-Mas, C., et al. (2016). Cortical thickness in obsessive-compulsive disorder: Multisite mega-analysis of 780 brain scans from six centres. *The British Journal of Psychiatry, 210*(1), 67–74.

Fouche, J. P., du Plessis, S., Hattingh, C., Roos, A., Lochner, C., Soriano-Mas, C., et al. (2017). Cortical thickness in obsessive-compulsive disorder: Multisite mega-analysis of 780 brain scans from six centres. *The British Journal of Psychiatry*, bjp-bp.

Fountoulakis, K. N., Nimatoudis, I., Iacovides, A., & Kaprinis, G. (2004). Off-label indications for atypical antipsychotics: A systematic review. *Annals of General Hospital Psychiatry, 18*, 4.

Fountoulakis, K. N., O'Hara, R., Iacovides, A., Camilleri, C. P., Kaprinis, S., Kaprinis, G., et al. (2003). Unipolar late-onset depression: A comprehensive review. *Annals of General Hospital Psychiatry, 2*, 11.

Fournier, J. C., DeRubeis, R. J., Hollon, S. D., Dimidjian, S., Amsterdam, J. D., Shelton, R. C., & Fawcett, J. (2010). Antidepressant drug effects and depression severity: A patient-level meta-analysis. *JAMA, 303*(1), 47–53.

Fowler, P. C., & O'Sullivan, N. C. (2016). ER-shaping proteins are required for ER and mitochondrial network organization in motor neurons. *Human Molecular Genetics, 25*(13), 2827–2837.

Francobandiera, G. (2001). Olanzapine augmentation of serotonin uptake inhibitors in obsessive-compulsive disorder: An open study. *Canadian Journal of Psychiatry, 46*, 356–358.

Frank, E., Kupfer, D. J., Perel, J. M., Cornes, C., Jarrett, D. B., Mallinger, A. G., et al. (1990). Three-year outcomes for maintenance therapies in recurrent depression. *Archives of Psychiatry, 47*, 1093–1099.

Frederikse, M. E., Lu, A., Aylward, E., Barta, P., Sharma, T., & Pearlson, G. (1999). Sex differences in inferior parietal lobule. *Cerebral Cortex, 9*, 896–901.

Freed, C. R., Greene, P. E., Breeze, R. E., Tsai, W. Y., DuMouchel, W., Kao, R., et al. (2001). Transplantation of embryonic dopamine neurons for severe Parkinson's disease. *New England Journal of Medicine, 344*, 710–719.

Freeman, E. D., Fast, D. K., Burd, L., Kerbeshian, J., Robertson, M. M., & Sandor, P. (2000). An international perspective on Tourette syndrome: Selected findings from 3,500 individuals in 22 countries. *Development in Medicine and Child Neurology, 42*, 436–447.

Freeman, M. P., Freeman, S. A., & McElroy, S. L. (2002). The comorbidity of bipolar and anxiety disorders: Prevalence, psychobiology, and treatment issues. *Journal of Affective Disorders, 68*, 1–23.

Frei, J. A., & Stoeckli, E. T. (2017). SynCAMs—From axon guidance to neurodevelopmental disorders. *Molecular and Cellular Neuroscience, 81*, 41–48.

Freitag, C. M., Agelopoulos, K., Huy, E., Rothermundt, M., Krakowitzky, P., Meyer, J., et al. (2010). Adenosine A 2A receptor gene (ADORA2A) variants may increase autistic symptoms and anxiety in autism spectrum disorder. *European Child & Adolescent Psychiatry, 19*(1), 67–74.

Frey, B. N., Andreazza, A. C., Nery, F. G., Martins, M. R., Quevedo, J., Soares, J. C., & Kapczinski, F. (2007). The role of hippocampus in the pathophysiology of bipolar disorder. *Behavioural Pharmacology, 18*(5–6), 419–430.

Frick, P. J., Lahey, B. B., Christ, M. A. G., Loeber, R., & Green, S. (1991). History of childhood behavior problems in biological relatives of boys with attention-deficit hyperactivity disorder and conduct disorder. *Journal of Clinical Child Psychology, 20*, 445–451.

Friedland, R. P., Jagust, W. J., Huesman, R. H., Koss, E., Knittel, B., Mathis, C. A., et al. (1989). Regional cerebral glucose transport and utilization in Alzheimer's disease. *Neurology, 39,* 1427–1434.

Friedman, E. S., Wisniewski, S. R., Gilmer, W., Nierenberg, A. A., Rush, A. J., Fava, M., et al. (2009). Sociodemographic, clinical, and treatment characteristics associated with worsened depression during treatment with citalopram: Results of the NIMH STAR* D trial. *Depression and Anxiety, 26*(7), 612–621.

Friedman, I., Dar, R., & Shilony, E. (2000). Compulsivity and obsessionality in opioid addiction. *Journal of Nervous and Mental Disease, 188,* 155–162.

Friedman, L. A., & Rapoport, J. L. (2015). Brain development in ADHD. *Current Opinion in Neurobiology, 30,* 106–111.

Friedrich, R. P., Tepper, K., Rönicke, R., Soom, M., Westermann, M., Reymann, K., et al. (2010). Mechanism of amyloid plaque formation suggests an intracellular basis of Aβ pathogenicity. *Proceedings of the National Academy of Sciences, 107*(5), 1942–1947.

Friedrichs-Maeder, C. L., Griffa, A., Schneider, J., Hüppi, P. S., Truttmann, A., & Hagmann, P. (2017). Exploring the role of white matter connectivity in cortex maturation. *PloS One, 12*(5), e0177466.

Fritschy, J. M., & Grzanna, R. (1992). Degeneration of rat locus coeruleus neurons is not accompanied by an irreversible loss of ascending projections. *Annals of the New York Academy of Sciences, 648,* 275–278.

Fritze, S., Spanagel, R., & Noori, H. R. (2017). Adaptive dynamics of the 5-HT systems following chronic administration of selective serotonin reuptake inhibitors: A meta-analysis. *Journal of Neurochemistry, 142*(5), 747–755.

Frizzo, M. E. (2017). Can a selective serotonin reuptake inhibitor act as a glutamatergic modulator? *Current Therapeutic Research, 87,* 9–12.

Frodl, T., Meisenzahl, E. M., Zetzsche, T., Born, C., Groll, C., Jäger, M., et al. (2002a). Hippocampal changes in patients with a first episode of major depression. *American Journal of Psychiatry, 159,* 1112–1118.

Frodl, T., Meisenzahl, E. M., Zetzsche, T., Born, C., Jäger, M., Groll, C., et al. (2003). Larger amygdala volumes in first depressive episode as compared to recurrent major depression and healthy control subjects. *Biological Psychiatry, 53,* 338–344.

Frodl, T., Meisenzahl, E., Zetzsche, T., Bottlender, R., Born, C., Groll, C., et al. (2002b). Enlargement of the amygdala in patients with a first episode of major depression. *Biological Psychiatry, 51,* 708–714.

Frost, J. J. (1992). Receptorimaging bypositron emission tomography and single-photon emission computed tomography. *Investigative Radiology, 27,* 54–58.

Fu, Q., Heath, A. C., Bucholz, K. K., Nelson, E., Goldberg, J., Lyons, M. J., et al. (2002). Shared genetic risk of major depression, alcohol dependence, and marijuana dependence: Contribution of antisocial personality disorder in men. *Archives of General Psychiatry, 59,* 1125–1132.

Fuchs, T., Birbaumer, N., Lutzenberger, W., Gruzelier, J. H., & Kaiser, J. (2003). Neurofeedback treatment for attentiondeficit/hyperactivity disorder in children: A comparison with methylphenidate. *Applied Psychophysiological Feedback, 28,* 1–12.

Fuhrer, T. E., Palpagama, T. H., Waldvogel, H. J., Synek, B. J., Turner, C., Faull, R. L., & Kwakowsky, A. (2017). Impaired expression of GABA transporters in the human Alzheimer's disease hippocampus, subiculum, entorhinal cortex and superior temporal gyrus. *Neuroscience, 351,* 108–118.

Fujii, K., Uchida, H., Suzuki, T., & Mimura, M. (2015). Dependence on benzodiazepines in patients with panic disorder: A cross-sectional study. *Psychiatry and Clinical Neurosciences, 69*(2), 93–99.

Fujiwara, A., Yoshida, T., Otsuka, T., Hayano, F., Asami, T., Narita, H., et al. (2011). Midbrain volume increase in patients with panic disorder. *Psychiatry and Clinical Neurosciences, 65*(4), 365–373.

Fusar-Poli, P., & Meyer-Lindenberg, A. (2012). Striatal presynaptic dopamine in schizophrenia, part I: Meta-analysis of dopamine active transporter (DAT) density. *Schizophrenia Bulletin, 39*(1), 22–32.

Fusar-Poli, P., Smieskova, R., Kempton, M. J., Ho, B. C., Andreasen, N. C., & Borgwardt, S. (2013). Progressive brain changes in schizophrenia related to antipsychotic treatment? A meta-analysis of longitudinal MRI studies. *Neuroscience & Biobehavioral Reviews, 37*(8), 1680–1691.

Fyer, A. J., Costa, R., Haghighi, F., Logue, M. W., Knowles, J. A., Weissman, M. M., . . . Hamilton, S. P. (2012). Linkage analysis of alternative anxiety phenotypes in multiply affected panic disorder families. *Psychiatric Genetics, 22*(3), 123–129.

Gabriëls, L., Cosyns, P., Nuttin, B., Demeulemeester, H., & Gybels, J. (2003). Deep brain stimulation for treatment-refractory obsessive-compulsive disorder: Psychopathological and neuropsychological outcome in three cases. *Acta Psychiatrica Scandinavica, 107*, 275–282.

Gaffney, G. R., Perry, P. J., Lund, B. C., Bever-Stille, K. A., Arndt, S., & Kuperman, S. (2002). Risperidone versus clonidine in the treatment of children and adolescents with Tourette's syndrome. *Journal of the American Academy of Child and Adolescent Psychiatry, 41*, 330–336.

Gagne, J. J., & Power, M. C. (2010). Anti-inflammatory drugs and risk of Parkinson disease A meta-analysis. *Neurology, 74*(12), 995–1002.

Gale, C. R., Čukić, I., Batty, G. D., McIntosh, A. M., Weiss, A., & Deary, I. J. (2017). When is higher neuroticism protective against death? Findings from UK Biobank. *Psychological Science, 28*(9), 1345–1357.

Galetto, V., & Sacco, K. (2017). Neuroplastic changes induced by cognitive rehabilitation in traumatic brain injury: A review. *Neurorehabilitation and Neural Repair, 31*(9), 800–813.

Galvez-Contreras, A. Y., Campos-Ordonez, T., Gonzalez-Castaneda, R. E., & Gonzalez-Perez, O. (2017). Alterations of growth factors in autism and attention-deficit/hyperactivity disorder. *Frontiers in Psychiatry, 8*, 126.

Ganguli, M., Chandra, V., Kamboh, M. I., Johnston, J. M., Dodge, H. H., Thelma, B. K., et al. (2000). Apolipoprotein E polymorphism and Alzheimer disease: The Indo-US Cross-National Dementia Study. *Archives of Neurology, 57*, 824–830.

Gao, S., Hendrie, H. C., Hall, K. S., & Hui, S. (1998). The relationships between age, sex, and the incidence of dementia and Alzheimer disease: A meta-analysis. *Archives of General Psychiatry, 55*(9), 809–815.

Garamendi-Ruiz, I., & Gómez-Esteban, J. C. (2017). Cardiovascular autonomic effects of vagus nerve stimulation. *Clinical Autonomic Research*, 1–12.

Garcia-Sevilla, J. A., Ventayol, P., Busquets, X., La Harpe, R., Walzer, C., & Guimon, J. (1997). Marked decrease of immunolabbelled 68 kDa neurofilament (NF-L) proteins in brains of opiate addicts. *Neuroreport, 6*, 1561–1565.

Garcia-Toro, M., Pascual-Leone, A., Romera, M., Gonz´alez, A., Micó, J., Ibarra, O., et al. (2001). Prefrontal repetitive transcranial magnetic stimulation as add on treatment in depression. *Journal of Neurology, Neurosurgery, and Psychiatry, 71*, 546–548.

Gardner, E. L. (2002). Addictive potential of cannabinoids: The underlying neurobiology. *Chemistry and Physics of Lipids, 121*, 267–290.

Gardner, J. (2013). A history of deep brain stimulation: Technological innovation and the role of clinical assessment tools. *Social Studies of Science, 43*(5), 707–728.

Gardner, R. C., Byers, A. L., Barnes, D. E., Li, Y., Boscardin, J., & Yaffe, K. (2018). Mild TBI and risk of Parkinson disease: A Chronic Effects of Neurotrauma Consortium Study. *Neurology*, 10–1212.

Garfinkel, B. D., Webster, C. D., & Sloman, L. (1975). Methylphenidate and caffeine in the treatment of children with minimal brain dysfunction. *The American Journal of Psychiatry, 132*(7), 723–728.

Garfinkel, B. D., Webster, C. D., & Sloman, L. (1981). Responses to methylphenidate and varied doses of caffeine in children with attention deficit disorder. *Canadian Journal of Psychiatry, 26*, 395–401.

Garre-Olmo, J., López-Pousa, S., Vilalta-Franch, J., Turon-Estrada, A., Lozano-Gallego, M., Hern´andez-Ferr´andiz, M., et al. (2004). Neuropsychological profile of Alzheimer's disease in women: Moderate and moderately severe cognitive decline. *Archives of Women's Mental Health, 7*, 27–36.

Garzon, D., Yu, G., & Fahnestock, M. (2002). A new brain-derived nerotrophic factor transcript and decrease in brain-derived neurotrophic factor transcripts 1, 2 and 3 in Alzheimer's disease parietal cortex. *Journal of Neurochemistry, 82*, 1058–1064.

Gasser, T., Rousson, V., & Schreiter Gasser, U. (2003). EEG power and coherence in children with educational problems. *Journal of Clinical Neurophysiology, 20*, 273–282.

Gassó, P., Sánchez-Gistau, V., Mas, S., Sugranyes, G., Rodríguez, N., Boloc, D., . . . Díaz-Caneja, C. M. (2016). Association of CACNA1C and SYNE1 in offspring of patients with psychiatric disorders. *Psychiatry Research, 245*, 427–435.

Gater, R., Tansella, M., Korten, A., Tiemens, B. G., Mavreas, V. G., & Olatawura, M. O. (1998). Sex differences in the prevalence and detection of depressive and anxiety disorders in general health care settings: Report from the World Health Organization collaborative study on psychological problems in general health care. *Archives of General Psychiatry, 55*, 405–413.

Gates, L., Clarke, J. R., Stokes, A., Somarjai, R., Jarmasz, M., Vandorpe, R., et al. (2004). Neuroanatomy of corpolalia in Tourette syndrome using functional magnetic resonance imaging. *Progress in Neuropsychopharmacolgoy and Biological Psychiatry, 28*, 397–400.

Gatov, E., Rosella, L., Chiu, M., & Kurdyak, P. A. (2017). Trends in standardized mortality among individuals with schizophrenia, 1993–2012: A population-based, repeated cross-sectional study. *Canadian Medical Association Journal, 189*(37), E1177-E1187.

Gatt, J. M., Burton, K. L., Williams, L. M., & Schofield, P. R. (2015). Specific and common genes implicated across major mental disorders: A review of meta-analysis studies. *Journal of Psychiatric Research, 60*, 1–13.

Gatz, M., Pedersen, N. L., Berg, S., Johansson, B., Johansson, K., Mortimer, J. A., et al. (1997). Heritability for Alzheimer's disease: The study of dementia in Swedish twins. *Journals of Gerontology, 52*, 117–125.

Gawrysiak, M. J., Jagannathan, K., Regier, P., Suh, J. J., Kampman, K., Vickery, T., & Childress, A. R. (2017). Unseen scars: Cocaine patients with prior trauma evidence heightened resting state functional connectivity (RSFC) between the amygdala and limbic-striatal regions. *Drug & Alcohol Dependence, 180*, 363–370.

Gazzaniga, M. S. (2005). Essay: Forty-five years of split-brain research and still going strong. *Nature Reviews Neuroscience, 6*(8), 653–659.

Gejman, P. V., Sanders, A. R., & Duan, J. (2010). The role of genetics in the etiology of schizophrenia. *Psychiatric Clinics, 33*(1), 35–66.

Gelder, M. G. (1998). Combined pharmacotherapy and cognitive behavior therapy in the treatment of panic disorder. *Journal of Clinical Psychopharmacology, 18, Supplement 2*, 2S-5S.

Gelfin, Y., Gorfine, M., & Lerer, B. (1998). Effect of clinical doses of fluoxetine on psychological variables in healthy volunteers. *American Journal of Psychiatry, 155*, 290–292.

Geller, B., Badner, J. A., Tillman, R., Christian, S. L., Bolhofner, K., & Cook, E. H. (2004). Linkage disequilibrium of the brain-derived neurotrophic factor Val66Met polymorphism in children with a prepubertal and early adolescent bipolar disorder phenotype. *American Journal of Psychiatry, 161*, 1698–1700.

Geller, D. A. (2004). Re-examining comorbidity of obsessive compulsive and attention-deficit hyperactivity disorder using an empirically derived taxonomy. *European Child & Adolescent Psychiatry, 13*, 83–91.

Geller, D. A., Biederman, J., Stewart, S. E., Mullin, B., Martin, A., Spencer, T., et al. (2003). Which SSRI? A meta-analysis of pharmacotherapy trials in pediatric obsessive-compulsive disorder. *American Journal of Psychiatry, 160*, 1919–1928.

Geng, X., Li, G., Lu, Z., Gao, W., Wang, L., Shen, D., et al. (2017). Structural and maturational covariance in early childhood brain development. *Cerebral Cortex*, 1795–1807.

Gennatas, E. D., Avants, B. B., Wolf, D. H., Satterthwaite, T. D., Ruparel, K., Ciric, R., et al. (2017). Age-related effects and sex differences in gray matter density, volume, mass, and cortical thickness from childhood to young adulthood. *Journal of Neuroscience, 37*(20), 5065–5073.

George, M. S., & Belmaker, R. H. (2000). *Transcranial magnetic stimulation in neuropsychiatry.* Washington, DC: American Psychiatric Press.

George, M. S., Costa, D. C., Kouris, K., Ring, H. A., & Ell, P. J. (1992). Cerebral blood flow abnormalities in adults with infantile autism. *Journal of Nervous and Mental Disease, 180,* 413–417.

George, M. S., Lisanby, S. H., Avery, D., McDonald, W. M., Durkalski, V., Pavlicova, M., et al. (2010). Daily left prefrontal transcranial magnetic stimulation therapy for major depressive disorder: A sham-controlled randomized trial. *Archives of General Psychiatry, 67*(5), 507–516.

George, M. S., Nahas, Z., Kozel, A. F., Li, X., Yamanaka, K., Mishory, A., et al. (2003). Mechanisms and the current state of transcranial magnetic stimulation. *CNS Spectrums, 8,* 496–514.

George, M. S., Sallee, F. R., Nahas, Z., Oliver, N. C., & Wassermann, E. M. (2001). Transcranial magnetic stimulation (TMS) as a research tool in Tourette syndrome and related disorders. *Advances in Neurology, 85,* 225–235.

George, M. S., Trimble, M. R., Costa, D. C., Robertson, M. M., Ring, H. A., & Ell, P. J. (1992). Elevated frontal cerebral blood flow in Gilles de la Tourette syndrome: a 99Tcm-HMPAO SPECT study. *Psychiatry Research: Neuroimaging, 45*(3), 143–151.

George, M. S., Trimble, M. R., Ring, H. A., Sallee, F. R., & Robertson, M. M. (1993). Obsessions in obsessive-compulsive disorder with and without Gilles de la Tourette's syndrome. *American Journal of Psychiatry, 150,* 93–97.

Georgievska, B., Kirik, D., Rosen, C., Lundberg, C., & Bjoerklund, A. (2002). Neuroprotection in the rat Parkinson model by intrastriatal GDNF gene transfer using a lentibiral vector. *NeuroReport, 13,* 75–82.

Gerber, P., Schlaffke, L., Heba, S., Greenlee, M., Schultz, T., & Schmidt-Wilcke, T. (2014). Juggling revisited—A voxel-based morphometry study with expert jugglers. *NeuroImage, 95,* 320–325.

Gervasi, N. M., Scott, S. S., Aschrafi, A., Gale, J., Vohra, S. N., MacGibeny, M. A., et al. (2016). The local expression and trafficking of tyrosine hydroxylase mRNA in the axons of sympathetic neurons. *RNA, 22,* 883–895.

Gevins, A. (1998). The future of electroencephalography in assessing neurocognitive functioning. *Electroencephalography and Clinical Neurophysiology, 106,* 165–172.

Ghaemi, S. N., Rosenquist, K. J., Ko, J. Y., Baldassano, C. F., Kontos, N. J., & Baldessarini, R. J. (2004). Antidepressant treatment in bipolar versus unipolar depression. *American Journal of Psychiatry, 161,* 163–165.

Ghaleiha, A., Entezari, N., Modabbernia, A., Najand, B., Askari, N., Tabrizi, M., et al. (2013). Memantine add-on in moderate to severe obsessive-compulsive disorder: Randomized double-blind placebo-controlled study. *Journal of Psychiatric Research, 47*(2), 175–180.

Ghaziuddin, M., Tsai, L. Y., Ghaziuddin, N., Eilers, L., Naylor, M., Alessi, N., et al. (1993). Utility of the head computerized tomography scan in child and adolescent psychiatry. *Journal of the American Academy of Child and Adolescent Psychiatry, 32,* 123–126.

Ghorayeb, I., Gamas, A., Mazurie, Z., & Mayo, W. (2017). Attention-deficit hyperactivity and obsessive-compulsive symptoms in adult patients with primary restless legs syndrome: Different phenotypes of the same disease? *Behavioral Sleep Medicine,* 1–8.

Gibbard, C. R., Ren, J., Skuse, D. H., Clayden, J. D., & Clark, C. A. (2018). Structural connectivity of the amygdala in young adults with autism spectrum disorder. *Human Brain Mapping, 39*(3), 1270–1282.

Gibbs, T. A., Okuda, M., Oquendo, M. A., Lawson, W. B., Wang, S., Thomas, Y. F., & Blanco, C. (2013). Mental health of African Americans and Caribbean blacks in the United States: Results from the national epidemiological survey on alcohol and related conditions. *American Journal of Public Health, 103*(2), 330–338.

Gibson, C. J., Logue, M., & Growdon, J. H. (1985). CSF monoamine metabolite levels in Alzheimer's and Parkinson's disease. *Archives of Neurology, 42,* 489–492.

Giedd, J. N., Castellanos, F. X., Casey, B. J., Kozuch, P., King, A. C., et al. (1994). Quantitative morphology of the corpus callosum in attention deficit hyperactivity disorder. *The American Journal of Psychiatry, 151*, 665–669.

Giedd, J. N., Jefferies, N. O., Blumenthal, J., Castellanos, F. X., Vaituzis, A. C., Fernandez, T., et al. (1999). Childhood-onset schizophrenia: Progressive brain changes during adolescence. *Biological Psychiatry, 46*, 892–898.

Giedd, J., Snell, J., Lange, N., Rajapakse, J., Casey, B., Kozuch, P., et al. (1996). Quantitative magnetic resonance imaging of human brain development: Ages 4–18. *Cerebral Cortex, 6*, 551–560.

Gilbert, A. R., Akkal, D., Almeida, J. R., Mataix-Cols, D., Kalas, C., Devlin, B., . . . Phillips, M. L. (2009). Neural correlates of symptom dimensions in pediatric obsessive-compulsive disorder: A functional magnetic resonance imaging study. *Journal of the American Academy of Child & Adolescent Psychiatry, 48*(9), 936–944.

Gilbert, A. R., Moore, G. J., Keshavan, M. S., Paulson, L. A., Narula, V., Mac Master, F. P., et al. (2000). Decrease in thalamic volumes of pediatric patients with obsessive-compulsive disorder who are taking paroxetine. *Archives of General Psychiatry, 57*, 449–456.

Gillberg, C. (1998). Chromosomal disorders and autism. *Journal of Autism and Developmental Disorders, 28*(5), 415–425.

Gillespie, N. A., Aggen, S. H., Gentry, A. E., Neale, M. C., Knudsen, G. P., Krueger, R. F., et al. (2018). Testing genetic and environmental associations between personality disorders and cocaine use: A population-based twin study. *Twin Research and Human Genetics, 21*(1), 24–32.

Gillman, M. A., & Sandyk, R. (1986). The endogenous opioid system in Gilles de la Tourette syndrome. *Medical Hypotheses, 19*, 371–378.

Gillman, P. K. (2011). Advances pertaining to the pharmacology and interactions of irreversible nonselective monoamine oxidase inhibitors. *Journal of Clinical Psychopharmacology, 31*(1), 66–74.

Gilman, S. E., Sucha, E., Kingsbury, M., Horton, N. J., Murphy, J. M., & Colman, I. (2017). Depression and mortality in a longitudinal study: 1952–2011. *Canadian Medical Association Journal, 189*(42), E1304-E1310.

Gippert, S. M., Switala, C., Bewernick, B. H., Kayser, S., Bräuer, A., Coenen, V. A., & Schlaepfer, T. E. (2017). Deep brain stimulation for bipolar disorder—Review and outlook. *CNS Spectrums, 22*(3), 254–257.

Giri, M., Shah, A., Upreti, B., & Rai, J. C. (2017). Unraveling the genes implicated in Alzheimer's disease. *Biomedical Reports, 7*(2), 105–114.

Giuliano, A., Saviozzi, I., Brambilla, P., Muratori, F., Retico, A., & Calderoni, S. (2018). The effect of age, sex and clinical features on the volume of Corpus Callosum in pre-schoolers with Autism Spectrum Disorder: A case–control study. *European Journal of Neuroscience, 47*(6), 568–578.

Gizatullin, R., Zaboli, G., Jönsson, E. G., Åsberg, M., & Leopardi, R. (2008). The tryptophan hydroxylase (TPH) 2 gene unlike TPH-1 exhibits no association with stress-induced depression. *Journal of Affective Disorders, 107*(1–3), 175–179.

Gjone, H., Stevenson, J., & Sundet, J. M. (1996). Genetic influence on parent-reported attention-related problems in a Norwegian general population twin sample. *Journal of the American Academy of Child and Adolescent Psychiatry, 35*, 588–598.

Glahn, A., Prell, T., Grosskreutz, J., Peschel, T., & Müller-Vahl, K. R. (2015). Obsessive-compulsive disorder is a heterogeneous disorder: Evidence from diffusion tensor imaging and magnetization transfer imaging. *BMC Psychiatry, 15*(1), 135.

Glantz, L. A., & Lewis, D. A. (2000). Decreased dendritic spine density on prefrontal cortical pyramidal neurons in schizophrenia. *Archives of General Psychiatry, 57*, 65–73.

Glaser, D. (2000). Child abuse and neglect and the brain—A review. *Journal of Child Psychology and Psychiatry and Allied Disciplines, 41*, 97–116.

Glatt, S. J., Faraone, S. V., & Tsuang, M. T. (2003). Association between a functional catechol O-methyltransferase gene polymorphism and schizophrenia: Meta-analysis of case-control and family-based studies. *American Journal of Psychiatry, 160*, 469–476.

Glenn, T. C., Kelly, D. F., Boscardin, W. J., McArthur, D. L., Vespa, P., Oetel, M., et al. (2003). Energy dysfunction as a predictor of outcome after moderate or severe head injury: Indices of oxygen, glucose, and lactate metabolism. *Journal of Cerebral Blood Flow Metabolism, 23*, 1239–1250.

Glosser, G. (2001). Neurobehavioral aspects of movement disorders. *Neurologic Clinics, 19*, 535–551.

Glover, G. H. (2011). Overview of functional magnetic resonance imaging. *Neurosurgery Clinics, 22*(2), 133–139.

Glover, M. E., & Clinton, S. M. (2016). Of rodents and humans: A comparative review of the neurobehavioral effects of early life SSRI exposure in preclinical and clinical research. *International Journal of Developmental Neuroscience, 51*, 50–72.

Glowinski, A. L., Madden, P. A., Bucholz, K. K., Lynskey, M. T., & Heath, A. C. (2003). Genetic epidemiology of self-reported lifetime DSM-IV major depressive disorder in a population-based twin sample of female adolescents. *Journal of Child Psychology and Psychiatry, and Allied Disciplines, 44*, 988–996.

Godar, S. C., & Bortolato, M. (2017). What makes you tic? Translational approaches to study the role of stress and contextual triggers in Tourette syndrome. *Neuroscience & Biobehavioral Reviews, 76*, 123–133.

Goedert, M., & Compston, A. (2018). Parkinson's disease—The story of an eponym. *Nature Reviews: Neurology, 14*(1), 47.

Goldberg, J. F., Burdick, K. E., & Endick, C. J. (2004). Preliminary randomized, double-blind, placebo-controlled trial of pramipexole added to mood stabilizers for treatment-resistant bipolar depression. *American Journal of Psychiatry, 161*, 564–566.

Goldman, D., Oroszi, G., O'Malley, S., & Anton, R. (2005). COMBINE genetics study: The pharmacogenetics of alcoholism treatment response: Genes and mechanisms. *Journal of Studies on Alcohol, Supplement*, (15), 56–64.

Goldschmidt, A. B., Crosby, R. D., Cao, L., Wonderlich, S. A., Mitchell, J. E., Engel, S. G., & Peterson, C. B. (2017). A preliminary study of momentary, naturalistic indicators of binge-eating episodes in adults with obesity. *International Journal of Eating Disorders.*

Goldstein, R. Z., & Volkow, N. D. (2002). Drug addiction and its underlying neurobiological basis: Neuroimaging evidence for the involvement of the frontal cortex. *American Journal of Psychiatry, 159*, 1642–1652.

Goldwurm, S., Di Fonzo, A., Simons, E. J., Rohe, C. F., Zini, M., Canesi, M., . . . Meucci, N. (2005). The G6055A (G2019S) mutation in LRRK2 is frequent in both early and late onset Parkinson's disease and originates from a common ancestor. *Journal of Medical Genetics, 42*(11), e65-e65.

Gomez-Sanchez, C. I., Riveiro-Alvarez, R., Soto-Insuga, V., Rodrigo, M., Tirado-Requero, P., Mahillo-Fernandez, I., et al. (2015). Attention deficit hyperactivity disorder: Geneticassociation study in a cohort of Spanish children. *Behavioral and Brain Functions, 12*(1), 2.

Gonçalves, Ó. F., Batistuzzo, M. C., & Sato, J. R. (2017). Real-time functional magnetic resonance imaging in obsessive-compulsive disorder. *Neuropsychiatric Disease and Treatment, 13*, 1825–1834.

Gonçalves, Ó. F., Carvalho, S., Leite, J., Fernandes-Gonçalves, A., Carracedo, A., & Sampaio, A. (2016). Gray matter morphological alteration in obsessive compulsive disorder: Evidence for an inhibitory control and emotional regulation disorder. *Principles and Practice of Clinical Research, 2*(2).

Gong, D., Ma, W., Gong, J., He, H., Dong, L., Zhang, D., et al. (2017). Action video game experience related to altered large-scale white matter networks. *Journal of Neural Plasticity*, 1–7.

Gong, L., He, C., Yin, Y., Ye, Q., Bai, F., Yuan, Y., . . . & Xie, C. (2017). Nonlinear modulation of interacting between COMT and depression on brain function. *European Psychiatry, 45*, 6–13.

Gonul, A. S., Coburn, K., & Kula, M. (2009). Cerebral blood flow, metabolic, receptor, and transporter changes in bipolar disorder: The role of PET and SPECT studies. *International Review of Psychiatry, 21*(4), 323–335.

Gonzalez-Rothi, L. J. (2001). Neurophysiologic basis of rehabilitation. *Journal of Medical Speech-Language Pathology, 9*, 117–127.

Gonzalez, S., Camarillo, C., Rodriguez, M., Ramirez, M., Zavala, J., Armas, R., et al. (2014). A genome-wide linkage scan of bipolar disorder in Latino families identifies susceptibility loci at 8q24 and 14q32. *American Journal of Medical Genetics Part B: Neuropsychiatric Genetics, 165*(6), 479–491.

Goodkind, M., Eickhoff, S. B., Oathes, D. J., Jiang, Y., Chang, A., Jones-Hagata, L. B., et al. (2015). Identification of a common neurobiological substrate for mental illness. *JAMA Psychiatry, 72*(4), 305–315.

Goodnick, P. J., Rush, A. J., George, M. S., Marangell, L. B., & Sackeim, H. A. (2001). Vagus nerve stimulation in depression. *Expert Opinions in Pharmacotherapy, 2*, 1061–1063.

Goodwin, G. M., Haddad, P. M., Ferrier, I. N., Aronson, J. K., Barnes, T. R. H., Cipriani, A., . . . Holmes, E. A. (2016). Evidence-based guidelines for treating bipolar disorder: Revised third edition recommendations from the British Association for Psychopharmacology. *Journal of Psychopharmacology, 30*(6), 495–553.

Goodwin, G., Price, J., Bodinat, C. D., & Laredo, J. (2017). Emotional blunting with antidepressant treatments: A survey among depressed patients. *Journal of Affective Disorders, 221*, 31–35.

Goodwin, R. D., Fergusson, D. M., & Horwood, L. J. (2004). Panic attacks and psychoticism. *American Journal of Psychiatry, 161*, 88–92.

Goodyer, I. M., Park, R. J., & Herbert, J. (2001). Psychosocial and endocrine features of chronic first-episode major depression in 8–16 year olds. *Society of Biological Psychiatry, 50*, 351–357.

Gordon, I., Grauer, E., Genis, I., Sehayek, E., & Michaelson, D. M. (1995). Memory deficits and cholinergic impairments in apolipoprotein E-deficient mice. *Neuroscience Letters, 199*(1), 1–4.

Gorell, J. M., Peterson, E. L., Rybicki, B. A., & Johnson, C. C. (2004). Multiple risk factors for Parkinson's disease. *Journal of the Neurological Sciences, 217*, 169–174.

Gorman, J. M. (2003). New methods of brain stimulation: What they tell us about the old methods and about the brain. *CNS Spectrums, 8*, 475.

Gorman, J. M., Kent, J. M, Sullivan, G. M., & Coplan, J. D. (2000). Neuroanatomical hypothesis of panic disorder, revised. *American Journal of Psychiatry, 157*, 493–505.

Gorman, J. M., Liebowitz, M. R., Fyer, A. J., & Stein, J. (1989). A neuroanatoimical hypothesis for panic disorder. *American Journal of Psychiatry, 146*, 148–161.

Gottesman, I. I. (1991). A series of book in psychology. *Schizophrenia genesis: The origins of madness.* New York, NY: WH Freeman/Times Books/Henry Holt & Co.

Gottesman, I. I., & Bertelsen, A. (1989). Confirming unexpressed genotypes for schizophrenia. *Archives of General Psychiatry, 46*, 867–872.

Goulet, K., Deschamps, B., Evoy, F., & Trudel, J. F. (2009). Use of brain imaging (computed tomography and magnetic resonance imaging) in first-episode psychosis: Review and retrospective study. *The Canadian Journal of Psychiatry, 54*(7), 493–501.

Gouvea, F., Lopes, A., Greenberg, B., Canteras, M., Taub, A., Mathis, M., & Miguel, E. (2010). Response to sham and active gamma ventral capsulotomy in otherwise intractable obsessive-compulsive disorder. *Stereotactic and Functional Neurosurgery, 88*(3), 177–182.

Gowing, L. R., Ali, R. L., Allsop, S., Marsden, J., Turf, E. E., West, R., & Witton, J. (2015). Global statistics on addictive behaviours: 2014 status report. *Addiction, 110*(6), 904–919.

Grace, A. A., Bunney, B. S., Moore, H., & Todd, C. L. (1997). Dopamine-cell depolarization block as a model for the therapeutic actions of antipsychotic drugs. *Trends in Neuroscience, 20*, 31–73.

Graeff, F. G. (2017). Translational approach to the pathophysiology of panic disorder: Focus on serotonin and endogenous opioids. *Neuroscience & Biobehavioral Reviews, 76*, 48–55.

Grammas, P., & Martinez, J. M. (2014). Targeting thrombin: An inflammatory neurotoxin in Alzheimer's disease. *Journal of Alzheimer's Disease, 42*(s4), S537-S544.

Grant, J. E., & Kim, S. W. (2001). A case of kleptomania and compulsive sexual behavior treated with naltrexone. *Annals of Clinical Psychiatry, 13*, 229–231.

Grassian, S. (1983). Psychopathological effects of solitary confinement. *American Journal of Psychiatry*, *140*, 1450–1454.

Gratacòs, M., Nadal, M., Martín-Santos, R., Pujana, M. A., Gago, J., Peral, B., et al. (2001). A polymorphic genomic duplication on human chromosome 15 is a susceptibility factor for panic and phobic disorders. *Cell*, *106*, 367–379.

Graves, A. B., Rosner, D., Echeverria, D., Mortimer, J. A., & Larson, E. B. (1998). Occupational exposures to solvents and aluminium and estimated risk of Alzheimer's disease. *Occupational and Environmental Medicine*, *55*, 627–633.

Graves, A. B., Rosner, D., Echeverria, D., Yost, M., & Larson, E. B. (1999). Occupational exposure to electromagnetic fields and Alzheimer disease. *Alzheimer Disease and Associated Disorders*, *13*, 165–170.

Gray, N. A., Milak, M. S., Delorenzo, C., Ogden, R. T., Huang, Y., Mann, J. J., & Parsey, R. V. (2013). Antidepressant treatment reduces serotonin-1A autoreceptor binding in major depressive disorder. *Biological Psychiatry*, *74*(1), 26–31.

Grazina, R., & Massano, J. (2013). Physical exercise and Parkinson's disease: Influence on symptoms, disease course and prevention. *Reviews in the Neurosciences*, *24*(2), 139–152.

Green, M. S., Kaye, J. A., & Ball, M. J. (2000). The Oregon brain aging study: Neuropathology accompanying healthy aging in the oldest old. *Neurology*, *54*, 105–113.

Greenberg, B. D. (2002). Update on deep brain stimulation. *Journal of ECT*, *18*, 193–196.

Greenberg, B. D., & Rezai, A. R. (2003). Mechanisms and the current state of deep brain stimulation in neuropsychiatry. *CNS Spectrums*, *8*, 522–526.

Greenberg, B. D., George, M. S., Martin, J. D., Benjamin, J., Schlaepfer, T. E., Altemus, M., et al. (1997). Effect of prefrontal repetitive transcranial magnetic stimulation in obsessive-compulsive disorder: A preliminary study. *American Journal of Psychiatry*, *154*, 867–869.

Greenberg, B. D., Price, L. H., Rauch, S. L., Friehs, G., Noren, G., Malone, D., et al. (2003). Neurosurgery for intractable obsessive-compulsive disorder and depression: Critical issues. *Neurosurgery Clinics of North America*, *14*, 199–212.

Greenberg, B. D., Rauch, S. L., & Haber, S. N. (2010). Invasive circuitry-based neurotherapeutics: Stereotactic ablation and deep brain stimulation for OCD. *Neuropsychopharmacology*, *35*(1), 317–336.

Greenberg, D., & Witztum, E. (1994). The influence of cultural factors on obsessive compulsive disorder: Religious symptoms in a religious society. *Israel Journal of Psychiatry, and Related Sciences*, *31*, 211–220.

Greenberg, P. E., Leong, S. A., Birnbaum, H. G., & Robinson, R. L. (2003). The economic burden of depression with painful symptoms. *The Journal of Clinical Psychiatry*, *64*, 17–23.

Greene, D. J., Williams III, A. C., Koller, J. M., Schlaggar, B. L., & Black, K. J. (2017). Brain structure in pediatric Tourette syndrome. *Molecular Psychiatry*, *22*(7), 972–980.

Greenfield, S. F., Manwani, S. G., & Nargiso, J. E. (2003). Epidemiology of substance use disorders in women. *Obstetric and Gynecological Clinics in North America*, *30*, 413–446.

Greengard, P. (2001). The neurobiology of slow synaptic transmission. *Science*, *24*, 1024–1030.

Greengard, P., Valtorta, F., Czernik, A. J., & Benfenati, B. (1993). Synaptic vesicle phosphoproteins and regulation of synaptic function. *Science*, *259*, 780–785.

Greenough, W. T., & Chang, F. F. (1988). Plasticity of synapse structure and pattern in the cerebral cortex. In A. Peters & E. G. Jones (Eds.), *Cerebral Cortex*, (Vol. 7, pp. 391–440). New York: Plenum Press.

Greenough, W. T., & Black, J. E. (1992). Induction of brain structure by experience: Substrates for cognitive development. In M. R. Gunnar & C. A. Nelson (Eds.), *Developmental behavioral neuroscience* (Minnesota symposia on child psychology, Vol. 24, pp. 155–200). Hillsdale, NJ: Lawrence Erlbaum Associates.

Greenough, W. T., & Chang, F. L. F. (1985). Synaptic structural correlates of information storage in mammalian nervous systems. In *Synaptic plasticity* (pp. 335–372). New York: Guilford Press.

Greenough, W. T., Withers, G. S., & Anderson, B. J. (1992). Experience dependent synaptogenesis as a plausible memory mechanism. In I. Gormezano & E. A. Wasserman (Eds.),

Learning and memory: The behavioral and biological substrates (pp. 209–299). Hillsdale, NJ: Lawrence Erlbaum Associates.

Greenwald, M. K., Schuh, K. J., Hopper, J. A., Schuster, C. R., & Johanson, C. E. (2002). Effects of buprenorphine sublingual tabler maintenance on opioid drug-seeking behavior in humans. *Psychopharmacology, 160*, 344–352.

Gregersen, N. O., Buttenschøn, H. N., Hedemand, A., Nielsen, M. N., Dahl, H. A., Kristensen, A. S., . . . Wang, A. G. (2016). Association between genes on chromosome 19p13. 2 and panic disorder. *Psychiatric Genetics, 26*(6), 287–292.

Griffin, C. E., Kaye, A. M., Bueno, F. R., & Kaye, A. D. (2013). PMC3684331Benzodiazepine pharmacology and central nervous system-mediated effects. *The Ochsner Journal, 13*(2), 214–223.

Griffin, J. W., & Bradshaw, P. C. (2017). Amino acid catabolism in alzheimer's disease brain: Friend or foe? *Oxidative Medicine and Cellular Longevity*, 1–15.

Griñan-Ferré, C., Pérez-Cáceres, D., Gutiérrez-Zetina, S. M., Camins, A., Palomera-Avalos, V., Ortuño- Sahagún, D., et al. (2015). Environmental enrichment improves behavior, cognition an brain functional markers in young Senescence-Accelerated Prone Mice (SAMP8). *Molecular Neurobiology, 53*(4), 2435–2450.

Griñan-Ferré, C., Pérez-Cáceres, D., Gutiérrez-Zetina, S. M., Camins, A., Palomera-Avalos, V., Ortuño- Sahagún, D., et al. (2016). Environmental enrichment improves behavior, cognition an brain functional markers in young Senescence-Accelerated Prone Mice (SAMP8). *Molecular Neurobiology, 53*(4), 2435–2450.

Griswold, A. J., Van Booven, D., Cuccaro, M. L., Haines, J. L., Gilbert, J. R., & Pericak-Vance, M. A. (2018). Identification of rare noncoding sequence variants in gamma-aminobutyric acid A receptor, alpha 4 subunit in autism spectrum disorder. *Neurogenetics, 19*(1), 17–26.

Groenewegen, H. J., van den Heuvel, O. A., Cath, D. C., Voorn, P., & Veltman, D. J. (2003). Does an imbalance between the dorsal and ventral striatopallidal systems play a role in Tourette's syndrome? A neuronal circuit approach. *Brain Development, 25*, S3–S14.

Grosshans, M., Mutschler, J., & Kiefer, F. (2015). Treatment of cocaine craving with as-needed nalmefene, a partial κ opioid receptor agonist: First clinical experience. *International Clinical Psychopharmacology, 30*(4), 237–238.

Grossman, M. (1999). Sentence processing in Parkinson's disease. *Brain and Cognition, 40*, 387–413.

Groth, C., Debes, N. M., Rask, C. U., Lange, T., & Skov, L. (2017). Course of Tourette syndrome and comorbidities in a large prospective clinical study. *Journal of the American Academy of Child & Adolescent Psychiatry, 56*(4), 304–312.

Grover, S., Hazari, N., Chakrabarti, S., & Avasthi, A. (2015). Relationship of obsessive compulsive symptoms/disorder with clozapine: A retrospective study from a multispeciality tertiary care centre. *Asian Journal of Psychiatry, 15*, 56–61.

Gruber, S. A., Sagar, K. A., Dahlgren, M. K., Gonenc, A., Smith, R. T., Lambros, A. M., et al. (2017). The grass might be greener: Medical marijuana patients exhibit altered brain activity and improved executive function after 3 months of treatment. *Frontiers in Pharmacology, 8*, 983.

Gruber, S. A., Sagar, K. A., Dahlgren, M. K., Gonenc, A., Smith, R. T., Lambros, A. M., et al. (2018). The grass might be greener: Medical marijuana patients exhibit altered brain activity and improved executive function after 3 months of treatment. *Frontiers in Pharmacology, 8*, 983.

Grünblatt, E., Marinova, Z., Roth, A., Gardini, E., Ball, J., Geissler, J., . . . Walitza, S. (2018). Combining genetic and epigenetic parameters of the serotonin transporter gene in obsessive-compulsive disorder. *Journal of Psychiatric Research, 96*, 209–217.

Grunder, G., Vernaleken I., Muller, M. J., Davids, E., Heydari, N., Buchholz, H. G., et al. (2003). Subchronic haloperidol downregulates dopamine synthesis capacity in the brain of schizophrenic patients in vivo. *Neuropsychopharmacology, 28*, 787–794.

Gruner, P., Vo, A., Ikuta, T., Mahon, K., Peters, B. D., Malhotra, A. K., et al. (2012). White matter abnormalities in pediatric obsessive-compulsive disorder. *Neuropsychopharmacology, 37*(12), 2730.

Grunhaus, L., Dannon, P. N., & Gershon, A. A. (2002). Transcranial magnetic stimulation: A new tool in the fight against depression. *Dialogues in Clinical Neuroscience, 4*(1), 93–103.

Grunze, H. C. (2010). Anticonvulsants in bipolar disorder. *Journal of Mental Health, 19*(2), 127–141.

Gruzelier, J. H., Galderisi, S., & Strik, W. (2002). Neurophysiological research in psychiatry. In J. J. Lopez-Ibor, W. Gaebel, M. Maj, & N. Sartorius (Eds.), *Psychiatry as a neuroscience* (pp. 125–180). New York: Wiley.

Gudmundsdottir, B. G., Weyandt, L., & Ernudottir, G. B. (2016). Prescription stimulant misuse and ADHD symptomatology among college students in Iceland. *Journal of Attention Disorders.* https://doi.org/10.1177/1087054716684379.

Guerrero, A. P., Hishinuma, E. S., Andrade, N. N., Bell, C. K., Kurahara, D. K., Lee, T. G., et al. (2003). Demographic and clinical characteristics of adolescents in Hawaii with obsessive-compulsive disorder. *Archives of Pediatrics & Adolescent Medicine, 157,* 665–670.

Guffanti, G., Gameroff, M. J., Warner, V., Talati, A., Glatt, C. E., Wickramaratne, P., & Weissman, M. M. (2016). Heritability of major depressive and comorbid anxiety disorders in multi-generational families at high risk for depression. *American Journal of Medical Genetics Part B: Neuropsychiatric Genetics, 171*(8), 1072–1079.

Gugliandolo, A., Bramanti, P., & Mazzon, E. (2017). Role of vitamin E in the treatment of Alzheimer's disease: Evidence from animal models. *International Journal of Molecular Sciences, 18*(12), 2504.

Guo, Q., Li, C., & Wang, J. (2017a). Updated review on the clinical use of repetitive transcranial magnetic stimulation in psychiatric disorders. *Neuroscience Bulletin,* 1–10.

Guo, Z., Cupples, L. A., Kurz, A., Auerbach, S. H., Volicer, L., Chui, H., et al. (2000). Head injury and the risk of AD in the MIRAGE study. *Neurology, 54,* 1316–1323.

Gupta, S. (2000). Immunological treatments for autism. *Journal of Autism and Developmental Disorders, 30,* 475–479.

Gur, E., Dremencov, E., Garcia, F., Van de Kar, L. D., Lerer, B., & Newman, M. E. (2002). Functional effects of chronic electroconvulsive shock on serotonergic 5-HT(1A) and 5-HT(1B) receptor activity in rat hippocampus and hypothalamus. *Brain Research, 952,* 52–60.

Gur, E., Lerer, B., & Newman, M. E. (1997). Chronic electroconvulsive shock and 5-HT autoreceptor activity in rat brain: An in vivo microdialysis study. *Journal of Neural Transmission, 104,* 795–804.

Gur, R. E., Petty, R. G., Turetsky, B. I., & Gur, R. C. (1996). Schizophrenia throughout life: Sex differences in severity and profile of symptoms. *Schizophrenia Research, 2,* 1–12.

Gusmão, R., Quintão, S., McDaid, D., Arensman, E., Van Audenhove, C., Coffey, C., et al. (2013). Antidepressant utilization and suicide in Europe: An ecological multi-national study. *PLoS One, 8*(6), e66455.

Gusnard, D. A., & Raichle, M. E. (2001). Searching for a baseline: Functional imaging and the resting human brain. *Nature Reviews, 2,* 685–694.

Guttman, M., Kish, S. J., & Furukawa, Y. (2003). Current concepts in the diagnosis and management of Parkinson's disease. *Canadian Medical Academy, 168,* 293–301.

Haaksma, M. L., Vilela, L. R., Marengoni, A., Calderón-Larrañaga, A., Leoutsakos, J. M. S., Rikkert, M. G. O., & Melis, R. J. (2017). Comorbidity and progression of late onset Alzheimer's disease: A systematic review. *PloS One, 12*(5), e0177044.

Haan, L. D., Bruggen, M. V., Lavalaye, J., Booij, J., Dingemans, P. M. A. J., & Linszen, D. (2003). Subjective experience and D2 receptor occupancy in patients with recent-onset schizophrenia treated with low-dose olanzapine or haloperidol: A randomized, double-blind study. *American Journal of Psychiatry, 160,* 303–309.

Haavik, J., Blau, N., & Thöny, B. (2008). Mutations in human monoamine-related neurotransmitter pathway genes. *Human mutation, 29*(7), 891–902.

Haghighi, M., Ludyga, S., Rahimi, B., Jahangard, L., Ahmadpanah, M., Torabian, S., et al. (2017). In patients suffering from major depressive disorders, quantitative EEG showed favorable changes in left and right prefrontal cortex. *Psychiatry Research*, *251*, 137–141.

Haig, G. M., Wang, D., Zhao, J., Othman, A. A., & Bain, E. E. (2018). Efficacy and Safety of the α7-Nicotinic Acetylcholine Receptor Agonist ABT-126 in the treatment of cognitive impairment associated with Schizophrenia: Results from a Phase 2b randomized controlled study in smokers. *The Journal of Clinical Psychiatry*, *79*(3).

Hálfdánarson, Ó., Zoëga, H., Aagaard, L., Bernardo, M., Brandt, L., Fusté, A. C., et al. (2017). International trends in antipsychotic use: A study in 16 countries, 2005–2014. *European Neuropsychopharmacol*, *27*(10), 1064–1076.

Hall, F. S., Drgonova, J., Jain, S., & Uhl, G. R. (2013). Implications of genome wide association studies for addiction: Are our a priori assumptions all wrong? *Pharmacology & Therapeutics*, *140*(3), 267–279.

Hall, G. B., Szechtman, H., & Nahmias, C. (2003). Enhanced salience and emotion recognition in autism: A PET study. *American Journal of Psychiatry*, *160*(8), 1439–1441.

Hall, K. S., Gao, S., Unverzagt, F. W., & Hendrie, H. C. (2000). Low education and childhood rural residence. Risk for Alzheimer's disease in African Americans. *Neurology*, *54*, 95–99.

Hall, M. G., Alhassoon, O. M., Stern, M. J., Wollman, S. C., Kimmel, C. L., Perez-Figueroa, A., & Radua, J. (2015). Gray matter abnormalities in cocaine versus methamphetamine-dependent patients: A neuroimaging meta-analysis. *The American Journal of Drug and Alcohol Abuse*, *41*(4), 290–299.

Hallett, J. J., Harling-Berg, C. J., Knopf, P. M., Stopa, E. G., & Kiessling, L. S. (2000). Anti-striatal antibodies in Tourette syndrome cause neuronal dysfunction. *Journal of Neuroimmunology*, *111*, 195–202.

Hallmayer, J., Cleveland, S., Torres, A., Phillips, J., Cohen, B., Torigoe, T., et al. (2011). Genetic heritability and shared environmental factors among twin pairs with autism. *Archives of General Psychiatry*, *68*(11), 1095–1102.

Halloway, S., Arfanakis, K., Wilbur, J., Schoeny, M. E., & Pressler, S. J. (2018). Accelerometer physical activity is associated with greater gray matter volumes in older adults without dementia or mild cognitive impairment. *The Journals of Gerontology: Series B*, gby010.

Hamani, C., Pilitsis, J., Rughani, A. I., Rosenow, J. M., Patil, P. G., Slavin, K. S., et al. (2014). Deep brain stimulation for obsessive-compulsive disorder: Systematic review and evidence-based guideline sponsored by the American Society for Stereotactic and Functional Neurosurgery and the Congress of Neurological Surgeons (CNS) and endorsed by the CNS and American Association of Neurological Surgeons. *Neurosurgery*, *75*(4), 327–333.

Hamilton, J. E., Heads, A. M., Cho, R. Y., Lane, S. D., & Soares, J. C. (2015). Racial disparities during admission to an academic psychiatric hospital in a large urban area. *Comprehensive Psychiatry*, *63*, 113–122.

Hamilton, S. P. (2011). A new lead from genetic studies in depressed siblings: Assessing studies of chromosome 3. *American Journal of Psychiatry*, *168*(8), 783–789.

Hamilton, S. P., Fyer, A. J., Durner, M., Heiman, G. A., De Leon, A. B., Hodge, S. E., . . . Weissman, M. M. (2003). Further genetic evidence for a panic disorder syndrome mapping to chromosome 13q. *Proceedings of the National Academy of Sciences*, *100*(5), 2550–2555.

Hamilton, S. P., Heiman, G. A., Haghighi, F., Mick, S., Klein, D. F., Hodge, S. E., . . . & Knowles, J. A. (1999). Lack of genetic linkage or association between a functional serotonin transporter polymorphism and panic disorder. *Psychiatric Genetics*, *9*(1), 1–6.

Hamilton, S. P., Slager, S. L., De Leon, A. B., Heiman, G. A., Klein, D. F., Hodge, S. E., et al. (2004). Evidence for genetic linkage between a polymorphism in the adenosine 2A receptor and panic disorder. *Neuropsychopharmacology*, *29*, 558–565.

Hamilton, S. P., Slager, S. L., Heiman, G. A., Deng, Z., Haghighi, F., Klein, D. F., et al. (2002). Evidence for a susceptibility locus for panic disorder near the catechol-O-methyltransferase gene on chromosome 22. *Biological Psychiatry*, *51*, 591–601.

Hamilton, S. P., Slager, S. L., Mayo, D., Heiman, G. A., Klein, D. F., Hodge, S. E., et al. (2004). Investigation of polymorphisms in the CREM gene in panic disorder. *American Journal of Medical Genetics, 126B*, 111–115.

Hammond, E. J., Uthman, B. M., Wilder, B. J., Ben-Menachem, E., Hamberger, A., Hedner, T., et al. (1992). Neuro-chemical effects of vagus nerve stimulation in humans. *Brain Research, 583*, 300–303.

Hamre, H. J., Witt, C. M., Kienle, G. S., Meinecke, C., Glockmann, A., Ziegler, R., et al. (2010). Anthroposophic therapy for attention deficit hyperactivity: A two-year prospective study in outpatients. *International Journal of General Medicine, 3*, 239.

Hamza, M., Halayem, S., Bourgou, S., Daoud, M., Charfi, F., & Belhadj, A. (2017). Epigenetics and ADHD: Toward an integrative approach of the disorder pathogenesis. *Journal of Attention Disorders*, https://doi.org/10.1177/1087054717696769.

Han, B., Olfson, M., & Mojtabai, R. (2017). Depression care among depressed adults with and without comorbid substance use disorders in the United States. *Depression and Anxiety, 34*(3), 291–300.

Han, E. J., Kim, Y. K., Hwang, J. A., Kim, S. H., Lee, H. J., Yoon, H. K., & Na, K. S. (2015). Evidence for association between the brain-derived neurotrophic factor gene and panic disorder: A novel haplotype analysis. *Psychiatry Investigation, 12*(1), 112–117.

Handen, B. L., Anagnostou, E., Aman, M. G., Sanders, K. B., Chan, J., Hollway, J. A., et al. (2017). A randomized, placebo-controlled trial of metformin for the treatment of overweight induced by antipsychotic medication in young people with Autism Spectrum Disorder: Open-label extension. *Journal of the American Academy of Child & Adolescent Psychiatry, 56*(10).

Handen, B. L., Johnson, C. R., & Lubetsky, M. (2000). Efficacy of methylphenidate among children with autism and symptoms of attention-deficit hyperactivity disorder. *Journal of Autism and Developmental Disorders, 30*, 245–255.

Haney, M., Cooper, Z. D., Bedi, G., Vosburg, S. K., Comer, S. D., & Foltin, R. W. (2013). Nabilone decreases marijuana withdrawal and a laboratory measure of marijuana relapse. *Neuropsychopharmacology, 38*(8), 1557.

Hänggi, J., Brütsch, K., Siegel, A. M., & Jäncke, L. (2014). The architecture of the chess player's brain. *Neuropsychologia, 62*, 152–162.

Hanna, G. L., Veenstra-VanderWeele, J., Cox, N. J., Boehnke, M., Himle, J. A., Curtis, G. C., et al. (2002). Genome-wide linkage analysis of families with obsessive-compulsive disorder ascertained through pediatric probands. *American Journal of Medical Genetics Part A, 114*(5), 541–552.

Hansen, B. H., Oerbeck, B., Skirbekk, B., Petrovski, B. É., & Kristensen, H. (2018). Neurodevelopmental disorders: Prevalence and comorbidity in children referred to mental health services. *Nordic Journal of Psychiatry*, 1–7.

Hansen, E. S., Hasselbalch, S., Law, I., & Bolwig, T. G. (2002). The caudate nucleus in obsessive-compulsive disorder. Reduced metabolism following treatment with paroxetine: A PET study. *International Journal of Neuropsychopharmacology, 5*, 1–10.

Hansen, K. B., Yi, F., Perszyk, R. E., Menniti, F. S., & Traynelis, S. F. (2017). NMDA receptors in the central nervous system. *Methods in Molecular Biology NMDA Receptors*, 1–80.

Hanyu, H., Shimizu, T., Tanaka, Y., Takasaki, M., Koizumi, K., & Abe, K. (2003). Regional cerebral blood flow patterns and response to donepezil treatment in patients with Alzheimer's disease. *Dementia and Geriatric Cognitive Disorders, 15*, 177–182.

Harasty, J., Double, K. L., Halliday, G. M., Kril, J. J., & McRitchie, D. A. (1997). Language-associated cortical regions are proportionately larger in the female brain. *Archives of Neurology, 54*, 171–176.

Harata, N. C., Aravanis, A. M., & Tsien, R. W. (2006). Kiss-and-run and full-collapse fusion as modes of exo-endocytosis in neurosecretion. *Journal of Neurochemistry, 97*(6), 1546–1570.

Harcherik, D. F., Cohen, D. J., Ort, S., Paul, R., Shaywitz, B. A., Volkmar, F. R., et al. (1985). Computed tomographic brain scanning in four neuropsychiatric disorders of childhood. *American Journal of Psychiatry, 142*, 731–734.

Harding, K. L., Judah, R. D., & Gant, C. (2003). Outcome-based comparison of Ritalin versus food supplement treated children with ADHD. *Alternative Medicine Review, 8,* 319–330.

Harmanci, H., Emre, M., Gurvit, H., Bilgic, B., Hanagasi, H., Gurol, E., et al. (2003). Risk factors for Alzheimer disease: A population-based case-control study in Istanbul, Turkey. *Alzheimer Disease and Associated Disorders, 17,* 139–145.

Harmer, C. J., Hill, S. A., Taylor, M. J., Cowen, P. J., & Goodwin, G. M. (2003). Toward a neuropsychological theory of antidepressant drug action: Increase in positive emotional bias after potentiation of norepinephrine activity. *American Journal of Psychiatry, 160,* 990–992.

Harper, C., Dixon, G., Sheedy, D., & Garrick, T. (2003). Neuropathological alterations in alcoholic brains. Studies arising from the New South Wales Tissue Resource Centre. *Programs in Neuropsychopharmacology and Biological Psychiatry, 27,* 951–961.

Harris, A. W., Bahramali, H., Slewa-Younan, S., Gordon, E., Williams, L., & Li, W. M. (2001). The topography of quantified electroencephalography in three syndromes of schizophrenia. *International Journal of Neuroscience, 107,* 265–278.

Harris, T. W., Hartwieg, E., Horvitz, H. R., & Jorensen, E. M. (2000). Mutations in synaptojanin disrupt synaptic vesicle recycling. *Journal of Cell Biology, 150,* 589–600.

Harrison, D. W., Demaree, H. A., Shenal, B. V., & Everhart, D. E. (1998). QEEG assisted neuropsychological evaluation of autism. *International Journal of Neuroscience, 93,* 133–140.

Harrison, P. J., Freemantle, N., & Geddes, J. R. (2003). Meta-analysis of brain weight in schizophrenia. *Schizophrenia Research, 64*(1), 25–34.

Harsing, L. G., Prauda. I., Barkoczy, J., Matyus, P., & Juranyi, Z. (2004). A 5-HT7 heteroreceptor-mediated inhibition of [3H] serotonin release in raphe nuclei slices of the rat: Evidence for a serotonergic-glutamateric interaction. *Neurochemistry Research, 29,* 1487–1497.

Hart, D. J., Craig, D., Compton, S. A., Critchlow, S., Kerrigan, B. M., McIlroy, S. P., et al. (2003). A retrospective study of the behavioural and psychological symptoms of mid and late phase Alzheimer's disease. *International Journal of Geriatric Psychiatry, 18,* 1037–1042.

Hartogs, B. M. A., Bartels-Velthuis, A., Van der Ploeg, K., & Bos, E. H. (2017). Heart rate variability biofeedback stress relief program for depression. *Methods of Information in Medicine, 56*(6), 419–426.

Harvey, R. C., James, A. C., & Shields, G. E. (2016). A systematic review and network meta-analysis to assess the relative efficacy of antipsychotics for the treatment of positive and negative symptoms in early-onset schizophrenia. *CNS Drugs, 30*(1), 27–39.

Hasbi, A., Perreault, M. L., Shen, M. Y., Fan, T., Nguyen, T., Alijaniaram, M., et al. (2017). Activation of dopamine D1-D2 receptor complex attenuates cocaine reward and reinstatement of cocaine-seeking through inhibition of DARPP-32, ERK, and ΔFosB. *Frontiers in Pharmacology, 8.*

Hasbi, A., Perreault, M. L., Shen, M. Y., Fan, T., Nguyen, T., Alijaniaram, M., et al. (2018). Activation of dopamine D1-D2 receptor complex attenuates cocaine reward and reinstatement of cocaine-seeking through inhibition of DARPP-32, ERK, and ΔFosB. *Frontiers in Pharmacology, 8.*

Hasler, G., Fromm, S., Carlson, P. J., Luckenbaugh, D. A., Waldeck, T., Geraci, M., et al. (2008). Neural response to catecholamine depletion in unmedicated subjects with major depressive disorder in remission and healthy subjects. *Archives of General Psychiatry, 65*(5), 521–531.

Hastings, J. E., & Barkley, R. A. (1978). A review of psychophysiological research with hyperkinetic children. *Journal of Abnormal Child Psychology, 6,* 413–447.

Haug, J. O. (1962). Pneumoencephalographic studies in mental disease. *Acta Psychiatrica Scandinavica, 38,* 1–114.

Haukvik, U. K., Tamnes, C. K., Söderman, E., & Agartz, I. (2018). Neuroimaging hippocampal subfields in schizophrenia and bipolar disorder: A systematic review and meta-analysis. *Journal of Psychiatric Research, 104,* 217–226.

Häusser, M., Spruston, N., & Stuart, G. J. (2000). Diversity and dynamics of dendritic signaling. *Science, 290,* 739–744.

Havassy, B. E., Alvidrez, J., & Owen, K. K. (2004). Comparisons of patients with comorbid psychiatric and substance use disorders: Implications for treatment and service delivery. *American Journal of Psychiatry*, *161*, 139–145.

Hawi, Z., Cummins, T. D. R., Tong, J., Johnson, B., Lau, R., Samarrai, W., & Bellgrove, M. (2015). The molecular genetic architecture of attention deficit hyperactivity disorder. *Molecular Psychiatry*, *20*(3), 289.

Hazlett, E. A., Buchsbaum, M. S., Hsieh, P., Haznedar, M. M., Platholi, J., LiCalzi, E. M., et al. (2004). Regional glucose metabolism within cortical Brodmann areas in healthy individuals and autistic patients. *Neuropsychobiology*, *49*, 115–125.

Hazlett, H. C., Gu, H., Munsell, B. C., Kim, S. H., Styner, M., Wolff, J. J., et al. (2017). Early brain development in infants at high risk for autism spectrum disorder. *Nature*, *542*(7641), 348–351.

Haznedar, M. M., Buchsbaum, M. S., Wei, T. C., Hof, P. R., Cartwright, C., Bienstock, C. A., et al. (2000). Limbic circuitry in patients with autism spectrum disorders studied with positron emission tomography and magnetic resonance imaging. *American Journal of Psychiatry*, *157*, 1994–2001.

Head, D., Buckner, R. L., Shimony, J. S., Williams, L. E., Akbudak, E., Conturo, T. E., et al. (2004). Differential vulnerability of anterior white matter in nondemented aging with minimal acceleration in dementia of the Alzheimer type: Evidence from diffusion tensor imaging. *Cerebral Cortex*, *14*, 410–423.

Health Quality Ontario. (2017). Pharmacogenomic testing for psychotropic medication selection: A systematic review of the assurex genesight psychotropic test. *Ontario Health Technology Assessment Series*, *17*(4), 1–39.

Healy, D. (2003). Lines of evidence on the risk of suicide with selective serotonin reuptake inhibitors. *Psychotherapy and Psychosomatics*, *72*, 71–79.

Hearing, M., Graziane, N., Dong, Y., & Thomas, M. J. (2018). Opioid and psychostimulant plasticity: Targeting overlap in nucleus accumbens glutamate signaling. *Trends in Pharmacological Sciences*, *39*(3), 276–294.

Hebb, D. (1949). *The organization of behavior*. New York: Wiley.

Hebert, M. A., Blanchard, D. C., & Blanchard, R. J. (1999). Intravenous cocaine precipitates panic-like flight responses and lasting hyperdefensiveness in laboratory rats. *Pharmacology, Biochemistry, and Behavior*, *63*, 349–360.

Heh, C. W., Smith, R., Wu, J., Hazlett, E., Russell, A., Asarnow, R., et al. (1989). Positron emission tomography of the cerebellum in autism. *American Journal of Psychiatry*, *146*, 242–245.

Heiligenstein, E., Guenther, G., Levy, A., Savino, F., & Fulwiler, J. (1999). Psychological and academic functioning in college students with attention deficit hyperactivity disorder. *Journal of American College Health*, *47*(4), 181–185.

Hedegaard, H., Warner, M., & Miniño, A. M. (2017). *Drug overdose deaths in the United States, 1999–2015*. US Department of Health and Human Services, Centers for Disease Control and Prevention. Hyattsville, MD: National Center for Health Statistics.

Heim, C., Shugart, M., Craighead, W. E., & Nemeroff, C. B. (2010). Neurobiological and psychiatric consequences of child abuse and neglect. *Developmental Psychobiology*, *52*(7), 671–690.

Heimer, L. (2003). A new anatomical framework for neuropsychiatric disorders and drug abuse. *American Journal of Psychiatry*, *160*, 1726–1739.

Heinz, A., Siessmeier, T., Wrase, J., Hermann, D., Klein, S., Gursser-Sinopoli, S. M., et al. (2004). Correlation between dopamine D2 receptors in the ventral striatum and central processing of alcohol cues and craving. *American Journal of Psychiatry*, *161*, 1783–1789.

Helenius, D., Munk-Jørgensen, P., & Steinhausen, H. C. (2012). Family load estimates of schizophrenia and associated risk factors in a nation-wide population study of former child and adolescent patients up to forty years of age. *Schizophrenia Research*, *139*(1), 183–188.

Helmes, E., & Hall, F. (2016). Performance of psychiatric diagnostic groups on measures and strategies of verbal fluency. *Applied Neuropsychology: Adult*, *23*(4), 284–294.

Helmreich, D. L., Parfitt, D. B., Lu, X. Y., Akil, H., & Watson, S. J. (2005). Relation between the hypothalamic-pituitary-thyroid (HPT) axis and the hypothalamic-pituitary-adrenal (HPA) axis during repeated stress. *Neuroendocrinology*, *81*(3), 183–192.

Hemmings, S. M., & Stein, D. J. (2006). The current status of association studies in obsessive-compulsive disorder. *Psychiatric Clinics, 29*(2), 411–444.

Hemmingsen, R., Madsen, A., Glenthoj, B., & Rubin, P. (1999). Cortical brain dysfunction in early schizophrenia: Secondary pathogenetic hierarchy of neuroplasticity psychopathology and social impairment. *Acta Psychiatrica Scandinavica, 99*, 80–88.

Henderson, A. S., Korten, A. E., Jorm, A. F., Jacomb, P. A., Christensen, H., Rodgers, B., et al. (2000). COMT and DRD3 polymorphisms, environmental exposures, and personality traits related to common mental disorders. *American Journal of Medical Genetics, 96*, 102–107.

Henderson, T. A., & Morries, L. D. (2017). Multi-Watt near-infrared phototherapy for the treatment of comorbid depression: An open-label single-arm study. *Frontiers in Psychiatry, 8*, 187.

Henricus, P., Van Domburg, H. J., & Donkelar, T. (1991). *The human substantia nigra and ventral tegmental area: A neuroanatomical study with notes on aging and aging diseases (advances in anatomy, embryolo)*. New York: Springer-Verlag.

Henry, M. E., Schmidt, M. E., Matochik, J. A., Stoddard, E. P., & Potter, W. Z. (2001). The effects of ECT on brain glucose: A pilot FDG PET study. *Journal of ECT, 17*, 33–40.

Henry, T. R. (2003). Vagus nerve stimulation for epilepsy: Anatomical, experimental and mechanistic investigations. In S. C. Schachter & D. Schmidt (Eds.), *Vagus nerve stimulation* (2nd ed., pp. 1–31). New York: Martin Dunitz, Taylor & Francis Group.

Henry, T. R., Bakay, R. A., Votaw, J. R., Pennell, P. B., Epstein, C. M., Faber, T. L., et al. (1998). Brain blood flow alterations induced by therapeutic vagus nerve stimulation in partial epilepsy: I. Acute effects at high and low levels of stimulation. *Epilepsia, 39*, 983–990.

Herb, E., & Thyen, U. (1992). Mutism after cerebellar medulloblastoma surgery. *Neuropediatrics, 23*, 144–146.

Hernan, M. A., Takkouche, B., Caamano-Isorna, F., & Gestal-Otero, J. J. (2002). A meta-analysis of coffee drinking, cigarette smoking, and the risk of Parkinson's disease. *Annals of Neurology, 52*, 276–284.

Herold, N., Uebelhack, K., Franke, L., Amthauer, H., Luedemann, L., Bruhn, H., et al. (2006). Imaging of serotonin transporters and its blockade by citalopram in patients with major depression using a novel SPECT ligand [123 I]-ADAM. *Journal of Neural Transmission, 113*(5), 659–670.

Heron, W. (1957). The pathology of boredom. *Scientific American, 196,* 52–56.

Herringshaw, A. J., Ammons, C. J., DeRamus, T. P., & Kana, R. K. (2016). Hemispheric differences in language processing in autism spectrum disorders: A meta-analysis of neuroimaging studies. *Autism Research, 9*(10), 1046–1057.

Hertz, L., Yu, A. C., Kala, G., & Schousboe, A. (2000). Neuronal-astrocytic and cytosolic-mitochondrial metabolite trafficking during brain activation, hyperammonemia and energy deprivation. *Neurochemistry International, 37*, 83–102.

Hesse, S., Müller, U., Lincke, T., Barthel, H., Villmann, T., Angermeyer, M. C., et al. (2005). Serotonin and dopamine transporter imaging in patients with obsessive-compulsive disorder. *Psychiatry Research: Neuroimaging, 140*(1), 63–72.

Hesse, S., Stengler, K., Regenthal, R., Patt, M., Becker, G. A., Franke, A., . . . Lobsien, D. (2011). The serotonin transporter availability in untreated early-onset and late-onset patients with obsessive–compulsive disorder. *International Journal of Neuropsychopharmacology, 14*(5), 606–617.

Hettema, J. M., Neale, M. C., & Kendler, K. S. (2001). A review and meta-analysis of the genetic epidemiology of anxiety disorders. *American Journal of Psychiatry, 158*, 1568–1578.

Heyman, I., Fombonne, E., Simmons, H., Ford, T., Meltzer, H., & Goodman, R. (2001). Prevalence of obsessive-compulsive disorder in the British nationwide survey of child mental health. *British Journal of Psychiatry, 179*, 324–329.

Heywood, C., & Beale, I. (2003). EEG biofeedback vs. placebo treatment for attention-deficit/hyperactivity disorder: A pilot study. *Journal of Attention Disorders, 7*, 43–55.

Hidalgo, R. B., & Sheehan, D. V. (2009). Benzodiazepines risk, abuse, and dependence: A tsunami in a tea cup. *Psychiatry (Edgmont), 6*(12), 13–15.

Hilker, R., Helenius, D., Fagerlund, B., Skytthe, A., Christensen, K., Werge, T. M., et al. (2018). Heritability of schizophrenia and schizophrenia spectrum based on the nationwide Danish twin register. *Biological Psychiatry, 83*(6), 492–498.

Hill, D. E., Yeo, R. A., Campbell, R. A., Hart, B., Vigil, J., & Brooks, W. (2003). Magnetic resonance imaging correlates of attention-deficit/hyperactivity disorder in children. *Neuropsychology, 17*(3), 496.

Hill, S. Y., Sharma, V., & Jones, B. L. (2016). Lifetime use of cannabis from longitudinal assessments, cannabinoid receptor (CNR1) variation, and reduced volume of the right anterior cingulate. *Psychiatry Research: Neuroimaging, 255*, 24–34.

Hirano, S., & Takeichi, M. (2012). Cadherins in brain morphogenesis and wiring. *Physiological Reviews, 92*(2), 597–634.

Hirasawa-Fujita, M., Tudor, L., Pekovic, M. N., Kozumplik, O., Erjavec, G. N., Uzun, S., . . . & Pivac, N. (2018). Genotypic and haplotypic associations of catechol-O-methyltransferase (COMT) rs4680 and rs4818 with salivary cortisol in patients with schizophrenia. *Psychiatry Research, 259*, 262–264.

Hirschfeld, R. M., & Schatzberg, A. F. (1994). Long-term management of depression. *American Journal of Medicine, 97*, 33–38.

Hirschtritt, M. E., Bloch, M. H., & Mathews, C. A. (2017). Obsessive-compulsive disorder: Advances in diagnosis and treatment. *Jama, 317*(13), 1358–1367.

Hirschtritt, M. E., Darrow, S. M., Illmann, C., Osiecki, L., Grados, M., Sandor, P., et al. (2018). Genetic and phenotypic overlap of specific obsessive-compulsive and attention-deficit/hyperactive subtypes with Tourette syndrome. *Psychological Medicine, 48*(2), 279–293.

Hirschtritt, M. E., Lee, P. C., Pauls, D. L., Dion, Y., Grados, M. A., Illmann, C., et al. (2015). Lifetime prevalence, age of risk, and genetic relationships of comorbid psychiatric disorders in Tourette syndrome. *JAMA Psychiatry, 72*(4), 325–333.

Hirsh, A. T., Dillworth, T. M., Ehde, D. M., & Jensen, M. P. (2010). Sex differences in pain and psychological functioning in persons with limb loss. *The Journal of Pain, 11*(1), 79–86.

Hjorth, S. (2016). Looking back (and in) to the future: A personal reflection on 'Serotonin autoreceptor function and antidepressant drug action' (Hjorth et al., 2000). *Journal of Psychopharmacology, 30*(11), 1129–1136.

Ho, B. C., Andreasen, N. C., Ziebell, S., Pierson, R., & Magnotta, V. (2011). Long-term antipsychotic treatment and brain volumes: A longitudinal study of first-episode schizophrenia. *Archives of General Psychiatry, 68*(2), 128–137.

Ho, P. S., Ho, K. K. J., Huang, W. S., Yen, C. H., Shih, M. C., Shen, L. H., et al. (2013). Association study of serotonin transporter availability and SLC6A4 gene polymorphisms in patients with major depression. *Psychiatry Research: Neuroimaging, 212*(3), 216–222.

Hoaken, P. C., & Schnurr, R. (1980). Genetic factors in obsessive-compulsive neurosis? A rare case of discordant monozygotic twins. *Canadian Journal of Psychiatry, 25*, 167–172.

Hodges, L. M., Fyer, A. J., Weissman, M. M., Logue, M. W., Haghighi, F., Evgrafov, O., . . . Hamilton, S. P. (2014). Evidence for linkage and association of GABRB3 and GABRA5 to panic disorder. *Neuropsychopharmacology, 39*(10), 2423–2431.

Hodges, L. M., Weissman, M. M., Haghighi, F., Costa, R., Bravo, O., Evgrafov, O., . . . Hamilton, S. P. (2009). Association and linkage analysis of candidate genes GRP, GRPR, CRHR1, and TACR1 in panic disorder. *American Journal of Medical Genetics Part B: Neuropsychiatric Genetics, 150*(1), 65–73.

Hoehn-Saric, R., Schlaepfer, T. E., Greenberg, B. D., McLeod, D. R., Pearlson, G. D., & Wong, S. H. (2001). Cerebral blood flow in obsessive-compulsive patients with major depression: Effect of treatment with sertraline or desipramine on treatment responders and non-responders. *Psychiatry Research, 108*, 89–100.

Hoekstra, P. J., Kallenberg, C. G. M., Korf, J., & Minderaa, R. B. (2002). Is Tourette's syndrome an autoimmune disease? *Molecular Psychiatry, 7*, 437–445.

Hoexter, M. Q., Diniz, J. B., Lopes, A. C., Batistuzzo, M. C., Shavitt, R. G., Dougherty, D. D., et al. (2015). Orbitofrontal thickness as a measure for treatment response prediction in obsessive-compulsive disorder. *Depression and Anxiety, 32*(12), 900–908.

Hoffmann, G., Linkowski, P., Kerkhofs, M., Desmedt, D., & Mendlewicz, J. (1985). Effects of ECT on sleep and CSF biogenic amines in affective illness. *Psychiatry Research, 16*, 199–206.

Hogarty, G. E., Flesher, S., Ulrich, R., Carter, M., Greenwald, D., Pogue-Geile, M., et al. (2004). Cognitive enhancement therapy for schizophrenia: Effects of a 2-year randomized trial on cognition and behavior. *Archives of General Psychiatry, 61*, 866–876.

Hohoff, C., Garibotto, V., Elmenhorst, D., Baffa, A., Kroll, T., Hoffmann, A., et al. (2014). Association of adenosine receptor gene polymorphisms and in vivo adenosine A 1 receptor binding in the human brain. *Neuropsychopharmacology, 39*(13), 2989.

Hohoff, C., Mullings, E. L., Heatherley, S. V., Freitag, C. M., Neumann, L. C., Domschke, K., . . . Unschuld, P. G. (2010). Adenosine A2A receptor gene: Evidence for association of risk variants with panic disorder and anxious personality. *Journal of Psychiatric Research, 44*(14), 930–937.

Hökfelt, T. (1991). Neuropeptides in perspective: The last ten years. *Neuron, 7*, 867–879.

Hollander, E., Bienstock, C. A., Koran, L. M., Pallanti, S., Marazziti, D., Rasmussen, S. A., et al. (2002). Refractory obsessive-compulsive disorder: State-of-the-art treatment. *Journal of Clinical Psychiatry, 63, Supplement 6*, 20–29.

Hollander, E., Kaplan, A., & Stahl, S. M. (2003). A double-blind, placebo-controlled trial of clonazepam in obsessive-compulsive disorder. *World Journal of Biological Psychiatry, 4*, 30–34.

Hollifield, M., Finley, M. R., & Skipper, B. (2003). Panic disorder phenomenology in urban self-identified Caucasian-Non-Hispanics and Caucasian-Hispanics. *Depression and Anxiety, 18*, 7–17.

Hollister, L. E., & Boutros, N. (1991). Clinical use of CT and MR scans in psychiatric patients. *Journal of Psychiatry and Neuroscience, 16*(4), 194–198.

Holloway, V., Gadian, D. G., Vargha-Khadem, F., Porter, D. A., Boyd, S. G., & Connelly, A. (2000). The reorganization of sensorimotor function in children after hemispherectomy: A functional MRI and somatosensory evoked potential study. *Brain, 123*, 2431–2444.

Holmans, P., Weissman, M. M., Zubenko, G. S., Scheftner, W. A., Crowe, R. R., DePaulo J. R., et al. (2007). Genetics of recurrent early-onset major depression (GenRED): Final genome scan report. *American Journal of Psychiatry, 164*(2), 248–258.

Holroyd, S., Currie, L., & Wooten, G. F. (2000). Prospective study of hallucinations and delusions in Parkinson's disease. *Journal of Neurology, Neurosurgery, and Psychiatry, 70*, 734–738.

Holroyd, S., Currie, L., & Wooten, G. F. (2001). Prospective study of hallucinations and delusions in Parkinson's disease. *Journal of Neurology, Neurosurgery, and Psychiatry, 70*, 734–738.

Holton, K. F., Johnstone, J. M., Brandley, E. T., & Nigg, J. T. (2018). Evaluation of dietary intake in children and college students with and without attention-deficit/hyperactivity disorder. *Nutritional neuroscience*, 1–14.

Holtz, K., Pané-Farré, C. A., Wendt, J., Lotze, M., & Hamm, A. O. (2012). Brain activation during anticipation of interoceptive threat. *Neuroimage, 61*(4), 857–865.

Holtzheimer, P. E., Husain, M. M., Lisanby, S. H., Taylor, S. F., Whitworth, L. A., McClintock, S., et al. (2017). Subcallosal cingulate deep brain stimulation for treatment-resistant depression: A multisite, randomised, sham-controlled trial. *The Lancet Psychiatry, 4*(11), 839–849.

Holzer, J. C., Goodman, W. K., McDougle, C. J., Baer, L., Boyarsky, B. K., Leckman, J. F., et al. (1994). Obsessive-compulsive disorder with and without a chronic tic disorder. A comparison of symptoms in 70 patients. *British Journal of Psychiatry, 164*, 469–473.

Holzer, K. J., Oh, S., Salas-Wright, C. P., Vaughn, M. G., & Landess, J. (2017). Gender differences in the trends and correlates of major depressive episodes among juvenile offenders in the United States. *Comprehensive Psychiatry, 80*, 72–80.

Holzman, P. S., & Matthysse, S. (1990). The genetics of schizophrenia: A review. *Psychological Science, 1*(5), 279–286.

Hong, E. R., Kawaminami, S., Neely, L., Morin, K., Davis, J. L., & Gong, L. Y. (2018). Tablet-based interventions for individuals with ASD: Evidence of generalization and maintenance effects. *Research in Developmental Disabilities*.

Hong, S. B., Kim, J. W., Cho, S. C., Shin, M. S., Kim, B. N., & Yoo, H. J. (2012). Dopaminergic and noradrenergic gene polymorphisms and response to methylphenidate in Korean children with attention-deficit/hyperactivity disorder: Is there an interaction? *Journal of Child and Adolescent Psychopharmacology, 22*(5), 343–352.

Hong, S. B., Shin, Y. W., Kim, S. H., Yoo, S. Y., Lee, J. M., Kim, I. Y., . . . Kwon, J. S. (2007). Hippocampal shape deformity analysis in obsessive-compulsive disorder. *European Archives of Psychiatry and Clinical Neuroscience, 257*(4), 185–190.

Hoozemans, J. J., Rozemuller, A. J., Veerhuis, R., & Eikelenboom, P. (2001). Immunological aspects of Alzheimer's disease: Therapeutic implications. *BioDrugs, Clinical Immunotherapeutics, Biopharmaceuticals and Gene Therapy, 15*, 325–337.

Hopf, F. W. (2017). Do specific NMDA receptor subunits act as gateways for addictive behaviors? *Genes, Brain and Behavior, 16*(1), 118–138.

Horga, G., Parellada, E., Lomeña, F., Fernández-Egea, E., Mané, A., Font, M., et al. (2011). Differential brain glucose metabolic patterns in antipsychotic-naive first-episode schizophrenia with and without auditory verbal hallucinations. *Journal of Psychiatry & Neuroscience: JPN, 36*(5), 312–321.

Horrigan, J. P., & Barnhill, L. J. (1999). Guanfacine and secondary mania in children. *Journal of Affective Disorders, 54*, 309–314.

Horváth, H. R., Fazekas, C. L., Balázsfi, D., Jain, S. K., Haller, J., & Zelena, D. (2017). Contribution of vesicular glutamate transporters to stress response and related psychopathologies: Studies in VGluT3 knockout mice. *Journal of Cellular and Molecular Neurobiology, 38*(1), 37–52.

Horwitz, B. (2003). The elusive concept of brain connectivity. *Neuroimage, 19*(2), 466–470.

Horwitz, B., Rumsey, J. M., Grady, C. L., & Rapoport, S. I. (1988). The cerebral metabolic landscape in autism: Intercorrelations of regional glucose utilization. *Archives of Neurology, 45*, 749–755.

Howe, A. S., Buttenschøn, H. N., Bani-Fatemi, A., Maron, E., Otowa, T., Erhardt, A., . . . Domschke, K. (2016). Candidate genes in panic disorder: Meta-analyses of 23 common variants in major anxiogenic pathways. *Molecular Psychiatry, 21*(5), 665.

Howell, E. M., Heiser, N., & Harrington, M. (1999). A review of recent findings on substance abuse treatment for pregnant women. *Journal of Substance Abuse Treatment, 16*, 195–219.

Howells, D. W., Porritt, M. J., Wong, J. Y., Batchelor, P. E., Kalnins, R., Hughes, A. J., et al. (2000). Reduced BDNF mRNA expression in the Parkinson's disease substantia nigra. *Experimental Neurology, 166*, 127–135.

Howes, O. D., Kambeitz, J., Kim, E., Stahl, D., Slifstein, M., Abi-Dargham, A., & Kapur, S. (2012). The nature of dopamine dysfunction in schizophrenia and what this means for treatment: Meta-analysis of imaging studies. *Archives of General Psychiatry, 69*(8), 776–786.

Hsieh, J. (2009). *Computed tomography: Principles, design, artifacts, and recent advances.* Bellingham, WA: SPIE.

Hu, X., Du, M., Chen, L., Li, L., Zhou, M., Zhang, L., et al. (2017). Meta-analytic investigations of common and distinct grey matter alterations in youths and adults with obsessive-compulsive disorder. *Neuroscience & Biobehavioral Reviews, 78*, 91–103.

Hu, X., Liu, Q., Li, B., Tang, W., Sun, H., Li, F., et al. (2016). Multivariate pattern analysis of obsessive—compulsive disorder using structural neuroanatomy. *European Neuropsychopharmacology, 26*(2), 246–254.

Hu, Y., Salmeron, B. J., Gu, H., Stein, E. A., & Yang, Y. (2015). Impaired functional connectivity within and between frontostriatal circuits and its association with compulsive drug use and trait impulsivity in cocaine addiction. *JAMA Psychiatry, 72*(6), 584–592.

Hua, F., Ying, J., Zhang, J., Wang, X., Hu, Y., Liang, Y., et al. (2016). Naringenin pre-treatment inhibits neuroapoptosis and ameliorates cognitive impairment in rats exposed to isoflurane anesthesia by regulating the PI3/Akt/PTEN signalling pathway and suppressing NF-κB-mediated inflammation. *International Journal of Molecular Medicine, 38*(4), 1271–1280.

Huang, C. W., Hsu, S. W., Chang, Y. T., Huang, S. H., Huang, Y. C., Lee, C. C., et al. (2018). Cerebral perfusion insufficiency and relationships with cognitive deficits in Alzheimer's disease: A multiparametric neuroimaging study. *Scientific Reports, 8*(1), 1541.

Huang, E. J., & Reichardt, L. F. (2001). Neurotrophins: Roles in neuronal development and function. *Annual Review of Neuroscience, 24*(1), 677–736.

Huang, Y. Z., Lu, M. K., Antal, A., Classen, J., Nitsche, M., Ziemann, U., et al. (2017). Plasticity induced by non-invasive transcranial brain stimulation: A position paper. *Clinical Neurophysiology, 128*(11), 2318–2329.

Huestis, R. D., Arnold, L. E., & Smeltzer, D. J. (1975). Caffeine versus methylphenidate and d-amphetamine in minimal brain dysfunction: A double-blind comparison. *American Journal of Psychiatry, 132*, 868–870.

Huff, M. O., Li, X., Ginns, E., & El-Mallakh, R. S. (2010). Effect of ethacrynic acid on the sodium- and potassium-activated adenosine triphosphatase activity and expression in Old Order Amish bipolar individuals. *Journal of Affective Disorders, 123*(1–3), 303–307.

Huhtaniska, S., Jääskeläinen, E., Hirvonen, N., Remes, J., Murray, G. K., Veijola, J., et al. (2017). Long-term antipsychotic use and brain changes in schizophrenia—A systematic review and meta-analysis. *Human Psychopharmacology: Clinical and Experimental, 32*(2).

Hui Poon, S., Sim, K., & J Baldessarini, R. (2015). Pharmacological approaches for treatment-resistant bipolar disorder. *Current Neuropharmacology, 13*(5), 592–604.

Hulshoff Pol, H. E., & Kahn, R. S. (2008). What happens after the first episode? A review of progressive brain changes in chronically ill patients with schizophrenia. *Schizophrenia Bulletin, 34*(2), 354–366.

Hung, J. C. (2013). Bringing New PET drugs to clinical practice-a regulatory perspective. *Theranostics, 3*(11), 885.

Hunt, G. (2000). A cellular perspective of neural networks. In E. Gordon (Ed.), *Integrative neuroscience: Bringing together biological, psychological, and clinical models of the human brain* (pp. 65–73). Amsterdam, Netherlands: Overseas Publishers Association.

Huppert, J. D., Siev, J., & Kushner, E. S. (2007). When religion and obsessive—Compulsive disorder collide: Treating scrupulosity in ultra-orthodox Jews. *Journal of Clinical Psychology, 63*(10), 925–941.

Huppi, P., Warfield, S., Kikinis, R., Barnes, P., Zientara, G., Jolesz, F., et al. (1998). Quantitative magnetic resonance imaging of brain development in premature and mature newborns. *Annals of Neurology, 43*, 224–235.

Hurley, M. J., Mash, D. C., & Jenner, P. (2003). Markers for dopaminergic neurotransmission in the cerebellum in normal individuals and patients with Parkinson's disease examined by RT-PCR. *European Journal of Neuroscience, 18*, 2668–2672.

Huttenlocher, J., Levine, S., & Vevea, J. (1998). Environmental input and cognitive growth: A study using time-period comparisons. *Child Development, 69*(4), 1012–1029.

Huttenlocher, P. R. (1979). Synaptic density in human frontal cortex—Developmental changes and effects of aging. *Brain Research, 163*, 195–205.

Huttenlocher, P. R. (1994). Synaptogenesis in human cerebral cortex. In G. Dawson & K. W. Fischer (Eds.), *Human behavior and the developing brain* (pp. 137–152). New York: Guilford.

Huttenlocher, P. R. (2002). *Neural plasticity: The effects of the environment on the development of the cerebral cortex.* Cambridge, MA: Harvard University Press.

Huys, D., Hardenacke, K., Poppe, P., Bartsch, C., Baskin, B., & Kuhn, J. (2012). Update on the role of antipsychotics in the treatment of Tourette syndrome. *Neuropsychiatric Disease and Treatment, 8*, 95.

Hviid, A., Stellfeld, M., Wohlfahrt, J., & Melbye, M. (2003). Association between thimerosal-containing vaccine and autism. *Journal of the American Medical Association, 290*, 1763–1766.

Hyde, C. L., Nagle, M. W., Tian, C., Chen, X., Paciga, S. A., Wendland, J. R., et al. (2016). Identification of 15 genetic loci associated with risk of major depression in individuals of European descent. *Nature genetics, 48*(9), 1031–1036.

Hyman, S. E. (2003). Diagnosing disorders. *Scientific American, Special Issue*, 99.

Hyman, S. E., & Malenka, R. C. (2001). Addiction and the brain: The neurobiology of compulsion and its persistence. *Neuroscience, 2*(10), 695–703.

Hynd, G. W., & Willis, W. G. (1988). *Pediatric neuropsychology.* Orlando, FL: Grune & Stratton.

Hynd, G. W., Hern, K. L., Novey, E. S., Eliopulos, D., Marshall, R., Gonzalez, J. J., & Voeller, K. K. (1993). Attention deficit-hyperactivity disorder and asymmetry of the caudate nucleus. *Journal of Child Neurology, 8*(4), 339–347.

Hynd, G. W., Semrud-Clikeman, M., Lorys, A. R., Novey, E. S., Eliopulos, D., & Lyytinen, H. (1991). Corpus callosum morphology in attention deficit-hyperactivity disorder: Morphometric analysis of MRI. *Journal of Learning Disabilities, 24*(3), 141–146.

Iacono, D., O'brien, R., Resnick, S. M., Zonderman, A. B., Pletnikova, O., Rudow, G., et al. (2008). Neuronal hypertrophy in asymptomatic Alzheimer disease. *Journal of Neuropathology & Experimental Neurology, 67*(6), 578–589.

Ibach, B., & Haen, E. (2004). Acetylcholinesterase inhibition in Alzheimer's disease. *Current Pharmaceutical Design, 10*, 231–251.

Ieong, H. F. H., & Yuan, Z. (2017). Resting-state neuroimaging and neuropsychological findings in opioid use disorder during abstinence: A review. *Frontiers in Human Neuroscience, 11*, 169.

Ilic, K., Hawke, R. L., Thirumaran, R. K., Schuetz, E. G., Hull, J. H., Kashuba, A. D., et al. (2013). The influence of sex, ethnicity, and CYP2B6 genotype on bupropion metabolism as an index of hepatic CYP2B6 activity in humans. *Drug Metabolism and Disposition, 41*(3), 575–581.

Ilic, M., Reinecke, J., Bohner, G., Röttgers, H. O., Beblo, T., Driessen, M., & Corrigan, P. W. (2013). Belittled, avoided, ignored, denied: Assessing forms and consequences of stigma experiences of people with mental illness. *Basic and Applied Social Psychology, 35*(1), 31–40.

Im, W. Y., Ha, J. H., Kim, E. J., Cheon, K. A., Cho, J., & Song, D. H. (2018). Impaired White Matter Integrity and Social Cognition in High-Function Autism: Diffusion Tensor Imaging Study. *Psychiatry Investigation, 15*(3): 292–299.

Imaizumi, Y. (1995). Geographical variations in mortality from Parkinson's disease in Japan, 1977–1985. *Acta Neurologica Scandinavica, 91*, 311–316.

Inturrisi, C. E. (2002). Clinical pharmacology of opioids for pain. *Clinical Journal of Pain, 18*, 3–13.

Ioannidis, K., Chamberlain, S. R., & Müller, U. (2014). Ostracising caffeine from the pharmacological arsenal for attention-deficit hyperactivity disorder–was this a correct decision? *A Literature Review: Journal of Psychopharmacology, 28*(9), 830–836.

Iseki, E. (2004). Dementia with Lewy bodies: Reclassification of pathological subtypes and boundary with Parkinson's disease or Alzheimer's disease. *Neuropathology, 24*, 72–78.

Ishihara, K., & Sasa, M. (2001). Potentiation of 5-HT(3) receptor functions in the hippocampal CA1 region of rats following repeated electroconvulsive shock treatments. *Neuroscience Letters, 307*, 37–40.

Ishihara, K., Amano, T., Hayakawa, H., Yamawaki, S., & Sasa, M. (1999). Enhancement of serotonin(1A) receptor function following repeated electroconvulsive shock in young rat hippocampal neurons in vitro. *International Journal of Neuropsychopharmacology, 2*, 101–104.

Ishii, T., & Eto, K. (2014). Fetal stem cell transplantation: Past, present, and future. *World Journal of Stem Cells, 6*(4), 404–420.

Issari, Y., Jakubovski, E., Bartley, C. A., Pittenger, C., & Bloch, M. H. (2016). Early onset of response with selective serotonin reuptake inhibitors in obsessive-compulsive disorder: A meta-analysis. *Journal of Clinical Psychiatry, 77*(5), e605-e611.

Isserles, M., Daskalakis, Z. J., Kumar, S., Rajji, T. K., & Blumberger, D. M. (2017). Clinical effectiveness and tolerability of electroconvulsive therapy in patients with neuropsychiatric symptoms of dementia. *Journal of Alzheimer's Disease, 57*(1), 45–51.

Itil, T. M. (1977). Qualitative and quantitative EEG findings in schizophrenia. *Schizophrenia Bulletin, 3*, 61–79.

Ito, H., Kawashima, R., Awata, S., Ono, S., Sato, K., Goto, R., et al. (1996). Hypoperfusion in the limbic system and prefrontal cortex in depression: SPECT with anatomic standardization technique. *Journal of Nuclear Medicine, 37*, 410–414.

Ito, K., Yoshida, K., Sato, K., Takahashi, H., Kamata, M., Higuchi, H., et al. (2002). A variable number of tandem repeats in the serotonin transporter gene does not affect the antidepressant response to fluboxamine. *Psychiatry Research, 111*, 235–239.

Ivanova, A., Zaidel, E., Salamon, N., Bookheimer, S., Uddin, L. Q., & Bode, S. D. (2017). Intrinsic functional organization of putative language networks in the brain following left cerebral hemispherectomy. *Brain Structure and Function, 222*(8), 3795–3805.

Iwamoto, K., Kakiuchi, C., Bundo, M., Ikeda, K., & Kato, T. (2004). Molecular characterization of bipolar disorder by comparing gene expression profiles of postmortem brains of major mental disorders. *Molecular Psychiatry, 9*, 406–416.

Iwata, N., Cowley, D. S., Radel, M., Roy-Byrne, P. P., & Goldman, D. (1999). Relationship between a GABAZ alpha 6 Pro385Ser substitution and benzodiazepine sensitivity. *American Journal of Psychiatry, 159*, 1447–1449.

Jablensky, A. (1997). The 100-year epidemiology of schizophrenia. *Schizophrenia Research, 28*, 111–125.

Jacob, T., Waterman, B., Heath, A., True, W., Bucholz, K. K., Haber, R., et al. (2003). Genetic and environmental effects on offspring alcoholism: New insights using offspring-of-twins design. *Archives of General Psychiatry, 60*, 1265–1272.

Jacobsen, L. K., Staley, J. K., Malison, R. T., Zoghbi, S. S., Seibyl, J. P., Kosten, T. R., et al. (2000). Elevated central serotonin transporter binding availability in acutely abstinent cocaine-dependent patients. *American Journal of Psychiatry, 157*, 1134–1140.

Jaisoorya, T. S., Reddy, Y. J., Nair, B. S., Rani, A., Menon, P. G., Revamma, M., et al. (2017). Prevalence and correlates of obsessive-compulsive disorder and subthreshold obsessive-compulsive disorder among college students in Kerala, India. *Indian Journal of Psychiatry, 59*(1), 56–62.

Jakobsen, J. C., Katakam, K. K., Schou, A., Hellmuth, S. G., Stallknecht, S. E., Leth-Møller, K., et al. (2017). Selective serotonin reuptake inhibitors versus placebo in patients with major depressive disorder. A systematic review with meta-analysis and Trial Sequential Analysis. *BMC Psychiatry, 17*(1), 58.

Jakubovski, E., Varigonda, A. L., Freemantle, N., Taylor, M. J., & Bloch, M. H. (2015). Systematic review and meta-analysis: Dose-response relationship of selective serotonin reuptake inhibitors in major depressive disorder. *American Journal of Psychiatry, 173*(2), 174–183.

Jamerson, M., Schmoyer, J. A., Park, J., Marciano-Cabral, F., & Cabral, G. A. (2017). Identification of Naegleria fowleri proteins linked to primary amoebic meningoencephalitis. *Microbiology, 163*(3), 322–332.

Jang, Y., Koo, J. H., Kwon, I., Kang, E. B., Um, H. S., Soya, H., et al. (2017). Neuroprotective effects of endurance exercise against neuroinflammation in MPTP-induced Parkinson's disease mice. *Brain Research, 1655*, 186–193.

Janicak, P. G., Dowd, S. M., Martis, B., Alam, D., Beedle, D., Krasuski, J., et al. (2002). Repetitive transcranial magnetic stimulation versus electroconvulsive therapy for major depression: Results of a randomized trial. *Biological Psychiatry, 51*, 659–667.

Janssen, J. C., Beck, J. A., Campbell, T. A., Dickinson, A., Fox, N. C., Harvey, R. J., et al. (2003). Early onset familial Alzheimer's disease Mutation frequency in 31 families. *Neurology, 60*(2), 235–239.

Janusis, G. M., & Weyandt, L. L. (2010). An exploratory study of substance use and misuse among college students with and without ADHD and other disabilities. *Journal of Attention Disorders, 14*(3), 205–215.

Järvenpää, T., Laakso, M. P., Rossi, R., Koskenvuo, M., Kaprio, J., Räihä, I., et al. (2004). Hippocampal MRI volumetry in cognitively discordant monozygotic twin pairs. *Journal of Neurology, Neurosurgery, and Psychiatry, 75*, 116–120.

Jarvis, B., & Figgitt, D. P. (2003). Memantine. *Drugs & Aging, 20*, 465–478.

Javanmard, M., Shlik, J., Kennedy, S. H., Vaccarino, F. J., Houle, S., & Bradwejn, J. (1999). Neuroanatomic correlates of CCK-4-induced panic attacks in healthy humans: A comparison of two time points. *Biological Psychiatry, 45*, 872–882.

Javitt, D., & Zukin, S. (1991). Recent advances in the phencyclidine mode of schizophrenia. *American Journal of Psychiatry, 148,* 1301–1308.

Jeffries, K. J., Schooler, C., Schoenbach, C., Herscovitch, P., Chase, T. N., & Braun, A. R. (2002). The functional neuroanatomy of Tourette's syndrome: An FDG PET study III: Functional coupling of regional cerebral metabolic rates. *Neuropsychopharmacology, 27,* 92–104.

Jenike, M. A., Baer, L., Ballentine, T., Martuza, R. L., Tynes, S., Giriunas, I., et al. (1991). Cingulotomy for refractory obsessive-compulsive disorder. A long-term follow-up of 33 patients. *Archives of General Psychiatry, 48,* 548–555.

Jenike, M. A., Breiter, H. C., Baer, L., Kennedy, D. N., Savage, C. R. Olivares, M. J, et al. (1996). Cerebral structural abnormalities in obsessive-compulsive disorder. A quantitative morphometric magnetic resonance imaging study. *Archives of General Psychiatry, 53,* 625–632.

Jensen, K. P. (2016). A review of genome-wide association studies of stimulant and opioid use disorders. *Molecular Neuropsychiatry, 2*(1), 37–45.

Jensen, S. K., Pangelinan, M., Björnholm, L., Klasnja, A., Leemans, A., Drakesmith, M., . . . Paus, T. (2017). Associations between prenatal, childhood, and adolescent stress and variations in white-matter properties in young men. *NeuroImage,* 31–38.

Jeong, Y. J., Yoon, H. J., & Kang, D. Y. (2017). Assessment of change in glucose metabolism in white matter of amyloid-positive patients with Alzheimer disease using F-18 FDG PET. *Medicine, 96*(48).

Jeppesen, S. S., Debes, N. M., Simonsen, H. J., Rostrup, E., Larsson, H. B. W., & Skov, L. (2014). Study of medication-free children with Tourette syndrome do not show imaging abnormalities. *Movement Disorders, 29*(9), 1212–1216.

Jest, D. V., Lacro, J. P., Palmer, B., Rockwell, E., Harris, J., & Caligiuri, M. P. (1999). Incidence of tardive dyskinesia in early stages of low-dose treatment with typical neuroleptics in older patients. *American Journal of Psychiatry, 156,* 309–311.

Ji, C., Tang, M., & Johnson, G. V. (2017). Assessing the degradation of tau in primary neurons: The röle of autophagy. *Methods in Tau Cell Biology Methods in Cell Biology,* 229–244.

Jia, P., Han, G., Zhao, J., Lu, P., & Zhao, Z. (2016). SZGR 2.0: A one-stop shop of schizophrenia candidate genes. *Nucleic Acids Research, 45*(D1), D915-D924.

Jiang, G., Yin, X., Li, C., Li, L., Zhao, L., Evans, A. C., et al. (2015). The plasticity of brain gray matter and white matter following lower limb amputation. *Journal of Neural Plasticity,* 1–10.

Jin, Z., Yang, Y., Liu, S., Huang, H., & Jin, X. (2018). Prevalence of DSM-5 autism spectrum disorder among school-based children aged 3–12 years in Shanghai, China. *Journal of Autism and Developmental Disorders, 48*(7), 2434–2443.

Joel, D., Avisar, A., & Doljansky, J. (2001). Enhancement of excessive lever-pressing after post-training signal attenuation in rats by repeated administration of the D1 antagonist SCH 23390 or the D2 agonist quinpirole, but not the D1 agonist SKF 38393 or the D2 antagonist haloperidol. *Behavioral Neuroscience, 115,* 1291–300.

Joensuu, M., Tolmunen, T., Saarinen, P. I., Tiihonen, J., Kuikka, J., Ahola, P., et al. (2007). Reduced midbrain serotonin transporter availability in drug-naïve patients with depression measured by SERT-specific [123 I] nor-β-CIT SPECT imaging. *Psychiatry Research: Neuroimaging, 154*(2), 125–131.

Johns, L. C., & van Os, J. (2001). The continuity of psychotic experiences in the general population. *Clinical Psychology Review, 21,* 1125–1141.

Johnson, J. W., & Kotermanski, S. E. (2006). Mechanism of action of memantine. *Current Opinion in Pharmacology, 6*(1), 61–67.

Johnson, K. R., & Johnson, S. L. (2014). Inadequate treatment of black Americans with bipolar disorder. *Psychiatric Services, 65*(2), 255–258.

Johnson, L., El-Khoury, A., Aberg-Wistedt, A., Stain-Malmgren, R., & Mathe, A. A. (2001). Tryptophan depletion in lithium-stabilized patients with affective disorder. *International Journal of Neuropsychopharmacology, 4,* 329–336.

Johnstone, E. C., Crow, T. J., Frith, C. D., Husband, J., & Kreel, L. (1976). Cerebral ventricular size and cognitive impairment in chronic schizophrenia. *Lancet, 2,* 924–926.

Joki, H., Higashiyama, Y., Nakae, Y., Kugimoto, C., Doi, H., Kimura, K., et al. (2018). White matter hyperintensities on MRI in dementia with Lewy bodies, Parkinson's disease with dementia, and Alzheimer's disease. *Journal of the Neurological Sciences, 385,* 99–104.

Jokic-Begic, N., & Begic, D. (2003). Quantitative electroencephalogram (qEEG) in combat veterans with post-traumatic stress disorder (PTSD). *Nordic Journal of Psychiatry, 57,* 351–355.

Jones, B. E. (1993). The organization of central cholinergic systems and their functional importance in sleep—Waking states. *Progress in Brain Research, 98,* 61–71.

Jonnal, A. H., Gardner, C. O., Prescott, C. A, & Kendler, K. S. (2000). Obsessive and compulsive symptoms in a general population sample of female twins. *American Journal of Medical Genetics, 96,* 791–796.

Jørgensen, H. S., Reith, J., Nakayama, H., Kammersgaard, L. P., Raaschou, H. O., & Olsen, T. S. (1999). What determines good recovery in patients with the most severe strokes?: The Copenhagen Stroke Study. *Stroke, 30*(10), 2008–2012.

Josephs, K. A., & Rossor, M. N. (2004). The alien limb. *Practical Neurology, 4*(1), 44–45.

Josephs, K. A., Dickson, D. W., Tosakulwong, N., Weigand, S. D., Murray, M. E., Petrucelli, L., et al. (2017). Rates of hippocampal atrophy and presence of post-mortem TDP-43 in patients with Alzheimer's disease: A longitudinal retrospective study. *The Lancet Neurology, 16*(11), 917–924.

Jovanovic, H., Lundberg, J., Karlsson, P., Cerin, Å., Saijo, T., Varrone, A., et al. (2008). Sex differences in the serotonin 1A receptor and serotonin transporter binding in the human brain measured by PET. *Neuroimage, 39*(3), 1408–1419.

Joyce, J. N., Lexow, N., Brid, E., & Winokur, A. (1988). Organization of dopamine D1 and D2 receptors in human striatum: Receptor autoradiographic studies in Huntington's disease and Schizophrenia. *Synapse, 2,* 546–557.

Joyce, J. N., & Millan, M. J. (2007). Dopamine D3 receptor agonists for protection and repair in Parkinson's disease. *Current Opinion in Pharmacology, 7*(1), 100–105.

Juan, D., Zhou, D. H., Li, J., Wang, J. Y., Gao, C., & Chen, M. (2004). A 2-year follow-up study of cigarette smoking and risk of dementia. *European Journal of Neurology, 11,* 277–282.

Julien, J., Joubert, S., Ferland, M. C., Frenette, L. C., Boudreau-Duhaime, M. M., Malo-Véronneau, L., & De Guise, E. (2017). Association of traumatic brain injury and Alzheimer disease onset: A systematic review. *Annals of Physical and Rehabilitation Medicine, 60*(5), 347–356.

Jullienne, A., Fukuda, A. M., Ichkova, A., Nishiyama, N., Aussudre, J., Obenaus, A., & Badaut, J. (2018). Modulating the water channel AQP4 alters miRNA expression, astrocyte connectivity and water diffusion in the rodent brain. *Scientific Reports, 8*(1), 4186.

Jung, E. J., Noh, J. Y., Choi, W. S., Seo, Y. B., Lee, J., Song, J. Y., et al. (2016). Perceptions of influenza vaccination during pregnancy in Korean women of childbearing age. *Human Vaccines & Immunotherapeutics, 12*(8), 1997–2002.

Just, M. A., Carpenter, P. A., Keller, T. A., Eddy, W. F., & Thulborn, K. R. (1996). Brain activation modulated by sentence comprehension. *Science, 274,* 114–116.

Juul-Dam, N., Townsend, J., & Courchesne, E. (2001). Prenatal, perinatal, and neonatal factors in autism, pervasive developmental disorder-not otherwise specified, and the general population. *Pediatrics, 107,* E63.

Ka, M., Chopra, D. A., Dravid, S. M., & Kim, W. (2016). Essential roles for ARID1B in dendritic arborization and spine morphology of developing pyramidal neurons. *Journal of Neuroscience, 36*(9), 2723–2742.

Kable, J. W., Caulfield, M. K., Falcone, M., McConnell, M., Bernardo, L., Parthasarathi, T., et al. (2017). No effect of commercial cognitive training on brain activity, choice behavior, or cognitive performance. *Journal of Neuroscience, 37*(31), 7390–7402.

Kageyama, Y., Kasahara, T., Morishita, H., Mataga, N., Deguchi, Y., Tani, M., et al. (2017). Search for plasma biomarkers in drug-free patients with bipolar disorder and schizophrenia using metabolome analysis. *Psychiatry and Clinical Neurosciences, 71*(2), 115–123.

Kahle, P. J., Jakowec, M., Teipel, S. J., Hampel, H., Petzinger, G. M., Di Monte, D. A., et al. (2000). Combined assessment of tau and neuronal thread protein in Alzheimer's disease CSF. *Neurology, 54,* 1498–1504.

Kaiser, R. H., Andrews-Hanna, J. R., Wager, T. D., & Pizzagalli, D. A. (2015). Large-scale network dysfunction in major depressive disorder: A meta-analysis of resting-state functional connectivity. *JAMA Psychiatry, 72*(6), 603–611.

Kajs-Wyllie, M. (2002). Ritalin revisited: Does it really help in neurological injury? *Journal of Neuroscience Nursing, 34*, 303–313.

Kalff, A. C., De Sonneville, L. M., Hurks, P. P., Hendriksen, J. G., Kroes, M., Feron, F. J., . . . Jolles, J. (2003). Low-and high-level controlled processing in executive motor control tasks in 5-6-year-old children at risk of ADHD. *Journal of Child Psychology and Psychiatry, 44*(7), 1049–1057.

Kalia, L. V., & Lang, A. E. (2015). Parkinson's disease. *Lancet, 386*(9996), 896–912.

Kalinderi, K., Bostantjopoulou, S., & Fidani, L. (2016). The genetic background of Parkinson's disease: Current progress and future prospects. *Acta Neurologica Scandinavica, 134*(5), 314–326.

Kaluzna-Czaplinska, J., Socha, E., & Rynkowski, J. (2010). Determination of homovanillic acid and vanillylmandelic acid in urine of autistic children by gas chromatography/mass spectrometry. *Medical Science Monitor, 16*(9), CR445-CR450.

Kambeitz, J. P., & Howes, O. D. (2015). The serotonin transporter in depression: Meta- analysis of in vivo and post mortem findings and implications for understanding and treating depression. *Journal of Affective Disorders, 186*, 358–366.

Kamboh, M. I. (2004). Molecular genetics of late-onset Alzheimer's disease. *Annals of Human Genetics, 68*(4), 381–404.

Kane, J. P., Surendranathan, A., Bentley, A., Barker, S. A., Taylor, J. P., Thomas, A. J., et al. (2018). Clinical prevalence of Lewy body dementia. *Alzheimer's Research & Therapy, 10*(1), 19.

Kanetaka, H., Matsuda, H., Asada, T., Ohnishi, T., Yamashita, F., Imabayashi, E. et al. (2004). Effects of partial volume correction on discrimination between very early Alzheimer's dementia and controls using brain perfusion SPECT. *European Journal of Nuclear Medicine and Molecular Imaging, 31*, 975–980.

Kang, D. H., Kim, J. J., Choi, J. S., Kim, Y. I., Kim, C. W., Youn, T., et al. (2004). Volumetric investigation of the frontal-subcortical circuitry in patients with obsessive-compulsive disorder. *The Journal of Neuropsychiatry and Clinical Neurosciences, 16*(3), 342–349.

Kang, D. H., Kwon, J. S., Kim, J. J., Youn, T., Park, H. J., Kim, M. S., et al. (2003). Brain glucose metabolic changes associated with neuropsychological improvements after 4 months of treatment in patients with obsessive-compulsive disorder. *Acta Psychiatrica Scandinavica, 107*, 291–297.

Kang, E., Choe, A. Y., Kim, B., Lee, J. Y., Choi, T. K., Na, H. R., & Lee, S. H. (2016). Serotonin transporter and COMT polymorphisms as independent predictors of health-related quality of life in patients with panic disorder. *Journal of Korean Medical Science, 31*(5), 757–763.

Kang, H. J., Lee, S. S., Lee, C. H., Shim, J. C., Shin, H. J., Liu, K. H., et al. (2006). Neurotoxic pyridinium metabolites of haloperidol are substrates of human organic cation transporters. *Drug Metabolism and Disposition, 34*(7), 1145–1151.

Kanouse, A. B., & Compton, P. (2015). The epidemic of prescription opioid abuse, the subsequent rising prevalence of heroin use, and the federal response. *Journal of Pain & Palliative Care Pharmacotherapy, 29*(2), 102–114.

Kaplan, B. J., McNicol, J., Conte, R. A., & Moghadam, H. K. (1989). Dietary replacement in preschool-aged hyperactive boys. *Pediatrics, 83*, 7–17.

Kaplan, B. J., Simpson, J. S., Ferre, R. C., Gorman, C. P., McMullen, D. M., & Crawford, S. G. (2001). Effective mood stabilization with a chelated mineral supplement: An open-label trial in bipolar disorder. *Journal of Clinical Psychiatry, 62*, 936–944.

Kapur, S. (2003). Psychosis as a state of aberrant salience: A framework for linking biology, phenomenology, and pharamcology in schizoprhenia. *American Journal of Psychiatry, 160*, 13–23.

Kapur, S., & Mann, J. J. (1993). Antidepressant action and the neurobiologic effects of ECT: Human studies. In C. E. Coffey (Ed.), *The clinical science of electroconvulsive therapy* (pp. 235–250). Washington, DC: American Psychiatric Press.

Kapur, S., & Seeman, P. (2001). Does fast dissociation from the dopamine D2 receptor explain the action of atypical antipsychotics?: A new hypothesis. *American Journal of Psychiatry, 158*, 360–369.

Kapur, S., Zipursky, R., Jones, C., Remington, G., & Hourle, S. (2000). Relationship between dopamine D2 occupancy, clinical response, and side effects: A double-blind PET study of first-episode schizophrenia. *American Journal of Psychiatry, 157*, 514–520.

Karajgi, B., Rifkin, A., Doddi, S., & Kolli, R. (1990). The prevalence of anxiety disorders in patients with chronic obstructive pulmonary disease. *American Journal of Psychiatry, 147*, 200–201.

Karayiorgou, M., Simon, T. J., & Gogos, J. A. (2010). 22q11. 2 microdeletions: Linking DNA structural variation to brain dysfunction and schizophrenia. *Nature Reviews Neuroscience, 11*(6), 402–416.

Karki, R., Pandya, D., Elston, R. C., & Ferlini, C. (2015). Defining "mutation" and "polymorphism" in the era of personal genomics. *BMC Medical Genomics, 8*(1), 37.

Karlović, D., & Serretti, A. (2013). Serotonin transporter gene (5-HTTLPR) polymorphism and efficacy of selective serotonin reuptake inhibitors—Do we have sufficient evidence for clinical practice. *Acta Clinica Croatica, 52*(3), 353–362.

Karno, M., Golding, J. M., Sorenson, S. B., & Burnam, A. (1988). The epidemiology of obsessive-compulsive. *Archives of General Psychiatry, 45*, 1094–1099.

Kas, A., Bottlaender, M., Gallezot, J. D., Vidailhet, M., Villafane, G., Grégoire, M. C., et al. (2017). Decrease of nicotinic receptors in the nigrostriatal system in Parkinson's disease. *Journal of Cerebral Blood Flow & Metabolism, 29*(9), 1601–1608.

Kaschka, W., Feistel, H., & Ebert, D. (1995). Reduced benzodiazepine receptor binding in panic disorders measured by iomazenil SPECT. *Journal of Psychiatric Research, 29*, 427–434.

Kashem, M. A., Ahmed, S., Sultana, N., Ahmed, E. U., Pickford, R., Rae, C., et al. (2016). Metabolomics of neurotransmitters and related metabolites in post-mortem tissue from the dorsal and ventral striatum of alcoholic human brain. *Neurochemical Research, 41*(1–2), 385–397.

Kasparek, P., Krausova, M., Haneckova, R., Kriz, V., Zbodakova, O., Korinek, V., & Sedlacek, R. (2014). Efficient gene targeting of the Rosa26 locus in mouse zygotes using TALE nucleases. *FEBS Letters, 588*(21), 3982–3988.

Kassubek, J., Juengling, F. D., Hellwig, B., Knauff, M., Spreer, J., & Lücking, C. H. (2001). Hypermetabolism in the ventrolateral thalamus in unilateral Parkinsonian resting tremor: A positron emission tomography study. *Neuroscience Letters, 304*, 17–20.

Katzan, I. L., Furlan, A. J., Lloyd, L. E., Frank, J. I., Harper, D. L., Hinchey, J. A., et al. (2000). Use of tissue-type plasminogen activator for acute ischemic stroke: The Cleveland area experience. *Journal of the American Medical Association, 283*, 1151–1158.

Kaur, C., Rathnasamy, G., & Ling, E. A. (2017). Biology of microglia in the developing brain. *Journal of Neuropathology and Experimental Neurology, 76*(9), 736–753.

Kawakami, K., Wake, R., Miyaoka, T., Furuya, M., Liaury, K., & Horiguchi, J. (2014). The effects of aging on changes in regional cerebral blood flow in schizophrenia. *Neuropsychobiology, 69*(4), 202–209.

Kazdin, A. E., & Marciano, P. L. (1998). Childhood and adolescent depression. In E. J. Mash & R. A. Barkley (Eds.), *Treatment of childhood disorders* (2nd ed.). New York: Guilford.

Kazhungil, F., Kumar, K. J., Viswanath, B., Shankar, R. G., Kandavel, T., Math, S. B., et al. (2017). Neuropsychological profile of schizophrenia with and without obsessive compulsive disorder. *Asian Journal of Psychiatry, 29*, 30–34.

Kebede, D., Alem, A., Shibre, T., Negash, A., Fekadu, A., Fekadu, D., et al. (2003). Onset and clinical course of schizophrenia in Butajira-Ethiopia. *Social Psychiatry and Psychiatric Epidemiology, 38*(11), 625–631.

Keers, R., & Aitchison, K. J. (2010). Gender differences in antidepressant drug response. *International Review of Psychiatry, 22*(5), 485–500.

Kefalopoulou, Z., Politis, M., Piccini, P., Mencacci, N., Bhatia, K., Jahanshahi, M., et al. (2014). Long-term clinical outcome of fetal cell transplantation for Parkinson disease: Two case reports. *JAMA Neurology, 71*(1), 83–87.

Keles, H. O., Radoman, M., Pachas, G. N., Evins, A. E., & Gilman, J. M. (2017). Using functional near-infrared spectroscopy to measure effects of delta 9-tetrahydrocannabinol on prefrontal activity and working memory in Cannabis users. *Frontiers in Human Neuroscience, 11*, 488.

Kelleher, R. J., & Shen, J. (2017). Presenilin-1 mutations and Alzheimer's disease. *Proceedings of the National Academy of Sciences, 114*(4), 629–631.

Keller, A., Castellanos, F. X., Jeffries, N. O., Giedd, J. N., & Rapoport, J. (2003). Progressive loss of cerebellar volume in childhood-onset schizophrenia. *American Journal of Psychiatry, 160*, 128–133.

Kellner, C. H., Knapp, R. G., Petrides, G., Rummans, T. A., Husain, M. M., Rasmussen, K., et al. (2006). Continuation electroconvulsive therapy vs pharmacotherapy for relapse prevention in major depression: A multisite study from the Consortium for Research in Electroconvulsive Therapy (CORE). *Archives of General Psychiatry, 63*(12), 1337–1344.

Kelly, C., Zuo, X. N., Gotimer, K., Cox, C. L., Lynch, L., Brock, D., et al. (2011). Reduced interhemispheric resting state functional connectivity in cocaine addiction. *Biological Psychiatry, 69*(7), 684–692.

Kelly, D. F., Martin, N. A, Kordestani, R., Counelis, G., Hovda, D. A., Bergsneider, M., et al. (1997). Cerebral blood flow as a predictor of outcome following traumatic brain injury. *Journal of Neurosurgery, 86*, 633–641.

Kelly, M. M., Reilly, E., Quiñones, T., Desai, N., & Rosenheck, R. (2017). Long-acting intramuscular naltrexone for opioid use disorder: Utilization and association with multi-morbidity nationally in the Veterans Health Administration. *Drug & Alcohol Dependence, 183*, 111–117.

Kemeny, A. A. (2003). Surgical technique in vagus nerve stimulation. In S. C. Schachter & D. Schmidt (Eds.), *Vagus nerve stimulation* (2nd ed., pp. 33–48). New York: Martin Dunitz, Taylor & Francis Group.

Kemp, J. A., & McKernan, R. M. (2002). NMDA receptor pathways as drug targets. *Nature Neuroscience, 5*, 1039–1042.

Kempton, M. J., Geddes, J. R., Ettinger, U., Williams, S. C., & Grasby, P. M. (2008). Meta-analysis, database, and meta-regression of 98 structural imaging studies in bipolar disorder. *Archives of General Psychiatry, 65*(9), 1017–1032.

Kendler, K. S., Gardner, C. O., & Prescott, C. A. (2001). Panic syndromes in a population-based sample of male and female twins. *Psychological Medicine, 31*, 989–1000.

Kendler, K. S., Jacobson, K. C., Prescott, C. A., & Neale, M. C. (2003). Specificity of genetic and environmental risk factors for use and abuse/dependence of cannabis, cocaine, hallucinogens, sedatives, stimulants, and opiates in male twins. *American Journal of Psychiatry, 160*, 687–695.

Kendler, K. S., Karkowski, L. M., Neale, M. C., & Prescott, C. A. (2000). Illicit psychoactive substance use, heavy use, abuse, and dependence in a US population-based sample of male twins. *Archives of General Psychiatry, 57*(3), 261–269.

Kendler, K. S., Neale, M. C., Kessler, R. C., Heath, A. C., & Eaves, L. J. (1993). Panic disorder in women: A population-based twin study. *Psychological Medicine, 23*, 397–406.

Kendler, K. S., Pedersen, N. L., Neale, M. C., & Mathe, A. A. (1995). A pilot Swedish twin study of affective illness including hospital- and population-ascertained subsamples: Results of model fitting. *Behavioral Genetics, 25*, 217–232.

Kendler, K. S., Prescott, C. A., Myers, J., & Neale, M. C. (2003). The structure of genetic and environmental risk factors for common psychiatric and substance use disorders in men and women. *Archives of General Psychiatry, 60*, 929–937.

Kennard, M. A. (1936). Age and other factors in motor recovery from precentral lesions in monkeys. *Journal of Neurophysiology, 1*, 477–496.

Kennedy, M. B. (2000). Signal-processing machines at the postsynaptic density. *Science, 290*, 750–754.

Kennedy, R., Mittal, D., & O'Jile, J. (2003). Electroconvulsive therapy in movement disorders: An update. *Journal of Neuropsychiatry and Clinical Neurosciences, 15*, 407–421.

Kennedy, S. H., Javanmard, M., & Vaccarino, F. J. (1997). A review of functional neuroimaging in mood disorders: Positron emission tomography and depression. *Canadian Journal of Psychiatry, 42,* 467–475.

Kerenyi, L., Ricaurte, G. A., Schretlen, D. J., McCann, U., Varga, J., Mathews, W. B., et al. (2003). Positron emission tomography of striatal serotonin transporters in Parkinson disease. *Archives of Neurology, 60,* 1223–1229.

Keshavarz, M. (2017). Glial cells as key elements in the pathophysiology and treatment of bipolar disorder. *Acta neuropsychiatrica, 29*(3), 140–152.

Kessler, J., Mielke, R., Grond, M., Herholz, K., & Heiss, W. D. (2000). Frontal lobe tasks do not reflect frontal lobe function in patients with probable Alzheimer's disease. *International Journal of Neuroscience, 104,* 1–15.

Kessler, R. C., Berglund, P., Demler, O., Jin, R., Koretz, D., Merikangas, K. R., et al. (2003). The epidemiology of major depressive disorder: Results from the national comorbidity survey replication (NCS-R). *Journal of the American Medical Association, 289,* 3095–3105.

Kessler, R. C., Birnbaum, H., Bromet, E., Hwang, I., Sampson, N., & Shahly, V. (2009). Age differences in major depression: Results from the National Comorbidity Survey Replication (NCS-R). *Psychological Medicine, 40*(2), 225–237.

Kessler, R. C., Ruscio, A. M., Shear, K., & Wittchen, H. U. (2009). Epidemiology of anxiety disorders. In *Behavioral neurobiology of anxiety and its treatment* (pp. 21–35). Springer, Berlin, Heidelberg.

Kestler, L. P., Walker, E., & Vega, E. M. (2001). Dopamine receptors in the brains of schizophrenia patients: A meta-analysis of the findings. *Behavioural Pharmacology, 12*(5), 355–371.

Kettenmann, H., & Ransom, B. R. (1995). *Neuroglia.* New York: Oxford University Press.

Ketter, T. A., Kimbrell, T. A., George, M. S., Dunn, R. T., Speer, A. M., Benson, B. E., et al. (2001). Effects of mood and subtype on cerebral glucose metabolism in treatment-resistant bipolar disorder. *Biological Psychiatry, 49,* 97–109.

Kety, S. S., Wender, P. H., Jacobsen, B., Ingraham, L. J., Jansson, L., Faber, B., et al. (1994). Mental illness in the biological and adoptive relatives of schizophrenic adoptees: Replication of the Copenhagen Study in the rest of Denmark. *Archives of General Psychiatry, 51,* 442–455.

Khan, A., Khan, S., Kolts, R., & Brown, W. A. (2003). Suicide rates in clinical trials of SSRIs, other antidepressants, and placebo: Analysis of FDA reports. *American Journal of Psychiatry, 160,* 790–792.

Khemakhem, A. M., Frye, R. E., El-Ansary, A., Al-Ayadhi, L., & Bacha, A. B. (2017). Novel biomarkers of metabolic dysfunction is autism spectrum disorder: Potential for biological diagnostic markers. *Metabolic Brain Disease, 32*(6), 1983–1997.

Khilnani, S., Field, T., Hernandez-Reif, M., & Schanberg, S. (2003). Massage therapy improves mood and behavior of students with attention-deficit/hyperactivity disorder. *Adolescence, 38,* 623–638.

Kieffer, B. L., & Simonin, F. (2003). Molecular mechanisms of opioid dependence by using knockout mice. In R. Maldonado (Ed.), *Molecular biology of drug addiction* (pp. 3–25). Totowa, NJ: Humana Press.

Kiessling, L. S. (1989). Tic disorders associated with evidence of invasive group A beta-hemolytic streptococcal disease. *Developmental Medicine and Child Neurology, 59,* 48.

Killgore, W. D., Britton, J. C., Schwab, Z. J., Price, L. M., Weiner, M. R., Gold, A. L., et al. (2014). Cortico-limbic responses to masked affective faces across PTSD, panic disorder, and specific phobia. *Depression and Anxiety, 31*(2), 150–159.

Killiany, R. J., Gomez-Isla, T., Moss, M., Kikinis, R., Sandor, T., Jolesz, F., et al. (2000). Use of structural magnetic resonance imaging to predict who will get Alzheimer's disease. *Annals of Neurology, 47,* 430–439.

Kilts, C. D., Gross, R. E., Ely, T. D., & Drexler, K. P. (2004). The neural correlates of cue-induced craving in cocaine-dependent women. *American Journal of Psychiatry, 161,* 233–241.

Kim, B., Kim, J. H., Kim, M. K., Lee, K. S., Kim, Y., Choi, T. K., et al. (2014). Frontal white matter alterations in short-term medicated panic disorder patients without comorbid conditions: A diffusion tensor imaging study. *PloS One, 9*(4), e95279.

Kim, B., Oh, J., Kim, M. K., Lee, S., Tae, W. S., Kim, C. M., et al. (2015). White matter alterations are associated with suicide attempt in patients with panic disorder. *Journal of Affective Disorders, 175*, 139–146.

Kim, C. K., & Rivier, C. L. (2000). Nitric oxide and carbon monoxide have a stimulatory role in the hypothalamicpituitary-adrenal response to physico-emotional stressors in rats. *Endocrinology, 141*, 2244–2253.

Kim, H. W., Kang, J. I., Lee, S. H., An, S. K., Sohn, S. Y., Hwang, E. H., et al. (2016). Common variants of HTR3 genes are associated with obsessive-compulsive disorder and its phenotypic expression. *Scientific Reports, 6*, 32564.

Kim, J. E., Dager, S. R., & Lyoo, I. K. (2012). The role of the amygdala in the pathophysiology of panic disorder: Evidence from neuroimaging studies. *Biology of Mood & Anxiety Disorders, 2*(1), 20.

Kim, J. J., Lee, M. C., Kim, J., Kim, I. Y., Kim, S. I., Han, M. H., et al. (2001). Grey matter abnormalities in obsessive-compulsive disorder: Statistical parametric mapping of segmented magnetic resonance images. *British Journal of Psychiatry, 179*, 330–334.

Kim, K. J., & Peterson, B. S. (2003). Cavum septi pellucidi in Tourette syndrome. *Biological Psychiatry, 54*, 76–85.

Kim, K. W., Jhoo, J. H., Lee, K. U., Lee, D. Y., Lee, J. H., Youn, J. Y., et al. (1999). Association between apolipoprotein E polymorphism and Alzheimer's disease in Koreans. *Neuroscience Letters, 277*, 145–148.

Kim, M. K., Kim, B., Choi, T. K., & Lee, S. H. (2017). White matter correlates of anxiety sensitivity in panic disorder. *Journal of Affective Disorders, 207*, 148–156.

Kim, S., Kaufman, M. J., Cohen, B. M., Jensen, J. E., Coyle, J. T., Du, F., & Öngür, D. (2017). In vivo brain glycine and glutamate concentrations in patients with first-episode psychosis measured by echo time—Averaged proton magnetic resonance spectroscopy at 4T. *Biological Psychiatry, 83*(6), 484–491.

Kim, Y., Santos, R., Gage, F. H., & Marchetto, M. C. (2017). Molecular mechanisms of bipolar disorder: Progress made and future challenges. *Frontiers in Cellular Neuroscience, 11* http://doi.org/10.3389/fncel.2017.00030.

Kimbrell, T. A., Ketter, T. A., George, M. S., Little, J. T., Benson, B. F., Willis, M. W., et al. (2002). Regional cerebral glucose utilization in patients with a range of severities of unipolar depression. *Biological Psychiatry, 51*, 237–252.

Kimura, H. (2002). Hydrogen sulfide as a neuromodulator. *Molecular Neurobiology, 26*, 13–19.

King, M. R., Heaton, M. B., & Walker, D. W. (2002). The effects of ethanol consumption on neurotrophins and their receptors in the rat hippocampus and basal forebrain. *Brain Research, 950*, 137–147.

Kinney, H. C., Brody, B. A., Kloman, A. S., & Gilles, F. H. (1988). Sequence of central nervous system myelination in human infancy. II. Patterns of myelination in autopsied infants. *Journal of Neuropathology and Experimental Neurology, 47*, 217–234.

Kirchhoff, F. (2017). Analysis of functional NMDA receptors in astrocytes. *Methods in Molecular Biology NMDA Receptors*, 241–251.

Kirino, E., & Inoue, R. (1999). The relationship mismatch negativity to quantitative EEG and morphological findings in schizophrenia. *Journal of Psychiatric Research, 33*, 445–456.

Kirkbride, J. B., Susser, E., Kundakovic, M., Kresovich, J. K., Smith, G. D., & Relton, C. L. (2012). Prenatal nutrition, epigenetics and schizophrenia risk: Can we test causal effects? *Epigenomics, 4*(3), 303–315.

Kirley, A., Lowe, N., Hawi, Z., Mullins, C., Daly, G., Waldman, I., et al. (2003). Association of the 480 bp DAT1 allele with methylphenidate response in a sample of Irish children with ADHD. *American Journal of Medical Genetics, 121B*, 50–54.

Kirmayer, L. J. (2001). Cultural variations in the clinical presentation of depression and anxiety: Implications for diagnosis and treatment. *Journal of Clinical Psychiatry, 62*, 22–30.

Kirov, G., Murphy, K. C., Arranz, M. J., Jones, I., McCandles, F., Kunugi, H., et al. (1998). Low activity allele of catechol-o-methyltransferase gene associated with rapid cycling bipolar disorder. *Molecular Psychiatry, 3*, 342–345.

Kirsch, I. (2003). St John's wort, conventional medicine, and placebo: An egregious double standard. *Complementary Therapies in Medicine, 11*, 193–195.

Klaassen, T., Klumperbeek, J., Deutz, N. E., Van Praag, H. M., & Griez, E. (1998). Effects of tryptophan depletion on anxiety and on panic provoked by carbon dioxide challenge. *Psychiatry Research, 77*, 167–174.

Klein, C., & Westenberger, A. (2012). Genetics of Parkinson's disease. *Cold Spring Harbor Perspectives in Medicine, 2*(1), a008888.

Klein, M., Berger, S., Hoogman, M., Dammers, J., Makkinje, R., Heister, A. J., et al. (2016). Meta-analysis of the DRD5 VNTR in persistent ADHD. *European Neuropsychopharmacology, 26*(9), 1527–1532.

Klimek, V., Roberson, G., Stockmeier, C. A., & Ordway, G. A. (2003). Serotonin transporter and MAO-B levels in monoamine nuclei of the human brainstem are normal in major depression. *Journal of Psychiatry Research, 37*, 387–397.

Klimesch, W. (1999). EEG alpha and theta oscillations reflect cognitive and memory performance: A review and analysis. *Brain Research Review, 29*, 169–195.

Klingberg, T., Vaidya, C. J., Gabrieli, J. D., Moseley, M. E., & Hedehus, M. (1999). Myelination and organization of the frontal white matter in children: A diffusion tensor MRI study. *Neuroreport, 10*(13), 2817–2821.

Klosinski, B. B., & Mithoefer, M. C. (2017). Potential psychiatric uses for MDMA. *Clinical Pharmacology & Therapeutics, 101*(2), 194–196.

Klünemann, H. H., Fronhöfer, W., Wurster, H., Fischer, W., Ibach, B., & Klein, H. E. (2002). Alzheimer's second patient: Johann F. and his family. *Annals of Neurology, 52*, 520–523.

Knoll, J. (1992). The pharmacological profile of (-)deprenyl (selegiline) and its relevance for humans: A personal view. *Pharmacology & Toxicology, 70*, 317–321.

Ko, A., Harada, M. Y., Barmparas, G., Thomsen, G. M., Alban, R. F., Bloom, M. B., . . . Ley, E. J. (2016). Early propranolol after traumatic brain injury is associated with lower mortality. *Journal of Trauma and Acute Care Surgery, 80*(4), 637–642.

Kobierska, M., Sitek, M., Gocyła, K., & Janik, P. (2014). Coprolalia and copropraxia in patients with Gilles de la Tourette syndrome. *Neurologia i neurochirurgia polska, 48*(1), 1–7.

Koch, G., Bonnì, S., Pellicciari, M. C., Casula, E. P., Mancini, M., Esposito, R., . . . Motta, C. (2018). Transcranial magnetic stimulation of the precuneus enhances memory and neural activity in prodromal Alzheimer's disease. *NeuroImage, 169*, 302–311.

Koch, K., Reeß, T. J., Rus, O. G., Zimmer, C., & Zaudig, M. (2014). Diffusion tensor imaging (DTI) studies in patients with obsessive-compulsive disorder (OCD): A review. *Journal of Psychiatric Research, 54*, 26–35.

Kodl, M. M., & Wakschlag, L. S. (2004). Does a childhood history of externalizing problems predict smoking during pregnancy? *Addictive Behavior, 29*, 273–279.

Koenders, L., Lorenzetti, V., de Haan, L., Suo, C., Vingerhoets, W. A. M., van den Brink, W., et al. (2017). Longitudinal study of hippocampal volumes in heavy cannabis users. *Journal of Psychopharmacology, 31*(8), 1027–1034.

Kogure, D., Matsuda, H., Ohnishi, T., Asada, T., Uno, M., Kunihiro, T., et al. (2000). Longitudinal evaluation of early Alzheimer's disease using brain perfusion SPECT. *Journal of Nuclear Medicine, 41*, 1155–1162.

Kohlrausch, F. B., Giori, I. G., Melo-Felippe, F. B., Vieira-Fonseca, T., Velarde, L. G. C., de Salles Andrade, J. B., & Fontenelle, L. F. (2016). Association of GRIN2B gene polymorphism and Obsessive Compulsive disorder and symptom dimensions: A pilot study. *Psychiatry Research, 243*, 152–155.

Kohls, G., Antezana, L., Mosner, M. G., Schultz, R. T., & Yerys, B. E. (2018). Altered reward system reactivity for personalized circumscribed interests in autism. *Molecular Autism, 9*(1), 9.

Kokkinou, M., Ashok, A. H., & Howes, O. D. (2018). The effects of ketamine on dopaminergic function: Meta-analysis and review of the implications for neuropsychiatric disorders. *Molecular Psychiatry, 23*(1), 59–69.

Kolb, B. (1989). Brain development, plasticity, and behavior. *American Psychologist, 44*, 1203–1212.

Kolb, B., & Elliott, W. (1987). Recovery from early cortical lesions in rats: II. Effects of experience on anatomy and behavior following frontal lesions at 1 or 5 days of age. *Behavioural Brain Research, 26,* 119–137.

Kolb, B., & Gibb, R. (2011). Brain plasticity and behaviour in the developing brain. *Journal of the Canadian Academy of Child Adolescent Psychiatry, 20,* 265–276.

Kolb, B., Mychasiuk, R., Muhammad, A., Li, Y., Frost, D. O., & Gibb, R. (2012). Experience and the developing prefrontal cortex. *Proceedings of the National Academy of Sciences of the United States of America, 109*(Suppl 2), 17186–17193. http://doi.org/10.1073/pnas.1121251109

Kolb, B., & Whishaw, I. Q. (1996). *Fundamentals of human neuropsychology.* New York: Freeman.

Kolb, B., & Whishaw, I. Q. (2001). *An introduction to brain and behavior.* New York: Worth.

Kole, M. H., & Stuart, G. J. (2012). Signal processing in the axon initial segment. *Neuron, 73*(2), 235–247.

Konishi, J., Asami, T., Hayano, F., Yoshimi, A., Hayasaka, S., Fukushima, H., et al. (2014). Multiple white matter volume reductions in patients with panic disorder: Relationships between orbitofrontal Gyrus volume and symptom severity and social dysfunction. *PloS One, 9*(3), e92862.

Konorski, J. (1948). *Conditioned reflexes and neuron organization.* Cambridge, England: Cambridge University Press.

Koob, G. F., & Nestler, E. J. (1997). The neurobiology of drug addiction. In S. Salloway, P. Malloy, & J. L. Cummings (Eds.), *The neuropsychiatry of limbic and subcortical disorders* (pp. 179–194). Washington, DC: American Psychiatric Press.

Koolschijn, P. C. M. P., van Haren, N. E., Lensvelt-Mulders, G. J., Pol, H., Hilleke, E., & Kahn, R. S. (2009). Brain volume abnormalities in major depressive disorder: A meta-analysis of magnetic resonance imaging studies. *Human Brain Mapping, 30*(11), 3719–3735.

Koran, L. M., Aboujaoude, E., Bullock, K. D., Franz, B., Gamel, N., & Elliott, M. (2005). Double-blind treatment with oral morphine in treatment-resistant obsessive-compulsive disorder. *The Journal of Clinical Psychiatry, 66*(3), 353–359.

Kordower, J. H., Emborg, M. E., Bloch, J., Ma, S. Y., Chu, Y., Leventhal, L., et al. (2000). Neurodegeneration prevented by lentiviral vector delivery of GDNF in primate models of Parkinson's disease. *Science, 290,* 767–773.

Kosel, M., & Schlaepfer, T. E. (2003). Beyond the treatment of epilepsy: New applications of vagus nerve stimulation in psychiatry. *CNS Spectrums, 8,* 515–521.

Kosel, M., Brockmann, H., Frick, C., Zobel, A., & Schlaepfer, T. E. (2011). Chronic vagus nerve stimulation for treatment-resistant depression increases regional cerebral blood flow in the dorsolateral prefrontal cortex. *Psychiatry Research: Neuroimaging, 191*(3), 153–159.

Kosel, M., Rudolph, U., Wielepp, P., Luginbuhl, M., Schmitt, W., Fisch, H. U., et al. (2004). Diminished GABA(A) receptor-binding capacity and a DNA base substitution in a patient with treatment-resistant depression and anxiety. *Neuropsychopharmacology, 29,* 347–350.

Koshiyama, D., Fukunaga, M., Okada, N., Yamashita, F., Yamamori, H., Yasuda, Y., et al. (2018). Role of subcortical structures on cognitive and social function in schizophrenia. *Scientific Reports, 8*(1), 1183.

Kosslyn, S. M. (1999). If neuroimaging is the answer, what is the question? *Philosophical Transactions of the Royal Society of London, Biological Sciences, 354,* 1283–1294.

Kossoff, E. H., & Singer, H. S. (2001). Tourette syndrome: Clinical characteristics and current management strategies. *Paediatric Drugs, 3,* 355–363.

Kostovic, I., Lukinovic, N., Judas, M., Bogdanovic, N., Mrzljak, L., Zecevic, N., et al. (1989). Structural basis of the developmental plasticity in the human cerebral cortex: The role of the transient subplate zone. *Metabolic Brain Diseases, 4,* 17–23.

Kotzbauer, P. T., Trojanowsk, J. Q., & Lee, V. M. (2001). Lewy body pathology in Alzheimer's disease. *Journal of Molecular Neuroscience, 17,* 225–232.

Kovelman, J. A., & Scheibel, A. B. (1984). A neurohistologic correlate of schizophrenia. *Biological Psychiatry, 19,* 1601–1621.

Kowalska, A. (2003). Amyloid precursor protein gene mutations responsible for early-onset autosomal dominant Alzheimer's disease. *Folia Neuropathologica, 41,* 35–40.

Kowalski, P. C., Dowben, J. S., & Keltner, N. L. (2017). My dad can beat your dad: Agonists, antagonists, partial agonists, and inverse agonists. *Perspectives in Psychiatric Care, 53*(2), 76–79.

Kowiański, P., Lietzau, G., Czuba, E., Waśkow, M., Steliga, A., & Moryś, J. (2017). BDNF: A key factor with multipotent impact on brain signaling and synaptic plasticity. *Cellular and Molecular Neurobiology, 38*(3), 579–593.

Kozuka, T., Chaya, T., Tamalu, F., Shimada, M., Fujimaki-Aoba, K., Kuwahara, R., . . . Furukawa, T. (2017). The TRPM1 channel is required for development of the rod ON bipolar cell-AII amacrine cell pathway in the retinal circuit. *Journal of Neuroscience*, 0824-17. doi: 10.1523/JNEUROSCI.0824-17.2017.

Krack, P., Poepping, M., Weinert, D., Schrader, B., & Deuschl, G. (2000). Thalamic, pallidal, or subthalamic surgery for Parkinson's disease? *Journal of Neurology, 247*, 122–134.

Kraehenmann, R., Pokorny, D., Aicher, H., Preller, K. H., Pokorny, T., Bosch, O. G., . . . Vollenweider, F. X. (2017). LSD increases primary process thinking via Serotonin 2A receptor activation. *Frontiers in Pharmacology, 8*, 814.

Krakauer, K., Nordentoft, M., Glenthøj, B. Y., Raghava, J. M., Nordholm, D., Randers, L., et al. (2017). White matter maturation during 12 months in individuals at ultra-high-risk for psychosis. *Acta Psychiatrica Scandinavica, 137*(1), 65–78.

Kranz, G. S., Kasper, S., & Lanzenberger, R. (2010). Reward and the serotonergic system. *Neuroscience, 166*(4), 1023–1035.

Krause, K. H., Dresel, S. H., Krause, J., Kung, H. F., & Tatsch, K. (2000). Increased striatal dopamine transporter in adult patients with attention deficit hyperactivity disorder: Effects of methylphenidate as measured by single photon emission computed tomography. *Neuroscience Letters, 285*(2), 107–110.

Krebs, E. E., Gravely, A., Nugent, S., Jensen, A. C., DeRonne, B., Goldsmith, E. S., et al. (2018). Effect of opioid vs nonopioid medications on pain-related function in patients with chronic back pain or hip or knee osteoarthritis pain: The SPACE randomized clinical trial. *JAMA, 319*(9), 872–882.

Kreczmanski, P., Heinsen, H., Mantua, V., Woltersdorf, F., Masson, T., Ulfig, N., et al. (2007). Volume, neuron density and total neuron number in five subcortical regions in schizophrenia. *Brain, 130*(3), 678–692.

Kreek, M. J., Levran, O., Reed, B., Schlussman, S. D., Zhou, Y., & Butelman, E. R. (2012). Opiate addiction and cocaine addiction: Underlying molecular neurobiology and genetics. *The Journal of Clinical Investigation, 122*(10), 3387–3393.

Krieg, J. C., Pirke, K. M., Lauer, C., & Backmund, H. (1988). Endocrine, metabolic, and cranial computed tomographic findings in anorexia nervosa. *Biological Psychiatry, 23*, 377–387.

Kubicki, M., Westin, C. F., Maier, S. E., Mamata, H., Frumin, M., Ersner-Hershfield, H., et al. (2002). Diffusion tensor imaging and its application to neuropsychiatric disorders. *Harvard Review of Psychiatry, 10*(6), 324–336.

Kuder, S. J., & Accardo, A. (2018). What works for college students with autism spectrum disorder. *Journal of Autism and Developmental Disorders, 48*(3), 722–773.

Kuhar, M. J. (1998). Recent biochemical studies of the dopamine transporter—A CNS drug target. *Life Sciences, 62*, 1573–1575.

Kuhl, D. E., Minoshima, S., Fessler, J. A., Frey, K. A., Foster, N. L., Ficaro, E. P., et al. (1996). In vivo mapping of cholinergic terminals in normal aging, Alzheimer's disease, and Parkinson's disease. *Annals of Neurology, 40*, 399–410.

Kuhn, J., Möller, M., Treppmann, J. F., Bartsch, C., Lenartz, D., Gründler, T. O., et al. (2014). Deep brain stimulation of the nucleus accumbens and its usefulness in severe opioid addiction. *Molecular Psychiatry, 19*(2), 145–146.

Kuikka, J. T., Pitkänen, A., Lepola, U., Partanen, K., Vainio, P., Bergström, K. A., et al. (1995). Abnormal regional benzodiazepine receptor uptake in the prefrontal cortex in patients with panic disorder. *Nuclear Medicine Communications, 16*, 273–280.

Kukull, W. A., Larson, E. B., Bowen, J. D., McCormick, W. C., Teri, L., Pfanschmidt, M. L., et al. (1995). Solvent exposure as a risk factor for Alzheimer's disease: A case-control study. *American Journal of Epidemiology, 141*, 1059–1079.

Kultas-Ilinsky, K., & Ilinsky, I. A. (2001). *Basal ganglia and thalamus in health and movement disorders*. New York: Kluwer Academic/Plenum.

Kumar, A., Schapiro, M. B., Grady, C., Haxby, J. V., Wagner, E., Salerno, J. A., et al. (1991). High-resolution PET studies in Alzheimer's disease. *Neuropsychopharmacology, 4*, 35–46.

Kumar, A., Trescher, W., & Byler, D. (2016). Tourette syndrome and comorbid neuropsychiatric conditions. *Current Developmental Disorders Reports, 3*(4), 217–221.

Kumar, A., Williams, M. T., & Chugani, H. T. (2015). Evaluation of basal ganglia and thalamic inflammation in children with pediatric autoimmune neuropsychiatric disorders associated with streptococcal infection and tourette syndrome: A positron emission tomographic (PET) study using 11C-[R]-PK11195. *Journal of Child Neurology, 30*(6), 749–756.

Kumar, B. A., Malhotra, S., Bhattacharya, A., Grover, S., & Batra, Y. K. (2017). Regional cerebral glucose metabolism and its association with phenotype and cognitive functioning in patients with autism. *Indian Journal of Psychological Medicine, 39*(3), 262–270.

Kumar, B. A., Malhotra, S., Bhattacharya, A., Grover, S., & Batra, Y. K. (2017). Regional cerebral glucose metabolism and its association with phenotype and cognitive functioning in patients with autism. *Indian Journal of Psychological Medicine, 39*(3), 262–270.

Kumar, K., Kumar, A., Keegan, R. M., & Deshmukh, R. (2018). Recent advances in the neurobiology and neuropharmacology of Alzheimer's disease. *Biomedicine & Pharmacotherapy, 98*, 297–307.

Kundu, B., Schrock, L., Davis, T., & House, P. A. (2017). Thalamic deep brain stimulation for essential tremor also reduces voice tremor. *Neuromodulation: Technology at the Neural Interface*. doi: 10.1111/ner.12739.

Kuniecki, M., Wołoszyn, K., Domagalik, A., & Pilarczyk, J. (2017). Disentangling brain activity related to the processing of emotional visual information and emotional arousal. *Brain Structure and Function*, 1–9.

Kunkel, A., Kopp, B., Muller, G., Villringer, K. Taub, E., & Flor, H. (1999). Constraint-induced movement therapy for motor recovery in chronic stroke patients. *Archives of Physical and Medical Rehabilitation, 80*, 624–628.

Kuopio, A. M., Marttila, R. J., Helenius, H., & Rinne, U. K. (1999). Environmental risk factors in Parkinson's disease. *Movement Disorders, 14*, 928–939.

Kupfer, D. J., Frank, E., Grochocinski, V. J., Cluss, P. A., Houck, P. R., & Stapf, D. A. (2002). Demographic and clinical characteristics of individuals in a bipolar disorder case registry. *Journal of Clinical Psychiatry, 63*, 120–125.

Kuppili, P. P., Manohar, H., & Menon, V. (2018). Current status of vaccines in psychiatry: A narrative review. *Asian Journal of Psychiatry, 31*, 112–120.

Kurian, P., Obisesan, T. O., & Craddock, T. J. A. (2017). Oxidative species-induced excitonic transport in tubulin aromatic networks: Potential implications for neurodegenerative disease. *Journal of Photochemistry and Photobiology B: Biology, 175*, 109–124.

Kurlan, R. (2004). Disabling repetitive behaviors in Parkinson's disease. *Movement Disorders, 19*, 433–437.

Kurlan, R., Kersun, J., Ballantine, H. T., Jr., & Caine, E. D. (1990). Neurosurgical treatment of severe obsessive-compulsive disorder associated with Tourette's syndrome. *Movement Disorders, 5*, 152–155.

Kuroki, N., Kashiwagi, H., Ota, M., Ishikawa, M., Kunugi, H., Sato, N., et al. (2017). Brain structure differences among male schizophrenic patients with history of serious violent acts: An MRI voxel-based morphometric study. *BMC Psychiatry, 17*(1), 105.

Kwak, C. H., & Jankovic, J. (2002). Tourettism and dystonia after subcortical stroke. *Movement Disorders, 17*, 821–825.

Kwak, C. H., Hanna, P. A., & Jankovic, J. (2000). Botulinum toxin in the treatment of tics. *Archives of Neurology, 57*, 1190–1193.

Kwok, C. S. N., & Lim, L. E. C. (2017). Mania following antidepressant discontinuation in depression: Two case reports. *Australasian Psychiatry, 25*(6), 617–621.

Kwon, J. S., McCarley, R. W., Hirayasu, Y., Anderson, J. E., Fischer, I. A., Kikinis, R., et al. (1999). Left planum temporale volume reduction in schizophrenia. *Archives of General Psychiatry, 56*, 142–148.

Kwon, J. S., Kim, J. J., Lee, D. W., Lee, J. S., Lee, D. S., Kim, M. S., et al. (2003a). Neural correlates of clinical symptoms and cognitive dysfunctions in obsessive-compulsive disorder. *Psychiatry Research: Neuroimaging, 122*(1), 37–47.

Kwon, J. S., Shin, Y. W., Kim, C. W., Kim, Y. I., Youn, T., Han, M. H., et al. (2003b). Similarity and disparity of obsessive-compulsive disorder and schizophrenia in MR volumetric abnormalities of the hippocampus-amygdala complex. *Journal of Neurology, Neurosurgery, and Psychiatry, 74*, 962–964.

Kyzar, E. J., Stewart, A. M., & Kalueff, A. V. (2016). Effects of LSD on grooming behavior in serotonin transporter heterozygous (Sert+/−) mice. *Behavioural Brain Research, 296*, 47–52.

Laakso, M. P., Frisoni, G. B., Könönen, M., Mikkonen, M., Beltramello, A., Geroldi, C., et al. (2000). Hippocampus and entorhinal cortex in frontotemporal dementia and Alzheimer's disease: A morphometric MRI study. *Biological Psychiatry, 47*, 1056–1063.

Laakso, M. P., Partanen, K., Riekkinen, P., Lehtovirta, M., Helkala, E. L., Hallikainen, M., et al. (1996). Hippocampal volumes in Alzheimer's disease, Parkinson's disease with and without dementia, and in vascular dementia: An MRI study. *Neurology, 46*, 678–681.

Laburn, H. P. (1996). How does the fetus cope with thermal challenges? *News in Physiological Sciences, 11*, 96–100.

Lacerda, A. L., Dalgalarrondo, P., Caetano, D., Camargo, E. E., Etchebehere, E. C., & Soares, J. C. (2003b). Elevated thalamic and prefrontal regional cerebral blood flow in obsessive-compulsive disorder: A SPECT study. *Psychiatry Research, 123*, 125–134.

Lacerda-Pinheiro, S. F., Junior, R. F. F. P., de Lima, M. A. P., da Silva, C. G. L., dos Santos, M. D. S. V., Júnior, A. G. T., et al. (2014). Are there depression and anxiety genetic markers and mutations? A systematic review. *Journal of Affective Disorders, 168*, 387–398.

Lachman, H. M., Morrow, B., Shprintzen, R., Veit, S., Parisa, S. S., Faedda, G., et al. (1996). Association of codon 108–158 catechol-o-methyltransferase gene polymorphism with the psychiatric manifestations of velo-cardio-facial syndrome. *American Journal of Medical Genetics, 67*, 468–472.

Lachman, H. M., Papolos, D. F., Saito, T., Yu, Y. M., Szumlanski, C. L., & Weinshilboum, R. M. (1996). Human catechol-o-methyltransferase pharmacogenetics: Description of a functional polymorphism and its potential application to neuropsychiatric disorders. *Pharmacogenetics, 6*, 243–250.

Lafaille-Magnan, M. E., Poirier, J., Etienne, P., Tremblay-Mercier, J., Frenette, J., Rosa-Neto, P., et al. (2017). Odor identification as a biomarker of preclinical AD in older adults at risk. *Neurology, 89*(4), 327–335.

Lagnaoui, R., Moore, N., Moride, Y., Miremont-Salamé, G., & Bégaud, B. (2003). Benzodiazepine utilization patterns in Alzheimer's disease patients. *Pharmacoepidemiology and Drug Safety, 12*, 511–515.

Lai, C. H., Hsu, Y. Y., & Wu, Y. T. (2010). First episode drug-naive major depressive disorder with panic disorder: Gray matter deficits in limbic and default network structures. *European Neuropsychopharmacology, 20*(10), 676–682.

Lai, C. H., & Wu, Y. T. (2013). Fronto-occipital fasciculus, corpus callosum and superior longitudinal fasciculus tract alterations of first-episode, medication-naive and late-onset panic disorder patients. *Journal of Affective Disorders, 146*(3), 378–382.

Lai, C. H., & Wu, Y. T. (2015). The gray matter alterations in major depressive disorder and panic disorder: Putative differences in the pathogenesis. *Journal of Affective Disorders, 186*, 1–6.

Lai, I. C., Hong, C. J., & Tsai, S. J. (2001). Association study of nicotinic-receptor variants and major depressive disorder. *Journal of Affective Disorders, 66*, 79–82.

Lai, Y. Y., & Siegel, J. M. (2003). Physiological and anatomical link between Parkinson-like disease and REM sleep behavior disorder. *Molecular Neurobiology, 27*, 137–152.

Laidi, C., Boisgontier, J., Chakravarty, M. M., Hotier, S., d'Albis, M. A., Mangin, J. F., et al. (2017). Cerebellar anatomical alterations and attention to eyes in autism. *Scientific Reports*, *7*(1), 12008.

Laihinen, A., Ruottinen, H., Rinne, J. O., Haaparanta, M., Bergman, J., Solin, O., et al. (2000). Risk for Parkinson's disease: Twin studies for the detection of asymptomatic subjects using [18F]6—fluorodopa PET. *Journal of Neurology*, *247*, 110–113.

Lajonchere, C., Nortz, M., & Finger, S. (1996). Gilles de la Tourette and the discovery of Tourette syndrome: Includes a translation of his 1884 article. *Archives of Neurology*, *53*(6), 567–574.

Lambert, R. A. (2012). Routine general practice care for panic disorder within the lifestyle approach to managing panic study. *Mental Illness*, *4*(2).

Lammert, D. B., & Howell, B. W. (2016). RELN mutations in autism spectrum disorder. *Frontiers in Cellular Neuroscience*, *10*, 84.

Lan, X., Zhang, M., Yang, W., Zheng, Z., Wu, Y., Zeng, Q., et al. (2014). Effect of treadmill exercise on 5-HT, 5-HT1A receptor and brain derived neurophic factor in rats after permanent middle cerebral artery occlusion. *Neurological Sciences*, *35*(5), 761–766.

Landau, A. M., Alstrup, A. K., Audrain, H., Jakobsen, S., Simonsen, M., Møller, A., et al. (2017). Elevated dopamine D1 receptor availability in striatum of Göttingen minipigs after electroconvulsive therapy. *Journal of Cerebral Blood Flow & Metabolism*, *38*(5), 881–887.

Lane, C., Kanjlia, S., Richardson, H., Fulton, A., Omaki, A., & Bedny, M. (2017). Reduced left lateralization of language in congenitally blind individuals. *Journal of Cognitive Neuroscience*, *29*(1), 65–78.

Lang, E., Mallien, A. S., Vasilescu, A., Hefter, D., Luoni, A., Riva, M. A., et al. (2017). Molecular and cellular dissection of NMDA receptor subtypes as antidepressant targets. *Neuroscience & Biobehavioral Reviews*, *84*, 352–358.

Langston, J. W., Ballard, P., Tetrud, J. W., & Irwin, I. (1983). Chronic Parkinsonism in humans due to a product of meperidine-analog synthesis. *Science*, *219*(4587), 979–980.

Lanoiselée, H. M., Nicolas, G., Wallon, D., Rovelet-Lecrux, A., Lacour, M., Rousseau, S., et al. (2017). APP, PSEN1, and PSEN2 mutations in early-onset Alzheimer disease: A genetic screening study of familial and sporadic cases. *PLoS Medicine*, *14*(3), e1002270.

Larisch, R., Klimke, A., Mayoral, F., Hamacher, K., Herzog, H. R., Vosberg, H., et al. (2001). Disturbance of serotonin 5HT2 receptors in remitted patients suffering from hereditary depressive disorder. *Nuklearmedizin*, *40*, 129–134.

Larøi, F., Luhrmann, T. M., Bell, V., Christian Jr, W. A., Deshpande, S., Fernyhough, C., . . . Woods, A. (2014). Culture and hallucinations: Overview and future directions. *Schizophrenia Bulletin*, *40*(Suppl_4), S213-S220.

Larsson, J. O., Larsson, H., & Lichtenstein, P. (2004). Genetic and environmental contributions to stability and change of ADHD symptoms between 8 and 13 years of age: A longitudinal twin study. *Journal of the American Academy of Child and Adolescent Psychiatry*, *43*, 1267–1275.

Laruelle, M., Abi-Dargham, A., van Dyck, C., Gil, R., D'Souza, C. D., Erdos, J., et al. (1996). Single photon emission computerized tomography imaging of amphetamine-induced dopamine release in drug-free schizophrenic subjects. *Proceedings of the National Academy of Science*, *93*, 9235–9240.

Laruelle, M., Abi-Dargham, A., van Dyck, C. H., Rosenblatt, W., Zea-Ponce, Y., Zoghbi, S. S., et al. (1995). SPECT imaging of striatal dopamine release after amphetamine challenge. *Journal of Nuclear Medicine*, *36*, 1182–1190.

Laurin, D., Masaki, K. H., Foley, D. J., White, L. R., & Launer, L. J. (2004). Midlife dietary intake of antioxidants and risk of late-life incident dementia: The Honolulu-Asia Aging Study. *American Journal of Epidemiology*, *159*, 959–967.

Lauterbach, E. C. (2016). Treatment resistant depression with loss of antidepressant response: Rapid-acting antidepressant action of dextromethorphan, A possible treatment bridging molecule. *Psychopharmacology Bulletin*, *46*(2), 53.

Lavalaye, J., Linszen, D. H., Booij, J., Dingemans, P. M. A. J., Reneman, L., Habraken, J. B. A., et al. (2001). Dopamine transporter density in young patients with schizophrenia assessed with [123I]FP-CIT SPECT. *Schizophrenia Research*, *47*, 59–67.

Laver, K., Dyer, S., Whitehead, C., Clemson, L., & Crotty, M. (2016). Interventions to delay functional decline in people with dementia: A systematic review of systematic reviews. *BMJ Open*, *6*(4), e010767.

Law, A. J., & Deakin, J. F. W. (2001). Asymmetrical reductions of hippocampal NMDARI glutamate receptor mRNA in the psychoses. *Neurochemistry*, *12*, 2971–2974.

Lawrie, S. M., & Abukmeil, S. S. (1998). Brain abnormality in schizophrenia. A systematic and quantitative review of volumetric magnetic resonance imaging studies. *British Journal of Psychiatry*, *172*, 110–120.

Laws, K. R., Irvine, K., & Gale, T. M. (2016). Sex differences in cognitive impairment in Alzheimer's disease. *World journal of psychiatry*, *6*(1), 54–65.

Lawson, J. S., Galin, H., Adams, S. J., Brunet, D. G., Criollo, M., & MacCrimmon, D. J. (2003). Artefacting reliability in QEEG topographic maps. *Clinical Neurophysiology*, *114*, 883–888.

Laxer, K. D., Sourkes, T. L., Fang, T. Y., Young, S. N., Gauthier, S. G., & Missala, K. (1979). Monoamine metabolites in the CSF of epileptic patients. *Neurology*, *29*, 1157–1161.

Leake, A., Fairbairn, A. F., McKeith, I. G., & Ferrier, I. N. (1991). Studies on the serotonin uptake binding site in major depressive disorder and control post-mortem brain: Neurochemical and clinical correlates. *Psychiatry Reseach*, *39*, 155–165.

Lebel, C., Treit, S., & Beaulieu, C. (2017). A review of diffusion MRI of typical white matter development from early childhood to young adulthood. *NMR in Biomedicine*, *47*, 50–58.

Lebowitz, M. S., & Appelbaum, P. S. (2017). Beneficial and detrimental effects of genetic explanations for addiction. *International Journal of Social Psychiatry*, *63*(8), 717–723.

Leckman, J. F., Cohen, D. J., Shaywitz, B. A., Caparulo, B. K., Heninger, G. R., & Bowers, M. B. Jr. (1980). CSF monoamine metabolites in child and adult psychiatric patients. *Archives of General Psychiatry*, *37*, 677–681.

Leckman, J. F., Hardin, M. T., Riddle, M. A., Stevenson, J., Ort, S. I., & Cohen, D. J. (1991). Clonidine treatment of Gilles de la Tourette's syndrome. *Archives of General Psychiatry*, *48*, 324–328.

Lecrubier, Y. (2001). The burden of depression and anxiety in general medicine. *Journal of Clinical Psychiatry*, *62*, 4–9.

LeDoux, J. (2002). *Synaptic self: How our brains become who we are*. New York: Viking.

Lee, H., Milev, R., & Paik, J. W. (2015). Comparison of stigmatizing experiences between Canadian and Korean patients with depression and bipolar disorders. *Asia-Pacific Psychiatry*, *7*(4), 383–390.

Lee, J. D., Nunes Jr, E. V., Novo, P., Bachrach, K., Bailey, G. L., Bhatt, S., et al. (2017). Comparative effectiveness of extended-release naltrexone versus buprenorphine-naloxone for opioid relapse prevention (X: BOT): A multicentre, open-label, randomised controlled trial. *The Lancet*, 309–318.

Lee, J., Kim, B. H., Kim, E., Howes, O. D., Cho, K. I. K., Yoon, Y. B., & Kwon, J. S. (2018). Higher serotonin transporter availability in early-onset obsessive—compulsive disorder patients undergoing escitalopram treatment: A [11C] DASB PET study. *Human Psychopharmacology: Clinical and Experimental*, *33*(1), e2642.

Lee, M., Martin-Ruiz, C., Graham, A., Court, J., Jaros, E., Perry, R., et al. (2002). Nicotinic receptor abnormalities in the cerebellar cortex in autism. *Brain*, *125*, 1483–1495.

Lee, Y. S., Hwang, J., Kim, S. J., Sung, Y. H., Kim, J., Sim, M. E., et al. (2006). Decreased blood flow of temporal regions of the brain in subjects with panic disorder. *Journal of Psychiatric Research*, *40*(6), 528–534.

Lefebvre, A., Beggiato, A., Bourgeron, T., & Toro, R. (2015). Neuroanatomical diversity of corpus callosum and brain volume in autism: Meta-analysis, analysis of the autism brain imaging data exchange project, and simulation. *Biological Psychiatry*, *78*(2), 126–134.

Leiknes, K. A., Schweder, L. J. V., & Høie, B. (2012). Contemporary use and practice of electroconvulsive therapy worldwide. *Brain and Behavior*, *2*(3), 283–344.

Leino, K., Mildh, L., Lertola, K., Seppala, T., & Kirvela, O. (1999). Time course of changes in breathing pattern in morphine- and oxycodone-induced respiratory depression. *Anaesthesia*, *54*, 835–840.

Leissring, M. A., LaFerla, F. M., Callamaras, N., & Parker, I. (2001). Subcellular mechanisms of presenilin-mediated enhancement of calcium signaling. *Neurobiology of Disease, 8*(3), 469–478.

Leite-Morris, K. A., Fukudome, E. Y., Shoeb, M. H., & Kaplan, G. B. (2004). GABAB receptor activation in the ventral tegmental area inhibits the acquisition and expression of opiate-induced motor sensitization. *Journal of Pharmacology and Experimental Therapy, 308*, 667–678.

Lemelson, R. (2003). Obsessive-compulsive disorder in Bali: The cultural shaping of a neuropsychiatric disorder. *Transcultural Psychiatry, 40*, 377–408.

Lencz, T., Guha, S., Liu, C., Rosenfeld, J., Mukherjee, S., DeRosse, P., et al. (2013). Genome-wide association study implicates NDST3 in schizophrenia and bipolar disorder. *Nature Communications, 4*, 2739.

Leng, G., & Ludwig, M. (2008). Neurotransmitters and peptides: Whispered secrets and public announcements. *The Journal of Physiology, 586*(23), 5625–5632.

Lenn, N. J., & Freinkel, A. J. (1989). Facial sparing as a feature of prenatal-onset hemiparesis. *Pediatric Neurology, 5*, 291–295.

Lenox, R. H., & Hahn, C. G. (2000). Overview of the mechanism of action of lithium in the brain: Fifty year update. *Journal of Clinical Psychiatry, 61*, 5–15.

Lenroot, R. K., Schmitt, J. E., Ordaz, S. J., Wallace, G. L., Neale, M. C., Lerch, J. P., et al. (2009). Differences in genetic and environmental influences on the human cerebral cortex associated with development during childhood and adolescence. *Human Brain Mapping, 30*(1), 163–174.

Leon, A. C., Solomon, D. A., Li, C., Fiedorowicz, J. G., Coryell, W. H., Endicott, J., & Keller, M. B. (2011). Antidepressants and risks of suicide and suicide attempts: A 27-year observational study. *The Journal of Clinical Psychiatry, 72*(5), 580.

Leonard, B. (2000). Stress, depression and the activation of the immune system. *World Journal of Biological Psychiatry, 1*, 17–25.

Leonard, H. L., & Rapoport, J. L. (1987). Relief of obsessive-compulsive symptoms by LSD and psilocin. *The American Journal of Psychiatry, 144*(9), 1239–1240.

Leonard, H. L., Topol, D., Bukstein, O., Hindmarsh, D., Allen, A. J., & Swedo, S. E. (1994). Clonazepam as an augmenting agent in the treatment of childhood-onset obsessive-compulsive disorder. *Journal of the American Academy of Child and Adolescent Psychiatry, 33*, 792–794.

Lepine, J. P. (2002). The epidemiology of anxiety disorders: Prevalence and societal costs. *Journal of Clinical Psychiatry, 63*, 4–8.

Leppamaki, S., Partonen, T., & Lonnqvist, J. (2002). Bright-light exposure combined with physical exercise elevates mood. *Journal of Affective Disorders, 72*, 139–144.

Leroi, I., O'Hearn, E., Marsh, L., Lyketsos, C. G., Rosenblatt, A., Ross, C. A., et al. (2002). Psychopathology in patients with degenerative cerebellar diseases: A comparison to Huntington's disease. *American Journal of Psychiatry, 159*, 1306–1314.

Lesch, K. P., Wiesmann, M., Hoh, A., Müller, T., Disselkamp-Tietze, J., Osterheider, M., & Schulte, H. M. (1992). 5-HT 1A receptor-effector system responsivity in panic disorder. *Psychopharmacology, 106*(1), 111–117.

Leshner, A. I. (1997). Addiction is a brain disease, and it matters. *Science, 278*(5335), 47–49.

Lesser, I. M., Myers, H. F., Lin, K. M., Bingham Mira, C., Joseph, N. T., Olmos, N. T., et al. (2010). Ethnic differences in antidepressant response: A prospective multi-site clinical trial. *Depression and Anxiety, 27*(1), 56–62.

Leuchter, A. F., Cook, I. A., Witte, E. A., Morgan, M., & Abrams, M. (2002). Changes in brain function of depressed subjects during treatment with placebo. *American Journal of Psychiatry, 159*, 122–129.

Leuchter, A. F., Hunter, A. M., Krantz, D. E., & Cook, I. A. (2014). Intermediate phenotypes and biomarkers of treatment outcome in major depressive disorder. *Dialogues in Clinical Neuroscience, 16*(4), 525–537.

Levin, H. S., & Robertson, C. S. (2012). Mild traumatic brain injury in translation. *Journal of Neurotrauma, 30*(8), 610–617.

Levine, D. S., Himle, J. A., Taylor, R. J., Abelson, J. M., Matusko, N., Muroff, J., & Jackson, J. (2013). Panic disorder among African Americans, Caribbean blacks and non-Hispanic whites. *Social Psychiatry and Psychiatric Epidemiology, 48*(5), 711–723.

Levine, J., Panchalingam, K., Rapoport, A., Gershon, S., McClure, R. J., & Pettegrew, J. W. (2000). Increased cerebrospinal fluid glutamine levels in depressed patients. *Biological Psychiatry, 47*(7), 586–593.

Levitan, I. B., & Kaczmarek, L. K. (1997). *The neuron: Cell and molecular biology.* New York: Oxford University Press.

Levy, S. E., & Hyman, S. L. (2015). Complementary and alternative medicine treatments for children with autism spectrum disorders. *Child and Adolescent Psychiatric Clinics, 24*(1), 117–143.

Levy, S. E., Mandell, D. S., Merhar, S., Ittenbach, R. F., & Pinto-Martin, J. A. (2003). Use of complementary and alternative medicine among children recently diagnosed with autistic spectrum disorder. *Journal of Developmental and Behavioral Pediatrics, 24*, 418–423.

Lewine, R. R., Hudgins, P., Brown, F., Caudle, J., & Risch, S. C. (1995). Differences in qualitative brain morphology findings in schizophrenia, major depression, bipolar disorder and normal volunteers. *Schizophrenia Research, 15*(3), 253–259.

Lewis, C. M., Ng, M. Y., Butler, A. W., Cohen-Woods, S., Uher, R., Pirlo, K., et al. (2010). Genome-wide association study of major recurrent depression in the UK population. *American Journal of Psychiatry, 167*(8), 949–957.

Lewis, D. A. (2000). GABAergic local circuit neurons and prefrontal dysfunction in schizophrenia. *Brain Research Reviews, 31*, 270–276.

Lewis, D. A., & González-Burgos, G. (2008). Neuroplasticity of neocortical circuits in schizophrenia. *Neuropsychopharmacology, 33*(1), 141–155.

Leyton, M., Boileau, I., Benkelfat, C., Diksic, M., Baker, G., & Dagher, A. (2002). Amphetamine-induced increases in extracellular dopamine, drug wanting, and novelty seeking: A PET/[11C]Raclopride study in healthy men. *Neuropsychopharmacology, 27*, 1027–1035.

Li, C. Y., Sung, F. C., & Wu, S. C. (2002). Risk of cognitive impairment in relation to elevated exposure to electromagnetic fields. *Journal of Occupational and Environmental Medicine, 44*, 66–72.

Li, D., Karnath, H. O., & Xu, X. (2017). Candidate biomarkers in children with autism spectrum disorder: A review of MRI studies. *Neuroscience Bulletin, 33*(2), 219–237.

Li, M., Chen, Z., Deng, W., He, Z., Wang, Q., Jiang, L., et al. (2012). Volume increases in putamen associated with positive symptom reduction in previously drug-naive schizophrenia after 6 weeks antipsychotic treatment. *Psychological Medicine, 42*(7), 1475–1483.

Li, N., Lee, B., Liu, R. J., Banasr, M., Dwyer, J. M., Iwata, M., . . . Duman, R. S. (2010). mTOR-dependent synapse formation underlies the rapid antidepressant effects of NMDA antagonists. *Science, 329*(5994), 959–964.

Li, P., Snyder, L. G., & Vanover, E. K. (2016). Dopamine targeting drugs for the treatment of schizophrenia: Past, present and future. *Current Topics in Medicinal Chemistry, 16*(29), 3385–3403.

Li, T., Liu, X., Zhao, J., Hu, X., Ball, D. M., Loh, E. W., et al. (2002). Allelic association analysis of the dopamine D2, D3, 5-HT2A, and GABA(A)gamma2 receptors and serotonin transporter genes with heroin abuse in Chinese subjects. *American Journal of Medical Genetics, 114*, 329–335.

Li, T., Vallada, H., Curtis, D., Arranz, M., Xu, K., Cai, G., et al. (1997). Catechol-O-methyltransferase Va1158Met polymorphism: Frequency analysis in Han Chinese subjects and allelic association of the low activity allele with bipolar affective disorder. *Pharmacogenetics, 7*, 349–353.

Li, T., Xu, K., Deng, H., Cai, G., Liu, J., Liu, X., et al. (1997). Association analysis of the dopamine D4 gene exon III VNTR and heroin abuse in Chinese subjects. *Molecular Psychiatry, 2*, 413–416.

Li, T., Zhu, Z. H., Liu, X., Hu, X., Zhao, J., Sham, P. C., et al. (2000). Association analysis of polymorphisms in the DRD4 gene and heroin abuse in Chinese subjects. *American Journal of Medical Genetics, 96*, 616–621.

Li, W., Yang, Y., Lin, J., Wang, S., Zhao, J., Yang, G., et al. (2013). Association of serotonin transporter gene (SLC6A4) polymorphisms with schizophrenia susceptibility and symptoms in a Chinese-Han population. *Progress in Neuro-Psychopharmacology and Biological Psychiatry, 44,* 290–295.

Liang, C. S., Ho, P. S., Yen, C. H., Yeh, Y. W., Kuo, S. C., Huang, C. C., et al. (2016). Reduced striatal dopamine transporter density associated with working memory deficits in opioid-dependent male subjects: A SPECT study. *Addiction Biology, 21*(1), 196–204.

Liao, X., Li, G., Wang, A., Liu, T., Feng, S., Guo, Z., et al. (2015). Repetitive transcranial magnetic stimulation as an alternative therapy for cognitive impairment in Alzheimer's disease: A meta-analysis. *Journal of Alzheimer's Disease, 48*(2), 463–472.

Librizzi, L., Losi, G., Marcon, I., Sessolo, M., Scalmani, P., Carmignoto, G., & Curtis, M. D. (2017). Interneuronal network activity at the onset of seizure-like events in entorhinal cortex slices. *The Journal of Neuroscience, 37*(43), 10398–10407

Lieb, R., Isensee, B., Hoefler, M., Pfister, H., & Wittchen, H. U. (2002). Parental major depression and the risk of depression and other mental disorders in offspring. *Archives of General Psychiatry, 59,* 365–374.

Lieberman, J. A., Tollefson, G., Tohen, M., Green, A., Gur, R. E., Kahn, R., et al. (2003). Comparative efficacy and safety of atypical and conventional antipsychotic drugs in first-episode psychosis: A randomized double-blind trial of olanzapine versus haloperidol. *American Journal of Psychiatry, 160,* 1396–1404.

Lile, J. A., Stoops, W. W., Allen, T. S., Glaser, P. E., Hays, L. R., & Rush, C. R. (2004). Baclofen does not alter the reinforcing, subject-rated or cardiovascular effects of intranasal cocaine in humans. *Psychopharmacology, 171,* 441–449.

Lim, K. O., Choi, S. J., Pomara, N., Wolkin, A., & Rotrosen, J. P. (2002). Reduced frontal white matter integrity in cocaine dependence: A controlled diffusion tensor imaging study. *Bilogical Psychiatry, 51,* 890–895.

Lim, K. O., Rosenbloom, M. J., Faustman, W. O., Sullivan, E. V., & Pfefferbaum, A. (1999). Cortical gray matter deficit in patients with bipolar disorder. *Schizophrenia Research, 40,* 219–227.

Lin, K. M., Smith, M. W., & Ortiz, V. (2001). Culture and psychopharmacology. *Psychiatric Clinics of North America, 24*(3), 523–538.

Lin, W. C., Chen, P. C., Huang, C. C., Tsai, N. W., Chen, H. L., Wang, H. C., et al. (2017). Autonomic function impairment and brain perfusion deficit in Parkinson's disease. *Frontiers in Neurology, 8,* 246.

Lindgren, E., Gray, K., Miller, G., Tyler, R., Wiers, C. E., Volkow, N. D., & Wang, G. J. (2018). Food addiction: A common neurobiological mechanism with drug abuse. *Frontiers in Bioscience (Landmark edition), 23,* 811–836.

Lindsley, C. W. (2016). Torn from the headlines: Surviving the "Brain Eating Amoeba". *ACS Chemical Neuroscience, 7*(10), 1313–1313.

Lindvall, O., Brundin, P., Widner, H., Rehncrona, S., Gustavii, B., Frackowiak, R., et al. (1990). Grafts of fetal dopamine neurons survive and improve motor function in Parkinson's disease. *Science, 247,* 574–577.

Lindvall, O., Sawle, G., Widner, H., Rothwell, J. C., Björklund, A., Brooks, D., et al. (1994). Evidence for long-term survival and function of dopaminergic grafts in progressive Parkinson's disease. *Annals of Neurology, 35,* 172–180.

Linnarsson, S., Bjorklund, A., & Ernfors, P. (1997). Learning deficits in BDNF mutant mice. *Journal of Neuroscience, 9,* 2581–2587.

Linterman, I., & Weyandt, L. (2001). Divided attention skills in college students with ADHD: Is it advantageous to have ADHD? *ADHD Report, 9,* 1–6.

Liotti, M., Mayberg, H. S., McGinnis, S., Brannan, S. L., & Jerabek, P. (2002). Unmasking disease-specific cerebral blood flow abnormalities: Mood challenge in patients with remitted unipolar depression. *American Journal of Psychiatry, 159,* 1830–1840.

Lishman, W. A. (1990). Alcohol and the brain. *British Journal of Psychiatry, 156,* 635–644.

List, J., Kübke, J. C., Lindenberg, R., Külzow, N., Kerti, L., Witte, V., & Flöel, A. (2013). Relationship between excitability, plasticity and thickness of the motor cortex in older adults. *Neuroimage, 83,* 809–816.

Little, J. T., Ketter, T. A., Kimbrell, T. A., Danielson, A., Benson, B., Willis, M. W., et al. (1996). Venlafaxine or bupropion responders but not nonresponders show baseline prefrontal and paralimbic hypometabolism compared with controls. *Psychopharmacology Bulletin*, *32*, 629–635.

Little, K. Y., McLaughlin, D. P., Ranc, J., Gilmore, J., Lopez, J. F., Watson, S. J., et al. (1997). Serotonin transporter binding sites and mRNA levels in depressed persons committing suicide. *Biological Psychiatry*, *41*, 1156–1164.

Liu, B., Liu, J., Wang, M., Zhang, Y., & Li, L. (2017). From serotonin to neuroplasticity: Evolvement of theories for major depressive disorder. *Frontiers in Cellular Neuroscience*, *11*, 305.

Liu, C. C., Kanekiyo, T., Xu, H., & Bu, G. (2013). Apolipoprotein E and Alzheimer disease: Risk, mechanisms and therapy. *Nature Reviews Neurology*, *9*(2), 106–118.

Liu, N., Cui, X., Bryant, D. M., Glover, G. H., & Reiss, A. L. (2015). Inferring deep-brain activity from cortical activity using functional near-infrared spectroscopy. *Biomedical Optics Express*, *6*(3), 1074–1089.

Liu, P., Wang, G., Liu, Y., Zeng, F., Lin, D., Yang, X., et al. (2017). Disrupted intrinsic connectivity of the periaqueductal gray in patients with functional dyspepsia: A resting-state fMRI study. *Neurogastroenterology & Motility*, *29*(8).

Liu, Q. R., Drgon, T., Johnson, C., Walther, D., Hess, J., & Uhl, G. R. (2006). Addiction molecular genetics: 639,401 SNP whole genome association identifies many "cell adhesion" genes. *American Journal of Medical Genetics Part B: Neuropsychiatric Genetics*, *141*(8), 918–925.

Liu, Y., Cheng, Z., Wang, J., Jin, C., Yuan, J., Wang, G., . . . Zhao, X. (2016). No association between the rs10503253 polymorphism in the CSMD1 gene and schizophrenia in a Han Chinese population. *BMC Psychiatry*, *16*(1), 206.

Liu, Z., Roosaar, A., Axéll, T., & Ye, W. (2017). Tobacco use, oral health, and risk of Parkinson's disease. *American journal of Epidemiology*, *185*(7), 538–545.

Livingston, G., Sommerlad, A., Orgeta, V., Costafreda, S. G., Huntley, J., Ames, D., et al. (2017). Dementia prevention, intervention, and care. *The Lancet*, *390*(10113), 2673–2734.

Lizarraga, L. E., Cholanians, A. B., Phan, A. V., Herndon, J. M., Lau, S. S., & Monks, T. J. (2014). Vesicular monoamine transporter 2 and the acute and long-term response to 3,4-(±)-Methylenedioxymethamphetamine. *Journal of Toxicological Sciences*, *143*(1), 209–219.

Locher, C., Koechlin, H., Zion, S. R., Werner, C., Pine, D. S., Kirsch, I., et al. (2017). Efficacy and safety of selective serotonin reuptake inhibitors, serotonin-norepinephrine reuptake inhibitors, and placebo for common psychiatric disorders among children and adolescents. *JAMA Psychiatry*, *74*(10), 1011.

Lochner, C., Hemmings, S. M., Kinnear, C. J., Moolman-Smook, J. C., Corfield, V. A., Knowles, J. A., et al. (2004). Gender in obsessive-compulsive disorder: Clinical and genetic findings. *European Neuropsychopharmacology*, *14*, 105–113.

Loepke, A. W., & Soriano, S. G. (2008). An assessment of the effects of general anesthetics on developing brain structure and neurocognitive function. *Anesthesia & Analgesia*, *106*(6), 1681–1707.

Logan, A. C. (2003). Neurobehavioral aspects of omega-3 fatty acids: Possible mechanisms and therapeutic value in major depression. *Alternative Medicine Review*, *8*, 410–425.

Lohani, S., Poplawsky, A. J., Kim, S. G., & Moghaddam, B. (2017). Unexpected global impact of VTA dopamine neuron activation as measured by opto-fMRI. *Molecular Psychiatry*, *22*(4), 585.

Lohoff, F. W. (2010a). Genetic variants in the vesicular monoamine transporter 1 (VMAT1/SLC18A1) and neuropsychiatric disorders. In *Membrane transporters in drug discovery and development* (pp. 165–180). New York: Humana Press.

Lohoff, F. W. (2010b). Overview of the genetics of major depressive disorder. *Current Psychiatry Reports*, *12*(6), 539–546.

Lohoff, F. W., Dahl, J. P., Ferraro, T. N., Arnold, S. E., Gallinat, J., Sander, T., & Berrettini, W. H. (2006). Variations in the vesicular monoamine transporter 1 gene (VMAT1/SLC18A1) are associated with bipolar i disorder. *Neuropsychopharmacology*, *31*(12), 2739–2747.

Lohr, J. B., & Braff, D. L. (2003). The value of referring to recently introduced antipsychotics as "second generation". *American Journal of Psychiatry, 160,* 1371–1372.

Loiselle, C. R., Wendlandt, J. T., Rohde, C. A., & Singer, H. S. (2003). Antistreptococcal, neuronal, and nuclear antibodies in Tourette syndrome. *Pediatric Neurology, 28,* 119–125.

Long, E. C., Aggen, S. H., Neale, M. C., Knudsen, G., Krueger, R. F., South, S. C., et al. (2017). The association between personality disorders with alcohol use and misuse: A population-based twin study. *Drug & Alcohol Dependence, 174,* 171–180.

Loo, C., Sachdev, P., Elsayed, H., McDarmont, B., Mitchell, P., Wilkinson, M., et al. (2001). Effects of a 2- to 4-week course of repetitive transcranial magnetic stimulation (rTMS) on neuropsychologic functioning, electroencephalogram, and auditory threshold in depressed patients. *Biological Psychiatry, 49,* 615–623.

Loo, S. K. (2003). EEG and neurofeedback findings in ADHD. *ADHD Report, 11,* 1–9.

Loonen, A. J., Kupka, R. W., & Ivanova, S. A. (2017). Circuits regulating pleasure and happiness in bipolar disorder. *Frontiers in Neural Circuits, 11.*

Looney, S. W., & El-Mallakh, R. S. (1997). Meta-analysis of erythrocyte, Na, K-ATPase activity in bipolar illness. *Depression and Anxiety, 5,* 53–65.

LoParo, D., & Waldman, I. D. (2015). The oxytocin receptor gene (OXTR) is associated with autism spectrum disorder: A meta-analysis. *Molecular Psychiatry, 20*(5), 640–646.

López-Muñoz, F., Alamo, C., Cuenca, E., Shen, W. W., Clervoy, P., & Rubio, G. (2005). History of the discovery and clinical introduction of chlorpromazine. *Annals of Clinical Psychiatry, 17*(3), 113–135.

Lopez, O. L., Becker, J. T., Sweet, R. A., Klunk, W., Kaufer, D. I., Saxton, J., et al. (2003). Psychiatric symptoms vary with the severity of dementia in probable Alzheimer's disease. *Journal of Neuropsychiatry and Clinical Neurosciences, 15,* 346–353.

Lopez, O. L., Becker, J. T., Wisniewski, S., Saxton, J., Kaufer, D. I., & DeKosky, S. T. (2002). Cholinesterase inhibitor treatment alters the natural history of Alzheimer's disease. *Journal of Neurology, Neurosurgery, and Psychiatry, 72,* 310–314.

Lorberboym, M., Watemberg, N., Nissenkorn, A., Nir, B., & Lerman-Sagie, T. (2004). Technetium 99m ethylcysteinate dimer single-photon emission computed tomography (SPECT) during intellectual stress test in children and adolescents with pure versus comorbid attention-deficit hyperactivity disorder (ADHD). *Journal of Child Neurology, 19*(2), 91–96.

Lorenzetti, V., Alonso-Lana, S., J Youssef, G., Verdejo-Garcia, A., Suo, C., Cousijn, J., et al. (2016). Adolescent cannabis use: What is the evidence for functional brain alteration? *Current pharmaceutical design, 22*(42), 6353–6365.

Lorenzetti, V., Solowij, N., & Yücel, M. (2016). The role of cannabinoids in neuroanatomic alterations in cannabis users. *Biological psychiatry, 79*(7), e17–e31.

Lotsch, J., Skarke, C., Grosch, S., Darimont, J., Schmidt, H., & Geisslinger, G. (2002). The polymorphism A118G of the human opioid receptor gene decreases the pupil constrictory effect of morphine-6-glucuronide but not that of morphine. *Pharmacogenetics, 12,* 3–9.

Lou, H. C., Henriksen, L., & Bruhn, P. (1984). Focal cerebral hypoperfusion in children with dysphasia and/or attention deficit disorder. *Archives of Neurology, 41*(8), 825–829.

Lou, H. C., Henriksen, L., Bruhn, P., Børner, H., & Nielsen, J. B. (1989). Striatal dysfunction in attention deficit and hyperkinetic disorder. *Archives of Neurology, 46*(1), 48–52.

Lou, H. C., Rosa, P., Pryds, O., Karrebæk, H., Lunding, J., Cumming, P., & Gjedde, A. (2004). ADHD: Increased dopamine receptor availability linked to attention deficit and low neonatal cerebral blood flow. *Developmental Medicine and Child Neurology, 46*(3), 179–183.

Louie, A. K., Lannon, R. A., Rutzick, E. A., Browne, D., Lewis, T. B., & Jones, R. (1996). Clinical features of cocaine-induced panic. *Biological Psychiatry, 40,* 938–940.

Love, S., & Miners, J. S. (2016). Cerebrovascular disease in ageing and Alzheimer's disease. *Acta Neuropathologica, 131*(5), 645–658.

Love, S., Chalmers, K., Ince, P., Esiri, M., Attems, J., Jellinger, K., . . . Kehoe, P. G. (2014). Development, appraisal, validation and implementation of a consensus protocol for the assessment of cerebral amyloid angiopathy in post-mortem brain tissue. *American Journal of Neurodegenerative Disease, 3*(1), 19–32.

Lozano, C. S., Tam, J., & Lozano, A. M. (2017). The changing landscape of surgery for Parkinson's Disease. *Movement Disorders, 33*(1), 36–47.

Lozza, C., Marié, R. M., & Baron, J. C. (2002). The metabolic substrates of bradykinesia and tremor in uncomplicated Parkinson's disease. *NeuroImage, 17*, 688–699.

Lübbert, M., Goral, R. O., Satterfield, R., Putzke, T., Maagdenberg, A. M., Kamasawa, N., & Young, S. M. (2017). A novel region in the CaV2.1 α1 subunit C-terminus regulates fast synaptic vesicle fusion and vesicle docking at the mammalian presynaptic active zone. *eLife Sciences, 6*, e28412.

Luby, J., Belden, A., Botteron, K., Marrus, N., Harms, M. P., Babb, C., . . . Barch, D. (2013). The effects of poverty on childhood brain development: The mediating effect of caregiving and stressful life events. *JAMA Pediatrics, 167*(12), 1135–1142.

Luby, J. L., Belden, A. C., Jackson, J. J., Lessov-Schlaggar, C. N., Harms, M. P., Tillman, R., et al. (2016). Early childhood depression and alterations in the trajectory of gray matter maturation in middle childhood and early adolescence. *JAMA Psychiatry, 73*(1), 31–38.

Lucassen, M. F., Stasiak, K., Samra, R., Frampton, C. M., & Merry, S. N. (2017). Sexual minority youth and depressive symptoms or depressive disorder: A systematic review and meta-analysis of population-based studies. *Australian & New Zealand Journal of Psychiatry, 51*(8), 774–787.

Lucey, J. V., Costa, D. C., Busatto, G., Pilowsky, L. S., Marks, I. M., Ell, P. J., et al. (1997). Caudate regional cerebral blood flow in obsessive-compulsive disorder, panic disorder and healthy controls on single photon emission computerised tomography. *Psychiatry Research, 74*, 25–33.

Luchsinger, J. A., Tang, M. X., Shea, S., & Mayeux, R. (2002). Caloric intake and the risk of Alzheimer disease. *Archives of Neurology, 59*, 1258–1263.

Lucki, I., & O'Leary, O. F. (2004). Distinguishing roles for norepinephrine and serotonin in the behavioral effects of antidepressant drugs. *Journal of Clinical Psychiatry, 65*, Supplement 4, 11–24.

Luders, E., & Toga, A. W. (2010). Sex differences in brain anatomy. *Sex Differences in the Human Brain, their Underpinnings and Implications Progress in Brain Research*, 3–12.

Luhrmann, T. M., Padmavati, R., Tharoor, H., & Osei, A. (2015). Differences in voice-hearing experiences of people with psychosis in the USA, India and Ghana: Interview-based study. *The British Journal of Psychiatry, 206*(1), 41–44.

Lung, F. W., Chen, N., & Shu, B. C. (2006). Dopamine D4 receptor gene and the– 521C> T polymorphism of the upstream region of the dopamine D4 receptor gene in schizophrenia. *Psychiatric Genetics, 16*(4), 139–143.

Luria, A. R. (1970). The functional organization of the brain. *Scientific American, 222*(3), 66–79.

Luria, A. R. (1973). *An introduction to neuro-psychology*. New York: Basic Books.

Lustman, P. J., Clouse, R. E., & Freedland, K. E. (1998). Management of major depression in adults with diabetes: Implications of recent clinical trials. *Seminars in Clinical Neuropsychiatry, 3*, 102–114.

Lutz, P., Tanti, A., Gasecka, A., Barnett-Burns, S., Kim, J. J., Zhou, Y., et al. (2017). Association of a history of child abuse with impaired myelination in the anterior cingulate cortex: Convergent epigenetic, transcriptional, and morphological evidence. *American Journal of Psychiatry, 174*(12), 1185–1194.

Lyall, K., Schweitzer, J. B., Schmidt, R. J., Hertz-Picciotto, I., & Solomon, M. (2017). Inattention and hyperactivity in association with autism spectrum disorders in the CHARGE study. *Research in Autism Spectrum Disorders, 35*, 1–12.

Lyon, L. (2017). Dead salmon and voodoo correlations: Should we be sceptical about functional MRI? *Brain, 140*(8), e53.

Ma, C., Liu, Y., Neumann, S., & Gao, X. (2017). Nicotine from cigarette smoking and diet and Parkinson disease: A review. *Translational Neurodegeneration, 6*(1), 18.

Ma, D., & Guest, P. C. (2017). Generation of the acute phencyclidine rat model for proteomic studies of schizophrenia. In *Proteomic methods in neuropsychiatric research* (pp. 257–261). Cham: Springer.

Ma, K., Xiong, N., Shen, Y., Han, C., Liu, L., Zhang, G., et al. (2018). Weight loss and malnutrition in patients with Parkinson's disease: Current knowledge and future prospects. *Frontiers in Aging Neuroscience, 10*(1).

Ma, L., Li, X. W., Zhang, S. J., Yang, F., Zhu, G. M., Yuan, X. B., & Jiang, W. (2014). Inter-leukin-1 beta guides the migration of cortical neurons. *Journal of Neuroinflammation, 11*(1), 114.

Ma, Y., Feigin, A., Dhawan, V., Fukunda, M., Shi, Q., Greene, P., et al. (2002). Dyskinesia after fetal cell transplantation for Parkinsonism: A PET study. *Annals of Neurology, 52*, 628–634.

Mac Master, F. P., Keshavan, M. S., Dick, E. L., & Rosenberg, D. R. (1999). Corpus callosal signal intensity in treatment-naive pediatric obsessive compulsive disorders. *Progress in Neuro-Psychopharmacology & Biological Psychiatry, 23*, 601–612.

Macerollo, A., & Martino, D. (2013). Pediatric autoimmune neuropsychiatric disorders associated with streptococcal infections (PANDAS): An evolving concept. *Tremor and Other Hyperkinetic Movements, 3.*

Machado, C., Estévez, M., Leisman, G., Melillo, R., Rodríguez, R., DeFina, P., et al. (2015). QEEG spectral and coherence assessment of autistic children in three different experimental conditions. *Journal of Autism and Developmental Disorders, 45*(2), 406–424.

Machado, S., Sancassiani, F., Paes, F., Rocha, N., Murillo-Rodriguez, E., & Nardi, A. E. (2017). Panic disorder and cardiovascular diseases: An overview. *International Review of Psychiatry, 29*(5), 436–444.

MacKinnon, D. F., Zandi, P. P., Cooper, J., Potash, J. B., Simpson, S. G., Gershon, E., et al. (2002). Comorbid bipolar disorder and panic disorder in families with a high prevalence of bipolar disorder. *American Journal of Psychiatry, 159*, 30–35.

Macpherson, H., Teo, W. P., Schneider, L. A., & Smith, A. E. (2017). A life-long approach to physical activity for brain health. *Frontiers in Aging Neuroscience, 9*, 147.

Madden, J. M., Lakoma, M. D., Lynch, F. L., Rusinak, D., Owen-Smith, A. A., Coleman, K. J., et al. (2017). Psychotropic medication use among insured children with autism spectrum disorder. *Journal of Autism and Developmental Disorders, 47*(1), 144–154.

Maestu, F., Quesney, M. F., Ortiz, A. T., Fernandez, L. A., Amo, C., Campo, P., et al. (2003). Cognition and neural networks, a new perspective based on functional neuroimaging. *Revista de neurologia, 37*, 962–966.

Maggini, C., Ampollini, P., Gariboldi, S., Cella, P. L., Peqlizza, L., & Marchesi, C. (2001). The parma high school epidemiological survey: Obsessive-compulsive symptoms. *Acta Psychiatrica Scandinavica, 103*, 441–446.

Magistretti, P. J., & Allaman, I. (2015). A cellular perspective on brain energy metabolism and functional imaging. *Neuron, 86*(4), 883–901.

Mah, S., Nelson, M. R., Delisi, L. E., Reneland, R. H., Markward, N., James, M. R., . . . Kammerer, S. (2006). Identification of the semaphorin receptor PLXNA2 as a candidate for susceptibility to schizophrenia. *Molecular Psychiatry, 11*(5), 471–478.

Mahendra, N., & Arkin, S. (2003). Effects of four years of exercise, language, and social interventions on Alzheimer discourse. *Journal of Communication Disorders, 36*, 395–422.

Maher, B. S., Marazita, M. L., Zubenko, W. N., Spiker, D. G., Giles, D. E., Kaplan, B. B., et al. (2002). Genetic segregation analysis of recurrent early-onset major depression: Evidence for single major locus transmission. *American Journal of Medical Genetics, 114*, 214–221.

Mahler, L. A., & Ramig, L. O. (2012). Intensive treatment of dysarthria secondary to stroke. *Clinical Linguistics & Phonetics, 26*(8), 681–694.

Mahley, R. W. (2016). Central nervous system LipoproteinsHighlights: ApoE and regulation of cholesterol metabolism. *Arteriosclerosis, Thrombosis, and Vascular Biology, 36*(7), 1305–1315.

Mahmood, T., & Silverstone, T. (2001). Serotonin and bipolar disorder. *Journal of Affective Disorders, 66*, 1–11.

Mak, E., Su, L., Williams, G. B., Firbank, M. J., Lawson, R. A., Yarnall, A. J., et al. (2017). Longitudinal whole-brain atrophy and ventricular enlargement in nondemented Parkinson's disease. *Neurobiology of Aging, 55*, 78–90.

Maletzky, B., McFarland, B., & Burt, A. (1994). Refractory obsessive compulsive disorder and ECT. *Convulsive Therapy, 10*, 34–42.

Malhi, G. S., Tanious, M., Das, P., Coulston, C. M., & Berk, M. (2013). Potential mechanisms of action of lithium in bipolar disorder. *CNS Drugs, 27*(2), 135–153.

Malison, R. T., McDougle, C. J., van Dyck, C. H., Scahill, L., Baldwin, R. M., Seibyl, J. P., et al. (1995). [123I]beta-CIT SPECT imaging of striatal dopamine transporter binding in Tourette's disorder. *American Journal of Psychiatry, 152*, 1359–1361.

Malison, R. T., Price, L. H., Berman, R., van Dyck, C. H., Pelton, G. H., Carpenter, L., et al. (1998). Reduced brain serotonin transporter availability in major depression as measured by [123I]-2-beta-carbomethoxy-3 beta-(4 iodophenyl)tropane and single photon emission computed tomography. *Biological Psychiatry, 44*, 1090–1098.

Malizia, A. L., Cunningham, V. J., Bell, C. J., Liddle, P. F., Jones, T., & Nutt, D. J. (1998). Decreased brain GABA(A)-benzodiazepine receptor binding in panic disorder: Preliminary results from a quantitative PET study. *Archives of General Psychiatry, 55*, 715–720.

Malla, A. K., Norman, R. M. G., Manchanda, R. M., Ahmed, R., Scholten, D., Harricharan, R., et al. (2002). One year outcome in first episode psychosis: Influence of DUP and other predictors. *Schizophrenia Research, 54*, 231–242.

Mallet, L., Mesnage, V., Houeto, J. L., Pelissolo, A., Yelnik, J., Behar, C., et al. (2002). Compulsions, Parkinson's disease, and stimulation. *Lancet, 360*, 1302–1304.

Malt'ete, D., Navarro, S., Welter, M. L., Roche, S., Bonnet, A. M., Houeto, J. L., et al. (2004). Subthalamic stimulation in Parkinson disease: With or without anesthesia? *Archives of Neurology, 61*, 390–392.

Mamo, D. C., Sweet, R. A., Chengappa, K. N. R., Reddy, R. R., & Jeste, D. V. (2002). The effect of age on the pharmacological management of ambulatory patients treated with depot neuroleptic medications for schizophrenia and related psychotic disorders. *International Journal of Geriatric Psychiatry, 17*, 1012–1017.

Mana, S., Martinot, M. L. P., & Martinot, J. L. (2010). Brain imaging findings in children and adolescents with mental disorders: A cross-sectional review. *European Psychiatry, 25*(6), 345–354.

Mancebo, M. C., Greenberg, B., Grant, J. E., Pinto, A., Eisen, J. L., Dyck, I., & Rasmussen, S. A. (2008). Correlates of occupational disability in a clinical sample of obsessive-compulsive disorder. *Comprehensive Psychiatry, 49*(1), 43–50.

Manchia, M., Carpiniello, B., Valtorta, F., & Comai, S. (2017). Serotonin dysfunction, aggressive behavior, and mental illness: Exploring the link using a dimensional approach. *ACS Chemical Neuroscience, 8*(5), 961–972.

Mandel, S., Grunblatt, E., Riederer, P., Gerlach, M., Levites, Y., & Youdim, M. B. (2003). Neuroprotective strategies in Parkinson's disease: An update on progress. *CNS Drugs, 17*, 729–762.

Manji, H. (2003). Depression, III. *American Journal of Psychiatry, 160*, 24.

Mann, D. M., Takeuchi, A., Sato, S., Cairns, N. J., Lantos, P. L., Rossor, M. N., et al. (2001). Cases of Alzheimer's disease due to deletion of exon 9 of the presenilin-1 gene show an unusual but characteristic beta-amyloid pathology known as "cotton wool" plaques. *Neuropathology and Applied Neurobiology, 27*, 189–196.

Maraganore, D. M., O'Connor, M. K., Bower, J. H., Kuntz, K. M., McDonnell, S. K., Schaid, D. J., et al. (1999). Detection of preclinical Parkinson disease in at-risk family members with use of [123I]beta-CIT and SPECT: An exploratory study. *Mayo Clinic Proclamations, 74,* 681–685.

Marangell, L. B., Rush, A. J., George, M. S., Sackeim, H. A., Johnson, C. R., Hussain, M. M., et al. (2002). Vagus nerve stimulation (VNS) for major depressive episodes: One year outcomes. *Biological Psychiatry, 51,* 280–287.

Marazziti, D., Albert, U., Mucci, F., & Piccinni, A. (2017). The glutamate and the immune systems: New targets for the pharmacological treatment of OCD. *Current Medicinal Chemistry, 24*(1).

Marceglia, S., Mrakic-Sposta, S., Rosa, M., Ferrucci, R., Mameli, F., Vergari, M., et al. (2016). Transcranial direct current stimulation modulates cortical neuronal activity in Alzheimer's disease. *Frontiers in Neuroscience, 10,* 134.

Marchand, W. R., Lee, J. N., Healy, L., Thatcher, J. W., Rashkin, E., Starr, J., & Hsu, E. (2009). An fMRI motor activation paradigm demonstrates abnormalities of putamen activation in females with panic disorder. *Journal of Affective Disorders, 116*(1), 121–125.

Marchesi, C., Tonna, M., & Maggini, C. (2009). Obsessive-compulsive disorder followed by psychotic episode in long-term ecstasy misuse. *The World Journal of Biological Psychiatry, 10*(4–2), 599–602.

Marcos de Souza Moura, A., Khede Lamego, M., Paes, F., Ferreira Rocha, N. B., Simoes-Silva, V., Almeida Rocha, S., et al. (2015). Effects of aerobic exercise on anxiety disorders: A systematic review. *CNS & Neurological Disorders-Drug Targets (Formerly Current Drug Targets-CNS & Neurological Disorders), 14*(9), 1184–1193.

Marcos-Vidal, L., Martínez-García, M., Pretus, C., Garcia-Garcia, D., Martínez, K., Janssen, J., . . . Carmona, S. (2018). Local functional connectivity suggests functional immaturity in children with attention-deficit/hyperactivity disorder. *Human Brain Mapping, 39*(6), 2442–2454.

Marder, K., Tang, M. X., Alfaro, B., Mejia, H., Cote, L., Louis, E., et al. (1999). Risk of Alzheimer's disease in relatives of Parkinson's disease patients with and without dementia. *Neurology, 52,* 719–724.

Marder, S. R., McQuade, R. D., Stock, E., Kaplita, S., Marcus, R., Safferman, A., et al. (2003). Aripiprazole in the treatment of schizophrenia: Safety and tolerability in short-term, placebo-controlled trials. *Schizophrenia Research, 61,* 123–136.

Marek, G. J. (2002). Preclinical pharmacology of mGlu2/3 receptor agonists: Novel agents for schizophrenia? *Current Drug Targets—CNS and Neurological Disorders, 1,* 215–225.

Maremmani, A. G., Maiello, M., Carbone, M. G., Pallucchini, A., Brizzi, F., Belcari, I., et al. (2018). Towards a psychopathology specific to substance use disorder: Should emotional responses to life events be included? *Comprehensive Psychiatry, 80,* 132–139.

Margolis, E. B., Hjelmstad, G. O., Bonci, A., & Fields, H. L. (2003). Kappa-opioid agonists directly inhibit midbrain dopaminergic neurons. *Journal of Neuroscience, 23,* 9981–9986.

Margolis, E. B., Hjelmstad, G. O., Fujita, W., & Fields, H. L. (2014). Direct bidirectional μ-opioid control of midbrain dopamine neurons. *Journal of Neuroscience, 34*(44), 14707–14716.

Margoob, M. A., & Mushtaq, D. (2011). Serotonin transporter gene polymorphism and psychiatric disorders: Is there a link? *Indian Journal of Psychiatry, 53*(4), 289–299.

Maria, K., Charalampos, T., Vassilakopoulou, D., Stavroula, S., Vasiliki, K., & Nikolaos, D. (2012). Frequency distribution of COMT polymorphisms in Greek patients with schizophrenia and controls: A study of SNPs rs737865, rs4680, and rs165599. *ISRN Psychiatry,* (2012)651613.

Marie-Claire, C., Courtin, C., Roques, B. P., & Noble, F. (2004). Cytoskeletal genes regulation by chronic morphine treatment in rat striatum. *Neuropsychopharmacology, 29*(12), 2208–2221.

Markota, M., Sin, J., Pantazopoulos, H., Jonilionis, R., & Berretta, S. (2014). Reduced dopamine transporter expression in the amygdala of subjects diagnosed with schizophrenia. *Schizophrenia Bulletin, 40*(5), 984–991.

Marković, I., Kresojević, N., & Kostić, V. S. (2016). Glucocerebrosidase and parkinsonism: Lessons to learn. *Journal of Neurology, 263*(5), 1033–1044.

Maron, E., Toru, I., Hirvonen, J., Tuominen, L., Lumme, V., Vasar, V., . . . Tiihonen, J. (2011). Gender differences in brain serotonin transporter availability in panic disorder. *Journal of Psychopharmacology, 25*(7), 952–959.

Marraccini, M. E., Weyandt, L. L., Rossi, J. S., & Gudmundsdottir, B. G. (2016). Neurocognitive enhancement or impairment? A systematic meta-analysis of prescription stimulant effects on processing speed, decision-making, planning, and cognitive perseveration. *Experimental and Clinical Psychopharmacology, 24*(4), 269–284.

Marshall, R. S., Asllani, I., Pavol, M. A., Cheung, Y. K., & Lazar, R. M. (2017). Altered cerebral hemodyamics and cortical thinning in asymptomatic carotid artery stenosis. *PloS One, 12*(12), e0189727.

Marston, L., Nazareth, I., Petersen, I., Walters, K., & Osborn, D. P. (2014). Prescribing of antipsychotics in UK primary care: A cohort study. *BMJ Open, 4*(12), e006135.

Martin, J. H. (1991). The collective electrical behavior of cortical neurons: The electroencephalogram and the mechanisms of epilepsy. In E. R. Kandel, J. H. Schwartz, & T. M. Jessell (Eds.), *Principles of neural science* (3rd ed., pp. 778–791). Norwalk, CT: Appleton & Lange.

Martin, J. L., Barbanoj, M. J., Schlaepfer, T. E., Thompson, E., Perez, V., & Kulisevsky, J. (2003). Repetitive transcranial magnetic stimulation for the treatment of depresssion. Systematic review and meta-analysis. *British Journal of Psychiatry, 182*, 480–491.

Martin, L., Latypova, X., Wilson, C. M., Magnaudeix, A., Perrin, M. L., Yardin, C., & Terro, F. (2013). Tau protein kinases: Involvement in Alzheimer's disease. *Ageing Research Reviews, 12*(1), 289–309.

Martin, P., & Albers, M. (1995). Cerebellum and schizophrenia: A selective review. *Schizophrenia Bulletin, 21*, 241–250.

Martinaud, O. (2017). Visual agnosia and focal brain injury. *Revue Neurologique, 173*(7–8), 451–460.

Martinez-Raga, J., Ferreros, A., Knecht, C., de Alvaro, R., & Carabal, E. (2017). Attention-deficit hyperactivity disorder medication use: Factors involved in prescribing, safety aspects and outcomes. *Therapeutic Advances in Drug Safety, 8*(3), 87–99.

Martinez-Ramirez, D., Jimenez-Shahed, J., Leckman, J. F., Porta, M., Servello, D., Meng, F. G., et al. (2018). Efficacy and safety of deep brain stimulation in Tourette syndrome: The international Tourette syndrome deep brain stimulation public database and registry. *JAMA Neurology, 75*(3), 353–359.

Martínez-Rivera, F. J., Rodriguez-Romaguera, J., Lloret-Torres, M. E., Do Monte, F. H., Quirk, G. J., & Barreto-Estrada, J. L. (2016). Bidirectional modulation of extinction of drug seeking by deep brain stimulation of the ventral striatum. *Biological Psychiatry, 80*(9), 682–690.

Martini, C., Trincavelli, M. L., Tuscano, D., Carmassi, C., Ciapparelli, A., Lucacchini, A., et al. (2004). Serotoninmediated phosphorylation of extracellular regulated kinases in platelets of patients with panic disorder versus controls. *Neurochemistry International, 44*, 627–639.

Martini, F. H. (1998). *Fundamentals of anatomy and physiology* (4th ed.). Upper Saddle River, NJ: Prentice-Hall.

Martis, B., Alam, D., Dowd, S. M., Hill, S. K., Sharma, R. P., Rosen, C., et al. (2003). Neurocognitive effects of repetitive transcranial magnetic stimulation in severe major depression. *Clinical Neurophysiology, 114*, 1125–1132.

Marwha, D., Halari, M., & Eliot, L. (2017). Meta-analysis reveals a lack of sexual dimorphism in human amygdala volume. *NeuroImage, 147*, 282–294.

Marzbani, H., Marateb, H. R., & Mansourian, M. (2016). Neurofeedback: A comprehensive review on system design, methodology and clinical applications. *Basic and Clinical Neuroscience, 7*(2), 143.

Maschke, M., Gomez, C. M., Tuite, P. J., & Konczak, J. (2003). Dysfunction of the basal ganglia, but not the cerebellum, impairs kinaesthesia. *Brain, 126*, 2312–2322.

Mason, B. J., Goodman, A. M., Dixon, R. M., Abdel Hameed, M. H., Hulot, T., Wesnes, K., et al. (2002). A pharmacokinetic and pharmacodynamic drug interaction study of acamprosate and naltrexone. *Neuropsychopharmacology, 27*, 596–606.

Mason, B. J., Quello, S., & Shadan, F. (2018). Gabapentin for the treatment of alcohol use disorder. *Expert Opinion on Investigational Drugs, (just-accepted) 27*(1), 113–124.

Massana, G., Serra-Grabulosa, J. M., Salgado-Pineda, P., Gastó, C., Junqué, C., Massana, J., et al. (2003a). Amygdalar atrophy in panic disorder patients detected by volumetric magnetic resonance imaging. *NeuroImage, 19*, 80–90.

Massou, J. M., Trichard, C., Attar-Levy, D., Feline, A., Corruble, E., Beaufils, B., et al. (1997). Frontal 5-HT2A receptors studied in depressive patients during chronic treatment by selective serotonin reuptake inhibitors. *Psychopharmacology, 133*, 99–101.

Mata, I. F., Lockhart, P. J., & Farrer, M. J. (2004). Parkin genetics: One model for Parkinson's disease. *Human Molecular Genetics, 13*(s1), R127–R133.

Mataix-Cols, D., Frans, E., Pérez-Vigil, A., Kuja-Halkola, R., Gromark, C., Isomura, K., . . . Rück, C. (2017). A total-population multigenerational family clustering study of autoimmune diseases in obsessive-compulsive disorder and Tourette's/chronic tic disorders. *Molecular Psychiatry, 23*, 1652–1658.

Mathalon, D. H., Sullivan, E. V., O., Lim, K., & Pfefferbaum, A. (2001). Progressive brain volume changes and the clinical course of schizophrenia in men: A longitudinal magnetic resonance imaging study. *Archives of General Psychiatry, 58*, 148–157.

Mathews, C. A., Badner, J. A., Andresen, J. M., Sheppard, B., Himle, J. A., Grant, J. E., et al. (2012). Genome-wide linkage analysis of obsessive-compulsive disorder implicates chromosome 1p36. *Biological Psychiatry, 72*(8), 629–636.

Matochik, J. A., Liebenauer, L. L., King, A. C., & Szymanski, H. V. (1994). Cerebral glucose metabolism in adults with attention deficit hyperactivity disorder after chronic stimulant treatment. *The American Journal of Psychiatry, 151*(5), 658.

Matochik, J. A., London, E. D., Eldreth, D. A., Cadet, J. L., & Bolla, K. I. (2003). Frontal cortical tissue composition in abstinent cocaine abusers: A magnetic resonance imaging study. *Neuroimage, 19*, 1095–1102.

Matsumoto, R., Ichise, M., Ito, H., Ando, T., Takahashi, H., Ikoma, Y., et al. (2010). Reduced serotonin transporter binding in the insular cortex in patients with obsessive-compulsive disorder: A [11C] DASB PET study. *Neuroimage, 49*(1), 121–126.

Matsunaga, H., Hayashida, K., Kiriike, N., Maebayashi, K., & Stein, D. J. (2010). The clinical utility of symptom dimensions in obsessive-compulsive disorder. *Psychiatry Research, 180*(1), 25–29.

Matsunaga, H., Kiriike, N., Iwasaki, Y., Miyata, A., Yamagami, S., & Kaye, W. H. (1999). Clinical characteristics in patients with anorexia nervosa and obsessive-compulsive disorder. *Psychological Medicine, 29*(2), 407–414.

Matsunaga, H., & Seedat, S. (2007). Obsessive-compulsive spectrum disorders: Cross-national and ethnic issues. *CNS Spectrums, 12*(5), 392–400.

Mattes, J. A., & Gittelman, R. (1981). Effects of artificial food colorings in children with hyperactive symptoms: A critical review and results of a controlled study. *Archives of General Psychiatry, 38*, 714–718.

Mattila, P. M., Röyttä, M., Lönnberg, P., Marjamäki, P., Helenius, H., & Rinne, J. O. (2001). Choline acetytransferase activity and striatal dopamine receptors in Parkinson's disease in relation to cognitive impairment. *Acta Neuropathologica, 102*, 160–166.

Mattson, B. J., & Morrell, J. I. (2005). Preference for cocaine-versus pup-associated cues differentially activates neurons expressing either Fos or cocaine- and amphetamine-regulated transcript in lactating, maternal rodents. *Neuroscience, 135*(2), 315–328.

Mattsson, N., Andreasson, U., Zetterberg, H., & Blennow, K. (2017). Association of plasma neurofilament light with neurodegeneration in patients with Alzheimer disease. *JAMA Neurology, 74*(5), 557–566.

Matus, A. (2000). Actin-based plasticity in dendritic spines. *Science, 290*, 754–758.

Mayberg, H. S., Brannan, S. K., Tekell, J. L., Silva, J. A., Mahurin, R. K., McGinnis, S., et al. (2000). Regional metabolic effects off luoxetine in major depression: Serial changes and relationship to clinical response. *Biological Psychiatry, 48*, 830–843.

Mayberg, H. S., Lozano, A. M., Voon, V., McNeely, H. E., Seminowicz, D., Hamani, C., et al. (2005). Deep brain stimulation for treatment-resistant depression. *Neuron, 45*(5), 651–660.

Mayberg, H. S., Silva, J. A., Brannan, S. K., Mahurin, R. K., McGinnis, S., & Jerabek, P. A. (2002). The functional neuroanatomy of the placebo effect. *American Journal of Psychiatry, 159*, 728–735.

Mayeda, E. R., Glymour, M. M., Quesenberry, C. P., & Whitmer, R. A. (2016). Inequalities in dementia incidence between six racial and ethnic groups over 14 years. *Alzheimer's & Dementia: The Journal of the Alzheimer's Association, 12*(3), 216–224.

Mazzone, L., Yu, S., Blair, C., Gunter, B. C., Wang, Z., Marsh, R., & Peterson, B. S. (2010). An FMRI study of frontostriatal circuits during the inhibition of eye blinking in persons with Tourette syndrome. *American Journal of Psychiatry, 167*(3), 341–349.

McCabe, S. (2000). Rapid detox: Understanding new treatment approaches for the addicted patient. *Perspectives in Psychiatric Care, 36*, 113–120.

Mccann, M. E., & Graaff, J. D. (2017). Current thinking regarding potential neurotoxicity of general anesthesia in infants. *Current Opinion in Urology, 27*(1), 27–33.

McCarley, R. W., Wible, C. G., Frumin, M., Hirayasu, Y., Levitt, J. J., Fischer, I. A., & Shenton, M. E. (1999). MRI anatomy of schizophrenia. *Biological Psychiatry, 45*, 1099–1119.

McCarthy, G. M., Farris, S. P., Blednov, Y. A., Harris, R. A., & Mayfield, R. D. (2018). Microglial-specific transcriptome changes following chronic alcohol consumption. *Neuropharmacology, 128*, 416–424.

McConville, B. J., Fogelson, M. H., Norman, A. B., Klykylo, W. M., Manderscheid, P. Z., Parker, K. W., et al. (1991). Nicotine potentiation of haloperidol in reducing tic frequency in Tourette's disorder. *American Journal of Psychiatry, 148*, 793–794.

McCracken, J. T., Smalley, S. L., McGough, J. J., Crawford, L., Del'Homme, M., Cantor, R. M., et al. (2000). Evidence for linkage of a tandem duplication polymorphism upstream of the dopamine D4 receptor gene (DRD4) with attention deficit hyperactivity disorder (ADHD). *Molecular Psychiatry, 5*, 531–536.

McCurry, S. M., Gibbons, L. E., Logsdon, R. G., & Teri, L. (2004). Anxiety and nighttime behavioral disturbances. Awakenings in patients with Alzheimer's disease. *Journal of Gerontological Nursing, 30*, 12–20.

McDonald, C., & Murphy, K. C. (2003). The new genetics of schizophrenia. *Psychiatric Clinics of North America, 26*(1), 41–63.

McDonald, C., Zanelli, J., Rabe-Hesketh, S., Ellison-Wright, I., Sham, P., Kalidindi, S., et al. (2004). Meta-analysis of magnetic resonance imaging brain morphometry studies in bipolar disorder. *Biological psychiatry, 56*(6), 411–417.

McDonald, W. M., Weiner, R. D., Fochtmann, L. J., & McCall, W. V. (2016). The FDA and ECT. *The Journal of ECT, 32*(2), 75–77.

McDonnell, A., Agius, M., & Zaytesva, Y. (2017). Is there an optimal cognitive application to be used for cognitive remediation in clinical psychiatric practice? *Psychiatria Danubina, 29*(3), 292–299.

McDougle, C. J., Epperson, C. N., Pelton, G. H., Wasylink, S., & Price, L. H. (2000). A double-blind, placebo-controlled study of risperidone addition in serotonin reuptake inhibitor-refractory obsessive-compulsive disorder. *Archives of General Psychiatry, 57*, 794–801.

McDougle, C. J., Kresch, L. E., Goodman, W. K., Naylor, S. T., Volkmar, F. R., Cohen, D. J., et al. (1995). A case-controlled study of repetitive thoughts and behavior in adults with autistic disorder and obsessive-compulsive disorder. *American Journal of Psychiatry, 152*, 772–777.

McEachern, J. C., & Shaw, C. A. (2001). Revisiting the LTP orthodoxy: Plasticity versus pathology. In C. Holscher (Ed.), *Neural mechanisms of memory formation: Concepts of long-term potentiation and beyond* (pp. 26–293). Cambridge, England: Cambridge University Press.

McEvoy, K., Osborne, L. M., Nanavati, J., & Payne, J. L. (2017). Reproductive affective disorders: A review of the genetic evidence for premenstrual dysphoric disorder and postpartum depression. *Current Psychiatry Reports, 19*(12), 94.

McEwen, B. S., & Sapolsky, R. M. (1995). Stress and cognitive function. *Current Opinion in Neurobiology, 5*, 205–216.

McFadden, K., & Minshew, N. (2013). Evidence for dysregulation of axonal growth and guidance in the etiology of ASD. *Frontiers in Human Neuroscience, 7*, 671.

McFie, J., & Zanwill, O. L. (1960). Visual-constructive disabilities associated with lesions of the left cerebral hemisphere. *Brain, 83*, 243–260.

McGrath, J. J., & Welham, J. L. (1999). Season of birth and schizophrenia: A systematic review and meta-analysis of data from the Southern Hemisphere. *Schizophrenia Research, 35*(3), 237–242.

McGrath, J., Saha, S., Chant, D., & Welham, J. (2008). Schizophrenia: A concise overview of incidence, prevalence, and mortality. *Epidemiologic Reviews, 30*(1), 67–76.

McGuffin, P., & Mawson, D. (1980). Obsessive-compulsive neurosis: Two identical twin pairs. *British Journal of Psychiatry, 137*, 285–287.

McGuffin, P., Knight, J., Breen, G., Brewster, S., Boyd, P. R., Craddock, N., . . . Mors, O. (2005). Whole genome linkage scan of recurrent depressive disorder from the depression network study. *Human Molecular Genetics, 14*(22), 3337–3345.

McGuffin, P., Rijsdijk, F., Andrew, M., Sham, P., Katz, R., & Cardno, A. (2003). The heritability of bipolar affective disorder and the genetic relationship to unipolar disorder. *Archives of General Psychiatry, 60*, 497–502.

McGuire, P. K., Paulesu, E., Frackowiak, R. S. J., & Frith, C. D. (1996). Brain activity during stimulus independent thought. *Neuroreport, 7*, 2095–2099.

McHugh, R. K., Votaw, V. R., Sugarman, D. E., & Greenfield, S. F. (2017). Sex and gender differences in substance use disorders. *Clinical Psychology Review*. doi: 10.1016/j.cpr.2017.10.012.

McIntire, S. L., Reimer, R. J., Schuske, K., Edwards, R. H., & Jorgensen, E. M. (1997). Identification and characterization of the vesicular GABA transporter. *Nature, 389*, 870–876.

McIntyre, C. C., Mori, S., Sherman, D. L., Thakor, N. V., & Vitek, J. L. (2004). Electric field and stimulating influence generated by deep brain stimulation of the subthalamic nucleus. *Clinical Neurophysiology, 115*, 589–595.

McKay, D., Abramovitch, A., Abramowitz, J. S., & Deacon, B. (2017). Association and causation in brain imaging: The case of OCD. *The American Journal of Psychiatry, 174*(6), 597.

McLaughlin, T., Geissler, E. C., & Wan, G. J. (2003). Comorbidities and associated treatment charges in patients with anxiety disorders. *Pharmacotherapy, 23*, 1251–1256.

McMahon, F. J., Akula, N., Schulze, T. G., Muglia, P., Tozzi, F., Detera-Wadleigh, S. D., Steele, C. J., Breuer, R., Strohmaier, J., Wendland, J. R., et al. (2010). Meta-analysis of genome-wide association data identifies a risk locus for major mood disorders on 3p21.1. *Nat Genet, 42*(2), 128–131.

McMahon, F. J., Simpson, S. G., McInnis, M. G., Badner, J. A., MacKinnon, D. F., & DePaulo, R. (2001). Linkage of bipolar disorder to chromosome 18q and the validity of bipolar II disorder. *Archives of General Psychiatry, 58*, 1025–1031.

McMahon, W. M., Carter, A. S., Fredine, N., & Pauls, D. L. (2003). Children at familial risk for Tourette's disorder: Child and parent diagnoses. *American Journal of Medical Genetics, 121B*, 105–111.

McNamara, B., Ray, J. L., Arthurs, O. J., & Boniface, S. (2001). Transcranial magnetic stimulation for depression and other psychiatric disorders. *Psychological Medicine, 31*, 1141–1146.

Mednick, S. A., Machon, R. A., & Huttunen, M. O. (1990). An update on Helsinki influenza project. *Archives of General Psychiatry, 47*, 292.

Meguro, K., Ishii, H., Yamaguchi, S., Ishizaki, J., Schimada, M., Sato, M., et al. (2002). Prevalence of dementia and dementing diseases in Japan: The Tajiri project. *Archives of Neurology, 59*, 1109–1114.

Mehta, K. M., & Yeo, G. W. (2017). Systematic review of dementia prevalence and incidence in United States race/ethnic populations. *Alzheimer's & Dementia: The Journal of the Alzheimer's Association, 13*(1), 72–83.

Meiser, J., Weindl, D., & Hiller, K. (2013). Complexity of dopamine metabolism. *Cell Communication and Signaling, 96*(50), 50–51.

Mellman, L. A., & Gorman, J. M. (1984). Successful treatment of obsessive-compulsive disorder with ECT. *American Journal of Psychiatry, 141*, 596–597.

Meltzer, H., & Kostakoglu, A. (2001). Treatment resistant schizophrenia. In J. Liberman & R. Murray (Eds.), *Comprehensive care of schizophrenia: A textbook of clinical management* (pp. 181–203). London: Martin Dunitz.

Meltzer, H. Y. (2017). New trends in the treatment of schizophrenia. *CNS & Neurological Disorders-Drug Targets (Formerly Current Drug Targets-CNS & Neurological Disorders), 16*(8), 900–906.

Melvin, G. A., Dudley, A. L., Gordon, M. S., Ford, S., Taffe, J., & Tonge, B. J. (2013). What happens to depressed adolescents? A follow-up study into early adulthood. *Journal of Affective Disorders, 151*(1), 298–305.

Mendez, M. F., O'Connor, S. M., & Lim, G. T. H. (2004). Hypersexuality after right pallidotomy for Parkinson's disease. *Journal of Neuropsychiatry and Clinical Neuroscience, 16*, 37–40.

Meng, Y., Li, G., Rekik, I., Zhang, H., Gao, Y., Lin, W., & Shen, D. (2017). Can we predict subject-specific dynamic cortical thickness maps during infancy from birth? *Human Brain Mapping, 38*(6), 2865–2874.

Menzies, L., Chamberlain, S. R., Laird, A. R., Thelen, S. M., Sahakian, B. J., & Bullmore, E. T. (2008). Integrating evidence from neuroimaging and neuropsychological studies of obsessive-compulsive disorder: The orbitofronto-striatal model revisited. *Neuroscience & Biobehavioral Reviews, 32*(3), 525–549.

Merali, Z., Du, L., Hrdina, P., Palkovits, M., Faludi, G., Poulter, M. O., et al. (2004). Dysregulation in the suicide brain: MRNA expression of corticotrophin-releasing hormone receptors and GABA(A) receptor subunits in frontal cortical brain region. *Journal of Neuroscience, 24*, 1478–1485.

Merikangas, K. R., He, J. P., Burstein, M., Swanson, S. A., Avenevoli, S., Cui, L., et al. (2010). Lifetime prevalence of mental disorders in US adolescents: Results from the National Comorbidity Survey Replication—Adolescent Supplement (NCS-A). *Journal of the American Academy of Child & Adolescent Psychiatry, 49*(10), 980–989.

Merikangas, K. R., Nakamura, E. F., & Kessler, R. C. (2009). Epidemiology of mental disorders in children and adolescents. *Dialogues in Clinical Neuroscience, 11*(1), 7–20.

Merikangas, K. R., Stolar, M., Stevens, D. E., Goulet, J., Preisig, M. A., Fenton, B., et al. (1998). Familial transmission of substance use disorders. *Archives of General Psychiatry, 55*(11), 973–979.

Merkl, A., Aust, S., Schneider, G. H., Visser-Vandewalle, V., Horn, A., Kühn, A. A., et al. (2018). Deep brain stimulation of the subcallosal cingulate gyrus in patients with treatment-resistant depression: A double-blinded randomized controlled study and long-term follow-up in eight patients. *Journal of Affective Disorders, 227*, 521–529.

Meruelo, A. D., Castro, N., Cota, C. I., & Tapert, S. F. (2017). Cannabis and alcohol use, and the developing brain. *Behavioural Brain Research, 325*, 44–50.

Mesman, E., Birmaher, B. B., Goldstein, B. I., Goldstein, T., Derks, E. M., Vleeschouwer, M., et al. (2016). Categorical and dimensional psychopathology in Dutch and US offspring of parents with bipolar disorder: A preliminary cross-national comparison. *Journal of Affective Disorders, 205*, 95–102.

Messaoudi, E., Bardsen, K., Srebro, B., & Bramham, C. R. (1998). Acute intrahippocampal infusion of BDNF induces lasting potentiation of synaptic transmission in the rat dentate gyrus. *Journal of Neurophysiology, 79*, 496–499.

Metaxas, A., Keyworth, H. L., Yoo, J. H., Chen, Y., Kitchen, I., & Bailey, A. (2012). The stereotypy-inducing and OCD-like effects of chronic 'binge'cocaine are modulated by distinct subtypes of nicotinic acetylcholine receptors. *British Journal of Pharmacology, 167*(2), 450–464.

Metin, O., Yazici, K., Tot, S., & Yazici, A. E. (2003). Amisulpride augmentation in treatment resistant obsessive-compulsive disorder: An open trial. *Human Psychopharmacology, 18*, 463–467.

Metz, V. E., Brown, Q. L., Martins, S. S., & Palamar, J. J. (2017). Characteristics of drug use among pregnant women in the United States: Opioid and non-opioid illegal drug use. *Drug & Alcohol Dependence, 183*, 261–266.

Meuret, A. E., Wilhelm, F. H., & Roth, W. T. (2004). Respiratory feedback for treating panic disorder. *Journal of Clinical Psychology, 60*, 197–207.

Meyer-Lindenberg, A., Miletich, R. S., Kohn, P. D., Esposito, G., Carson, R. E., Quarantelli, M., et al. (2002). Reduced prefrontal activity predicts exaggerated striatal dopaminergic function in schizophrenia. *Nature Neuroscience, 5*(3), 267.

Meyer, J. H., Cho, R., Kennedy, S., & Kapur, S. (2001). The effects of single dose nefazodone and paroxetine upon 5-HT 2A binding potential in humans using [18 F]-setoperone PET. *Psychopharmacology, 144*(3), 279–281.

Meyer, J. H., Kapur, S., Houle, S., DaSilva, J., Owczarek, B., Brown, G. M., et al. (1999). Prefrontal cortex 5-HT2 receptors in depression: An [18F]setoperone PET imaging study. *American Journal of Psychiatry, 156*, 1029–1034.

Meyer, J. H., Swinson, R., Kennedy, S. H., Houle, S., & Brown, G. M. (2000). Increased left posterior parietal-temporal cortex activation after D-fenfluramine in women with panic disorder. *Psychiatry Research, 98*, 133–143.

Meyers, J. L., Sartor, C. E., Werner, K. B., Koenen, K. C., Grant, B. F., & Hasin, D. (2018). Childhood interpersonal violence and adult alcohol, cannabis, and tobacco use disorders: Variation by race/ethnicity? *Psychological Medicine*, 1–11.

Micallef, J., & Blin, O. (2001). Neurobiology and clinical pharmacology of obsessive-compulsive disorder. *Clinical Neuropharmacology, 24*, 191–207.

Michael, N., Erfurth, A., Ohrmann, P., Gossling, M., Arolt, V., Heindel, W., et al. (2003). Acute mania is accompanied by elevated glutamate/glutamine levels within the left dorsolateral prefrontal cortex. *Psychopharmacology, 168*, 344–346.

Michelini, S., Cassano, G. B., Frare, F., & Perugi, G. (1996). Long-term use of benzodiazepines: Tolerance, dependence and chemical problems in anxiety and mood disorders. *Pharmacopsychiatry, 29*, 127–134.

Middeldorp, C. M., Hammerschlag, A. R., Ouwens, K. G., Groen-Blokhuis, M. M., Pourcain, B. S., Greven, C. U., . . . Vilor-Tejedor, N. (2016). A genome-wide association meta-analysis of attention-deficit/hyperactivity disorder symptoms in population-based pediatric cohorts. *Journal of the American Academy of Child & Adolescent Psychiatry, 55*(10), 896–905.

Mielke, R., Zerres, K., Uhlhaas, S., Kessler, J., & Heiss, W. D. (1998). Apolipoprotein E polymorphism influences the cerebral metabolic pattern in Alzheimer's disease. *Neuroscience Letters, 254*, 49–52.

Mihailescu, S., & Drucker-Colin, R. (2000). Nicotine, brain nicotinic receptors, and neuropsychiatric disorders. *Archives of Medical Research, 31*, 131–144.

Miller, A. H., Maletic, V., & Raison, C. L. (2009). Inflammation and its discontents: The role of cytokines in the pathophysiology of major depression. *Biological Psychiatry, 65*(9), 732–741.

Miller, A. L. (2008). The methylation, neurotransmitter, and antioxidant connections between folate and depression. *Alternative Medicine Review, 13*(3), 216–226.

Miller, E. (2003). Measles-mumps-rubella vaccine and the development of autism. *Seminars in Pediatric Infectious Diseases, 14*, 199–206.

Miller, H. L., Delgado, P. L., Salomon, R. M., Berman R., Krystal, J. H., Heninger, G. R., et al. (1996). Clinical and biochemical effects of catecholamine depletion on antidepressant-induced remission of depression. *Archives of General Psychiatry, 53*, 117–128.

Miller, M., Pate, V., Swanson, S. A., Azrael, D., White, A., & Stürmer, T. (2014). Antidepressant class, age, and the risk of deliberate self-harm: A propensity score matched cohort study of SSRI and SNRI users in the USA. *CNS Drugs, 28*(1), 79–88.

Millet, B., Chabane, N., Delorme, R., Leboyer, M., Leroy, S., Poirier, M. F., et al. (2003). Association between the dopamine receptor D4 (DRD4) gene and obsessive-compulsive disorder. *American Journal of Medical Genetics, 116B*, 55–59.

Millier, A., Horváth, M., Ma, F., Kóczián, K., Götze, A., & Toumi, M. (2017). Healthcare resource use in schizophrenia, EuroSC findings. *Journal of Market Access & Health Policy, 5*(1), 1372027.

Mills, D. L., Coffey-Corina, S. A., & Neville, H. J. (1993). Language acquisition and cerebral specialization in 20-month old infants. *Journal of Cognitive Neuroscience, 5*, 317–334.

Milo, T. J., Kaufman, G. E., Barnes, W. E., Konopka, L. M., Crayton, J. W. Ringelstein, J. G., et al. (2001). Changes in regional cerebral blood flow after electroconvulsive therapy for depression. *Journal of ECT, 17*, 15–21.

Mimmack, M. L., Ryan, M., Baba, H., Navarro-Ruiz, J., Iritani, S., Faull, R. L. M., et al. (2002). Gene expression analysis in schizophrenia: Reproducible up-regulation of several members of the apolipoprotein L family located in a high-susceptibility locus for schizophrenia on chromosome 22. *Proceedings of the National Academy of the Sciences, 99,* 4680–4685.

Minozzi, S., Cinquini, M., Amato, L., Davoli, M., Farrell, M. F., Pani, P. P., & Vecchi, S. (2015). Anticonvulsants for cocaine dependence. *Cochrane Database of Systematic Reviews,* (4).

Minshawi, N. F., Hurwitz, S., Fodstad, J. C., Biebl, S., Morriss, D. H., & McDougle, C. J. (2014). The association between self-injurious behaviors and autism spectrum disorders. *Psychology Research and Behavior Management, 7,* 125.

Minzer, K., Lee, O., Hong, J. J., & Singer, H. S. (2004). Increased prefrontal D2 protein in Tourette syndrome: A postmortem analysis of frontal cortex and striatum. *Journal of Neurological Science, 219,* 55–61.

Mirkovic, B., Cohen, D., Laurent, C., Lasfar, M., Marguet, C., & Gerardin, P. (2017). A case- control association study of 12 candidate genes and attempted suicide in French adolescents. *International Journal of Adolescent Medicine and Health.* doi: 10.1515/ijamh-2017-0089.

Miron, J., Picard, C., Nilsson, N., Frappier, J., Dea, D., Théroux, L., et al. (2018). CDK5RAP2 gene and tau pathophysiology in late-onset sporadic Alzheimer's disease. *Alzheimer's & Dementia: The Journal of the Alzheimer's Association, 13*(7), 654.

Misiak, B., Stramecki, F., Gawęda, Ł., Prochwicz, K., Sąsiadek, M. M., Moustafa, A. A., & Frydecka, D. (2017). Interactions between variation in candidate genes and environmental factors in the etiology of schizophrenia and bipolar disorder: A systematic review. *Molecular Neurobiology,* 1–26.

Miskowiak, K. W., Kjærstad, H. L., Støttrup, M. M., Svendsen, A. M., Demant, K. M., Hoeffding, L. K., et al. (2017). The catechol-O-methyltransferase (COMT) Val158Met genotype modulates working memory-related dorsolateral prefrontal response and performance in bipolar disorder. *Bipolar Disorders. 19*(3), 214–224.

Mistry, S., Harrison, J. R., Smith, D. J., Escott-Price, V., & Zammit, S. (2017). The use of polygenic risk scores to identify phenotypes associated with genetic risk of schizophrenia: Systematic review. *Schizophrenia Research, 197,* 2–8.

Mitelman, S. A., Bralet, M. C., Haznedar, M. M., Hollander, E., Shihabuddin, L., Hazlett, E. A., & Buchsbaum, M. S. (2017). Positron emission tomography assessment of cerebral glucose metabolic rates in autism spectrum disorder and schizophrenia. *Brain Imaging and Behavior,* 1–15.

Miyamoto, S., Miyake, N., Jarskog, L. F., Fleischhacker, W. W., & Lieberman, J. A. (2012). Pharmacological treatment of schizophrenia: A critical review of the pharmacology and clinical effects of current and future therapeutic agents. *Molecular Psychiatry, 17*(12), 1206–1227.

Mizuno, Y., Hattori, N., Mori, H., Suzuki, T., & Tanaka, K. (2001). Parkin and Parkinson's disease. *Current Opinion in Neurology, 14*(4), 477–482.

Mo, B., Feng, N., Renner, K., & Forster, G. (2008). Restraint stress increases serotonin release in the central nucleus of the amygdala via activation of corticotropin-releasing factor receptors. *Brain Research Bulletin, 76*(5), 493–498.

Moceri, V. M., Kukull, W. A., Emanuel, I., van Belle, G., & Larson, E. B. (2000). Early-life risk factors and the development of Alzheimer's disease. *Neurology, 54,* 415–420.

Modabbernia, A., Yaghoubidoust, M., Lin, C. Y., Fridlund, B., Michalak, E. E., Murray, G., & Pakpour, A. H. (2016). Quality of life in Iranian patients with bipolar disorder: A psychometric study of the Persian Brief Quality of Life in Bipolar Disorder (QoL. BD). *Quality of Life Research, 25*(7), 1835–1844.

Mohammadi, M. R., Davidian, H., Noorbala, A. A., Malekafzali, H., Naghavi, H. R., Pouretemad, H. R., et al. (2005). An epidemiological survey of psychiatric disorders in Iran. *Clinical Practice and Epidemiology in Mental Health, 1*(1), 16.

Mohler-Kuo, M., Lee, J. E., & Wechsler, H. (2003). Trends in marijuana and other illicit drug use among college students: Results from 4 Harvard School of Public Health College Alcohol Study surveys: 1993–2001. *Journal of American College Health, 52,* 17–24.

Mojsa-Kaja, J., Golonka, K., & Gawlowska, M. (2016). Preliminary analyses of psychometric characteristics of the Polish version of the Obsessive-Compulsive Inventory-Revised (OCI-R) in a non-clinical sample. *International Journal of Occupational Medicine and Environmental Health, 29*(6), 1011–1021.

Mojtabai, R., & Olfson, M. (2011). Proportion of antidepressants prescribed without a psychiatric diagnosis is growing. *Health Affairs, 30*(8), 1434–1442.

Molendijk, M. L., Bus, B. A., Spinhoven, P., Penninx, B. W., Kenis, G., Prickaerts, J., et al. (2011). Serum levels of brain-derived neurotrophic factor in major depressive disorder: State-trait issues, clinical features and pharmacological treatment. *Molecular Psychiatry, 16*(11), 1088–1095.

Molfese, D. (1984). Auditory evoked responses recorded from 16-month-old human infants to words they did and did not know. *Brain and Language, 22*, 109–127.

Molfese, D. L., Molfese, U. J., Key, A. F., & Kelly, S. D. (2003). Influence of environment on speech-sound discrimination: Findings from a longitudinal study. *Developmental Nuropsychology, 24*, 541–558.

Molina, V., Montz, R., Perez-Castejon, M. J., Carreras, J. L., Calcedo, A., & Rubia, F. J. (1995). Cerebral perfusion, electrical activity and effects of serotonergic treatment in obsessive-compulsive disorder. A preliminary study. *Neuropsychobiology, 32*, 423–430.

Möller, H. J. (2006). Is there evidence for negative effects of antidepressants on suicidality in depressive patients? A systematic review. *European Archives of Psychiatry and Clinical Neuroscience, 256*, 476. https://doi-org.uri.idm.oclc.org/10.1007/s00406-006-0689-8.

Momose, Y., Murata, M., Kobayashi, K., Tachikawa, M., Nakabayashi, Y., Kanazawa, I., & Toda, T. (2002). Association studies of multiple candidate genes for Parkinson's disease using single nucleotide polymorphisms. *Annals of Neurology: Official Journal of the American Neurological Association and the Child Neurology Society, 51*(4), 534–534.

Monastra, V. J., Monastra, D. M., & George, S. (2002). The effects of stimulant therapy, EEG, biofeedback, and parenting style on the primary symptoms of attention-deficit/hyperactivity disorder. *Applied Psychophysiological Biofeedback, 27*, 231–249.

Moniz, E. (1994). Prefrontal leucotomy in the treatment of mental disorders. 1937. *American Journal of Psychiatry, 151*, Supplement, 236–239.

Monnig, M. A., Thayer, R. E., Caprihan, A., Claus, E. D., Yeo, R. A., Calhoun, V. D., & Hutchison, K. E. (2014). White matter integrity is associated with alcohol cue reactivity in heavy drinkers. *Brain and Behavior, 4*(2), 158–170.

Monteggia, L. M., & Nestler, E. J. (2003). Opiate addiction. In R. Maldonado (Ed.), *Molecular biology of drug addiction* (pp. 37–44). Totowa, NJ: Humana.

Montgomery, Jr, E. B., & Gale, J. T. (2008). Mechanisms of action of deep brain stimulation (DBS). *Neuroscience & Biobehavioral Reviews, 32*(3), 388–407.

Monti, M. M., Vanhaudenhuyse, A., Coleman, M. R., Boly, M., Pickard, J. D., Tshibanda, L., et al. (2010). Willful modulation of brain activity in disorders of consciousness. *New England Journal of Medicine, 362*(7), 579–589.

Montoya, A., Bruins, R., Katzman, M., & Blier, P. (2016). The noradrenergic paradox: Implications in the management of depression and anxiety. *Neuropsychiatric Disease and Treatment, 541.*

Montoya, A., Weiss, A. P., Price, B. H., Cassem, E. H., Dougherty, D. D., Nierenberg, A. A., Rauch, S. L., & Cosgrove, G. R. (2002). Magnetic resonance imaging-guided limbic leucotomy for treatment of intractable psychiatric disease. *Neurosurgery, 50*, 1049–1052.

Moon, C. M., & Jeong, G. W. (2017). Associations of neurofunctional, morphometric and metabolic abnormalities with clinical symptom severity and recognition deficit in obsessive-compulsive disorder. *Journal of Affective Disorders, 227*, 603–612.

Moore, T. J., & Mattison, D. R. (2017). Adult utilization of psychiatric drugs and differences by sex, age, and race. *JAMA Internal Medicine, 177*(2), 274–275.

Moorman, D. E. (2018). The role of the orbitofrontal cortex in alcohol use, abuse, and dependence. *Progress in Neuro-Psychopharmacology and Biological Psychiatry*, (17), 30813–30818.

Morales, A. M., Kohno, M., Robertson, C. L., Dean, A. C., Mandelkern, M. A., & London, E. D. (2015). Gray-matter volume, midbrain dopamine D2/D3 receptors and drug craving in methamphetamine users. *Molecular Psychiatry, 20*(6), 764–771.

Moretto, E., Murru, L., Martano, G., Sassone, J., & Passafaro, M. (2017). Glutamatergic synapses in neurodevelopmental disorders. *Progress in Neuro-Psychopharmacology and Biological Psychiatry, 84*(B), 328–342.

Moriarty, J., Eapen, V., Coasta, D. C., Gacinovic, S., Trimble, M., Ell, P. J., & Robertson, M. M. (1997). HMPAO SPET does not distinguish obsessive-compulsive and tic syndromes in families multiply affected with Gilles de la Tourette's syndrome. *Psychological Medicine, 27*, 737–740.

Morgan, C. M., Mefeez, A., Brandner, B., Bromley, L., & Curran, H. V. (2003). Acute effects of ketamine on memory systems and psychotic symptoms in healthy volunteers. *Neuropsychopharmacology, 29*, 208–218.

Morgan, C., Webb, R. T., Carr, M. J., Kontopantelis, E., Green, J., Chew-Graham, C. A., et al. (2017). Incidence, clinical management, and mortality risk following self harm among children and adolescents: Cohort study in primary care. *British Medical Journal, 359*, j4351.

Moriguchi, S., Takano, H., Kimura, Y., Nagashima, T., Takahata, K., Kubota, M., et al. (2017). Occupancy of norepinephrine transporter by duloxetine in human brains measured by positron emission tomography with (S,S)-[18F]FMeNER-D2. *International Journal of Neuropsychopharmacology, 20*(12), 957–962.

Morimoto, S., Takao, M., Hatsuta, H., Nishina, Y., Komiya, T., Sengoku, R., et al. (2017). Homovanillic acid and 5-hydroxyindole acetic acid as biomarkers for dementia with Lewy bodies and coincident Alzheimer's disease: An autopsy-confirmed study. *Public Library of Science One, 12*(2), e0171524.

Morris, J. S., Smith, K. A., Cowen, P. J., Friston, K. J., & Dolan, R. J. (1999). Covariation of activity in habenula and dorsal raphé nuclei following tryptophan depletion. *Neuroimage, 10*, 163–172.

Morris, R. L., & Hollenbeck, P. J. (1995). Axonal transport of mitochondria along microtubules and F-actin in living vertebrate neurons. *Journal of Cell Biology, 131*, 1315–1326.

Morrison, J. R., & Stewart, M. A. (1973). The psychiatric status of the legal families of adopted hyperactive children. *Archives of General Psychiatry, 28*, 888–891.

Mortby, M. E., Burns, R., Eramudugolla, R., Ismail, Z., & Anstey, K. J. (2017). Neuropsychiatric symptoms and cognitive impairment: Understanding the importance of co-morbid symptoms. *Journal of Alzheimer's Disease, 59*(1), 141–153.

Morton, R. A., Yanagawa, Y., & Fernando Valenzuela, C. (2015). Electrophysiological Assessment of Serotonin and GABA Neuron Function in the Dorsal Raphe during the Third Trimester Equivalent Developmental Period in Mice. *eNeuro, 2*(6), ENEURO.0079-15.2015. http://doi.org/10.1523/ENEURO.0079-15.2015

Mostofsky, S. H., Reiss, A. L., Lockhart, P., & Denckla, M. B. (1998). Evaluation of cerebellar size in attention-deficit hyperactivity disorder. *Journal of Child Neurology, 13*(9), 434–439.

Mostofsky, S. H., Wendlandt, J., Cutting, L., Denckla, M. B., & Singer, H. S. (1999). Corpus callosum measurements in girls with Tourette syndrome. *Neurology, 53*, 1345–1347.

Motoi, Y., Shimada, K., Ishiguro, K., & Hattori, N. (2014). Lithium and autophagy. *American Chemical Society Chemical Neuroscience, 5*(6), 434–442.

Mottram, P. G., Wilson, K., & Strobl, J. J. (2006). Antidepressants for depressed elderly. *Cochrane Database of Systematic Reviews,* (1).

Mozley, L. H., Gur, R. C., Mozley, P. D., & Gur, R. E. (2001). Striatal dopamine transporters and cognitive functioning in healthy men and women. *American Journal of Psychiatry, 158*, 1492–1499.

Muangpaisan, W., Mathews, A., Hori, H., & Seidel, D. (2011). A systematic review of the worldwide prevalence and incidence of Parkinson's disease. *Journal of the Medical Association of Thailand, 94*(6), 749–755.

Mueller, B. K. (1999). Growth cone guidance: First steps towards a deeper understanding. *Annual Reviews of Neuroscience, 22*, 351–388.

Mueller, N., Riedel, M., Straube, A., Guenther, W., & Wilske, B. (2000). Increased anti-streptococcal antibodies in patients with Tourette's syndrome. *Psychiatry Research, 94*, 43–49.

Mueller-Vahl, K. R., Schneider, U., Koblenz, A., Joebges, M., Kolbe, H., Daldrup, T., et al. (2002). Treatment of Tourette's syndrome with Δ9-tetrahydrocannabinol (THC): A randomized crossover trial. *Pharmacopsychiatry, 35*, 57–61.

Mueller-Vahl, K. R., Schneider, U., Prevedel, H., Theloe, K., Kolbe, H., Daldrup, T., et al. (2003). Δ9-tetrahydrocannabinol (THC) is effective in the treatment of tics in Tourette syndrome: A 6-week randomized trial. *Journal of Clinical Psychiatry, 64*, 459–465.

Muellner, J., Delmaire, C., Valabrégue, R., Schüpbach, M., Mangin, J. F., Vidailhet, M., et al. (2015). Altered structure of cortical sulci in gilles de la Tourette syndrome: Further support for abnormal brain development. *Movement Disorders, 30*(5), 655–661.

Muguruza, C., Miranda-Azpiazu, P., Díez-Alarcia, R., Morentin, B., González-Maeso, J., Callado, L. F., & Meana, J. J. (2014). Evaluation of 5-HT2A and mGlu2/3 receptors in postmortem prefrontal cortex of subjects with major depressive disorder: Effect of antidepressant treatment. *Neuropharmacology, 86*, 311–318.

Mulia, N., Karriker-Jaffe, K. J., Witbrodt, J., Bond, J., Williams, E., & Zemore, S. E. (2017). Racial/ethnic differences in 30-year trajectories of heavy drinking in a nationally representative US sample. *Drug & Alcohol Dependence, 170*, 133–141.

Müller-Vahl, K., Dodel, I., Müller, N., Münchau, A., Reese, J. P., Balzer-Geldsetzer, M., . . . Oertel, W. H. (2010). Health-related quality of life in patients with Gilles de la Tourette's syndrome. *Movement Disorders, 25*(3), 309–314.

Müller, H. H., Lücke, C., Moeller, S., Philipsen, A., & Sperling, W. (2017). Efficacy and long-term tuning parameters of vagus nerve stimulation in long-term treated depressive patients. *Journal of Clinical Neuroscience, 44*, 340–341.

Muller, M. B., Lucassen, P. J., Yassaouridis, A., Hoogendijk, W. J., Holsboer, F., & Swaab, D. F. (2001). Neither major depression nor glucocorticoid treatment affects the cellular integrity of the hippocampus. *European Journal of Neuroscience, 14*, 1603–1612.

Müller, U. J., Sturm, V., Voges, J., Heinze, H. J., Galazky, I., Büntjen, L., et al. (2016). Nucleus accumbens deep brain stimulation for alcohol addiction—Safety and clinical long-term results of a pilot trial. *Pharmacopsychiatry, 49*(04), 170–173.

Mundo, E., & Kennedy, J. L. (2002). Genetics of mental disorders. *Journal of Psychiatry and Neuroscience, 27*(4), 291–292.

Mullins, N., & Lewis, C. M. (2017). Genetics of depression: Progress at last. *Current Psychiatry Reports, 19*(8), 43.

Mundo, E., Tharmalingham, S., Neves-Pereia, M., Dalton, E. J., Macciardi, F., Parikh, S. V., et al. (2003). Evidence that the N-methyl-D-aspartate subunit 1 receptor gene (GRIN1) confers susceptibility to bipolar disorder. *Molecular Psychiatry, 8*, 241–245.

Mundo, E., Walker, M., Cate, T., Macciardi, F., & Kennedy, J. L. (2001). The role of serotonin transporter protein gene in antidepressant-induced mania in bipolar disorder. *Archives of General Psychiatry, 58*, 539–544.

Munn, M. A., Alexopoulos, J., Nishino, T., Babb, C. M., Flake, L. A., Singer, T., et al. (2007). Amygdala volume analysis in female twins with major depression. *Biological Psychiatry, 62*(5), 415–422.

Munro, B. A., Weyandt, L. L., Hall, L. E., Oster, D. R., Gudmundsdottir, B. G., & Kuhar, B. G. (2017). Physiological substrates of executive functioning: A systematic review of the literature. *ADHD Attention Deficit and Hyperactivity Disorders, 10*(1), 1–20.

Munro, B. A., Weyandt, L. L., Marraccini, M. E., & Oster, D. R. (2017). The relationship between nonmedical use of prescription stimulants, executive functioning and academic outcomes. *Addictive Behaviors, 65*, 250–257.

Murata, T., Suziki, R., Higuchi, T., & Oshima, A. (2000). Regional cerebral blood flow in the patients with depressive disorders. *Keio Journal of Medicine, 49*, 112–113.

Murer, M. G., Yan, Q., & Raisman-Vozari, R. (2001). Brain-derived neurotrophic factor in the control human brain, and in Alzheimer's disease and Parkinson's disease. *Progress in Neurology, 63*, 71–124.

Murphy, D. D., Rueter, S. M., Trojanowski, J. Q., & Lee, V. M. Y. (2000). Synucleins are developmentally expressed, and alpha-synuclein regulates the size of the presynaptic vesicular pool in primary hippocampal neurons. *Journal of Neuroscience, 20*, 3214–3200.

Murphy, M. L., & Pichichero, M. E. (2002). Prospective identification and treatment of children with pediatric autoimmune neuropsychiatric disorder associated with group A streptococcal infection (PANDAS). *Archives of Pediatrics & Adolescent Medicine, 156*, 356–361.

Murray, R. M., Bhavsar, V., Tripoli, G., & Howes, O. (2017). 30 years on: How the neurodevelopmental hypothesis of schizophrenia morphed into the developmental risk factor model of psychosis. *Schizophrenia Bulletin, 43*(6), 1190–1196.

Murthy, N. V., Selvaraj, S., Cowen, P. J., Bhagwagar, Z., Riedel, W. J., Peers, P., et al. (2010). Serotonin transporter polymorphisms (SLC6A4 insertion/deletion and rs25531) do not affect the availability of 5-HTT to [11 C] DASB binding in the living human brain. *Neuroimage, 52*(1), 50–54.

Myer, N. M., Boland, J. R., & Faraone, S. V. (2017). Pharmacogenetics predictors of methylphenidate efficacy in childhood ADHD. *Molecular Psychiatry*.

N'songo, A., Carrasquillo, M. M., Wang, X., Burgess, J. D., Nguyen, T., Asmann, Y. W., et al. (2017). African American exome sequencing identifies potential risk variants at Alzheimer disease loci. *Neurology Genetics, 3*(2), e141.

Na, K. S., Ham, B. J., Lee, M. S., Kim, L., Kim, Y. K., Lee, H. J., & Yoon, H. K. (2013). Decreased gray matter volume of the medial orbitofrontal cortex in panic disorder with agoraphobia: A preliminary study. *Progress in Neuro-Psychopharmacology and Biological Psychiatry, 45*, 195–200.

Nahas, Z., Molloy, M., Risch, S. C., & George, M. S. (2000). TMS in schizophrenia. In M. S. George & R. H. Belmaker (Eds.), *Transcranial magnetic stimulation in neuropsychiatry* (pp. 237–252). Washington, DC: American Psychiatric Press.

Nahas, Z., Speer, A., Molloy, M., Arana, G. W., Risch, S. C., & George, M. S. (1998). Frequency and intensity in the antidepressant effect of left prefrontal rTMS. *Biological Psychiatry, 43*, 94–95.

Najafi, K., Najafi, T., Fakour, Y., Zarrabi, H., Heidarzadeh, A., Khalkhali, M., et al. (2017). Efficacy of transcranial direct current stimulation in the treatment-resistant patients who suffer from severe obsessive-compulsive disorder. *Indian Journal of Psychological Medicine, 39*(5), 573–578.

Naji, L., Dennis, B. B., Bawor, M., Varenbut, M., Daiter, J., Plater, C., et al. (2017). The association between age of onset of opioid use and comorbidity among opioid dependent patients receiving methadone maintenance therapy. *Addiction Science & Clinical Practice, 12*(1), 9.

Nakamae, T., Narumoto, J., Shibata, K., Matsumoto, R., Kitabayashi, Y., Yoshida, T., . . . Fukui, K. (2008). Alteration of fractional anisotropy and apparent diffusion coefficient in obsessive-compulsive disorder: A diffusion tensor imaging study. *Progress in Neuro-Psychopharmacology and Biological Psychiatry, 32*(5), 1221–1226.

Nakano, S., Asada, T., Matsuda, H., Uno, M., & Takasaki, M. (2001). Donepezil hydrochloride preserves regional cerebral blood flow in patients with Alzheimer's disease. *Journal of Nuclear Medicine, 42*, 1441–1445.

Nakao, T., Okada, K., & Kanba, S. (2014). Neurobiological model of obsessive-compulsive disorder: Evidence from recent neuropsychological and neuroimaging findings. *Psychiatry and Clinical Neurosciences, 68*(8), 587–605.

Nandra, K. S., & Agius, M. (2012). The differences between typical and atypical antipsychotics: The effects on neurogenesis. *Psychiatria Danubina, 24*(Suppl 1), S95–S99.

Narayan, S., Liew, Z., Bronstein, J. M., & Ritz, B. (2017). Occupational pesticide use and Parkinson's disease in the Parkinson Environment Gene (PEG) study. *Environment International, 107*, 266–273.

Narayana, P. A., Herrera, J. J., Bockhorst, K. H., Esparza-Coss, E., Xia, Y., Steinberg, J. L., & Moeller, F. G. (2014). Chronic cocaine administration causes extensive white matter damage in brain: Diffusion tensor imaging and immunohistochemistry studies. *Psychiatry Research: Neuroimaging, 221*(3), 220–230.

Narayanaswamy, J. C., Jose, D. A., Kalmady, S. V., Venkatasubramanian, G., & Reddy, Y. J. (2012). Clinical correlates of caudate volume in drug-naïve adult patients with obsessive-ompulsive disorder. *Psychiatry Research: Neuroimaging, 212*(1), 7–13.

Narushima, K., Kosier, J. T., & Robinson, R. G. (2003). A reappraisal of poststroke depression, intra- and interhemispheric lesion location using meta-analysis. *Journal of Neuropsychiatry and Clinical Neuroscience, 15*, 422–430.

Nash, J. R., & Nutt, D. J. (2005). Pharmacotherapy of anxiety. In *Anxiety and anxiolytic drugs* (pp. 469–501). Berlin, Heidelberg: Springer.

Nazemi, H., & Dager, S. R. (2003). Coping strategies of panic and control subjects undergoing lactate infusion during magnetic resonance imaging confinement. *Comprehensive Psychiatry, 44*, 190–197.

Neerakal, I., & Srinivasan, K. (2003). A study of the phenomenology of panic attacks in patients from India. *Psychopathology, 36*, 92–97.

Neighbors, H. W., Caldwell, C., Williams, D. R., Nesse, R., Taylor, R. J., Bullard, K. M., et al. (2007). Race, ethnicity, and the use of services for mental disorders: Results from the National Survey of American Life. *Archives of General Psychiatry, 64*(4), 485–494.

Nejati, V., Salehinejad, M. A., Nitsche, M. A., Najian, A., & Javadi, A. H. (2017). Transcranial direct current stimulation improves executive dysfunctions in ADHD: Implications for inhibitory control, interference control, working memory, and cognitive flexibility. *Journal of Attention Disorders*, 1087054717730611.

Neligh, G., Baron, A. E., Braun, P., & Czarnecki, M. (1990). Panic disorder among American Indians: A descriptive study. *American Indian and Alaska Native Mental Health Research: The Journal of the National Center, 4*(2), 43–54.

Nelson, J. C., Mazure, C. M., Jatlow, P. I., Bowers, M. B., & Price, L. H. (2004). Combining norepinephrine and serotonin reuptake inhibition mechanisms for treatment of depression: A double-blind, randomized study. *Biological Psychiatry, 55*, 296–300.

Nemani, K. L., Greene, M. C., Ulloa, M., Vincenzi, B., Copeland, P. M., Al-Khadari, S., & Henderson, D. C. (2017). Clozapine, diabetes mellitus, cardiovascular risk and mortality: Results of a 21-year naturalistic study in patients with schizophrenia and schizoaffective disorder. *Clinical Schizophrenia & Related Psychoses*.

Nemeroff, C. B. (1998). Psychopharmacology of affective disorders in the 21st century. *Biological Psychiatry, 44*, 517–525.

Nenert, R., Allendorfer, J. B., Martin, A. M., Banks, C., Vannest, J., Holland, S. K., & Szaflarski, J. P. (2017). Age-related language lateralization assessed by fMRI: The effects of sex and handedness. *Brain Research, 1674*, 20–35.

Nestadt, G., Samuels, J., Riddle, M. A., Liang, K. Y., Bienvenu, O. J., Hoehn-Saric, R., et al. (2001). The relationship between obsessive-compulsive disorder and anxiety and affective disorders: Results from the Johns Hopkins OCD Family Study. *Psychological Medicine, 31*, 481–487.

Nestler, E. J. (2002). Common molecular and cellular substrates of addiction and memory. *Neurobiology of Learning and Memory, 78*, 637–647.

Nestler, E. J. (2004). Cellular and molecular mechanisms of drug addiction. In D. S. Charney & E. J. Nestler (Eds.), *Neurobiology of mental illness* (2nd ed., pp. 698–709). New York: Oxford University Press.

Nestler, E. J., Barrot, M., & Self, D. W. (2001). ΔFosB: A sustained molecular switch for addiction. *Proceedings for the National Academy of Science, 98*, 11042–11046.

Netherland, J., & Hansen, H. (2017). White opioids: Pharmaceutical race and the war on drugs that wasn't. *BioSocieties, 12*(2), 217–238.

Neumeister, A., Bain, E., Nugent, A. C., Carson, R. E., Bonne, O., Luckenbaugh, D. A., . . . Drevets, W. C. (2004). Reduced serotonin type 1A receptor binding in panic disorder. *Journal of Neuroscience, 24*(3), 589–591.

Neville, H. J., Schmidt, A., & Kutas, M. (1983). Altered visual-evoked potentials in congenitally deaf adults. *Brain Research, 266,* 127–132.

Newberg, A. B., Moss, A. S., Monti, D. A., & Alavi, A. (2011). Positron emission tomography in psychiatric disorders. *Annals of the New York Academy of Sciences, 1228*(1), 13–25.

Newton, J. N., Briggs, A. D., Murray, C. J., Dicker, D., Foreman, K. J., Wang, H., . . . Vos, T. (2015). Changes in health in England, with analysis by English regions and areas of deprivation, 1990–2013: A systematic analysis for the Global Burden of Disease Study 2013. *The Lancet, 386*(10010), 2257–2274.

Ng, Q. X., Venkatanarayanan, N., & Ho, C. Y. X. (2017). Clinical use of Hypericum perforatum (St John's wort) in depression: A meta-analysis. *Journal of Affective Disorders, 210,* 211–221.

Ngan, E. T., Yatham, L. N., Ruth, T. J., & Liddle, P. F. (2000). Decreased serotonin 2A receptor densities in neuroleptic-naive patients with schizophrenia: A PET study using [(18)F] setoperone. *American Journal of Psychiatry, 157,* 1016–1018.

Nguyen, J. P., Suarez, A., Kemoun, G., Meignier, M., Le Saout, E., Damier, P., et al. (2017). Repetitive transcranial magnetic stimulation combined with cognitive training for the treatment of Alzheimer's disease. *Neurophysiologie Clinique/Clinical Neurophysiology, 47*(1), 47–53.

Niccolini, F., Su, P., & Politis, M. (2014). Dopamine receptor mapping with PET imaging in Parkinson's disease. *Journal of Neurology, 261*(12), 2251–2263.

Nicholson, L. F. B., & Faull, R. L. M. (2002). *The basal ganglia VII.* New York: Kluwer Academic/Plenum.

Nicolaidis, S. (2017). Neurosurgery of the future: Deep brain stimulations and manipulations. *Metabolism-Clinical and Experimental, 69,* S16-S20.

Nicoll, R. A., & Malenka, R. C. (1999). Expression mechanisms underlying NMDA receptor-dependent long-term potentiation. *Annals of the New York Academy of Sciences, 868*(1), 515–525.

Nicolson, R., & Rapport, J. L. (2000). Childhood-onset schizophrenia: What can it teach us? In J. L. Rapoport (Ed.), *Childhood onset of "adult" psychopathology.* Washington, DC: American Psychiatric Press.

NIDA. (2016, October 1). *Media Guide.* Retrieved August 29, 2018 from https://www.drug-abuse.gov/publications/media-guide

NIDA. (2018, January 17). *Prescription opioids and heroin.* Retrieved from https://www.drug-abuse.gov/publications/research-reports/prescription-opioids-heroin

NIDA. (2018, June 7). *Heroin.* Retrieved from https://www.drugabuse.gov/publications/drugfacts/heroin

Nikolaus, S., Antke, C., Beu, M., & Müller, H. W. (2010). Cortical GABA, striatal dopamine and midbrain serotonin as the key players in compulsive and anxiety disorders-results from in vivo imaging studies. *Reviews in the Neurosciences, 21*(2), 119–139.

Nischal, A., Tripathi, A., Nischal, A., & Trivedi, J. K. (2012). Suicide and antidepressants: What current evidence indicates. *Mens Sana Monographs, 10*(1), 33–44.

Nishijima, H., Ueno, T., Funamizu, Y., Ueno, S., & Tomiyama, M. (2017). Levodopa treatment and dendritic spine pathology. *Movement Disorders, 33*(6): 877–888.

Nishizawa, S., Benkelfat, C., Young, S. N., Leyton, M., Mzengeza, S., de Montigny, C., et al. (1997). Differences between males and females in rates of serotonin synthesis in human brain. *Proceedings of the National Academy of Sciences of the United States of America, 94,* 5308–5313.

Nitsche, M. A., Fricke, K., Henschke, U., Schlitterlau, A., Liebetanz, D., Lang, N., et al. (2003). Pharmacological modulation of cortical excitability shifts induced by transcranial direct current stimulation in humans. *The Journal of Physiology, 553*(1), 293–301.

Nobili, F., Vitali, P., Canfora, M., Girtler, N., De Leo, C., Mariani, G., et al. (2002). Effects of long-term Donepezil therapy on rCBF of Alzheimer's patients. *Clinical Neurophysiology, 113,* 1241–1248.

Noble, E. P. (2003). D2 dopamine receptor gene in psychiatric and neurologic disorders and its phenotypes. *American Journal of Medical Genetics Part B: Neuropsychiatric Genetics, 116*(1), 103–125.

Nobler, M. S., Olvet, K. R., & Sackeim, H. A. (2002). Effects of medication on cerebral blood flow in late-life depression. *Current Psychiatry Reports, 4,* 51–58.

Nobler, M. S., Oquendo, M. A., Kegeles, L. S., Malone, K. M., Campbell, C. C., Sackeim, H. A., et al. (2001). Decreased regional brain metabolism after ECT. *American Journal of Psychiatry, 158,* 305–308.

Nobler, M. S., Sackheim, H. A., Prohovnik, I., Moeller, J. R., Mukherjee, S., Schnur, D. B., et al. (1994). Regional cerebral blood flow in mood disorders, III. Treatment and clinical response. *Archives of General Psychiatry, 51,* 884–897.

Nomura, Y., & Segawa, M. (2003). Neurology of Tourette's syndrome (TS) TS as a developmental dopamine disorder: A hypothesis. *Brain Development, 25,* 37–42.

Noonan, A. S., Velasco-Mondragon, H. E., & Wagner, F. A. (2016). Improving the health of African Americans in the USA: An overdue opportunity for social justice. *Public Health Reviews, 37*(1), 12.

Nordahl, T. E., Semple, W. E., Gross, M., Mellman, T. A., Stein, M. B., Goyer, P., et al. (1990). Cerebral glucose metabolic differences in patients with panic disorder. *Neuropsychopharmacology, 3,* 261–272.

Nørgaard, A., Jensen-Dahm, C., Gasse, C., Hansen, E. S., & Waldemar, G. (2017). Psychotropic polypharmacy in patients with dementia: Prevalence and predictors. *Journal of Alzheimer's Disease, 56*(2), 707–716.

Noyce, A. J., Bestwick, J. P., Silveira-Moriyama, L., Hawkes, C. H., Giovannoni, G., Lees, A. J., & Schrag, A. (2012). Meta-analysis of early nonmotor features and risk factors for Parkinson disease. *Annals of Neurology, 72*(6), 893–901.

Nuntamool, N., Ngamsamut, N., Vanwong, N., Puangpetch, A., Chamnanphon, M., Hongkaew, Y., et al. (2017). Pharmacogenomics and efficacy of risperidone long-term treatment in Thai Autistic children and adolescents. *Basic & Clinical Pharmacology & Toxicology, 121*(4), 316–324.

Nutt, D. J., & Malizia, A. L. (2004). Structural and functional brain changes in posttraumatic stress disorder. *Journal of Clinical Psychiatry, 65,* 11–17.

Nutt, D., King, L. A., Saulsbury, W., & Blakemore, C. (2007). Development of a rational scale to assess the harm of drugs of potential misuse. *The Lancet, 369*(9566), 1047–1053.

Nuttin, B., Cosyns, P., Demeulemeester, H., Gybels, J., & Meyerson, B. (1999). Electrical stimulation in anterior limbs of internal capsules in patients with obsessive-compulsive disorder. *Lancet, 354,* 1526.

Nuttin, B. J., Gabriëls, L. A., Cosyns, P. R., Meyerson, B. A., Andréewitch, S., Sunaert, S. G., et al. (2003). Long-term electrical capsular stimulation in patients with obsessive-compulsive disorder. *Neurosurgery, 52,* 1263–1274.

Nuwer, M. R., Lehmann, D., Lopes Da Silva, F., Matusuoka, S., Sutherling, W., & Vibert, J. F. (1994). IFCN guidelines for topographic and frequency analysis of EEGs and EPs. Report of an IFCN committee. *Electroencephalography and Clinical Neurophysiology, 91,* 1–5.

Nyberg, F. (2014). Structural plasticity of the brain to psychostimulant use. *Neuropharmacology, 87,* 115–124.

Nyegaard, M., Børglum, A. D., Bruun, T. G., Collier, D. A., Russ, C., Mors, O., . . . Kruse, T. A. (2002). Novel polymorphisms in the somatostatin receptor 5 (SSTR5) gene associated with bipolar affective disorder. *Molecular Psychiatry, 7*(7), 745.

Nystrom, C., Matousek, M., & Hallstrom, T. (1986). Relationships between EEG and clinical characteristics in major depressive disorder. *Acta Psychiatrica Scandinavica, 73,* 390–394.

O'sullivan, S. S., Djamshidian, A., Evans, A. H., Loane, C. M., Lees, A. J., & Lawrence, A. D. (2010). Excessive hoarding in Parkinson's disease. *Movement Disorders, 25*(8), 1026–1033.

O'Brien, J. T., Metcalfe, S., Swann, A., Hobson, J., Jobst, K., Ballard, C., et al. (2000). Medial temporal lobe width on CT scanning in Alzheimer's disease: Comparison with vascular dementia, depression, and dementia with Lewy bodies. *Dementia Geriatric Cognitive Disorders, 11*, 114–118.

O'Bryant, S. E., Mielke, M. M., Rissman, R. A., Lista, S., Vanderstichele, H., Zetterberg, H., . . . Fong, Y. L. (2017). Blood-based biomarkers in Alzheimer disease: Current state of the science and a novel collaborative paradigm for advancing from discovery to clinic. *Alzheimer's & Dementia: The Journal of the Alzheimer's Association, 13*(1), 45–58.

O'Connell, R. A., Van Heertum, R. L., Luck, D., Yudd, A. P., Cueva, J. E., Billick, S. B., et al. (1995). Single-photon emission computed tomography of the brain in acute mania and schizophrenia. *Journal of Neuroimaging, 5*, 101–104.

O'Hare, J. K., Li, H., Kim, N., Gaidis, E., Ade, K., Beck, J., et al. (2017). Striatal fast-spiking interneurons selectively modulate circuit output and are required for habitual behavior. *eLife, 6*, e26231.

Oakley, H., Cole, S. L., Logan, S., Maus, E., Shao, P., Craft, J., et al. (2006). Intraneuronal β-amyloid aggregates, neurodegeneration, and neuron loss in transgenic mice with five familial Alzheimer's disease mutations: Potential factors in amyloid plaque formation. *Journal of Neuroscience, 26*(40), 10129–10140.

Obadia, Y., Rotily, M., Degrand-Guillaud, A., Guelain, J., Ceccaldi, M., Severo, C., et al. (1997). The PREMAP Study: Prevalence and risk factors of dementia and clinically diagnosed Alzheimer's disease in Provence, France. Prevalence of Alzheimer's disease in Provence. *European Journal of Epidemiology, 13*, 247–253.

Oberlander, T. F., & Miller, A. R. (2011). Antidepressant use in children and adolescents: Practice touch points to guide paediatricians. *Paediatrics & Child Health, 16*(9), 549–553.

Obeso, J. A., Rodriguez, M. C., Guridi, J., Alvarez, L., Alvarez, E., Macias, R., et al. (2001). Lesion of the basal ganglia and surgery for Parkinson disease. *Archives of Neurology, 58*, 1165–1166.

Odaka, H., Adachi, N., & Numakawa, T. (2017). Impact of glucocorticoid on neurogenesis. *Neural Regeneration Research, 12*(7), 1028.

Ogawa, M., Fukuyama, H., Ouchi, Y., Yamauchi, H., & Kimura, J. (1996). Altered energy metabolism in Alzheimer's disease. *Journal of the Neurological Sciences, 139*, 78–82.

Ogden, J. A. (1996). Phological dyslexia and phonological dysgraphia following left and right hemispherectomy. *Neuropsychologia, 34*, 905–918.

Oh, J. Y., Yu, B. H., Heo, J. Y., Yoo, I., Song, H., & Jeon, H. J. (2015). Plasma catecholamine levels before and after paroxetine treatment in patients with panic disorder. *Psychiatry Research, 225*(3), 471–475.

Oh, S. W., Shin, N., Lee, J. J., Lee, S., Lee, P. H., Lim, S. M., & Kim, J. W. (2016). Correlation of 3D FLAIR and dopamine transporter imaging in patients with Parkinsonism. *American Journal of Roentgenology, 207*(5), 1089–1094.

Ohara, K., Nagai, M., Suzuki, Y., Ochiai, M., & Ohara, K. (1998). No association between anxiety disorders and catechol-O-methyltransferase polymorphism. *Psychiatry Research, 80*, 145–148.

Ohara, K., Nagai, M., Suzuki, Y., & Ohara, K. (1998). Low activity allele of catechol-o-methyltransferase gene and Japanese unipolar depression. *Neuroreport, 9*, 1305–1308.

Ohnishi, T., Matsuda, H., Hashimoto, T., Kunihiro, T., Nishikawa, M., Uema, T., et al. (2000). Abnormal regional cerebral blood flow in childhood autism. *Brain, 123*, 1838–1844.

Ohta, H., Yamagata, B., Tomioka, H., Takahashi, T., Yano, M., Nakagome, K., & Mimura, M. (2008). Hypofrontality in panic disorder and major depressive disorder assessed by multi-channel near-infrared spectroscopy. *Depression and Anxiety, 25*(12), 1053–1059.

Ohye, C., Shibazaki, T., Zhang, J., & Andou, Y. (2002). Thalamic lesions produced by gamma thalamotomy for movement disorders. *Journal of Neurosurgery, 97*, 600–606.

Ojemann, G. A., & Schoenfield-McNeill, J. (1999). Activity in neurons in human temporal cortex during identification and memory for names and words. *Journal of Neuroscience, 19*, 5674–5682.

Ojo, J. O., Mouzon, B., Algamal, M., Leary, P., Lynch, C., Abdullah, L., et al. (2016). Chronic repetitive mild traumatic brain injury results in reduced cerebral blood flow, axonal injury, gliosis, and increased T-Tau and Tau oligomers. *Journal of Neuropathology & Experimental Neurology, 75*(7), 636–655.

Okasha, A., Saad, A., Khalil, A. H., el Dawla, A. S., & Yehia, N. (1994). Phenomenology of obsessive-compulsive disorder: A transcultural study. *Comprehensive Psychiatry, 35,* 191–197.

Okugawa, G., Sedvall, G. C., & Agartz, I. (2003). Smaller cerebellar vermis but not hemisphere volume in patients with chronic schizophrenia. *American Journal of Psychiatry, 160,* 1614–1617.

Okugawa, G., Sedvall, G., Nordstrom, M., Andreasen, N., Pierson, R., Magnotta, V., et al. (2002). Selective reduction of posterior superior vermis in men with chronic schizophrenia. *Schizophrenia Research, 55,* 61–67.

Olanow, C. W., Goetz, C. G., Kordower, J. H., Stoessl, A. J., Sossi, V., Brin, M. F., et al. (2003). A double-blind controlled trial of bilateral fetal nigral transplantation in Parkinson's disease. *Annals of Neurology, 54*(3), 403–414.

Olbrich, S., & Arns, M. (2013). EEG biomarkers in major depressive disorder: Discriminative power and prediction of treatment response. *International Review of Psychiatry, 25*(5), 604–618.

Olds, J., & Milner, P. (1954). Positive reinforcement produced by electrical stimulation of septal area and other regions of rat brain. *Journal of Comparative and Physiological Psychology, 47*(6), 419.

Oleskevich, S., Leck, K. J., Matthaei, K., & Hendry, I. A. (2005). Enhanced serotonin response in the hippocampus of Gαz protein knock-out mice. *Neuroreport, 16*(9), 921–925.

Olfson, M., Gameroff, M. J., Marcus, S. C., & Jensen P. S. (2003). National trends in the treatment of attention deficit hyperactivity disorder. *The American Journal of Psychiatry, 160,* 1071–1077.

Oliveira, T. V. H. F. D., Francisco, A. N., Demartini Junior, Z., & Stebel, S. L. (2017). The role of vagus nerve stimulation in refractory epilepsy. *Arquivos de neuro-psiquiatria, 75*(9), 657–666.

Olney, J. W., & Farber, N. B. (1995). Glutamate receptor dysfunction and schizophrenia. *Archives of General Psychiatry, 52,* 998–1007.

Olson, L. (2000). Combating Parkinson's disease—Step three. *Science, 290,* 721–772.

Oluboka, O. J., Stewart, S. L., Sharma, V., Mazmanian, D., & Persad, E. (2002). Preliminary assessment of intrahemispheric QEEG measures in bipolar mood disorders. *Canadian Journal of Psychiatry, 47,* 368–374.

Omura, T., Kimura, M., Kim, K., Mishina, M., Mizunari, T., Kobayashi, S., & Morita, A. (2018). Acute poststroke depression is associated with thalamic lesions and clinical outcomes: A case—Control study. *Journal of Stroke and Cerebrovascular Diseases, 27*(2), 499–505.

Ongur, D., Drevets, W. C., & Price, J. L. (1998). Glial reduction in the subgenual prefrontal cortex in mood disorders. *Proclamations of the National Academy of Science, U.S.A., 95,* 13290–13295.

Onitsuka, T., Shenton, M. E., Salisbury, D. F., Dickey, C. C., Kasai, K., et al. (2004). Middle and inferior temporal gyrus gray matter volume abnormalities in chronic schizophrenia: An MRI study. *American Journal of Psychiatry, 161,* 1603–1611.

Ontiveros, A., Fontaine, R., Breton, G., Elie, R., Fontaine, S., & Déry, R. (1989). Correlation of severity of panic disorder and neuroanatomical changes on magnetic resonance imaging. *Journal of Neuropsychiatry and Clinical Neurosciences, 1,* 404–408.

Opel, N., Redlich, R., Zwanzger, P., Grotegerd, D., Arolt, V., Heindel, W., et al. (2014). Hippocampal atrophy in major depression: A function of childhood maltreatment rather than diagnosis? *Journal of Neuropsychopharmacology, 39*(12), 2723–2731.

Ophoff, R. A., Escamilla, M. A., Service, S. K., Spesny, M., Meshi, D. B., Poon, W., et al. (2002). Genomewide linkage disequilibrium mapping of severe bipolar disorder in a population isolate. *American Journal of Human Genetics, 71,* 565–574.

Opmeer, E. M., Kortekaas, R., & Aleman, A. (2010). Depression and the role of genes involved in dopamine metabolism and signalling. *Progress in Neurobiology, 92*(2), 112–133.

Oquendo, M. A., Ellis, S. P., Greenwald, S., Malone, K. M., Weissman, M. M., & Mannm, J. J. (2001). Ethnic and sex differences in suicide rates relative to major depression in the United States. *American Journal of Psychiatry, 158,* 1652–1658.

Orosz, A., Jann, K., Federspiel, A., Horn, H., Höfle, O., Dierks, T., et al. (2012). Reduced cerebral blood flow within the default-mode network and within total gray matter in major depression. *Brain connectivity, 2*(6), 303–310.

Orr-Urtreger, A., Shifrin, C., Rozovski, U., Rosner, S., Bercovich, D., Gurevich, T., et al. (2007). The LRRK2 G2019S mutation in Ashkenazi Jews with Parkinson disease: Is there a gender effect? *Neurology, 69*(16), 1595–1602.

Ortega, J. A., Sirois, C. L., Memi, F., Glidden, N., & Zecevic, N. (2017). Oxygen levels regulate the development of human cortical radial glia cells. *Cerebral Cortex, 27*(7), 3736–3751.

Orvidas, L. J., & Slattery, M. J. (2001). Pediatric autoimmune neuropsychiatric disorders and streptococcal infections: Role of otolaryngologist. *Laryngoscope, 111,* 1515–1519.

Oswald, P., Souery, D., & Medlewicz, J. (2003). Molecular genetics of affective disorders. *International Journal of Neuropsychopharmacology, 6,* 155–169.

Otero, G. A., Pliego-Rivero, F. B., Fernandez, T., & Ricardo, J. (2003). EEG development in children with sociocultural disadvantages: A follow-up study. *Clinical Neurophysiology, 114,* 1918–1925.

Otowa, T., Kawamura, Y., Nishida, N., Sugaya, N., Koike, A., Yoshida, E., et al. (2012). Meta-analysis of genome-wide association studies for panic disorder in the Japanese population. *Translational Psychiatry, 2*(11), e186.

Ouhaz, Z., Fleming, H., & Mitchell, A. S. (2018). Cognitive functions and neurodevelopmental disorders involving the prefrontal cortex and mediodorsal thalamus. *Frontiers in Neuroscience, 12,* 33.

Overall, K. L., & Dunham, A. E. (2002). Clinical features and outcome in dogs and cats with obsessive-compulsive disorder: 126 cases (1989–2000). *Journal of the American Veterinary Medical Association, 221,* 1445–1452.

Overmeyer, S., Simmons, A., Santosh, J., Andrew, C., Williams, S. C. R., Taylor, A., . . . Taylor, E. (2000). Corpus callosum may be similar in children with ADHD and siblings of children with ADHD. *Developmental Medicine and Child Neurology, 42*(1), 8–13.

Ovesen, P., Krøner, K., Ørnsholt, J., & Bach, K. (1991). Phantom-related phenomena after rectal amputation: Prevalence and clinical characteristics. *The Journal of Pain, 44*(3), 289–291.

Owley, T., McMahon, W., Cook, E. H., Laulhere, T., South, M., Mays, L. Z., Shernoff, E. S., et al. (2001). Multisite, double-blind, placebo-controlled trial of porcine secretin in autism. *Journal of the American Academy of Child and Adolescent Psychiatry, 40,* 1293–1299.

Ozaki, N., Goldman, D., Kaye, W. H., Plotnicov, K., Greenberg, B. D., Lappalainen, J., et al. (2003). Serotonin transporter missense mutation associated with a complex neuropsychiatric phenotype. *Molecular Psychiatry, 8,* 933–936.

Ozonoff, S., Young, G. S., Carter, A., Messinger, D., Yirmiya, N., Zwaigenbaum, L., et al. (2011). Recurrence risk for autism spectrum disorders: A Baby Siblings Research Consortium study. *Pediatrics, 128*(3), e488–e495.

Packer, A. (2016). Neocortical neurogenesis and the etiology of autism spectrum disorder. *Journal of Neuroscience & Biobehavioral Reviews, 64,* 185–195.

Padberg, F., Zwanzger, P., Thoma, H., Kathmann, N., Haag, C., Greenberg, B. D., et al. (1999). Repetitive transcranial magnetic stimulation (rTMS) in pharmacotherapy-refractory major depression: Comparative study of fast, slow and sham rTMS. *Psychiatry Research, 88,* 163–171.

Padilha, S. C., Virtuoso, S., Tonin, F. S., Borba, H. H., & Pontarolo, R. (2018). Efficacy and safety of drugs for attention deficit hyperactivity disorder in children and adolescents: A network meta-analysis. *European Child & Adolescent Psychiatry,* 1–11.

Pagliaroli, L., Vető, B., Arányi, T., & Barta, C. (2016). From genetics to epigenetics: New perspectives in Tourette syndrome research. *Frontiers in Neuroscience, 10,* 277.

Paiva, R. R., Batistuzzo, M. C., McLaughlin, N. C., Canteras, M. M., de Mathis, M. E., Requena, G., et al. (2018). Personality measures after gamma ventral capsulotomy in intractable OCD. *Progress in Neuro-Psychopharmacology and Biological Psychiatry, 81,* 161–168.

Pal, P. K., Thennarasu, K., Fleming, J., Schulzer, M., Brown, T., & Calne, S. M. (2004). Nocturnal sleep disturbances and daytime dysfunction in patients with Parkinson's disease and in their caregivers. *Parkinsonism & Related Disorders, 10,* 157–168.

Pałasz, E., Bąk, A., Gąsiorowska, A., & Niewiadomska, G. (2017). The role of trophic factors and inflammatory processes in physical activity-induced neuroprotection in Parkinson's disease. *Postepy higieny i medycyny doswiadczalnej (Online), 71*(1), 713–726.

Pallanti, S., & Bernardi, S. (2009). Neurobiology of repeated transcranial magnetic stimulation in the treatment of anxiety: A critical review. *International Clinical Psychopharmacology, 24*(4), 163–173.

Pallanti, S., & Mazzi, D. (1992). MDMA (Ecstasy) precipitation of panic disorder. *Biological Psychiatry, 32,* 91–95.

Pallanti, S., & Quercioli, L. (2006). Treatment-refractory obsessive-compulsive disorder: Methodological issues, operational definitions and therapeutic lines. *Progress in Neuro-Psychopharmacology and Biological Psychiatry, 30*(3), 400–412.

Pallathra, A. A., Calkins, M. E., Parish-Morris, J., Maddox, B. B., Perez, L. S., Miller, J., et al. (2018). Defining behavioral components of social functioning in adults with autism spectrum disorder as targets for treatment. *Autism Research, 11*(3), 488–502.

Pallier, C., Dehaene, S., Poline, J. B., & LeBihan, D. (2003). Brain imaging of language plasticity in adopted adults: Can a second language replace the first? *Cerebral Cortex, 2,* 155–161.

Pålsson, E., Jakobsson, J., Södersten, K., Fujita, Y., Sellgren, C., Ekman, C. J., et al. (2015). Markers of glutamate signaling in cerebrospinal fluid and serum from patients with bipolar disorder and healthy controls. *European Neuropsychopharmacology, 25*(1), 133–140.

Pandey, G. N. (2013). Biological basis of suicide and suicidal behavior. *Bipolar Disorders, 15*(5), 524–541.

Pandey, S., Srivanitchapoom, P., Kirubakaran, R., & Berman, B. D. (2018). Botulinum toxin for motor and phonic tics in Tourette's syndrome. *The Cochrane Library* Vol. 1, Article ID CD012285.

Panegyres, P. K., & Chen, H. Y. (2013). Differences between early and late onset Alzheimer's disease. *American Journal of Neurodegenerative Disease, 2*(4), 300–306.

Panizzon, M. S., Hoff, A. L., Nordahl, T. E., Kremen, W. S., Reisman, B., Wieneke, M., et al. (2003). Sex differences in the corpus callosum of patients with schizophrenia. *Schizophrenia Research, 62,* 115–122.

Pantazopoulos, H., Wiseman, J. T., Markota, M., Ehrenfeld, L., & Berretta, S. (2017). Decreased numbers of somatostatin-expressing neurons in the amygdala of subjects with bipolar disorder or schizophrenia: Relationship to circadian rhythms. *Biological Psychiatry, 81*(6), 536–547.

Papakostas, G. I., Petersen, T., Mahal, Y., Mischoulon, D., Nierenberg, A. A., & Fava, M., (2004). Quality of life assessments in major depressive disorder: A review of the literature. *General Hospital Psychiatry, 26,* 13–17.

Papanicolaou, A. C. (1998). *Fundamentals of functional brain imaging: A guide to the methods and their applications to psychology and behavioral neuroscience.* CRC Press. Exton, PA: Swets & Zeitlinger.

Papapetropoulos, S., Ellul, J., Argyriou, A. A., Talelli, P., Chroni, E., & Papapetropoulos, T. (2004). The effect of vascular disease on late onset Parkinson's disease. *European Journal of Neurology, 11,* 231–235.

Papes, F., Surpili, M. J., Langone, F., Trigo, J. R., & Arruda, P. (2001). The essential amino acid lysine acts as precursor of glutamate in the mammalian central nervous system. *FEBS Letters, 488*(1–2), 34–38.

Paradiso, S., Andreasen, N. C., Crespo-Facorro, B., O'Leary, D. S., Watkins, G. L., Boles Ponto, L. L., et al. (2003). Emotions in unmedicated patients with schizophrenia during evaluation with positron emission tomography. *American Journal of Psychiatry, 160,* 1775–1783.

Parain, K., Murer, M. G., Yan, Q., Faucheux, B., Agid, Y., Hirsch, E., et al. (1999). Reduced expression of brain-derived neurotrophic factor protein in Parkinson's disease substantia nigra. *Neuroreport, 10*, 557–561.

Parboosing, R., Bao, Y., Shen, L., Schaefer, C. A., & Brown, A. S. (2013). Gestational influenza and bipolar disorder in adult offspring. *JAMA Psychiatry, 70*(7), 677–685.

Pardo, R., Andreolotti, A. G., Ramos, B., Picatoste, F., & Claro, E. (2003). Opposed effects of lithium on the MEK-ERK pathway in neural cells: Inhibition in astrocytes and stimulation in neurons by GSK3 independent mechanisms. *Journal of Neurochemistry, 87*, 417–426.

Parham, W. A., Mahdirad, A. A., Biermann, K. M., & Fredman, C. S. (2006). Hyperkalemia revisited. *Texas Heart Institute Journal, 33*, 40–47.

Park, M., & Unützer, J. (2011). Geriatric depression in primary care. *Psychiatric Clinics, 34*(2), 469–487.

Park, S. H., Park, H. S., & Kim, S. E. (2016). Regional cerebral glucose metabolism in novelty seeking and antisocial personality: A positron emission tomography study. *Experimental Neurobiology, 25*(4), 185–190.

Park, S., Lee, J., Baik, Y., Kim, K., Yun, H. J., Kwon, H., et al. (2015). A preliminary study of the effects of an arts education program on executive function, behavior, and brain structure in a sample of nonclinical school-aged children. *Journal of Child Neurology, 30*(13), 1757–1766.

Park, T. W., Yoon, K. S., Kim, J. H., Park, W. Y., Hirvonen, A., & Kang, D. (2002). Functional catechol-O-methyltransferase gene polymorphism and susceptibility to schizophrenia. *European Neuropsychopharmacology, 12*, 299–303.

Park, Y. D. (2003). The effects of vagus nerve stimulation on patients with intractable seizures and either Landau-Kleffner syndrome or autism. *Epilepsy and Behavior, 4*, 286–290.

Parkinson, J. (1817). *An essay on the Shaking Palsy*. London: Whittingham & Rowland for Sherwood, Neely, and Jones.

Parsey, R. V., & Mann, J. J. (2003). Applications of positron emission tomography in psychiatry. In *Seminars in nuclear medicine* (Vol. 33, No. 2, pp. 129–135). Elsevier.

Pary, R., Matuschka, P. R., Lewis, S., Caso, W., & Lippmann, S. (2003). Generalized anxiety disorder. *Southern Medical Journal, 96*, 581–586.

Pascual-Leone, A., Freitas, C., Oberman, L., Horvath, J. C., Halko, M., Eldaief, M., et al. (2011). Characterizing brain cortical plasticity and network dynamics across the age-span in health and disease with TMS-EEG and TMS-fMRI. *Brain Topography, 24*(3–4), 302–315.

Pascual-Leone, A., Tarazona, F., Keenan, J., Tormos, J. M., Hamilton, R., & Catala, M. D. (1999). Transcranial magnetic stimulation and neuroplasticity. *Neuropsychologia, 37*, 207–217.

Patel, K. R., Cherian, J., Gohil, K., & Atkinson, D. (2014). Schizophrenia: Overview and treatment options. *Pharmacy and Therapeutics, 39*(9), 638–645.

Patel, T., Brookes, K. J., Turton, J., Chaudhury, S., Guetta-Baranes, T., Guerreiro, R., et al. (2017). Whole-exome sequencing of the BDR cohort: Evidence to support the role of the PILRA gene in Alzheimer's disease. *Neuropathology and Applied Neurobiology, 44*(5), 506–521.

Patorno, E., Glynn, R. J., Levin, R., Lee, M. P., & Huybrechts, K. F. (2017). Benzodiazepines and risk of all cause mortality in adults: Cohort study. *British Medical Journal, 358*, j2941.

Patterson, P. H. (1978). Environmental determination of autonomic neurotransmitter functions. *Annual Review of Neuroscience, 1*, 1–17.

Pauls, D. L., Fernandez, T. V., Mathews, C. A., & Scharf, J. M. (2014). The inheritance of Tourette disorder: A review. *Journal of Obsessive-Compulsive and Related Disorders, 3*(4), 380–385.

Paulus, M. P., Hozack, N. E., Zauscher, B. E., Frank, L., Brown, G. G., Braff, D. L., et al. (2002). Behavioral and functional neuroimaging evidence for prefrontal dysfunction in methamphetamine-dependent subjects. *Neuropsychopharmacology, 26*, 53–63.

Paunio, T., Tuulio-Henriksson, A., Hiekkalinna, T., Perola, M., Varilo, T., Partonen, T., . . . Peltonen, L. (2004). Search for cognitive trait components of schizophrenia reveals a locus for verbal learning and memory on 4q and for visual working memory on 2q. *Human Molecular Genetics, 13*(16), 1693–1702.

Pavlova, E. L., Menshikova, A. A., Semenov, R. V., Bocharnikova, E. N., Gotovtseva, G. N., Druzhkova, T. A., et al. (2017). Transcranial direct current stimulation of 20-and 30-minutes combined with sertraline for the treatment of depression. *Progress in Neuro-Psychopharmacology and Biological Psychiatry, 47*(1), 1–7.

PDR Staff. (2018). *PDR Drug Information Handbook 2018.* Montvale, NJ: PDR Network.

Pearce, A. J., Lum, J. A., Seth, S., Rafael, O., Hsu, C. M. K., Drury, H. G., & Tooley, G. A. (2014). Multiple bout rTMS on spatial working memory: A comparison study of two cortical areas. *Biological Psychology, 100,* 56–59.

Pearlson, G. D., Wong, D. F., Tune, L. E., Ross, C. A., Chase, G. A., Links, J. M., et al. (1995). In vivo D2 dopamine receptor density in psychotic and nonpsychotic patients with bipolar disorder. *Archives of General Psychiatry, 52,* 471–477.

Peavy, G. M., Jacobson, M. W., Salmon, D. P., Gamst, A. C., Patterson, T. L., Goldman, S., et al. (2012). The influence of chronic stress on dementia-related diagnostic change in older adults. *Alzheimer Disease and Associated Disorders, 26*(3), 260–266.

Pedersen, N. L., Gatz, M., Berg, S., & Johansson, B. (2004). How heritable is Alzheimer's disease late in life? Findings from Swedish twins. *Annals of Neurology, 55,* 180–185.

Pedrinolla, A., Venturelli, M., Fonte, C., Munari, D., Benetti, M. V., Rudi, D., et al. (2018). Exercise training on locomotion in patients with Alzheimer's disease: A feasibility study. *Journal of Alzheimer's Disease, 61*(4), 1599–1609.

Pelphrey, K. (2017). Charting a course for autism biomarkers. *Biological Psychiatry, 82*(3), 155–156.

Pena-Bravo, J. I., Reichel, C. M., & Lavin, A. (2017). Abstinence from cocaine-induced conditioned place preference produces discrete changes in glutamatergic synapses onto deep layer 5/6 neurons from prelimbic and infralimbic cortices. *eNeuro, 4*(6), ENEURO-0308.

Penadés, R., González-Rodríguez, A., Catalán, R., Segura, B., Bernardo, M., & Junqué, C. (2017). Neuroimaging studies of cognitive remediation in schizophrenia: A systematic and critical review. *World Journal of Psychiatry, 7*(1), 34–43.

Penfield, W. (1958). Some mechanisms of consciousness discovered during electrical stimulation of the brain. *Proceedings of the National Academy of Sciences, 44*(2), 51–66.

Peng, Q., Gizer, I. R., Wilhelmsen, K. C., & Ehlers, C. L. (2017). Associations between genomic variants in alcohol dehydrogenase genes and alcohol symptomatology in American Indians and European Americans: Distinctions and convergence. *Alcoholism: Clinical and Experimental Research, 41*(10), 1695–1704.

Peng, Z., Lui, S. S., Cheung, E. F., Jin, Z., Miao, G., Jing, J., & Chan, R. C. (2012). Brain structural abnormalities in obsessive-compulsive disorder: Converging evidence from white matter and grey matter. *Asian Journal of Psychiatry, 5*(4), 290–296.

Peng, Z., Li, G., Shi, F., Shi, C., Yang, Q., Chan, R. C., & Shen, D. (2015). Cortical asymmetries in unaffected siblings of patients with obsessive-compulsive disorder. *Psychiatry Research: Neuroimaging, 234*(3), 346–351.

Penn, D. L., Meuser, K. T., Tarrier, N., Gloege, A., Cather, C., Serrano, D., et al. (2004). Supportive therapy for schizophrenia: Possible mechanisms and implications for adjective psychosocial treatments. *Schizophrenia Bulletin, 30,* 101–112.

Péran, P., Barbagallo, G., Nemmi, F., Sierra, M., Galitzky, M., Traon, A. P. L., et al. (2018). MRI supervised and unsupervised classification of Parkinson's disease and multiple system atrophy. *Movement Disorders, 33*(4), 600–608.

Perani, D., Garibotto, V., Gorini, A., Moresco, R. M., Henin, M., Panzacchi, A., et al. (2008). In vivo PET study of 5HT2A serotonin and D2 dopamine dysfunction in drug-naive obsessive-compulsive disorder. *Neuroimage, 42*(1), 306–314.

Pereira, L. P., Köhler, C. A., de Sousa, R. T., Solmi, M., de Freitas, B. P., Fornaro, M., . . . Stubbs, B. (2017). The relationship between genetic risk variants with brain structure and function in bipolar disorder: A systematic review of genetic-neuroimaging studies. *Neuroscience & Biobehavioral Reviews, 79,* 87–109.

Perini, G. I., Toffanin, T., Pigato, G., Ferri, G., Follador, H., Zonta, F., et al. (2017). Hippocampal gray volumes increase in treatment-resistant depression responding to vagus nerve stimulation. *The Journal of ECT, 33*(3), 160–166.

Perl, D. P., Olanow, C. W., & Calne, D. (1998). Alzheimer's disease and Parkinson's disease: Distinct entities or extremes of a spectrum of neurodegeneration? *Annals of Neurology, 44,* 19–31.

Perlis, R. H., Mischoulon, D., Smoller, J. W., Wan, Y. J., Lamon-Fava, S., Lin, K. M., et al. (2003). Serotonin transporter polymorphisms and adverse effects with fluoxetine treatment. *Biological Psychiatry, 54,* 879–883.

Perlman, G., Kotov, R., Fu, J., Bromet, E. J., Fochtmann, L. J., Medeiros, H., et al. (2016). Symptoms of psychosis in schizophrenia, schizoaffective disorder, and bipolar disorder: A comparison of African Americans and Caucasians in the Genomic Psychiatry Cohort. *American Journal of Medical Genetics Part B: Neuropsychiatric Genetics, 171*(4), 546–555.

Perrine, D. M. (1996). *The chemistry of mind-altering drugs: History, pharmacology, and cultural context.* Washington, DC: American Chemical Society.

Persico, A. M., Reich, S., Henningfield, J. E., Kuhar, M. J., & Uhl, G. R. (1998). Parkinsonian patients report blunted subjective effects of methylphenidate. *Experimental and Clinical Psychopharmacology, 6,* 54–63.

Perugi, G., Medda, P., Toni, C., Mariani, M. G., Socci, C., & Mauri, M. (2017). The role of electroconvulsive therapy (ECT) in bipolar disorder: Effectiveness in 522 patients with bipolar depression, mixed-state, mania and catatonic features. *Current Neuropharmacology, 15*(3), 359–371.

Perugi, G., Toni, C., Frare, F., Travierso, M. C., Hantouche, E., & Akiskal, H. S. (2002). Obsessive-compulsive-bipolar comorbidity: A systematic exploration of clinical features and treatment outcome. *Journal of Clinical Psychiatry, 63,* 1129–1134.

Petanceska, S. S., DeRosa, S., Sharma, A., Diaz, N., Duff, K., & Tint, S. G. (2003). Changes in apolipoprotein E expression in response to dietary and pharmacological modulation of cholesterol. *Journal of Molecular Neuroscience, 20,* 395–406.

Petanjek, Z., Judaš, M., Šimić, G., Rašin, M. R., Uylings, H. B., Rakic, P., & Kostović, I. (2011). Extraordinary neoteny of synaptic spines in the human prefrontal cortex. *Proceedings of the National Academy of Sciences, 108*(32), 13281–13286.

Peters, L., & Smedt, B. D. (2017). Arithmetic in the developing brain: A review of brain imaging studies. *Journal of Developmental Cognitive Neuroscience, 30,* 265–279.

Petersen, R. C., Wiste, H. J., Weigand, S. D., Rocca, W. A., Roberts, R. O., Mielke, M. M., et al. (2016). Association of elevated amyloid levels with cognition and biomarkers in cognitively normal people from the community. *JAMA Neurology, 73*(1), 85–92.

Peterson, B. S., Leckman, J. F., Duncan, J. S., Wetzles, R., Riddle, M. A., Hardin, M. T., et al. (1994). Corpus callosum morphology from magnetic resonance images in Tourette's syndrome. *Psychiatry Research, 55,* 85–99.

Peterson, B. S., Leckman, J. F., Tucker, D., Scahill, L., Staib, L., Zhang, H., et al. (2000). Preliminary findings of antistreptococcal antibody titers and basal ganglia volumes in tic, obsessive-compulsive, and attention deficit/hyperactivity disorders. *Archives of General Psychiatry, 57,* 364–372.

Peterson, B. S., Skudlarski, P., Anderson, A. W., Zhang, H., Gatenby, J. C., Lacadie, C. M., et al. (1998). A functional magnetic resonance imaging study of tic suppression in Tourette syndrome. *Archives of General Psychiatry, 55,* 326–333.

Peterson, B. S., Staib, L., Scahill, L., Zhang, H., Anderson, C., Leckman, J. F., et al. (2001). Regional brain and ventricular volumes in Tourette syndrome. *Archives of General Psychiatry, 58,* 427–440.

Peterson, B. S., Thomas, P., Kane, M. J., Scahill, L., Zhang, H., Bronen, R., et al. (2003). Basal ganglia volumes in patients with Gilles de la Tourette syndrome. *Archives of General Psychiatry, 60,* 415–424.

Peterson, B., Riddle, M. A., Cohen, D. J., Katz, L. D., Smith, J. C., Hardin, M. T., et al. (1993). Reduced basal ganglia volumes in Tourette's syndrome using three-dimensional reconstruction techniques from magnetic resonance images. *Neurology, 43,* 941–949.

Peterson, K., Dieperink, E., Anderson, J., Boundy, E., Ferguson, L., & Helfand, M. (2017). Rapid evidence review of the comparative effectiveness, harms, and cost-effectiveness of pharmacogenomics-guided antidepressant treatment versus usual care for major depressive disorder. *Psychopharmacology*, 1–13.

Petit, M., Astruc, J. M., Sarry, J., Drouilhet, L., Fabre, S., Moreno, C., & Servin, B. (2017). Variation in recombination rate and its genetic determinism in sheep populations. *Genetics*, *207*(2), 767–784.

Petok, J. R., Myers, C. E., Pa, J., Hobel, Z., Wharton, D. M., Medina, L. D., et al. (2018). Impairment of memory generalization in preclinical autosomal dominant Alzheimer's disease mutation carriers. *Neurobiology of Aging*, *65*, 149–157.

Petralia, R. S., Al-Hallaq, R. A., & Wenthold, R. J. (2009). Trafficking and targeting of NMDA receptors. *Biology of the NMDA Receptor*, *1*, 149–200.

Pettmann, B., & Henderson, C. E. (1998). Neuronal cell death. *Neuron*, *20*, 633–647.

Petty, F., Kramer, G. L., Fulton, M., Moeller, F. G., & Rush, A. J. (1993). Low plasma GABA is a trait-like marker for bipolar illness. *Neuropsychopharmacology*, *9*(2), 125.

Petty, R. G., Barta, P. W., Pearlson, G. D., McGilchrist, I. K., Lewis, R. W., Tien, A. Y., et al. (1995). Reversal of asymmetry of the planum temporale in schizophrenia. *American Journal of Psychiatry*, *152*, 715–721.

Pfefferbaum, A., Sullivan, E. V., Mathalon, D. H., & Lim, K. O. (1997). Frontal lobe volume loss observed with magnetic resonance imaging in older chronic alcoholics. *Alcoholism: Clinical and Experimental Research*, *21*(3), 521–529.

Pfleiderer, B., Zinkirciran, S., Arolt, V., Heindel, W., Deckert, J., & Domschke, K. (2007). fMRI amygdala activation during a spontaneous panic attack in a patient with panic disorder. *The World Journal of Biological Psychiatry*, *8*(4), 269–272.

Phelan, A. T. (2002). MMR and autism: An overview of the debate to date. *British Journal of Nursing*, *11*, 621–625.

Philadelphia Department of Public Health. (2017). 2016 overdoses from opioids in Philadelphia. *CHART*, *2*(7), 1–3.

Philip, R. C., Dauvermann, M. R., Whalley, H. C., Baynham, K., Lawrie, S. M., & Stanfield, A. C. (2012). A systematic review and meta-analysis of the fMRI investigation of autism spectrum disorders. *Neuroscience & Biobehavioral Reviews*, *36*(2), 901–942.

Phillips, C. (2017). Brain-derived neurotrophic factor, depression, and physical activity: Making the neuroplastic connection. *Neural Plasticity* Vol. 2017, Article ID 7260130.

Phillips, M. L., & Swartz, H. A. (2014). A critical appraisal of neuroimaging studies of bipolar disorder: Toward a new conceptualization of underlying neural circuitry and a road map for future research. *American Journal of Psychiatry*, *171*(8), 829–843.

Physician' desk reference (71st ed.). (2017). Montvale, NJ: PDR Network.

Piacentini, J., Woods, D. W., Scahill, L., Wilhelm, S., Peterson, A. L., Chang, S., et al. (2010). Behavior therapy for children with Tourette disorder: A randomized controlled trial. *JAMA*, *303*(19), 1929–1937.

Pickar, D., Breir, A., Hsiao, J. K., Doran, A. R., Wolkowitz, O. M., Pato, C. N., et al. (1990). Cerebrospinal fluid and monoamine metabolites and their relation to psychosis: Implications for regional brain dysfunction in schizophrenia. *Archives of General Psychiatry*, *47*, 641–648.

Pieribone, V. A., Shupliakov, O., Brodin, L., Hilfiker-Rothenfluh, S., Czernik, A. J., & Greengard, P. (1995). Distinct pools of synaptic vesicles in neurotransmitter release. *Nature*, *375*, 493–497.

Pierot, L., Desnos, C., Blin, J., Raisman, R., Scherman, D., Javoy-Agid, F., et al. (1988). D1 and D2—Type dopamine receptors in patients with Parkinson's disease and progressive supranuclear palsy. *Journal of the Neurological Sciences*, *86*, 291–306.

Pignon, B., du Montcel, C. T., Carton, L., & Pelissolo, A. (2017). The place of antipsychotics in the therapy of anxiety disorders and obsessive-compulsive disorders. *Current Psychiatry Reports*, *19*(12), 103.

Pigott, T. A., & Seay, S. M. (1999). A review of the efficiency of selective serotonin reuptake inhibitors in obsessive-compulsive disorder. *Journal of Clinical Psychiatry*, *60*, 101–106.

Pilotto, A., Premi, E., Caminiti, S. P., Presotto, L., Turrone, R., Alberici, A., et al. (2018). Single-subject SPM FDG-PET patterns predict risk of dementia progression in Parkinson disease. *Neurology*, *90*(12), e1029–e1037.

Pilowsky, L. S., Costa, D. C., & Eli, P. J. (1992). Clozapine single photo emissiontomography and the D2 receptor blockade hypothesis of schizophrenia. *Lancet, 340*, 199–202.

Pinho, T. D., Manz, P. H., DuPaul, G. J., Anastopoulos, A. D., & Weyandt, L. L. (2017). Predictors and moderators of quality of life among college students with ADHD. *Journal of Attention Disorders*.

Pino-Gutiérrez, A., Jiménez-Murcia, S., Fernández-Aranda, F., Agüera, Z., Granero, R., Hakansson, A., et al. (2017). The relevance of personality traits in impulsivity-related disorders: From substance use disorders and gambling disorder to bulimia nervosa. *Journal of Behavioral Addictions, 6*(3), 396–405.

Pinto-Sanchez, M. I., Hall, G. B., Ghajar, K., Nardelli, A., Bolino, C., Lau, J. T., et al. (2017). Probiotic Bifidobacterium longum NCC3001 reduces depression scores and alters brain activity: A pilot study in patients with irritable bowel syndrome. *Gastroenterology, 153*(2), 448–459.

Pinto, S., Thobois, S., Costes, N., Le Bars, D., Benabid, A. L., Broussolle, E., et al. (2004). Subthalamic nucleus stimulation and dysarthia in Parkinson's disease: A PET study. *Brain, 127*, 602–615.

Piras, F., Piras, F., Caltagirone, C., & Spalletta, G. (2013). Brain circuitries of obsessive compulsive disorder: A systematic review and meta-analysis of diffusion tensor imaging studies. *Neuroscience & Biobehavioral Reviews, 37*(10), 2856–2877.

Piras, F., Piras, F., Chiapponi, C., Girardi, P., Caltagirone, C., & Spalletta, G. (2015). Widespread structural brain changes in OCD: A systematic review of voxel-based morphometry studies. *Cortex, 62*, 89–108.

Pisula, E., & Ziegart-Sadowska, K. (2015). Broader autism phenotype in siblings of children with ASD: A review. *International Journal of Molecular Sciences, 16*(6), 13217–13258.

Pittenger, C. (2015). Glutamatergic agents for OCD and related disorders. *Current Treatment Options in Psychiatry, 2*(3), 271–283.

Pittenger, C., Adams, T. G., Gallezot, J. D., Crowley, M. J., Nabulsi, N., Ropchan, J., et al. (2016). OCD is associated with an altered association between sensorimotor gating and cortical and subcortical 5-HT1b receptor binding. *Journal of Affective Disorders, 196*, 87–96.

Pittenger, C., Bloch, M. H., Wasylink, S., Billingslea, E., Simpson, R., Jakubovski, E., . . . Coric, V. (2015). Riluzole augmentation in treatment-refractory obsessive-compulsive disorder: A pilot placebo-controlled trial. *The Journal of Clinical Psychiatry, 76*(8), 1075–1084.

Piven, J., Arndt, S., Bailey, J., & Andreasen, N. (1996). Regional brain enlargement in autism: A magnetic resonance imaging study. *Journal of the American Academy of Child and Adolescent Psychiatry, 35*, 530–536.

Piven, J., Bailey, J., Ranson, B. J., & Arndt, S. (1998). No difference in hippocampus volume detected on magnetic resonance imaging in autistic individuals. *Journal of Autism and Developmental Disorders, 28*, 105–110.

Pizzagalli, D. A., Oakes, T. R., Fox, A. S., Chung, M. K., Larson, C. L., Larson, C. L., et al. (2003). Functional but not structural subgenual prefrontal cortex abnormalities in melancholia. *Molecular Psychiatry, 9*, 393–405.

Plag, J., Gaudlitz, K., Zschucke, E., Yassouridis, A., Pyrkosch, L., Wittmann, A., et al. (2012). Distinct panicogenic activity of sodium lactate and cholecystokinin tetrapeptide in patients with panic disorder. *Current Pharmaceutical Design, 18*(35), 5619–5626.

Plassman, B. L., Havlik, R. J., Steffens, D. C., Helms, M. J., Newman, T. N., Drosdick, D., et al. (2000). Documented head injury in early adulthood and risk of Alzheimer's disease and other dementias. *Neurology, 55*, 1158–1166.

Playford, E. D., Jenkins, I. H., Passingham, R. E., Nutt, J., Frackowiak, R. S., & Brooks, D. J. (1992). Impaired mesial frontal and putamen activation in Parkinson's disease: A positron emission tomography study. *Annals of Neurology, 32*, 151–161.

Pogarell, O., Hamann, C., Pöpperl, G., Juckel, G., Chouk'er, M., Zaudig, M., et al. (2003). Elevated brain serotonin transporter availability in patients with obsessive-compulsive disorder. *Biological Psychiatry, 54*, 1406–1413.

Pohlabeln, H., Rach, S., De Henauw, S., Eiben, G., Gwozdz, W., Hadjigeorgiou, C., . . . Pigeot, I. (2017). Further evidence for the role of pregnancy-induced hypertension and other early life influences in the development of ADHD: Results from the IDEFICS study. *European Child & Adolescent Psychiatry, 26*(8), 957–967.

Polanczyk, G., De Lima, M. S., Horta, B. L., Biederman, J., & Rohde, L. A. (2007). The worldwide prevalence of ADHD: A systematic review and metaregression analysis. *American Journal of Psychiatry, 164*(6), 942–948.

Poldrack, R. A. (2012). The future of fMRI in cognitive neuroscience. *Neuroimage, 62*(2), 1216–1220.

Poldrack, R. A., Laumann, T. O., Koyejo, O., Gregory, B., Hover, A., Chen, M. Y., . . . Hunicke-Smith, S. (2015). Long-term neural and physiological phenotyping of a single human. *Nature Communications, 6,* 8885.

Poletti, S., Myint, A. M., Schüetze, G., Bollettini, I., Mazza, E., Grillitsch, D., et al. (2016). Kynurenine pathway and white matter microstructure in bipolar disorder. *European Archives of Psychiatry and Clinical Neuroscience,* 1–12.

Pollack, M. H., Allgulander, C., Bandelow, B., Cassano, G. B., Greist, J. H., Hollander, E., et al. (2003). WCA recommendations for the long-term treatment of panic disorder. *CNS Spectrums, 8, Supplement 1,* 17–30.

Poluzzi, E., Motola, D., Silvani, C., De Ponti, F., Vaccheri, A., & Montanaro, N. (2004). Prescriptions of antidepressants in primary care in Italy: Pattern of use after admission of selective serotonin reuptake inhibitors for reimbursement. *European Journal of Clinical Pharmacology, 59*(11), 825–831.

Pompili, M., Giordano, G., Luciano, M., Lamis, D. A., Del Vecchio, V., Serafini, G., et al. (2017). Unmet needs in schizophrenia. *CNS & Neurological Disorders-Drug Targets (Formerly Current Drug Targets-CNS & Neurological Disorders), 16*(8), 870–884.

Ponnusamy, R., Nissim, H. A., & Barad, M. (2005). Systemic blockade of D2-like dopamine receptors facilitates extinction of conditioned fear in mice. *Learning & Memory, 12*(4), 399–406.

Porta, M., Maggioni, G., Ottaviani, F., & Schindler, A. (2004). Treatment of phonic tics in patients with Tourette's syndrome using botulinum toxin type A. *Neurological Science, 24,* 420–423.

Porter, R. J., Mulder, R. T., Joyce, P. R., Miller, A. L., & Kennedy, M. (2008). Tryptophan hydroxylase gene (TPH1) and peripheral tryptophan levels in depression. *Journal of Affective Disorders, 109*(1–2), 209–212.

Posener, J. A., Wang, L., Price, J. L., Gado, M. H., Province, M. A., Miller, M. I., et al. (2003). High-dimensional mapping of the hippocampus in depression. *American Journal of Psychiatry, 160,* 83–89.

Posner, J., Marsh, R., Maia, T. V., Peterson, B. S., Gruber, A., & Simpson, H. B. (2014). Reduced functional connectivity within the limbic cortico-striato-thalamo-cortical loop in unmedicated adults with obsessive-compulsive disorder. *Human Brain Mapping, 35*(6), 2852–2860.

Post, R. M. (2017 oct 4). The New News about Lithium: An Underutilized Treatment in the United States. *Neuropsychopharmacology.*

Post, R. M., Altshuler, L. L., Leverich, G. S., Frye, M. A., Suppes, T., McElroy, S. L., et al. (2014). More medical comorbidities in patients with bipolar disorder from the United States than from the Netherlands and Germany. *The Journal of Nervous and Mental Disease, 202*(4), 265–270.

Potash, J. B., Zandi, P. P., Willour, V. L., Lan, T. H., Huo, Y., Avramopoulos, D., et al. (2003). Suggestive linkage to chromosomal regions 13q31 and 22q12 in families with psychotic bipolar disorder. *American Journal of Psychiatry, 160,* 680–686.

Potter, W. Z., Hsiao, J. K., & Goldman, S. M. (1989). Effects of renal clearance on plasma concentrations of homovanillic acid. Methodological cautions. *Archives of General Psychiatry, 46,* 558–562.

Poulakis, K., Pereira, J. B., Mecocci, P., Vellas, B., Tsolaki, M., Kłoszewska, I., et al. (2018). Heterogeneous patterns of brain atrophy in Alzheimer's disease. *Neurobiology of Aging, 65,* 98–108.

Pratt, L. A., Brody, D. J., & Gu, Q. (2011). Antidepressant use in persons aged 12 and over: United States, 2005–2008. US Department of Health and Human Services, Centers for Disease Control and Prevention, National Center for Health Statistics, (76), 1–8.

Praveen, K. T., Law, F., O'Shea, J., & Melichar, J. (2011). Opioid dependence. *BMJ Clinical Evidence*, 2011, 1015.

Prescott, J. W. (2013). Quantitative imaging biomarkers: The application of advanced image processing and analysis to clinical and preclinical decision making. *Journal of Digital Imaging*, *26*(1), 97–108.

Preux, P. M., Condet, A., Anglade, C., Druet-Cabanac, M., Debrock, M., Macharia, W., et al. (2000). Parkinson's disease and environmental factors. Matched case-control study in the Limousin region, France. *Neuroepidemiology*, *19*, 333–337.

Price, D., Burris, D., Cloutier, A., Thompson, C. B., Rilling, J. K., & Thompson, R. R. (2017). Dose-dependent and lasting influences of intranasal vasopressin on face processing in men. *Frontiers in Endocrinology*, *8*.

Price, R. A., Kidd, K. K., Cohen, D. J., Paulus, D. L., & Leckman, J. F. (1985). A twin study of Tourette syndrome. *Archives of General Psychiatry*, *42*, 815–820.

Price, R. A., Leckman, J. F., Pauls, D. L., Cohen, D. J., Kidd, K. K. (1986). Gilles de la Tourette's syndrome: Tics and central nervous system stimulants in twins and nontwins. *Neurology*, *36*, 232–237.

Prince, M., Comas-Herrera, A., Knapp, M., Guerchet, M., & Karagiannidou, M. (2016). World Alzheimer report 2016: Improving healthcare for people living with dementia: Coverage, quality and costs now and in the future. London: Alzheimer's Disease International.

Pringsheim, T., Doja, A., Gorman, D., McKinlay, D., Day, L., Billinghurst, L., et al. (2012). Canadian guidelines for the evidence-based treatment of tic disorders: Pharmacotherapy. *The Canadian Journal of Psychiatry*, *57*(3), 133–143.

Pringsheim, T., Jette, N., Frolkis, A., & Steeves, T. D. (2014). The prevalence of Parkinson's disease: A systematic review and meta-analysis. *Movement Disorders*, *29*(13), 1583–1590.

Priyadarshi, A., Khuder, S. A., Schaub, E. A., & Shrivastava, S. (2000). A meta-analysis of Parkinson's disease and exposure to pesticides. *Neurotoxicity*, *21*, 435–440.

Priyadarshi, A., Khuder, S. A., Schaub, E. A., & Priyadarshi, S. S. (2001). Environmental risk factors and Parkinson's disease: A metaanalysis. *Environmental Research*, *86*(2), 122–127.

Prom-Wormley, E. C., Ebejer, J., Dick, D. M., & Bowers, M. S. (2017). The genetic epidemiology of substance use disorder: A review. *Drug & Alcohol Dependence*, *180*, 241–259.

Protopopescu, X., Pan, H., Tuescher, O., Cloitre, M., Goldstein, M., Engelien, A., et al. (2006). Increased brainstem volume in panic disorder: A voxel-based morphometric study. *Neuroreport*, *17*(4), 361–363.

Pubill, D., Canudas, A. M., Pallàs, M., Camins, A., Camarasa, J., & Escubedo, E. (2003). Different glial response to methamphetamine- and methylenedioxymethamphetamine-induced neurotoxicity. *Naunyn-Schmiedeberg's Archives of Pharmacology*, *367*(5), 490–499.

Pujol, C. N., Paasche, C., Laprevote, V., Trojak, B., Vidailhet, P., Bacon, E., & Lalanne, L. (2018). Cognitive effects of labeled addictolytic medications. *Progress in Neuro-Psychopharmacology and Biological Psychiatry*, 306–332. doi: 10.1016/j.pnpbp.2017.09.008. Epub 2017 Sep 14

Pujol, J., Soriano-Mas, C., Alonso, P., Cardoner, N., Menchón, J. M., Deus, J., & Vallejo, J. (2004). Mapping structural brain alterations in obsessive-compulsive disorder. *Archives of General Psychiatry*, *61*(7), 720–730.

Pulver, A. E. (2000). Search for schizophrenia susceptibility genes. *Biological Psychiatry*, *47*(3), 221–230.

Qi, Y., Zheng, Y., Li, Z., & Xiong, L. (2017). Progress in genetic studies of Tourette's syndrome. *Brain Sciences*, *7*(10), 134.

Quansah, E., Ruiz-Rodado, V., Grootveld, M., Probert, F., & Zetterström, T. S. (2017). 1H NMR-based metabolomics reveals neurochemical alterations in the brain of adolescent rats following acute methylphenidate administration. *Neurochemistry international*, *108*, 109–120.

Quezada, J., & Coffman, K. A. (2018). Current approaches and new developments in the pharmacological management of Tourette syndrome. *CNS Drugs*, 33–45.

Quirk, G. J., & Gehlert, D. R. (2003). Inhibition of the amygdala: Key to pathological states? *Annals of the New York Academy of Sciences*, *985*, 263–272.

Quitkin, F. M., Petkova, E., McGrath, P. J., Taylor, B., Beasley, C., Stewart, J., et al. (2003). When should a trial of fluoxetine for major depression be declared failed? *American Journal of Psychiatry, 160*, 734–740.

Rabinowitz, J., Cohen, H., & Atias, S. (2002). Outcomes of naltrexone maintenance following ultra rapid opiate detoxification versus intensive inpatient detoxification. *The American Journal on Addictions, 11*(1), 52–56.

Radua, J., & Mataix-Cols, D. (2009). Voxel-wise meta-analysis of grey matter changes in obsessive—Compulsive disorder. *The British Journal of Psychiatry, 195*(5), 393–402.

Raedler, T. J., Knable, M. B., Jones, D. W., Urbina. R. A., Corey, J. G., Lee, K. S., et al. (2003). In vivo determination of muscarinic acetylcholine receptor availability in schizophrenia. *American Journal of Psychiatry, 160*, 118–127.

Ragonese, P., Salemi, G., Morgante, L., Aridon, P., Epifanio, A., Buffa, D., et al. (2003). A case-control study on cigarette, alcohol, and coffee consumption preceding Parkinson's disease. *Neuroepidemiology, 22*, 297–304.

Raichle, M. E. (2000). A brief history of human functional brain mapping. In A. W. Toga & J. C. Mazziotta (Eds.), *Brain mapping: The systems* (pp. 33–76). Los Angeles, CA: Academic Press.

Raichle, M. E., MacLeod, A. M., Snyder, A. Z., Powers, W. J., Gusnard, D. A., & Shulman, G. L. (2001). A default mode of brain function. *Proceedings of the National Academy of Sciences, 98*(2), 676–682.

Raiteri, M. (2001). Presynaptic autoreceptors. *Journal of Neurochemistry, 78*, 673–675.

Raja, M., & Bentivoglio, A. (2012). Impulsive and compulsive behaviors during dopamine replacement treatment in Parkinson's disease and other disorders. *Current Drug Safety, 7*(1), 63–75.

Rajagopal, V. M., Rajkumar, A. P., Jacob, K. S., & Jacob, M. (2018). Gene-gene interaction between DRD4 and COMT modulates clinical response to clozapine in treatment-resistant schizophrenia. *Pharmacogenetics and Genomics, 28*(1), 31–35.

Rajendram, R., Kronenberg, S., Burton, C. L., & Arnold, P. D. (2017). Glutamate genetics in obsessive-compulsive disorder: A review. *Journal of the Canadian Academy of Child and Adolescent Psychiatry, 26*(3), 205.

Rajkowska, G., Halaris, A., & Selemon, L. D. (2001). Reductions in neuronal and glial density characterize the dorsolateral prefrontal cortex in bipolar disorder. *Biological Psychiatry, 49*, 741–752.

Rajkumar, A. P., Christensen, J. H., Mattheisen, M., Jacobsen, I., Bache, I., Pallesen, J., et al. (2015). Analysis of t (9; 17)(q33. 2; q25. 3) chromosomal breakpoint regions and genetic association reveals novel candidate genes for bipolar disorder. *Bipolar Disorders, 17*(2), 205–211.

Rakic, P. (1995). A small step for the cell, a giant leap for mankind—A hypothesis of neocortical expansion during evolution. *Trends in Neuroscience, 18*, 383–388.

Ramachandran, V. S. (1993). Behavioral and magnetoencephalographic correlates of plasticity in the adult human brain. *Proceedings of the National Academy of the Sciences, USA, 90*, 10413–10420.

Ramachandran, V. S., & McGeoch, P. D. (2007). Occurrence of phantom genitalia after gender reassignment surgery. *Medical Hypotheses, 69*(5), 1001–1003.

Ramachandran, V. S., & Rogers-Ramachandran, D. (2000). Phantom limbs and neural plasticity. *Archives of Neurology, 57*, 317–320.

Ramesh, D., & Haney, M. (2015). Treatment of Cannabis use disorders. *Textbook of Addiction Treatment: International Perspectives*, 367–380.

Rao, M. L., Hawellek, B., Papassotiropoulos, A., Deister, A., & Frahnert, C. (1998). Upregulation of the platelet serotonin 2A receptor and low blood serotonin in suicidal psychiatric patients. *Neuropsychobiology, 38*, 84–98.

Rao, S., Leung, C. S. T., Lam, M. H., Wing, Y. K., Waye, M. M. Y., & Tsui, S. K. W. (2017). Resequencing three candidate genes discovers seven potentially deleterious variants susceptibility to major depressive disorder and suicide attempts in Chinese. *Gene, 603*, 34–41.

Rapoport, J., Giedd, J., Blumenthal, J., Hamburger, S., Jeffries, N., Fernandez, T., et al. (1999). Progressive cortical change during adolescence in childhood-onset schizophrenia. A longitudinal magnetic resonance imaging study. *Archives of General Psychiatry, 56*, 649–654.

Rapoport, M., Feder, V., & Sandor, P. (1998). Response of major depression and Tourette's syndrome to ECT: A case report. *Psychosomatic Medicine, 60*, 528–529.

Rapoport, S. I. (2003). Coupled reductions in brain oxidative phosphorylation and synaptic function can be quantified and staged in the course of Alzheimer disease. *Neurotoxicity Research, 5*, 385–398.

Rapoport, S. I., Horwitz, B., Grady, C. L., Haxby, J. V., DeCarli, C., & Schapiro, M. B. (1991). Abnormal brain glucose metabolism in Alzheimer's disease, as measured by position emission tomography. *Advances in Experimental Medicine and Biology, 291*, 231–248.

Rapoport, S. I., Pettigrew, K. D., & Schapiro, M. B. (1991). Discordance and concordance of dementia of the Alzheimer type (DAT) in monozygotic twins indicate heritable and sporadic forms of Alzheimer's disease. *Neurology, 41*, 1549–1553.

Rasenick, M. M. (2016). Depression and adenylyl cyclase: Sorting out the signals. *Biological Psychiatry, 80*(11), 812–814.

Rasgon, A., Lee, W. H., Leibu, E., Laird, A., Glahn, D., Goodman, W., & Frangou, S. (2017). Neural correlates of affective and non-affective cognition in obsessive compulsive disorder: A meta-analysis of functional imaging studies. *European Psychiatry, 46*, 25–32.

Rasmussen, K., Almvik, R., & Levander, S. (2001). Attention deficit hyperactivity disorder, reading disability, and personality disorders in a prison population. *Journal of the American Academy of Psychiatry and Law, 29*, 186–193.

Rasmussen, S. A., & Tsuang, M. T. (1984). The epidemiology of obsessive compulsive disorder. *The Journal of Clinical Psychiatry, 45*(11).

Rauch, S. L., Shin, L. M., & Wright, C. I. (2003). Neuroimaging studies of amygdala function in anxiety disorders. *Annals of the New York Academy of Sciences, 985*, 389–410.

Rauch, S. L., Shin, L. M., Dougherty, D. D., Alpert, N. M., Fischman, A. J., & Jenike, M. A. (2002). Predictors of fluvoxamine response in contamination-related obsessive compulsive disorder: PET symptom provocation study. *Neuropsychopharmacology, 27*, 782–791.

Ravaglia, G., Forti, P., Maioli, F., Sacchetti, L., Mariani, E., Nativio, V., et al. (2002). Education, occupation, and prevalence of dementia: Findings from the Conselice study. *Dementia and Geriatric Cognitive Disorders, 14*, 90–100.

Rayburn, N. R., & Otto, M. W. (2003). Cognitive-behavioral therapy for panic disorder: A review of treatment elements, strategies, and outcomes. *CNS Spectrums, 8*, 356–362.

Razza, L. B., Moffa, A. H., Moreno, M. L., Carvalho, A. F., Padberg, F., Fregni, F., & Brunoni, A. R. (2018). A systematic review and meta-analysis on placebo response to repetitive transcranial magnetic stimulation for depression trials. *Progress in Neuro-Psychopharmacology and Biological Psychiatry, 81*, 105–113.

Read, J., & Bentall, R. (2010). The effectiveness of electroconvulsive therapy: A literature review. *Epidemiology and Psychiatric Sciences, 19*(4), 333–347.

Reba, R. C. (1993). PET and SPECT: Opportunities and challenges for psychiatry. *Journal of Clinical Psychiatry, 54, Supplement*, 26–32.

Reess, T. J., Rus, O. G., Gürsel, D. A., Schmitz-Koep, B., Wagner, G., Berberich, G., & Koch, K. (2017). Association between hippocampus volume and symptom profiles in obsessive-compulsive disorder. *NeuroImage: Clinical, 17*, 474–480.

Reiman, E. M., Raichle, M. E., Robins, E., Mintun, M. A., Fusselman, M. J., Fox, P. T., et al. (1989). Neuroanatomical correlates of a lactate-induced anxiety attack. *Archives of General Psychiatry, 46*(6), 493–500.

Reimer, R. J., Fon, E. A., & Edwards, R. H. (1998). Vesicular neurotransmitter transport and the presynaptic regulation of quantal size. *Current Opinion in Neurobiology, 8*, 405–412.

Reimherr, F. W., Amsterdam, J. D., Quitkin, F. M., Rosenbaum, F., Fava, M., Zajecka, J., et al. (1998). Optimal length of continuation therapy in depression: A prospective assessment during long-term fluoxetine treatment. *American Journal of Psychiatry, 15*, 1247–1253.

Reimold, M., Smolka, M. N., Zimmer, A., Batra, A., Knobel, A., Solbach, C., et al. (2007). Reduced availability of serotonin transporters in obsessive-compulsive disorder correlates with symptom severity—A [11 C] DASB PET study. *Journal of Neural Transmission, 114*(12), 1603–1609.

Reinares, M., Bonnín, C. M., Hidalgo-Mazzei, D., Colom, F., Solé, B., Jiménez, E., et al. (2016). Family functioning in bipolar disorder: Characteristics, congruity between patients and relatives, and clinical correlates. *Psychiatry Research, 245*, 66–73.

Remington, G., & Kapur, S. (1999). D_2 and 5-HT_2 receptor effects of antipsychotics: Bridging basic and clinical findings using PET. *The Journal of Clinical Psychiatry*, 15–19.

Ren, D., Bi, Y., Xu, F., Niu, W., Zhang, R., Hu, J., et al. (2017). Common variants in GRIK4 and major depressive disorder: An association study in the Chinese Han population. *Neuroscience Letters, 653*, 239–243.

Renn, B. N., & Areán, P. A. (2017). Psychosocial treatment options for major depressive disorder in older adults. *Current Treatment Options in Psychiatry, 4*(1), 1–12.

Reshma Jabeen Taj, M. J., Ganesh, S., Shukla, T., Deolankar, S., Nadella, R. K., Sen, S., Purushottam, M., Reddy, Y. C. J., Jain, S., Viswanath, B. (2017). BDNF gene and obsessive compulsive disorder risk, symptom dimensions and treatment response, *Asian Journal of Psychiatry*, https://doi.org/10.1016/j.ajp.2017.10.014.

Retico, A., Giuliano, A., Tancredi, R., Cosenza, A., Apicella, F., Narzisi, A., et al. (2016). The effect of gender on the neuroanatomy of children with autism spectrum disorders: A support vector machine case-control study. *Molecular Autism, 7*(1), 5.

Reynolds, C. F. (1992). Treatment of depression in special populations. *Journal of Clinical Psychiatry, 53*, 45–53.

Rhew, I. C., Fleming, C. B., Stoep, A. V., Nicodimos, S., Zheng, C., & McCauley, E. (2017). Examination of cumulative effects of early adolescent depression on cannabis and alcohol use disorder in late adolescence in a community-based cohort. *Addiction, 112*(11), 1952–1960.

Rice, F., Harold, G., & Thapar, A. (2002). The genetic aetiology of childhood depression: A review. *Journal of child Psychology and Psychiatry, 43*(1), 65–79.

Richardson, A. J., & Puri, B. K. (2002). A randomized double-blind, placebo-controlled study of the effects of supplementation with highly unsaturated fatty acids on ADHD-related symptoms in children with specific learning difficulties. *Progress in Neuropsychopharmacology and Biological Psychiatry, 26*, 233–239.

Richer, P., & Fernandez, T. V. (2015). Tourette syndrome: Bridging the gap between genetics and biology. *Molecular Neuropsychiatry, 1*(3), 156–164.

Riedel, G., Platt, B., & Micheau, J. (2003). Glutamate receptor function in learning and memory. *Behavioural Brain Research, 140*, 1–47.

Rietveld, M. J., Hudziak, J. J., Bartels, M., van Beijsterveldt, C. E., & Boomsma, D. I. (2003). Heritability of attention problems in children: I. Cross-sectional results from a study of twins, age 3–12 years. *American Journal of Medical Genetics, 117B*, 102–113.

Rinne, J. O., Laihinen, A., Lönnberg, P., Marjamäki, P., & Rinne, U. K. (1991). A postmortem study on striatal dopamine receptors in Parkinson's disease. *Brain Research, 556*, 117–122.

Rioux, L., Nissanov, J., Lauber, K., Bilker, W. B., & Arnold, S. E. (2003). Distribution of microtubule-associated protein MAP2—Immunoreactive interstitial neurons in the parahippocampal white matter in subjects with schizophrenia. *American Journal of Psychiatry, 160*, 149–155.

Ripke, S., Wray, N. R., Lewis, C. M., Hamilton, S. P., Weissman, M. M., Breen, G., et al. (2013). A mega-analysis of genome-wide association studies for major depressive disorder. *Molecular Psychiatry, 18*(4), 497–511.

Risinger, R. C., Salmeron, B. J., Ross, T. J., Amen, S. L., Sanfilipo, M., Hoffmann, R. G., et al. (2005). Neural correlates of high and craving during cocaine self-administration using BOLD fMRI. *Neuroimage, 26*(4), 1097–1108.

Ritvo, E. R., Freeman, B. J., Scheibel, A. B., Duong, T., Robinson, H., Guthrie, D., et al. (1986). Lower Purkinje cell counts in the cerebella of four autistic subjects: Initial findings of the UCLA-NSAC Autopsy Research Report. *American Journal of Psychiatry, 143*, 862–866.

Ritz, M. C., Lamb, R. J., Goldberg, S. R., & Kuhar, M. J. (1987). Cocaine receptors on dopamine transporters are related to self-administration of cocaine. *Science, 237*, 1219–1223.

Riva, D., Taddei, M., & Sara, B. (2018). The neuropsychology of basal ganglia. *European Journal of Paediatric Neurology, 22*(2), 321–326.

Rivera, P., Miguéns, M., Coria, S. M., Rubio, L., Higuera-Matas, A., Bermúdez-Silva, F. J., et al. (2013). Cocaine self-administration differentially modulates the expression of endogenous cannabinoid system-related proteins in the hippocampus of Lewis vs. Fischer 344 rats. *International Journal of Neuropsychopharmacology, 16*(6), 1277–1293.

Rivkin, M. J., Davis, P. E., Lemaster, J. L., Cabral, H. J., Warfield, S. K., Mulkern, R. V., et al. (2008). Volumetric MRI study of brain in children with intrauterine exposure to cocaine, alcohol, tobacco, and marijuana. *Pediatrics, 121*(4), 741–750.

Roberts, R. C., Roche, J. K., Conley, R. R., & Lahti, A. C. (2009). Dopaminergic synapses in the caudate of subjects with schizophrenia: Relationship to treatment response. *Synapse, 63*(6), 520–530.

Robertson, M. M. (2015). A personal 35 year perspective on Gilles de la Tourette syndrome: Prevalence, phenomenology, comorbidities, and coexistent psychopathologies. *The Lancet Psychiatry, 2*(4), 291.

Robertson, M. M., & Eapen, V. (2014). Tourette's: Syndrome, disorder or spectrum? Classificatory challenges and an appraisal of the DSM criteria. *Asian Journal of Psychiatry, 11*, 106–113.

Robertson, M. M., Eapen, V., Singer, H. S., Martino, D., Scharf, J. M., Paschou, P., et al. (2017). Gilles de la Tourette syndrome. *Nature Reviews Disease Primers, 2*(3), 16097.

Robins, L. N. (1993). Vietnam veterans' rapid recovery from heroin addiction: A fluke or normal expectation? *Addiction, 88*(8), 1041–1054.

Robins, L. N., & Slobodyan, S. (2003). Post-Vietnam heroin use and injection by returning US veterans: Clues to preventing injection today. *Addiction, 98*(8), 1053–1060.

Robinson, D., Wu, H., Munne, R. A., Ashtari, M., Alvir, J. M., Lerner, G., et al. (1995). Reduced caudate nucleus volume in obsessive-compulsive disorder. *Archives of General Psychiatry, 52*, 393–398.

Robinson, T. E., & Kolb, B. (2004). Structural plasticity associated with exposure to drugs of abuse. *Neuropharmacology, 47*, 33–46.

Robinson, T. E., Gorny, G., Mitton, E., & Kolb, B. (2001). Cocaine self-administration alters the morphology of dendrites and dendritic spines in the nucleus accumbens and neocortex. *Synapse, 39*, 257–266.

Robitaille, A., van den Hout, A., Machado, R. J., Bennett, D. A., Čukić, I., Deary, I. J., et al. (2018). Transitions across cognitive states and death among older adults in relation to education: A multistate survival model using data from six longitudinal studies. *Alzheimer's & Dementia, 14*(4), 462–472.

Rodriguez, G., Nobili, F., Rocca, G., De Carli, F., Gianelli, M. V., & Rosadini, G. (1998). Quantitative electroencephalography and regional cerebral blood flow: Discriminant analysis between Alzheimer's patients and healthy controls. *Dementia and Geriatric Cognitive Disorders, 9*, 274–283.

Roessner, V., Becker, A., Banaschewski, T., Freeman, R. D., Rothenberger, A., & Tourette Syndrome International Database Consortium. (2007). Developmental psychopathology of children and adolescents with Tourette syndrome-impact of ADHD. *European Child & Adolescent Psychiatry, 16*(9), 24–35.

Roessner, V., Schoenefeld, K., Buse, J., Bender, S., Ehrlich, S., & Münchau, A. (2013). Pharmacological treatment of tic disorders and Tourette syndrome. *Neuropharmacology, 68*, 143–149.

Rogers, J. C., & De Brito, S. A. (2016). Cortical and subcortical gray matter volume in youths with conduct problems: A meta-analysis. *JAMA Psychiatry, 73*(1), 64–72.

Roh, S. C., Park, E. J., Shim, M., & Lee, S. H. (2016). EEG beta and low gamma power correlates with inattention in patients with major depressive disorder. *Journal of Affective Disorders, 204*, 124–130.

Rohde, L. A., Roman, T., Szobot, C., Cunha, R. D., Hutz, M. H., & Biederman, J. (2003). Dopamine transporter gene, response to methylphenidate and cerebral blood flow in attention-deficit/hyperactivity disorder: A pilot study. *Synapse, 48*(2), 87–89.

Roizen, N. J., Blondis, T. A., Irwin, M., Rubinoff, A., Kieffer, J., & Stein, M. A. (1996). Psychiatric and developmental disorders in families of children with attention-deficit hyperactivity disorder. *Archives of Pediatric and Adolescent Medicine, 150*, 203–208.

Roizen, N. J., & Patterson, D. (2003). Down's syndrome. *Lancet, 361*(9365), 1281–1289.

Roman, T., Schmitz, M., Polanczyk, G. V., Eizirik, M., Rohde, L. A., & Hutz, M. H. (2003). Is the alpha-2A adrenergic receptor gene (ADRA2A) associated with attention-deficit/hyperactivity disorder? *American Journal of Human Genetics, 120B*, 116–120.

Romero, A. M., Renau-Piqueras, J., Marin, M. P., Timoneda, J., Berciano, M. T., Lafarga, M., & Esteban-Pretel, G. (2013). Chronic alcohol alters dendritic spine development in neurons in primary culture. *Neurotoxicity Research, 24*(4), 532–548.

Rosenberg, D. R., Benazon, N. R., Gilbert, A., Sullivan, A., & Moore, G. J. (2000). Thalamic volume in pediatric obsessive-compulsive disorder patients before and after cognitive behavioral therapy. *Biological Psychiatry, 48*, 294–300.

Rosenberg, D. R., Keshavan, M. S., Dick, E. L., Bagwell, W. W., MacMaster, F. P., & Birmaher, B. (1997). Corpus callosal morphology in treatment-naive pediatric obsessive compulsive disorder. *Progress in Neuro-Psychopharmacology & Biological Psychiatry, 21*, 1269–1283.

Rosenberg, D. R., Keshavan, M. S., O'Hearn, K. M., Dick, E. L., Bagwell, W. W., Seymour, A. B., et al. (1997). Frontostriatal measurement in treatment-naive children with obsessive-compulsive disorder. *Archives of General Psychiatry, 54*, 824–830.

Rosenberg, G. (2007). The mechanisms of action of valproate in neuropsychiatric disorders: Can we see the forest for the trees? *Cellular and Molecular Life Sciences, 64*(16), 2090–2103.

Rosenblat, J. D., & McIntyre, R. S. (2018). Efficacy and tolerability of minocycline for depression: A systematic review and meta-analysis of clinical trials. *Journal of Affective Disorders, 227*, 219–225.

Roslin, M., & Kurian, M. (2003). Vagus nerve stimulation in the treatment of morbid obesity. In S. C. Schachter & D. Schmidt (Eds.), *Vagus nerve stimulation* (2nd ed., pp. 113–121). New York: Martin Dunitz, Taylor & Francis Group.

Ross, G. W., Abbott, R. D., Petrovitch, H., Morens, D. M., Grandinetti, A., Tung, K. H., et al. (2000). Association of coffee and caffeine intake with the risk of Parkinson disease. *Journal of the American Medical Association, 283*, 2674–2679.

Ross, J., Badner, J., Garrido, H., Sheppard, B., Chavira, D. A., Grados, M., et al. (2011). Genome-wide linkage analysis in Costa Rican families implicates chromosome 15q14 as a candidate region for OCD. *Human Genetics, 130*(6), 795–805.

Rossi, A., Barraco, A., & Donda, P. (2004). Fluoxetine: A review on evidence based medicine. *Annals of General Hospital Psychiatry, 12*, 2.

Rossi, R., Pievani, M., Järvenpää, T., Testa, C., Koskenvuo, M., Räihä, I., et al. (2016). Voxel-based morphometry study on monozygotic twins discordant for Alzheimer's disease. *Acta Neurologica Scandinavica, 133*(6), 427–433.

Rostami, R., Kazemi, R., Nitsche, M. A., Gholipour, F., & Salehinejad, M. A. (2017). Clinical and demographic predictors of response to rTMS treatment in unipolar and bipolar depressive disorders. *Clinical Neurophysiology, 128*(10), 1961–1970.

Rotge, J. Y., Guehl, D., Dilharreguy, B., Cuny, E., Tignol, J., Bioulac, B., et al. (2008). Provocation of obsessive—Compulsive symptoms: A quantitative voxel-based meta-analysis of functional neuroimaging studies. *Journal of Psychiatry & Neuroscience: JPN, 33*(5), 405–412.

Rothwell, C. M., Hoog, E. D., & Spencer, G. E. (2017). The role of retinoic acid in the formation and modulation of invertebrate central synapses. *Journal of Neurophysiology, 117*(2), 692–704.

Rotondo, A., Mazzanti, C., Dell'Osso, L., Rucci, P., Sullivan, P., Bouanani, S., et al. (2002). Catechol omethyltransferase, serotonin transporter, and tryptophan hydroxylase gene polymorphism in bipolar disorder patiens with and without comorbid panic disorder. *American Journal of Psychiatry, 159*, 23–29.

Rowland, A. S., Lesesne, C. A., & Abramowitz, A. J. (2002). The epidemiology of attention-deficit/hyperactivity disorder (ADHD): A public health view. *Mental Retardation and Developmental Disabilities Research Reviews, 8*, 162–170.

Roy, A., Dejong, J., & Ferraro, T. (1991). CSF GABA in depressed patients and normal controls. *Psychological Medicine, 21*, 613–618.

Rozin, P., Millman, L., & Nemeroff, C. (1986). Operation of the laws of sympathetic magic in disgust and other domains. *Journal of Personality and Social Psychology, 50*(4), 703.

Rubia, K., Overmeyer, S., Taylor, E., Brammer, M., Williams, S. C., Simmons, A., & Bullmore, E. T. (1999). Hypofrontality in attention deficit hyperactivity disorder during higher-order motor control: A study with functional MRI. *American Journal of Psychiatry, 156*(6), 891–896.

Rubin, E., Sackeim, H. A., Prohovnik, I., Moeller, J. R., Schnur, D. B., & Mukherjee, S. (1995). Regional cerebral blood flow in mood disorders: IV. Comparison of mania and depression. *Psychiatry Research, 61*, 1–10.

Rubino, A., Roskell, N., Tennis, P., Mines, D., Weich, S., & Andrews, E. (2007). Risk of suicide during treatment with venlafaxine, citalopram, fluoxetine, and dothiepin: Retrospective cohort study. *British Medical Journal, 334*(7587), 242.

Rubio, J. M., Sanjuán, J., Flórez-Salamanca, L., & Cuesta, M. J. (2012). Examining the course of hallucinatory experiences in children and adolescents: A systematic review. *Schizophrenia Research, 138*(2), 248–254.

Rück, C., Andréewitch, S., Flyckt, K., Edman, G., Nyman, H., Meyerson, B. A., et al. (2003). Capsulotomy for refractory anxiety disorders: Long-term follow-up of 26 patients. *American Journal of Psychiatry, 160*, 513–521.

Rudorfer, M. V., & Potter, W. Z. (1997). The role of metabolites of antidepressants in the treatment of depression. *CNS Drugs, 7*(4), 273–312.

Ruhé, H. G., Khoenkhoen, S. J., Ottenhof, K. W., Koeter, M. W., Mocking, R. J., & Schene, A. H. (2015). Longitudinal effects of the SSRI paroxetine on salivary cortisol in major depressive disorder. *Psychoneuroendocrinology, 52*, 261–271.

Rui, Q., Ni, H., Li, D., Gao, R., & Chen, G. (2018). The role of LRRK2 in neurodegeneration of Parkinson disease. *Current Neuropharmacology, 16*(9), 1348–1357.

Ruland, T., Domschke, K., Schütte, V., Zavorotnyy, M., Kugel, H., Notzon, S., et al. (2015). Neuropeptide S receptor gene variation modulates anterior cingulate cortex Glx levels during CCK-4 induced panic. *European Neuropsychopharmacology, 25*(10), 1677–1682.

Rumsey, J. M., Duara, R., Grady, C., Rapoport, J. L., Margolin, R. A., Rapoport, S. I., et al. (1985). Brain metabolism in autism: Resting cerebral glucose utilization rates as measured with positron emission tomography. *Archives of General Psychiatry, 42*, 448–455.

Runeson, B., & Åsberg, M. (2003). Family history of suicide among suicide victims. *American Journal of Psychiatry, 160*, 1525–1526.

Rus, O. G., Reess, T. J., Wagner, G., Zaudig, M., Zimmer, C., & Koch, K. (2017). Structural alterations in patients with obsessive-compulsive disorder: A surface-based analysis of cortical volume, surface area and thickness. *Journal of Psychiatry & Neuroscience: JPN, 42*(6), 395–403.

Rus, O. G., Reess, T. J., Wagner, G., Zimmer, C., Zaudig, M., & Koch, K. (2017). Functional and structural connectivity of the amygdala in obsessive-compulsive disorder. *NeuroImage: Clinical, 13*, 246–255.

Ruscio, A. M., Stein, D. J., Chiu, W. T., & Kessler, R. C. (2010). The epidemiology of obsessive-compulsive disorder in the National Comorbidity Survey Replication. *Molecular Psychiatry, 15*(1), 53.

Russell, P. S., Tharyan, P., Arun Kumar, K., & Cherian, A. (2002). Electro convulsive therapy in a pre-pubertal child with severe depression. *Journal of Postgraduate Medicine, 48*, 290–291.

Ryan, J. M., Kidder, S. W., Daiello, L. A., & Tariot, P. N. (2002). Mental health services in nursing homes: Psychopharmacologic interventions in nursing homes: What do we know and where should we go? *Psychiatric Services, 53*, 1407–1413.

Ryan, N. S., & Rossor, M. N. (2010). Correlating familial Alzheimer's disease gene mutations with clinical phenotype. *Biomarkers in Medicine, 4*(1), 99–112.

Rybicki, B. A., Johnson, C. C., Peterson, E. L., Kortsha, G. X., & Gorell, J. M. (1999). A family history of Parkinson's disease and its effect on other PD risk factors. *Neuroepidemiology, 18,* 270–278.

Rydell, M., Taylor, M. J., & Larsson, H. (2017). Genetic and environmental contributions to the association between ADHD and affective problems in early childhood: A Swedish population-based twin study. *American Journal of Medical Genetics Part B: Neuropsychiatric Genetics, 174*(5), 538–546.

Sabec, M. H., Wonnacott, S., Warburton, E. C., & Bashir, Z. I. (2018). Nicotinic acetylcholine receptors control encoding and retrieval of associative recognition memory through plasticity in the medial prefrontal cortex. *Cell Reports, 22*(13), 3409–3415.

Sacco, R., Gabriele, S., & Persico, A. M. (2015). Head circumference and brain size in autism spectrum disorder: A systematic review and meta-analysis. *Psychiatry Research: Neuroimaging, 234*(2), 239–251.

Sachdev, P. S., McBride, R., Loo, C. K., Mitchell, P. B., Malhi, G. S., & Croker, V. M. (2001). Right versus left prefrontal transcranial magnetic stimulation for obsessive-compulsive disorder: A preliminary investigation. *Journal of Clinical Psychiatry, 62,* 981–984.

Sachdev, P., Trollor, J., Walker, A., Wen, W., Fulham, M., Smith, J. S., et al. (2001). Bilateral orbitomedial leucotomy for obsessive-compulsive disorder: A single-case study using positron emission tomography. *Australian and New Zealand Journal of Psychiatry, 35,* 684–690.

Sackeim, H. A., Prohovnik, I., Moeller, J. R., Mayeux, R., Stern, Y., & Devanand, D. P. (1993). Regional cerebral blood flow in mood disorders. II. Comparison of major depression and Alzheimer's disease. *Journal of Nuclear Medicine, 34,* 1090–1101.

Sackeim, H. A., Rush, A. J., George, M. S., Marangell, L. B., Husain, M. M., Nahas, Z., et al. (2001). Vagus nerve stimulation (TNS) for treatment-resistant depression: Efficacy, side effects, and predictors of outcome. *Neuropsychopharmacology, 25,* 713–728.

Sackheim, H. A. (1997). What's new with ECT. *American Society of Clinical Psychopharmacology Progress Notes, 8,* 27–33.

Sadato, N., Okada, T., Honda, M., & Yonekura, Y. (2002). Critical period for cross-modal plasticity in blind humans: A functional MRI study. *Neuroimage, 16*(2), 389–400.

Sadato, N., Pascual-Leone, A., Grafman, J., Deibe, M. P., Ibanez, V., & Hallett, M. (1998). Neural networks for Braille reading by the blind. *Brain, 121,* 1213–1229.

Safer, D. J. (1973). A familial factor in minimal brain dysfunction. *Behavioral Genetics, 3,* 175–186.

Safer, D. J. (2016). Recent trends in stimulant usage. *Journal of Attention Disorders, 20*(6), 471–477.

Safer, D. J. (2017). Differing antidepressant maintenance methodologies. *Contemporary Clinical Trials, 61,* 87–95.

Safer, D. J., Zito, J. M., & dosReis, S. (2003). Concomitant psychotropic medication for youths. *American Journal of Psychiatry, 160,* 438–449.

Saha, S., Chant, D., & Mcgrath, J. (2008). Meta-analyses of the incidence and prevalence of schizophrenia: Conceptual and methodological issues. *International Journal of Methods in Psychiatric Research, 17*(1), 55–61.

Saify, K., & Saadat, M. (2015). Association between variable number of tandem repeats (VNTR) polymorphism in the promoter region of monoamine oxidase A (MAOA) gene and susceptibility to heroin dependence. *Psychiatry Research, 229*(3), 1055–1056.

Saito, M., Nishio, Y., Kanno, S., Uchiyama, M., Hayashi, A., Takagi, M., et al. (2011). Cognitive profile of idiopathic normal pressure hydrocephalus. *Dementia and Geriatric Cognitive Disorders Extra, 1*(1), 202–211.

Salcedo, S., McMaster, K. J., & Johnson, S. L. (2017). Disparities in treatment and service utilization among hispanics and non-hispanic whites with bipolar disorder. *Journal of Racial and Ethnic Health Disparities, 4*(3), 354–363.

Salery, M., Dos Santos, M., Saint-Jour, E., Moumné, L., Pagès, C., Kappès, V., et al. (2017). Activity-regulated cytoskeleton-associated protein accumulates in the nucleus in response to cocaine and acts as a brake on chromatin remodeling and long-term behavioral alterations. *Biological Psychiatry, 81*(7), 573–584.

Sallee, F. R., Nesbitt, L., Jackson, C., Sine, L., & Sethuraman, G. (1997). Relative efficiency of halo-peridol and pimozide in children and adolescents with Tourette's disorder. *American Journal of Psychiatry, 154,* 1057–1062.

Salloway, S., Malloy, P., Kohn, R., Gillard, E., Duffy, J., Rogg, J., et al. (1996). MRI and neuropsychological differences in early- and late-life-onset geriatric depression. *Neurology, 46,* 1567–1574.

Salokangas, R. K. R., Honkonen, T., Stengard, E., Koivisto, A. M., & Hietala, J. (2002). Negative symptoms and neuroleptics in catatonic schizophrenia. *Schizophrenia Research, 59,* 73–76.

Salter, M. W., & Stevens, B. (2017). Microglia emerge as central players in brain disease. *Nature Medicine, 23*(9), 1018.

Salvadore, G., Quiroz, J. A., Machado-Vieira, R., Henter, I. D., Manji, H. K., & Zarate Jr, C. (2010). The neurobiology of the switch process in bipolar disorder: A review. *The Journal of Clinical Psychiatry, 71*(11), 1488.

Samara, M. T., Cao, H., Helfer, B., Davis, J. M., & Leucht, S. (2014). Chlorpromazine versus every other antipsychotic for schizophrenia: A systematic review and meta-analysis challenging the dogma of equal efficacy of antipsychotic drugs. *European Neuropsychopharmacology, 24*(7), 1046–1055.

Samartzis, L., Dima, D., Fusar-Poli, P., & Kyriakopoulos, M. (2014). White matter alterations in early stages of schizophrenia: A systematic review of diffusion tensor imaging studies. *Journal of Neuroimaging, 24*(2), 101–110.

Samartzis, L., Dimopoulos, S., Tziongourou, M., Koroboki, E., Kyprianou, T., & Nanas, S. (2013). SSRIs versus exercise training for depression in chronic heart failure: A meta- analysis of randomized controlled trials. *International Journal of Cardiology, 168*(5), 4956–4958.

Sanberg, P. R., Silver, A. A., Shytle, R. D., Philipp, M. K., Cahill, D. W., Fogelson, H. M., et al. (1997). Nicotine for the treatment of Tourette's syndrome. *Pharmacological Therapy, 74,* 21–25.

Sanchez, J. L., Buritica, O., Pineda, D., Santiago Uribe, C., & Guillermo Palacio, L. (2004). Prevalence of Parkinson's disease and parkinsonism in a Colombian population using the capture-recapture method. *International Journal of Neuroscience, 114*(2), 175–182.

Sand, P. G., Mori, T., Godau, C., Stöber, G., Flachenecker, P., Franke, P., et al. (2002). Norepinephrine transporter gene (NET) variants in patients with panic disorder. *Neuroscience Letters, 333,* 41–44.

Sand, T., Bjørk, M. H., & Vaaler, A. E. (2013). Is EEG a useful test in adult psychiatry? *Tidsskrift for den Norske laegeforening: Tidsskrift for praktisk medicin, ny raekke, 133*(11), 1200–1204.

Sanders, A. R., Duan, J., Levinson, D. F., Shi, J., He, D., Hou, C., et al. (2008). No significant association of 14 candidate genes with schizophrenia in a large European ancestry sample: Implications for psychiatric genetics. *American Journal of Psychiatry, 165*(4), 497–506.

Sandin, S., Lichtenstein, P., Kuja-Halkola, R., Larsson, H., Hultman, C. M., & Reichenberg, A. (2014). The familial risk of autism. *Jama, 311*(17), 1770–1777.

Sandoval, V., Riddle, E. L., Hanson, G. R., & Fleckenstein, A. E. (2003). Methylphenidate alters vesicular monoamine transport and prevents methamphetamine-induced dopaminergic deficits. *Journal of Pharmacology and Experimental Therapeutics, 304*(3), 1181–1187.

Sankaranarayanan, S., De Angelis, D., Rothman, J. E., & Ryan, T. A. (2000). The use of pHluorins for optical measurements of presynaptic activity. *Biophysical Journal, 79*(4), 2199–2208.

Sano, M., Ernesto, C., Thomas, R. G., Klauber, M. R., Schafer, K., Grundman M., et al. (1997). A controlled trial of selegiline, alpha-tocopherol, or both as treatment for Alzheimer's disease. The Alzheimer's Disease Cooperative Study. *New England Journal of Medicine, 336,* 1216–1222.

Santiago, J. A., Bottero, V., & Potashkin, J. A. (2017). Biological and clinical implications of comorbidities in Parkinson's disease. *Frontiers in Aging Neuroscience, 9,* 394.

Santos, M., D'Amico, D., & Dierssen, M. (2015). From neural to genetic substrates of panic disorder: Insights from human and mouse studies. *European Journal of Pharmacology, 759,* 127–141.

Sanyal, J., Chakraborty, D. P., Sarkar, B., Banerjee, T. K., Mukherjee, S. C., Ray, B. C., & Rao, V. R. (2010). Environmental and familial risk factors of Parkinsons disease: Case-control study. *Canadian Journal of Neurological Sciences, 37*(5), 637–642.

Sargent, P. A., Kjaer, K. H., Bench, C. J., Rabiner, E. A., Messa, C., Meyer, J., et al. (2000). Brain serotonin1A receptor binding measured by positron emission tomography with [11C] WAY-100635: Effects of depression and antidepressant treatment. *Archives of General Psychiatry, 57*, 174–180.

Sarup, A., Larsson, O. M., & Schousboe, A. (2003). GABA transporters and GABA-transaminase as drug targets. *Current Drug Targets—CNS and Neurological Disorders, 2*, 269–277.

Satel, S., & Lilienfeld, S. O. (2014). Addiction and the brain-disease fallacy. *Frontiers in Psychiatry, 4*, 141.

Savitz, J. B., & Drevets, W. C. (2013). Neuroreceptor imaging in depression. *Neurobiology of Disease, 52*, 49–65.

Sawchuk, C. N., Roy-Byrne, P., Noonan, C., Bogart, A., Goldberg, J., Manson, S. M., et al. (2015). The association of panic disorder, posttraumatic stress disorder, and major depression with smoking in American Indians. *Nicotine & Tobacco Research, 18*(3), 259–266.

Sawle, G. V., Bloomfield, P. M., Bjorklund, A., Brooks, D. J., Brundin, P., Leenders, K. L., et al. (1992). Transplantation of fetal dopamine neurons in Parkinson's disease: PET [18F]6-L-fluorodopa studies in two patients with putaminal implants. *Annals of Neurology, 31*, 166–173.

Saxena, S., Brody, A. L., Ho, M. L., Alborzian, S., Ho, M. K., Maidment, K. M., et al. (2001). Cerebral metabolism in major depression and obsessive-compulsive disorder occurring separately and concurrently. *Biological Psychiatry, 50*, 159–170.

Saxena, S., Brody, A. L., Ho, M. L., Alborzian, S., Maidment, K. M., Zohrabi, N., et al. (2002). Differential cerebral metabolic changes with paroxetine treatment of obsessive-compulsive disorder vs major depression. *Archives of General Psychiatry, 59*, 250–261.

Saxena, S., Brody, A. L., Ho, M. L., Zohrabi, N., Maidment, K. M., & Baxter L. R. Jr. (2003). Differential brain metabolic predictors of response to paroxetine in obsessive-compulsive disorder versus major depression. *American Journal of Psychiatry, 160*, 522–532.

Saxena, S., Brody, A. L., Schwartz, J. M., & Baxter, L. R. (1998). Neuroimaging and frontal-subcortical circuitry in obsessive-compulsive disorder. *British Journal of Psychiatry, Supplement*, 26–37.

Scahill, L., Leckman, J. F., Schultz, R. T., Katsovich, L., & Peterson, B. S. (2003). A placebo-controlled trial of risperidone in Tourette syndrome. *Neurology, 60*, 1130–1135.

Scarmeas, N., & Stern, Y. (2003). Cognitive reserve and lifestyle. *Journal of Clinical and Experimental Neuropsychology, 25*(5), 625–633.

Scharre, D. W., Weichart, E., Nielson, D., Zhang, J., Agrawal, P., Sederberg, P. B., et al. (2018). Deep brain stimulation of frontal lobe networks to treat Alzheimer's disease. *Journal of Alzheimer's Disease*, (Preprint), 1–13.

Schefft, C., Kilarski, L. L., Bschor, T., & Köhler, S. (2017). Efficacy of adding nutritional supplements in unipolar depression: A systematic review and meta-analysis. *European Neuropsychopharmacology, 27*(11), 1090–1109.

Scheibler, F., Zumbé, P., Janssen, I., Viebahn, M., Schröer-Günther, M., Grosselfinger, R., et al. (2012). Randomized controlled trials on PET: A systematic review of topics, design, and quality. *Journal of Nuclear Medicine, 53*(7), 1016–1025.

Scheinost, D., Holmes, S. E., DellaGioia, N., Schleifer, C., Matuskey, D., Abdallah, C. G., et al. (2017). Multimodal investigation of network level effects using intrinsic functional connectivity, anatomical covariance, and structure-to-function correlations in unmedicated major depressive disorder. *Neuropsychopharmacology, 43*(5), 1119.

Schel, M. A., & Klingberg, T. (2016). Specialization of the right intraparietal sulcus for processing mathematics during development. *Cerebral Cortex, 27*(9), 4436–4446.

Scherf, K. S., Elbich, D. B., & Motta-Mena, N. V. (2017). Investigating the influence of biological sex on the behavioral and neural basis of face recognition. *eNeuro, 4*(3). doi: 10.1523/ENEURO.0104-17.2017.

Schermerhorn, A. C., Bates, J. E., Puce, A., & Molfese, D. L. (2017). Socio-emotionally significant experience and children's processing of irrelevant auditory stimuli. *International Journal of Psychophysiology, 112*, 52–63.

Schiffer, H. H. (2002). Glutamate receptor genes: Susceptibility factors in schizophrenia and depressive disorders? *Molecular Neurobiology, 25,* 191–212.

Schildkaut, J. J. (1965). The catecholamine hypothesis of affective disorders: A review of supporting evidence. *American Journal of Psychiatry, 122,* 509–522.

Schindler, S., Geyer, S., Strauß, M., Anwander, A., Hegerl, U., Turner, R., & Schönknecht, P. (2012). Structural studies of the hypothalamus and its nuclei in mood disorders. *Psychiatry Research: Neuroimaging, 201*(1), 1–9.

Schirinzi, T., Martella, G., D'Elia, A., Di Lazzaro, G., Imbriani, P., Madeo, G., et al. (2016). Outlining a population "at risk" of Parkinson's disease: Evidence from a case-control study. *Parkinson's Disease.* http://doi.org/10.1155/2016/9646057.

Schlaepfer, T. E., Harris, G. J., Tien, A. Y., Peng, L., Lee, S., & Pearlson, G. (1995). Structural differences in the cerebral cortex of healthy female and male subjects: A magnetic resonance imaging study. *Psychiatry Research: Neuroimaging, 61,* 129–135.

Schlaepfer, T. E., Pearlson, G. D., Wong, D. F., Marenco, S., & Dannals, R. F. (1997). PET study of competition between intravenous cocaine and [11C]-raclopride at dopamine receptors in human subjects. *American Journal of Psychiatry, 154,* 1209–1213.

Schlaggar, B. L., & O'Leary, D. D. (1991). Potential of visual cortex to develop an array of functional units unique to somatosensory cortex. *Science, 252*(5012), 1556–1560.

Schlicker, E., & Feuerstein, T. (2017). Human presynaptic receptors. *Pharmacology & Therapeutics, 172,* 1–21.

Schlicker, E., & Gothert, M. (1998). Interactions between the presynaptic alpha2-autoreceptor and presynaptic inhibitory heteroreceptors on noradrenergic neurones. *Brain Research Bulletin, 15,* 129–132.

Schloss, P., & Williams, D. C. (1998). The serotonin transporter: A primary target for antidepressant drugs. *Journal of Psychopharmacology, 12,* 115–121.

Schmahl, C. G., Vermetten, E., Elzinga, B. M., & Bremner, D. J. (2003). Magnetic resonance imaging of hippocampal and amygdala volume in women with childhood abuse and borderline personality disorder. *Psychiatry Research, 122,* 193–198.

Schmauss, C., Haroutunian, V., Davis, K. L., & Davidson, M. (1993). Selective loss of dopamine D3-type receptor mRNA expression in parietal and motor cortices of patients with chronic schizophrenia. *Proceedings of the National Academy of Sciences of the United States of America, 90,* 8942–8946.

Schmitt, A., Steyskal, C., Bernstein, H. G., Schneider-Axmann, T., Parlapani, E., Schaeffer, E. L., et al. (2009). Stereologic investigation of the posterior part of the hippocampus in schizophrenia. *Acta Neuropathologica, 117*(4), 395–407.

Schmitt, A., Weber, S., Jatzko, A., Braus, D. F., & Henn, F. A. (2004). Hippocampal volume and cell proliferation after acute and chronic clozapine or haloperidol treatment. *Journal of Neural Transmission, 111,* 91–100.

Schneeweiss, S., Patrick, A. R., Solomon, D. H., Dormuth, C. R., Miller, M., Mehta, J., et al. (2010). Comparative safety of antidepressant agents for children and adolescents regarding suicidal acts. *Pediatrics, 125*(5), 876–888.

Schneider, M., Debbané, M., Bassett, A. S., Chow, E. W., Fung, W. L. A., Van Den Bree, M. B., et al. (2014). Psychiatric disorders from childhood to adulthood in 22q11. 2 deletion syndrome: Results from the International Consortium on Brain and Behavior in 22q11. 2 Deletion Syndrome. *American Journal of Psychiatry, 171*(6), 627–639.

Schrag, A., Ben-Shlomo, Y., & Quinn, N. (2002). How valid is the clinical diagnosis of Parkinson's disease in the community? *Journal of Neurology, Neurosurgery, and Psychiatry, 73,* 529–534.

Schrag, A., Jahanshahi, M., & Quinn, N. P. (2001). What contributes to depression in Parkinson's disease? *Psychological Medicine, 31,* 65–73.

Schulte, C., & Gasser, T. (2011). Genetic basis of Parkinson's disease: Inheritance, penetrance, and expression. *The Application of Clinical Genetics, 4,* 67–80.

Schultz, W., Stauffer, W. R., & Lak, A. (2017). The phasic dopamine signal maturing: From reward via behavioural activation to formal economic utility. *Current Opinion in Neurobiology, 43,* 139–148.

Schulz, K. P., Bédard, A. C. V., Fan, J., Hildebrandt, T. B., Stein, M. A., Ivanov, I., et al. (2017). Striatal activation predicts differential therapeutic responses to methylphenidate and atomoxetine. *Journal of the American Academy of Child & Adolescent Psychiatry, 56*(7), 602–609.

Schulz, K. P., Fan, J., Tang, C. Y., Newcorn, J. H., Buchsbaum, M. S., Cheung, A. M., & Halperin, J. M. (2004). Response inhibition in adolescents diagnosed with attention deficit hyperactivity disorder during childhood: An event-related FMRI study. *American Journal of Psychiatry, 161*(9), 1650–1657.

Schuman, E. M. (1999). Neurotrophin regulation of synaptic transmission. *Current Opinion in Neurobiology, 9*, 105–109.

Schutter, D. J. (2016). A cerebellar framework for predictive coding and homeostatic regulation in depressive disorder. *The Cerebellum, 15*(1), 30–33.

Schwartz, G., Amor, L. B., Grizenko, N., Lageix, P., Baron, C., Boivin, D., et al. (2004). Actigraph monitoring during sleep of children with ADHD on methylphenidate and placebo. *Journal of the American Academy of Child and Adolescent Psychiatry, 43*, 1267–1282.

Schweitzer, J. B., Lee, D. O., Hanford, R. B., Tagamets, M. A., Hoffman, J. M., Grafton, S. T., & Kilts, C. D. (2003). A positron emission tomography study of methylphenidate in adults with ADHD: Alterations in resting blood flow and predicting treatment response. *Neuropsychopharmacology, 28*(5), 967.

Scoville, W. B., & Miller, B. (1957). Loss of recent memory after bilateral hippocampal lesions. *Journal of Neurology, Neurosurgery, and Psychiatry, 20*, 11–21.

Sebat, J., Levy, D. L., & McCarthy, S. E. (2009). Rare structural variants in schizophrenia: One disorder, multiple mutations; One mutation, multiple disorders. *Trends in Genetics, 25*(12), 528–535.

Sedvall, G., Farde, L., Persson, A., & Wiesel, F. A. (1986). Imaging of neurotransmitter receptors in the living human brain. *Archives of General Psychiatry, 43*, 995–1005.

Seeman, P., Guan, H. C., & Van Tol, H. H. (1995). Schizophrenia: Elevation of dopamine D4-like sites, using [3H]nemonapride and [125I]epidepride. *European Journal of Pharmacology, 286*, 3–5.

Seeman, P., & Tallerico, T. (1999). Rapid release of antipsychotic drugs from dopamine D2 receptors: An explanation for low receptor occupancy and early clinical relapse upon withdrawal of clozapine or quetiapine. *American Journal of Psychiatry, 156*, 876–884.

Segawa, M. (2003). Neurophysiology of Tourette's syndrome: Pathophysiological considerations. *Brain Development, 25*, supplement, 62–69.

Seibyl, J. P., Marek, K. L., Quinlan, D., Sheff, K., Zoghbi, S., Zea-Ponce, Y., et al. (1995). Decreased single-photon emission computed tomographic [123I]beta-CIT striatal uptake correlates with symptom severity in Parkinson's disease. *Annals of Neurology, 38*, 589–598.

Seidman, L. J., Faraone, S. V., Goldstein, J. M., Goodman, J. M., Kremen, W. S., Matsuda, G., et al. (1997). Reduced subcortical brain volumes in nonpsychotic siblings of schizophrenic patients: A pilot MRI study. *American Journal of Medical Genetics, Neuropsychiatric Genetics, 74*, 507–514.

Seidman, L. J., Faraone, S. V., Goldstein, J. M., Kremen, W. S., Horton, N. J., Makris, N., et al. (2002). Left hippocampal volume as a vulnerability indicator for schizophrenia: A magnetic resonance imaging morphometric sudy of nonpsychotic first-degree relatives. *Archives of General Psychiatry, 9*, 839–849.

Seino, Y., Kawarabayashi, T., Wakasaya, Y., Watanabe, M., Takamura, A., Yamamoto-Watanabe, Y., et al. (2010). Amyloid β accelerates phosphorylation of tau and neurofibrillary tangle formation in an amyloid precursor protein and tau double-transgenic mouse model. *Journal of Neuroscience Research, 88*(16), 3547–3554.

Sekar, A., Bialas, A. R., De Rivera, H., Davis, A., Hammond, T. R., Kamitaki, N., et al. (2016). Schizophrenia risk from complex variation of complement component 4. *Nature, 530*(7589), 177–183.

Sekino, Y., Koganezawa, N., Mizui, T., & Shirao, T. (2017). Role of drebrin in synaptic plasticity. *Advances in Experimental Medicine and Biology Drebrin*, 183–201.

Selemon, L. D., & Goldman-Rakic, P. S. (1999). The reduced neuropil hypothesis: A circuit based model of schizophrenia. *Biological Psychiatry, 45*, 17–25.

Selemon, L. D., Kleinman, J. E., Herman, M. M., & Goldman-Rakic, P. S. (2002). Smaller frontal gray matter volume in postmortem schizophrenic brains. *American Journal of Psychiatry, 159*(12), 1983–1991.

Selemon, L. D., Rajkowska, G., & Goldman-Rakic, P. S. (1995). Abnormally high neuronal density in the schizophrenic cortex. *Archives of General Psychiatry, 52*, 805–818.

Self, D. (2004). Drug dependence and addiction. *American Journal of Psychiatry, 161*, 223.

Sell, L. A., Morris, J., Bearn, J., Frackowiak, R. S. J., Friston, K. J., & Dolan, R. J. (1999). Activation of reward circuitry in human opiate addicts. *European Journal of Neuroscience, 11*, 1042–1048.

Selten, J. P., & Termorshuizen, F. (2017). The serological evidence for maternal influenza as risk factor for psychosis in offspring is insufficient: Critical review and meta-analysis. *Schizophrenia Research, 183*, 2–9.

Seltzer, B., & Sherwin, I. (1983). A comparison of clinical features in early- and late-onset primary degenerative dementia: One entity or two? *Archives of Neurology, 40*(3), 143–146.

Semrud-Clikeman, M., Filipek, P. A., Biederman, J., Steingard, R., Kennedy, D., Renshaw, P., & Bekken, K. (1994). Attention-deficit hyperactivity disorder: Magnetic resonance imaging morphometric analysis of the corpus callosum. *Journal of the American Academy of Child & Adolescent Psychiatry, 33*(6), 875–881.

Senanarong, V., Harnphadungkit, K., Lertrit, P., Mitrpant, C., Udompunthurak, S., Limwong, C., et al. (2001). Experience of ApoE study in Thai elderly. *Journal of the Medical Association of Thailand, 84*, 182–187.

Seo, J. Y., & Chao, Y. Y. (2017). Effects of exercise interventions on depressive symptoms among community-dwelling older adults in the united states: A systematic review. *Journal of Gerontological Nursing, 44*(3), 31–38.

Sepkuty, J. P., Cohen, A. S., Eccles, C., Rafiq, A., Behar, K., Ganel, R., et al. (2002). A neuronal glutamate transporter contributes to neurotransmitter GABA synthesis and epilepsy. *Journal of Neuroscience, 22*, 6372–6379.

Sepulveda, P., Sitaram, R., Rana, M., Montalba, C., Tejos, C., & Ruiz, S. (2016). How feedback, motor imagery, and reward influence brain self-regulation using real-time fMRI. *Human Brain Mapping, 37*(9), 3153–3171.

Serby, M. (2003). Methylphenidate-induced obsessive-compulsive symptoms in an elderly man. *CNS Spectrums, 8*, 612–613.

Sestito, S., Nesi, G., Pi, R., Macchia, M., & Rapposelli, S. (2017). Hydrogen sulfide: A worthwhile tool in the design of new multitarget drugs. *Frontiers in Chemistry, 5*, 72.

Shafran, R., Ralph, J., & Tallis, F. (1995). Obsessive-compulsive symptoms and the family. *Bulletin of the Menninger Clinic, 59*, 472–492.

Shagass, C., Roemer, R. A., Straumanis, J. J., & Josiassen, R. C. (1984). Psychiatric diagnostic discriminations with combinations of quantitative EEG variables. *British Journal of Psychiatry, 144*, 581–592.

Shah, D., Chand, P., Bandawar, M., Benegal, V., & Murthy, P. (2017). Cannabis induced psychosis and subsequent psychiatric disorders. *Asian Journal of Psychiatry, 30*, 180–184.

Shakeri, J., Farnia, V., Karimi, A. R., Tatari, F., Juibari, T. A., Alikhani, M., . . . Brand, S. (2016). The prevalence and clinical features of amphetamine-induced obsessive compulsive disorder. *Drug & Alcohol Dependence, 160*, 157–162.

Shang, J., Fu, Y., Ren, Z., Zhang, T., Du, M., Gong, Q., et al. (2014). The common traits of the ACC and PFC in anxiety disorders in the DSM-5: Meta-analysis of voxel-based morphometry studies. *PloS One, 9*(3), e93432.

Sharma, N., & Singh, A. N. (2016). Exploring biomarkers for Alzheimer's disease. *Journal of Clinical and Diagnostic Research: JCDR, 10*(7), KE01-KE06.

Sharma, V. (2017). Relationship of bipolar disorder with psychiatric comorbidity in the postpartum period—A scoping review. *Archives of Women's Mental Health*, 1–7.

Sharp, S. I., Lange, J., Kandaswamy, R., Daher, M., Anjorin, A., Bass, N. J., & McQuillin, (2017). Identification of rare nonsynonymous variants in SYNE1/CPG2 in bipolar affective disorder. *Psychiatric Genetics*, 27(3), 81–88.

Shaw, P., Eckstrand, K., Sharp, W., Blumenthal, J., Lerch, J. P., Greenstein, D. E. E. A., . . . Rapoport, J. L. (2007). Attention-deficit/hyperactivity disorder is characterized by a delay in cortical maturation. *Proceedings of the National Academy of Sciences*, 104(49), 19649–19654.

Shaywitz, B. A., Shaywitz, S. E., Pugh, K. R., Constable, R. T., Skudlarski, P., Fulbright, R. K., et al. (1995). Sex differences in the functional organization of the brain for language. *Nature*, 373, 607–609.

Sheehan, D. V. (2002). The management of panic disorder. *Journal of Clinical Psychiatry*, 63, Supplement 14, 17–21.

Shekhar, A., Sajdyk, T. J., Gehlert, D. R., & Rainnie, D. G. (2003). The amygdala, panic disorder, and cardiovascular responses. *Annals of the New York Academy of Sciences*, 985, 308–325.

Sheline, Y., Bardgett, M. E., & Csernansky, J. G. (1997). Correlated reductions in cerebrospinal fluid 5-HIAA and MHPG concentrations after treatment with selective serotonin reuptake inhibitors. *Journal of Clinical Psychopharmacology*, 17, 11–14.

Sheline, Y. I., Mokhtar, H. G., & Price, J. L. (1998). Amygdala core nuclei volumes are decreased in recurrent major depression. *NeuroReport*, 9, 2023–2028.

Sheline, Y. I., Wang, P. W., Gado, M. H., Csernansky, J. G., & Vannier, M. W. (1996). Hippocampal atrophy in recurrent major depression. *Proceedings of the National Academy of Sciences of the United States of America*, 93, 3908–3913.

Shen, K., & Bargmann, C. I. (2003). The immunoglobulin superfamily protein SYG-1 determines the location of specific synapses in C. elegans. *Cell*, 112, 619–630.

Sheng, M. H. T. (2001). The postsynaptic specialization. In M. W. Cowan, T. C. Sudhof, & C. F. Stevens (Eds.), *Synapses* (pp. 315–356). Baltimore: Johns Hopkins University Press.

Shenton, M. E., Dickey, C. C., Frumin, M., & McCarley, R. W. (2001). A review of MRI findings in schizophrenia. *Schizophrenia Research*, 49, 1–52.

Sherrington, C. S. (1897). The central nervous system. In M. Foster (Ed.), *A textbook of physiology* (7th ed., Part III, p. 929). London: Macmillan.

Shi, J., Gershon, E. S., & Liu, C. (2008). Genetic associations with schizophrenia: Meta-analyses of 12 candidate genes. *Schizophrenia Research*, 104(1), 96–107.

Shiino, A., Chen, Y. W., Tanigaki, K., Yamada, A., Vigers, P., Watanabe, T., et al. (2017). Sex-related difference in human white matter volumes studied: Inspection of the corpus callosum and other white matter by VBM. *Scientific Reports*, 7, 39818.

Shimada-Sugimoto, M., Otowa, T., & Hettema, J. M. (2015). Genetics of anxiety disorders: Genetic epidemiological and molecular studies in humans. *Psychiatry and Clinical Neurosciences*, 69(7), 388–401.

Shimizu, S., Kanetaka, H., Hirose, D., Sakurai, H., & Hanyu, H. (2015). Differential effects of acetylcholinesterase inhibitors on clinical responses and cerebral blood flow changes in patients with Alzheimer's disease: A 12-month, randomized, and open-label trial. *Dementia and Geriatric Cognitive Disorders Extra*, 5(1), 135–146.

Shin, J. H., Adrover, M. F., & Alvarez, V. A. (2017). Distinctive Modulation of Dopamine Release in the Nucleus Accumbens Shell Mediated by Dopamine and Acetylcholine Receptors. *The Journal of Neuroscience*, 37(46).

Shine, J. M., Koyejo, O., & Poldrack, R. A. (2016). Temporal metastates are associated with differential patterns of time-resolved connectivity, network topology, and attention. *Proceedings of the National Academy of Sciences*, 113(35), 9888–9891.

Shinoura, N., Yamada, R., Tabei, Y., Otani, R., Itoi, C., Saito, S., & Midorikawa, A. (2011). Damage to the right dorsal anterior cingulate cortex induces panic disorder. *Journal of Affective Disorders*, 133(3), 569–572.

Shizukuishi, T., Abe, O., & Aoki, S. (2013). Diffusion tensor imaging analysis for psychiatric disorders. *Magnetic Resonance in Medical Sciences*, 12(3), 153–159.

Shoirah, H., & Hamoda, H. M. (2011). Electroconvulsive therapy in children and adolescents. *Expert Review of Neurotherapeutics*, *11*(1), 127–137.

Shoptaw, S., Yang, X., Rotheram-Fuller, E. J., Hsieh, Y. C., Kintaudi, P. C., Charuvastra, V. C., et al. (2003). Randomized placebo-controlled trial of baclofen for cocaine dependence: Preliminary effects for individuals with chronic patterns of cocaine use. *Journal of Clinical Psychiatry*, *64*, 1440–1448.

Short, E. J., Manos, M. J., Findling, R. L., & Schubel, E. A. (2004). A prospective study of stimulant response in preschool children: Insights from ROC analyses. *Journal of the American Academy of Child and Adolescent Psychiatry*, *43*, 251–259.

Shorter, E. (2009). Sakel versus Meduna: Different strokes, different styles of scientific discovery. *The Journal of ECT*, *25*(1), 12–14.

Shugart, Y. Y., Samuels, J., Willour, V. L., Grados, M. A., Greenberg, B. D., Knowles, J. A., . . . Pinto, A. (2006). Genomewide linkage scan for obsessive-compulsive disorder: Evidence for susceptibility loci on chromosomes 3q, 7p, 1q, 15q, and 6q. *Molecular Psychiatry*, *11*(8), 763–770.

Shulman, R. B. (2003). Maintenance ECT in the treatment of PD. Therapy improves psychotic symptoms, physical function. *Geriatrics*, *58*, 43–45.

Sibon, I., Benkelfat, C., Gravel, P., Aznavour, N., Costes, N., Mzengeza, S., et al. (2008). Decreased [18 F] MPPF binding potential in the dorsal raphe nucleus after a single oral dose of fluoxetine: A positron-emission tomography study in healthy volunteers. *Biological Psychiatry*, *63*(12), 1135–1140.

Siegel, B. V., Nuechterlein, K. H., Abel, L., Wu, J. C., & Buchsbaum, M. S. (1995). Glucose metabolic correlates of continuous performance test performance in adults with a history of infantile autism, schizophrenics, and controls. *Schizophrenia Research*, *17*(1), 85–94.

Siegle, G. J., Steinhauer, S. R., Thase, M. E., Stenger, V. A., & Carter, C. S. (2002). Can't shake that feeling: Event-related fMRI assessment of sustained amygdala activity in response to emotional information in depressed individuals. *Biological Psychiatry*, *51*, 693–707.

Silbert, L. C., Quinn, J. F., Moore, M. M., Corbridge, E., Ball, M. J., Murdoch, G., et al. (2003). Changes in premorbid brain volume predict Alzheimer's disease pathology. *Neurology*, *61*, 487–492.

Silfverskiold, P., & Risberg, J. (1989). Regional cerebral blood flow in depression and mania. *Archives of General Psychiatry*, *46*, 253–259.

Silver, A. A., Shytle, R. D., Philipp, M. K., Wilkinson, B. J., McConville, B., & Sanberg, P. R. (2001). Transdermal nicotine and haloperidol in Tourette's disorder: A double-blind placebo-controlled study. *The Journal of Clinical Psychiatry*, *62*(9), 707–714.

Silver, H. (2003). Selective serotonin reuptake inhibitor augmentation in the treatment of negative symptoms of schizophrenia. *International Clinical Psychopharmacology*, *18*, 305–313.

Silverman, J. M., Smith, C. J., Marin, D. B., Mohs, R. C., & Propper, C. B. (2003). Familial patterns of risk in very late-onset Alzheimer disease. *Archives of General Psychiatry*, *60*, 190–197.

Simchon-Tenenbaum, Y., Weizman, A., & Rehavi, M. (2015). Alterations in brain neurotrophic and glial factors following early age chronic methylphenidate and cocaine administration. *Behavioural Brain Research*, *282*, 125–132.

Simeone, J. C., Ward, A. J., Rotella, P., Collins, J., & Windisch, R. (2015). An evaluation of variation in published estimates of schizophrenia prevalence from 1990–2013: A systematic literature review. *BMC Psychiatry*, *15*(1), 193.

Simoes, E. L., Bramati, I., Rodrigues, E., Franzoi, A., Moll, J., Lent, R., & Tovar-Moll, F. (2012). Functional expansion of sensorimotor representation and structural reorganization of callosal connections in lower limb amputees. *Journal of Neuroscience*, *32*(9), 3211–3220.

Simonoff, E. (1998). Genetic counseling in autism and pervasive developmental disorders. *Journal of Autism and Developmental Disorders*, *28*(5), 447–456.

Simor, A., Györffy, B. A., Gulyássy, P., Völgyi, K., Tóth, V., Todorov, M. I., et al. (2017). The short- and long-term proteomic effects of sleep deprivation on the cortical and thalamic synapses. *Molecular and Cellular Neuroscience*, *79*, 64–80.

Simpson, H. B., Lombardo, I., Slifstein, M., Huang, H. Y., Hwang, D. R., Abi-Dargham, A., et al. (2003). Serotonin transporters in obsessive-compulsive disorder: A positron emission tomography study with [(11)C]McN 5652. *Biological Psychiatry, 54*, 1414–1421.

Simpson, H. B., Slifstein, M., Bender, J., Xu, X., Hackett, E., Maher, M. J., & Abi-Dargham, A. (2011). Serotonin 2A receptors in obsessive-compulsive disorder: A positron emission tomography study with [11C] MDL 100907. *Biological Psychiatry, 70*(9), 897–904.

Singer, H. S., Hahn, I. H., & Moran, T. H. (1991). Abnormal dopamine uptake sites in postmortem striatum from patients with Tourette's syndrome. *Annals of Neurology, 30*, 558–562.

Singer, H. S., Reiss, A. L., Brown, J. E., Aylward, E. H., Shih, B., Chee, E., et al. (1993). Volumetric MRI changes in basal ganglia of children with Tourette's syndrome. *Neurology, 43*, 950–956.

Singer, H. S., Szymanski, S., Giuliano, J., Yokoi, F., Dogan, A. S., Brasic, J. R., et al. (2002). Elevated intrasynaptic dopamine release in Tourette's syndrome measured by PET. *American Journal of Psychiatry, 159*, 1329–1336.

Singhal, A. B., Caviness, V. S., Begleiter, A. F., Mark, E. J., Rordorf, G., & Koroshetz, W. J. (2002). Cerebral vasoconstriction and stroke after use of serotonergic drugs. *Neurology, 58*, 130–133.

Singham, T., Viding, E., Schoeler, T., Arseneault, L., Ronald, A., Cecil, C. M., et al. (2017). Concurrent and longitudinal contribution of exposure to bullying in childhood to mental health: The role of vulnerability and resilience. *JAMA Psychiatry, 74*(11), 1112–1119.

Singleton, R. H. (2004). Identification and characterization of heterogeneous neuronal injury and death in regions of diffuse brain injury: Evidence for multiple independent injury phenotypes. *Journal of Neuroscience, 24*(14), 3543–3553.

Sinha, R. (2011). New findings on biological factors predicting addiction relapse vulnerability. *Current Psychiatry Reports, 13*(5), 398–405.

Sinopoli, V. M., Burton, C. L., Kronenberg, S., & Arnold, P. D. (2017). A review of the role of serotonin system genes in obsessive-compulsive disorder. *Neuroscience & Biobehavioral Reviews, 80*, 372–381.

Sit, D. (2004). Women and bipolar disorder across the life span. *Journal of the American Medical Women's Association (1972), 59*(2), 91.

Siuda, J., Patalong-Ogiewa, M., Żmuda, W., Targosz-Gajniak, M., Niewiadomska, E., Matuszek, I., . . . Rudzińska-Bar, M. (2017). Cognitive impairment and BDNF serum levels. *Neurologia i neurochirurgia polska, 51*(1), 24–32.

Skalabrin, E. J., Laws, E. R. Jr., & Bennett, J. P. Jr. (1998). Pallidotomy improves motor responses and widens the levodopa therapeutic window in Parkinson's disease. *Movement Disorders, 13*, 775–781.

Skapinakis, P., Caldwell, D. M., Hollingworth, W., Bryden, P., Fineberg, N. A., Salkovskis, P., et al. (2016). Pharmacological and psychotherapeutic interventions for management of obsessive-compulsive disorder in adults: A systematic review and network meta-analysis. *The Lancet Psychiatry, 3*(8), 730–739.

Sklair-Tavron, L., Shi, W. X., Lane, S. B., Harris, H. W., Bunney, B. S., & Nestler, E. J. (1996). Chronic morphine induces visible changes in the morphology of mesolimbic dopamine neurons. *Proceedings of the National Academy of Sciences, 93*, 11202–11207.

Skre, I., Onstad, S., Torgersen, S., Lygren, S., & Kringlen, E. (1993). A twin study of DSM-III-R anxiety disorders. *Acta Psychiatrica Scandinavica, 88*, 85–92.

Slykerman, R., Hood, F., Wickens, K., Thompson, J., Barthow, C., Murphy, R., et al. (2017). Effect of lactobacillus rhamnosus HN001 in pregnancy on postpartum symptoms of depression and anxiety: A randomised double-blind placebo-controlled trial. *EBioMedicine, 24*, 159–165.

Small, D. M., Zatorre, R. J., Dagher, A., Evans, A. C., & Jones-Gotman, M. (2001). Changes in brain activity related to eating chocolate: From pleasure to aversion. *Brain, 124*, 1720–1733.

Smart, D., Smith, G., & Lambert, D. G. (1994). Mu-opioid receptor stimulation of inositol (1, 4, 5) triphosphate formation via a pertussis toxin-sensitive G protein. *Journal of Neurochemistry, 62*, 1009–1014.

Smiley, J. F., Rosoklija, G., Mancevski, B., Pergolizzi, D., Figarsky, K., Bleiwas, C., et al. (2011). Hemispheric comparisons of neuron density in the planum temporale of schizophrenia and nonpsychiatric brains. *Psychiatry Research: Neuroimaging, 192*(1), 1–11.

Smith, A., & Sugar, O. (1975). Development of above normal language and intelligence 21 years after left hemispherectomy. *Neurology, 25*, 813–818.

Smith, R., Chen, K., Baxter, L., Fort, C., & Lane, R. D. (2013). Antidepressant effects of sertraline associated with volume increases in dorsolateral prefrontal cortex. *Journal of Affective Disorders, 146*(3), 414–419.

Smoller, J. W., & Finn, C. T. (2003). Family, twin, and adoption studies of bipolar disorder. *American Journal of Medical Genetics, Part C, 123*, 48–58.

Smoller, J. W., Pollack, M. H., Wassertheil-Smoller, S., Barton, B., Hendrix, S. L., Jackson, R. D., et al. (2003). Prevalence and correlates of panic attacks in postmenopausal women: Results from an ancillary study to the Women's Health Initiative. *Archives of Internal Medicine, 163*, 2041–2050.

Smucny, J., Lesh, T. A., Newton, K., Niendam, T. A., Ragland, J. D., & Carter, C. S. (2017). Levels of cognitive control: A functional magnetic resonance imaging-based test of an RDoC domain across bipolar disorder and schizophrenia. *Neuropsychopharmacology, 43*(3), 598.

Snider, L. A., & Swedo, S. E. (2003). Post-streptococcal autoimmune disorders of the central nervous system. *Current Opinion in Neurology, 16*, 359–365.

Snow, D., & Anderson, C. (2000). Exploring the factors influencing relapse and recovery among drug and alcohol addicted women. *Journal of Psychosocial Nursing and Mental Health Service, 38*, 8–19.

Snyder, S. H., & Ferris, C. D. (2000). Novel neurotransmitters and their neuropsychiatric relevance. *Am J Psychiatry, 157*(11), 1738–1751.

Snyder, S. H., Jaffrey, S. R., & Zakhary, R. (1998). Nitric oxide and carbon monoxide: Parallel roles and neural messengers. *Brain Research Reviews, 26*, 167–175.

Soares, J. C., & Innis, R. B. (1999). Neurochemical brain imaging investigations of schizophrenia. *Biological Psychiatry, 46*, 600–615.

Soares, J. C., & Mann, J. J. (1997). The functional neuroanatomy of mood disorders. *Journal of Psychiatric Research, 31*, 393–432.

Sobanski, T., & Wagner, G. (2016). Functional neuroanatomy in panic disorder: Status quo of the research. *World Journal of Psychiatry, 7*(1), 12.

Sodhi, M. S., & Sanders-Bush, E. (2004). Serotonin and brain development. *International Review of Neurobiology, 59*, 111–174.

Sokol, D. K., Dunn, D. W., Edwards-Brown, M., & Feinberg, J. (2002). Hydrogen proton magnetic resonance spectroscopy in autism: Preliminary evidence of elevated choline/creatine ratio. *Journal of Child Neurology, 17*, 245–249.

Sokoloff, L. (1989). Circulation and energy metabolism of the brain. In G. J. Siegel (Ed.), *Basic neurochemistry: Molecular, cellular, and medical aspects* (4th ed., pp. 565–590). New York: Raven.

Soloff, P. H., Meltzer, C. C., Becker, C., Greer, P. J., Kelly, T. M., & Constantine, D. (2003). Impulsivity and prefrontal hypometabolism in borderline personality disorder. *Psychiatric Research, 123*, 153–163.

Solomon, R., Rich, C. L., & Darko, D. F. (1990). Antidepressant treatment and occurrence of mania in bipolar patients admitted for depression. *Journal of Affective Disorders, 18*, 253–257.

Sommer, M., Döhnel, K., Jarvers, I., Blaas, L., Singer, M., Nöth, V., et al. (2018). False belief reasoning in adults with and without autistic spectrum disorder: Similarities and differences. *Frontiers in Psychology, 25*(6), 345–354.

Soomro, G. M., Altman, D. G., Rajagopal, S., & Browne, M. O. (2008). Selective serotonin re-uptake inhibitors (SSRIs) versus placebo for obsessive compulsive disorder (OCD). *Cochrane database of systematic reviews*, (1).

Sosic-Vasic, Z., Abler, B., Grön, G., Plener, P., & Straub, J. (2017). Effects of a brief cognitive behavioural therapy group intervention on baseline brain perfusion in adolescents with major depressive disorder. *Neuroreport, 28*(6), 348–353.

Sousa, M. B., Reis, T., Reis, A., & Belmonte-de-Abreu, P. (2015). New-onset panic attacks after deep brain stimulation of the nucleus accumbens in a patient with refractory obsessive-compulsive and bipolar disorders: A case report. *Revista Brasileira de Psiquiatria, 37*(2), 182–183.

Sowell, E., Thompson, P., Holmes, C., Batth, R., Jernigan, T., & Toga, A. (1999). Localizing age-related changes in brain structure between childhood and adolescence using statistical parametric mapping. *Neuroimage, 9,* 587–597.

Spalletta, G., Pasini, A., Pau, F., Guido, G., Menghini, L., & Caltagirone, C. (2001). Prefrontal blood flow dysregulation in drug naive ADHD children without structural abnormalities. *Journal of Neural Transmission, 108*(10), 1203–1216.

Spanagel, R. (2017). Animal models of addiction. *Dialogues in Clinical Neuroscience, 19*(3), 247–258.

Spence, D. W., Kayumov, L., Chen, A., Lowe, A., Jain, U., Katzman, M. A., et al. (2004). Acupuncture increases nocturnal melatonin secretion and reduces insomnia and anxiety: A preliminary report. *Journal of Neuropsychiatry and Clinical Neurosciences, 16,* 19–28.

Spencer, D. W., Marshall, J., Post, B., Kulakodlu, M., Newschaffer, C., Dennen, T., et al. (2013). Psychotropic medication use and polypharmacy in children with autism spectrum disorders. *Pediatrics, 132*(5), 833–840.

Spencer, T. J. (2004). ADHD treatment across the life cycle. *Journal of Clinical Psychiatry, 65,* 22–26.

Spencer, T. J., & Biederman, J. (2002). Non-stimulant treatment for attention-deficit/hyperactivity disorder. *Journal of Attention Disorders, 6,* 109–119.

Spencer, T. J., Biederman, J., Harding, M., O'Donnell, D., Wilens, T., Faraone, S., et al. (1998). Disentangling the overlap between Tourette's disorder and ADHD. *Journal of Child Psychology and Psychiatry, 39,* 1037–1044.

Sperry, R. W. (1974). Lateral specialization in the surgically separated hemispheres. In F. Schmitt & F. Worden (Eds.), *The neurosciences: Third study program.* Cambridge, MA: MIT Press.

Spiegel, D. A., & Bruce, T. J. (1997). Benzodiazepines and exposure-based cognitive behavior therapies for panic disorder: Conclusions from combined treatment trials. *American Journal of Psychiatry, 154,* 773–781.

Spiegelhalder, K., Hornyak, M., Kyle, S. D., Paul, D., Blechert, J., Seifritz, E., et al. (2009). Cerebral correlates of heart rate variations during a spontaneous panic attack in the fMRI scanner. *Neurocase, 15*(6), 527–534.

Spiga, S., Puddu, M. C., Pisano, M., & Diana, M. (2005). Morphine withdrawal-induced morphological changes in the nucleus accumbens. *European Journal of Neuroscience, 22*(9), 2332–2340.

Spinello, C., Laviola, G., & Macrì, S. (2016). Pediatric autoimmune disorders associated with streptococcal infections and Tourette's syndrome in preclinical studies. *Frontiers in Neuroscience, 10,* 310.

Spofford, C. M., McLaughlin, N. C., Penzel, F., Rasmussen, S. A., & Greenberg, B. D. (2014). OCD behavior therapy before and after gamma ventral capsulotomy: Case report. *Neurocase, 20*(1), 42–45.

Sponheim, S. R., Clementz, B. A., Iacono, W. G., & Beiser, M. (2000). Clinical and biological concomitants of resting state EEG power abnormalities in schizophrenia. *Biological Psychiatry, 48,* 1088–1097.

Springer, S. P., & Deutsch, G. (1993). *Left brain right brain* (4th ed.). New York: Freeman.

Squarcina, L., Fagnani, C., Bellani, M., Altamura, C. A., & Brambilla, P. (2016). Twin studies for the investigation of the relationships between genetic factors and brain abnormalities in bipolar disorder. *Epidemiology and Psychiatric Sciences, 25*(6), 515–520.

Squire, L. R. (2017). Memory for relations in the short term and the long term after medial temporal lobe damage. *Hippocampus, 27*(5), 608–612.

St. James-Roberts, I. (1981). A reinterpretation of hemispherectomy data without functional plasticity of the brain. *Brain and Language, 13,* 31–53.

Staff, R. T., Gemmell, H. G., Shanks, M. F., Murray, A. D., & Venneri, A. (2000). Changes in the rCBF images of patients with Alzheimer's disease receiving Donepezil therapy. *Nuclear Medicine Communications, 21,* 37–41.

Stahl, S. M. (1998). Mechanism of action of serotonin selective reuptake inhibitors. Serotonin receptors and pathways mediate therapeutic effects and side effects. *Journal of Affective Disorders, 51,* 215–235.

Stahl, S. M. (2000a). Blue genes and the mechanism of action of antidepressants. *Journal of Clinical Psychiatry, 6,* 164–165.

Stahl, S. M. (2000b). *Essential psychopharmacology of depression and bipolar disorder.* New York: Cambridge University Press.

Stamenkovic, M., Schindler, S. D., Asenbaum, S., Neumeister, A., Willeit, M., Willinger, U., et al. (2000). No change in striatal dopamine re-uptake site density in psychotropic drug naïve and in current treated Tourette's disorder patients: A [123I]-β-CIT SPECT study. *European Neuropsychopharmacology, 11,* 69–74.

Stanford, S. C. (2001a). Anxiety. In R. A. Webster (Ed.), *Neurotransmitters, drugs, and brain function* (pp. 395–423). New York: Wiley.

Stanford, S. C. (2001b). 5-Hydroxytryptamine. In R. A. Webster (Ed.), *Neurotransmitters, drugs, and brain function* (pp. 187–209). New York: Wiley.

Stanford, S. C. (2001c). Depression. In R. A. Webster (Ed.), *Neurotransmitters, drugs, and brain function* (pp. 425–452). New York: Wiley.

Stein, D. G., Brailowsky, S., & Will, B. (1995). *Brain repair* (pp. 41–45). New York: Oxford University Press.

Stein, L. (1962). Effects and interactions of imipramine, chlorpromazine, resperine and amphetamine on self-stimulation: Possible neurophysiological basis of depression. In J. Wortis (Ed.), *Recent advances in biological psychiatry* (pp. 288–308). New York: Plenum.

Steiner, M., Dunn, E., & Born, L. (2003). Hormones and mood: From menarche to menopause and beyond. *Journal of Affective Disorders, 74,* 67–83.

Stepanova, E., Dowling, S., Phelps, M., & Findling, R. L. (2017). Pharmacotherapy of emotional and behavioral symptoms associated with autism spectrum disorder in children and adolescents. *Dialogues in Clinical Neuroscience, 19*(4), 395–402.

Stern, E., Silbersweig, D. A., Chee, K. Y., Holmes, A., Robertson, M. M., Trimble, M., et al. (2000). A functional neuroanatomy of tics in Tourette syndrome. *Archives of General Psychiatry, 57,* 741–748.

Sterr, A., Elbert, T., & Rockstroh, B. (2002). Functional reorganization of human cerebral cortex and its perceptual concomitants. In M. Fahle & T. Poggio (Eds.), *Perceptual learning* (pp. 125–144). Cambridge, MA: MIT Press.

Stewart, J. L., Flagan, T. M., May, A. C., Reske, M., Simmons, A. N., & Paulus, M. P. (2013). Young adults at risk for stimulant dependence show reward dysfunction during reinforcement-based decision making. *Biological Psychiatry, 73*(3), 235–241.

Stewart, R. J., Chen, B., Dowlatshahi, D., MacQueen, G. M., & Young, T. (2001). Abonormalities in the camp signaling pathway in post-mortem brain tissue from the Stanley Neuropathology Consortium. *Brain Research Bulletin, 55,* 625–629.

Stickel, F., Moreno, C., Hampe, J., & Morgan, M. Y. (2017). The genetics of alcohol dependence and alcohol-related liver disease. *Journal of Hepatology, 66*(1), 195–211.

Stiles, J. (2000). Neural plasticity and cognitive development. *Developmental Neuropsychology, 18,* 237–272.

Stimpson, N., Agrawal, N., & Lewis, G. (2002). Randomised controlled trials investigating pharmacological and psychological interventions for treatment-refractory depression. *British Journal of Psychiatry, 181,* 284–294.

Stolf, A. R., Müller, D., Schuch, J. B., Akutagava-Martins, G. C., Guimaraes, L. S., Szobot, C. M., et al. (2017). Association between the Intron 8 VNTR Polymorphism of the DAT1 gene and crack cocaine addiction. *Neuropsychobiology, 75*(3), 141–144.

Stoner, R., Chow, M. L., Boyle, M. P., Sunkin, S. M., Mouton, P. R., Roy, S., . . . Courchesne, E. (2014). Patches of disorganization in the neocortex of children with autism. *New England Journal of Medicine, 370*(13), 1209–1219.

Storch, E. A., Merlo, L. J., Lack, C., Milsom, V. A., Geffken, G. R., Goodman, W. K., & Murphy, T. K. (2007). Quality of life in youth with Tourette's syndrome and chronic tic disorder. *Journal of Clinical Child and Adolescent Psychology, 36*(2), 217–227.

Strafella, A. P., Paus, T., Barrett, J., & Dagher, A. (2001). Repetitive transcranial magnetic stimulation of the human prefrontal cortex induces dopamine release in the caudate nucleus. *Journal of Neuoscience, 21,* 1–4.

Strafella, A. P., Paus, T., Fraraccio, M., & Dagher, A. (2003). Striatal dopamine release induced by repetitive transcranial magnetic stimulation of the human cortex. *Brain, 12,* 2609–2615.

Strange, P. G. (2001). Antipsychotic drugs: Importance of dopamine receptors for mechanisms of therapeutic actions and side effects. *Pharmacological Reviews, 45,* 119–134.

Stratmann, M., Konrad, C., Kugel, H., Krug, A., Schöning, S., Ohrmann, P., et al. (2014). Insular and hippocampal gray matter volume reductions in patients with major depressive disorder. *PLoS One, 9*(7), e102692.

Straube, B., Reif, A., Richter, J., Lueken, U., Weber, H., Arolt, V., . . . Konrad, C. (2014). The functional– 1019C/G HTR1A polymorphism and mechanisms of fear. *Translational Psychiatry, 4*(12), e490.

Strickland, D., & Bertoni, J. M. (2004). Parkinson's prevalence estimated by a state registry. *Movement Disorders, 19,* 318–323.

Strimbu, K., & Tavel, J. A. (2010). What are biomarkers? *Current Opinion in HIV and AIDS, 5*(6), 463–466.

Ströhle, A., & Holsboer, F. (2003). Stress responsive neurohormones in depression and anxiety. *Pharmacopsychiatry, 36, Supplement 3,* S207–214.

Ströhle, A., Romeo, E., di Michele, F., Pasini, A., Yassouridis, A., Holsboer, F., et al. (2002). GABA(A) receptor-modulating neuroactive steroid composition in patients with panic disorder before and during paroxetine treatment. *American Journal of Psychiatry, 159,* 145–147.

Struble, R. G., Ala, T., Patrylo, P. R., Brewer, G. J., & Yan, X. X. (2010). Is brain amyloid production a cause or a result of dementia of the Alzheimer's type? *Journal of Alzheimer's Disease, 22*(2), 393–399.

Stubberfield, T., & Parry, T. (1999). Utilization of alternative therapies in attention-deficit hyperactivity disorder. *Journal of Pediatrics and Child Health, 35,* 450–453.

Stuber, G. D., Hopf, F. W., Tye, K. M., Chen, B. T., & Bonci, A. (2010). Neuroplastic alterations in the limbic system following cocaine or alcohol exposure. In *Behavioral neuroscience of drug addiction* (pp. 3–27). Berlin, Heidelberg: Springer.

Sturm, V., Lenartz, D., Koulousakis, A., Treuer, H., Herholz, K., Klein, J. C., et al. (2003). The nucleus accumbens: A target for deep brain stimulation in obsessive-compulsive and anxiety disorders. *Journal of Chemical Neuroanatomy, 26,* 293–299.

Sturman, N., Deckx, L., & van Driel, M. L. (2017). Methylphenidate for children and adolescents with autism spectrum disorder. *The Cochrane Library, 11,* CD011144.

Subcommittee on Attention-Deficit. (2011). ADHD: Clinical practice guideline for the diagnosis, evaluation, and treatment of attention-deficit/hyperactivity disorder in children and adolescents. *Pediatrics,* peds-2011–2654.

Substance Abuse and Mental Health Services Administration, *Results from the 2013 National Survey on Drug Use and Health: Summary of National Findings,* NSDUH Series H-48, HHS Publication No. (SMA) 14–4863. Rockville, MD: Substance Abuse and Mental Health Services Administration, 2014.

Suddath, R. L., Christison, G. W., Torrey, E. F., Casanova, M. F., & Weinberger, D. R. (1990). Anatomical abnormalities in the brains of monozygotic twins discordant for schizophrenia. *New England Journal of Medicine, 322*(12), 789–794.

Südof, T. C. (2001). The synaptic cleft and synaptic cell adhesion. In *Synapses* (pp. 275–313). Baltimore, MD: Johns Hopkins University Press.

Sugimoto, T., Nakamura, A., Kato, T., Iwata, K., Saji, N., Arahata, Y., et al. (2017). Decreased glucose metabolism in medial prefrontal areas is associated with nutritional status in patients with prodromal and early Alzheimer's disease. *Journal of Alzheimer's Disease, 60*(1), 225–233.

Sukhodolsky, D. G., Scahill, L., Zhang, H., Peterson, B. S., King, R. A., Lombroso, P. J., et al. (2003). Disruptive behavior in children with Tourette's syndrome: Association with ADHD comorbidity, tic severity, and functional impairment. *Journal of the American Academy of Child and Adolescent Psychiatry, 42*(1), 98–105.

Sullivan, A. M., & O'Keeffe, G. W. (2016). Neurotrophic factor therapy for Parkinson's disease: Past, present and future. *Neural Regeneration Research, 11*(2), 205–207.

Sullivan, G. M., Oquendo, M. A., Milak, M., Miller, J. M., Burke, A., Ogden, R. T., . . . Mann, J. J. (2015). Positron emission tomography quantification of serotonin1A receptor binding in suicide attempters with major depressive disorder. *JAMA Psychiatry, 72*(2), 169–178.

Sullivan, P. F., Neale, M. C., & Kendler, K. S. (2000). Genetic epidemiology of major depression: Review and meta-analysis. *American Journal of Psychiatry, 157,* 1552–1562.

Sultzer, D. L., Brown, C. V., Mandelkern, M. A., Mahler, M. E., Mendez, M. F., Chen, S. T., & Cummings, J. L. (2003). Delusional thoughts and regional frontal/temporal cortex metabolism in Alzheimer's disease. *American Journal of Psychiatry, 160*(2), 341–349.

Sultzer, D. L., Leskin, L. P., Melrose, R. J., Harwood, D. G., Narvaez, T. A., Ando, T. K., & Mandelkern, M. A. (2014). Neurobiology of delusions, memory, and insight in Alzheimer's disease. *The American Journal of Geriatric Psychiatry: Official Journal of the American Association for Geriatric Psychiatry, 22*(11), 1346–1355.

Sun, Y., Nadal-Vicens, M., Misono, S., Lin, M. Z., Zubiaga, A., Hua, X., et al. (2001). Neurogenin promotes neurogenesis and inhibits glial differentiation by independent mechanisms. *Cell, 104,* 365–376.

Sun, Y., Sun, X., Qu, H., Zhao, S., Xiao, T., & Zhao, C. (2017). Neuroplasticity and behavioral effects of fluoxetine after experimental stroke. *Restorative Neurology and Neuroscience, 35*(5), 457–468.

Surget, A., Leman, S., Griebel, G., Belzung, C., & Yalcin, I. (2006). Neuropeptides in psychiatric diseases: An overview with a particular focus on depression and anxiety disorders. *CNS & Neurological Disorders—Drug Targets, 5*(2), 135–145.

Surguladze, S. A., Marshall, N., Schulze, K., Hall, M. H., Walshe, M., Bramon, E., . . . McDonald, C. (2010). Exaggerated neural response to emotional faces in patients with bipolar disorder and their first-degree relatives. *Neuroimage, 53*(1), 58–64.

Suzuki, T., Remington, G., Mulsant, B. H., Uchida, H., Rajji, T. K., Graff-Guerrero, A., et al. (2012). Defining treatment-resistant schizophrenia and response to antipsychotics: A review and recommendation. *Psychiatry Research, 197*(1), 1–6.

Swanberg, M. M., Tractenberg, R. E., Mohs, R., Thal, L. J., & Cummings, J. L. (2004). Executive dysfunction in Alzheimer disease. *Archives of Neurology, 61,* 556–560.

Swann, A. C., Secunda, S., Davis, J. M., Robbins, E., Hanin, I., Koslow, S. H., et al. (1983). CSF monoamine metabolites in mania. *American Journal of Psychiatry, 140,* 396–400.

Swanson, J. M., Flodman, P., Kennedy, J., Spence, M. A., Moyzis, R., Schuck, S., et al. (2000). Dopamine genes and ADHD. *Neuroscience and Biobehavior Reviews, 24,* 21–25.

Swanson, L. W. (2003). *Brain architecture: Understanding the basic plan.* New York: Oxford University Press.

Swedo, S. E., Leonard, H. L., Garvey, M., Mittleman, B., Allen, A. J., Perlmutter, S., et al. (1998). Pediatric autoimmune neuropsychiatric disorders associated with streptococcal infections: Clinical description of the first 50 cases. *American Journal of Psychiatry, 155,* 264–271.

Sykova, Poulain, & Oliet. (2004). Glial cells.

Szeszko, P. R., Ardekani, B. A., Ashtari, M., Malhotra, A. K., Robinson, D. G., Bilder, R. M., & Lim, K. O. (2005). White matter abnormalities in obsessive-compulsive disorder: A diffusion tensor imaging study. *Archives of General Psychiatry, 62*(7), 782–790.

Szeszko, P. R., Robinson, D., Alvir, J. M., Bilder, R. M., Lencz, T., Ashtari, M., et al. (1999). Orbital frontal and amygdala volume reductions in obsessive-compulsive disorder. *Archives of General Psychiatry, 56,* 913–919.

Tabet, N., Birks, J., & Grimley Evans, J. (2000). Vitamin E for Alzheimer's disease. *Cochrane Database of Systematic Reviews,* CD002854.

Tafet, G. E., Idoyaga-Vargas, V. P., Abulafia, D. P., Calandria, J. M., Roffman, S. S., Chiovetta, A., et al. (2001). Correlation between cortisol level and serotonin uptake in patients with chronic stress and depression. *Cognitive, Affective, and Behavioral Neuroscience, 1*, 388–393.

Taft, C. E., & Turrigiano, G. G. (2014). PSD-95 promotes the stabilization of young synaptic contacts. *Philosophical Transactions of the Royal Society B: Biological Sciences, 369*(1633).

Takagi, Y., Sakai, Y., Lisi, G., Yahata, N., Abe, Y., Nishida, S. C., et al. (2017). A neural marker of obsessive-compulsive disorder from whole-brain functional connectivity. *Scientific Reports, 7*(1), 7538.

Takahashi, H., Suzumura, S., Shirakizawa, F., Wada, N., Tanaka-Taya, K., Arai, S., et al. (2003). An epidemiological study on Japanese autism concerning routine childhood immunization history. *Japanese Journal of Infectious Disorders, 56*, 114–117.

Takakusaki, K. (2017). Functional neuroanatomy for posture and gait control. *Journal of Movement Disorders, 10*(1), 1.

Takamiya, A., Hirano, J., Ebuchi, Y., Ogino, S., Shimegi, K., Emura, H., et al. (2017). High-dose antidepressants affect near-infrared spectroscopy signals: A retrospective study. *NeuroImage: Clinical, 14*, 648–655.

Takei, K., Mundigl, O., Daniell, L., & De Camilli, P. (1996). The synaptic vesicle cycle: A single vesicle budding step involving clathrin and dynamin. *The Journal of Cell Biology, 133*(6), 1237–1250.

Takeuchi, H., Fervaha, G., Lee, J., Agid, O., & Remington, G. (2015). Effectiveness of different dosing regimens of risperidone and olanzapine in schizophrenia. *European Neuropsychopharmacology, 25*(3), 295–302.

Takizawa, R., Fukuda, M., Kawasaki, S., Kasai, K., Mimura, M., Pu, S., et al. (2014). Neuroimaging-aided differential diagnosis of the depressive state. *Neuroimage, 85*, 498–507.

Tam, W. C. C., & Sewell, K. W. (1995). Seasonality of birth in schizophrenia in Taiwan. *Schizophrenia Bulletin, 21*(1), 117–127.

Tamnes, C. K., Herting, M. M., Goddings, A. L., Meuwese, R., Blakemore, S. J., Dahl, R. E., et al. (2017). Development of the cerebral cortex across adolescence: A multisample study of inter-related longitudinal changes in cortical volume, surface area, and thickness. *Journal of Neuroscience, 37*(12), 3402–3416.

Tan, A., Ma, W., Vira, A., Marwha, D., & Eliot, L. (2016). The human hippocampus is not sexually-dimorphic: Meta-analysis of structural MRI volumes. *NeuroImage, 124*, 350–366.

Tan, E. K., Tan, C., Fook-Chong, S. M., Lum, S. Y., Chai, A., Chung, H., et al. (2003). Dose-dependent protective effect of coffee, tea, and smoking in Parkinson's disease: A study in ethnic Chinese. *Journal of Neurological Science, 216*, 163–167.

Tan, Z. S., Seshadri, S., Beiser, A., Wilson, P. W., Kiel, D. P., Tocco, M., et al. (2003). Plasma total cholesterol level as a risk factor for Alzheimer disease: The Framingham Study. *Archives of Internal Medicine, 163*, 1053–1057.

Tanahashi, H., Asada, T., & Tabira, T. (2004). Association between tau polymorphism and male early-onset Alzheimer's disease. *Neuroreport, 15*, 175–179.

Tanaka, S., Matsunaga, H., Kimura, M., Tatsumi, K., Hidaka, Y., Takano, T., et al. (2003). Autoantibodies against four kinds of neurotransmitter receptors in psychiatric disorders. *Journal of Neuroimmunology, 141*, 155–164.

Tang, L., Shafer, A. T., & Ofen, N. (2017). Prefrontal cortex contributions to the development of memory formation. *Cerebral Cortex*, 1–14.

Tang, M. X., Stern, Y., Marder, K., Bell, K., Gurland, B., Lantigua, R., et al. (1998). The *APOE-ε4* allele and the risk of Alzheimer's disease among African Americans, whites, and Hispanics. *Journal of the American Medical Association, 279*, 751–755.

Tanti, A., & Belzung, C. (2010). Open questions in current models of antidepressant action. *British Journal of Pharmacology, 159*(6), 1187–1200.

Tardif, S., & Simard, M. (2011). Cognitive stimulation programs in healthy elderly: A review. *International Journal of Alzheimer's Disease, 2011*. Article ID 378934, 13 pages, 2011.

Tass, P. A., Klosterdotter, J., Schneider, F., Lenartz, D., Koulousakis, A., & Sturm, V. (2003). Obsessive-compulsive disorder: Development of demand-controlled deep brain stimulation with methods from stochastic phase resetting. *Neuropsychopharmacology, 28,* 27–34.

Taub, E., Miller, N. E., Novack, T. A., Cook, E. W., III, Fleming, W. C., Nepomuncen, C. S., et al. (1993). Technique to improve chronic motor deficit after stroke. *Archives of Physical and Medical Rehabilitation, 74,* 347–354.

Taub, E., Uswatte, G., & Elbert, T. (2002). New treatments in neurorehabilitation founded on basic research. *Nature Reviews in Neuroscience, 3,* 228–236.

Tauscher, J., Hussain, T., Agid, O., Verhoeff, P., Wilson, A. A., Houle, S., et al. (2004). Equivalent occupancy of dopamine D1 and D2 receptors with clozapine: Differentiation from other atypical antipsychotics. *American Journal of Psychiatry, 161,* 1620–1625.

Tauscher, J., Kapur, S., Verhoeff, P. L. G., Hussey, D. F., Daskalakis, Z. J., Tauscher-Wisniewski, S., et al. (2002). Brain serotonin 5-HT1A receptor binding in schizophrenia measured by positron emission tomography and [11C]WAY-100635. *Archives of General Psychiatry, 59,* 514–520.

Taylor, H. G., Yeates, K. O., Wade, S. L., Drotar, D., Stancin, T., & Minich, N. (2002). A prospective study of short-and long-term outcomes after traumatic brain injury in children: Behavior and achievement. *Neuropsychology, 16*(1), 15.

Taylor, S. (2011). Etiology of obsessions and compulsions: A meta-analysis and narrative review of twin studies. *Clinical Psychology Review, 31*(8), 1361–1372.

Taylor, S. (2016). Disorder-specific genetic factors in obsessive-compulsive disorder: A comprehensive meta-analysis. *American Journal of Medical Genetics Part B: Neuropsychiatric Genetics, 171*(3), 325–332.

Taylor, S. (2018). Association between COMT Val158Met and psychiatric disorders: A comprehensive meta-analysis. *American Journal of Medical Genetics Part B: Neuropsychiatric Genetics, 177*(2), 199–210.

Taylor, T. A., Bell, J. M., Breiding, M. J., & Xu, L. (2017). Traumatic brain injury-related emergency department visits, hospitalizations, and deaths—United States, 2007 and 2013. *MMWR Surveill Summ 2017, 66,* 1–16.

Teicher, M. H., Anderson, C. M., Polcari, A., Glod, C. A., Maas, L. C., & Renshaw, P. F. (2000). Functional deficits in basal ganglia of children with attention-deficit/hyperactivity disorder shown with functional magnetic resonance imaging relaxometry. *Nature Medicine, 6*(4), 470.

Teicher, M. H., Glod, C. A., & Cole, J. O. (1993). Antidepressant drugs and the emergence of suicidal tendencies. *Drug Safety, 8,* 186–212.

Teixeira, F. G., Gago, M. F., Marques, P., Moreira, P. S., Magalhães, R., Sousa, N., & Salgado, A. J. (2018). Safinamide: A new hope for Parkinson's disease? *Drug Discovery Today, 23*(3), 736–744.

Tek, C., & Ulug, B. (2001). Religiosity and religious obsessions in obsessive-compulsive disorder. *Psychiatry Research, 104,* 99–108.

Temple, E., Deutsche, G. K., Poldrack, R. A., Miller, S. L., Tallal, P., Merzenich, M. M., & Gabrieli, J. D. E. (2003). Neural deficits in children with dyslexia ameliorated by behavioral remediation: Evidence from functional MRI. *Proceedings of the National Academy of Sciences, 100,* 2860–2865.

Tendler, A., Barnea Ygael, N., Roth, Y., & Zangen, A. (2016). Deep transcranial magnetic stimulation (dTMS)-beyond depression. *Expert Review of Medical Devices, 13*(10), 987–1000.

Teri, L., Gibbons, L. E., McCurry, S. M., Logsdon, R. G., Buchner, D. M., Barlow, W. E., et al. (2003). Exercise plus behavioral management in patients with Alzheimer disease: A randomized controlled trial. *Journal of the American Medical Association, 290,* 2015–2022.

Terman, J. R., & Kolodkin, A. L. (1999). Attracted or repelled? Look within. *Neuron, 23,* 193–195.

Termine, C., Selvini, C., Rossi, G., & Balottin, U. (2013). Emerging treatment strategies in Tourette syndrome: What's in the pipeline? In *International Review of Neurobiology, 112,* 445–480.

Thaker, U., McDonagh, A. M., Iwatsubo, T., Lendon, C. L., Pickering-Brown, S. M., & Mann, D. M. (2003). Tau load is associated with apolipoprotein E genotype and the amount of amyloid beta protein, Abeta40, in sporadic and familial Alzheimer's disease. *Neuropathology and Applied Neurobiology, 29,* 35–44.

Thapar, A., Cooper, M., Eyre, O., & Langley, K. (2013). Practitioner review: What have we learnt about the causes of ADHD? *Journal of Child Psychology and Psychiatry, 54*(1), 3–16.

Thayer, R. E., YorkWilliams, S., Karoly, H. C., Sabbineni, A., Ewing, S. F., Bryan, A. D., & Hutchison, K. E. (2017). Structural neuroimaging correlates of alcohol and cannabis use in adolescents and adults. *Addiction, 112*(12), 2144–2154.

Thibault, R. T., Lifshitz, M., & Raz, A. (2016). The self-regulating brain and neurofeedback: Experimental science and clinical promise. *Cortex, 74*, 247–261.

Thies, W., & Bleiler, L. (2013). Alzheimer's disease facts and figures. *Alzheimer's & Dementia, 9*(2), 208–245.

Thirumala, P., Hier, D. B., & Patel, P. (2002). Motor recovery after stroke: Lessons from functional brain imaging. *Neurological Research, 24*, 453–458.

Thoenen, H., Zafra, F., Hengerer, B., & Lindholm, D. (1991). The synthesis of nerve growth factor and brain-derived neurotrophic factor in hippocampal and cortical neurons is regulated by specific transmitter systems. *Annual of the New York Academy Science, 640*, 86–90.

Thomas, K. M., Drevets, W. C., Dahl, R. E, Ryan, N. D., Birmaher, B., Eccard, C. H., et al. (2001). Amygdala response to fearful faces in anxious and depressed children. *Archives of General Psychiatry, 58*, 1057–1063.

Thomas, S. G., & Kellner, C. H. (2003). Remission of major depression and obsessive-compulsive disorder after a single unilateral ECT. *Journal of ECT, 19*, 50–51.

Thompson, R. F. (2000). *The brain: A neuroscience primer* (3rd ed.). New York: Worth.

Tick, B., Bolton, P., Happé, F., Rutter, M., & Rijsdijk, F. (2016). Heritability of autism spectrum disorders: A meta-analysis of twin studies. *Journal of Child Psychology and Psychiatry, 57*(5), 585–595.

Tiemeier, H. (2003). Biological risk factors for late life depression. *European Journal of Epidemiology, 18*, 745–750.

Tiexeira, F. G., Gago, M. F., Marques, P., Moreira, P. S., Magalhães, R., Sousa, N., & Salgado, A. J. (2018). Safinamide: a new hope for Parkinson's disease? *Drug Discovery Today.*

Tiihomem, J., Kuikka, J., Bergstrom, K., Hakola, P., Karhu, J., Ryynanen, O. P., et al. (1995). Altered striatal dopamine re-uptake site densities in habitually violent and non-violent alcoholics. *National Medicine, 1*, 654–657.

Tiihonen, J., Vilkman, H., Rasanen, P., Ryynanen, O. P., Hakko, H., Bergman, J., et al. (1998). Striatal presynaptic dopamine function in type 1 alcoholics measured with positron emission tomography. *Molecular Psychiatry, 3*, 156–161.

Tiili, E. M., Mitiushkina, N. V., Sukhovskaya, O. A., Imyanitov, E. N., & Hirvonen, A. P. (2017). The genotypes and methylation of MAO genes as factors behind smoking behavior. *Pharmacogenetics and Genomics, 27*(11), 394–401.

Titova, N., Martinez-Martin, P., Katunina, E., & Chaudhuri, K. R. (2017). Advanced Parkinson's or "complex phase" Parkinson's disease? Re-evaluation is needed. *Journal of Neural Transmission, 124*(12), 1529–1537.

Tizabi, Y., Louis, V. A., Taylor, C. T., Waxman, D., Culver, K. E., & Szechtman, H. (2002). Effect of nicotine on quinpirole-induced checking behavior in rats: Implications for obsessive-compulsive disorder. *Biological Psychiatry, 51*, 164–171.

Tokumaru, A. M., Barkovich, A. J., O'ichi, T., Matsuo, T., & Kusano, S. (1999). The evolution of cerebral blood flow in the developing brain. Evaluation with iodine-123 iodoamphetamine SPECT and correlation with MR imagin. *American Journal of Neuroradiology, 20*, 845–852.

Tomasi, D., Volkow, N. D., Wang, R., Carrillo, J. H., Maloney, T., Alia-Klein, N., et al. (2010). Disrupted functional connectivity with dopaminergic midbrain in cocaine abusers. *PloS One, 5*(5), e10815.

Toni, N., Buchs, P. A., Nikonenko, I., Bron, C. R., & Muller, D. (1999). LTP promotes formation of multiple spine synapses between a single axon terminal and a dendrite. *Nature, 402*, 421–425.

Tonini, G., Shanks, M. F., & Venneri, A. (2003). Short-term longitudinal evaluation of cerebral blood flow in mild Alzheimer's disease. *Neurological Sciences, 24*, 24–30.

Tononi, G., & Cirelli, C. (2014). Sleep and the price of plasticity: From synaptic and cellular homeostasis to memory consolidation and integration. *Neuron, 81*(1), 12–34.

Torres, A. R. (2003). Is fever suppression involved in the etiology of autism and neurodevelopmental disorders? *BMC Pediatrics, 3*, 9.

Torres, M. D., Garcia, O., Tang, C., & Busciglio, J. (2017). Dendritic spine pathology and thrombospondin-1 deficits in Down syndrome. *Free Radical Biology and Medicine, 114*, 10–14.

Torres, U. S., Duran, F. L., Schaufelberger, M. S., Crippa, J. A., Louzã, M. R., Sallet, P. C., et al. (2016). Patterns of regional gray matter loss at different stages of schizophrenia: A multisite, cross-sectional VBM study in first-episode and chronic illness. *NeuroImage: Clinical, 12*, 1–15.

Torrey, E. F., Miller, J., Rawlings, R., & Yoken, R. H. (1997). Seasonality of births in schizophrenia and bipolar disorder: A review of the literature. *Schizophrenia Research, 28*, 1–38.

Torvik, F. A., Rosenström, T. H., Ystrom, E., Tambs, K., Røysamb, E., Czajkowski, N., . . . Reichborn-Kjennerud, T. (2017). Stability and change in etiological factors for alcohol use disorder and major depression. *Journal of Abnormal Psychology, 126*(6), 812.

Tot, S., Ozge, A., Comelekoglu, U., Yazici, K., & Bal, N. (2002). Association of QEEG findings with clinical characteristics of OCD: Evidence of left frontotemporal dysfunction. *Canadian Journal of Psychiatry, 47*, 538–545.

Treffert, D. A. (2014). Savant syndrome: Realities, myths and misconceptions. *Journal of Autism and Developmental Disorders, 44*(3), 564–571.

Trenton, A., Currier, G., & Zwemer, F. (2003). Fatalities associated with therapeutic use and overdose of atypical antipsychotics. *CNS Drugs, 17*, 307–324.

Trevizol, A. P., Shiozawa, P., Cook, I. A., Sato, I. A., Kaku, C. B., Guimarães, F. B., . . . Cordeiro, Q. (2016). Transcranial magnetic stimulation for obsessive-compulsive disorder: An updated systematic review and meta-analysis. *The Journal of ECT, 32*(4), 262–266.

Trivedi, H. K., Mendelowitz, A. J., & Fink, M. (2003). Gilles de la Tourette form of catatonia: Response to ECT. *Journal of ECT, 19*, 115–117.

Trivedi, M. H., Greer, T. L., Church, T. S., Carmody, T. J., Grannemann, B. D., Galper, D. I., . . . Blair, S. N. (2011). Exercise as an augmentation treatment for nonremitted major depressive disorder: A randomized, parallel dose comparison. *Journal of Clinical Psychiatry, 72*(5), 677.

Trott, C. T., Fahn, S., Greene, P., Dillon, S., Winfield, H., Winfield, L., et al. (2003). Cognition following bilateral implants of embryonic dopamine neurons in PD: A double blind study. *Neurology, 60*, 1938–1943.

Tsang, K. M., Croen, L. A., Torres, A. R., Kharrazi, M., Delorenze, G. N., Windham, G. C., et al. (2013). A genome-wide survey of transgenerational genetic effects in autism. *PloS One, 8*(10), e76978.

Tsang, R. S., Mather, K. A., Sachdev, P. S., & Reppermund, S. (2017). Systematic review and meta-analysis of genetic studies of late-life depression. *Neuroscience & Biobehavioral Reviews, 75*, 129–139.

Tsuang, M. T., Bar, J. L., Harley, R. M., & Lyons, M. J. (2001). The Harvard twin study of substance abuse: What we have learned. *Harvard Review of Psychiatry, 9*(6), 267–279.

Tsuang, M. T., Lyons, M. J., Eisen, S. A., Golberg, J., True, W., Lin, W., et al. (1996). Genetic influences on DSM-III-R drug abuse and dependence: A study of 3, 372 twin pairs. *American Journal of Medical Genetics, 67*, 473–477.

Tunbridge, E., Burnet, P. W., Sodhi, M. S., & Harrison, P. J. (2004). Catechol-o-methyltransferase (COMT) and praline dehydrogenase (PRODH) mRNAs in the dorsolateral prefrontal cortex in schizophrenia, bipolar disorder, and major depression. *Synapse, 51*, 112–118.

Tupala, E., Hall, H., Bergstrom, K., Mantere, T., Rasanen, P., Sarkioja, T., et al. (2003a). Different effect of age on dopamine transporters in the dorsal and ventrical striatum of controls and alcoholics. *Synapse, 48*, 205–211.

Tupala, E., Hall, H., Bergstrom, K., Mantere, T., Rasanen, P., Sarkioja, T., et al. (2003b). Dopamine D2 receptors and transporters in type 1 and 2 alcoholics measured with human whole hemisphere autoradiography. *Human Brain Mapping, 20*, 91–102.

Turjanski, N., Sawle, G. V., Playford, E. D., Weeks, R., Lammerstma, A. A., Lees, A. J., et al. (1994). PET studies of the presynaptic and ppostsynaptic dopaminergic system in Tourette's syndrome. *Journal of Neurology, Neurosurgery, and Psychiatry, 57*, 688–692.

Turner, R. S., Grafton, S. T., McIntosh, A. R., DeLong, M. R, & Hoffman, J. M. (2003). The functional anatomy of Parkinsonian bradykinesia. *NeuroImage, 19*, 163–179.

Tutus, A., Simek, A., Sofuoglu, S., Nardali, M., Kugu, N., Karaaslan, F., & Gonul, A. S. (1998). Changes in regional cerebral blood flow demonstrated by single photon emission computed tomography in depressive disorders: Comparison of unipolar vs. bipolar subtypes. *Psychiatry Research, 83*, 169–177.

Twelves, D., Perkins, K. S., & Counsell, C. (2003). Systematic review of incidence studies of Parkinson's disease. *Movement Disorders, 18*, 19–31.

Tyas, S. L., Manfreda, J., Strain, L. A., & Montgomery, P. R. (2001). Risk factors for Alzheimer's disease: A population-based, longitudinal study in Manitoba, Canada. *International Journal of Epidemiology, 30*, 590–597.

Tyson, P. J., Roberts, K. H., & Mortimer, A. M. (2004). Are the cognitive effects of atypical antipsychotics influenced by their affinity to 5HT-2A receptors? *International Journal of Neuroscience, 114*(6), 593–611.

Uboga, N. V., & Price, J. L. (2000). Formation of diffuse and fibrillar tangles in aging and early Alzheimer's disease. *Neurobiology of Aging, 21*, 1–10.

Uchida, R. R., Del-Ben, C. M., Santos, A. C., Araujo, D., Crippa, J. A., Guimaraes, F. S., & Graeff, F. G. (2003). Decreased left temporal lobe volume of panic patients measured by magnetic resonance imaging. *Brazilian Journal of Medical and Biological Research, 36*(7), 925–929.

Uchino, S., & Waga, C. (2015). Novel therapeutic approach for autism spectrum disorder: Focus on SHANK3. *Current Neuropharmacology, 13*(6), 786–792.

Udina, M., Hidalgo, D., Navinés, R., Forns, X., Solà, R., Farré, M., et al. (2014). Prophylactic antidepressant treatment of interferon-induced depression in chronic hepatitis C. *The Journal of Clinical Psychiatry*, 1113–1121.

Uesugi, H., Toyoda, J., & Iio, M. (1995). Positron emission tomography and plasma biochemistry findings in schizophrenic patients before and after electroconvulsive therapy. *Psychiatry Clinical Neuroscience, 49*, 131–135.

Uhde, T. W., & Kellner, C. H. (1987). Cerebral ventricular size in panic disorder. *Journal of Affective Disorders, 12*(2), 175–178.

Ulbricht, C. M., Rothschild, A. J., Hunnicutt, J. N., & Lapane, K. L. (2017). Depression and cognitive impairment among newly admitted nursing home residents in the USA. *International Journal of Geriatric Psychiatry, 32*(11), 1172–1181.

Ullman, R. K., & Sleator, E. K. (1986). Responders, nonresponders, and placebo responders among children with attention deficit disorder: Importance of a blinded placebo evaluation. *Clinical Pediatrics, 25*, 594–599.

Ulrich, J. D., Ulland, T. K., Colonna, M., & Holtzman, D. M. (2017). Elucidating the role of TREM2 in Alzheimer's disease. *Neuron, 94*(2), 237–248.

Upadhyay, J., Maleki, N., Potter, J., Elman, I., Rudrauf, D., Knudsen, J., et al. (2010). Alterations in brain structure and functional connectivity in prescription opioid-dependent patients. *Brain, 133*(7), 2098–2114.

Uranova, N. A., Vostrikov, V. M., Orlovskaya, D. D., & Rachmanova, V. I. (2004). Oligodendroglial density in the prefrontal cortex in schizophrenia and mood disorders: A study from the Stanley Neuropathology Consortium. *Schizophrenia Research, 67*(2), 269–275.

Uribe, C., Segura, B., Baggio, H. C., Abos, A., Garcia-Diaz, A. I., Campabadal, A., et al. (2018). Cortical atrophy patterns in early Parkinson's disease patients using hierarchical cluster analysis. *Parkinsonism & Related Disorders*, 30042–30047.

Uthayathas, S., Parameshwaran, K., Karuppagounder, S. S., Ahuja, M., Dhanasekaran, M., & Suppiramaniam, V. (2013). Selective inhibition of phosphodiesterase 5 enhances glutamatergic synaptic plasticity and memory in mice. *Synapse, 67*(11), 741–747.

Uytun, M. C., Karakaya, E., Oztop, D. B., Gengec, S., Gumus, K., Ozmen, S., et al. (2017). Default mode network activity and neuropsychological profile in male children and adolescents with attention deficit hyperactivity disorder and conduct disorder. *Brain Imaging and Behavior, 11*(6), 1561–1570.

Vaccarino, F. J., Bloom F. E., & Koob, G. F. (1985). Blockade of nucleus accumbens opiate receptors attenuates heroin reward in the rat. *Psychopharmacology, 86*, 37–42.

Vaidya, C. J., Austin, G., Kirkorian, G., Ridlehuber, H. W., Desmond, J. E., Glover, G. H., & Gabrieli, J. D. (1998). Selective effects of methylphenidate in attention deficit hyperactivity disorder: A functional magnetic resonance study. *Proceedings of the National Academy of Sciences, 95*(24), 14494–14499.

Vakili, K., Pillay, S. S., Lafer, B., Fava, M., Renshaw, P. F., Bonello-Cintron, C. M., et al. (2000). Hippocampal volume in primary unipolar major depression: A magnetic resonance imaging study. *Biological Psychiatry, 47*, 1087–1090.

Valk, S. L., Bernhardt, B. C., Trautwein, F., Böckler, A., Kanske, P., Guizard, N., et al (2017). Structural plasticity of the social brain: Differential change after socio-affective and cognitive mental training. *Science Advances, 3*(10).

Van Beek, J. H., Willemsen, G., De Moor, M. H., Hottenga, J. J., & Boomsma, D. I. (2010). Associations between ADH gene variants and alcohol phenotypes in Dutch adults. *Twin Research and Human Genetics, 13*(1), 30–42.

Van Bogaert, P., Wikler, D., Damhaut, P., Szliwowski, H. B., & Goldman, S. (1998). Cerebral glucose metabolism and centrotemporal spikes. *Epilepsy Research, 29*(2), 123–127.

van de Giessen, E., Weinstein, J. J., Cassidy, C. M., Haney, M., Dong, Z., Ghazzaoui, R., et al. (2017). Deficits in striatal dopamine release in cannabis dependence. *Molecular Psychiatry, 22*(1), 68–75.

Van der Auwera, S., Teumer, A., Hertel, J., Homuth, G., Völker, U., Lucht, M. J., . . . John, U. (2016). The inverse link between genetic risk for schizophrenia and migraine through NMDA (N-methyl-D-aspartate) receptor activation via D-serine. *European Neuropsychopharmacology, 26*(9), 1507–1515.

Van Der Wee, N. J., Stevens, H., Hardeman, J. A., Mandl, R. C., Denys, D. A., Van Megen, H. J., . . . & Westenberg, H. M. (2004). Enhanced dopamine transporter density in psychotropic-naive patients with obsessive-compulsive disorder shown by [123I] β-CIT SPECT. *American Journal of Psychiatry, 161*(12), 2201–2206.

VanDongen, A. M. (Ed.). (2009). *Biology of the NMDA receptor.* Boca Raton: CRC Press.

van Dongen, Y. C., & Groenewegen, H. J. (2002). Core and shell of the nucleus accumbens are interconnected via intrastriatal projections. In L. F. B. Nicholson & R. L. M. Faull (Eds.), *The basal ganglia VII* (pp. 191–200). New York: Kluwer Academic/Plenum.

Van Doren, J., Arns, M., Heinrich, H., Vollebregt, M. A., Strehl, U., & Loo, S. K. (2018). Sustained effects of neurofeedback in ADHD: A systematic review and meta-analysis. *European Child & Adolescent Psychiatry*, 1–13.

Van Dyck, C. H., Malison, R. T., Seibyl, J. P., Laruelle, M., Klumpp, H., Zoghbi, S. S., et al. (2000). Age-related decline in central serotonin transporter availability with [(123)I]beta-CIT SPECT. *Neurobiology of Aging, 21*, 497–501.

van Dyck, C. H., Quinlan, D. M., Cretella, L. M., Staley, J. K., Malison, R. T., Baldwin, R. M., . . . Innis, R. B. (2002). Unaltered dopamine transporter availability in adult attention deficit hyperactivity disorder. *American Journal of Psychiatry, 159*(2), 309–312.

van Haren, N. E., Pol, H. E. H., Schnack, H. G., Cahn, W., Mandl, R. C., Collins, D. L., et al. (2007). Focal gray matter changes in schizophrenia across the course of the illness: A 5-year follow-up study. *Neuropsychopharmacology, 32*(10), 2057–2066.

van Hecke, O., Hocking, L. J., Torrance, N., Campbell, A., Padmanabhan, S., Porteous, D. J., et al. (2017). Chronic pain, depression and cardiovascular disease linked through a shared genetic predisposition: Analysis of a family-based cohort and twin study. *PloS One, 12*(2), e0170653.

van Os, J., Hanssen, M., Bijl, R. V., & Vollebergh, W. (2001). Prevalence of psychotic disorder and community level of psychotic symptoms. *Archives of General Psychiatry, 58*, 663–668.

Van Rooij, D., Anagnostou, E., Arango, C., Auzias, G., Behrmann, M., Busatto, G. F., et al. (2017). Cortical and subcortical brain morphometry differences between patients with autism spectrum disorder and healthy individuals across the lifespan: Results from the ENIGMA ASD working group. *American Journal of Psychiatry, 175*(4), 359–369.

van Tol, M. J., van der Wee, N. J., van den Heuvel, O. A., Nielen, M. M., Demenescu, L. R., Aleman, A., . . . Veltman, D. J. (2010). Regional brain volume in depression and anxiety disorders. *Archives of General Psychiatry, 67*(10), 1002–1011.

Varrone, A., Marek, K. L, Jennings, D., Innis, R. B., & Seibyl, J. P. (2001). [123I]beta-CIT SPECT imaging demonstrates reduced density of striatal dopamine transporters in Parkinson's disease and multiple system atrophy. *Movement Disorders, 16*, 1023–1032.

Vassalle, C., Sabatino, L., Pingitore, A., Chatzianagnostou, K., Mastorci, F., & Ceravolo, R. (2017). Antioxidants in the diet and cognitive function: Which role for the mediterranean life-style? *The Journal of Prevention of Alzheimer's Disease, 4*(1), 58–64.

Vázquez-Bourgon, J., Martino, J., Sierra, M. P., Infante, J. C., Martínez, M. M., Ocón, R., et al. (2017). Deep brain stimulation and treatment-resistant obsessive-compulsive disorder: A systematic review. *Revista de psiquiatria y salud mental*, 30076–30079.

Veale, D., & Roberts, A. (2014). Obsessive-compulsive disorder. *BMJ, 348*, g2183.

Veijola, J., Guo, J. Y., Moilanen, J. S., Jääskeläinen, E., Miettunen, J., Kyllönen, M., et al. (2014). Longitudinal changes in total brain volume in schizophrenia: Relation to symptom severity, cognition and antipsychotic medication. *PloS One, 9*(7), e101689.

Veliz, P., McCabe, S. E., Eckner, J. T., & Schulenberg, J. E. (2017). Prevalence of concussion among US adolescents and correlated factors. *JAMA, 318*(12), 1180–1182.

Velthorst, E., Reichenberg, A., Kapra, O., Goldberg, S., Fromer, M., Fruchter, E., . . . Weiser, M. (2016). Developmental trajectories of impaired community functioning in schizophrenia. *JAMA Psychiatry, 73*(1), 48–55.

Verdi, G., Weyandt, L. L., & Zavras, B. M. (2016). Non-medical prescription stimulant use in graduate students: Relationship with academic self-efficacy and psychological variables. *Journal of Attention Disorders, 20*(9), 741–753.

Verhulst, F. C., Achenbach, T. M., van der Ende, J., Erol, N., Lambert, M. C., Leung, P. W. L., et al. (2003). Comparison of problems reported by youths from seven countries. *American Journal of Psychiatry, 160*, 1479–1485.

Vermeire, S., Audenaert, K., De Meester, R., Vandermeulen, E., Waelbers, T., De Spiegeleer, B., et al. (2012). Serotonin 2A receptor, serotonin transporter and dopamine transporter alterations in dogs with compulsive behaviour as a promising model for human obsessive-compulsive disorder. *Psychiatry Research: Neuroimaging, 201*(1), 78–87.

Vermeulen, T. (1998). Distribution of paroxetine in three postmortem cases. *Journal of Analytical Toxicology, 22*, 541–544.

Verstreken, P., Koh, T. W., Schulze, K. L., Zhai, R. G., Hiesinger, P. R., Zhou, Y., . . . Bellen, H. J. (2003). Synaptojanin is recruited by endophilin to promote synaptic vesicle uncoating. *Neuron, 40*(4), 733–748.

Vlček, P., Polák, J., Brunovský, M., & Horáček, J. (2017). Role of glutamatergic system in obsessive-compulsive disorder with possible therapeutic implications. *Pharmacopsychiatry.*

Videbech, P., & Ravnkilde, B. (2004). Hippocampal volume and depression: A meta-analysis of MRI studies. *American Journal of Psychiatry, 161*, 1957–1966.

Vingerhoets, F. J., Villemure, J. G., Temperli, P., Pollo, C., Pralong, E., & Ghika, J. (2002). Subthalamic DBS replaces levodopa in Parkinson's disease: Two-year follow-up. *Neurology, 58*, 396–401.

Visser, A. K., van Waarde, A., Willemsen, A. T., Bosker, F. J., Luiten, P. G., den Boer, J. A., . . . & Dierckx, R. A. (2011). Measuring serotonin synthesis: From conventional methods to PET tracers and their (pre) clinical implications. *European Journal of Nuclear Medicine and Molecular Imaging, 38*(3), 576–591.

Visser, A. K., Waarde, A. V., Willemsen, A. T., Bosker, F. J., Luiten, P. G., Boer, J. A., et al. (2014). Measuring serotonin synthesis: From conventional methods to PET tracers and their (pre) clinical implications. *European Journal of Nuclear Medicine and Molecular Imaging, 38*(3), 576–591.

Visser, S. N., Danielson, M. L., Bitsko, R. H., Holbrook, J. R., Kogan, M. D., Ghandour, R. M., . . . Blumberg, S. J. (2014). Trends in the parent-report of health care provider-diagnosed and medicated attention-deficit/hyperactivity disorder: United States, 2003–2011. *Journal of the American Academy of Child & Adolescent Psychiatry, 53*(1), 34–46.

Visser-Vandewalle, V., Temel, Y., Boon, P., Vreeling, F., Colle, H., Hoogland, G., et al. (2003). Chronic bilateral thalamic stimulation: A new therapeutic approach in intractable Tourrette syndrome. Report of three cases. *Journal of Neurosurgery, 99*, 1094–1100.

Vizi, E., Fekete, A., Karoly, R., & Mike, A. (2010). Non-synaptic receptors and transporters involved in brain functions and targets of drug treatment. *British Journal of Pharmacology, 160*(4), 785–809.

Vlček, P., Polák, J., Brunovský, M., & Horáček, J. (2017). Role of glutamatergic system in obsessive-compulsive disorder with possible therapeutic implications. *Pharmacopsychiatry, 50*(5).

Vles, J. S. H., Feron, F. J. M., Hendriksen, J. G. M., Jolles, J., van Kroonenburgh, M. J. P. H., & Weber, W. E. J. (2003). Methylphenidate down-regulates the dopamine receptor and transporter system in children with attention deficit hyperkinetic disorder (ADHD). *Neuropediatrics, 34*(2), 77–80.

Voigt, R. G., Llorente, A. M., Jensen, C. L., Fraley, J. K., Berretta, M. C., & Heird, W. C. (2001). A randomized, double-blind, placebo-controlled trial of docosahexaenoic acid supplementation in children with attention-deficit/hyperactivity disorder. *Journal of Pediatrics, 139*, 189–196.

Voineskos, D., & Daskalakis, Z. J. (2013). A primer on the treatment of schizophrenia through repetitive transcranial magnetic stimulation. *Expert Review of Neurotherapeutics, 13*(10), 1079–1082.

Vokaer, M., Bier, J. C., Elincx, S., Claes, T., Paquier, P., Goldman, S., et al. (2002). The cerebellum may be directly involved in cognitive functions. *Neurology, 58*, 967–970.

Volkow, N. D. (2014). America's addiction to opioids: Heroin and prescription drug abuse. Senate Caucus on International Narcotics Control, 14.

Volkow, N. D., Chang, L., Wang, G. J., Fowler, J. S., Ding, Y. S. Sedler, M., et al. (2001). Low level of brain dopamine D2 receptors in methamphetamine abusers: Association with metabolism in the orbitofrontal cortex. *American Journal of Psychiatry, 158*, 2015–2021.

Volkow, N. D., Fowler, J. S., & Wang, G. J. (2002). Roles of dopamine in drug reinforcement and addiction in humans: Results from imaging studies. *Behavioral Pharmacology, 13*(5), 355–366.

Volkow, N. D., Fowler, J. S., & Wang, G. J. (2003). Positron emission tomography and single-photon emission computed tomography in substance abuse. *Seminars in Nuclear Medicine, 33*, 114–128.

Volkow, N. D., Fowler, J. S., Wolf, A. P., & Gillespi, H. (1991). Metabolic studies of drugs of abuse. *NIDA Research Monograph, 105*, 47–53.

Volkow, N. D., Koob, G. F., & McLellan, A. T. (2016). Neurobiologic advances from the brain disease model of addiction. *New England Journal of Medicine, 374*(4), 363–371.

Volkow, N. D., Koob, G. F., Croyle, R. T., Bianchi, D. W., Gordon, J. A., Koroshetz, W. J., et al. (2017). The conception of the ABCD study: From substance use to a broad NIH collaboration. *Developmental Cognitive Neuroscience, 32*, 4–7.

Volkow, N. D., Wang, G. J., Fowler, J. S., & Ding, Y. S. (2005). Imaging the effects of methylphenidate on brain dopamine: New model on its therapeutic actions for attention-deficit/hyperactivity disorder. *Biological Psychiatry, 57*(11), 1410–1415.

Volkow, N. D., Wang, G. J., Fowler, J. S., Fischman, M., Foltin, R., Abumrad, N. N., et al. (1999). Methylphenidate and cocaine have a similar in vivo potency to block dopamine transporters in the human brain. *Life Science, 65*, 7–12.

Volkow, N. D., Wang, G. J., Fowler, J. S., Logan, J., Franceschi, D., Maynard, L., et al. (2002). Relationship between blockade of dopamine transporters by oral methylphenidate and the increase in extracellular dopamine: Therapeutic implications. *Synapse, 43*, 181–187.

Volkow, N. D., Wang, G. J., Fowler, J. S., Logan, J., Hitzemann, R., Ding, Y. S., et al. (1996). Decreases in dopamine receptors but not in dopamine transporters in alcoholics. *Alcoholism: Clinical and Experimental Research, 20*, 1594–1598.

Volkow, N. D., Wang, G. J., Maynard, L., Fowler, J. S., Jayne, B., Telang, F., et al. (2002). Effects of alcohol detoxification on dopamine D2 receptors in alcoholics: A preliminary study. *Psychiatry Research, 116,* 163–172.

Volkow, N. D., Wang, G. J., Telang, F., Fowler, J. S., Logan, J., Childress, A. R., et al. (2006). Cocaine cues and dopamine in dorsal striatum: Mechanism of craving in cocaine addiction. *Journal of Neuroscience, 26*(24), 6583–6588.

Vollenweider, F. X., Vontobel, P., Hell, D., & Leenders, K. L. (1999). 5-HT modulation of dopamine release in basal ganglia in psilocybin-induced psychosis in man—A PET study with [11C]raclopride. *Neuropsychopharmacology, 20,* 424–433.

von Bartheld, C. S., Bahney, J., & Herculano-Houzel, S. (2016). The search for true numbers of neurons and glial cells in the human brain: A review of 150 years of cell counting. *Journal of Comparative Neurology, 524*(18), 3865–3895.

von Bohlen und Halbach, O., & Dermietzel, R. (2002). *Neurotransmitters and neuromodulators: Handbook of receptors and biological effects.* Wenheim, Germany: Wiley-VCH.

Von Bohlen, O., & Dermietzel, R. (2006). *Neurotransmitters and neuromodulators: Handbook of receptors and biological effects.* Weinheim, Germany: Wiley-VCH.

Vossel, S., Weiss, P. H., Eschenbeck, P., Saliger, J., Karbe, H., & Fink, G. R. (2012). The neural basis of anosognosia for spatial neglect after stroke. *Stroke, 43*(7), 1954–1956.

Voyiaziakis, E., Evgrafov, O., Li, D., Yoon, H. J., Tabares, P., Samuels, J., et al. (2011). Association of SLC6A4 variants with obsessive-compulsive disorder in a large multicenter US family study. *Molecular Psychiatry, 16*(1), 108–120.

Vrontakis, M. E. (2002). Galanin: A biologically active peptide. *Current Drug Targets—CNS and Neurological Disorders, 1,* 531–541.

Vuksan, C. B., Klepac, N., Jakšic, N., Bradaš, Z., Božicevic, M., Palac, N., & Šagud, M. (2018). The effects of electroconvulsive therapy augmentation of antipsychotic treatment on cognitive functions in patients with treatment-resistant schizophrenia. *The Journal of ECT, 34*(1), 31–34.

Vul, E., Harris, C., Winkielman, P., & Pashler, H. (2009). Puzzlingly high correlations in fMRI studies of emotion, personality, and social cognition. *Perspectives on Psychological Science, 4*(3), 274–290.

Vythilingam, M., Anderson, E. R., Goddard, A., Woods, S. W., Staib, L. H., Charney, D. S., et al. (2000). Temporal lobe volume in panic disorder: A quantitative magnetic resonance imaging study. *Psychiatry Research, 99,* 75–82.

Vythilingam, M., Charles, H. C., Tupler, L. A., Blitchington, T., Kelly, L., & Krishnan, K. R. (2003). Focal and lateralized subcortical abnormalities in unipolar major depressive disorder: An automated multivoxel proton magnetic resonance spectroscopy study. *Biological Psychiatry, 54,* 744–750.

Wagner, J. P., Black, I. B., & DiCicco-Bloom, E. (1999). Stimulation of neonatal and adult brain neurogenesis by subcutaneous injection of basic fibroblast growth factor. *Journal of Neuroscience, 19,* 6006–6016.

Wake, R., Miyaoka, T., Araki, T., Kawakami, K., Furuya, M., Limoa, E., . . . Horiguchi, J. (2016). Regional cerebral blood flow in late-onset schizophrenia: A SPECT study using 99mTc-ECD. *European Archives of Psychiatry and Clinical Neuroscience, 266*(1), 3–12.

Waldie, K. E., Wilson, A. J., Roberts, R. P., & Moreau, D. (2017). Reading network in dyslexia: Similar, yet different. *Brain and Language, 174,* 29–41.

Walkup, J. T., LaBuda, M. C., Singer, H. S., Brown, J., Riddle, M. A., & Hurko, O. (1996). Family study and segregation analysis of Tourette syndrome: Evidence for a mixed model of inheritance. *American Journal of Human Genetics, 59,* 684–693.

Wallace, G. L., Happé, F., & Giedd, J. N. (2009). A case study of a multiply talented savant with an autism spectrum disorder: Neuropsychological functioning and brain morphometry. *Philosophical Transactions of the Royal Society B: Biological Sciences, 364*(1522), 1425–1432.

Walsh, E., Buchanan, A., & Fahy, T. (2001). Violence and schizophrenia: Examining the evidence. *British Journal of Psychiatry, 180,* 490–495.

Walsh, L. E., & Garg, B. P. (1997). Ischemic strokes in children. *Indian Journal of Pediatrics, 64*, 613–623.

Wamulugwa, J., Kakooza, A., Kitaka, S. B., Nalugya, J., Kaddumukasa, M., Moore, S., . . . Katabira, E. (2017). Prevalence and associated factors of attention deficit hyperactivity disorder (ADHD) among Ugandan children: A cross-sectional study. *Child and Adolescent Psychiatry and Mental Health, 11*(1), 18.

Wang, C. H., Wang, L. S., & Zhu, N. (2016). Cholinesterase inhibitors and non-steroidal anti-inflammatory drugs as Alzheimer's disease therapies: An updated umbrella review of systematic reviews and meta-analyses. *European Review for Medical and Pharmacological Sciences., 20*(22), 4801–4817.

Wang, C. T., Grishanin, R., Earles, C. A., Chang, P. Y., Martin, T. F., Chapman, E. R., et al. (2001). Synaptotagmin modulation of fusion pore kinetics in regulated exocytosis of dense-core vesicles. *Science, 294*, 1111–1115.

Wang, C., & Zhang, Y. (2017). Season of birth and schizophrenia: Evidence from China. *Psychiatry Research, 253*, 189–196.

Wang, H. S., & Kuo, M. F. (2003). Tourette's syndrome in Taiwan: An epidemiological study of tic disorder in an elementary school at Taipei County. *Brain Development, 25*, S29–S31.

Wang, L., Swank, J. S., Glick, I. E., Gado, M. H., Miller, M. I., Morris, J. C., et al. (2003). Changes in hippocampal volume and shape across time distinguish dementia of the Alzheimer type from healthy aging. *NeuroImage, 20*, 667–682.

Wang, R. (2002). Two's company, three's a crowd: Can H2S be the third endogenous gaseous transmitter? *Federation of American Societies of Experimental Biology Journal, 16*, 1792–1798.

Wang, S., Mims, P. N., Roman, R. J., & Fan, F. (2016). Is beta-amyloid accumulation a cause or consequence of Alzheimer's disease? *Journal of Alzheimer's Parkinsonism & Dementia, 1*(2).

Wang, Y. M., Li, N., Yang, L. L., Song, M., Shi, L., Chen, W. H., et al. (2017). Randomized controlled trial of repetitive transcranial magnetic stimulation combined with paroxetine for the treatment of patients with first-episode major depressive disorder. *Psychiatry Research, 254*, 18–23.

Wang, Y., Wang, H., Li, W., Zhu, J., Gold, M. S., Zhang, D., et al. (2014). Reduced responses to heroin-cue-induced craving in the dorsal striatum: Effects of long-term methadone maintenance treatment. *Neuroscience Letters, 581*, 120–124.

Wang, Y., Wang, J., Jia, Y., Zhong, S., Niu, M., Sun, Y., et al. (2017). Shared and specific intrinsic functional connectivity patterns in unmedicated bipolar disorder and major depressive disorder. *Scientific Reports, 7*(1), 3570.

Wani, A. L., Bhat, S. A., & Ara, A. (2015). Omega-3 fatty acids and the treatment of depression: A review of scientific evidence. *Integrative Medicine Research, 4*(3), 132–141.

Warden, D., Rush, A. J., Trivedi, M. H., Fava, M., & Wisniewski, S. R. (2007). The STAR* D Project results: A comprehensive review of findings. *Current Psychiatry Reports, 9*(6), 449–459.

Warkentin, S., Ohlsson, M., Wollmer, P., Edenbrandt, L., & Minthon, L. (2004). Regional cerebral blood flow in Alzheimer's disease: Classification and analysis of heterogeneity. *Dementia and Geriatric Cognitive Disorders, 17*, 207–214.

Warner, L. A., Kessler, R. C., Hughes, M., Anthony, J. C., & Nelson, C. B. (1995). Prevalence and correlates of drug use and dependence in the United States: Results from the National Comorbidity Survey. *Archives of General Psychiatry, 52*(3), 219–229.

Watanabe, K., Kudo, Y., Sugawara, E., Nakamizo, T., Amari, K., Takahashi, K., et al. (2018). Comparative study of ipsilesional and contralesional repetitive transcranial magnetic stimulations for acute infarction. *Journal of the Neurological Sciences, 384*, 10–14.

Watanabe, S., & Boucrot, E. (2017). Fast and ultrafast endocytosis. *Current Opinion in Cell Biology, 47*, 64–71.

Watanabe, T. K., Miller, M. A., & McElligott, J. M. (2003). Congenital and acquired brain injury: Outcomes after acquired brain injury. *Archives of Physical and Medical Rehabilitation, 84*, 23–31.

Watanabe, T., Ishiguro, S., Aoki, A., Ueda, M., Hayashi, Y., Akiyama, K., et al. (2017). Genetic Polymorphism of 1019C/G (rs6295) promoter of serotonin 1A receptor and catechol-O-methyltransferase in panic disorder. *Psychiatry Investigation, 14*(1), 86–92.

Watkins, K. E., Paus, T., Lerch, J. P., Zijdenbos, A., Collins, D. L., Neelin, P., et al. (2001). Structural asymmetries in the human brain: A voxel-based statistical analysis of 142 MRI scans. *Cerebral Cortex, 9*, 868–877.

Watkins, P. B., Zimmerman, H. J., Knapp, M. J., Gracon, S. I., & Lewis, K. W. (1994). Hepatotoxic effects of tacrine administration in patients with Alzheimer's disease. *Journal of the American Medical Association, 271*, 992–998.

Webb, S. J., Monk, C. S., & Nelson, C. A. (2001). Mechanisms of postnatal neurobiological development: Implications for human development. *Developmental Neuropsychology, 19*, 147–171.

Webster, R. A. (2001). Diseases of the basal ganglia. In R. A. Webster (Ed.), *Neurotransmitters, drugs and brain function* (pp. 299–323). New York: John Wiley & Sons.

Webster, R. A. (2001a). Dopamine (DA). In R. A. Webster (Ed.), *Neurotransmitters, drugs, and brain function* (pp. 137–161). New York: Wiley.

Webster, R. A. (2001b). Neurotransmitter systems and function: Overview. In R. A. Webster (Ed.), *Neurotransmitters, drugs, and brain function* (pp. 3–32). New York: Wiley.

Webster, R. A. (2001c). Schizophrenia. In R. A. Webster (Ed.), *Neurotransmitters, drugs, and brain function* (pp. 351–373). New York: Wiley.

Weerts, E. M., Kim, Y. K., Wand, G. S., Dannals, R. F., Lee, J. S., Frost, J. J., & McCaul, M. E. (2008). Differences in δ- and μ-opioid receptor blockade measured by positron emission tomography in naltrexone-treated recently abstinent alcohol-dependent subjects. *Neuropsychopharmacology, 33*(3), 653–665.

Wehr, T. A., Muscettola, G., & Goodwin, F. K. (1980). Urinary 3-methoxy-4-hydroxyphenylglycol circadian rhythm. Early timing (phase-advance) in manic-depressives compared with normal subjects. *Archives of General Psychiatry, 37*, 257–263.

Wei, L., Zhong, S., Nie, S., & Gong, G. (2018). Aberrant development of the asymmetry between hemispheric brain white matter networks in autism spectrum disorder. *European Neuropsychopharmacology, 28*(1), 48–62.

Weiland, B. J., Thayer, R. E., Depue, B. E., Sabbineni, A., Bryan, A. D., & Hutchison, K. E. (2015). Daily marijuana use is not associated with brain morphometric measures in adolescents or adults. *Journal of Neuroscience, 35*(4), 1505–1512.

Weinberger, A. H., Gbedemah, M., Martinez, A. M., Nash, D., Galea, S., & Goodwin, R. D. (2017). Trends in depression prevalence in the USA from 2005 to 2015: Widening disparities in vulnerable groups. *Psychological Medicine*, 1–10.

Weinberger, D. R. (1987). Implications of normal brain development for the pathogenesis of schizophrenia. *Archives of General Psychiatry, 44*, 600–669.

Weinberger, D. R. (1995). From neuropathology to neurodevelopment. *Lancet, 346*, 552–557.

Weinberger, D. R. (1996). On the plausibility of "the neurodevelopmental hypothesis" of schizophrenia. *Neuropsychopharmacology, 14*, 1–11.

Weinberger, D. R., & Lipska, B. K. (1995). Cortical maldevelopment, antipsychotic drugs and schizophrenia: A search for common ground. *Schizophrenia Research, 16*, 87–110.

Weiner, M. F., de la Plata, C. M., Fields, J., Womack, K. B., Rosenberg, R. N., Gong, Y. H, et al. (2009). Brain MRI, apoliprotein E genotype, and plasma homocysteine in American Indian Alzheimer disease patients and Indian controls. *Current Alzheimer Research, 6*(1), 52–58.

Weiner, M. W., Crane, P. K., Montine, T. J., Bennett, D. A., & Veitch, D. P. (2017). Traumatic brain injury may not increase the risk of Alzheimer disease. *Neurology, 89*(18), 1923–1925.

Weintraub, D., & Claassen, D. O. (2017). Impulse control and related disorders in Parkinson's disease. *International Review of Neurobiology, 133*, 679–717.

Weiskopf, N. (2012). Real-time fMRI and its application to neurofeedback. *Neuroimage, 62*(2), 682–692.

Weiss, H. D., & Marsh, L. (2012). Impulse control disorders and compulsive behaviors associated with dopaminergic therapies in Parkinson disease. *Neurology: Clinical Practice, 2*(4), 267–274.

Weissman, M. M. (1993). Family genetic studies of panic disorder. *Journal of Psychiatric Research, 27, Supplement 1*, 69–78.

Welch, J. M., Lu, J., Rodriguiz, R. M., Trotta, N. C., Peca, J., Ding, J. D., et al. (2007). Cortico-striatal synaptic defects and OCD-like behaviours in Sapap3-mutant mice. *Nature, 448*(7156), 894–900.

Welter, D., MacArthur, J., Morales, J., Burdett, T., Hall, P., Junkins, H., . . . Parkinson, H. (2013). The NHGRI GWAS Catalog, a curated resource of SNP-trait associations. *Nucleic Acids Research, 42*(D1), D1001–D1006.

Wender, E. H. (1986). The food additive-free diet in the treatment of behavior disorders: A review. *Journal of Development and Behavioral Pediatrics, 7*, 35–42.

Werman, R. (1966). Criteria for identification of a central nervous system transmitter. *Comparative Biochemistry and Physiology, 18*, 745–766.

Werner, C., & Engelhard, K. (2007). Pathophysiology of traumatic brain injury. *British Journal of Anaesthesia, 99*(1), 4–9.

West, S. L., Graham, C. W., & Temple, P. (2017). Rates and correlates of binge drinking among college students with disabilities, United States, 2013. *Public Health Reports, 132*(4), 496–504.

Westbrook, C. (2016). *MRI at a Glance.* West Sussex, UK: John Wiley & Sons.

Weyandt, L. L. (2001). *Attention deficit hyperactivity disorder: An ADHD primer* (2nd ed.). New York: Lawrence Erlbaum Associates.

Weyandt, L. L. (2004). Alternative interventions: Nontraditional treatments for attention disorders. In *Helping children at home and school: Handouts from your school psychologist.* Bethesda, MD: National Association of School Psychologists.

Weyandt, L. L. (2005). Neuropsychological performance in adults with ADHD. In D. Gozal & D. Molfese (Eds.), *Attention deficit hyperactivity disorder: From genes to animal models to patients.* Totowa, NJ: Humana.

Weyandt, L. L. (2006). *The physiological bases of cognitive and behavioral disorders.* Routledge.

Weyandt, L. L. (2007). *An ADHD primer* (2nd ed.). Mahwah, NJ, US: Lawrence Erlbaum Associates Publishers.

Weyandt, L. L., & DuPaul, G. J. (2012). *College students with ADHD: Current issues and future directions.* New York, NY: Springer Science & Business Media.

Weyandt, L. L., Janusis, G., Wilson, K. G., Verdi, G., Paquin, G., Lopes, J., et al. (2009). Non-medical prescription stimulant use among a sample of college students: Relationship with psychological variables. *Journal of Attention Disorders, 13*(3), 284–296.

Weyandt, L. L., Iwaszuk, W., Fulton, K., Ollerton, M., Beatty, N., Fouts. H., et al. (2003). The internal restlessness scale: Performance of college students with and without ADHD. *Journal of Learning Disabilities, 36*, 382–389.

Weyandt, L. L., Marraccini, M. E., Gudmundsdottir, B. G., Zavras, B. M., Turcotte, K. D., Munro, B. A., & Amoroso, A. J. (2013). Misuse of prescription stimulants among college students: A review of the literature and implications for morphological and cognitive effects on brain functioning. *Experimental and Clinical Psychopharmacology, 21*(5), 385–407.

Weyandt, L. L., Mitzlaff, L., & Thomas, L. (2002). The relationship between intelligence and performance on the Test of Variables of Attention (TOVA). *Journal of Learning Disabilities, 35*, 114–120.

Weyandt, L. L., Oster, D. R., Gudmundsdottir, B. G., DuPaul, G. J., & Anastopoulos, A. D. (2017). Neuropsychological functioning in college students with and without ADHD. *Neuropsychology, 31*(2), 160–172.

Weyandt, L. L., Oster, D. R., Marraccini, M. E., Gudmundsdottir, B. G., Munro, B. A., Rathkey, E. S., & McCallum, A. (2016). Prescription stimulant medication misuse: Where are we and where do we go from here? *Experimental and Clinical Psychopharmacology, 24*(5), 400–414.

Whalen, P. J., Shin, L. M., McInerney, S. C., Fischer, H., Wright, C. I., & Rauch, S. L. (2001). A functional MRI study of human amygdala responses to facial expressions of fear versus anger. *Emotion, 1,* 70–83.

Whitall, J., McCombe-Waller, S., Silver, K. H. C., & Macko, R. F. (2000). Repetitive bilateral arm training with rhythmic auditory cueing improves motor function in chronic hemiparetic stroke. *Stroke, 31,* 2390–2397.

White, B. L., & Held, R. (1966). Plasticity of sensorimotor development. In J. F. Rosenblith & W. Allinsmith (Eds.), *The causes of behavior.* Boston: Allyn & Bacon.

White, F. J., & Kalivas, P. W. (1998). Neuroadaptations involved in amphetamine and cocaine addiction. *Drug and Alcohol Dependence, 51,* 141–153.

White, T. L., Monnig, M. A., Walsh, E. G., Nitenson, A. Z., Harris, A. D., Cohen, R. A., et al. (2018). Psychostimulant drug effects on glutamate, Glx, and creatine in the anterior cingulate cortex and subjective response in healthy humans. *Neuropsychopharmacology, 1.*

Whitehouse, P. J., Martino, A. M., Marcus, K. A., Zweig, R. M., Singer, H. S., Price, D. L., et al. (1988). Reductions in acetylcholine and nicotine binding in several degenerative diseases. *Archives of Neurology, 45,* 722–724.

Wiedemann, G., Pauli, P., Dengler, W., Lutzenberger, W., Birbaumer, N., & Buchkremer, G. (1999). Frontal brain asymmetry as a biological substrate of emotions in patients with panic disorders. *Archives of General Psychiatry, 56,* 78–84.

Wilcox, J. A. (2014). Psilocybin and obsessive compulsive disorder. *Journal of Psychoactive Drugs, 46*(5), 393–395.

Wilcox, J. A., Tsuang, M. T., Ledger, E., Algeo, J., & Schnurr, T. (2002). Brain perfusion in autism varies with age. *Biological Psychiatry, 46,* 13–16.

Wilens, T. E. (2004). Attention-deficit/hyperactivity disorder and the substance use disorders: The nature of the relationship, subtypes at risk, and treatment issues. *Psychiatric Clinics, 27*(2), 283–301.

Wilkinson, B. J., Newman, M. B., Shytle, R. D., Silver, A. A., Sanberg, P. R., & Sheehan, D. (2002). Family impact of Tourette's syndrome. *Journal of Child and Family Studies, 10,* 477–483.

Wilkinson, S. T., Sanacora, G., & Bloch, M. H. (2017). Hippocampal volume changes following electroconvulsive therapy: A systematic review and meta-analysis. *Biological Psychiatry: Cognitive Neuroscience and Neuroimaging, 2*(4), 327–335.

Williams, R. S., Hauser, S. L., Purpura, D. P., DeLong, G. R., & Swisher, C. N. (1980). Autism and mental retardation: Neuropathologic studies performed in four retarded persons with autistic behavior. *Archives of Neurology, 37,* 749–753.

Willcutt, E. G., Pennington, B. F., & DeFries, J. C. (2000). Twin study of the etiology of comorbidity between reading disability and attention-deficit/hyperactivity disorder. *American Journal of Medical Genetics, 96,* 293–301.

Wille-Bille, A., de Olmos, S., Marengo, L., Chiner, F., & Pautassi, R. M. (2017). Long-term ethanol self-administration induces ΔFosB in male and female adolescent, but not in adult, Wistar rats. *Progress in Neuro-Psychopharmacology and Biological Psychiatry, 74,* 15–30.

Williams, H. J., Owen, M. J., & O'donovan, M. C. (2007). Is COMT a susceptibility gene for schizophrenia? *Schizophrenia Bulletin, 33*(3), 635–641.

Williams, N. R., Bentzley, B. S., Sahlem, G. L., Pannu, J., Korte, J. E., Revuelta, G., et al. (2017). Unilateral ultra-brief pulse electroconvulsive therapy for depression in Parkinson's disease. *Acta Neurologica Scandinavica, 135*(4), 407–411.

Williams, S. E., Ris, M. D., & Ayangar, R. (1998). Recovery in pediatric brain injury: Is psychostimulant medication beneficial? *Journal of Head Trauma, 13,* 73–81.

Willis, W. G., & Weiler, M. D. (2005). Neural substrates of childhood attention-deficit/hyperactivity disorder: Electroencephalographic and magnetic resonance imaging evidence. *Developmental Neuropsychology, 27,* 135–187.

Willis, W. G., Weyandt, L. L., Lubiner, A. G., & Schubart, C. D. (2011). Neurofeedback as a treatment for attention-deficit/hyperactivity disorder: A systematic review of evidence for practice. *Journal of Applied School Psychology, 27*(3), 201–227.

Wilson, R. S., Evans, D. A., Bienias, J. L., Mendes de Leon, C. F., Schneider, J. A., & Bennett, D. A. (2003). Proneness to psychological distress is associated with risk of Alzheimer's disease. *Neurology, 61,* 1479–1485.

Wilson, R. S., Mendes de Leon, C. F., Barnes, L. L., Schneider, J. A., Bienias, J. L., Evans, D. A., et al. (2002). Participation in cognitively stimulating activities and risk of incident Alzheimer's disease. *Journal of the American Medical Association, 287,* 742–748.

Wimalasena, K. (2011). Vesicular monoamine transporters: Structure-function, pharmacology, and medicinal chemistry. *Medicinal Research Reviews, 31*(4), 483–519.

Wimberley, T., Gasse, C., Meier, S. M., Agerbo, E., MacCabe, J. H., & Horsdal, H. T. (2017). Polygenic risk score for schizophrenia and treatment-resistant schizophrenia. *Schizophrenia Bulletin, 43*(5), 1064–1069.

Wintermann, G. B., Donix, M., Joraschky, P., Gerber, J., & Petrowski, K. (2013). Altered olfactory processing of stress-related body odors and artificial odors in patients with panic disorder. *PLoS One, 8*(9), e74655.

Wirdefeldt, K., Gatz, M., Reynolds, C. A., Prescott, C. A., & Pedersen, N. L. (2011). Heritability of Parkinson disease in Swedish twins: A longitudinal study. *Neurobiology of Aging, 32*(10), e1-e8.

Wisden, W., Yu, X., & Franks, N. P. (2017). GABA receptors and he pharmacology of sleep. *Handbook of Experimental Pharmacology, 164.*

Wise, R. A., & Gardner, E. L. (2004). Animal models of addiction. In D. S. Charney & E. J. Nestler (Eds.), *Neurobiology of mental illness* (2nd ed., pp. 683–697). New York: Oxford University Press.

Wise, R. A., Leeb, K., Pocock, D., Newton, P., Burnette, B., & Justice, J. B. (1995). Fluctuations in nucleus accumbens dopamine concentration during intravenous cocaine self-administration in rats. *Psychopharmacology, 120*(1), 10–20.

Wise, T., Radua, J., Via, E., Cardoner, N., Abe, O., Adams, T. M., et al. (2017). Common and distinct patterns of grey-matter volume alteration in major depression and bipolar disorder: Evidence from voxel-based meta-analysis. *Molecular Psychiatry, 22*(10), 1455–1463.

Witelson, S. F. (1989). Hand and sex differences in the isthmus and genu of the human corpus callosum. *Brain, 112,* 799–835.

Wittchen, H. U. (2002). Generalized anxiety disorder: Prevalence, burden, and cost to society. *Depression and Anxiety, 16,* 162–171.

Wolf, M. E., & Ferrario, C. R. (2010). AMPA receptor plasticity in the nucleus accumbens after repeated exposure to cocaine. *Neuroscience & Biobehavioral Reviews, 35*(2), 185–211.

Wolf, S. S., Jones, D. W., Knable, M. B., Gorey, J. G., Lee, K. S., Hyde, T. M., et al. (1996). Tourette syndrome: Prediction of phenotypic variation in monozygotiz twins by caudate nucleus D2 receptor. *Science, 273,* 1225–1227.

Wolfe, B. E., Metzger, E. D., Levine, J. M., Finkeltein, D. M., Cooper, T. B., & Jimerson, D. C. (2000). Serotonin function following remission from bulimia nervosa. *Neuropsychopharmacology, 22,* 257–263.

Wolfe, F. H., Auzias, G., Deruelle, C., & Chaminade, T. (2015). Focal atrophy of the hypothalamus associated with third ventricle enlargement in autism spectrum disorder. *NeuroReport, 26*(17), 1017–1022.

Wolff, N., Luehr, I., Sender, J., Ehrlich, S., Schmidt-Samoa, C., Dechent, P., & Roessner, V. (2016). A DTI study on the corpus callosum of treatment-naïve boys with "pure" Tourette syndrome. *Psychiatry Research: Neuroimaging, 247,* 1–8.

Wolraich, M. L., McKeown, R. E., Visser, S. N., Bard, D., Cuffe, S., Neas, B., et al. (2014). The prevalence of ADHD: Its diagnosis and treatment in four school districts across two states. *Journal of Attention Disorders, 18*(7), 563–575.

Wong, D. F., Brašić, J. R., Singer, H. S., Schretlen, D. J., Kuwabara, H., Zhou, Y., . . . Rousset, O. (2007). Mechanisms of dopaminergic and serotonergic neurotransmission in Tourette syndrome: Clues from an in vivo neurochemistry study with PET. *Neuropsychopharmacology, 33*(6), 1239.

Wong, D. F., Wanger, H. N., Tune, L. E., Dannals, R. F., Pearlson, G. D., Links, J. M., et al. (1986). Positron emission tomography reveals elevated D2 dopamine receptors in drug-naive schizophrenics. *Science, 234*, 1558–1563.

Woo, J. M., Yoon, K. S., & Yu, B. H. (2002). Catechol-O-methyltransferase genetic polymorphism in panic disorder. *American Journal of Psychiatry, 159*, 1785–1787.

Woo, J., Lau, E., Ziea, E., & Chan, D. K. (2004). Prevalence of Parkinson's disease in a Chinese population. *Acta Neurologica Scandinavica, 109*, 228–231.

Woodruff, P., McManus, I., & David, A. (1995). A meta-analysis of corpus callosum size in schizophrenia. *Journal of Neurology, Neurosurgery, and Psychiatry, 58*, 457–461.

Woods, A. J., Antal, A., Bikson, M., Boggio, P. S., Brunoni, A. R., Celnik, P., et al. (2016). A technical guide to tDCS, and related non-invasive brain stimulation tools. *Clinical Neurophysiology, 127*(2), 1031–1048.

Worbe, Y., Lehericy, S., & Hartmann, A. (2015). Neuroimaging of tic genesis: Present status and future perspectives. *Movement Disorders, 30*(9), 1179–1183.

World Health Organization. (2018, March 22). *Depression*. Retrieved from http://www.who.int/news-room/fact-sheets/detail/depression

Wray, N. R., Pergadia, M. L., Blackwood, D. H. R., Penninx, B. W. J. H., Gordon, S. D., Nyholt, D. R., . . . Smit, J. H. (2012). Genome-wide association study of major depressive disorder: New results, meta-analysis, and lessons learned. *Molecular Psychiatry, 17*(1), 36.

Wright, I. C., Rabe-Hesketh, S., Woodruff, P. W., David, A. S., Murray, R. M., & Bullmore, E. T. (2000). Meta-analysis of regional brain volumes in schizophrenia. *American Journal of Psychiatry, 157*(1), 16–25.

Wu, K., Taki, Y., Sato, K., Qi, H., Kawashima, R., & Fukuda, H. (2013). A longitudinal study of structural brain network changes with normal aging. *Frontiers in Human Neuroscience, 7*, 113.

Wu, L. T., Kouzis, A. C., & Schlenger, W. E. (2003). Substance use, dependence, and service utilization among US uninsured nonelderly population. *American Journal of Public Health, 93*, 2079–2085.

Wu, T., Chen, C., Yang, L., Zhang, M., Zhang, X., Jia, J., . . . Guo, X. (2015). Distinct lncRNA expression profiles in the prefrontal cortex of SD rats after exposure to methylphenidate. *Biomedicine & Pharmacotherapy, 70*, 239–247.

Wu, Y., Yao, Y. G., & Luo, X. J. (2017). SZDB: A database for schizophrenia genetic research. *Schizophrenia Bulletin, 43*(2), 459–471.

Wulsin, L., Alterman, T., Bushnell, P. T., Li, J., & Shen, R. (2014). Prevalence rates for depression by industry: A claims database analysis. *Social Psychiatry and Psychiatric Epidemiology, 49*(11), 1805–1821.

Wurthmann, C., Bogerts, B., Gregor, J., Baumann, B., Effenberger, O., & Döhring, W. (1997). Frontal CSF enlargement in panic disorder: A qualitative CT-scan study. *Psychiatry Research: Neuroimaging, 76*(2), 83–87.

Xiong, Y., Zhang, Y., Mahmood, A., & Chopp, M. (2015). Investigational agents for treatment of traumatic brain injury. *Expert Opinion on Investigational Drugs, 24*(6), 743–760.

Xu, G., Strathearn, L., Liu, B., & Bao, W. (2018). Prevalence of autism spectrum disorder among US children and adolescents, 2014–2016. *Jama, 319*(1), 81–82.

Xu, L., Qin, W., Zhuo, C., Liu, H., Zhu, J., & Yu, C. (2017). Combination of volume and perfusion parameters reveals different types of grey matter changes in schizophrenia. *Scientific Reports, 7*(1), 435.

Yamada, K., Watanabe, A., Iwayama-Shigeno, Y., & Yoshikawa, T. (2003). Evidence of association between gamma-aminobutyric acid type A receptor genes located on 5q34 and female patients with mood disorders. *Neuroscience Letters, 349*, 9–12.

Yamamoto, D. J., Banich, M. T., Regner, M. F., Sakai, J. T., & Tanabe, J. (2017). Behavioral approach and orbitofrontal cortical activity during decision-making in substance dependence. *Drug & Alcohol Dependence, 180*, 234–240.

Yamashita, Y., Fujimoto, C., Nakajima, E., Isagai, T., & Matsuishi, T. (2003). Possible association between congenital cytomegalovirus infection and autistic disorder. *Journal of Autism and Developmental Disorders, 33*, 455–459.

Yanagisawa, K., Nakamura, N., Tsunashima, H., & Narita, N. (2016). Proposal of auxiliary diagnosis index for autism spectrum disorder using near-infrared spectroscopy. *Neurophotonics, 3*(3), 031413.

Yang, B. Z., Han, S., Kranzler, H. R., Palmer, A. A., & Gelernter, J. (2017). Sex-specific linkage scans in opioid dependence. *American Journal of Medical Genetics Part B: Neuropsychiatric Genetics, 174*(3), 261–268.

Yang, D. Y. J., Beam, D., Pelphrey, K. A., Abdullahi, S., & Jou, R. J. (2016). Cortical morphological markers in children with autism: A structural magnetic resonance imaging study of thickness, area, volume, and gyrification. *Molecular Autism, 7*(1), 11.

Yang, H. C., Liu, C. M., Liu, Y. L., Chen, C. W., Chang, C. C., Fann, C. S., et al. (2013). The DAO gene is associated with schizophrenia and interacts with other genes in the Taiwan Han Chinese population. *PloS One, 8*(3), e60099.

Yang, J., & Li, M. D. (2016). Converging findings from linkage and association analyses on susceptibility genes for smoking and other addictions. *Molecular Psychiatry, 21*(8), 992–1008.

Yang, X., Si, T., Gong, Q., Qiu, L., Jia, Z., Zhou, M., et al. (2016). Brain gray matter alterations and associated demographic profiles in adults with autism spectrum disorder: A meta-analysis of voxel-based morphometry studies. *Australian & New Zealand Journal of Psychiatry, 50*(8), 741–753.

Yang, Y. K., Yu, L., Yeh, T. L., Chiu, N. T., Chen, P. S., & Lee, I. H. (2004). Associated alterations of striatal dopamine D2/D3 receptor and transporter binding in drug-naive patients with schizophrenia: A dual-isotope SPECT study. *American Journal of Psychiatry, 161*(8), 1496–1498.

Yao, J., Chen, A., Kuiken, T., Carmona, C., & Dewald, J. (2015). Sensory cortical re mapping following upper-limb amputation and subsequent targeted reinnervation: A case report. *NeuroImage: Clinical, 8*, 329–336.

Yapici, E. H., Bora, H. A., & Kuruoglu, A. (2017). Depression and Parkinson disease: Prevalence, temporal relationship, and determinants. *Turkish Journal of Medical Sciences, 47*(2), 499–503.

Yatham, L. N., Clark, C. C., & Zis, A. P. (2000). A preliminary study of the effects of electroconvulsive therapy on regional brain glucose metabolism in patients with major depression. *Journal of ECT, 16*, 171–176.

Yatham, L. N., Sossi, V., Ding, Y. S., Vafai, N., Arumugham, S. S., Dhanoa, T., . . . Puyat, J. (2017). A positron emission tomography study of norepinephrine transporter occupancy and its correlation with symptom response in depressed patients treated with quetiapine xr. *International Journal of Neuropsychopharmacology, 21*(2), 108–113.

Yelamanchi, S. D., Jayaram, S., Thomas, J. K., Gundimeda, S., Khan, A. A., Singhal, A., . . . Gowda, H. (2016). A pathway map of glutamate metabolism. *Journal of Cell Communication and Signaling, 10*(1), 69–75.

Yildiz, A., & Sachs, G. S. (2003). Age of onset of psychotic versus non-psychotic bipolar illness in men & in women. *Journal of Affective Disorders, 74*, 197–201.

Yildiz, A., Sachs, G. S., Dorer, D. J., & Renshaw, P. F. (2001). 31P nuclear magnetic resonance spectroscopy findings in bipolar illness: A meta-analysis. *Psychiatry Research: Neuroimaging Section, 106*, 181–191.

Yin, Y., Wang, M., Wang, Z., Xie, C., Zhang, H., Zhang, H., et al. (2018). Decreased cerebral blood flow in the primary motor cortex in major depressive disorder with psychomotor retardation. *Progress in Neuro-Psychopharmacology and Biological Psychiatry, 81*, 438–444.

Yip, S. W., Worhunsky, P. D., Xu, J., Morie, K. P., Constable, R. T., Malison, R. T., et al. (2018). Gray-matter relationships to diagnostic and transdiagnostic features of drug and behavioral addictions. *Addiction Biology, 23*(1), 394–402.

Yoon, D. Y., Gause, C. D., Leckman, J. F., & Singer, H. S. (2007). Frontal dopaminergic abnormality in Tourette syndrome: A postmortem analysis. *Journal of the Neurological Sciences, 255*(1), 50–56.

Yoon, S., Kim, J. E., Kim, G. H., Kang, H. J., Kim, B. R., Jeon, S., et al. (2016). Subregional shape alterations in the amygdala in patients with panic disorder. *PloS One, 11*(6), e0157856.

Yoshida, K. Y., Takahashi, H., Higuchi, H., Kamata, M., Ito, K., Sato, K., et al. (2004). Prediction of antidepressant response to milnacipran by norepinephrine transporter gene polymorphisms. *American Journal of Psychiatry, 161*, 1575–1580.

Young, L. T. (2001). Postreceptor pathways for signaling transduction in depression and bipolar disorder. *Journal of Psychiatry and Neuroscience, 26*, 17–22.

Young, L. T., Li, P. P., Kish, S. J., Siu, K. P., Kamble, A., Hornykiewicz, O., et al. (1993). Cerebral cortex Gs alpha protein levels and forskolin-stimulated cyclic AMP formation are increased in bipolar affective disorder. *Journal of Neurochemistry, 61*, 890–898.

Young, L. T., Warsh, J. J., Kish, S. J., Shannak, K., & Hornykeiwicz, O. (1994). Reduced brain 5-HT and elevated NE turnover and metabolites in bipolar affective disorder. *Biological Psychiatry, 35*, 121–127.

Young, R. F., Jacques, S., Mark, R., Kopyov, O., Copcutt, B., Posewitz, A., et al. (2000). Gamma knife thalamotomy for treatment of tremor: Long-term results. *Journal of Neurosurgery, 93*, 128–135.

Yrondi, A., Sporer, M., Péran, P., Schmitt, L., Arbus, C., & Sauvaget, A. (2018). Electroconvulsive therapy, depression, the immune system and inflammation: A systematic review. *Brain Stimulation: Basic, Translational, and Clinical Research in Neuromodulation, 11*(1), 29–51.

Yuan, A., Su, L., Yu, S., Li, C., Yu, T., & Sun, J. (2015). Association between DRD2/ANKK1 TaqIA polymorphism and susceptibility with Tourette syndrome: A meta-analysis. *PloS one, 10*(6), e0131060.

Yuen, R. K., Merico, D., Bookman, M., Howe, J. L., Thiruvahindrapuram, B., Patel, R. V., et al. (2017). Whole genome sequencing resource identifies 18 new candidate genes for autism spectrum disorder. *Nature neuroscience, 20*(4), 602–611.

Yuen, R. K., Thiruvahindrapuram, B., Merico, D., Walker, S., Tammimies, K., Hoang, N., et al. (2015). Whole-genome sequencing of quartet families with autism spectrum disorder. *Nature Medicine, 21*(2), 185–191.

Yu-Feng, L., Li, J., & Faraone, S. (2004). Association of norepinephrine transporter gene with methylphenidate response. *Journal of the American Academy of Child and Adolescent Psychiatry, 43*, 1154–1158.

Ystrom, E., Reichborn-Kjennerud, T., Neale, M. C., & Kendler, K. S. (2014). Genetic and environmental risk factors for illicit substance use and use disorders: Joint analysis of self and co-twin ratings. *Behavior Genetics, 44*(1), 1–13.

Yu, C., Baune, B. T., Wong, M. L., & Licinio, J. (2018). Investigation of short tandem repeats in major depression using whole-genome sequencing data. *Journal of Affective Disorders, 232*, 305–309.

Yu, J., Yan, Y., Li, K. L., Wang, Y., Huang, Y. H., Urban, N. N., et al. (2017). Nucleus accumbens feedforward inhibition circuit promotes cocaine self-administering. *Proceedings of the National Academy of the Sciences of the United States of America, 4*, E8750–E8759.

Yu, X., Qiu, Z., & Zhang, D. (2017). Recent research progress in autism spectrum disorder. *Neuroscience Bulletin, 33*(2), 125–129.

Yulug, B., Hanoglu, L., & Kilic, E. (2017). Does sleep disturbance affect the amyloid clearance mechanisms in alzheimer's disease? *Psychiatry and clinical neurosciences 71*(10), 673–677.

Yusufov, M., Weyandt, L. L., & Piryatinsky, I. (2017). Alzheimer's disease and diet: A systematic review. *International Journal of Neuroscience, 127*(2), 161–175.

Zaffanello, M., Zamboni, G., Fontana, E., Zoccante, L., & Tato, L. (2003). A case of partial biotinidase deficiency associated with autism. *Child Neuropsychology, 9*, 184–188.

Zaldy, S. T., Seshadri, S., Beiser, A., Wilson, P. W. F., Kiel, D. P., Tocco, M., et al. (2003). Plasma total cholesterol level as a risk factor for Alzheimer's disease. *Archives of Internal Medicine*, *163*, 1053–1057.

Zaman, R., & Robbins, T. W. (2017). Is there potential for repetitive Transcranial Magnetic Stimulation (rTMS) as a treatment of OCD? *Psychiatria Danubina*, *29*(3), 672–678.

Zametkin, A. J., Liebenauer, L. L., Fitzgerald, G. A., King, A. C., Minkunas, D. V., Herscovitch, P., . . . Cohen, R. M. (1993). Brain metabolism in teenagers with attention-deficit hyperactivity disorder. *Archives of General Psychiatry*, *50*(5), 333–340.

Zametkin, A. J., Nordahl, T. E., Gross, M., King, A. C., Semple, W. E., Rumsey, J., . . . Cohen, R. M. (1990). Cerebral glucose metabolism in adults with hyperactivity of childhood onset. *New England Journal of Medicine*, *323*(20), 1361–1366.

Zandi, P. P., Anthony, J. C., Khachaturian, A. S., Stone, S. V., Gustafson, D., Tschanz, J. T., et al. (2004). Reduced risk of Alzheimer disease in users of antioxidant vitamin supplements: The Cache County Study. *Archives of Neurology*, *61*, 82–88.

Zhang, C., Li, D., Jin, H., Zeljic, K., & Sun, B. (2017). Target-specific deep brain stimulation of the ventral capsule/ventral striatum for the treatment of neuropsychiatric disease. *Annals of Translational Medicine*, *5*(20).

Zhang, G., Zhang, Z., Liu, L., Yang, J., Huang, J., Xiong, N., & Wang, T. (2014). Impulsive and compulsive behaviors in Parkinson's disease. *Frontiers in Aging Neuroscience*, *6*, 318.

Zhang, K., Jiang, H., Zhang, Q., Du, J., Wang, Y., & Zhao, M. (2016). Brain-derived neurotrophic factor serum levels in heroin-dependent patients after 26 weeks of withdrawal. *Comprehensive Psychiatry*, *65*, 150–155.

Zhang, L., Chang, S., Li, Z., Zhang, K., Du, Y., Ott, J., & Wang, J. (2011). ADHDgene: A genetic database for attention deficit hyperactivity disorder. *Nucleic Acids Research*, *40*(D1), D1003–D1009.

Zhang, Q., Liu, Q., Li, T., Liu, Y., Wang, L., Zhang, Z., et al. (2016). Expression and colocalization of NMDA receptor and FosB/ΔFosB in sensitive brain regions in rats after chronic morphine exposure. *Neuroscience Letters*, *614*, 70–76.

Zhang, R. L., Chopp, M., Roberts, C., Wei, M., Wang, X., Liu, X., et al. (2012). Sildenafil enhances neurogenesis and oligodendrogenesis in Ischemic brain of middle-aged mouse. *PLoS One*, *7*(10).

Zhang, R., Wang, Y., Zhang, L., Zhang, Z., Tsang, W., Lu, M., et al. (2002). Sildenafil (Viagra) induces neurogenesis and promotes functional recovery after stroke in rats. *Stroke*, *33*, 2675–2680.

Zhang, X., Lee, M. R., Salmeron, B. J., Stein, D. J., Hong, L. E., Geng, X., et al. (2013). Prefrontal white matter impairment in substance users depends upon the catechol-o-methyl transferase (COMT) val158met polymorphism. *Neuroimage*, *69*, 62–69.

Zhao, H., & Nyholt, D. R. (2017). Gene-based analyses reveal novel genetic overlap and allelic heterogeneity across five major psychiatric disorders. *Human Genetics*, *136*(2), 263–274.

Zheng, C., Shen, Y., & Xu, Q. (2012). Association of intron 1 variants of the dopamine transporter gene with schizophrenia. *Neuroscience Letters*, *513*(2), 137–140.

Zhou, F. M., Wilson, C., & Dani, J. A. (2003). Muscarinic and nicotinic cholinergic mechanisms in the mesostriatal dopamine systems. *The Neuroscientist*, *9*, 23–36.

Zhu, J., Klein-Fedyshin, M., & Stevenson, J, M. (2017). Serotonin transporter gene polymorphisms and selective serotonin reuptake inhibitor tolerability: Review of pharmacogenetic evience. *Pharmacotherapy*, *37*(9), 1089–1104.

Ziemann, U., Corwell, B., & Cohen, L. G. (1998). Modulation of plasticity in human motor cortex after forearm ischemic nerve block. *Journal of Neuroscience*, *18*, 1115–1123.

Zilberman, T., Tavares, H., & el-Guebaly, N. (2003). Gender similarities and differences: The prevalence and course of alcohol and other substance-related disorders. *Journal of Addiction Disorders*, *22*, 61–74.

Zilbovicius, M., Boddaert, N., Belin, P., Poline, J. B., Remy, P., Mangin, J. F., et al. (2000). Temporal lobe dysfunction in childhood autism: A PET study: Positron emission tomography. *American Journal of Psychiatry, 157*, 1988–1993.

Zilbovicius, M., Garreau, B., Samson, Y., Remy, P., Barthélémy, C., Syrota, A., et al. (1995). Delayed maturation of the frontal cortex in childhood autism. *American Journal of Psychiatry, 152*, 248–252.

Zilhão, N. R., Olthof, M. C., Smit, D. J., Cath, D. C., Ligthart, L., Mathews, C. A., et al. (2017). Heritability of tic disorders: A twin-family study. *Psychological Medicine, 47*(6), 1085–1096.

Zilles, D., Lewandowski, M., Vieker, H., Henseler, I., Diekhof, E., Melcher, T., & Gruber, O. (2016). Gender differences in verbal and visuospatial working memory performance and networks. *Neuropsychobiology, 73*(1), 52–63.

Zilles, D., Meyer, J., Schneider-Axmann, T., Ekawardhani, S., Gruber, E., Falkai, P., & Gruber, O. (2012). Genetic polymorphisms of 5-HTT and DAT but not COMT differentially affect verbal and visuospatial working memory functioning. *European Archives of Psychiatry and Clinical Neuroscience, 262*(8), 667–676.

Zimmerman, A. M., Abrams, M. T., Giuliano, J. D., Denckla, M. B., & Singer, H. S. (2000). Subcortical volumes in girls with Tourette syndrome: Support for a gender effect. *Neurology, 54*, 2224–2229.

Zimmerman, M., Chelminski, I., & McDermut, W. (2002). Major depressive disorder and axis I diagnostic comorbidity. *Journal of Clinical Psychiatry, 63*, 187–193.

Zink, M., Sartorius, A., Lederbogen, F., & Henn, F. A. (2002). Electroconvulsive therapy in patient receiving rivastigmine. *Journal of ECT, 18*, 162–164.

Zipursky, R. B., Seeman, M. V., Bury, A., Langevin, R., Wortzman, G., & Katz, R. (1997). Deficits in gray matter volume are present in schizophrenia but not bipolar disorder. *Schizophrenia Research, 26*, 85–92.

Zis, P., & Strydom, A. (2017). Clinical aspects and biomarkers of Alzheimers disease in Down syndrome. *Free Radical Biology and Medicine, 114*, 3–9.

Zito, K. A., Vickers, G., & Roberts, D. C. (1985). Disruption of cocaine and heroin self-administration following kainic acid lesions of the nucleus accumbens. *Pharmacology Biochemistry and Behavior, 23*(6), 1029–1036.

Zotev, V., Yuan, H., Misaki, M., Phillips, R., Young, K. D., Feldner, M. T., & Bodurka, J. (2016). Correlation between amygdala BOLD activity and frontal EEG asymmetry during real-time fMRI neurofeedback training in patients with depression. *NeuroImage: Clinical, 11*, 224–238.

Zubieta, J. K., Greenwald, M. K., Lombardi, U., Woods, J. H., Kilbourn, M. R., Jewett, D. M., et al. (2000). Buprenorphine-induced changes in mu-opioid receptor availability in male heroin-dependent volunteers: A preliminary study. *Neuropsychopharmacology, 23*, 326–334.

Zuvekas, S. H., & Vitiello, B. (2012). Stimulant medication use in children: A 12-year perspective. *American Journal of Psychiatry, 169*(2), 160–166.

Index

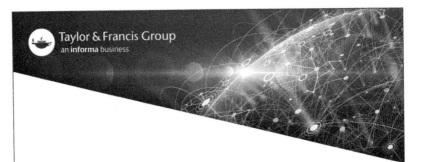